The **Rough Guide** to

The Baltic States

written and researched by

Jonathan Bousfield

with additional contributions by
Shafik Meghji

**ROUGH
GUIDES**

NEW YORK • LONDON • DELHI

www.roughguides.com

Contents

The great outdoors
colour section following
p.152

Baltic food & drink
colour section following
p.344

3

◀ Tallinn Old Town

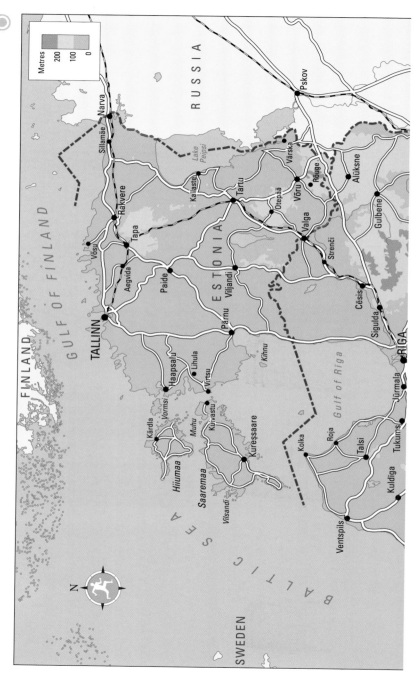

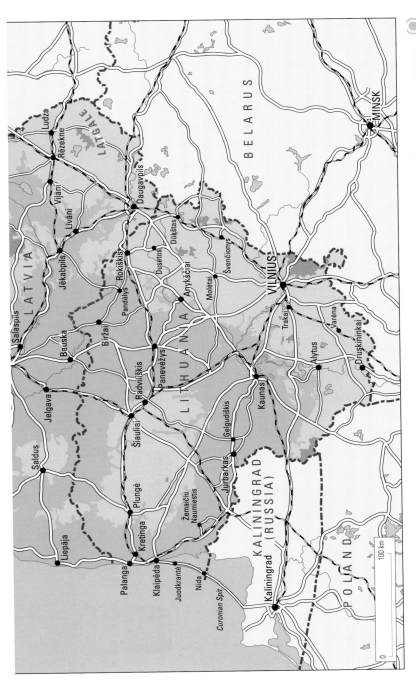

Introduction to the

Baltic States

The Baltic States – Lithuania, Latvia and Estonia – are graced by three of the most enthralling national capitals in Eastern Europe, each highly individual in character and boasting an extraordinary wealth of historic buildings, as well as an expanding and energetic nightlife and cultural scene. Outside the cities lie great swathes of unspoiled countryside, with deep, dark pine forests punctuated by stands of silver birch, calm blue lakes and a wealth of bogs and wetlands, all bordered by literally hundreds of kilometres of silvery beach. Peppering the landscape are villages that look like something out of the paintings of Marc Chagall, their dainty churches and wonky timber houses leaning over narrow, rutted streets. As you'd expect from a region periodically battered by outside invaders, there are dramatic historical remains aplenty, from the grizzled ruins of the fortresses thrown up by land-hungry Teutonic Knights in the thirteenth century, to the crumbling military installations bequeathed by Soviet occupiers some seven hundred years later.

Although the half-century spent under Soviet rule has left Lithuanians, Latvians and Estonians with a great deal in common, they're each fiercely proud of their separate status and tend to regard the "Baltic States" label as a matter of geographical convenience rather than a real indicator of shared culture. The Latvians and Lithuanians do at least have similar **origins**, having emerged from the Indo-European tribes who settled in the area some two thousand years before Christ, and they still speak closely related languages. The Estonians, on the other hand, have lived here at least three millennia longer and speak a Finno-Ugric tongue that has more in common with Finnish than with the

Song Festivals

Each of the Baltic States holds a truly massive national Song Festival once every four or five years, when choirs from all over the country assemble to sing traditional songs on huge, outdoor stages. These festivals have played a crucial role in Baltic life ever since the nineteenth century, when the rediscovery of folk songs was an important step in rejuvenating indigenous cultures weakened by centuries of foreign domination. During the Soviet period, Song Festivals nurtured feelings of national solidarity at a time when any other expression of patriotic sentiment was severely frowned upon. In June 1988, the Song Festival Grounds in Tallinn became the focus of mass demonstrations against the Soviet regime, and the phrase "Singing Revolution" was coined to describe the independence movements in all three Baltic States. These struggles may be over, but the sight and sound of thousands of performers singing in unison still carries unique emotional power.

languages of their next-door neighbours. In historical and religious terms, it's the Lithuanians that are a nation apart – having carved out a huge, independent empire in medieval times, they then converted to the Catholic faith in order to cement an alliance with Poland. In contrast, the Latvians and Estonians were conquered by Teutonic Knights in the thirteenth century and subjected to a German-speaking feudal culture that had become solidly Protestant by the mid-1500s. From the eighteenth century onwards, the destinies of the three Baltic peoples began to converge, with most Latvians and Estonians being swallowed up by the **Tsarist Empire** during the reign of Peter the Great, and the Lithuanians following several decades later. Despite their common predicament, no great tradition of Baltic cooperation emerged, and when the three Baltic States became independent democracies in 1918–20 – only to lose

▲ Traditional fisherman's cottage, Nida, western Lithuania

A love for the countryside, coupled with a contemplative, almost mystical feeling for nature, still runs in the blood.

their independence to the USSR and Nazi Germany two decades later – they did so as isolated units rather than as allies.

The one occasion on which the Baltic nations truly came together was in the 1988–1991 period, when a shared sense of injustice at the effects of Soviet occupation produced an outpouring of **inter-Baltic solidarity**. At no time was this more evident than when an estimated two million people joined hands to form a human chain stretching from Tallinn to Vilnius on 23 August, 1989, the fiftieth anniversary of the 1939 Molotov-Ribbentrop pact – the cynical Soviet–Nazi carve-up that had brought the curtain down on inter-war Baltic independence. Baltic fellow feeling became less pronounced in the post-Soviet period when each country began to focus on its own problems, and it's now the differences – rather than the similarities – between the Baltic peoples that most locals seem eager to impress upon visitors.

How different they actually are remains open to question, with both locals and outsiders resorting to a convenient collection of clichés whenever the question of **national identity** comes under discussion: the Lithuanians are thought to be warm and spontaneous, the Estonians distant and difficult to get to know, while the Latvians belong somewhere in between. In truth there are plenty of ethnographic similarities linking the three nationalities. A century ago the majority of Lithuanians, Latvians and Estonians lived on isolated farmsteads or small villages, and a **love for the countryside**, coupled with a contemplative, almost mystical feeling for nature, still runs in the blood. Shared historical experiences – especially the years of Soviet occupation and the sudden reimposition of capitalism that followed it – have produced people with broadly similar outlooks and, wherever you are in the Baltic States, you'll come across older people marked by fatalism and lack of initiative and younger generations characterized by ambition, impatience and adaptability to change.

The Baltic peoples today are also united by gnawing concerns about whether such relatively small countries can preserve their distinct identities in a rapidly globalizing world. The rush to join NATO and the EU has been broadly welcomed in all three countries, not least because membership of both organizations promises protection against any

Midsummer's Eve

Given the shortness of the Baltic summer, it's no great surprise that the arrival of the longest day of the year is celebrated with much enthusiasm in all three Baltic States. Although the festival is known by the Christian name of St John's Day (Jaanipäev in Estonian, Jāņi in Latvian, Joninės in Lithuanian), it's an unashamedly pagan affair, with families or groups of friends lighting a bonfire on the night of June 23 and waiting up to see the sunrise, often fortified by large quantities of alcohol. As well as being the last chance for a booze-up before the hard work of the harvest season began, Midsummer's Eve was traditionally a fertility festival in which the bounty of nature was celebrated in all its forms. Folk wisdom still maintains that herbs, grasses and even morning dew collected early on the 24th can have magical medicinal powers. Above all it was – and still is – a great opportunity for young members of the community to get together and do what comes naturally, with couples setting off into the forest supposedly in search of the mythical fern flower (which, rather like the four-leafed clover, will bring untold good fortune to whoever succeeds in actually finding it).

▲ Turaida Castle, eastern Latvia

Storks

If there's one thing that characterizes the Baltic countryside in spring and early summer it's the sight of large numbers of white storks, nesting atop telegraph poles and farmyard buildings, or poking around in recently tilled land looking for tasty insects. Arriving in late March or early April, the birds hatch their young in May, then spend a couple of months filling up on bugs and frogs before returning to their wintering grounds towards the end of August. While the twentieth century saw a dramatic decrease in the stork population in Western Europe, their numbers are actually on the rise in the Baltics – the unspoilt expanses of food-rich wetlands combined with the comparatively low use of pesticides in Baltic agriculture having made the region into something of a haven for the creatures. With folk wisdom maintaining that the presence of a stork's nest promises good fortune and protection from fire and lightning, their presence is much appreciated by the locals.

▲ Tallinn

future resurgence of Russian power. However, locals remain keenly aware that they can only be bit-part players in any future Europe. Lithuania has a **population** of 3.8 million, Latvia 2.3 million and Estonia only 1.4 million – hardly the stuff of economic or cultural superpowers. Combined with this is a looming fear of population decline in countries that share some of the lowest birth rates in the world. Such anxieties are particularly strong in Estonia and Latvia, where the indigenous populations are in many towns and cities outnumbered by other **ethnic groups** – particularly Russians – who were encouraged to move here during the Soviet period. Only 55 percent of Latvia's inhabitants are ethnic Latvians, and the figure in Estonia, at 65 percent, isn't much better. Eager to immerse themselves in the new Europe and yet profoundly concerned with the need to preserve their national uniqueness, the Baltic States find themselves at a challenging crossroads.

Travel in the Baltic States presents no real hardships, providing you're prepared to put up with badly surfaced roads or don't mind travelling in rural buses that look as if they belong in a transport museum. Gloomy, Soviet-era hotels are everywhere outnumbered by spanking-new establishments offering high standards of **accommodation** at slightly less than Western-standard prices. Even though the three national capitals are beginning to take off as popular city-break destinations, the volume of visitors remains low by Western European standards, leaving you with the feeling that there's still much to be discovered.

When to go

ate spring and summer are the best times to visit the Baltic States, when there's usually enough fine weather to allow you to stroll around the cities and make significant forays into the great outdoors. On the whole though, the only thing that's predictable about the Baltic climate is the deep, dark winters – in all other seasons the weather can be changeable in the extreme.

▲ Pärnu beach

▲ Cathedral of Alexander Nevsky, Tallinn

Summers are relatively short (roughly mid-June to late August), and although you may well experience a string of hot, dry days during this period, showers and chilly nights are equally likely. Remember to pack a waterproof jacket and warm sweater alongside your T-shirts.

Temperatures cool down rapidly from mid-September onwards, although **autumn** can be an extraordinarily beautiful season in which to visit, with the golden brown leaves of deciduous trees contrasting with the dark-green pines.

▲ Estonian nightlife

The first snowfalls can come as early as mid-November, and by early to mid-December **winter** sets in with a vengeance. Average daytime temperatures can remain below zero right through until March, plummeting to minus 15–20°C in particularly cold spells. Winter can of course be a magical time, with lakes, rivers and large expanses of the Baltic Sea freezing over, and crunchy snow cover adding an air of enchantment to medieval city centres. However, rural areas can be difficult to get to without a four-wheel-drive vehicle (only the main highways are showploughed), and you'll have to be well togged up in order to endure anything but the shortest of walks. Wherever you are in winter, some form of hat or head covering is absolutely essential.

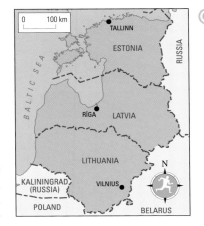

Even when the **spring** thaw sets in, the countryside can remain grey and barren until well into April (or even May in northern Estonia), when a sudden explosion of colour transforms the landscape. The countryside takes on a green lushness, drawing cattle and horses out from their winter barns, while city-dwellers indulge in a frenzied stampede for the pavement cafés.

Average daily maximum temperatures in degrees centigrade

	Jan	Feb	Mar	Apr	May	Jun	Jul	Aug	Sep	Oct	Nov	Dec
Vilnius	-5	-3	1	12	18	21	23	22	17	11	4	-3
Rīga	-4	-3	2	10	16	21	22	21	17	11	4	-2
Tallinn	-4	-4	0	7	14	19	20	19	15	10	3	-1

27

things not to miss

It's not possible to see everything the Baltic States have to offer in one trip – and we don't suggest you try. What follows, in no particular order, is a selective taste of the region's highlights – unforgettable cities, outstanding architecture and natural wonders. You can browse through to find the very best things to see, do and experience, arranged in five colour-coded categories. All highlights have a page reference to take you straight into the guide, where you can find out more.

01 Erratic boulders Page **132** • Enigmatic lumps of rock left behind long ago by retreating glaciers lie scattered along the shores of the Lahemaa National Park.

02 Bogs Page **39** • The Baltic region is especially rich in these bewitchingly barren landscapes of squelchy mosses and stunted trees.

04 Rīgas melnais balzams
Page **174** • Many locals swear by the elixir-like qualities of the gloopy, herb-flavoured spirit that is Rīga Black Balsam – just don't be surprised if it turns out to be something of an acquired taste.

03 Hill of Crosses Page **393** • Bristling with crosses, statues and wood-carved shrines, this otherworldly pilgrimage site packs a powerful spiritual punch.

05 **Rīga** Page **181** • The Baltic States' one true metropolis, Rīga can muster the kind of architectural monuments that any capital city would be proud of – including one of the biggest collections of Art Nouveau buildings in Europe.

06 **Vilsandi National Park** Page **116** • Pebble-strewn shores, juniper thickets and lonely lighthouses on Saaremaa's northwestern coast.

07 Potato pancakes Page **289**
• Served with lashings of sour cream and bacon bits, these delicious pancakes are the perfect introduction to the Lithuanian love of the potato.

09 Going to jail in Liepāja
Page **251** • Take a tour of the cells, or even spend a night in them, at the former Soviet naval prison at Karosta, Liepāja.

08 Vilnius Old Town Page **309** •
Every one of Vilnius's cobbled alleys seems to have a magnificent church at the end of it, and the Baroque masterpiece that is St John's is no exception.

10 Piusa sand caves Page
166 • These eerie man-made caverns make for one of the more offbeat attractions of southeast Estonia.

11 **Tallinn** Page **64** • Tallinn's Old Town is an addictive warren of maze-like alleys and medieval squares.

12 Kumu Art Museum Page **86** • As well as showcasing Estonian past and present, Tallinn's bold new art museum is an attraction in itself.

13 Skamba skamba kankliai Page **291** • The most intimate and accessible of Baltic folk festivals, with performances in the streets and courtyards of Vilnius's Old Town.

14 Rīga Open-air Ethnographic Museum Page **212** • For an insight into how nineteenth-century Latvians used to live, visit this vast ensemble of timber-built farmhouses gathered from all over the country.

15 Trakai Page **342** • This wonderfully restored island fortress recalls the grandeur of Lithuania's medieval empire, which once stretched from the Baltic to the Black Sea.

16 Saaremaa Page **106** • Enjoy weather-beaten coastal wilderness, castles and windmills on Estonia's most enchanting island.

18 The Madonna of the Gate of Dawn Page **318** •
This mysterious and much-revered image has watched over the people of Vilnius for over three centuries.

19 Rundāle Palace, western Latvia Page **226** •
The Baltic aristocracy certainly knew a thing or two about interiors, as the beautifully restored ballrooms and bedchambers of this Rococo country palace attest.

17 Gauja National Park Page **257** • Dramatic sandstone cliffs and virgin forests combine to make the unspoilt Gauja Latvia's most beautiful valley.

21

20 **Jewish heritage** Page **210** • Both Lithuania and Latvia were home to a flourishing Jewish civilization before World War II. The Holocaust memorial in Rīga's Bikernieki forest is a fitting and eloquent monument to its disappearance.

21 **Pape** Page **253** • A magnificently unspoilt stretch of coastal heath in southern Latvia, famous for its free-roaming herd of wild horses.

22 **Āraiši lake village** Page **268** • This quietly impressive replica of a ninth-century log-built settlement evokes the simplicity and harshness of life in ancient Latvia.

23 **Tartu** Page **142** • An invitingly easy-going university town with an attractive jumble of historic buildings and plenty of student-filled pubs.

27 **Nida** Page **408** • Silky-smooth beaches and towering dunes add an air of Saharan grandeur to this popular summer resort on the Curonian Spit.

Basics

Basics

Getting there

From the UK and Ireland the most convenient way of getting to the Baltic States is to fly – there's a reasonable choice of direct and non-direct flights taking from three to five hours respectively, whereas the overland journey by car, train or coach can easily run to two or three days. While there are no direct flights to the Baltic capitals from North America or Australasia, plenty of airlines offer one- or two-stop connections. Budget deals from either continent are often hard to find however – it may work out cheaper to get a bargain flight to a Western European destination and continue your journey by land. It's relatively easy to combine a visit to the Baltic States with a more general trip around northeastern Europe, with Poland to the west and Scandinavia to the north providing plenty in the way of bus and ferry links respectively.

When it comes to buying **flights**, it's worth bearing in mind that while some airlines have fixed return fares which don't change from one month to the next, others depend very much on the **season**, with high season being from early June to mid-September, when the weather is at its best; fares drop during the "shoulder" seasons – mid-September to the end of October and mid-April to early June – and you'll get the best prices during the low season, November to mid-April (excluding Christmas and New Year when prices are hiked up and seats are at a premium). Note also that flying at weekends is generally more expensive; price ranges quoted below assume midweek travel, unless otherwise stated.

You can often cut costs by going through a specialist flight agent – either a **consolidator**, who buys up blocks of tickets from the airlines and sells them at a discount, or a **discount agent**, who in addition to dealing with discounted flights may also offer special student and youth fares, as well as a range of other travel-related services such as travel insurance, rail passes, car rentals, tours and the like.

Flights from the UK and Ireland

The Latvian capital of **Rīga** is the easiest to get to from the UK and Ireland, with direct flights from London, Liverpool, Glasgow and Dublin. Good transport connections between Rīga and other Baltic cities ensure that it is perfectly feasible to fly into Rīga and continue

your journey to another Baltic State by land. In addition, the Estonian capital **Tallinn**, the Lithuanian capital **Vilnius** and Lithuania's second city **Kaunas** are served by daily direct flights from London. Competition between airlines is fierce, and cheap deals to all the above cities are not difficult to come by, providing you book over the Internet at least a month in advance.

Low-cost airline Ryanair flies to Rīga from London Stansted (daily), Liverpool (three times weekly), Glasgow (three times weekly) and Dublin (daily); and to Kaunas from London Stansted and Dublin (both daily). Easyjet flies daily from London Stansted to Tallinn. **Fares** with both of these airlines can be very cheap indeed if you book well in advance and avoid the summer season. If you book at peak times or at short notice, one-way prices on these flights can rise to £150/€220.

The **national carriers** are also worth considering. Latvian carrier Air Baltic flies daily from London Gatwick to Rīga and Vilnius, and from Dublin to Rīga. Lithuanian carrier FlyLal also flies daily from London Gatwick to Vilnius and from Dublin to Vilnius, while Estonian Air operates daily flights from London Gatwick to Tallinn and from Dublin to Tallinn. Booking out-of-season flights well in advance can get you return **fares** for as little as £80/€120 on the above routes – although in summer you could well be paying in advance of £300/€435 return.

Depending on where in the UK or Ireland you live, you might save money by shopping around for **indirect flights**, which involve changing planes at a European hub. Peak-season flights from Manchester to the Baltic capitals (with CSA via Prague, for example, or with Lufthansa via Frankfurt) weigh in at around £250; while services from Glasgow to Vilnius and Tallinn (with KLM via Amsterdam or SAS via Copenhagen) would cost in the region of £300. Flights from Belfast are more expensive, and it makes sense to head for Dublin or London and pick up a flight from there.

Flights to the Baltics are rarely advertised in the travel pages of newspapers and magazines, so your best sources of information will be discount flight agents (see p.33) or the airlines themselves (see p.32).

An increasing number of tour operators are including Vilnius, Rīga and Tallinn in their city-break brochures. This is an excellent way of getting a flight-plus-accommodation **package** at a reasonable price – the comfortable three- to four-star hotels used by tour operators would probably work out more expensive if you tried to book them independently. A **three-night city break** in one of the Baltic capitals costs somewhere in the region of £320–370 in the low season, rising to £400–470 in high season, with additional nights costing £40–60 depending on the hotel. Prices assume that you're departing from London – add-on fares for Birmingham, Manchester and elsewhere can be pretty hefty.

In addition, several specialist companies offer **general Baltic tours** taking in all three capitals and a few outlying attractions. Prices vary according to group size and hotel quality, but expect to pay upwards of £900 for a week-long tour taking in a little of all three states, and from £1200 for a two-week trip. **Baltic specialists** (see p.34), such as Regent Holidays and Baltic Holidays, are the best places to enquire about tailor-made itineraries and special-interest tours.

Flights from the US and Canada

Although there are no direct flights **from North America** to the Baltic States, there are plenty of indirect routings to choose from. If you're departing from one of North America's gateway cities you'll probably only have to change planes once – otherwise,

a two-stop flight seems more likely. Flying **from Canada**, airlines such as CSA, KLM, LOT and Lufthansa offer one-stop connections with Baltic capitals.

Fares vary widely according to which Baltic capital you're flying to and which city you're setting out from, and it might make sense to fly to whichever Baltic destination offers the cheapest return fares, then continue your trip by land. One money-saving option is to fly to the UK with a low-cost airline, and continue your journey to the Baltics with another budget carrier such as Ryanair or easyJet (see p.27). The best fares tend to be with north European airlines with frequent Baltic connections: flying **from New York** to Vilnius, Rīga or Tallinn with Finnair (via Helsinki) or SAS (via Copenhagen), for example, currently costs around US$900 in low season, US$1250 high. Return fares **from Chicago** to the Baltic capitals with SAS or LOT (via Warsaw) cost around US$1000 and US$1500 respectively. From elsewhere in North America, the cheapest scheduled fares to the Baltic capitals fluctuate between US$1500 and US$2000 return – although it's always worth looking out for special seasonal fares. A typical peak-season return fare **from Toronto** to Rīga, Tallinn or Vilnius weighs in at Can$1550.

A small but growing number of companies operate **organized tours** to the Baltic States, ranging from city breaks to two-week cultural tours of the whole region. Booking a flights-plus-accommodation deal through a specialist travel agent (see p.34) can often work out cheaper than organizing things yourself. Group tours tend to be more expensive, ranging in price from US$1500 for seven days to US$2200 for a fortnight, not including flights from North America.

Flights from Australia and New Zealand

Although one-stop flights **from Australia** to the Baltics do exist (typical routings involve European hubs such as London, Frankfurt or Vienna), they tend to be expensive, with the average return fare from Sydney/Melbourne/Perth to Tallinn, Rīga or Vilnius hovering around the Aus$4000 mark. Cheaper deals involve a combination of airlines and two stops en route. Australia–Kuala Lumpur–Amsterdam–Vilnius, or Australia–Bangkok–Helsinki–Tallinn are two typical routings. **Fares** on these routes range from Aus$2200 in low season to Aus$2700 in high season.

From New Zealand, Air New Zealand operates daily flights from Auckland to London and Frankfurt, where you can pick up connecting flights to the Baltic capitals. All other flights from New Zealand involve at least two stops. Return fares start at around NZ$4000 in low season, rising to NZ$4900 in high season.

You might save money by picking up a budget flight to the UK and continuing your journey with a low-cost airline from there (see "Flights from the UK and Ireland", p.27, for some suggestions); if you want to see the country as part of a wider trip across Europe, it might be worth your while considering a European rail pass (see p.30).

There's a small number of **package-tour operators** (see p.34) offering holidays in the Baltic States from Australia and New Zealand, including accommodation, sightseeing packages and rail passes.

Fly less – stay longer! Travel and climate change

Climate change is the single biggest issue facing our planet. It is caused by a build-up in the atmosphere of carbon dioxide and other greenhouse gases, which are emitted by many sources – including planes. Already, flights account for around 3–4 percent of human-induced global warming: that figure may sound small, but it is rising year on year and threatens to counteract the progress made by reducing greenhouse emissions in other areas.

Rough Guides regards travel, overall, as a global benefit, and feels strongly that the advantages to developing economies are important, as are the opportunities for greater contact and awareness among peoples. But we all have a responsibility to limit our personal "carbon footprint". That means giving thought to how often we fly and what we can do to redress the harm that our trips create.

Flying and climate change

Pretty much every form of motorized travel generates CO_2, but planes are particularly bad offenders, releasing large volumes of greenhouse gases at altitudes where their impact is far more harmful. Flying also allows us to travel much further than we would contemplate doing by road or rail, so the emissions attributable to each passenger become truly shocking. For example, one person taking a return flight between Europe and California produces the equivalent impact of 2.5 tonnes of CO_2 – similar to the yearly output of the average UK car.

Less harmful planes may evolve but it will be decades before they replace the current fleet – which could be too late for avoiding climate chaos. In the meantime, there are limited options for concerned travellers: to reduce the amount we travel by air (take fewer trips, stay longer!), to avoid night flights (when plane contrails trap heat from Earth but can't reflect sunlight back to space) and to make the trips we do take "climate neutral" via a carbon offset scheme.

Carbon offset schemes

Offset schemes run by climatecare.org, carbonneutral.com and others allow you to "neutralize" the greenhouse gases that you are responsible for releasing. Their websites have simple calculators that let you work out the impact of any flight. Once that's done, you can pay to fund projects that will reduce future carbon emissions by an equivalent amount (such as the distribution of low-energy light bulbs and cooking stoves in developing countries). Please take the time to visit our website and make your trip climate neutral.

Ⓦ**www.roughguides.com/climatechange**

By train

Travelling to the Baltic States **by train from the UK** is more expensive than flying, but it gives you the option of stopping off in other parts of Europe on the way. From Western Europe there's only one route into the Baltics – the line from Warsaw in Poland to Vilnius in Lithuania. Beyond Vilnius, the Baltic rail network itself is pretty limited, and onward travel to Rīga and Tallinn will most likely be by bus.

The main **London–Vilnius** itinerary runs via Brussels, Cologne, Berlin and Warsaw, and takes about 45 hours if you're lucky with connections – somewhat longer if you cross the Channel by ferry rather than taking the Eurostar. Buying a through ticket for this route isn't easy: most major UK train stations can sell tickets as far as Brussels, but are rarely equipped to deal with destinations beyond. The agents who specialize in international train journeys (see "Rail Contacts" p.34) may be able to book your passage as far as Warsaw, but are unlikely to sell tickets further east. The price of a return ticket from London to Warsaw using Eurostar hovers around the £220 mark – to this you'll need to add a further £30–40 to cover the Warsaw–Vilnius leg. The trip will work out slightly cheaper if you cross the Channel by ferry, but as none of the ticket agents sells through tickets on continental journeys not using Eurostar, you'll have to buy tickets as you go.

Rail passes

If you're travelling across Europe by train, it's worth considering one of the many **rail passes** available, covering regions as well as individual countries. None of them actually extends to the Baltic States themselves, but they're a useful way of getting across most of the other countries on the way. Some passes have to be bought before leaving home, while others can only be bought in the country for which they're valid. For rail ticket agents, see p.34.

Inter-Rail passes are only available to European residents, and you'll be asked to provide proof of residency before being allowed to purchase one. They come in over-26 and (cheaper) under-26 versions, and cover 31 countries. Lithuania, Latvia and Estonia are not covered by Inter-Rail, but it does include Belgium, Germany and Poland.

A pass for five days' travel in a ten-day period (£175 for adults, £110 for the under-26s) will get you to the Baltic States and back but won't give you much time to look around while you're there; it may be preferable to purchase a pass for ten days' travel within a 22-day period (£225 and £168 respectively) or a pass for one month's continuous travel (£425 and £282). Inter-Rail passes do not include travel between Britain and the Continent, although pass holders are eligible for discounts on rail travel in the UK and cross-Channel ferries.

Non-European residents qualify for the **Eurail Global pass**, which must be purchased before arrival in Europe (or from Rail Europe in London by non-residents who were unable to get it at home). The pass allows unlimited free first-class train travel in seventeen European countries, including Belgium and Germany but not Poland or the Baltic States – so you'll have to buy a regular ticket to cover the last leg of the journey. The pass is available in increments of fifteen

Useful publications

The red-covered Thomas Cook European Timetables details schedules of over 50,000 trains in Europe, as well as timings of over two hundred ferry routes and rail-connecting bus services. It's updated and issued every month; the main changes are in the June edition (published end of May), which has details of the summer European schedules, and the October one (published end of Sept), which includes winter schedules; some have advance summer/winter timings also. The book can be purchased online (which gets you a ten percent discount) at ⓦ www.thomascooktimetables.com or from branches of Thomas Cook (see ⓦ www.thomascook.co.uk for your nearest branch), and costs £11.50. Their useful Rail Map of Europe (regular price £8.95) also comes with an online discount.

days ($675), 21 days ($877) and one month ($1088). A **Eurail Global Flexi pass** will give you ten days' first-class travel in a two-month period for $798. If you're under 26, you can save money with a **Eurail Global Youthpass** ($440 for fifteen days, $708 for one month, or $519 for ten days' travel in a two-month period). Further details of these passes and other Eurail permutations can be found on ⓦ www.raileurope.com.

By bus

Given the increased number of low-cost airlines flying to the Baltic States, attempting the journey by bus is unlikely to save you a great deal of money. **Eurolines** (see p.35) operates daily services from London to Rīga, taking something in the order of 45 hours. Some services are direct, others involve a change in either Antwerp or Brussels. It's not as gruelling an experience as you might think, with drivers making refreshment stops at regular intervals, although the experience of spending the best part of two days in the same seat will not be to everyone's taste. Tickets to Rīga cost £149 return, with a ten percent reduction for under-26s and seniors.

If you're travelling **from Ireland**, there are Eurolines services to London from Dublin, Cork, Killarney, Limerick, Tralee and Belfast.

By car and ferry

Driving to the Baltic States involves a long haul of 1800km from Calais or Ostend to the Lithuanian border, followed by a further 170km, 360km or 660km to Vilnius, Rīga or Tallinn respectively. Using the motorways of Belgium, Holland and northern Germany, you'll find the first 1000km of the journey are reasonably straightforward and might easily be covered in a couple of days' hard driving. From the Polish border onwards however, roads are mostly single carriageway and are not always in the best state of repair – you'll have to adopt a leisurely approach to the Polish leg of the journey if you want to arrive with your nerves intact.

The most convenient **Channel crossings** are on the P&O Stena services from Dover/Folkestone to Calais, Hoverspeed to Ostend, or Eurotunnel's Le Shuttle Channel Tunnel

option from Folkestone to Calais. Once in Calais or Ostend, you can pick up the main motorway route east through Belgium and beyond, bypassing Brussels, Düsseldorf, Hannover and Berlin on the way.

You can cut down the driving distance by taking one of the thrice-weekly Scandinavian Seaways **sailings from Harwich to Hamburg** (19hr), or the nightly P&O Ferries service **from Hull to Rotterdam** (14hr).

If you don't fancy driving across Poland, you could consider a handful of **ferry options from northern Europe** that would cut the country out of your itinerary. Scandline operate a weekly sailing **from Arhus** in Denmark to Klaipėda in Lithuania (45hr) and a four-times-weekly ferry from Rostock in Germany to Ventspils in Latvia. There are also thrice-weekly sailings operated by Lisco **from Kiel** to Klaipėda (20hr), **Sassnitz** (a small port northeast of Rostock) to Klaipėda (21hr) and **Lübeck** to Rīga (32hr). Finally, **Rostock** is the departure point for twice-weekly Scandlines services to Liepāja in Latvia (19hr).

A more time-consuming but undoubtedly rewarding way of getting to the Baltic States is to cross the North Sea to Scandinavia, before catching a Baltic-bound ferry from the Swedish ports of Stockholm or Karlshamn. DFDS operates a twice-weekly service from **Newcastle to Stavanger** (20hr) and **Bergen** (27hr) in Norway, from where it's a 700-kilometre drive to Stockholm. For details of ferries from Stockholm and Karlshamn to the Baltic States, see p.32.

From Poland

Travelling overland from Poland to the Baltics is very cheap, with train and bus tickets from Warsaw to the Lithuanian capital Vilnius rarely exceeding €30/£20/US$38 each way. Daily **bus services** operate from Warsaw's Warszawa Zachodnia terminal to Vilnius (8–10hr). There are also services from Gdańsk to Vilnius daily (12hr; overnight), Olsztyn to Vilnius five days a week (8hr; overnight) and Kraków to Vilnius twice a week (16hr; overnight). A daily bus from Warsaw travels to Rīga via Białystok (18hr).

A direct **train** runs from **Warsaw to Vilnius** daily; otherwise head for the near-border town of Suwałki, from where there are two trains a day to Šeštokai on the Lithuanian side of the frontier, each of which is met by a connecting service to Kaunas and Vilnius.

There are **flights** too, though at around €180/£125/US$240, they're not much of a bargain. The Polish national carrier LOT operates daily flights from Warsaw to Vilnius and Rīga.

From Finland

One of the most popular jumping-off points for travel into the Baltic States is the Finnish capital **Helsinki**, with five **ferry** companies – Eckerö Line, Lindaline, Tallink, Silja Line and Nordic Jet Line – offering daily services to the Estonian capital **Tallinn**. The 85-kilometre crossing takes three and a half hours in the older, larger ferries operated by Eckerö and Tallink, and about half that time in the more modern catamarans (note that catamarans only run when the sea is free of ice – usually mid-March to late December).

All services depart from Helsinki's South Harbour, an easy ten-minute walk from central train and bus stations. The terminals for Eckerö Line, Lindaline, Tallink and Silja Line are located on the western side of the harbour; Nordic Jet Line is on the east.

From Sweden

Sweden enjoys ferry links with all three Baltic States and, although crossings involve spending one night on the boat, fares are reasonable enough to make this a good budget alternative to flying.

From Stockholm, Tallink operates overnight ferries to both Tallinn and Rīga. The port of **Karlshamn**, 350km southwest of Stockholm, is the departure point for both Lisco's thrice-weekly ferry to Liepāja in Latvia and Scandlines' thrice-weekly services to Ventspils in Latvia. Note that Karlshamn ferry terminal is 4km west of town, and there's no public transport – so foot passengers should budget for the cost of a taxi.

Airlines, agents and operators

Online booking

Ⓦ **www.expedia.co.uk** Discount airfares and daily deals. Search and book flights, hotels, cars

and packages worldwide (UK only; for US Ⓦ www.expedia.com; for Canada, Ⓦ www.expedia.ca).

Ⓦ **www.lastminute.com** Offers good last-minute holiday package and flight-only deals (UK only; for Australia, Ⓦ www.lastminute.com.au).

Ⓦ **www.opodo.co.uk** UK site offering flight, hotel and car deals, as well as city-break and last-minute deals.

Ⓦ **www.orbitz.com** US site with packages, and individual trips, flight and hotel deals worldwide.

Ⓦ **www.travelocity.co.uk** Destination guides and deals on car rental, accommodation and lodging, as well as fares. (UK only; for US, Ⓦ www.travelocity.com; for Canada Ⓦ www.travelocity.ca).

Ⓦ **www.zuji.com.au** Australian website searching airlines, hotels and package deals for the best prices. (Australia only; for New Zealand, Ⓦ www.zuji.co.nz).

Airlines

Air Baltic UK ☎ 01293/555 700, Ⓦ www.airbaltic.com. Flights from London Gatwick to Rīga and Vilnius; flights from Dublin to Riga.

Air Canada ☎ 1-888/247-2262, Ⓦ www.aircanada.com. Flights from Canada to major European hubs, with onward connections to the Baltics handled by a partner airline.

Air New Zealand Australia ☎ 13 24 76, New Zealand ☎ 0800/737 000, Ⓦ www.airnz.co.nz. Daily flights from Auckland to London via Los Angeles, then onward connections to Rīga, Tallinn and Vilnius.

American Airlines ☎ 1-800/433-7300, Ⓦ www.aa.com. Flights from North American cities to major European hubs.

Austrian Airlines US ☎ 1-800/843-0002, Canada ☎ 1888-8174/444, UK ☎ 0870/124 2625, Republic of Ireland ☎ 1800/509 142, Australia ☎ 1800/642 438 or 02/9251 6155, Ⓦ www.aua.com. Flights from London, Toronto, Montreal, New York and Washington to Vilnius, changing planes in Vienna. Also Melbourne and Sydney to Vilnius via Vienna.

bmi US ☎ 1-800/788-0555 Ⓦ www.flybmi.com. Flights from Washington and Chicago to Manchester, with onward connections to the Baltic capitals.

British Airways US and Canada ☎ 1-800/AIRWAYS, UK ☎ 0870/850 9850, Republic of Ireland ☎ 1890/626 747, Australia ☎ 1300/767 177, New Zealand ☎ 09/966 9777, Ⓦ www.ba.com. Daily to London from several North American cities, and from Sydney, Melbourne or Perth with onward connections to the Baltic capitals.

Continental Airlines US and Canada ☎ 1-800/523-3273, UK ☎ 0845/607 6760,

International ☏1800/231 0856, 🖒www
.continental.com. Daily flights from various North
American cities to most major European hubs, with
onward connections to Baltic capitals.
CSA (Czech Airlines) US ☏1-800/223-2365,
Canada ☏416-363/3174, UK ☏0870/444 3747,
Republic of Ireland ☏0818/200 014, Australia
☏61/82480 000, 🖒www.czechairlines.co.uk.
Flights to Rīga and Vilnius from UK airports such
as Birmingham, London and Manchester, changing
in Prague. Also to Rīga and Vilnius from New York,
Washington and Toronto, changing in Prague.
Delta Air Lines US and Canada ☏1-800/221-
1212, UK ☏0845/600 0950, Republic of Ireland
☏1850/882 031 or 01/407 3165, Australia
☏1300/302 849, New Zealand ☏09/9772232,
🖒www.delta.com. Flights to Stockholm, London
and other European hubs with onward connections to
Tallinn, Rīga and Vilnius.
easyJet UK ☏0905/821 0905, 🖒www.easyjet
.com. Daily flights from London Stansted to Tallinn.
Also from Berlin to Tallinn and Rīga.
Estonian Airlines UK ☏020/7333 0196, Ireland
☏01/8444 300, 🖒www.estonian-air.ee. Direct
fights from London Gatwick and Dublin to Tallinn.
Finnair US ☏1-800/950-5000, UK ☏0870/241
4411, Republic of Ireland ☏01/844 6565, Australia
☏02/9244 2299, SA ☏11/339 4865/9, 🖒www
.finnair.com. Direct flights from Dublin, Heathrow
and Manchester to Helsinki, from where there are
connecting flights to Vilnius, Rīga and Tallinn. Also
flights from New York and Toronto to Tallinn, Rīga
and Vilnius, changing at Helsinki; and flights from
Australia via Bangkok or Singapore to Helsinki, with
onward connections to Tallinn, Rīga and Vilnius.
flyLAL (Lithuanian Airlines) ☏+370 5 252
5555, 🖒www.flylal.com. Direct flights from London
Gatwick to Vilnius.
KLM US and Canada ☏1-800/225-2525, UK
☏0870/507 4074, Republic of Ireland ☏1850/747
400, Australia ☏1300/392 192, New Zealand
☏09/921 6040, SA ☏11/961 6727, 🖒www
.klm.com. Flights from a range of UK, Irish, North
American and Australian airports to Amsterdam,
followed by connections to Tallinn, Rīga and Vilnius.
LOT (Polish Airlines) US ☏212-789/0970,
Canada ☏616-236/4242, UK ☏0845/601 0949,
Republic of Ireland ☏1890/359 568, 🖒www
.lot.com. Direct flights from London, Manchester,
New York, Chicago and Toronto to Warsaw, with
connecting flights to Vilnius and Rīga.
Lufthansa US ☏1-800/3995-838, Canada
☏1-800/563-5954, UK ☏0870/837 7747,
Republic of Ireland ☏01/844 5544, Australia
☏1300/655 727, New Zealand ☏0800-945 220,
SA ☏0861/842 538, 🖒www.lufthansa.com.

Flights from various UK, Irish, North American and
Australian airports to Frankfurt or Munich, with onward
connections to all three Baltic capitals.
Qantas Australia ☏13 13 13, New Zealand
☏0800/808 767 or 09/357 8900, SA ☏11/441
8550, 🖒www.qantas.com. Flights from Sydney to
Frankfurt with onward connections to Vilnius and Rīga.
Ryanair UK ☏0871/246 0000, Republic of Ireland
☏0818/303 030, 🖒www.ryanair.com. Low-cost
flights to Rīga from London Stansted, Liverpool,
Glasgow and Dublin. Also flights to Kaunas (Lithuania)
from Stansted and Dublin.
SAS Scandinavian Airlines US and Canada
☏1-800/221-2350, UK ☏0870/6072 7727,
Republic of Ireland ☏01/844 5440, Australia
☏1300/727 707, 🖒www.scandinavian.net.
Flights to all three Baltic capitals from UK, Irish, North
American and Australian airports, changing at either
Copenhagen or Stockholm.
Singapore Airlines Australia ☏13 10 11,
New Zealand ☏0800/808 909, 🖒www
.singaporeair.com. Flights from New Zealand and
Australia to major European hubs via Singapore, with
onward connections to Baltic capitals.
Thai Airways Australia ☏1300/651 960,
New Zealand ☏09/377 3886, 🖒www.thaiair
.com. Flights from Auckland to Bangkok with onward
connections to Baltic cities via Copenhagen, London,
Frankfurt or Amsterdam.
US Airways US and Canada ☏1-800/428-4322,
🖒www.usair.com. Flights from North America to
London, Frankfurt and Amsterdam, with onward
connections to the Baltic capitals.
Virgin Atlantic US ☏1-800/821-5438, 🖒www
.virgin-atlantic.com. Flights from North America to
London.
Zoom US ☏1-866-359-9666, 🖒www.flyzoom
.com. Low-cost flights from Canada and the US to
London.

Agents and operators

ebookers UK ☏0800/082 3000, Republic of
Ireland ☏01/488 3507, 🖒www.ebookers.com.
🖒www.ebookers.ie. Low fares on an extensive
selection of scheduled flights and package deals.
North South Travel UK ☏01245/608 291,
🖒www.northsouthtravel.co.uk. Friendly,
competitive travel agency, offering discounted fares
worldwide. Profits are used to support projects in
the developing world, especially the promotion of
sustainable tourism.
Trailfinders UK ☏0845/058 5858, Republic of
Ireland ☏01/677 7888, Australia ☏1300/780 212,
🖒www.trailfinders.com. One of the best-informed
and most efficient agents for independent travellers.

STA Travel US ☎1-800/781-4040, UK
☎0871/2300 040, Australia ☎134 STA, New
Zealand ☎0800/474 400, SA ☎0861/781 781,
Ⓦwww.statravel.com. Worldwide specialists in
independent travel; also student IDs, travel insurance,
car rental, rail passes and more. Good discounts for
students and under-26s.

Specialist tour operators

Adventure Center US ☎1-800/228-8747 or
510/654-1879, Ⓦwww.adventurecenter.com.
Two-week Baltic tours.
Adventures Abroad US ☎1-800/665-3998,
Ⓦwww.adventures-abroad.com. A range of seven-
to twenty-day tours of the Baltic capitals, with optional
visits to St Petersburg and Warsaw thrown in.
Baltic Holidays UK ☎0870/757 9233, Ⓦwww
.lithuanianholidays.com. City breaks to the Baltic
capitals, seven- to fourteen-day tours of Lithuania,
Latvia and Estonia (either individually or in combination)
and tailor-made accommodation-plus-flights packages.
Bentours Australia ☎02/9521 1574, Ⓦwww
.bentours.com.au. Seven-day tours incorporating
the Baltic capitals, with an optional extra seven
days in Scandinavia. Also flights to the Baltics and
Scandinavia.
Eastern Eurotours Australia ☎07/5526 2855 or
1800/242 353, Ⓦwww.easterneurotours.com.au.

Flights, hotel accommodation and city breaks in the
Baltic States.
Estonia Holidays UK ☎01773/850222,
Ⓦwww.estoniaholidays.com. City breaks to Tallinn.
Explore Worldwide UK ☎0870 333 4001,
Ⓦwww.explore.co.uk. Two-week tours of Baltic
cities and national parks.
Gateway Travel Australia ☎02/9745 3333,
Ⓦwww.russian-gateway.com.au. Eastern European
and Russian specialists.
Go To Russia Travel US ☎1-888/263-0023,
Ⓦwww.gotorussia.com. City breaks in Tallinn, Rīga
and Vilnius, and tailor-made arrangements.
Isram World of Travel US ☎1-800/223-7460,
Ⓦwww.isram.com. City breaks in the Baltic capitals
and wide-ranging Baltic tours.
Martin Randall Travel UK ☎020/8742 3355,
Ⓦwww.martinrandall.com. Seven- and twelve-day
cultural tours with expert guides, taking in the main
urban sights of all three Baltic states.
Passport Travel Australia ☎03/9867 3888,
Ⓦwww.travelcentre.com.au. City breaks and Baltic
tours.
Regent Holidays UK ☎0117/921 1711, Ⓦwww
.regent-holidays.co.uk. City breaks to Tallinn, Rīga
and Vilnius. Accompanied ten- and fifteen-day tours
through the Baltics, nine-day cycling holidays on
the Estonian island of Saaremaa and tailor-made
arrangements for individual tourists.
Russian Gateway Australia ☎02/9745 3333 and
1800 700 333, Ⓦwww.russian-gateway.com.au.
City breaks, Baltic tours and tailor-made flight-
plus-accommodation packages.
Russian Travel Company UK ☎0870/366 5454,
Ⓦwww.russiantravel.co.uk. City breaks in Tallinn,
Rīga and Vilnius.
Scantours UK ☎020/7554 3530, Ⓦwww
.scantoursuk.com; US ☎1-800/223-7226,
Ⓦwww.scantours.com. City breaks in Vilnius, Rīga
and Tallinn, general Baltic tours, plus bicycle tours in
Lithuania. Also agents for European rail passes.
Travel Editions UK ☎020/7251 0045, Ⓦwww
.traveleditions.co.uk. City breaks to Tallinn and
three-city tours of the Baltic capitals.
Travellers Cities UK ☎01959/540700, Ⓦwww
.travellerscities.com. City breaks to Tallinn, Rīga
and Vilnius.
Vytis Tours US ☎1-718/423-6161, Ⓦwww
.vytistours.com. Baltic specialist offering tailor-made
accommodation-plus-flights packages, tours and
car rental.

Rail contacts

CIT World Travel Australia ☎1300 361 500,
Ⓦwww.cittravel.com.au. Eurail and Europass rail
passes.

Deutsche Bahn UK ☎08718 808 066, ⓦwww
.bahn.co.uk. Timetable information and through
ticketing on European routes.

Europrail International Canada ☎1-888/667-
9734, ⓦwww.europrail.net. Eurail, Europass and
individual country passes.

Eurostar UK ☎08705 186 186, ⓦwww.eurostar
.com. Passenger train which goes from St Pancras
International station in central London to Paris
(2hr 15min) and to Brussels (1hr 51min), and from
Ebbsfleet International station, off Junction 2 of the
M25 (journey times 10min shorter). You can get
through tickets – including the tube journey to
St Pancras International – from Eurostar itself, from
most travel agents or from mainline train stations
in Britain. Inter-Rail passes give discounts on the
Eurostar service.

Rail Europe UK ☎0870/584 8848, ⓦwww
.raileurope.co.uk; US ☎1-877/257-2887, Canada
☎1-800/361-RAIL; ⓦwww.raileurope.com/us.
Agents for Eurail, Inter-Rail and Eurostar.

Rail Plus Australia ☎1300/555 003 or 03/9642
8644, ⓦwww.railplus.com.au. Sells Eurail,
Europass, Britrail and Amtrak passes.

The Man in Seat 61 ⓦwww.seat61.com.
Enthusiast-run site packed with information on all
aspects of international rail travel, including tips on
how best to enjoy the trip to the Baltic States. Far
more reliable than many official sites.

Trailfinders Australia ☎02/9247 7666, ⓦwww
.trailfinder.com.au. All Europe passes.

Trainseurope UK ☎871 700 7722, ⓦwww
.trainseurope.co.uk. Tickets from the UK to Poland.
Inter-Rail and other individual country passes.

Channel tunnel

Eurotunnel UK ☎0870/535 3535, ⓦwww
.eurotunnel.com. Shuttle train via the Channel Tunnel
for vehicles and their passengers only. The service
runs continuously between Folkestone and Coquelles,
near Calais, with up to four departures per hour (only
one per hour midnight–6am) and takes 35min (45min
for some night departure times), though you must
arrive at least 30min before departure. It is possible
to turn up and buy your ticket at the toll booths (after
exiting the M20 at junction 11a), though at busy
times booking is advisable. Rates depend on the time
of year, time of day and length of stay; it's cheaper
to travel between 10pm and 6am, while the highest
fares are reserved for weekend departures and
returns in July and August.

Bus contacts

Eurolines UK ☎0870/580 8080, ⓦwww
.eurolines.co.uk; Republic of Ireland ☎01/836
6111, ⓦwww.eurolines.ie.

Ferry contacts

DFDS Seaways UK ☎0871 582 9955, ⓦwww
.dfds.co.uk. Harwich to Esbjerg (Denmark); Newcastle
to Bergen, Stavanger and Haugesund (Norway); and
Newcastle to Amsterdam.

Eckerö Line Finland ☎09/228 8544, ⓦwww
.eckeroline.ee. One daily Helsinki–Tallinn ferry
(3hr 30min).

Irish Ferries UK ☎0870 517 1717, Northern
Ireland ☎0818 300 400; ⓦwww.irishferries.com.
Dublin to Holyhead; Rosslare to Pembroke.

Lindaline Finland ☎09/668 9700, ⓦwww
.lindaline.fi. Six daily services from Helsinki to Tallinn
(1hr 30min).

Lisco Lithuania ☎8-46/395 051, ⓦwww.lisco
.lt. Kiel to Klaipėda; Sassnitz to Klaipėda; Lübeck to
Riga; Lübeck to Ventspils.

Nordic Jet Line Finland ☎09/681770, ⓦwww
.njl.info. Helsinki to Tallinn three times daily
(1hr 40min).

Norfolk Line UK ☎0870 1642 114, ⓦwww
.norfolkline-ferries.com. Dover to Dunkerque.

P&O UK ☎08705 980 303, ⓦwww.poferries
.com. Dover to Calais; Hull to Rotterdam; Hull to
Zeebrugge; Dublin to Liverpool.

Scandlines Denmark ☎33 15 15 15,
ⓦwww.scandlines.dk; Germany ☎01805 116
688, ⓦwww.scandlines.de; Sweden ☎042
186100, ⓦwww.scandlines.se. Arhus to Klaipėda;
Rostock to Ventspils; Karlshamn to Ventspils;
Rostock to Liepāja.

Sea Cat UK ☎0870/5523 523, Republic of Ireland
☎1800/805055; ⓦwww.seacat.co.uk. Belfast to
Stranraer, Heysham and Troon; Dublin to Liverpool.

Sea France UK ☎0870 443 1653, ⓦwww
.seafrance.com. Dover to Calais.

Stena Line UK ☎0870/570 7070, Northern Ireland
☎0870/520 4204, Republic of Ireland ☎1/204
7777, ⓦwww.stenaline.co.uk. Harwich to the Hook
of Holland.

Tallink ☎+358 600 174 552, ⓦwww.tallinksilja
.com. Car ferries (3hr 30min) and catamarans
(1hr 40min) from Helsinki to Tallinn. Also overnight
ferries from Stockholm to Riga and Stockholm to
Tallinn.

BASICS | Getting there

Getting around

The public transport network in the Baltic States is fairly comprehensive, although some of the vehicles used by bus and train companies may be rather more decrepit than their Western European counterparts. In general, buses are both more frequent and quicker than trains; trains are restricted to commuter lines around the major cities and a meagre handful of inter-city routes. International rail and bus passes (see pp.30–31) are not valid for the Baltic States, but regular ticket prices are reasonably cheap. A one-way bus ticket from Tallinn to Vilnius costs around £20/€30/$38; Rīga–Vilnius or Rīga–Tallinn comes to around £10/€15/$19; inter-city routes within each country are considerably cheaper.

Buses are your best means of getting from one Baltic state to another, with express services taking about five hours to travel from Tallinn to Rīga and the same again from Rīga to Vilnius. **Flights** between the capitals take only 45 minutes, but are ten times more expensive than buses. For further information about public transport, see each country's "Getting around" section and the "Travel details" at the end of every chapter.

Car rental in the Baltic States works out at about £41–48/€60–70/US$78–90 a day and £240–275/€350–400/US$450–525 a week for a small car with unlimited mileage if you go through one of the big firms, slightly less if you go through a smaller local operator. You may well find it more convenient to arrange car rental before setting off; the big international operators have agents throughout the Baltic States.

Car rental agencies

Avis US and Canada ☏ 1-800/331-1212, UK ☏ 0870/606 0100, Republic of Ireland ☏ 021/428 1111, Australia ☏ 13 63 33 or 02/9353 9000, New Zealand ☏ 09/526 2847 or 0800/655 111, ⓦ www.avis.com.

Budget US ☏ 1-800/527-0700, Canada ☏ 1-800/268-8900, UK ☏ 0870/156 5656, Australia ☏ 1300/362 848, New Zealand ☏ 0800/283 438, ⓦ www.budget.com.

Europcar US & Canada ☏ 1-877/940 6900, UK ☏ 0870/607 5000, Republic of Ireland ☏ 01/614 2800, Australia ☏ 393/306 160, ⓦ www.europcar.com.

Hertz US & Canada ☏ 1-800/654-3131, UK ☏ 020/7026 0077, Republic of Ireland ☏ 01/870 5777, New Zealand ☏ 0800/654 321, ⓦ www.hertz.com.

Holiday Autos US ☏ 866-392/9288, UK ☏ 0870/400 4461, Republic of Ireland ☏ 01/872 9366, Australia ☏ 299/394 433, SA ☏ 11/2340 597, ⓦ www.holidayautos.co.uk.

SIXT US ☏ 1-877/347-3227, UK ☏ 0800/4747 4227, Republic of Ireland ☏ 1850/206 088, ⓦ www.irishcarrentals.ie.

Accommodation

The hotel market has witnessed a considerable shake-up in recent years, with the construction of new business-oriented hotels and the arrival of international franchises, alongside the privatization and refurbishment of old state-run establishments. There are plenty of budget options in the form of family-run B&Bs, backpacker-related hostels and some enjoyably rough-and-ready campsites.

Hotels

These days, the standard and range of **hotel accommodation** in the major cities and resorts of the Baltic States approaches that of Western Europe. With Vilnius, Rīga and Tallinn becoming popular city-break destinations, hotels often offer special weekend deals, while establishments in coastal areas drop their prices dramatically outside the peak summer season – it always pays to ask.

In provincial towns the quality of accommodation is much more unpredictable, with smart hotels aimed at the modern business traveller rubbing shoulders with Soviet-era establishments that rejoice in gloomy furnishings and mildewed shower curtains. Many of the best deals are in family-run **guesthouses and B&Bs**, especially in rural areas, where down-on-the-farm **homestays** are increasingly being promoted by local tourist authorities. More details, together with a guide to prices, are given under each country's "Accommodation" section.

Hostels and camping

There is a growing number of backpacker-friendly **hostels** in the Baltic capitals – especially in Rīga, where new hostels are opening up all the time. The quantity – and quality – of hostels in the provinces is much more unpredictable. Many of the hostel-type establishments In Vilnius, Tallinn and Rīga are affiliated to the **Hostelling International (HI)** organization, membership of which will get you a discount of ten percent or more on the price of accommodation.

You can join Hostelling International before leaving home (for contact details, see below) or when you get to the Baltic States; the addresses of the relevant national hostelling organizations are given in each country's "Accommodation" section.

There are only a handful of **campsites** in the Baltic States equipped with washing facilities, toilet blocks and other amenities. Others have primitive earth toilets and – if you're lucky – a tap for drinking water, while many are simply fields with tent space and clearings for lighting fires, but no other facilities.

Youth hostel associations

UK and Ireland

Youth Hostel Association (YHA) ☎0870/770 8868, ⓦ www.yha.org.uk. England and Wales.
Scottish Youth Hostel Association ☎01786/891 400, ⓦ www.syha.org.uk.
Irish Youth Hostel Association ☎01/830 4555, ⓦ www.irelandyha.org. Republic of Ireland.
Hostelling International Northern Ireland ☎028/9031 5435, ⓦ www.hini.org.uk.

US and Canada

Hostelling International-American Youth Hostels US ☎1-301/495-1240, ⓦ www.hiayh.org.
Hostelling International Canada ☎1-800/663-5777, ⓦ www.hihostels.ca.

Australia and New Zealand

Australia Youth Hostels Association Australia ☎02/9565 1699, ⓦ www.yha.com.au.
Youth Hostelling Association New Zealand ☎0800/278 299 or 03/379 9970, ⓦ www.yha.co.nz.

The media

Specific information on Estonian, Latvian and Lithuanian newspapers, magazines and TV can be found under each individual country's "Media" section.

A small number of useful English-language publications are available Baltic-wide. Prime among these is the *Baltic Times* (ⓦwww.baltictimes.com), a pan-Baltic weekly newspaper based in Rīga. Published every Thursday, it carries a mixture of local news, features and business info, and also contains entertainment listings for the coming weekend. It is sold in newspaper kiosks in all three Baltic capitals and in a few provincial cities like Kaunas in Lithuania and Tartu in Estonia, but is hard to get hold of elsewhere.

Other handy publications are the small-format city guides produced by *In Your Pocket* (ⓦwww.inyourpocket.com). Incorporating information on accommodation, eating, drinking and sightseeing, their separate publications on Tallinn, Rīga and Vilnius

(each updated every two months) are lively, opinionated and up-to-date – and are also an invaluable source of Yellow-Pages-style information. The same company produces guides to Tartu and Pärnu in Estonia and Kaunas and Klaipēda in Lithuania, each of which is updated annually. The guides are on sale in big bookshops in the three Baltic capitals, but can be hard to find in the provinces.

The main international English-language **radio** broadcasters can be picked up on long wave throughout the region, but frequencies change from one time of day to the next: check the websites of the BBC (ⓦwww.bbc.co.uk/worldservice), Radio Canada (ⓦwww.rcinet.ca) and Voice of America (ⓦwww.voa.gov) for further information.

Outdoor activities

For many visitors, the wide range of outdoor pursuits that the Baltic States have to offer constitutes the region's chief allure. Indeed, if you like the outdoors it's a truly wonderful place, abounding in dense forests, secluded lakes, long, sandy beaches and large tracts of wilderness rich in wildlife. Best of all, you won't find the countryside overcrowded – there's plenty of space to get away from it all.

Hiking

Despite the absence of anything remotely resembling a mountain, the low-lying Baltic States offer a rich menu of hiking possibilities. If you like forests, then you'll love the **woodland trails** on offer in Estonia's Lahemaa National Park (see p.130) or the Dzūkija National Park in Lithuania (see p.380), where it's possible to walk for miles without

seeing another soul. The Gauja National Park in Latvia (see p.257) probably offers the most exciting terrain, with lush woodland, knobbly hills and twisting riverbanks overlooked by ruddy sandstone cliffs.

The forests support a variety of **fauna** – you're certain to catch sight of roe deer during your stay, beavers abound wherever there are streams, and if you're lucky you might also see wild boar, moose, elk or even bears.

It's easy to combine a forest hike with traditional activities like **berry-picking** in summer and **mushrooming** in autumn – although for the latter activity you really need to know what you're looking for. You're usually banned from picking the cranberries that cover the region's **peat bogs**, a number of which have become important nature conservation areas. Many of these regions of mosses, stunted conifers and marshy pools can be explored via specially constructed wooden walkways – most notably in the Soomaa National Park in Estonia (see p.123), the Ķemeri National Park in Latvia (see p.235) and the Čepkelių Nature Reserve in Lithuania (see p.383).

If a short, non-strenuous nature walk is what you're after, then there are plenty of well-maintained paths through areas of natural beauty, with signboards along the route detailing the local flora and fauna – good examples are the Slītere Nature Trail near Cape Kolka in Latvia (see p.233), Tervete Nature Park in southern Latvia (see p.230) and the Šeirė Nature Trail in western Lithuania (see p.421).

If you do want to climb a hill, then consider **Suur-Munamägi** in southern Estonia, which at 318m above sea level is the highest point in the Baltic States, and the vicinity offers plenty of other wooded heights to explore.

Finally, the glorious expanses of sand that run almost uninterruptedly along the Baltic coast provide any number of opportunities for **beach walking**. While the Sahara-esque dunescapes around Nida in Lithuania can't be matched in terms of spectacle, the wild beauty of Cape Kolka in Latvia shouldn't be overlooked. Beach walkers can try their luck hunting for amber, especially after storms, when tiny nuggets of the stuff are washed up along the coast – especially the stretch between Liepāja and Ventspils in Latvia.

Canoeing

Large stretches of the Baltic landscape are dotted with lakes, and it's relatively easy to rent a variety of watercraft. The number of navigable waterways ensures that there's a host of **canoeing and kayaking** itineraries to choose from, often involving overnight stops at campsites en route. The most popular routes involve the Gauja and Abava rivers

in Latvia, the lakes of the Aukštaitija National Park in northeastern Lithuania and the Ūla and Merkys rivers in southern Lithuania. In Estonia's Soomaa National Park, you can try your hand at paddling a *haabja*, a traditional canoe hewn from a single trunk of aspen.

Cycling

Although few places in the Baltic States are equipped with cycle paths or cycle lanes, the flat, quiet country roads of many rural areas are ideally suited to exploration by bike. Unfortunately, the business of **bike rental** has yet to be developed in many areas, but it shouldn't be too difficult to pick up a bicycle from agencies in the major national parks and in regions where cycling is beginning to take off – notably the islands of Saaremaa and Hiiumaa in Estonia and the Curonian Spit in Lithuania.

Birdwatching

Occupying a key position on north–south migration routes, the Baltic States are visited by hundreds of **bird species** every year. Most visible of these are white storks, which arrive in their thousands every spring and proceed to set up home on roofs and telegraph poles all over the region – with many birds returning to the same nesting spot year after year. Fish-rich wetland areas bordering the Baltic coast attract many migrating birds that have been all but squeezed out of Western Europe by intensive farming – bitterns, corncrakes, black storks, cranes, mute swans and all manner of geese, among them. Many wetland areas have been declared protected zones, some of which are totally off-limits to visitors, although you'll usually be able to make use of observation towers on the edges of these reserves.

Key areas for birdwatching **in Estonia** include the Lahemaa National Park (🌐www.lahemaa.ee), Vilsandi National Park on the island of Saaremaa (🌐www.saaremaa.ee) and the Matsalu Nature Reserve (🌐www.matsalu.ee) south of Haapsalu. **In Latvia**, reed-shrouded lakes at Engure and Pape (🌐www.wwf.lv) are well worth visiting; the website 🌐www.putni.lv is a useful source of information on other locations. **In Lithuania**, the Curonian Spit National Park and the

Nemunas Delta Regional Park are the best places to spot wading birds.

Skiing

Despite the largely flat landscape, the Baltic States can boast a handful of **downhill skiing** opportunities, although pistes tend to be short in length. The Baltic climate does at least ensure that snow cover is guaranteed for a good four months of the year. The most versatile of all the Baltic winter resorts is Õtepää in southern Estonia: it has a wide range of downhill slopes and endless opportunities for **cross-country skiing**, as well as a lively nightlife. If an undemanding day out on the slopes is all you're after, you could do worse than head for the Gauja Valley in Latvia, where resorts like Sigulda (see p.259) and Cīrulīši (just outside Cēsis; p.268) are within easy day-trip range of the capital, Rīga. It's pretty easy to rent gear on arrival; a day's use of skis and boots rarely costs over €15/£10/$19.

Travel essentials

Crime and personal safety

Despite an increase in theft, corruption and mafia-style organized crime in the years following the collapse of communism, the three Baltic States are relatively unthreatening countries in which to travel, and most tourists will have little or no contact with the local police. Technically, everyone is required to carry ID at all times, so it's a good idea to have your passport (or other form of photo ID) handy in case of random police checks.

The principal crimes to which visitors are likely to be exposed are **petty theft** and **mugging**. Your main defence against these is to exercise common sense and refrain from flaunting luxury items, expensive cameras and snazzy mobile phones. Beware of pickpockets in markets, bus stations and areas popular with tourists – especially the historic quarters of the three capital cities and busy beach resorts like Palanga and Jūrmala.

Take out an insurance policy before you leave home (see p.42) and always stow a photocopy of the last page of your passport in a safe place – this will enable your consulate to issue you with new travel documents in the event of your passport being stolen.

Car theft (either its contents, or the whole vehicle) is an ever-present danger. It's worth paying to leave your car in a guarded car park (hotels will either have one of their own or tell you where the nearest one is), and avoid leaving your car on the street unless it's equipped with immobilizers. Never leave anything of value in your car if you park it in unguarded car parks, near isolated beaches or in rural beauty spots (especially national parks) – all high-risk areas for theft.

Although younger policemen are likely to understand at least some English, Russian is more common among their older colleagues. **Police** are usually courteous and businesslike in their dealings with foreigners, but may be slow to fill out reports should you be unlucky enough to have anything stolen. A mixture of patience and persistence should be enough to resolve most problems.

Disabled travellers

Many public places in the Baltic States are wheelchair-accessible, especially in larger cities, though in general, access to public transport and tourist sites still leaves a lot to be desired.

Spa visits, rest cures and mud baths have been an important aspect of Baltic tourism ever since the mid-nineteenth century, and it's in the **spa resorts** that you're most likely to find hotels used to receiving guests with disabilities. In Estonia, Haapsalu, Kuressaare and Pärnu have a particularly good range of facilities. Forest-fringed Druskininkai, Lithuania's oldest health resort, also caters well to disabled visitors.

Elsewhere, especially in the capital cities, there's a growing number of **wheelchair-accessible hotels**, though these tend to be in the more expensive price brackets. Tourist offices throughout the Baltics will usually find out whether there are any suitable accommodation facilities in their region if you ring in advance, but be sure to double-check the information they give you – some hotels advertise disabled facilities, but haven't got round to building them yet.

Read your **travel insurance** small print carefully to make sure that people with a pre-existing medical condition are not excluded, and use your travel agent to make your journey simpler: airline or bus companies can cope better if they are expecting you, with a wheelchair provided at airports and staff primed to help. A **medical certificate** of your fitness to travel, provided by your doctor, is also extremely useful; some airlines or insurance companies may insist on it. Make sure that you have extra supplies of drugs – carried with you if you fly – and a prescription including the generic name in case of emergency.

Electricity

220 volts. Round, two-pin plugs are used, so it's best to get hold of an adaptor before leaving home.

Entry requirements

Citizens of the US, EU member states, Australia, New Zealand and Canada are allowed visa-free entry into Latvia, Estonia and Lithuania. Nationals of other countries should check on visa regulations at the relevant embassy or consulate before setting out.

Visitors are allowed to stay in each Baltic State for a total of ninety days in any given calendar year. If you wish to stay longer than this you'll need to apply for a residence or work permit – simply crossing the border and re-entering again every ninety days won't work. Up-to-date information on entrance regulations and visa costs can be found on the websites of the relevant foreign ministry: Ⓦ www.vm.ee for Estonia, Ⓦ www.mfa.gov.lv or Ⓦ www.am.gov.lv for Latvia and Ⓦ www.urm.lt for Lithuania.

Baltic embassies and consulates

Australia and New Zealand Latvia: PO Box 457, Strathfield, NSW 2135 ☏ 02/9744 5981, Ⓔ dalins @optusnet.com.au; Lithuania: 40B Fiddlers Wharf Rd, Killara, Sydney, NSW 2071 ☏ 02/9498 2571.
Canada Estonia: 260 Dalhousie St, Suite 210, Ottawa, Ontario K1N 7E4 ☏ 613/789 4222, Ⓦ www.estemb.ca; Lithuania: 130 Albert St, Suite 204, Ottawa, Ontario K1P 5G4 ☏ 613/567 5458, Ⓦ www.lithuanianembassy.ca.
Ireland Estonia: Riversdale House, St Anne's, Ailesbury Rd, Dublin 4 ☏ 01/219 6730, Ⓔ embassy.dublin@mfa.ee; Latvia: 92 St Stephen's Green, Dublin 2 ☏ 01/428 3320, Ⓔ embassy.ireland@mfa.gov.lv; Lithuania: 90 Merrion Rd, Ballsbridge, Dublin 4 ☏ 01/668 8292, Ⓦ ie.mfa.lt.
UK Estonia: 16 Hyde Park Gate, London SW7 5DG ☏ 020/7589 3428, Ⓦ www.estonia.gov.uk; Latvia: 45 Nottingham Place, London W1U 5LV ☏ 020/7312 0040, Ⓔ embassy.uk@mfa.gov.lv; Lithuania: 84 Gloucester Place, London W1U 6AU ☏ 020/7486 6401, Ⓦ uk.mfa.lt.
US Estonia: 2131 Massachusetts Ave, NW, Washington DC 20008 ☏ 202/588-0101, Ⓦ www.estemb.org; Latvia: 2306 Massachusetts Ave, NW, Washington DC 20008 ☏ 202/328-2840, Ⓦ www.latvia.usa.org; Lithuania: 4590 McArthur Boulevard. NW, Suite 200, Washington, DC 20007 ☏ 202/234 5860, Ⓦ www.ltembassyus.org.

Gay and lesbian travellers

Although homosexuality is legal in the Baltic States, social attitudes remain conservative. Generally speaking, young, educated urban-dwellers are increasingly open-minded on questions of sexual preference, but few other sections of society can muster much in the way of tolerance. The Estonian capital Tallinn boasts a broad range of openly gay bars and clubs, whereas Lithuania's main city Vilnius has only a couple. The Latvian capital Rīga is somewhere in between. Outside the capital cities, the scene is either non-existent or so far underground that you won't be able to find it without local knowledge. Good general sources of information are Ⓦ www.gay.lv in Latvia; Ⓦ www.gayline.lt and Ⓦ www.gay.lt in Lithuania.

Health

The health risks of travelling in the Baltic States are minimal, and no immunizations are required before you visit. If you plan to do a lot of walking in woodland areas between March and October, it's worth considering getting vaccinated against tick-borne encephalitis, though the chance of contracting the disease from a single tick-bite is very low.

The local **tap water** is safe to drink, despite frequently being somewhat less than palatable.

Minor complaints can be treated at a **pharmacy** (*apteek* in Estonia, *aptieka* in Latvia, *vaistinė* in Lithuania), most of which stock a wide range of international drugs. Pharmacy **opening hours** vary widely, but generally they're Mon–Fri 8am–8pm, Sat 8/10am–3pm; some city-centre establishments open on Sundays as well. Big cities will have at least one pharmacy with a night counter; details of where to find the nearest one are posted in the windows of most other pharmacies.

For serious complaints, head for the nearest **hospital** (*haigla* in Estonia, *slimnīca* in Latvia, *ligoninė* in Lithuania) or call an ambulance (☎112 in Estonia, ☎03 in Latvia and Lithuania). Emergency treatment is free in all three Baltic States, but in the event of your being admitted to hospital, you'll be charged a small fee for your bed space and for drugs. Although the standard of medical training in the region is high, public hospitals are underfunded and staff are unlikely to speak much English. **Private clinics** with English-speaking doctors exist in the major cities – and are a much better bet if you have a decent travel insurance policy (see "Insurance" below). Always check what the fee covers

when booking an appointment with a private practitioner – many of them assume that all Westerners are insured to the hilt and will happily pay through the nose for unnecessary treatment.

Insurance

Even though EU healthcare privileges apply in Estonia, Latvia and Lithuania, you'd do well to take out an insurance policy before travelling to cover against theft, loss and illness or injury. Before paying for a new policy, however, it's worth checking whether you are already covered: some all-risks home insurance policies may cover your possessions when overseas, and many private medical schemes include cover when abroad. In Canada, provincial health plans usually provide partial cover for medical mishaps overseas, while holders of official student/teacher/youth cards in Canada and the US are entitled to meagre accident coverage and hospital in-patient benefits. Students will often find that their student health coverage extends during the vacations and for one term beyond the date of last enrolment.

After exhausting the possibilities above, you might want to contact a specialist travel insurance company, or consider the travel insurance deal we offer (see box below). A typical travel insurance policy usually provides cover for the loss of baggage, tickets and – up to a certain limit – cash or cheques, as well as cancellation or curtailment of your journey. Most of them exclude so-called dangerous sports unless an extra premium is paid: in the Baltic States dangerous sports can include skiing, though probably not kayaking. Many policies can be chopped and changed to exclude coverage you don't need – for example, sickness and accident benefits can often be excluded or included at will. If you do take medical coverage, ascertain whether benefits will be paid as treatment proceeds or only after return home, and whether there is a 24-hour medical emergency number.

When securing baggage cover, make sure that the per-article limit – typically under £500 – will cover your most valuable possession. If you need to make a claim, you should keep receipts for medicines and medical treatment, and in the event you have anything stolen, you must obtain an official statement from the police.

Mail

Information on post office opening hours and postage costs is given under each individual country's "Basics" at "Mail".

You can have letters sent **poste restante** to any post office in the Baltic States: simply mark them "Poste Restante", followed by the name of the town and country. When picking up mail you'll need to take your passport; make sure you check under middle names and initials, as letters often get misfiled.

Maps

The **maps** in this book should be adequate for most purposes, but drivers, cyclists and hikers will require something more detailed. The city plans and regional maps stocked by local tourist offices tend towards the rudimentary and are rarely given away free.

Latvian publishers **Jāņa Sēta**, who themselves run a lovely travel bookshop in Rīga, provide the most comprehensive coverage of the Baltics with regularly updated maps. The three countries are available separately at 1:500,000, or combined into a pocket-size atlas at the same scale, with 72 street plans in addition. Jāņa Sēta also produces the best individual fold out maps of the three Baltic capitals, as well as most other cities and provincial towns in Latvia and Lithuania.

If you intend to do some serious **hiking** you'll need to get hold of more detailed maps. In **Latvia**, Jāņa Sēta produces indispensable maps of the national parks, while

other areas are covered by the 1:50,000 maps in the Latvijas republikas satelitkarte series, though they're hard to get hold of – the Jāņa Sēta bookshop (see p.219) is the most likely outlet.

In **Lithuania**, local firm Briedis publishes a series of 1:130,000 regional road maps that cover just about every country lane and farmstead. Lithuania's national park areas are badly served, and you might have to rely on the rough-and-ready maps provided by local tourist offices.

In **Estonia**, the highly detailed 1:50,000 Eesti baaskart series, based on satellite photographs, are useful for walking, although not all shops stock them. Also handy are the Regio 1:100,000 maps of national parks and islands.

Money

The national currencies of Estonia, Latvia and Lithuania are all pegged to the euro, ensuring fairly stable exchange rates for the foreseeable future. The Estonian kroon (EEK) works out at about 15.65EEK to €1, 22EEK to £1 and 11.5EEK to US$1; the Latvian lats (Ls) at about 0.70Ls to €1, 1Ls to £1 and 0.55Ls to US$1; and the Lithuanian litas (Lt) at about 3.45Lt to €1, 5Lt to £1, 2.65Lt to $1.

The safest way to carry money is in the form of **traveller's cheques**, in either dollars, euros or pounds sterling; they're insured, and in the event of theft or loss are reimbursed in full. They're relatively easy to cash in city-centre banks in the Baltic States, though the transaction can take an inordinately long time in provincial towns, where banking staff may be unsure of the correct procedure.

The major **credit and charge cards** – Visa, MasterCard, American Express and Diners Club – are accepted in the bigger hotels, restaurants and shops throughout the Baltic States, although most medium- and small-sized businesses only take cash.

Phones

Phone boxes offering international direct dialling are plentiful; English instructions are often posted inside. Phone cards are most commonly available from newspaper and tobacco kiosks, although post offices and supermarket checkouts often sell them as well.

Calling home from abroad

One of the most convenient ways of phoning home from abroad is via a telephone charge card from your phone company back home. Using a PIN number, you can make calls from most hotel, public and private phones and the calls are charged to your account; contact your phone company for information.

International dialling codes

To phone the Baltic States, dial your country's international access code, then:

Estonia ☎372

Latvia ☎371

Lithuania ☎370

When calling the UK, Ireland, Australia and New Zealand from abroad, note that the initial zero is omitted from the area code. To phone from Estonia, Latvia and Lithuania, dial:

Australia ☎0061

Britain ☎0044

Ireland ☎00353

New Zealand ☎0064

US & Canada ☎001

GSM **mobile phone** networks enjoy almost blanket coverage in the Baltic States – and the absence of high mountains helps ensure that there are very few blind spots. Check with your phone provider whether your mobile will work abroad, and what the call charges are; getting your international access switched on may depend upon payment of a hefty deposit. If you want to retrieve messages while you're away, you'll have to ask your provider for a new access code, as your home one is unlikely to work abroad.

For information on pre-paid SIM cards, see each individual country's "Basics" section.

Saunas

Most Baltic hotels will have a sauna on site. Usually it costs money to use them, though they're often free to guests at certain times of the day. Many people have saunas built into their homes, visitors are often invited to share one – it's a sure sign that they value your friendship and the offer should not be refused lightly. In the countryside, look out for old-style, log-fired saunas – smokey, pungent and usually followed by a dip in an ice-cold lake.

Time

Estonia and Latvia are two hours ahead of the UK, and seven hours ahead of New York,

with clocks going backwards and forwards in March and October respectively. In Lithuania, however, the time stays the same all year round – which means that in summer Lithuania is one hour ahead of the UK (and six hours ahead of New York), and in winter two hours ahead of the UK (and seven hours ahead of New York).

Tourist information

Each of the Baltic States has a national tourist board, and is in the process of setting up information centres in other European capitals. If there is no Lithuanian, Latvian or Estonian tourist information office in your home country, you can contact their central offices (in Vilnius, Rīga and Tallinn respectively).

Almost every major city and resort in the Baltic States has a **tourist office** where you can pick up information on sights, public transport and accommodation; most can also book hotels and B&Bs on your behalf. Staff usually have a working knowledge of English; German and Russian are the other most frequently spoken languages. **Opening hours** are usually Mon–Fri 9am–5pm, although tourist offices in more popular areas may open for a few hours at weekends, especially during the summer. You'll find details of individual offices throughout the guide.

National tourist boards

Estonian National Tourist Association
ⓦ www.visitestonia.com.
Latvian Tourism Development Agency
ⓦ www.latviatourism.lv.
Lithuanian State Department of Tourism
☎ +370 5 210 8796, ⓦ www.tourism.lt or
ⓦ www.travel.lt.

Tourist offices in the UK

Latvian Tourism Bureau 72 Queensborough Terrace, London W2 3SH ☎ 020/7229 8271, ⓔ london@latviatourism.lv.
Lithuanian Tourist Information Centre 86 Gloucester Place, London W1U 6HP ☎ 020/7034 1222, ⓦ www.lithuaniatourism.co.uk.

Work and study

Casual **work** in the Baltic States is hard to find unless you know one of the local languages, and wages are in any case low – anything above €600/£415/$780 a month is generous. The back pages of the *Baltic Times* (see p.38) occasionally advertise vacancies for English-speaking job-seekers, but opportunities are thin on the ground.

Teaching English is probably your best bet: there's a growing demand for native-language English teachers in the private language schools that have recently sprung up all over the region. However, you'll need a **CELTA** (Certificate in English Language Teaching to Adults) qualification in order to secure a job at any but the most fly-by-night organizations. Vacancies are sometimes advertised in the education supplements of Western newspapers; otherwise it's a question of touting your CV around the language schools and making use of local contacts once you arrive.

A handful of organizations run **volunteer work camps** in the Baltic States, most of which are concerned with environmental or social issues – Earthwatch and Volunteers for Peace (see p.46) might provide some pointers.

There are several **language-learning** opportunities in the Baltic States. In Lithuania, Vilnius University organizes two- and four-week intensive **Lithuanian courses** in summer, as well as a one-year programme spanning two university semesters. Full details are available from the Department of Lithuanian Studies, Vilnius University, Universiteto 5, 2734 Vilnius (☎ +370 5/687 214 and 687 215, ⓦ www.lsk.flf.vu.lt or ⓦ www.vu.lt/en).

Lithuania is also a good place to learn **Yiddish**: the local Jewish community, in association with Vilnius University, organizes intensive four-week language courses in August, as well as year-long university courses. Full details are available on ⓦ www.judaicvilnius.com.

In Latvia, the Valodu Mācību Centrs ("Language Study Centre"), Smilšu iela 1/3 1050 Rīga (☎ 6721 2251; ⓦ www.vmc.lv), offers tuition in **Latvian**, while Rīga Technical University runs beginners' Latvian language courses throughout the academic year, as well as an intensive Latvian course in summer. They're primarily intended for foreign exchange students, although other interested parties can take part – for details, contact the university's International Relations office (☎ +371 6708 9021, ⓦ www.rtu.lv or ⓦ www.summerschool.rtu.lv).

In Estonia, Tartu University runs a year-long **Estonian** language course for foreign students and has been known in the past to organize short-term intensive courses – consult ⓦ www.ut.ee/english for details. The same university also organizes a two-semester **Baltic Studies** programme (ⓦ www.baltic.ut.ee), taught in English and featuring a pick-and-mix menu of politics-, history- and culture-related courses.

Work and study contacts

In the UK and Ireland

British Council ☎ 0161 957 7755. Produces a free leaflet which details study opportunities abroad. The Council also recruits TEFL teachers for posts worldwide.
Erasmus ⓦ www.erasmus.ac.uk. EU-run student exchange programme enabling students at participating universities in Britain and Ireland to study in one of 26 European countries (including Estonia, Latvia and Lithuania). Mobility grants available for three months to a full academic year.
International House ☎ 020/7611 2400, ⓦ www.ihlondon.com. Reputable English-teaching organization which offers TEFL training leading to the

award of a CELTA, and recruits for teaching positions in Britain and abroad.

In the US

Note that most universities have semester- or year-abroad programmes to certain countries; the following are independent organizations that run programmes in lots of countries.
Earthwatch Institute ☎ 1-800/776-0188 or 978/461-0081, ⓦ www.earthwatch.org. International non-profit organization. 50,000 members and

supporters spread across the US, Europe, Africa, Asia and Australia volunteer their skills to work on field research projects all around the world, including one in Estonia.
Volunteers for Peace ☎ 802/259-2759, ⓦ www .vfp.org. Non-profit organization with links to a network of "workcamps", two- to four-week programmes organized around community projects, most in summer, with registration in April–May. Programmes worldwide, including Lithuania, Latvia and Estonia.

Guide

Guide

1

Estonia

Estonia highlights

✳ Tallinn Old Town A tightly-packed maze of narrow streets overlooked by proud merchants' houses and medieval church spires. See p.72

✳ Kadriorg, Tallinn This leafy park, laid out by Peter the Great for his mistress, is now home to the finest art museum in the Baltics. See p.84

✳ Saaremaa This popular holiday island offers the best of Estonia's maritime landscape, its starkly beautiful heathland dotted with windmills, lighthouses and even the odd meteorite crater. See p.106

✳ Pärnu A glorious white-sand beach and vibrant, summertime nightlife. See p.116

✳ Lahemaa National Park An unparalleled variety of unspoilt natural environments, from dense pine forests to bogs and desolate, boulder-strewn shores. See p.130

✳ Tartu An easy-going university town with plenty in the way of handsome historic architecture, quirky museums and a vibrant after-dark drinking scene. See p.142

✳ Setumaa Home to the Setu, a dwindling branch of the Estonian people attached to the Orthodox Church, Setumaa is one of the most rewarding and mysterious corners of the country, with bucolic villages set amid rippling hills. See p.164

△ Raekoja plats, Tallinn

Introduction and basics

It's a tribute to the resilience of the Estonians that during the short years since the Declaration of Independence in August 1991 they've transformed their country from a dour outpost of the former Soviet Union into a forward-looking, economically stable nation that boasts the highest rates of computer and mobile-phone ownership in the Baltic region. A higher proportion of Estonians use the Internet to vote in local elections, settle their tax affairs and manage their bank accounts than in any other European country. The creation of a go-ahead, technologically advanced nation-state is even more impressive in light of the fact that Estonians have ruled their own country for barely thirty years out of the past eight hundred. A Finno-Ugric people related to the Finns, the Estonians have had the misfortune to be surrounded by powerful, warlike neighbours. The first to conquer Estonia were the Danes, who arrived at the start of the thirteenth century; they were succeeded in turn by German crusading knights, Swedes and then Russians. Following a mid-nineteenth-century cultural and linguistic revival known as the National Awakening, the collapse of Germany and Tsarist Russia allowed the Estonians to snatch their independence in 1918. Their brief freedom between the two world wars was extinguished by the Soviets in 1940 and Estonia disappeared from view again. When the country re-emerged from the Soviet shadow in 1991, some forty percent of its population were Russians who had been encouraged to settle there during the Soviet era.

Where to go

Estonia's capital, **Tallinn**, is a fascinating combination of quaint medieval town and glitzy, go-ahead metropolis, with a choice of restaurants, bars and clubs wide enough to bring out the hedonist in anyone. By way of complete contrast, the **Lahemaa National Park**, east of Tallinn, possesses one of the most enticing mixtures of forests, fishing villages and manorial estates in the Baltics, its deeply indented coastline pebble-dashed with an enigmatic collection of boulders.

Of the east Estonian cities, the gruff border city of **Narva** is worth visiting for its superb fortress, although it's the historic university town of **Tartu**, full of inviting museums, pubs and parks, that exerts most appeal. Tartu is also a great base from which to visit the unspoilt countryside of the south, with ski-resort **Otepää** and small-town **Võru** providing access to a rolling landscape of pudding-shaped hills – one of which, Suur-Munamägi, is the highest point in the Baltics at a cloud-scraping 300m above sea level. In the far southeast,

bucolic villages inhabited by the Russian sect of Old Believers and the Orthodox Estonian Setu provide an insight into the country's racial and cultural diversity.

Most beach tourism is located on the west coast, where laid-back, genteel **Haapsalu** and boisterous, party-hard **Pärnu** are the main places to aim for. For a taste of the Estonian coast's desolate beauty, head for islands like **Hiiumaa** and **Saaremaa**, their landscape of lighthouse-scattered shores and inland juniper heaths perfect for hiking and cycling. As well as being a popular spa resort, Saaremaa's capital **Kuressaare** is home to one of the finest castles in the Baltics.

Getting around

Given the relative lack of fast, two-lane highways, Estonia can be a slow country to get around. For all that, if you're relying on **public transport** you're more likely to use the well-organized and extensive bus network than Estonia's trains, which have been cut

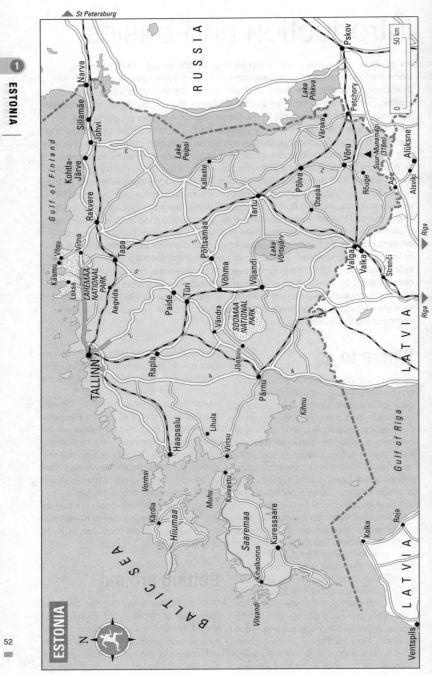

back so drastically in recent years that there are few useful passenger routes left.

Buses

Although car ownership in Estonia is on the increase, **bus transport** is still crucial to the lives of many citizens, and there's hardly a town in the country that isn't served by at least one daily bus from Tallinn. Buses linking the main cities are frequent, fast and comfortable, while those operating rural routes often look like museum pieces and rarely exceed speeds of 30km/hr. Express buses (marked with a red "E" on timetables) stop at fewer places en route and cost slightly more than regular services.

Tickets (*pilet*) can be bought from the driver or from the bus-station ticket office in advance – buying tickets in advance is wise if you're travelling on a popular inter-city route at a weekend, when buses fill up quickly. Normally, luggage is taken on board – if you have a large bag you may have to pay 10–15EEK extra to have it stowed in the luggage compartment.

Prices differ according to the operating company, but are unlikely to put a major dent in your budget. Expect to pay around 125EEK for major **inter-city journeys** such as Tallinn–Tartu and Tallinn–Pärnu, much less for shorter trips in the provinces. Buses from the mainland to the islands are more expensive, but the price of the ferry crossing is included in your ticket – expect to pay around 200EEK for the Tallinn–Kuressaare journey, 250EEK for Tartu–Kuressaare.

Estonian **bus timetables** (*sõiduplaan*) are quite complicated at first glance, incorporating lots of specific annotations that are important to get the hang of if you want to be sure that a particular service is travelling on a particular day. Days of the week on which a service runs are usually denoted by a letter (eg "E" for *esmaspäev* or Monday; see p.466 for the days of the week in Estonian). The abbreviation "v.a." before a particular letter means "runs every day except...". *Iga päev* means "every day"; *tööpäev* means "working day" (ie Mon–Sat).

The Estonian for "departure" is *väljub*, and "arrival" is *saabub*. Some timetables simply list a departure time and nothing else; others may have four columns of timings, denoting time of departure, time of arrival at destination, time of departure back to original starting point, time of arrival back at original starting point – very useful if you're planning a day out.

Although a few bus-station employees speak English (especially in Tallinn), it's best to have a pen and paper handy to ease communication. The English-speaking **information line** on ☎1182 handles **inter-city bus information**, while timetables for most of the **national network** are available on the Internet at ⊛www.bussireisid.ee – simply enter your point of departure under *lähtekoht*, intended destination under *sihtkoht*, then click on *otsi!* ("search!").

Trains

Estonia's **train network** has been cut back to such an extent that Tallinn is now the only place in the country that has a permanently manned station – all the rest either have sporadically open ticket windows or are simply unstaffed. The destinations you can reach by train are somewhat limited: regular **commuter trains** run south from Tallinn to Rapla and Türi, and there are less frequent **long-distance services** to Tartu, Pärnu, Rakvere and Viljandi. Moscow (daily) and St Petersburg (daily) are the only **international destinations** covered. Trains are on the whole slower, less frequent and only slightly cheaper than buses, so unless you have a particular preference for rail travel, there's no compelling reason to use them.

For international services, **tickets** (*pilet*) should be bought in advance. For domestic services, you should buy them in advance if you're beginning your journey from a station with a working ticket office – otherwise, pay the conductor. Trains to Tartu contain first-class as well as second-class carriages; all others just have second class. **Train timetables** use pretty much the same terminology as those displayed in bus stations (see above).

Driving

Driving in Estonia is not too nerve-racking, with main roads in reasonable condition and traffic fairly light outside the towns. Reckless driving is the exception rather than the rule, but watch out for people showing off in BMWs and four-wheel drives. There's no motorway to speak of – just a few stretches of two-lane highway either side of Tallinn and another near Pärnu.

To bring a car into Estonia you need a valid Green Card. **Speed limits** are 50kph in built-up areas and 90kph on the open road – some sections of highway allow speeds of 100kph or 110kph. The wearing of seatbelts is compulsory for the driver and all passengers, and headlights should be switched on at all times. In towns it's forbidden to overtake stationary trams so that passengers can alight in safety, and it's against the law to drive after drinking any alcohol whatsoever. Petrol stations can be a little thin on the ground in rural areas, so it's advisable to carry a spare can.

For information on **car rental**, see "Basics", p.36.

Ferries

Roll-on, roll-off ferries operated by the state shipping line (ⓦ www.laevakompanii.ee) connect the Estonian mainland with the main islands, with services from Rohuküla near Haapsalu to **Hiiumaa** (5–7 daily) and **Vormsi** (2–4 daily), and sailings from Virtsu serving **Saaremaa** (hourly).

Prices are very reasonable: if you're travelling by bus, the cost of the crossing will be included in your ticket; otherwise, expect to pay 45–60EEK per person one-way for these services, with an additional 80–120EEK for a car, 30–50EEK for a motorbike and 15–30EEK for a bike. Although journey times are short (about 90 minutes to Hiiumaa, less than an hour to Saaremaa and Vormsi), ferries have a well-stocked cafeteria on board.

The small island of **Kihnu**, off Estonia's southern coast, is served by a couple of daily, privately operated ferries from the port of Munalaiu, northwest of Pärnu. Prices for these services are around 50EEK per person, 130EEK per car.

Cycling

Estonia, being predominantly flat, makes perfect cycling terrain, although there aren't any cycle lanes and – on the mainland at least – you can't expect much consideration from other road users. Things are slightly better on the **islands**, where cyclists are a common sight in summer and there's more in the way of prepared routes and signage. While motor traffic can still be a problem on the roads of the two biggest islands, Saaremaa and Hiiumaa, cyclists will have the country lanes to themselves on Vormsi and Kihnu, where there are far fewer cars.

Flights

Although there are no domestic services linking Estonia's inland cities, flying can be a quick way of getting to the islands. Avies (ⓣ 605 8022; ⓦ www.avies.ee) operates flights from Tallinn to Kärdla and Kuressaare.

Accommodation

Tallinn can muster a growing stock of modern, comfortable hotels on a par with those in any Western European city, and similar establishments are also sprouting up in provincial cities. In addition, most towns have one or two reasonable budget hotels, and an increasing number of inexpensive guesthouses and B&Bs exist in rural areas and on the islands. Other cheap options include a handful of hostels, a few private rooms (mostly in Tallinn) and a healthy scattering of campsites – though the majority of these are basic in the extreme.

Hotels

Estonian hotels (*hotell*) come in all shapes and sizes, from the international-style blocks mushrooming all over Tallinn to the more characterful, mid-size places you're more likely to find in small towns and on the islands.

Addresses

In Estonian addresses the name of the street or square comes first, the number second. The following terms or their abbreviations are commonly encountered: *väljak* – square; tee or *mantee* (mnt) – road; *puistee* (pst) – avenue; and *tänav* (tn) – street.

Accommodation price codes

The hotels and guesthouses listed in the Estonian chapters of this guide have been graded according to the following price bands, based on the cost of the least expensive double room in summer.

- ❶ Under 450EEK
- ❷ 450–600EEK
- ❸ 600–800EEK
- ❹ 800–1100EEK
- ❺ 1100–1500EEK
- ❻ 1500–2000EEK
- ❼ 2000–3000EEK
- ❽ Over 3000EEK

Most of Estonia's hotel stock has been either refurbished or built from scratch in the last ten to fifteen years, and swish interior design and gleaming bathrooms tend to be the rule rather than the exception. A few unrenovated, Soviet-era establishments still exist here and there, and worn carpets and chipped furniture aside, they're still perfectly habitable.

A buffet **breakfast** is included in the price in almost all but the cheapest hotels, where you'll probably have to buy your own in a nearby café. **Prices** of plain, but clean, double rooms, often in old Soviet-era places or converted student hostels, range from 500 to 800EEK. For this, you're likely to get a basic en-suite shower unit and WC, although some of the cheaper places have one shower/WC shared between every two or three rooms. If you want newer furnishings and a TV in the room you'll be paying more like 700–1200EEK. Anything more than this will buy you comforts equivalent to international three- or four-star standard.

Hotel prices in the **main cities** and towns are the same all year round – although many offer weekend discounts and it never hurts to ask. In **coastal areas**, hotels are often twenty- to thirty percent cheaper in the off-season (Oct–April) – even hotels that don't publicly advertise an off-peak rate will usually be open to bargaining during this period. Note that many hotels quote their prices in euros, though you can still pay in kroon.

Small hotels in rural areas may close altogether from October to April. Even those that claim to stay open during the winter may refuse to take bookings from individuals or groups of less than four or five – it's not worth their while turning the heating on if only one or two rooms are occupied.

Families are better catered for in Estonia than its Baltic neighbours: children under the age of 3 usually stay for free, while those under 14 (sometimes 16) get a thirty- to fifty percent discount if sleeping in the same room as their parents. Many hotels offer two-room suites featuring a bedroom and a living room with fold-down beds – perfect for three- or four-member families.

One feature that all travellers will enjoy is the **sauna** – all hotels of any size will have one or more of these on site. They cost from 180 to 300EEK an hour to use, although guests might be allowed to use them for free during off-peak hours (ie early in the morning).

Provision of **no-smoking rooms** is standard throughout the hotel industry and the vast majority of small and medium-sized hotels are non-smoking throughout.

Guesthouses, B&Bs and private rooms

In Tallinn's suburbs, provincial towns and rural areas there's a growing number of small, family-run establishments offering homely bed-and-breakfast accommodation for lower prices than those offered by the hotels. If one of these places has five rooms or more, it's classified as a **guesthouse** (*külalistemaja*); otherwise it's a **B&B** (*kodumajutus*). Standards in these places are hard to predict: the snazzier ones will have en-suite rooms with TV; others will offer simply furnished, but cosy, rooms with communal WC/shower in the hallway. Guesthouses and B&Bs based on working farms often go under the name of *turismitalu* or "tourist farmstead" – such places offer an excellent opportunity to observe rural life at first hand and may also offer horse riding and other activities as part of the package. **Prices** for guesthouses and B&Bs range from 400 to 800EEK for a double, depending on location and facilities.

Local tourist offices throughout Estonia provide **information** on local guesthouses and B&Bs and will in most cases make reservations on your behalf. You can also book rural B&Bs in Estonia through Latvian agency Lauku ceļotājs, Kuģu 11, Rīga (☎+371 783 0041, ⓦwww.celotajs.lv). The Estonian Rural Travel Association, Vilmsi 53B, 10147 Tallinn (☎600 9999, ⓦwww.maaturism.ee) is another source of information on rural B&Bs, but doesn't offer an on-line booking service as yet.

In Tallinn, Tartu and Pärnu, another cheap alternative to hotels are **private rooms**. These usually involve staying in the spare room of an apartment-block dweller and sharing their WC/bathroom. Although you'll usually be greeted by a spick-and-span room and a friendly host, be aware that these standards can't be guaranteed. **Prices** are around 300EEK for a single, 550EEK for a double. The Rasastra agency in Tallinn (see p.70) can fix you up with rooms in all three cities; otherwise contact the tourist office in Tartu (p.147).

Hostels and campsites

Estonia has a modest network of **hostels**, ranging from large, concrete buildings, with a multitude of three- to four-bed rooms, to small (often privately owned) establishments offering an unpredictable range of sleeping quarters – from sparsely furnished, bunk-packed dormitories to cosy doubles. **Prices** range from 200 to 300EEK per person.

The geographical distribution of hostels is somewhat haphazard: there's a good choice in Tallinn, a couple in the Lahemaa National Park, a couple in Pärnu – and a handful elsewhere. Most (but not all) hostels are members of the **Estonian Youth Hostel Association** (Narva mnt 16–25, 10120 Tallinn, ☎646 1455, ⓦwww.hostels.ee and ⓦwww.balticbookings.com/eyha), which can provide information and make bookings.

The most basic form of **campsite** (*kämping*) in Estonia is a simple patch of ground where you're allowed to pitch a tent for 50–60EEK. Earth toilets may be provided, but running water usually isn't. These sites are particularly common in the **Lahemaa National Park** (where camping is actually free, provided you stick to the official, park-run sites) – wardens call round every day to collect rubbish and drop off free supplies of firewood. Many small hotels and guesthouses in rural Estonia allow camping in the garden for about 60EEK – in these places you'll be allowed access to a toilet and running water.

Some **larger campsites** are equipped with toilets and washing facilities and also provide accommodation in three- to four-bed **cabins** for around 200 to 300EEK per person. **Caravans** are something of a novelty in Estonia, although there are at least a couple of sites (at Pärnu and near Võsu in the Lahemaa National Park) that have electricity points for **trailers**.

Food and drink

For centuries, **rye bread**, **salted herring** and **beer** formed the Estonians' staple diet, with **roast pork** making an appearance on festive occasions. Such staples are still the backbone of the eating and drinking scene, although nowadays there's a great deal else besides. As in much of northern Europe, calorific meat dishes and dairy products set the tone of Estonia's national cuisine, although you can find plenty in the way of salads and ethnic foods – especially in Tallinn and other cities.

Where to eat

Eating in towns and cities usually takes place in **restaurants** (*restoran*) with menus and table service, or in **cafés** (*kohvik*) where you order and pay at the counter. Cafés often provide a simpler repertoire of main courses than restaurants and are usually much cheaper – they're also good places to tuck into snacks and sweets. In rural or well-touristed areas you'll come across traditional **inns** (*kõrts*), which cater for both eaters and drinkers and concentrate on standard Estonian meat-and-potato dishes. In addition, a lot of **pubs and bars** (see "Drinking", opposite) offer a full menu of cooked food.

Restaurants and inns are usually **open** till 10pm in small towns and rural areas, 11pm or midnight in cities and resorts. Cafés usually close at around 7/8pm, earlier on Sundays.

By and large, you should be able to have a decent meal (two courses and a drink) for around 200EEK in restaurants, 125EEK in cafés, although prices in Tallinn are creeping ever upwards. Watch out for restaurants and cafés offering excellent deals on a dish of the day (*päevapraad*), details of which are usually chalked up on a board outside.

For **self-catering** and picnicking, basics like bread, cheese, smoked meat and tinned fish can be picked up in supermarkets, while the full range of fruit and vegetables is available at outdoor markets in most towns of any size. Most high streets have a bakery (*pagariäri*) where you can pick up bread and pastries.

Snacks, starters and salads

The most characteristic Estonian **starter** is *sült*, a mixture of pork bits set in jelly that is definitely an acquired taste; a family meal or festive occasion would be unthinkable without a big bowl of the stuff on the table. Salted herring (*heeringas* or *räim*), smoked eel (*angerjas*) and sliced sausage (*voorst*) frequently feature as restaurant starters or bar snacks and invariably come with a few slices of delicious dark rye bread (*leib*).

Soup (*supp*) is eaten either as a starter or a lunchtime snack in its own right; available pretty much everywhere is *seljanka*, a broth of Russian origin featuring meat, pickled vegetables and sometimes (in its Estonian version at least) fish. Other light meals that you'll come across – in cafés more often than in restaurants – include *pelmenid* (ravioli-like parcels of minced meat), *pirukas* (dough stuffed with bacon, cabbage or other fillings) and *pankoogid* (pancakes) which can come with cheese, meat or mushrooms.

Many cafés offer salads (*salat*), which can range from a sorry-looking bowl of peas and gherkins drenched in sour cream to a healthy platter of greens and other ingredients, substantial enough to serve as a light meal in its own right – tuna salad (*tuunikasalat*) is one of the most common.

Main courses

The quintessential Estonian main course comprises **pork** (*sia*), **potatoes** (*kartulid*) and

sauerkraut (*mulgikapsad*) – and during the Soviet era this was all that most restaurants ever bothered serving. Pork is most commonly served roasted or pan-fried in the form of a *karbonaad* – a chop coated in tasty batter. Cuts of pork usually come with a healthy rind of fat which, when properly cooked, can be quite delicious. Other meats that crop up regularly on menus are chicken (*kana*), steak (*biifsteik*) and a locally produced form of blood sausage known as *verevoorst*. Lamb (*lamba*) is much less common unless you're eating in a grill restaurant devoted to Caucasian cooking, in which case it will probably feature in a *šašlõkk* (shish kebab). Freshwater **fish** (*kala*) figures strongly on restaurant menus, with pan-fried trout (*forell*), perch (*ahven*) or pike (*haug*) being the most popular. Main courses are usually served with potatoes and seasonal vegetables and frequently come with lashings of sour cream (*hapukoor*).

Vegetarians are not well catered for, though a few places make a token effort – especially the growing number of (generally pretty good) ethnic restaurants in Tallinn.

Desserts

Estonian cafés serve up a mouth-watering array of sweets, most of which crop up on restaurant menus, too. The satisfyingly smooth *mannapuder* (semolina pudding) rules the roost as far as indigenous desserts are concerned – it often comes garnished with local fruits and berries. Pancakes, usually filled with jam, are also ubiquitous. If you want a daytime nibble to go with your coffee then you can choose between a sticky bun (*sai*) or a slice of cake (*kook*) – the latter is a blanket term covering everything from chocolate cake and cheesecake to fruit flan. One local delicacy you'll see in the best bakeries and delicatessens is *kringel*, a sweet loaf filled with dried fruit.

Drinking

An ever-increasing range of **pubs and bars** – most of which imitate Irish or American models – are beginning to take over the Estonian drinking scene, especially in Tallinn and other major centres. Many **cafés** (*kohvik*) only serve soft drinks and are closed by mid-evening, although some stay open later and offer alcohol too.

Estonians are enthusiastic drinkers, with **beer** (*õlu*) being the most popular tipple. The principal local brands are Saku and A. Le Coq, both of which are rather tame, lager-style brews, although both companies also produce stronger porters (*tume*). The strong-est beers are found on the islands – best known is the deceptively sweet Saaremaa õlu (widely available in supermarkets, less so in bars), which has twice the alcohol content of regular brands. Inland, a number of smaller breweries continue to supply the pubs in their local areas, notably Wiru in the northeast – their Palmse porter is well worth trying. Beer is sold in measures of 0.3 or 0.5 of a litre, although many establishments outside Tallinn only stock 0.5 litre glasses, believing the consumption of lesser quanti-ties to be an affectation.

Most common of the **spirits** is **vodka** (*viin*) – either the locally made Viru Valge or Rus-sian brands – which is usually drunk with juice or a fizzy-drink mixer. Local alcoholic specialities include *hõõgvein* (mulled wine) and Vana Tallinn, a syrupy, medicinal-looking liqueur, best mixed with blackcurrant juice or black coffee.

Coffee (*kohv*) sometimes comes as espresso or cappuccino in the better cafés, although filter coffee is more common and it's usually served black, unless you specify *koorega* (with cream).

The media

Given a national population of 1,370,000 (of which only 67 percent are native Esto-nian speakers), the range of newspapers and magazines cluttering up Estonia's street kiosks is absolutely staggering, with titles covering every conceivable interest group from computer nerds to dog breeders and gardeners.

The most prestigious of the national daily **newspapers** is *Eesti Postimees* (ⓦwww.postimees.ee), founded in Tartu in 1867 and still required reading for the politi-cal and business elite – the Friday edition carries good cultural listings, too. Mass-market tabloids *Eesti Päevaleht* and

Sõnumileht make up for lightweight news coverage with racy showbiz gossip. Best of the weeklies is *Eesti Ekspress*, which mixes political reporting with extensive cul-tural coverage and carries by far the best "what's on" information (found at the end of the TV section under the heading *Vaba aeg* – "Free Time").

The locally produced Russian daily *Molo-dezh Estonii* (ⓦwww.moles.ee) is a reliable and readable guide to what's happening in politics and society. There's also a huge array of Moscow-published newspapers and magazines in the kiosks, including the seductively stylish Russian-language editions of major international fashion and design monthlies.

Locally produced **English-language** pub-lications are thin on the ground, although there's a decent selection if you're interested in the visual arts: *kunst.ee* is a superbly designed art monthly with a mixture of intel-ligent articles in Estonian and English; while *cheese.ee* covers contemporary photogra-phy in similar fashion.

As far as **television** is concerned, the state-run Eesti TV and the privately owned TV1, Kanal 2 and TV3 offer a pretty varied diet of home-grown and imported program-ming, although many Estonians (and most Estonian hotels) have cable packages offering a range of English, German, Finn-ish and Russian channels. All the Estonian stations show imported films and dramas in the original language with Estonian subtitles. For details of pan-Baltic media in the English language, see p.38.

Festivals

Although traditional festivities and folk practices don't fill the Estonian calendar in the same way as they do in Latvia and Lithuania, there are several major seasonal events, many of which are closely related to the traditional work-cycle of the agricultural year.

As elsewhere in Europe, **Easter** is both a Christian feast and a much more general cel-ebration of the coming spring, with painted eggs and general over-consumption of festive food setting the tone. Easter is celebrated

Calendar of festivals and events

Jazzkaar Tallinn and Tartu, April. Top-name jazz concerts; ®www.jazzkaar.ee.

Soup City Days (Supilinna päevad) Tartu, last weekend in April. Three days of art and music in Tartu's run-down bohemian suburb.

University Spring Days (Ülikooli kevadpäevad) Tartu, late April/early May. Five days of partying and feasting, straddling May 1.

International Dance Festival (Rahvusvahelisel tantsufestival) Tartu, late May/early June. Contemporary dance from all over Europe.

Old Town Days Tallinn, late May early June. Medieval parades and jousting tournaments.

Pühajärve Beach Party Otepää, June. Pop festival with live bands and DJs on the shores of Lake Pühajärve; ®www.beachparty.ee.

Early Music Festival Haapsalu Haapsalu, early July. Local and international ensembles perform in Haapsalu's cathedral; ®www.concertogrosso.ee.

Summer Music Festival Tartu, early June to late August. Classical, contemporary and jazz concerts at venues all over town.

Hansa Days Tartu, late June. Medieval-style fair with street musicians and tournaments; ®www.tartu.ee/hansa.

Folklore Festival Viljandi (Viljandi pärimuusika festival) Viljandi, July. Estonia's biggest ethno bash; ®www.folk.ee.

Folklore Festival Võru, mid-July. Estonian and international ensembles; ®www.werro.ee/folkloor.

Days of the Setu Kingdom (Setokuningriik) Obinitsa, August. Folk festival celebrating the culture of the Setu people in Estonia's far southeast; ®www.hot.ee/setokuningriik.

Days of the White Lady Haapsalu, mid-August. Drinking and dancing in the castle courtyard; ®www.daam.haapsalu.ee.

Dark Nights Film Festival (Pimedate Ööde) Tallinn, December. Contemporary art-house film festival; ®www.poff.ee.

with more gusto by Estonia's Orthodox minority, who mark the event by processing around churches with lighted candles at midnight on Easter Saturday – Orthodox Easter takes place anything up to five weeks after the Catholic/Protestant event.

Until recently, the other great springtime festival was **St George's Day** (Jüripäev) on April 23, traditionally the last chance to indulge in feasting and drinking before the sowing season – sadly it's not much observed nowadays. Celebrations of **St John's Day** (Jaanipäev) on June 24 have proved more enduring. Originally the last chance for a knees-up before the hard work of the harvesting season began, St John's Day is still associated with hedonistic abandon – and for working Estonians it's the most important day off of the summer. On June 23 most people head for the countryside with family and friends and spend the night drinking and carousing, staying up long enough

to greet the sunrise on the longest day of the year.

Before World War II, late October was marked by the four-day holiday known as *kliistripühad* ("shutting the windows"), when people mended cracked window frames and sealed up draughty cavities in preparation for the coming winter. Early November is traditionally a period of remembrance roughly analogous to All Souls' Day in Catholic Europe, when families visit cemeteries to tidy graves and lay flowers. This period traditionally comes to an end on **St Martin's Day** (Mardipäev) on November 11, when – in some areas – children dressed as beggars do the rounds of neighbourhood houses asking for treats. **Christmas** (Jõulud) is pretty much the same as in the rest of Europe, with children hassling a fat, bearded bloke (Jõuluvana) for gifts while their parents pig out on roast pork (*seapraad*), gingerbread (*piparkoogid*) and mulled wine (*hõõgvein*).

Entertainment

Estonians take their leisure time seriously, and there's a correspondingly wide range of classical music and serious theatre on offer, especially in the capital. Tallinn can also muster a huge choice of clubs, cinemas and venues offering live jazz, rock and pop.

Classical music

Estonia's principal musical institutions – national symphony orchestra, chamber orchestra, opera and ballet – are all based in Tallinn, although they frequently perform in the provinces, most notably at Tartu and Pärnu. The Ⓦ www.concert.ee site carries schedule details.

Contemporary classical music occupies an important place in the regular Estonian repertoire, thanks in large part to local-born composer **Arvo Pärt** (b.1935), whose sparsely orchestrated, meditative pieces have earned him a towering international reputation. Having spent the 1960s experimenting with serialism and other modernist techniques, the devoutly religious Pärt began to develop a much more personal style in the 1970s, with works like *Summa* (1977), the *St John Passion* (1982) and *Stabat Mater* (1986) being acclaimed as classics of spiritually inspired minimalism. Clearly no stranger to the Estonian choral tradition, Pärt has also used German-language evensong and medieval Latin in his works.

Considerably more rooted in indigenous folk tradition is Pärt's near-contemporary **Veljo Tormis** (b.1930), whose choral works take their inspiration from the mesmeric, chant-like runic songs that form such an important part in Estonian musical heritage. The best known of Tormis's works are *Curse Upon Iron* (1972), which combines sweeping orchestral passages with archaic, shamanistic drum beats, and *Karelian Destiny* (1989), a cycle of fairytale-esque narrative songs drawing on the heritage of Estonians, Finns and other related Finno-Ugric peoples.

Archaic sounds of another sort feature in the repertoire of **Hortus Musicus**, a world-renowned early music ensemble that is based in Tallinn and performs regularly in the city. Specializing in the music of the Renaissance and Baroque periods, they often dress up in the clothes of the period as well as playing as-authentic-as-possible instruments.

Clubbing and pop music

There's a growing and increasingly sophisticated choice of **club culture** to be sampled in **Tallinn**, where you'll find everything from heaving discos playing mainstream chart music to ironic retro clubs and all manner of niche DJ styles. There's a lot of activity outside the capital too, with the student-filled town of **Tartu** offering a particularly enjoyable range of clubs and the beach resort of **Pärnu** coming to life in the summer.

Some clubs in Tallinn and Tartu host **live gigs** by local pop-rock acts and there are a couple of music bars in the capital where you can hear competent cover bands churning out blues and R&B standards. The jazz scene is hampered by a lack of regular venues, although the **Jazzkaar festival** (held in Tallinn every spring; see p.92) is arguably the best such event in the Baltics, attracting major international names.

Few Estonian pop-rock acts have made much of an impression internationally, save perhaps for the manufactured duo of Tanel Pader and Dave Benton, who had the dubious honour of winning the Eurovision Song Contest in 2001. Pader has subsequently re-emerged as a reasonably respectable rock-pop solo artist.

Cinema

Cinemas in Estonia show mainstream movies pretty much immediately after their release in Western Europe. They're shown in the original language, with Estonian subtitles.

During the Soviet period, the Tallinn Film Studio churned out several workmanlike films a year, many of which were made in Russian to appeal to a wider Soviet market. As far as the locals are concerned, the outstanding product of this era was the Estonian-language *The Last Relic* (*Viimne Reliikvia*; 1969), a cross between swashbuckler, sex comedy and musical, set amidst the religious struggles of the sixteenth century and intended to demonstrate that Estonian cinema was as capable of producing lavish historical epics as anyone. It's still great to look at, and some of the countryside scenes could almost pass for an advertisement for the Estonian Tourist Board. There's certainly been nothing like it since, although Kristjan Taska's intelligent historical drama *Names in Marble* (*Nimed Marmortahvlil*; 2002), set in the post-World War I struggles between Estonians and Bolsheviks, points towards a rosier future for the industry.

Internationally, Estonia is known less for its full-length features than for its animated films, thanks largely to the efforts of the Tallinn-based studio Nukufilm (ⓦ www.nukufilm .ee). Established in 1957 by Elbert Tuganov, the studio has garnered a global reputation for its use of superbly fashioned dolls and puppets. Most of its output is intended for children, although some of the studio's more surreal products – especially recent work by Riho Unt and Mait Laas – go down equally well with the European art-house crowd.

Sport

Few Estonian teams have tasted success in the international arena, which probably explains the lack of excitement generated by even the most popular sports, **basketball** and **football**. The Estonian football team play their home matches in Tallinn and these are your best bet if you're looking for a modicum of atmosphere and a decent-sized crowd; domestic league games rarely attract more than a few hundred paying fans.

Estonia is not entirely without its sporting heroes, however: decathlete Erki Nool put the country on the map when he won Olympic gold in 2000, while cross-country skier Andrus Veerpalu brought back one gold and one silver medal from the 2002 Winter Olympics in Salt Lake City.

Culture and etiquette

Tipping is only expected in Estonia if you're in a restaurant or smart café with table service, or if you've had a meal and/or big round of drinks in a bar. In these cases, round up your bill by ten to fifteen percent.

Public toilets (*tualettid*) can usually be found in bus stations. Gents are marked with a letter "M" or a ▼ symbol; ladies with an "N" or an ▲ symbol.

The best place to find **contraceptives** is at a pharmacy (*apteek*).

Travel essentials

Costs

Although costs are on the rise in Estonia's capital, **Tallinn**, it's still a reasonably inexpensive destination compared with cities in Western Europe – a day's sightseeing followed by a fun evening out is unlikely to break the bank. Things are cheaper still outside the capital, where a little money can go a long way.

Accommodation is likely to prove your biggest expense in Estonia. In Tallinn, Tartu and resort areas, hostel beds cost between €15/£10/$19 and €22/£15/$27, private rooms around €36/£25/$47 for a double. The cheaper hotels start at about the €45/£30/$57 mark for a double, with comfortable, mid-range choices costing around €70/£48/$90 – anything more stylish will be considerably more than this. In rural areas you won't find much in the way of hostels, but the price of a double room can fall to €30/£20/$38 in a rustic B&B, €55/£38/$72 in a hotel.

Public transport costs are comparatively low: an inter-city bus journey from Tallinn to Pärnu or Tartu will be somewhere in the region of €7.50/£5/$9.50, while a one-way ticket from Tallinn to Kuressaare on the island of Saaremaa costs €15/£10/$19.

If you're shopping in markets for picnic ingredients during the daytime and sticking to the cheaper cafés and bars in the evening, then €20/£14/$26 per person per day will suffice for **food and drink**. In order to cover a sit-down lunch and a decent dinner followed by a couple of night-time drinks, you'll need at least €45/£30/$57 per person per day in Tallinn, €30/£20/$38 outside the capital.

Estonia is one Baltic country in which it's well worth having a **student discount card**: ISIC cardholders get discounts of ten percent in many hotels, reduced entry in museums and often up to thirty percent off theatre and concert tickets.

Internet

You'll find plenty of **Internet cafés** (*interneti kohvik*) in Tallinn and Tartu, but they're somewhat thin on the ground elsewhere in the country. Expect to pay 40–60EEK for an hour's surfing. Public libraries all have at least one Internet terminal available for public use free of charge, although they're often booked up in advance by the locals. Most cafés, bars and hotel lobbies in Tallinn, Tartu and Pärnu are Wi-Fi-equipped.

Left luggage

There's usually a left-luggage office (*pakihõid*) in big-town bus stations, charging 10–15EEK per item.

Mail

Estonian **post offices** (*postkontor*) are in the main efficient, easy to use, and often staffed by English-speakers. They are usually open Monday to Friday 9am–6/7pm and Saturday 9am–3pm. You can buy **stamps** (*postmark*) at post offices and at most newspaper kiosks. Sending a letter or postcard will cost 4.40EEK within Estonia, 6.50EEK to the rest of Europe, 8EEK to North America, Canada or Australasia.

Money

Estonia's unit of currency is the **kroon**, normally abbreviated to EEK (Eesti kroon – "Estonian Crown"), and is divided into 100 sents. Notes come in 1, 2, 5, 10, 25, 50, 100 and 500EEK denominations and coins in 0.05, 0.10, 0.20, 0.50, 1 and 5EEK denominations.

The kroon is currently pegged to the euro at a rate of 15.65EEK to €1 and exchange rates are likely to remain reasonably stable. At the time of writing there are around 22EEK to £1, 11.5EEK to $1.

With plenty of **ATMs** scattered around Estonia's town centres, you should have no problem drawing instant cash with a valid debit or credit card. Major banks (*pank*) such as Ühispank, Hansapank and Sampo Pank can change cash for a commission, cash traveller's cheques (Thomas Cook and American Express preferred) and give cash advances on most major credit cards for a commission of around three percent. **Banks** are usually open Monday to Friday 9am–4/6pm; major banks in the cities often open on Saturday from 9am to 2 or 3pm. **Exchange offices** (*Valuuta vahetus*) usually work longer hours and open on Sundays, too, and in many cases offer lower commission rates than the banks for cash transactions.

Credit cards can be used in some of the more expensive hotels, restaurants and stores and in some petrol stations in Tallinn, and although you will find places that accept cards outside Tallinn, it's best not to count on it.

Opening hours and public holidays

Most **shops** are open Monday to Friday 9/10am–6/7pm and Saturday 10am–2/3pm. Some food shops stay open until 10pm or later and are also open on Sundays. The opening hours of **museums** and galleries vary greatly from one place to the next, although they're usually closed on Mondays and frequently on Tuesdays as

---

Public holidays

Most shops, banks and museums close on the following public holidays:

Jan 1 New Year's Day
Feb 24 Independence Day
Good Friday
May 1 May Day
Whitsun
June 23 Victory Day
June 24 St John's Day
August 20 Day of Restoration of Independence
Dec 25 & 26 Christmas

well. Estonia's Protestant **churches** generally close outside Mass times unless they're of historical or artistic importance, in which case their opening hours will be similar to those of museums. Orthodox churches frequented by Estonia's Russian minority are much more likely to be open all day for the benefit of devout locals.

For post office and bank opening hours, see "Mail" (opposite) and "Money" (opposite) respectively.

Phones

You shouldn't have any difficulty using Estonia's smooth, problem-free **telephone system**. Direct international calls are possible from all phones – simply dial ☎00 followed by the country code. **Public telephones** (*telefoniputka*) all use magnetic cards (available in denominations of 30, 50 and 100EEK from post offices and newspaper kiosks) for both local and long-distance calls; a 50EEK card should be sufficient to call Western Europe, a 100EEK card to call the US. For English-language **directory enquiries** dial ☎1182 or ☎1184.

For general information on using **mobile phones** in the Baltic States, see p.44. If you have a GSM mobile phone you can cut the cost of local calls by buying a pre-paid SIM card from Estonian operators like EMT or Tele2. For 150EEK you'll get an Estonian phone number and a few minutes of call time – which you can top up by buying cards (available from newspaper kiosks) in increments of 100, 200 and 500EEK.

Emergencies

Police ☎110; ambulance and fire ☎112.

1.1
Tallinn

One of the most beautiful and best-preserved medieval towns in northern Europe, **TALLINN** never fails to make a positive first impression. "Of all the Baltic capitals, [it has] least of the vices of a town and most of the virtues of a village," wrote the British author and 1920s resident Arthur Ransome – a statement that still rings true today: Tallinn boasts myriad cultural attractions, historical sights and entertainment options, but retains an absorbing intimacy and is easy to explore on foot.

The striking cobblestone alleyways, slender steeples and barrel-shaped towers of the **Old Town** – a UNESCO World Heritage site – could have jumped straight out of the pages of a medieval illustrated manuscript. However, Tallinn is no historical theme park, but rather the commercial and political heart of a rapidly changing nation, which boasts one of the fastest-growing economies in the European Union and a booming property market. Brand new business parks, designer clothes shops, stylish lounge bars and the ubiquitous Wi-Fi access signs provide the backdrop to a work-hard-play-hard culture that imbues the city with a palpable, restless energy.

Despite being the capital of an independent Estonia from 1918 to 1940 and again from 1991, modern-day Tallinn is more of a hybrid creation than many Estonians would care to admit. The city's name, derived from the Estonian *taani linnus*, meaning "Danish Fort", is a reminder of the fact that the city was founded by the Danes at

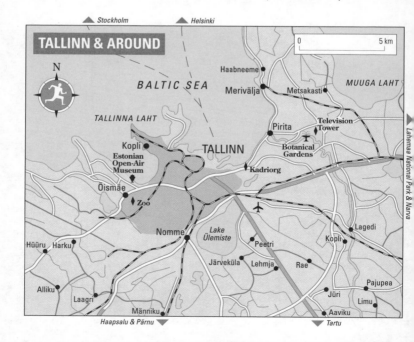

the beginning of the thirteenth century, and since then political control has been for lengthy periods in the hands of foreigners – Swedes and particularly Germans have left lasting influences. Russians, meanwhile, continue to make up around 45 percent of the population, and the Russian language persists as an ever-present shadow culture, heard constantly on the streets and in neighbourhood bars.

A popular destination for Scandinavians for many years, Tallinn now draws holiday-makers from all across Europe and beyond. The advent of budget flights has helped to lure ever-increasing numbers of city-breakers, while stag parties also make an appearance – particularly on summer weekends – but are a far less common sight than in, say, Rīga or Prague. June, July and August are the most popular times to visit Tallinn, but the city's year-round cultural attractions and vibrant nightlife ensure that it's a rewarding weekend destination whatever time of year you choose to visit.

Specific seasonal attractions include the Advent period, when there's a **Christmas Market** selling handicrafts, gingerbread and other treats on the town hall square (Raekoja plats); and the **Old Town Days**, which run for a week from the end of May through to the start of June, when locals parade around in medieval garb, a knights' tournament is held to choose the May Count, and there's a "rat race" in which contestants run round the streets carrying briefcases and mobile phones.

Some history

Tallinn began life as a trading post where Vikings came to buy furs and wax from Estonian tribes. It only became a defensible settlement with a permanent population in 1219, when it was conquered by empire-building Danish **King Valdemar II**, nicknamed "the Victorious", who had been given free licence by the pope to subjugate the heathen Estonians. Valdemar built a castle and a cathedral on the rock known as Toompea, and a town of merchants and craftsmen soon grew up at its foot. Most of those who chose to settle in Danish-ruled Tallinn were of German or Flemish stock and they called the town Reval – a name that stuck until 1918. Estonians, drawn to the city to work as servants and labourers, were allowed to reside there, but were not given full citizens' rights.

With the **Teutonic Knights** gobbling up more and more of Estonia from the 1220s onwards, the Danes hung on to Tallinn (save for one short period of Teutonic overlordship in 1227–38) until 1347, when cash-strapped King Valdemar III sold it – along with the rest of his remaining possessions in Estonia – to the Livonian Order for 19,000 silver marks. By this time the town had already become a member of the **Hanseatic League** (see box, p.66), which united German-speaking cities throughout northern Europe in a trading alliance – stimulating the emergence of a boisterous, self-confident mercantile culture. The townsfolk of Tallinn, resentful of the power wielded by the knights and bishops on Toompea, enthusiastically adopted Protestantism in the early sixteenth century; riots in September 1524 destroyed most of the town's medieval altarpieces and put monks and clergy to flight.

Weakened by the Reformation and squeezed by neighbouring powers, the Livonian Order dissolved itself in 1561, leaving Tallinn to be fought over by Russians and Swedes. The resulting **Livonian Wars** led to a decline in trade, and despite serving the victorious Swedes as an important military and administrative centre, Tallinn's days as a mercantile powerhouse were over. Swedish control came to an end in 1710, when Peter the Great's armies took the city. For the next two centuries Tallinn was part of the **Russian Empire**. By the early nineteenth century it had established itself as the most fashionable bathing resort in the region, with the cream of St Petersburg society taking up residence in town for the whole month of July. The arrival of the railway in 1870, however, transformed Tallinn into an important port and industrial centre, effectively ending its days as a seaside resort (Baltic folk trooped off to the beaches of Pärnu and Haapsalu instead).

Industrialization also changed Tallinn's **ethnic profile**, with more and more workers being drawn from the surrounding countryside. At the start of the nineteenth century barely one third of Tallinn's population had been Estonian, yet a hundred years later

The Hanseatic League

In the thirteenth century, maritime traffic in the Baltic was controlled by the Danes, prompting cities across northern Europe to band together in an attempt to protect their trading and fishing rights. Gradually, a group of cities, centred on the German port of Lübeck, developed a common set of trading standards and ostracized those who didn't sign up to them. Delegates from these cities occasionally met at Lübeck to debate issues of common concern and their association became known as "Hansa", meaning "union" or "guild". Despite being subject to the Danish crown throughout much of the thirteenth century, Tallinn eagerly signed up to the Hanseatic League in 1285. Other Baltic members included Tartu, Pärnu, Rīga, Ventspils and Cēsis.

The league was initially a loose alliance whose members could join and leave as they pleased, but in the fourteenth century the need to defend trade routes bound the Hansa members into a tighter union. The Hanseatic cities held annual assemblies and organized common defence, successfully prosecuting a war against the Danes in the 1360s. However, it remained a politically loose organization, with most of its member-cities owing allegiance to a variety of different north European rulers, whose interests often overrode those of the league.

The league's influence faded in the fifteenth century, when the exhaustion of the Baltic's herring stocks led to a slump in fishing, and Hanseatic cities began competing amongst themselves for access to the same markets. With its members no longer tied to a common agenda, the league slowly folded.

this proportion had more than doubled. Estonian-language parties won a majority of seats on the town council for the first time in 1904, turning Tallinn into the obvious focus of the Estonian national movement. The Germans, who had for so long formed the city's elite, now numbered less than ten percent of the total and were outnumbered by Russians.

Soviet rule after World War II led to further industrialization and the construction of dour, high-rise suburbs to accommodate a workforce imported from other parts of the USSR. The population mushroomed from a pre-war figure of 170,000 to a total of just under 420,000 in 1991, with Estonians outnumbered by Russian-speakers. The spire-studded skyline of the medieval Old Town survived Soviet rule largely intact, bequeathing the city a tourist potential that was readily exploited when Estonia finally regained its independence. Indeed, since 1991, the Estonian capital has established itself as a popular city-break destination, stimulating a rash of architectural renovation work and an explosion in the number of hotels, restaurants, bars and clubs. Membership of the EU and an influx of foreign investment brought about by the **return to capitalism** has also changed the face of the city, with glass-and-steel office blocks sprouting up on the fringes of the Old Town – an eloquent statement of the capital's new self-image as a young, dynamic society ready to deal with Western Europe on equal terms.

Arrival, information and city transport

Tallinn's **airport** (Lennujaam) is 4km southeast of the city centre and linked to Viru väljak, just east of the Old Town, by bus #2 (Mon–Sat every 20min; Sun every 30min; journey time 10min; 15EEK). A **taxi** from the airport to the centre should cost around 70EEK. **Trains** arrive at the **Balti Jaam** (Baltic Station) on Toompuiestee, a five-minute walk northwest of the Old Town. The **long-distance bus station** (Autobussijaam) is 2km south east at Lastekodu 46 – trams #2 and #4 run from nearby Tartu mnt to Viru väljak, right on the eastern fringes of the Old Town. Tallinn's **local bus terminal** is below the Viru Keskus shopping centre at Viru väljak 4/6. The passenger **port** (Reisisadam) is northeast of the centre at the end of Sadama.

Tallinn's main **tourist office**, a few steps south of Raekoja plats at Nigulste 2/Kullasseppa 4 (May & June Mon–Fri 9am–7pm, Sat & Sun 10am–5pm; July & Aug

Mon–Fri 9am–8pm, Sat & Sun 10am–6pm; Sept Mon–Fri 9am–6pm, Sat & Sun 10am–5pm; Oct–April Mon–Fri 9am–5pm, Sat 10am–3pm; ☏ 645 7777, ⊛ www.tourism .tallinn.ee), provides well-informed advice about the city and a free sightseeing map, and also sells a selection of more detailed maps and guides. There is a smaller tourist information booth with longer opening hours in Viru Keskus (daily 9am–9pm; ☏ 610 1557).

During the summer, opposite the main official tourist office is the determinedly unofficial **Traveller Info Tent** (daily 10am–9.30pm). Set up by local students and aimed at backpackers, it gives the lowdown on Tallinn's more offbeat attractions and the local nightlife, as well as running fun, budget tours.

The **Tallinn Card** (⊛ www.tallinncard.ee), which can be bought from the official tourist offices, entitles you to free use of public transport, entrance to all museums and major sights, a city tour, discounted car rental, and savings in some shops and cafés. A 24-hour card costs 350EEK; a 48-hour one 400EEK; and a 72-hour one 450EEK – worth it if you're seriously planning to blitz your way round the museums. The excellent *Tallinn in Your Pocket* city guide (35EEK; ⊛ www.inyourpocket.com) carries informed restaurant and bar **listings**, as well as plenty of info on local services and shopping, and is available from shops and hotels.

Most of Tallinn's sights can be covered on foot; those slightly further out are served by an extensive **tram, bus and trolleybus** network. Services are frequent and cheap, though usually crowded, with tickets common to all three systems available from kiosks near stops for 10EEK (a book of ten is 85EEK) or from the driver for 15EEK.

Moving on from Tallinn

Tallinn is the Baltic Sea's main gateway to Scandinavia, with a host of ferries, hydro-foils and catamarans travelling across the Gulf of Finland to **Helsinki**. Ferries take 3hr 15min–4hr; hydrofoils and catamarans are faster, taking on average 1hr 30min–1hr 40min, but only run when the gulf isn't frozen over – roughly from early March to late December, although beware that some winters last longer than others. There's a daily ferry to **Stockholm** (16hr; overnight) and at the time of writing there were also discussions about relaunching a direct service to **St Petersburg**. An easy ten-minute walk northeast of the Old Town, the **Passenger Port** (Reisisadam) is divided into four terminals: A, B, C and D. A, B and C are grouped together on the northern side of the port, at the end of Sadama; D is on the south side, an extra ten-minute walk round the dock: bus #2 goes there every twenty to thirty minutes. Terminals A and D are equipped with cafés, exchange offices, and luggage lockers (Estonian coins required).

Most travel agents (see p.96) in the Old Town sell **tickets** to Helsinki and Stockholm, and the main operators have offices in the harbour-front terminals. The leading operators for Helsinki are Eckerö Lines at Terminal B (car ferries; ☏ 631 8606, ⊛ www.eckeroline.ee); Nordic Jet Line at Terminal C (catamarans; ☏ 613 7000, ⊛ www.njl.info); and Tallink at Terminal A (car ferries and catamarans; ☏ 640 9808, ⊛ www.tallink.ee). Tallink's service to Stockholm is at Terminal D. It's worth bearing in mind also that getting an onward connection from Helsinki to Stockholm may be quicker than going direct from Tallinn.

All domestic and international **bus routes** are served by the long-distance bus station (Autobussijaam), 2km southeast of the Old Town at Lastekodu 46 (tram #2 from Mere pst or #4 from Pärnu mnt to the Autobussijaam stop). In summer and on weekends throughout the year it's worth booking international bus tickets in advance – as there are no agencies in the centre of town handling reservations, you'll have to trek out to the bus station itself to do this.

Train services from the Balti Jaam (Baltic Station), right on the west side of the Old Town, are less frequent and take longer than buses – St Petersburg and Moscow are the only international destinations offered. Tickets are sold from windows in the main hall.

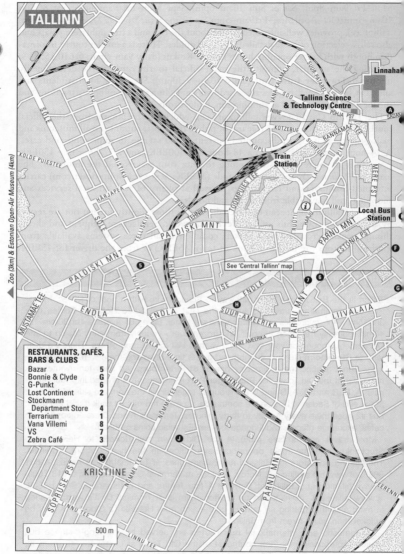

Zoo (3km) & Estonian Open-Air Museum (4km)

RESTAURANTS, CAFÉS, BARS & CLUBS

Bazar	5
Bonnie & Clyde	G
G-Punkt	6
Lost Continent	2
Stockmann Department Store	4
Terrarium	1
Vana Villemi	8
VS	7
Zebra Café	3

Tickets need to be validated using the on-board punches. In theory, **taxis** are reasonably cheap – however they are also notorious for overcharging. The best way to avoid getting ripped off is to order one in advance from a recommended taxi company (see p.96) and fix a rough price beforehand; you can also find taxi ranks at all major entrances to the pedestrianized Old Town. Most companies have a minimum charge of at least 25EEK.

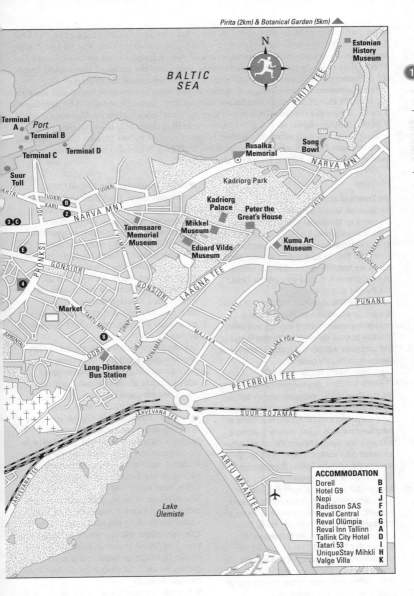

ACCOMMODATION

Dorell	B
Hotel G9	E
Nepi	J
Radisson SAS	F
Reval Central	C
Reval Olümpia	G
Reval Inn Tallinn	A
Tallink City Hotel	D
Tatari 53	I
UniqueStay Mihkli	H
Valge Villa	K

Accommodation

Barely a month goes by without a new **hotel** opening up in Tallinn, ensuring that there's no shortage of modern, high-standard accommodation. Most of the hotels in the Old Town are in the luxury bracket or just below, although over the last couple of years several new **hostels** have also sprung up, the majority of which are pretty good.

Most mid-range choices are located in the inner-city areas south and east of the Old Town, within easy walking distance of most sights and amenities. The budget hotels tend to be Soviet-era establishments, many of which haven't been renovated since the 1980s; they're likely to be a tram or bus ride away from the action. There's also a handful of homely **B&Bs**, mostly in Kristiine and outer residential districts.

Private rooms are another good option if you want somewhere cheap and close to the heart of things, although conditions vary widely: in most cases you'll be sleeping in a small, minimally furnished room and sharing your host's bathroom. Rasastra at Mere 4 (daily 9.30am–6pm; ☎661 6291, ⓦwww.bedbreakfast.ee), is an accommodation-finding service which offers the widest range of central rooms (singles from 260EEK, doubles from 460EEK and apartments from 850EEK). It can also fix up similar accommodation in Tartu, Pärnu, Haapsalu and Viljandi.

Hotels

Old Town and around

Baltic Hotel Vana Wiru Viru 11 (entrance round the corner on Müürivahe) ☎669 1500, ⓦwww .baltichotelgroup.com. A swish, four-star hotel with an enticing combination of top-level comfort, and a superb Old Town location and competitive prices. Rooms are tastefully decorated in pale yellows, blues or greens, and come with satellite TV and free Internet access. ⑥

Domina Inn City Vana-Posti 11/13 ☎681 3900, ⓦwww.dominahotels.com. Stylish rooms in a restored eighteenth-century building, with plenty of classy touches like marble bathroom fittings and computers with Internet access in every room. Service is particularly good. ⑦

🏃 **Merchant's House** Dunkri 4/6 ☎697 7500, ⓦwww.merchantshousehotel .ee. In a three-storey, fourteenth-century building a few steps from the town square, this boutique hotel is a perfect blend of old and new. Some of the chicest rooms in Tallinn come with exposed brickwork and wooden beams; the opulent suites are wonderful. Excellent Internet deals. ⑥–⑦

Meriton Grand Hotel Tallinn Toompuiestee 27 ☎667 7000, ⓦwww.meritonhotels.com. Just down the hill from the Old Town, this four-star hotel's uninspiring, functionalist exterior doesn't make a good first impression. Inside, however, you find spacious, recently renovated rooms; those facing east have great views of Toompea. ⑦

Meriton Old Town Hotel Lai 49 ☎614 1300, ⓦwww.meritonhotels.com. Set in a restored nineteenth-century building which contains part of the old city wall, rooms at the *Meriton*, though small, have all modern comforts. ⑥

Metropol Roseni 13 ☎ 667 4500, ⓦwww .metropol.ee. A big, mid-range establishment not far from the port, the *Metropol* has decent en suites with faintly 1970s decor and a casino. At the time of writing, however, there was a lot of building work going on nearby – the area can be noisy. ⑥

OldHouse Guesthouse Uus 22 ☎641 1464, ⓦwww.oldhouse.ee. This friendly, six-room B&B has an intimate feel. Rooms with shared facilities are bright and pristine, while the owners also rent out two- and four-person private apartments (1100–1600EEK per night) in buildings close by. ③

Old Town Maestro's Suur-Karja 10 ☎626 2000, ⓦwww.maestrohotel.ee. This smallish four-star hotel – there are only 23 rooms – is in a tall, narrow building on a central street packed with bars and pubs, so late-night noise can be an issue. En-suite rooms, with 1930s-style touches, are spacious and comfortable, but not especially exciting. ⑥

Scandic Palace Vabaduse väljak 3 ☎640 7300, ⓦwww.scandic-hotels.com. A handsome inter-war building overlooking a lively downtown square, offering sizeable, comfortable rooms, with deep-pile carpets and pastel tones. ⑦

Schlössle Pühavaimu 13/15 ☎699 7777, ⓦwww.schlossle-hotels.com. The five-star luxury of this impeccably restored fifteenth-century building attracts the great and the good – and from the medieval charm of the entrance to the artfully decorated rooms to the intimate atmosphere, it's easy to see why. Doubles start at 5900EEK. ⑧

Sokos Hotel Viru Viru väljak 4 ☎630 1390, ⓦwww.viru.ee. All the big-hotel facilities – beauty centre, several bars and restaurants, three saunas – make this 22-storey place on the edge of the Old Town very popular with tour groups, particularly those from Finland. Modern en suites come with satellite TV, minibar and subtle blue or cream colour schemes. Great views of the Old Town from the upper floors. ⑦

St Petersbourg Rataskaevu 7 ☎628 6500, ⓦwww.schlossle-hotels.com. The oldest continually operating hotel in Tallinn has smart, bright rooms (with features like DVD players) and a few Art Deco touches in the common areas. Only marginally less luxurious than sister-hotel *Schlössle*. ⑧

Three Sisters Pikk 71 ☎630 6300, ⓦwww .threesistershotel.com. A wonderfully renovated trio of neighbouring medieval merchants' houses, dating back 450 years, the award-winning *Three Sisters* has fantastic rooms. Painted ceilings, exposed brickwork and wooden beams blend seamlessly with tasteful, modern designer furnishings. Unsurprisingly, all the rooms are suites, from 5039EEK. **⑧**

Taanilinna Hotell Uus 6 ℡ 640 6700, ⓦ www.taanilinna.ee. Rooms are on the small side in this former nineteenth-century town house, but come with chic decoration and wooden floors. The wine cellar is an added bonus. **⑦**

UniqueStay Tallinn Paldiski mnt 1/3 ℡ 660 0700, ⓦ www.uniquestay.com. A hyper-modern hotel within spitting distance of the Old Town. Standard rooms are stylishly minimalist and feature desktop computers with free Internet access; more expensive "Zen" rooms add to this whirlpool baths and NASA-designed chairs. **⑥–⑦**

East and south of the Old Town

Dorell Karu 39 (entrance through a passage on Narva mnt) ℡ 666 4333, ⓦ www.dorell.ee. This cheapie has an unprepossessing location amid drab grey housing blocks, but is in walking distance from the Old Town. Rooms are spacious but garish; the cheaper ones are without en-suite bathroom. **❸**

🏃 **Hotel G9** Gonsiori 9 ℡ 626 7100, ⓦ www.hotelg9.ee. A simple place on the third floor of an office block five minutes' walk from the Old Town, with spotless, airy singles, doubles, triples and quads, all with bathroom and TV. No breakfast, but staff are welcoming and help make *G9* an excellent-value option. Book ahead. **❸**

Radisson SAS Rävala pst 3 ℡ 669 0000, ⓦ www.tallinn.radissonsas.com. One of the tallest structures in Tallinn, the *Radisson SAS* is in a sleek modern building, a ten-minute walk outside the Old Town. Rooms, which have Scandinavian, Oriental, Italian or nautical decor and furnishings, deliver high standards of comfort and quality. Geared towards the business traveller. **⑦**

Reval Central Narva mnt 7C ℡ 633 9800, ⓦ www.revalhotels.com. Recently renovated, this modern three-star with 200-plus rooms is a bit lacking in atmosphere, but the compact, uncluttered rooms are good value. **④–⑤**

Reval Inn Tallinn Sadama 1 ℡ 667 8700, ⓦ www.revalinn.com. A busy, impersonal, box-like hotel close to the harbour that nevertheless delivers the goods: smart en suites with TV within easy walking distance of all the sights. **④**

Reval Olümpia Liivalaia 33 ℡ 669 0690, ⓦ www.revalhotels.com. Glass-and-steel slab built in 1980 (when Tallinn hosted the Olympic yachting events),

with levels of comfort and service that fully justify its four-star status. The top-floor sauna, swimming pool and gym boast stunning views of the city. 500m from the Old Town. **⑦**

Tallink City Hotel Laikmaa 5 ℡ 630 0808, ⓦ www.tallink.com. It's hard to miss this looming, shiny, mirror-plated hotel, owned by the Tallink ferry company and located behind Viru Keskus. Rooms are modern but lack the charm of some of the other hotels in this price range. There's a restaurant, bar and nightclub downstairs. **⑦**

Tatari 53 Tatari 53 (entrance is behind Pärnu mnt 69) ℡ 640 5150, ⓦ www.tatari53.ee. A straightforward, no-frills mid-range choice a fifteen-minute walk from the Old Town, *Tatari 53* has comfortable en suites with TV and smooth service. **④**

UniqueStay Mihkli Endla 23 ℡ 666 4800, ⓦ www.uniquestay.com. The sister hotel to *Unique-Stay Tallinn* has the same state-of-the-art rooms at a slightly cheaper price, as a result of a location 450m from the Old Town. **⑤**

Kristiine

Nepi Nepi 10 ℡ 655 1665 or 655 2254, ⓦ www.nepihotell.ee. This small and welcoming B&B has plain, brown-carpeted rooms with en-suite shower and TV. A couple of apartment-style rooms come with more tasteful, if vaguely 1970s-era, furnishings. Bus #17 or #17A to Koolimaja, or bus #23 to Ööbiku. **❷–❸**

Valge Villa Kännu 26/2 ℡ 654 2302, ⓦ www.white-villa.com. The "White Villa" is a homely B&B tucked away on a quiet suburban street. Comfy en-suite rooms have wood-panelled walls and plenty of character. The family who own and run it provide the warmest of welcomes. Bus #17 or #17A to the Rääqu stop, or trolleybus #2, #3 or #4 to the Tedre stop. **❸**

Hostels

City Guesthouse Pärnu mnt 10 ℡ 628 2236, ⓦ www.cityguesthouse.ee. Spread over three floors of a large building just outside the Old Town, *City Guesthouse* is a good budget choice, with comfortable three- to five-bed dorms (300EEK), and neat and tidy private rooms with shared facilities (**❹**). Bathrooms are clean and breakfast is included in the price.

Eurohostel Nunne 2 ℡ 644 7788, ⓦ www.eurohostel.ee. Through the sturdy, carved-wood door and up a creaky staircase you find airy three- to eight-bed dorms (280EEK), as well as plain doubles with high ceilings (**❸**). The location – just a few steps from the town square – is hard to beat.

Old Town Alur Lai 20 ℡ 646 6210, ⓦ www.alur.ee. A new hostel in a renovated town house in the

Old Town, *Alur* is a friendly place with bunk-bed dorms (230–260EEK), plus a number of singles, doubles, triples and quads (❸). Bathrooms are modern and clean, and there's a kitchen, common room and free Wi-Fi access for guests.

🏃 **OldHouse Hostel** Uus 26 ☎641 1464, Ⓦwww.oldhouse.ee. Run by the folks at *OldHouse Guesthouse* (see p.70), this high-quality hostel on the northern edge of the Old Town has six-bed dorms (290EEK), immaculate bathrooms and a TV room. Homely singles, doubles, triples and quads (all with shared facilities) are also available (❸).
Tallinn Backpackers Lai 10 ☎644 0298, Ⓦwww.tallinnbackpackers.com. A few doors along

from *Alur* is an equally welcoming but more basic hostel, with six- and ten-bed dorms (200–225EEK). It's run by backpackers and as a result has a fun atmosphere: films are shown on a big screen and cheap day-trips to places like Lahemaa are on offer. It also has a handful of private rooms in an adjacent building (❸).
Vana Tom Väike-Karja 1 ☎631 3252, Ⓦwww.hostel.ee. It does share an entrance with a strip club, but don't let that put you off; this hostel in the heart of the Old Town has a decent collection of smallish dorms (200EEK) and good-value private rooms (❷), all with kitchen access. If you're an HI member you can knock 15EEK off the price.

The City

The heart of Tallinn and location of most of its sights is the **Old Town** (Vanalinn), once enclosed by medieval walls, significant stretches of which still exist. Above it looms **Toompea**, hilltop stronghold of the German knights and bishops who nominally controlled the city during the Middle Ages. Beyond the medieval core, much of Tallinn is bland and uninteresting, with notable exceptions, namely the park and palace at **Kadriorg** and the **Botanical Gardens** above the beach resort of **Pirita** – all located in the eastern suburbs. The **Estonian Open–Air Museum** in Rocca al Mare is the one unmissable attraction in the western part of town.

The Old Town

Tallinn's largely pedestrianized Old Town is an enjoyable, atmospheric and ultimately addictive jumble of medieval churches, cobbled streets and gabled merchants' houses. With a street plan that comprises a confusion of curving streets and interconnecting passageways, there are few obvious itineraries to follow, although the **Raekoja plats** provides an obvious point of reference. From here, your best plan is to amble down any of the adjacent alleyways that take your fancy, emerging onto sinuous streets like **Pikk**, **Lai** and **Vene** – each of which is lined with tall, quietly imperious medieval warehouses. Must-visit attractions include the entertaining history displays at the **Tallinn City Museum** and the show-stopping medieval artworks in **St Nicholas's Church**.

Raekoja plats and around

The cobbled and gently sloping **Raekoja plats** (Town Hall Square) is as old as Tallinn itself. Surrounded by a handsome ensemble of pastel-coloured houses, the square has become a trademark of both the city and Estonia as a whole, reproduced on innumerable souvenirs and tourist posters. It is also a popular rallying point and a focus for displays of Estonian patriotic feeling: over 10,000 people packed the square in February 2002 to salute Andrus Veerpalu, the cross-country skier who had just struck gold in the Winter Olympics at Salt Lake City, while eight months earlier it had been the site of a vast open-air reception for Tanel Padar and Dave Benton, winners of the 2001 Eurovision Song Contest – it was on this occasion that the then Prime Minister Mart Laar made a since oft-quoted remark about Estonia singing its way out of the Soviet Union and into the EU.

On the square's southern side stands an imposing reminder of the city's Hanseatic past: the fifteenth-century **Town Hall** (Tallinna raekoda), boasting an elegant arcade of Gothic arches and a delicate, slender steeple. Look out for the waterspouts in the shape of green dragons just below the roof. Near the summit of the steeple you'll spy Vana Toomas (Old Thomas), a sixteenth-century weather vane in the form of a stout, spear-wielding sentry. According to legend, the real-life model for the weather vane was a local lad who excelled at the springtime "parrot-shooting" contests (which involved firing crossbow bolts at a painted wooden bird on top of a pole) organized by Tallinn's German-speaking elite. Unable to receive a prize owing to his low-born status, Toomas was instead rewarded with the job of town guard for life. Subsequently immortalized in copper, Toomas continues to watch over Tallinn and its citizens. Inside the Town Hall, the two main chambers – the Citizens' Hall and the Council Hall – are almost devoid of ornamentation, save for the latter's elaborately carved benches, the oldest surviving woodcarvings in the country.

Of the other old buildings lining the square, the most venerable is the **Town Council Pharmacy** (Raeapteek) in the northeastern corner; its cream-coloured facade dates from the seventeenth century, though the building is known to have existed in 1422 and may be much older. It's still a working pharmacy – which is probably a good job judging by the rather half-hearted attempt at creating a museum (Mon–Fri 9am–7pm, Sat 9am–5pm; free) in one of its corners. If the Raeapteek leaves you underwhelmed, head for the former jail (Raevangla) behind the Town Hall at Raekoja 4/6, now home to the **Museum of Photography** (Fotomuuseum; daily except Wed: March–Oct 10.30am–6pm; Nov–Feb 10.30am–5pm; 15EEK), an entertaining little photographic collection with views of Tallinn from the days when it was still known as Reval and portraits of Estonians in traditional costume (captions in English).

The Church of the Holy Ghost

Next to the Raeapteek, a small passage named Saiakang leads through to Pühavaimu tänav and one of the city's most appealing churches, the **Church of the Holy Ghost** (Pühavaimu kirik; Jan–April Mon–Sat 9.30am–5.30pm, Sun 10am–4pm; May–Aug Mon–Sat 9.30am–6.30pm, Sun 10am–6.30pm; Sept–Dec daily 10am–5.30pm; 10EEK). A small Gothic building with stepped gables, it originally served as the Town Hall chapel before becoming the main church of Tallinn's Estonian-speaking population. In 1535, priests from the church compiled an Estonian-language Lutheran catechism, an important affirmation of identity at a time when most Estonians had been reduced to serfdom. The ornate clock set into the wall above the entrance dates from 1680 and is Tallinn's oldest public timepiece. The slender, verdigris-coated spire was almost totally wrecked by fire in May 2002 and underwent a year-long period of restoration. The interior of the church – dark-veneered wood and cream-painted walls – has an intimate beauty and contains one of the city's most significant pieces of religious art, an extraordinary triptych centred on an intricately rendered grouping of painted wooden statuettes representing the *Descent of the Holy Ghost* (1483) by the Lübeck master Berndt Notke (1430–1509).

Along Pikk tänav

At the northern end of Raekoja plats sprouts a sequence of small alleyways crammed with cafés and souvenir shops. Most of them emerge onto medieval Tallinn's main thoroughfare, **Pikk tänav** ("Long Street"), cutting northeast to southwest through the town. It would have been an important link between the ecclesiastical and military buildings of Toompea and the port area, traversing the main business district on the way. Along the street's 800-metre length lie some of the city's most important secular buildings from the Hanseatic period, kicking off with the forbidding Gothic facade of the **House of the Great Guild** (Suurgildi hoone) at Pikk 17. Completed in 1430, this provided a home for the most powerful of the city's guilds, uniting the city's German-speaking mercantile elite into an organization that effectively controlled commerce in the city. The Great Guild's doors were closed to Tallinn's petty merchants and artisans, who were instead organized into lesser institutions, such as the largely Estonian-speaking Guild of Corpus Christi. The Great Guild was the focus of many of medieval Tallinn's social events, notably the traditional springtime tournaments, when the so-called May Count was chosen – a practice recently revived to form the centrepiece of the Old Town Days festival, a tourist-oriented piece of pageantry which now takes place in late May and early June.

RESTAURANTS & CAFÉS

African Kitchen	1	Kuldse Notsu Körts	19
Anneli Vikk Handmade Chocolates Café	7	Le Bonaparte	3
Artemis Souvlaki	8	Leiburi Pagariäri	43
Bocca	2	Maiasmokk	10
Bogapott	29	Mata Hari	35
Buongiorno	36	Möökkala	39
Coffer	24	Must Lammas	33
Controvento	17	Olde Hansa	20
Eesti Maja	47	Pegasus	32
Elevant	18	Pizza Americana	42
Elsebet	26	Robert's Coffee	25
Gloria	41	St Michael Juusturestoran	9
Golden Dragon	4	Tristan ja Isolde	21
Karl Friedrich	16	Troika	14
Kehrwieder	12	Vanaema Juures	22

BARS, PUBS & CLUBS

Angel	28	Karja Kelder	O
Basso	11	Kompressor	15
Beer House	23	Molly Malone's	13
BonBon	5	Moskva	45
Café Amigo	N	Nimega Baar	37
Deja Vu	30	Nimeta Baar	31
Guitar Safari	38	Privé	46
Hell Hunt	6	St Patrick's	34
Hollywood	40	Stereo Lounge	44
Hookah House	48	X Baar	27
Ice Bar	K		

Map labels: POHJA PUIESTEE · Train Station · RANNAMÄE TEE · Tornide Väljak · Church of the Transfiguration · OLD TOWN · NUNNE · Nukuteater · Snelli Pond · TOOMPUIES TEE · Toompark · Lutheran Cathedral · Von Krahl Theatre · RAATSKAEVU · DUNKRI · PIKK JALG · Adamson-Eric Museum · NIGULISTE · St Nicholas's Church · TOOM-KOOLI · Aleksander Nevsky Cathedral · TOOMPEA · Väravatorn · RUUTLI · HARJU · LOSSI PLATS · Kiek-in-de-kök · FALGI TEE · KOMANDANDI · TOOMPEA · Lindamägi · VABADUSE VALJAK · Hirvepark · WISMARI · The Museum of Occupation & of The Fight for Freedom · LUISE · ENDLA · City Council Building

0 — 200 m

74

Energy Centre ▲

▲ Ferry Port (200m)

ACCOMMODATION

Baltic Hotel Vana Wiru	M
City Guesthouse	T
Domina Inn City	R
Eurohostel	I
Merchant's House	K
Meriton Grand Hotel Tallinn	Q
Meriton Old Town Hotel	B
Metropol	G
OldHouse Guesthouse	F
OldHouse Hostel	C
Old Town Alur	D
Old Town Maestro's	P
Scandic Palace	U
Schlössle	H
Sokos Hotel Viru	N
St Petersbourg	L
Taanilinna Hotell	J
Tallinn Backpackers	E
Three Sisters	A
UniqueStay Tallinn	S
Vana Tom	O

Estonia Ferry Monument

Great Sea Gate

Maritime Museum

St Olaf's Church

Applied Art & Design Museum

Linnateater

Health Museum

House of the Blackheads

City Museum

Great Guild

Church of the Holy Ghost Raeapteek

Dominican Monastery

Theatrum

Town Hall

Photography Museum

Viru Gate

Viru Väljak

Salt Storage Warehouse

THE ROTERMANN QUARTER

Museum of Theatre & Music

Tallinn Art Hall

St John's Church

Estonian Drama Theatre

Estonia Theatre & Concert Hall

Kaubamaja Department Store

Russian Drama Theatre

Boy of Bronze

Sakala Concert Hall

Vanalinnastudio

Bus station & Airport ▶

CENTRAL TALLINN

SUURTÜKI

GÜMNAASIUMI

PIKK TANAV

LAI

UUS

RANNAMÄE TEE

MERE PUIESTEE

PÜHAVAIMU

VENE

APTEEGI

KATARINA KÄIK

KULLASEPPA

VIRU

VANA-POSTI

SUUR-KARJA

VÄIKE-KARJA

MUURIVAHE

PÄRNU MNT

G. OTSA

ESTONIA PST

SAKALA

75

The Great Guild's gloomy exterior now fronts the **Estonian History Museum** (Eesti ajaloomuuseum; daily except Wed 11am–6pm; 10EEK; ⓦwww.eam.ee), where the history of Estonia from the Stone Age to the eighteenth century is traced via an uninspiring and predictable array of weapons, domestic objects and jewellery. An assortment of bracelets and necklaces from twelfth-century graves and a scale model of Narva in the eighteenth century do their best to enliven the proceedings. Another branch of the museum, on the outskirts of the city beyond Kadriorg Park, has a rather more inspiring collection; see p.87.

If the appearance of their headquarters is anything to go by, the guild that occupied the **House of the Blackheads** (Mustpeade maja), Pikk 26, was a more exuberant bunch than the merchants of the Great Guild. The Renaissance facade of their building, inset with an elaborate stone portal and richly decorated door, cuts a bit of dash amid the stolidity of Pikk. Like its namesake in Rīga, Tallinn's Brotherhood of the Blackheads was formed to accommodate visiting bachelor merchants and took the North African St Maurice as its patron – hence the name of the organization. Unlike in Rīga, however, the Blackheads here also served a military purpose, organizing defence detachments (Blackheads fought off Russian besiegers during the Livonian Wars) and honouring visiting dignitaries with parades. Legend has it that the guild was founded to defend Tallinn during the Estonian uprising of St George's Day in 1343, though in later years it seems to have degenerated into a drinking club. The Brotherhood moved here in 1531 and stayed until 1940, when the Soviets turfed out a dwindling crew of survivors. Nowadays, the house's main first-floor hall is the venue for regular chamber concerts – attending one of these is probably your best chance of getting to see the elegant, wood-panelled interior.

Continuing along Pikk brings you to **St Olaf's Church** (Oleviste kirik), first mentioned in 1267 and named in honour of King Olaf II of Norway, who was canonized for massacring pagans in Scandinavia. This slab-towered Gothic structure would not be particularly eye-catching were it not for the height of its **spire**, which reaches 124m and used to be even taller. According to local legend, the citizens of Tallinn wanted the church to have the highest spire in the world in order to attract passing ships and bring trade into the city. Whether Tallinn's prosperity in the Middle Ages had anything to do with the visibility of the church spire is not known, but between 1625 and 1820 the church burnt down eight times as a result of lightning striking it. Occupying a niche low down on the rear exterior wall of the church is the tombstone of plague victim Johann Ballivi, an outstanding piece of fifteenth-century stone-carving, featuring a deliciously macabre depiction of a decaying body surrounded by delicately rendered mourners. The church's interior is relatively unexceptional, the product of extensive renovation between 1829 and 1840.

Most striking of the Old Town's gabled merchants' houses are the **Three Sisters** (Kolm õde), just beyond St Olaf's Church at Pikk 71. Among the city's best-preserved Hanseatic buildings, these supremely functional buildings, with loading hatches and winch-arms set into their facades, would have been dwelling places, warehouses and offices all rolled into one. Recently, they have been converted into an upmarket hotel (see p.70) and painted in snazzy, citrus colours, giving them the appearance of a monumental trio of ready-to-lick Gothic lollies.

Fat Margaret and the Maritime Museum

At its northern end Pikk is straddled by the **Great Sea Gate** (Suur rannavärav), a sixteenth-century arch flanked by two towers. The larger of these, the barrel-shaped "**Fat Margaret**" (Paks Margareeta), has walls 4m thick. Pressed into use as the city jail, the tower witnessed Tallinn's first outbreak of violence during the Revolution of March 1917, when striking workers joined mutineering soldiers and sailors in an assault on the prison, murdering the warders and setting the tower alight. It now houses the **Estonian Maritime Museum** (Eesti meremuuseum; Wed–Sun 10am–6pm; 25EEK; Estonian, Russian and some English captions), a diverting collection of model boats and nautical ephemera spread out over several floors. Sounding a poignant note, one of the exhibits is a scale model of the *Estonia*, the car ferry that sank midway between Tallinn and Stockholm on September 28, 1994, with the loss of 852 lives.

The area on the far side of Fat Margaret, now occupied by a road junction and a few scrappy bits of park, used to be known as the Parrot Garden in honour of the "parrot shooting" contests (see p.73) held here every spring in medieval times. Victors were presented with a silver salver and then borne in triumphal procession along Pikk to the Great Guild.

Along Lai tänav

Southwest of Fat Margaret, **Lai tänav** ("Broad Street") is another of the Old Town's set-piece thoroughfares, with rows of high-gabled merchants' houses haughtily presiding over the cobbled streets below, their cast-iron weather vanes creaking in the wind. Occupying a courtyard behind Lai 17, the **Applied Art and Design Museum** (Tarbekunstimuuseum; Wed–Sun 11am–6pm; 30EEK) pays tribute to Estonia's strong design traditions with a well-presented collection of textiles, jewellery and ceramics; one of the highlights is the highly desirable "caveman" tea-set designed in 1937 by Adamson-Eric (see p.79), with spindly human figures chasing mammoths and other beasts around the cups and saucers. Diagonally opposite, the **Health Museum** at Lai 28 (Tervishoiu muuseum; Tues–Sat 11am–6pm; 20EEK) was clearly designed with local schoolchildren in mind, and has didactic diagrams and grisly photographs detailing the horrors that will result from unprotected sex or recreational drugs (rock 'n' roll for some reason fails to feature).

The city walls

Just beyond the Health Museum, Suur-Kloostri strikes off westwards past the **Church of the Transfiguration** (Issanda muutlise kirik), the centrepiece of a sizeable Cistercian convent until the Reformation. It was given to the Orthodox Church during the reign of Peter the Great. At the end of the street, Vaike-Kloostri threads its way below one of the longest surviving sections of Tallinn's medieval **city wall**, here featuring nine complete towers and three gates. Passing through any one of the gates and crossing the park-like expanse of Tornide väljak on the other side, provides a wonderful view back towards the towers, which look like a series of squat crimson crayons. The walls were largely constructed during the fourteenth century, then added to over the years until improvements in artillery rendered them obsolete during the eighteenth century. Citizens of medieval Tallinn were each obliged to do a stint of guard duty – one of the annual exercises required them all to gather on the walls in full armour and shake their weapons as a sign of military readiness. Once you've had your fill of turrets you can re-enter the Old Town along Nunne or alternatively continue southwest towards the **Toompark**, a relaxing expanse of lawns and flowerbeds draped around the western slopes of the Toompea. In the middle of the park is the Snelli Pond, a W-shaped stretch of former moat that becomes a hugely popular outdoor skating rink in winter.

Along Vene: the City Museum and the Dominican Monastery

Another way of returning to the centre from Fat Margaret's end of town is to zig-zag your way east from Pikk, via the narrow streets of Sulevimägi and Olevimägi, onto Vene, another of the Old Town's main arteries, that heads south to join up with Viru. Occupying a handsomely restored merchant's house at Vene 17 is the **Tallinn City Museum** (Tallinna linnamuuseum; daily except Tues: March–Oct 10.30am–6pm; Nov–Feb 10.30am–5pm; 35EEK; ⓦ www.linnamuuseum.ee), a superbly arranged collection over three floors brought to life by the inclusion of costumed wax figures, medieval street sounds and illuminating English-language texts. A cutaway model of a sixteenth-century merchant's house reveals how these buildings once functioned, with vast cranes jutting from facades hauling merchandise to the upper storeys, where it was warehoused before being re-exported or sold in the shop space at ground level. Original furnishings and costumes feature in a display of nineteenth-century interiors, while events of the twentieth century unfold through a collection of posters and photographs (including one of an enormous Stalin poster draped incongruously over the facade of the Town Hall), and videos document the growth of the independence movement.

Diagonally opposite the museum at Vene 16, the **Dominican Monastery** was one of the most powerful institutions in medieval Tallinn – until it was comprehensively trashed by anti-Catholic rioters in 1525. The site was subsequently used as a school, hospital and arsenal before a new church was built in the mid-nineteenth century, which remains the main Catholic place of worship in the city. Some of the former monastery buildings now accommodate the **Dominican Monastery Museum** (Dominiiklaste kloostri muuseum; mid-May to mid-Sept daily 10am–6pm, at other times by prior arrangement; 90EEK; ⓦwww.kloostri.ee), home to an extensive collection of medieval and Renaissance stone-carving, including some intricate fourteenth-century tombstones. Look out for a delightful relief of an angel set in a triangular frame courtesy of Arendt Passer – the doyen of sixteenth-century stone masonry who also worked on the portal of the House of the Blackheads (see p.76) and the tomb of Pontus de la Gardie in Tallinn Cathedral (p.81).

Immediately south of the monastery, a narrow alleyway known as **Katariina kaik** ("Catherine's Passage") runs round the surviving wall of the original monastery church, passing a string of craft workshops where you can observe potters, bookbinders and glaziers at work (see "Shopping", p.94).

St Nicholas's Church

Heading south from Raekoja plats along Kullaseppa leads to a patch of raised open ground, upon which sits the imposing **St Nicholas's Orthodox Church** (Niguliste kirik; Wed–Sun 10am–5pm; 35EEK; English-language pamphlets available). A three-aisled basilica fashioned from huge chunks of limestone, this was initially put up by Westphalian merchants in the thirteenth century, although most of what can be seen today dates from the fifteenth – especially the apse and the sturdy tower, built with defence in mind. Extensively restored following Soviet bombing raids at the end of World War II, it's now a **museum**, gathering together the surviving crop of Tallinn's medieval artworks – most of which perished in the Protestant riots of September 1524. St Nicholas's itself was saved from a thorough ransacking by the quick thinking of the warden, who – so the story goes – poured lead in the locks to prevent the raiders from gaining access. Standing

△ St Nicholas's Church

out among a clutch of Gothic altarpieces is a spectacular double-winged altar by Herman Rode of Lübeck from 1481, in which scenes featuring the life of St Nicholas figure prominently, although St George is also shown effortlessly skewering a dragon on one panel, and getting his head chopped off in another. Standing to the left of the altar is a sixteenth-century Crucifixion scene by an anonymous Bruges painter, in which Jerusalem is embellished with the kind of medieval towers and bastions that wouldn't look out of place in a north European city like Tallinn. Over on the right, the so-called **Altar of the Blackheads** was painted for the Brotherhood by a Bruges master, who depicted robed Blackhead members kneeling in prayer on the inner sides of the wings. The central panel shows a golden-tressed Madonna flanked by S George and Maurice.

Occupying pride of place at the rear of the church is a largish fragment from a fifteenth-century *Dance of Death* frieze by Berndt Notke. It's an outstanding example of the genre, with skeletal figures swaying gracefully to a bagpipe ditty while cajoling a bishop, king and noblewoman to join in the fun – unsurprisingly, they look less than enthusiastic. Elsewhere around the sides of the nave lie a series of striking seventeenth-century tomb-top effigies: note the delicate floral pillow upon which rests Berndt Reinhold von Delung (died 1699), and the stiff handlebar moustache and full body armour of Hermann Neuroth (died 1641).

A side chapel near the main entrance used to hold the mummified form of Duke Charles-Eugène de Croy, who commanded the Russian army at Narva in 1701 and, electing to stand and fight rather than flee like his troops, was taken prisoner by Charles XII of Sweden. He died a year later and ended up being propped up here because nobody was prepared to pay for a decent burial (he wasn't the only one to endure this fate either: Tallinn's church wardens were notorious for demanding funeral expenses upfront). Protected from decay by dry weather, de Croy's corpse soon became an attraction, and remained on display until 1897, when the authorities finally saw fit to stick it in the ground.

The church's sonorous **organ** is put through its paces every Saturday and Sunday, with **recitals** starting at around 4 or 5pm: details of the current week's performance are posted at the entrance.

The Adamson-Eric Museum

A few steps west of the church entrance, Lühike jalg climbs uphill to Toompea (see p.80). The medieval merchant's house at no. 3 now houses the **Adamson-Eric Museum** (Wed–Sun 11am–6pm; 15EEK), charting the career of Estonian art's most talented all-rounder. Born Erich Carl Hugo Adamson, Adamson-Eric (1902–68) drifted through various art and design schools in Tartu, Berlin and Paris before settling in Tallinn in the 1920s. He quickly garnered a reputation for producing accessible figurative paintings, while simultaneously churning out unabashedly abstract designs for tapestries, book-bindings and ceramics – all showcased here to good effect. The most popular of his paintings on display here, *In Summer* (1938), is also one of his most mischievous, subverting traditional Estonian ideas of rural wholesomeness by portraying a female subject clad in national costume – but only from the waist down. Like many nonconformists of his generation, Adamson-Eric supported the Soviet Union in the 1940s (his fawning portrait of Stalin entitled *On the Coast of the Baltic Sea* is sadly not on display here), but fell out of favour with the regime in the 1950s and was banned from exhibiting until the 1960s – by which time he'd retaught himself to paint with his left hand after a stroke had put paid to his right. Later works – Cubist designs for café murals, and rows of irregularly shaped ceramic tiles bearing primitive animal forms – show that he remained at the peak of his powers right to the last.

Along Harju to the Museum of Theatre and Music

On the eastern side of St Nicolas's Church, Harju tänav leads past a vacant lot filled with grassed-over ruins – a reminder of the night of 9 March, 1944, when the Soviet air force pummelled central Tallinn, destroying an estimated "53% of the city's living space", according to the accompanying signboard. On the opposite side of the street, the snazzy *Pegasus* eatery at Harju 1 (see "Restaurants", p.90) began life as a hip writers' and artists' café in the early 1960s and its super-cool, Modernist interior still survives in something approaching its original form. The café's most famous feature is the spiral staircase topped by Edgar Viies's sleek *Pegasus* – supposedly the first piece of abstract sculpture ever to appear in Soviet Estonia. Notwithstanding its small size, this graceful, three-pronged piece of aluminium is still as eloquent a statement of 1960s optimism as you'll find anywhere, and it's well worth stopping off for a drink here in order to see it.

Taking the next left brings you onto Müürivahe, a narrow street running east then north alongside what were once the city walls – chunks of medieval masonry still pepper the walls of many of the buildings around here. The **Museum of Theatre and Music** at Müürivahe 12 (Teatri-ja muusikamuuseum; Wed–Sun 10am–6pm; 20EEK) boasts publicity stills of stage stars in its stairwell and a motley collection of keyboards, music boxes and folk instruments upstairs – most striking of which is the *põispill*, a stringed instrument incorporating an animal-skin soundbox which looks like the result of an unnatural union between a cello and a bagpipe. More glamorous by half is the frilly black dress once worn by Meliza Korjus (1909–80), the soprano who made her name singing in the Estonia Concert Hall before emigrating to Hollywood – her appearance in the 1938 film *The Great Waltz* seemed to promise great things, until a car accident brought her career to a premature end.

Toompea

Looming over the Old Town to the southwest is the limestone outcrop known as **Toompea**, the site of an Estonian stockade fort until the Danes took it over in 1219 and built a stone castle, later wrested from them by the Livonian Order. As the nerve centre of the Christian effort to convert the pagan Estonians, Toompea (from the German word "Domberg", meaning "Cathedral Hill") often led a separate life from the rest of Tallinn below – which was much more interested in trade than ideology. The seat of several state and religious institutions, it still stands apart from the rest of central Tallinn – a somewhat secretive lair of bureaucrats and ministers rather than the happy-go-lucky habitat of shoppers and drinkers.

The most atmospheric approach to Toompea from the Old Town is through the sturdy gate tower – built by the Livonian Order to contain the Old Town's inhabitants in times of unrest – at the foot of Pikk jalg (Long Leg). This is the cobbled continuation of Pikk, the Old Town's main street, and climbs up to Lossi plats (Castle Square), dominated by the onion-domed Russian Orthodox **Cathedral of Alexander Nevsky**

△ Cathedral of Alexander Nevsky

(Aleksander Nevski katedraal; daily 8am–7pm; free). Built in 1900 to remind the local Estonians of their subservient position in the Tsarist scheme of things, this gaudy concoction has always had the slightly inappropriate appearance of an over-iced cake at a funeral feast. Inside, however, an aura of spiritual calm reigns supreme, with incense wafting over a lofty, icon-packed interior.

At the head of Lossi plats is **Toompea Castle** (Toompea loss), on the site of the original Danish fortification. The castle has been altered by every conqueror who raised his flag above it since then; these days it wears a shocking-pink Baroque facade, the result of an eighteenth-century rebuild under Catherine the Great. The northern and western walls are the oldest part of the castle and include three defensive towers, the most impressive of which is the fifty-metre Tall Hermann (Pikk Hermann) at the southwestern corner, dating from 1371.

As the home to the **Riigikogu**, Estonia's Parliament, Toompea witnessed many of the events leading up to the re-establishment of Estonia's independence – most notably on May 15, 1990, when citizens gathered to defend the building against followers of the pro-Soviet Intermovement, who were attempting to storm it.

The Cathedral

From Lossi plats, Toomkooli leads north to the **Cathedral of St Mary the Virgin** (Toomkirik; Tues–Sun 9am–4pm; English-language leaflet 10EEK), a homely, white-washed structure that, despite numerous rebuildings, doesn't appear to have changed much since the first stone church built by Danes here in 1240. Inside, set apart from the ordinary ranks of pews are glass-enclosed family boxes that would have been reserved for local notables, enabling them to keep their distance from the hoi polloi. Presiding over the pews is an ornate seventeenth-century pulpit by Christian Ackerman, who also carved many of the 107 coats of arms of noble families that adorn the white walls of the vaulted nave and choir. Stealing all the attention on the right-hand side of the main altar is the tomb of Pontus de la Gardie, the French-born mercenary who captured Narva for the Swedes in 1578, before massacring, it is said, 6000 of its inhabitants. The sarcophagus bears tender likenesses of Pontus and his wife, a fine piece of sculpture by local master Arendt Passer. Look out, too, for Giacomo Quarenghi's Neoclassical memorial to Admiral Samuel Greigh (died 1788) halfway down the aisle, ordered by Catherine the Great as a tribute to the Scots-born seadog who commanded Russian ships in the Black Sea.

Kiek-in-de-Kök and around

South of Lossi plats, a sloping park abuts another impressive stretch of town wall. Among the towers here is a gruff, grey blockhouse that once served as a prison for prostitutes – ironically named the Neitsitorn ("Virgins' Tower"); it's now home to one of the few café-bars popular in Soviet-era Tallinn that is still going strong today. Immediately south of the Neitsitorn is the impregnable-looking bastion known as **Kiek-in-de-Kök** (Tues–Sun: March–Oct 10.30am–6pm; Nov–Feb 10.30am–5pm; ☎644 6686; 25EEK), built in 1475 to provide a home for Toompea's main gun battery. Named in honour of a Low-German expression meaning "look in the kitchen" (the bastion's sentries could see straight into the parlours of downtown Tallinn), it now contains an entertaining, if sparse, collection of artefacts linked to the town's defences. There are suits of armour, rusty-looking weapons and replicas of the cannon once stationed here, variously nicknamed Lion, Fat Girl and Bitter Death – this last being engraved with the following cheerful rhyme:

Bitter Death is my name
Thus I travel everywhere
Killing the rich and the poor
To me, who I slay is all the same.

Staff at Kiek-in-de-Kök can also organize atmospheric tours of the recently rediscovered network of **seventeenth-century tunnels** within Toompea (Tues, Wed, Thurs, Fri & Sun; 5hr; advance booking necessary; 50EEK).

Originally built by the Swedes so they could hide from Russian attacks, they were used during World War II as air raid shelters and subsequently modernized by the Soviets, before slowly falling out of use.

Some 250m south of Kiek-in-de-Kök at Toompea 8 is the **Museum of Occupation and of the Fight for Freedom** (Okupatsiooni ja Vabadusvoitluse Muuseum; Tues–Sun 11am–6pm; 10EEK; Ⓦ www.okupatsioon.ee), which gives a fascinating insight into the 1939–91 period and the occupations of Estonia by first the German Reich and then the Soviet Union. A modern structure houses exhibits (including surveillance equipment, prison doors and military uniforms), art displays and audiovisual testimonies (in both Estonian and English).

Returning to Kiek-in-de-Kök, head immediately west to the paths that climb a wooded knoll known as **Lindamägi** ("Linda's Hill") after the woman in sculptural form who squats pensively at its summit. According to Estonian folk myth, Linda was the loving wife of Kalev and mother of superhuman hero Kalevipoeg. On the death of Kalev, Linda laboured to build a mound of rocks in his honour – Toompea is said to be the result. The statue is the work of August Weizenberg (1837–1921), a cabinet-maker who paid his way through art college in St Petersburg and Munich to become Estonia's first professional sculptor. Below Lindamägi to the south lies the leafy **Hirvepark**, scene of a 2000-strong gathering to mark the fiftieth anniversary of the Molotov-Ribbentrop Pact on August 23, 1987, one of the first big anti-Soviet demonstrations in the Baltics.

Round the fringes of the Old Town

Just outside the Old Town are some fine nineteenth- and twentieth-century buildings, housing theatres and concert halls, offices and department stores. The main thoroughfare here is **Pärnu mnt** and its northbound extension **Mere pst**.

Vabaduse väljak

East of Kiek-in-de-Kök, Komandandi tänav slopes downhill to **Vabaduse väljak**, a large open space formerly used for parades on May Day and other Soviet holidays. Laid out in the 1920s and 1930s, the square survives as something of an architectural tribute to the achievements of the inter-war state. Hugging the southeast corner of the square, the *Scandic Palace* hotel was the best place to stay in town during Estonia's first period of independence, and has re-emerged to become one of the more desirable tourist *pieds-à-terre* in the second. Standing on the same side of the square is a vivacious red-brick building built for the EKA insurance company in 1931 and now serving as the seat of Tallinn City Council; its facade is enlivened by chevrons and other zany brickwork patterns. More austere in appearance, but no less impressive, is the seven-storey Modernist cube standing roughly opposite on the northern side of the square, erected by an Estonian building society in 1934 and clearly intended as a muscular statement of the republic's self-confidence. Also dating from the 1930s – and a major institution ever since – is the next-door **Tallinn Art Hall**, Vabaduse väljak 6 (Tallinna Kunstihoone; Wed–Sun noon–6pm; price depends on exhibition), whose high-profile exhibitions showcase the best in contemporary Estonian art.

From Vabaduse väljak to Viru väljak

Running northeast from Vabaduse väljak, Pärnu mnt and Estonia pst follow roughly parallel paths round the eastern fringes of the Old Town. Presiding over Pärnu mnt at no. 4, the eye-catching **Estonian Drama Theatre** (Eesti draamateater), built in 1910 as the city's main German-language theatre, mixes Art Nouveau with Nordic folk motifs to produce a wealth of quirky detail: roofs resemble the shingles of village huts, and ancient bards in frieze form preside over the main entrance. Behind the theatre looms the much grander, but less engaging, **Estonia Theatre and Concert Hall**, financed by public contributions and completed in 1913 to provide Tallinn's Estonian-speaking majority with a cultural institution superior to anything that the city's Germans or Russians could muster. With the Estonian Philharmonic Orchestra occupying one wing and the opera and ballet performing in the other, it's still very much the nation's cultural flagship. On the southwestern side of the Concert Hall, just across G. Otsa tänav, a sculpture of a nude youth – the so-called "**Boy of Bronze**" – honours the high-school pupils who fell in the post-World War I struggle for independence. When Tallinn was in danger of falling to the Bolsheviks in the winter of 1918–19, the Estonian Commander-in-Chief General Laidoner was so starved of manpower that he had no choice but to appeal to the patriotic instincts of local schoolboys: equipped with improvised uniforms and obsolete rifles, they somehow managed to save the city.

The area northwest of the Concert Hall, nowadays a grassy park leading back to Pärnu mnt, used to be the site of the **town market** (now found 1.5km further east). It was here that Russian troops fired on left-wing protesters on October 16, 1905, killing 90 and wounding over 200. Four days later, an estimated 40,000 people (a staggering figure if true: it represents almost one in four of the entire city population) gathered in the market for the start of a mass funeral procession – one of the biggest anti-Tsarist demonstrations of the era. The market remained the focus of Tallinn life well into the 1920s – when British author Arthur Ransome marvelled at "pike still alive in bath-tubs" and "hunks of meat wrapped in newspaper and dripping blood and printers' ink".

Further northeast, beyond Tammsaare Park, Pärnu mnt and Estonia pst converge at **Viru väljak**, a bustling interchange and shopping area overlooked by the huge grey slab of the **Sokos Viru Hotel**. Built in the 1970s to accommodate holidaying Finns, the *Viru* long enjoyed the reputation of being the most Westernized hotel in the USSR – and was the automatic honeymoon venue of choice for any Soviet couple who could afford it.

The Rotermann Quarter

Due north of Viru, Mere pst heads south towards the port area, skirting the eastern ramparts of the Old Town on the way. On the eastern side of Mere lies the so-called **Rotermann Quarter**, an area of decaying factories and warehouses established by nineteenth-century industrialist Christian Abraham Rotermann. Neglected during much of the Soviet era, it's now prime inner-city redevelopment territory – a number of bars and cafés have already moved into the big warehouses running along the side of Mere. The most impressive of the quarter's buildings is the **Salt Storage Warehouse** at Ahtri 2 (Soololadu; mid-May to Sept Wed–Fri noon–8pm, Sat & Sun 11am–6pm; Oct to mid-May Wed–Sun 11am–6pm; 30EEK; ⓦwww.arhitektuurimuuseum.ee), built by Christian Abraham's grandson, Christian Barthold Rotermann, in 1908, and renovated in the mid-1990s to serve as an exhibition space. Shared by the Estonian Architecture and Art museums, it hosts all manner of top-notch exhibitions, often featuring visiting artists from abroad – shown to advantage in the warehouse's minimalist limestone-and-steel interior.

Towards the northern end of Mere pst, Rannamäe tee and Põhja pst break off to run round the northern tip of the Old Town. Here you can either re-enter the Old Town along Pikk, or venture over to the far side of Põhja, where the old power station at no. 29 has been transformed into the **Tallinn Science and Technology Centre** (Tallinna tehnika-ja teaduskeskus; July Mon–Fri 10am–6pm; Aug–June Mon–Fri 10am–6pm, Sat noon–5pm; 35EEK; ⓦwww.energiakeskus.ee). An enjoyable hands-on museum, it features endless halls full of strange-looking machines – many of which you can play around on if you can make any sense of the Estonian-language instructions.

The eastern outskirts

Tallinn's eastern outskirts are dotted with a number of worthwhile attractions that could easily take up a day or two of sightseeing. The nearest, just 2km east of the Old Town, is the heavily wooded area of **Kadriorg Park**, with its lavishly decorated Baroque palace, built by Peter the Great. Beyond Kadriorg, the broad shoreline boulevard, Pirita tee, extends along the Bay of Tallinn, passing one of the city's better history museums at **Maaramäe Palace**, before arriving at the haunting ruins of **Pirita Convent**. Uphill from here, the luxuriant **Botanical Gardens** and the **TV Tower**, with its unbeatable views of the city, are sufficiently distant from central Tallinn to have the feel of a rural excursion.

Kadriorg is a ten-minute tram ride from Viru väljak, while the other destinations in eastern Tallinn are only a slightly longer bus trip from the same spot – by combining public **transport** with a bit of walking, you can link up several (conceivably all) of the attractions below in a single day-trip.

Kadriorg Park

A grassy expanse stretching for some 1.5km from southwest to northeast, generously planted with oak, chestnut and lime trees and criss-crossed with avenues, **Kadriorg** is Tallinn's favourite **park**, built, together with the **palace** at its centre, for the Russian Tsar Peter the Great. After conquering Estonia in 1711, Peter began planning the park and palace as a gift to his mistress Marta Skavronskaya. A serving girl of Lithuanian origin, Skavronskaya was taken as war booty by General Sheremetiev during one of

Kadriorg literary museums

The sedate streets south and west of Kadriorg are the setting for memorial museums honouring two of twentieth-century Estonia's literary giants – well worth a detour if you've a passion for Estonian culture or an interest in well-preserved inter-war interiors.

The first is the **Eduard Vilde Museum**, just south of the Kreuzwald monument at Roheline 3 (Edvard Vilde memoriaalmuuseum; daily except Tues: March–Oct 11am–6pm; Nov–Feb 11am–5pm; 10EEK), located in the house presented to him by the government in honour of his life's work. Inspired by the naturalist novels of Emile Zola, Vilde (1865–1933) was the first Estonian novelist to write about recent Estonian history in realist, documentary style. As well as being filled with social analysis and economic statistics, his narratives were also the popular, page-turning blockbusters of their time. His most famous novel *Mahtra sõda* ("The War in Mahtra"; 1902), dealing with peasant rebellions of the 1850s, began life as a serial in the newspaper *Teataja* – readers hungry for the latest instalment would queue up outside the editorial offices on the day of publication. An opponent of the Tsarist autocracy as well as Estonia's German-speaking landowning classes, Vilde spent long periods of exile in Western Europe following the failed 1905 Revolution – first-hand experience of cosmopolitan cities like Paris and Berlin lent his writing a modern, urban edge unique for Estonian literature at the time. Not surprisingly, Vilde's battered travelling trunks are given pride of place in this charmingly reverent display of authorial heirlooms and period furnishings.

Heading west from the Vilde Museum along Koidula tänav soon brings you to the **Anton Hansen Tammsaare Memorial Museum** at Koidula 12A (A.H. Tammsaare memoriaalmuuseum; daily except Tues 10am–5pm; 10EEK), occupying the handsome timber house where this dour novelist lived for the last decade of his life. Tammsaare (1878–1940) was born into a farming family in Järvamaa, central Estonia, and went on to study law at Tartu University, although he never graduated because of poor health. His literary reputation rests primarily on the five-volume, semi-autobiographical *Tõde ja Õigus* ("Truth and Justice"), a panorama of Estonian life from the 1870s to the 1930s that still forms the staple fodder of Estonian schoolchildren. It's famous (or infamous) both for its enormously long sentences, some of which last half a page, and for an oft-quoted line from volume 2, said to sum up the mixture of doggedness and resignation that defines the Estonian character: "Work hard, sweat hard, and then love will come". Alongside manuscripts and first editions, the museum displays some charming old postcards of Tallinn (including a mesmerizing 1930s vista of a zeppelin floating over St Olaf's Church), and a startlingly lifelike dummy of Tammsaare staring out of his study window.

his campaigns in Livonia and used as human currency at the Russian court – Sher-emetiev gave her to Prince Menschikov, who in turn presented her to Peter in 1703. She remained the Tsar's companion thereafter, becoming Empress Catherine in 1724, hence the name of the park – Kadriorg is Estonian for "Catherine's Valley". Peter, who personally supervised the planting of the trees, always intended the park to be open to the public, and a stroll in Kadriorg soon became an essential fixture of the Tallinn social round. In the mid-nineteenth century, when Tallinn was one of the Russian Empire's most popular seaside resorts, Kadriorg was the place all the summer visitors gravitated towards, enjoying a constant round of what German writer J.G. Kohl called "prom-enades, balls, illuminations and pleasure parties".

The **main entrance** to the park is at the junction of Weizenbergi tänav and J. Poska (tram #1 or #3 from Viru väljak). Weizenbergi cuts southeastwards through the park, passing first of all a small lake bordered by formal flowerbeds and patronized by a fair number of ducks and swans. Presiding over the eastern shore of the lake is a statue of Friedrich Reinhold Kreuzwald (see p.161), the Võru doctor who kickstarted the Estonian literary renaissance by publishing *Kalevipoeg* ("The Son of Kalev"), an epic poem composed of original fragments of folk material and Tolkien-esque episodes made up by Kreuzwald himself. Before Kreuzwald's time the Estonian language had been regarded as an uncultured country dialect by the German-speaking Baltic elite, and *Kalevipoeg* was hugely influential in inspiring a new generation of native-born intellectuals to start writing in their own tongue. Round the base of the statue, plaques depicting harp-strumming bards and heroic warriors convey the required tone of myth and mystery.

From here, Wizenbergi ascends gently towards **Kadriorg Palace** (Kadrioru loss), a late-Baroque residence designed by the Italian architect Niccolo Michetti to provide Empress Catherine with a comfy Baltic pad and used as an imperial residence right up until 1918. These days the palace's opulent staterooms accommodate the **Kadriorg Art Museum** (Kadrioru kunstimuuseum; May–Sept Tues–Sun 10am–5pm; Oct–April Wed–Sun 10am–5pm; ⓦwww.ekm.ee; 55EEK), an impressive collection of European painting and sculpture over the centuries. The display opens on an exuberant note with Pieter Brueghel the Younger's *Wedding Feast*, followed by a room of seventeenth-century Dutch still lifes – the glistening, ready-to-eat surface of Hans van Essen's *Still Life with Lobster* being an obvious highlight. The Main Hall of the palace is an artwork in its own right, with chunky fireplaces topped by trumpet-blowing angels and two-headed eagles. A central ceiling painting illustrates the legend of Diana and Actaeon, in which the latter is transformed into a stag for having surprised Diana while bath-ing, and is hunted and killed by his dogs (Diana here represents the Russian Empire of Peter the Great, Actaeon the impudent and over-ambitious Swedish king, Charles XII). The adjoining lime-green Banqueting Hall is in fact a large conservatory tacked on in the 1930s – packed with soft furnishings and plants, it provides a suitably sensu-ous environment in which to admire the aptly named *Venus of the Beautiful Buttocks*, a nineteenth-century sculpture based on a Classical Greek original. If you can tear yourself away, there follows a room full of pictures by followers of Caravaggio and a representative sample of nineteenth-century Russian Realists like Ivan Shishkin and Ilya Repin – although Aleksey Bogolyubov's *Port of Tallinn* (1853) provides most in the way of local interest.

In the Kadriorg Palace's former kitchen building is the **Mikkel Museum** (Weizen-bergi 28; Wed–Sun 10am–5pm; 20EEK; 65EEK joint ticket covering entrance to the Kadriorg Art Museum also available), home to artwork donated by prominent Estonian collector Johannes Mikkel. The collection features paintings, engravings and sculptures from Estonia, Western Europe, Russia and the Far East, dating back to the sixteenth century; intricate Chinese porcelain from the Qianlong period (1736–95) is one of the highlights.

Behind the palace, an eighteenth-century **ornamental garden** is being restored to its former glory. The peach-coloured building just beyond it houses Estonia's current head of state.

Peter the Great's House

Between 1714 and 1716, Peter the Great lived in the so-called Dutch House, a small cottage about 200m uphill from Kadriorg Palace. Today this simple building harbours the **Peter the Great House Museum** (Peeter I majamuuseum; May–Aug 11am–7pm; Sept–April Wed–Sun 11am–4pm; 15EEK), comprising a hall, drawing room, dining room and bedroom decked out in the kind of utilitarian furnishings that practical-minded Peter favoured. Little in the house is original, save for a pair of slippers beside the bed, said to be the Tsar's own.

Kumu Art Museum

Close to Peter's cottage is the new home of the **Kumu Art Museum**, the main gallery of the Art Museum of Estonia (Kumu Kunstimuuseum; Valge 1/Weizenbergi 34; May–Sept Tues–Sun 11am–6pm; Oct–April Wed–Sun 11am–6pm; 75EEK; ⓦwww .ekm.ee). Opened in February 2006, this dynamic stony-grey and blue glass structure houses one of the best art collections in the Baltics, tracing Estonian art from its awakenings in the eighteenth century, through the "Socialist Realism" of the Soviet period, to contemporary works. The permanent collection features work by prominent Estonian artists like Kristjan Raud, Johannes Köler and Konrad Mägi, as well as the influential Pallas art school. There are also ever-changing temporary exhibitions, both local and international, as well as regular lectures and film screenings, the latter often in English.

The Song Bowl and the Rusalka Memorial

Heading north from Kumu leads, after around fifteen minutes, to Narva mnt. On the other side of this busy road is the **Song Bowl** (Lauluväljak), a vast amphitheatre that has been the venue for Estonia's Song Festivals ever since its construction in the 1960s. These gatherings, featuring massed choirs thousands strong, take place every two years and have been an important form of national expression in Estonia ever since the first all-Estonia Song Festival was held in Tartu in 1869. The present structure, which can accommodate 15,000 singers (with room for a further 30,000 or so performers on the platform in front of the stage and countless thousands of spectators on the banked field beyond it), was filled to capacity for the June 1988 festival, when up to 100,000 people

△ Kumu Art Museum

a night came here to express their longing for independence from Soviet rule, giving rise to the epithet "Singing Revolution". Since then the Song Bowl has hosted concerts by numerous representatives of Western urban folklore – the Rolling Stones (1998) and Metallica (2006) among them. In winter-the grassy slope where spectators usually stand is transformed into an impromptu winter-sports arena, with scores of kids hurling themselves down the incline on sleds, old tyres or bits of cardboard.

A tree-lined avenue runs downhill from the amphitheatre to Pirita tee, which follows the seashore. A left turn here brings you to the **Rusalka Memorial**, built in 1902 in memory of the *Rusalka*, a Russian ship that had gone down nine years earlier. Designed by Amandus Adamson, the leading Estonian sculptor of the day, it comprises a rocky pillar on which an angel stands on tiptoe, waving an Orthodox cross in the direction of the Gulf of Finland.

The Estonian History Museum

Turning right at the bottom of the Song Bowl access road and following the coastal Pirita tee brings you after 1km or so to a balustraded stairway leading up to the Maarjamäe Palace (Maarjamäe loss), a neo-Gothic residence built for an aide of the Tsar, Count Anatoli Orlov-Davidov, in 1873. Long considered a beauty spot on account of its position overlooking Tallinn Bay, the building now houses a branch of the **Estonian History Museum** (Eesti ajaloomuuseum; Wed–Sun: March–Oct 11am–6pm; Nov–Feb 10am–5pm; 10EEK; ⓦwww.eam.ee), covering the mid-nineteenth century onwards, and is far more interesting and imaginative than its city-centre counterpart (see p.73). The display starts with a section on urban and rural life in nineteenth-century Estonia, including a few re-created domestic interiors, before moving on to the political and social upheavals of the early twentieth century, including grainy photographs of the volunteers who fought against Bolsheviks, White Russians and Germans to win Estonian independence in the aftermath of World War I. Later sections have a display on the Molotov-Ribbentrop "secret protocols", which effectively handed the Baltic Republics to Stalin, leading into material about the fate of Estonia during World War II, and the activities of the "Forest Brothers", Estonian partisans who carried on the battle against Soviet occupation into the 1950s. Ironically, Maarjamäe Palace was earmarked as the site of a "Museum of Soviet Friendship" during the 1980s, a project which never got off the ground owing to the untimely demise of the state it was intended to celebrate. However, Evald Okas's 1987 frescoes, featuring cosmonauts, scientists, gymnasts and other symbols of communist achievement, can still be admired in the main hall.

Just beyond Maarjamäe Palace, a huge concrete needle marks the site of a Soviet-era war memorial honouring the dead of World War II – intended to symbolize the Soviet role in "liberating" Estonia in 1944–5, it has long been nicknamed "Pinocchio's Grave" by locals.

Pirita

Two kilometres northeast of Maarjamäe, Pirita tee enters the suburb of **Pirita** (buses #1, #1A, #34 and #38 from Viru väljak), site of a huge yachting marina at the point where the Pirita River flows into the Baltic Sea. The sailing events of the 1980 Moscow Olympics were held here, which explains the presence of an ungainly concrete hotel and an under-used complex of port buildings. The main reasons to visit nowadays are the forest-backed **Pirita beach**, which stretches for some 2km on the far side of the marina and offers great views west towards Tallinn's port, and the **St. Bridget's Convent Ruins** (Pirita klooster; daily: Jan–March, Nov & Dec noon–4pm; April, May, Sept & Oct 10am–6pm; June–Aug 9am–7pm; 20EEK), which loom above the landward side of the main road. Founded in 1407 by Tallinn merchants, the convent was unusual in admitting both male and female novices, who resided in different wings under the strict rule of a single abbess. The convent was destroyed and abandoned during the Livonian Wars and all that survives now is the shell of its church, whose hugely impressive facade recalls the gabled merchants' houses of Tallinn's Old Town. Studded with tiny windows, it looks like an unearthly advent calendar.

During the summer you can also take one of the regular boat trips from Pirita harbour to the islands of **Aegna** and **Naissaar** – check timetable information with the Tallinn tourist office; the journey to either island takes around an hour. Aegna (just three square kilometres in size) is a protected nature area, while the significantly larger Naissaar has numerous military ruins and a nineteenth-century cemetery for soldiers who died in the Crimean War; both islands have appealing sandy beaches.

The Botanical Gardens and the Television Tower

Just beyond Pirita Convent, buses #34 and #38 turn sharp right into Kloostrimetsa tee and begin climbing into the hilly Kloostrimets ("Convent Wood"), a peaceful area of thick pine forest and suburban cottages that seems a world away from the city. On the north side of the road, tracks lead into the Forest cemetery (Metsakalmistu), Tallinn's most desirable final resting place. On the south side, just beyond the Kloostrimetsa bus stop, paths head to the **Botanical Gardens** (Botaanikaaed; daily: May–Sept 11am–7pm; Oct–April 11am–4pm; 45EEK), a landscaped area of woodland centred on a rather wonderful palm house, with tall trees in the octagonal central hall and smaller specimens in the numerous side chambers. Just beyond it are alpine and rose gardens, although you'll have to come in late spring or summer to enjoy them at their best.

Half a kilometre further along Kloostrimetsa tee, beside the Motoklubi bus stop, a side road leads off to the **Television Tower** (Teletorn; daily 10am–midnight; 60EEK), where a lift whisks you to a twenty-first-floor observation platform with superb views back towards the church spires and port cranes of central Tallinn. The pleasingly Soviet-kitsch bar-restaurant is a relaxing spot for a drink.

The Zoo and the Estonian Open-Air Museum

Tallinn's western outskirts offer much less in the way of sights, the one must-see attraction here being the **Estonian Open-Air Museum**, 6km west of town in the upmarket suburb of Rocca al Mare (Italian for "Rock by the Sea") – thus christened by a merchant who built himself a mansion here during the late nineteenth century. Buses #21 and #21B make the trip here from the Baltic Station every twenty to thirty minutes.

Just before arriving in Rocca al Mare you'll pass **Tallinn Zoo** at Paldiski mnt 145 (daily: March, April, Sept & Oct 9am–5pm; May–Aug 9am–7pm; Nov–Feb 9am–3pm; 50EEK), founded in 1937 to accommodate the baby lynx won by the Estonian Riflemen's Society at the World Championships in Helsinki. There's now a much wider range of mammals on show, as well as a croc-filled tropical house.

The Estonian Open-Air Museum

Arranged in a spacious wooded park overlooking the sea, the **Estonian Open-Air Museum** at Vabaõhumuuseumi tee 12 (Eesti vabaõhumuuseum; daily: May–Sept 10am–8pm; 70EEK; Oct–April 10am–5pm; 35EEK; ⓦwww.evm.ee) brings together over a hundred eighteenth- and nineteenth-century village buildings from different parts of the country. The exhibits illustrate how Estonian dwellings developed from single longhouses in which humans and animals lived cheek by jowl, to more sophisticated farmsteads, in which barns and other outbuildings were built to accommodate the beasts. Estonian living rooms were traditionally built around open hearths with no chimneys – the resulting fug facilitated the drying of grain and the curing of meat and fish. Until the twentieth century most Estonian houses were built from spruce or pine – except on Saaremaa, where stone walls were sometimes used – as evidenced by a pair of farmsteads on display here. The museum also includes an appealing wooden church, taken from the village of Sutlepa north of Haapsalu – traditionally an area of Swedish settlement – its roof supported by swelling, cigar-shaped pillars. An additional attraction is the *Kolu Kõrts* café, which serves up traditional bean soup and beer.

If you're interested in studying the ethnography of contemporary Estonia you could do worse than catch bus #21 back into town – before making for the centre, it loops through a swathe of well-heeled suburbia northwest of Rocca al Mare, taking you past some of the most expensive real estate in the country.

Eating

Tallinn has an ever-expanding array of **restaurants**, many of which serve up high-quality food. International cuisines, particularly French, Italian, Russian, Chinese and Indian, are increasingly popular; most other establishments feature the solid meat-and-potatoes fare common to many north European countries. The Old Town's more expensive restaurants pull this off with considerable panache, usually offering a number of global dishes in addition. In the more modest eateries, however, the pork chop still rules the roost.

As you'd expect, meals work out more expensive in Tallinn than elsewhere in the country – you'll rarely get away with paying less than 90–100EEK for a main course in a restaurant. However, cafés, bars and pubs often have a quite substantial menu of full meals, generally at much cheaper prices than in full-blown restaurants, which also often offer good-value lunch specials.

Restaurants are **open** daily from noon until 11pm or midnight unless otherwise stated. Cafés are a law unto themselves, with the more old-fashioned places closing at 6–8pm, the trendier joints working until 11pm or later.

Cafés and snacks

Anneli Vikk Handmade Chocolates Café Pikk 30. Dozens of tempting handmade chocolates, as well as Illy coffee, draw in the crowds, who can even watch the chocolatiers at work through a glass screen. Mon–Sat 11am–11pm, Sun 11am–7pm.

Bogapott Pikk jalg 9. This curious, quirky café on Toompea, located in a ceramicists' workshop (see p.94), has delicious homemade cakes and pastries. Daily 10am–6pm.

Coffer Vanaturu Kael 8. Big breakfasts (with beer), salads, steaks and other light meals are on offer at this low-key café, marginally less swamped with tourists than others in the centre. Daily 8.30am–10pm.

Elsebet Viru 2. An old-fashioned café above the *Peppersack* restaurant with a genteel atmosphere and cakes and snack dishes on the menu. Daily 8am–8pm.

Kehrwieder Saiakang 1. A relaxing coffee house on the main square, with low ceilings, wooden tables and a succulent range of cakes. The outdoor terrace quickly fills up during the summer. Daily 11am–midnight.

Le Bonaparte Pikk 45. In a lovely seventeenth-century building, this French café has crisp white tablecloths, smart service and great food: the quiche in particular is delicious. There's a more expensive restaurant attached (see p.90). Mon–Sat 8am–10pm, Sun 10am–6pm.

Leiburi Pagariäri Suur Karja 18. This central bakery has a satisfying range of cheap pastries, sandwiches and cakes to eat in or take away. Mon–Fri 8am–7pm, Sat 8am–6pm, Sun 9am–4pm.

Maiasmokk Pikk 16. The city's most venerable café – founded in 1864 – with a beautiful

wood-panelled interior. You may have to queue for a seat, however, as it's hugely popular with elderly ladies and tour groups. Mon–Sat 8am–7pm, Sun 10am–6pm.

Mata Hari Suur Karja 11. If you're not put off by the fact that it turns into a strip bar after 9pm, this café, complete with kitsch soft furnishings, has some of the best soups, crepes and pancakes in town at dirt-cheap prices. Opens daily 10am.

Pizza Americana Müürivahe 2. A satisfying range of cheap deep-pan pizzas served up in antiseptic surroundings. Daily 11.30am–10.30pm.

Robert's Coffee Viru 13/15. Good coffee, cakes and sandwiches in this Finnish chain on the top floor of a shopping mall. The highlight, however, is the majestic view from the terrace. Daily 10am–8pm.

Stockmann Department Store Liivala 53. This fifth-floor self-service restaurant is a good spot for a cheap and filling hot meal, sandwich or salad. Mon–Thurs, Sun 9am–10pm, Fri & Sat 9am–9pm.

Tristan ja Isolde Raekoja plats 1. A dark, poky and atmospheric café in the Town Hall with a full range of drinks and tasty salads and cakes. Daily 10am–10pm.

Restaurants

Estonian and north European cuisine

Eesti Maja Lauteri 1. A relaxed Estonian restaurant just southeast of the Estonia Concert Hall with plenty of pork-based local favourites and excellent freshwater-fish dishes. Main courses around 150EEK. Daily 11am–11pm.

Karl Friedrich Raekoja plats 5. This "pepper restaurant" – pepper being a key flavour in all dishes – has fish specialities and succulent steaks, served in an elegant, olde-worlde interior. Some of the starters cost as much as main courses in other restaurants, but they're probably worth it. Daily noon–midnight.

Kuldse Notsu Kõrts Dunkri 8. The "Little Piggy Inn" has Estonian country dishes in a suite of rooms decked out with rustic textiles and wooden benches. Go for the roast pork or try wild boar in juniper sauce. Mains around 170EEK. Daily noon–midnight.

Le Bonaparte Pikk 45. Like its attached café (see p.89), *Le Bonaparte* provides a high-quality French dining experience, with delicious food (particularly the cheeses) and stylish decor. Prices, however, are very steep – main courses around the 300EEK mark – and portions can be on the small side. Daily noon–midnight.

Mõõkkala Rüütli 16/18. An excellent, if a little pricey (mains from 160EEK), seafood place in the cellar of what used to be the Tallinn executioner's house. Daily noon–midnight.

Olde Hansa Vanaturg 1. The longest-established and best of Tallinn's medieval-themed restaurants, with wooden benches set out in a sequence of atmospherically lit rooms in the Town Hall. Meaty dishes based on medieval recipes, appropriately costumed staff and live minstrels. Main courses from 150EEK. Daily 11am–midnight.

Vanaema Juures Rataskaevu 10 ☎ 626 9080. "Grandma's Place", a cosy cellar restaurant decorated with sepia-tinged photos and antique candle-holders, has some of the best Estonian food in Tallinn, including mouth-wateringly tender pork, elk, wild boar and salmon; mains around 160EEK. A warm welcome is guaranteed. Reservations necessary. Mon–Sat noon–midnight, Sun noon–6pm.

International cuisine

African Kitchen Uus 34. Leopard-print cushions, tribal masks and mini palm trees make this a fun and atmospheric experience. Tasty, well-priced African food, including chicken peri-peri and good vegetarian options. Sun–Thurs noon–1am, Fri & Sat noon–2am.

Artemis Souvlaki Pikk 35. Greek owners and cooks ensure this small and friendly taverna serves up authentic dishes like moussaka and *pasticcio*, with mains around 110EEK. Good-value lunch specials. Daily 10am–midnight.

Bazar Tulika põik 3/Madara 14. Hidden away in a colourful refurbished warehouse 1.5km west of Toompea, this restaurant has a wide-ranging menu of Middle Eastern specialities, and Arab-influenced background music. Turns into a club at weekends. Daily Sun–Thurs noon–11pm, Fri & Sat noon–2am.

Bocca Olevimägi 9 ☎ 641 2610. This designer restaurant draws a well-heeled, fashionable

crowd with its excellent, and predictably expensive, Italian cuisine. Mains from 200EEK. Daily noon–midnight.

Buongiorno Müürivahe 17. Reasonably priced soups, pastas and specials are the lunchtime options in this relaxed cellar restaurant, with more substantial Italian-themed fare in the evenings. Daily 10am–11pm.

Controvento Vene 12 ☎ 644 0470. A fourteenth-century granary is the location for this tasteful and authentic Italian restaurant, with a good selection of pizza and pasta dishes and a decent wine list. Main courses from around 120EEK. Reservations advised. Daily noon–11.30pm.

Elevant Vene 5. A chic Indian restaurant with mellow decor and a wide range of authentic dishes, including plenty for vegetarians. Daily noon–11pm.

Gloria Müürivahe 2 ☎ 644 6950. *Gloria* has been producing top-quality French cuisine since 1937 which, combined with the Art Nouveau decor and the best wine list in the country, makes for a memorable dining experience. Frequently voted the best restaurant in Estonia; mains from 250EEK. Daily noon–11pm.

Golden Dragon Pikk 37. Squeezed into a small and intimate cellar space, this is a highly recommended Chinese restaurant with a bewildering array of fish and vegetarian option, mains from 80EEK. Daily noon–11pm.

Must Lammas Sauna 2. The "Black Sheep" – a Georgian restaurant – specializes in superbly spicy stews and grills, served up in stylish surroundings with a few ethnic touches. Mains from 170EEK. Mon–Sat noon–11pm, Sun noon–11pm.

Pegasus Harju 1 ☎ 631 4040. Exquisite international eats, including plenty of vegetarian choices, in a three-storey temple to 1960s Modernism in the heart of the Old Town. Mains around the 200EEK mark, but quick-lunch soups and salads are significantly cheaper. The ground-floor bar attracts a hip, young crowd. Mon–Thurs 8am–1am, Fri 8am–2pm, Sat 10am–2am.

St Michael Juusturestoran Nunne 14. This medieval-style restaurant dedicated to cheese is based in a former nunnery. Waiters dressed as monks serve up slightly heavy meals like spinach and cottage cheese ravioli, and foie gras with blue cheese sauce. Mon–Fri 5pm–midnight, Sat & Sun 3pm–midnight.

Troika Raekoja plats 15. An atmospheric cellar restaurant on the main square with excellent Russian food, including caviar served on blini and *pelmeni* with mushroom sauce; mains around 160EEK. Folk singers and free-flowing vodka provide a lively atmosphere in the evenings. Daily 10am–11.30pm.

Zebra Café Narva mnt 7. A stylish, modern space with slick service and fashionable patrons. The international menu includes Italian and Japanese cuisine with main courses from 150EEK. Daily 11am–midnight.

Drinking

Most young Tallinn folk are enthusiastic and sociable drinkers, ensuring the Old Town area remains lively most nights of the week. At weekends the drinking scene can be particularly raucous, with bars filling up with holidaying Finns and city-break tourists from all across Europe – stag parties included – drawn by the comparatively cheap prices.

Tallinn's Old Town could have been made for drinking, its narrow, winding streets lending themselves perfectly to all manner of smoky dens, stylish lounge bars and laid-back pubs. Most of them offer a full range of main meals, making it possible to hunker down for a whole evening's drinking while appeasing your hunger pangs at the same time. Many bars feature DJs and/or live bands at the weekends, making them a good alternative to the city's pay-to-enter clubs (see "Clubs and live music", p.92). Most bars and pubs open around 11am and don't close until 1/2am at the earliest. All bars listed below are in the Old Town unless otherwise stated.

Basso Pikk 13. An attractive, burgundy-coloured space with a floral theme and attentive staff give *Basso* a more chilled-out ambience than some of the other bars in the Old Town. Good food, some unusual drinks (like chocolate beer) and occasional live jazz. Sun & Mon 11am–midnight, Tues–Thurs 11am–1am, Fri & Sat 11am–3am.

Beer House Dunkri 5. A roomy, German-style beer hall with bench seating, cheerful oom-pah music, a wide range of ales (many of which are brewed on the premises), and moderately priced pork dishes. Sun–Tues 10am–midnight, Wed & Thurs 10am–2am, Fri & Sat 10am–4am.

Deja Vu Sauna 1. Hyper-trendy lounge bar with a huge list of cocktails, a style-conscious crowd, lengthy opening hours and an icy attitude. Sun–Thurs 11.30am–1am, Fri & Sat 11.30am–7am.

G-Punkt Pärnu mnt 23 (entrance via courtyard on Tatari). The "G Spot" can be hard to find, but this lounge bar, with a loyal gay and lesbian following, is worth the search for its warm welcome and relaxed ambience. A ten-minute walk south of the Old Town. Sun–Tues & Thurs noon–1am, Wed, Fri & Sat till 4am.

Hell Hunt Pikk 39. Don't be put off by the name - it means "Gentle Wolf" - *Hell Hunt* is a low-key pub, relatively untouched by the tourist scene. Locals are drawn in by the cheap drinks and hearty meals. Daily noon–2am.

Hookah House Roosikrantsi 3. A stylish night-time venue, with *shisha* pipes and inviting sofas on which to enjoy them, drawing a twenty-something crowd. The food, however, can be hit-and-miss. Sun–Thurs 10am–11pm, Fri & Sat 10am–2am.

Ice Bar Dunkri 6. The tiny bar at *Merchant's House* is a similarly chic blend of old and new: space-age bar stools, stained-glass windows and a fourteenth-century painted ceiling. Even the drinks are stylish – cocktails or vodka in a shot glass made of ice – and there's also a quality restaurant and a café with great milkshakes and lunch specials. Sun–Thurs 9am–midnight, Fri & Sat 9am–2am.

Karja Kelder Väike-Karja 1 (beneath *Vana Tom* hostel. A good bet if you're looking for an Old Town location but a predominantly local crowd. Competitive prices are an added bonus. Sun & Mon 11am–1am, Tues–Thurs 11am–2am, Fri & Sat 11am–4am.

Kompressor Rataskaevu 3. A young crowd flocks to this café-bar by day for its famous, wonderfully stodgy pancakes, returning in the evening for the economical drinks and lively atmosphere. Sun–Thurs 11am–1am, Fri & Sat 11am–3am.

Lost Continent Narva mnt 19. A large and loud Australian pub, 1km east of the Old Town, with pool tables, occasional live music and decent global cuisine. Sun–Tues 11.30am–1pm, Wed till midnight, Thurs till 1am, Fri & Sat till 2am.

Molly Malone's Mündi 2. With a prime, main-square position, sport on TV, pub grub and live music at the weekend, *Molly Malone's* pulls in a mix of ex-pats, tourists and locals. Sun–Thurs 9am–1am, Fri & Sat 9am–4am.

Moskva Vabaduse väljak 10. A glass-fronted square-side café-bar, with a loungey design theme, cool customers and DJs at weekends. Mon–Thurs 9am–midnight, Fri 9am–4am, Sat 11am–4am, Sun 11am–midnight.

Nimega Baar Suur-Karja 13. "The Pub with a Name" has a long, narrow bar with plenty of half-price and two-for-one drinks promotions, plus

DJs at the weekend, and attracts plenty of tourists and ex-pats. Mon–Thurs 11am–2am, Fri & Sat 11am–4am, Sun noon–2am.

Nimeta Baar Suur-Karja 4/6. With a similar crowd to *Nimega*, the ever-busy *Nimeta* ("The Pub with no Name") has numerous TV screens showing live sport and a pool table out back. Staff are quick to let you know if they think you're not drinking enough. Sun–Thurs 11am–2am, Fri & Sat 11am–4am.

Stereo Lounge Harju 6. A blindingly white interior, icicle-like hangings in the window and a glass bar lit up by multicoloured lights make this the most visually arresting bar in Tallinn. Popular with both locals and foreigners. Mon–Thurs 9am–1am, Fri & Sat 9am–4am.

St Patrick's Suur-Karja 8. The most popular of the four *St Patrick's* pubs is in a wonderful medieval building. Every fourth Saku is free and the substantial Estonian staples on the menu are

surprisingly authentic. Sun–Thurs 11am–2am, Fri & Sat 11am–4am.

Vana Villemi Tartu mnt 52. A welcoming, wood-furnished pub with a largely local clientele, full range of beers and good-value Estonian food on the menu. Somewhat off the beaten track, 2km east of the Old Town, just round the corner from the bus station. Sun–Tues 11am–midnight, Wed & Thurs 11am–1am, Fri & Sat 11am–2am.

VS Pärnu mnt 28. A hip DJ bar some 200m south of the Old Town, featuring industrial decor and restaurant-quality food (including some mouth-watering Indian dishes); mains around 120EEK. Try to bag one of the purple sofas by the window. Mon 10am–midnight, Tues–Thurs 10am–1am, Fri 10am–3am, Sat noon–3am, Sun noon–1am.

X Baar Sauna 1. Tallinn's first gay bar is still going strong. A smallish venue with a friendly vibe, cheap drinks and a tiny, but energetic, dance floor. Sun–Thurs 2pm–1am, Fri & Sat 2pm–3am.

Entertainment

As well as offering the range of classical music and theatre that you would expect from a capital city, Tallinn is also a burgeoning nightlife centre, with clubs of all shapes and sizes offering a hedonistic menu of entertainment every night of the week – apart from Monday, when everybody takes time off to recharge their batteries.

Tickets for all events are usually obtained from the venues themselves, although Piletimaailin, Gonsiori 2, and Piletilevi, in the Viru Keskus shopping centre, handle bookings for many of the bigger music and theatre spectacles. *Tallinn in Your Pocket* (see p.67) carries advance information on classical music, opera and ballet performances, although the *Baltic Times* is much better for weekly cinema, concert and club listings. If your language skills are up to it, the *Eesti Ekspress* magazine, which comes out every Thursday, carries exhaustive listings (under the heading *Vaba Aeg*, or "Free Time"; they're currently to be found at the back of the TV supplement). Major cultural **festivals** include **Jazzkaar** (Ⓦwww.jazzkaar.ee), when big names in world jazz visit Tallinn in April; and the **Dark Nights Film Festival** (see p.59).

Clubs and live music

Tallinn's popularity as a weekend-break city has led to an explosion in the number of nightlife venues over the last few years. Mainstream discos churning out top-40 hits, house and techno remain the rule, although a strong upsurge in the local DJ culture ensures that you'll come across all genres of dance music most nights of the week, if you know where to look. Dedicated clubbers should look out for street posters or pick up flyers in Internet cafés and record shops to get an idea of what's going on in any given week. For advance details of major DJ-led events, check out the websites of Ⓦwww.vibe.ee and Ⓦwww.mutantdisco.com. Expect to pay 75EEK and up for **admission** to clubs and 150–200EEK for weekend events with big-name DJs. Clubs generally open 9pm–11pm, and close 3am–6am.

Tallinn is never likely to become the rock 'n' roll capital of the universe, although you'll find a motley collection of alternative musicians, middle-of-the-road rockers and cover bands playing in clubs, or in some of the drinking venues listed on p.91. The Linnahall (see opposite) hosts some of the more adult-oriented pop-rock acts. Big gigs featuring international touring bands take place at the brand-new, 10,000-capacity **Saku Suurhall**, 5km west of the centre at Paldiski mnt 104B in the suburb of Rocca al Mare (@www.sakusuurhall.ee; bus #21 from Balti Jaam); and at the outdoor **Song Bowl** (Lauluväljak; see p.86) near Kadriorg Park.

Angel Sauna 1. Tallinn's best gay club has a strict "face control" policy; if you get in, however, you're virtually guaranteed a raucous night. The attached café is almost as popular, drawing a mixed gay and straight crowd. Wed–Sat till 5am.

BonBon Mere pst 6E @www.bonbon.ee. One of the hottest tickets in town, *BonBon*'s exclusive feel continues to pull in the fashionable set, who come to dance under the chandeliers and sip expensive cocktails. Wed, Fri & Sat till 6am (sometimes later).

Bonnie & Clyde in the *Olümpia Hotel*, Liivalaia 33. Busy at the weekends, and with fewer of the teens that populate many of Tallinn's clubs, *Bonnie & Clyde* lures people to its circular dance floor with a mixture of pop and 1960s, '70s and '80s favourites. Fri & Sat till 5am.

Café Amigo beneath the *Viru Hotel*, Viru väljak 4. Locals and (particularly Finnish) tourists flock to this cheesy but likeable disco, which alternates live bands with mainstream dance music. Estonian pop-rock acts make regular appearances. Sun–Thurs 9pm–4am, Fri & Sat 9pm–5am.

Guitar Safari Müürivahe 22 @www.guitarsafari .ee. A cellar venue specializing in live rock and blues music acts for a more mature clientele. Daily till 3am.

Hollywood Vana-Posti 8 @www .clubhollywood.ee. Housed in a former cinema in the heart of the Old Town, *Hollywood* has become a Tallinn nightlife institution. Tourists and youthful locals tear it up on a huge dance floor, whilst DJs play anything from house to hip-hop. Wed & Thurs 10pm–4am, Fri & Sat 10pm–5am.

Privé Harju 6 @www.clubprive.ee. Trendy club with higher-than-average prices and a fairly strict door policy, attracting well-known, predominantly dance-music DJs from the Baltic and beyond. Wed & Thurs 10pm–4am, Fri & Sat 10pm–5am.

Terrarium Sadama 6 @www.terrarium.ee. A youthful, energetic portside warehouse, with an outdoor terrace in the summer and a largely mainstream music policy. Fri & Sat till 5am, closed Sun–Tues.

Classical music, opera and ballet

Both the Estonian National Symphony Orchestra and the National Opera have solid reputations and attract their fair share of big-name conductors and soloists from abroad. There's also an impressive choice of chamber music on offer, much of it taking place in Tallinn's suitably atmospheric collection of medieval churches and halls; @www .concert.ee is a useful website for finding out what's on in the bigger concert venues. The **box office** at the Estonia Concert Hall, Estonia pst 4 (T614 7760), sells tickets for some, but not all, of the classical concerts around town.

Estonia Concert Hall (Estonia kontserdisaal) Estonia pst 4 T614 7760, @www.concert.ee. Prestige venue for classical music and choral works, including performances by the Estonian National Symphony Orchestra. Box office Mon–Fri noon–7pm, Sat noon–5pm, Sun one hour before performance.

Estonia Theatre (Estonia teater) Estonia pst 4. Immediately next door to the Estonia Concert Hall, home of the National Opera (Rahvusooper; @www .opera.ee), ballet and musicals. Same box office as the Estonia Concert Hall.

Estonian Music Academy (Eesti muusikaakadeemia) Rävala 16 T667 5768, @www.ema.edu .ee. Chamber music several times a week.

House of the Blackheads (Mustpeademaja) Pikk 26 T631 3199, @www.mustpeademaja.ee.

Frequent chamber music and solo recitals. Box office 1hr before performance.

Linnahall Mere 20 T641 1500/641 1600, @www.linnahall.ee. Several comfortable auditoria inside an unloved concrete cultural centre, hosting classical concerts and musicals. Box office Mon–Sat 11am–7pm.

St Nicholas's Church (Niguliste kirik) Niguliste 3 T631 4330, @www.ekm.ee. Organ recitals at weekends; details are usually posted outside.

Town Hall (Raekoda) Raekoja plats 1 T645 7900. Solo recitals and chamber concerts.

Väravatorn Lühike jalg 9 T614 7760. This is the HQ of internationally acclaimed early music ensemble Hortus Musicus – they play here once or twice a month.

Theatre

There's a great deal of top-quality **theatre** in Tallinn, but with most of it performed in Estonian, your best bet is to stick to major productions and concentrate

on the stage-craft – or simply treat the whole experience as a social event. ⓦwww
.estoniatheatre.info is a good source of information on performances.

Estonian Drama Theatre (Draamateater) Pärnu
mnt 5 ☎680 5555, ⓦwww.draamateater.ee. The
country's flagship theatrical institution, offering
classical drama in a wonderful building. Box office
daily noon–7pm.
Linnateater Lai 23 ☎665 0800, ⓦwww
.linnateater.ee. Top-quality contemporary work. Box
office Mon–Fri 9am–6pm, Sat 10am–6pm.
Nukuteater Lai 1 ☎667 9555, ⓦwww.nukuteater
.ee. Puppet theatre, with most productions kicking
off at lunchtime.

Russian Drama Theatre (Vene teater)
Vabaduse väljak 5 ☎611 4911, ⓦwww.veneteater
.ee. Drama from the classical Russian canon, as
well as contemporary international work in Russian
translation.
Theatrum Vene 14 ☎644 6889, ⓦwww.theatrum
.ee. Youth and student productions.
Von Krahli Teater Rataskaevu 10 ☎626 9090,
ⓦwww.vonkrahl.ee. Modern, challenging work in a
lovely old-fashioned theatre.

Cinemas

There's a dwindling number of **cinemas** in central Tallinn – a trend that looks likely
to continue as smaller city-centre movie theatres are replaced by modern multiscreens.
Films are shown in the original language with Estonian subtitles. One event that
attracts cineastes from all over the Baltic is the November–December **Dark Nights
Film Festival** (Pimedate ööde festivaal; ⓦwww.poff.ee), celebrating contemporary
art-house movie production.

Coca-Cola Plaza Hobujaama 5 ☎1182, ⓦwww
.superkinod.ee. State-of-the-art multiplex with
eleven screens and a healthy sprinkling of cafés
and restaurants on the ground floor.

Kosmos Pärnu mnt 45 ☎1182, ⓦwww.superkinod
.ee. Mainstream Hollywood fare. Closed Mon.
Sõprus Vana-Posti 8 ☎644 1919, ⓦwww.kino.ee.
Mixture of art-house and mainstream films.

Shopping

The streets of the Old Town are perfect for **souvenir shopping**; linen, patchwork
quilts, amber jewellery, woolly jumpers and mittens are the main items on offer in a
string of outlets along Pikk and Dunkri. The best place to browse for woollens is the
open-air jumper market on Müürivahe, right beneath the stretch of city walls immediately north of the Viru Gate.

Viru Keskus, Viru väljak 4/6 (daily 9am–9pm), is Tallinn's most prominent shopping
centre, with international chains like Body Shop, Zara, Hugo Boss and Mango, a range
of local stores, several coffee shops and a well-stocked supermarket in the basement.

From Viru Keskus you can also access Tallinn Kaubamaja, Gonsiori 2 (Mon–Sun
9am–9pm, Sun 10am–7pm), one of Tallinn's main **department stores**, which stocks
everything from cosmetics to electronics. A ten-minute walk away is Stockmann,
Liivalaia 53 (Mon–Fri 9am–9pm, Sat & Sun 9am–8pm), a popular Finnish import,
which alongside the usual department-store items also sells a decent range of international magazines and newspapers.

Souvenir and specialist shops
Bogapott Pikk jalg 9. A small, elegant pottery
studio with an attached café where you watch the
potters at work before making a purchase.
Galerii Vanaturu kael 3. Prints and small-scale
paintings by contemporary Estonian artists and
classy greetings cards.
Jardin Apteegi 3. A cosy little souvenir shop with
a good mixture of linen, wooden kitchen utensils
and woollens.

Katariina Gild Vene 12/Katariina käik. An ensemble
of craft workshops squeezed into Katariina käik
(Catherine's Passage), where you can watch applied
artists at work and check out their wares. Experts
in stained glass, ceramics, patchwork, leatherwork,
millinery and jewellery all get a studio each.
Keraamika Atelje Pikk 33. Weird and wonderful
ceramic creations, most of which are far too arty to
qualify as simple souvenirs.
Kuld ja Hõbeehted Pikk 27. Classy jewellery,
glassware and ceramics, including repro tea-sets

designed by Adamson-Eric (see p.79) in the 1930s.

Lühikese Jala Galerii Lühike jalg 6. An art gallery with modern tapestry, textiles, jewellery, sculptures and other items.

Master's Courtyard Vene 6. Jewellery, handicrafts and tempting handmade chocolates in a medieval courtyard, which also often stages art exhibitions.

Myy Art Müürivahe 36. Ceramics, textiles, glasswork and graphic art works are on sale in this gallery-shop.

Sepa Ari Olevimägi 11. Traditional and contemporary blacksmith work, including accessories for the kitchen and garden.

Veta Pikk 4. Best of a whole line of linen shops on Pikk, selling tablecloths as well as the kind of linen clothes that you won't be ashamed to wear when you get back home.

Zizi Vene 12. Classy textiles for the home, with a few ethnographic touches.

Bookshops

Apollo Viru 23. Tallinn's biggest and brightest bookstore, offering plentiful maps, guidebooks and English-language classics in paperback.

Rahva Raamat Pärnu mnt 10 and in Viru Keskus.

Estonia's oldest bookshop has a solid selection of maps and some English-language novels and magazines.

Clothes shops

Nu Nordik Vabaduse väljak 8. Stocks the latest clothes by Estonia's most promising young fashion designers.

Reet Aus Müürivahe 19. The eponymous shop of Estonia's leading designer has both her signature collection and her ReUse label, which uses entirely recycled materials. Also strung along Müürivahe are numerous other trendy boutiques.

Food & drink

Ararat Viru 23. If you've developed a taste for Vana Tallinn or the local Viru Valge vodka, this is a central place to stock up.

Kalev Viru Keskus. Stocks a cavity-inducing range of sweet treats from Estonia's famous confectioner.

Music shops

Lasering Pärnu mnt 38. Big selection of Estonian and international pop and rock.

Listings

Airlines Estonian Air, Vabaduse väljak 10 ☏631 3302, ⓦwww.estonian-air.ee; Finnair, Roosikrantsi 2 ☏611 0950, ⓦwww.finnair.com; SAS, Rävala 2 ☏666 3030, ⓦwww.flysas.com.

Airport (Lennujaam) 3km east of the centre; reached by bus #2 from Gonsiori. Flight information ☏605 8888.

Car rental Avis, Liivalaia 13/15 ☏667 1515, and at the airport ☏605 8222, ⓦwww.avis.ee; Budget, at the airport ☏605 8600, ⓦwww.budget.ee; Hertz, at the airport ☏605 8923, ⓦwww.hertz .com; National, at the airport ☏605 8071, ⓦwww .nationalcar.ee.

Embassies and consulates Australia, Marja 9 ☏650 9308, ⓔmati@standard.ee; Canada, Toom-Kooli 13 ☏627 3311, ⓔtallinn@canada .ee; Finland, Kohtu 4 ☏610 3200, ⓦwww.finland .ee; Latvia, Tõnismägi 10 ☏627 7850; Lithuania, Uus 15 ☏631 4030; Russia, Pikk 19 ☏646 4175; UK, Wismari 6 ☏667 4700, ⓦwww .britishembassy.ee; US, Kentmanni 20 ☏668 8100, ⓦwww.usemb.ee. Citizens of Ireland, New Zealand and South Africa should contact one of the English-speaking embassies to find out who is currently representing their interests.

Exchange Outside banking hours, try Tavid, Aia 5, which is open all night, or the Kaubamaja or Stockmann department stores (both daily 9am–8pm).

Gay and Lesbian The Gay and Lesbian Information Centre (GLIK) is on Tartu mnt 29 ☏645 4545, ⓦwww.gay.ee.

Hospital The main hospital is at Ravi 18 ☏620 7015; for an ambulance call ☏112.

Internet access Kaubamaja department store, 5th floor (35EEK for 1hr; Mon–Sat 9am–9pm, Sun 10am–7pm); *Revel Café*, Aia 3 (25EEK for 1hr; daily 10am–11pm); Handicraft Store, Kuninga 13 (30EEK for one hour; daily 9am–9pm). If you have a laptop almost all hotels, and many cafés, restaurants, bars and pubs have Wi-Fi networks, often for free.

Laundry Sauberland, Maakri 23; Seebimull, Liivalaia 7.

Left luggage In the basement of the bus station (Mon–Sat 6.30am–10.20pm, Sun 7.45am–8.20pm; 4–10EEK); and at the train station (even-numbered dates 9am–10pm; odd-numbered dates 9am–5pm). There are also lockers in Viru Keskus.

Libraries British Council, Vana-Posti 7 (Tues–Fri noon–6pm, Sat 10am–3pm).

Newspapers Some of the larger city-centre kiosks stock English-language newspapers and magazines; otherwise try the newsagent in the Stockmann department store, Liivalaia 53.

Pharmacies Centrally located pharmacies which are open seven days a week include Raeapteek, Raekoja plats 11; Tallinna Linna Apteek, Pärnu mnt

10; Tõnismäe Apteek, Tõnismägi 5. The latter has a 24hr emergency counter (ring the buzzer).
Photo developing Fotoluks, Viru Keskus (daily 9am–9pm).
Police Pärnu mnt 11 ☎ 644 5266.
Post office Narva mnt 1, opposite the *Sokos Viru Hotel* (Mon–Fri 8am–8pm, Sat 8am–6pm).
Taxis Ranks on Vabaduse väljak or just outside the Viru gate. Otherwise call Tulika ☎ 612 0000 or Linnatakso ☎ 644 2442.

Telephones Next to the post office on Narva mnt 1 (Mon–Fri 8am–7pm, Sat 9am–4pm).
Travel agents Baltic Tours, Pikk 31 (☎ 630 0430, ⓦ www.baltictours.ee), deals in international plane tickets and hotel reservations within Estonia. Estravel, Suur-Karja 15 (☎ 626 6266, ⓦ www .estravel.ee), sells tickets for all the major ferry lines and is agent for American Express. City Bike Tours, Uus 33 (☎ 511 1819, ⓦ www.citybike.ee), runs bicycle tours.

Travel details

Trains

Tallinn to: Narva (2 daily; 3hr 30min); Paldiski (10 daily; 1hr 15min); Pärnu (2 daily; 3hr); Tartu (4 daily; 2hr 30min); Viljandi (2 daily; 3hr).

Buses

Tallinn to: Haanja (2 daily; 5hr); Haapsalu (every 1hr; 1hr 45min); Kärdla (3 daily; 4hr 30min); Kuressaare (every 2hr; 4hr 30min); Narva (hourly; 3hr 40min); Pärnu (hourly; 1hr 45min); Tartu (every 30min; 2hr 20min); Viljandi (hourly; 2hr 15min); Võru (12 daily; 3hr 45min).

International trains

Tallinn to: Moscow (1 daily; 14hr); St Petersburg (3 weekly; 7hr).

International buses

Tallinn to: Berlin (1–2 daily; 30hr); Rīga (9 daily; 5–6hr); St Petersburg (5 daily; 5hr); Vilnius (5 daily; 10hr).

International flights

Tallinn to: Copenhagen (up to 3 daily; 1hr 40min); Frankfurt (7 weekly; 2hr 40min); Helsinki (up to 8 daily; 1hr); London (2–3 daily; 3hr); Moscow (3 weekly; 3hr); Paris (1 daily; 3hr 30min); Rīga (up to 3 daily; 1hr); Stockholm (up to 5 daily; 2hr); Vilnius (up to 4 daily; 1hr 30min).

1.2
Western Estonia

With its jutting coastline, archipelago of islands and hinterland of thick forest and heaths, **western Estonia** is a microcosm of the country. Many locals maintain that it's in this region's juniper-covered heaths, quaint country towns and wave-battered shores watched over by solitary lighthouses, that the true soul of the nation ultimately lies. Although many of the coastal towns have been resorts since the nineteenth century, when the cream of the Baltic aristocracy came to bathe their weary limbs in medicinal coastal mud, much of western Estonia was treated as a sensitive border area during the Soviet period and tourism didn't really get going again until the 1990s. Happily, the desire to develop western Estonia has been tempered by the realization that the region's wealth of unspoilt natural landscapes is its

most valuable asset. The area also boasts a rich variety of wildlife, including sizeable communities of deer, moose, elk and beaver, as well as thousands of migrating birds in the spring and autumn.

The main gateway to the northwestern coast is the resort of **Haapsalu**, an endearing mixture of *belle époque* gentility and contemporary chic, and a convenient staging post en route to the tranquil islands of **Vormsi** and **Hiiumaa**. Immediately south of Hiiumaa, **Saaremaa** is the biggest and most popular of Estonia's islands, its enjoyably animated capital Kuressaare providing access to a beautiful hinterland of forest, heath and swamp. The southwestern coast is dominated by **Pärnu**, Estonia's one true beach resort. Inland from Pärnu, the laid-back provincial town of **Viljandi** is one of Estonia's prettiest and provides access to the beautiful, desolate peat bogs of the **Soomaa National Park**.

Western Estonia is easy to access, with frequent **buses** from Tallinn to the coast's principal towns, Haapsalu and Pärnu. The islands are all served by regular **ferry** services from the mainland. In addition, express buses run from Tallinn to Hiiumaa and Saaremaa, with the ferry crossing included as part of the deal. Local transport on the islands themselves is pretty scarce, and unless you have access to a car you'll need to adopt a leisurely approach to exploring the countryside.

Haapsalu and around

Straddling a three-kilometre-long strip of land pointing out into the Baltic Sea, **HAAPSALU** is an appealing mix of traditional seaside resort and modern spa town. Surrounded on three sides by water, it has been optimistically dubbed by some locals as the "Nordic Venice". This requires a significant degree of imagination, but Haapsalu has an undeniable charm, with narrow, winding streets of haphazard wooden fisherman's cottages, stately neo-Gothic villas gazing proudly out to sea and an imposing thirteenth-century castle.

The town has been popular with holidaymakers since the early nineteenth century, when local doctor Carl Abraham Hunnius (1797–1851) began to publicize the curative properties of the local mud. The town soon became a magnet for St Petersburg high society, attracting royalty by the end of the century – both Tsar Alexander II and son Alexander III were regular visitors. By the mid-twentieth century, Haapsalu was a mass-market bucket-and-spade resort, although tourism was subsequently wound down by the security-conscious Soviet regime, which regarded northwestern Estonia as one vast military installation. Since independence, it has become increasingly popular again, not least for the attractive stretch of sand just west of town at Paralepa. Meanwhile, many of the hotels offer the kind of mud treatments that first made the town famous.

Haapsalu is 10km from the Rohuküla ferry terminal, which serves the islands of Hiiumaa and Vormsi. The latter is an easy day-trip from town, as is the bird-rich nature reserve of **Matsalu** on the mainland to the south.

Arrival, information and accommodation

Buses arrive in the forecourt of the old train station on the southwestern side of town, ten minutes' walk from the **tourist office** at Posti tänav 37 (mid-May to mid–Sept Mon–Fri 9am–6pm, Sat & Sun 10am–3pm; mid-Sept to mid-May 14 Mon–Fri 9am–5pm; ☏473 3248, ⊛www.haapsalu.ee); staff can book you into local **B&Bs** (❶–❷). Some Haapsalu **hotels** drop their prices from October to April, and those that don't officially do so may still be open to bargaining. There are two **campsites** in town, one in Paralepa forest (*Paralepa Camping*, ☏515 5666, ⊛www .paralepacamping.ee) and another south of the centre at Monniku 32 (*Camping Pikseke*, ☏475 5779, ⊛www.albinet.com/camping). *Vanalinna Hostel* (Jaani 4, ☏473 4900, ⊛www.vanalinnabowling.ee), opened in 2006 – the only **hostel** in Estonia with a bowling alley downstairs – offers bright and spotlessly clean singles, doubles and triples, some en-suite (❶), but no dorm beds.

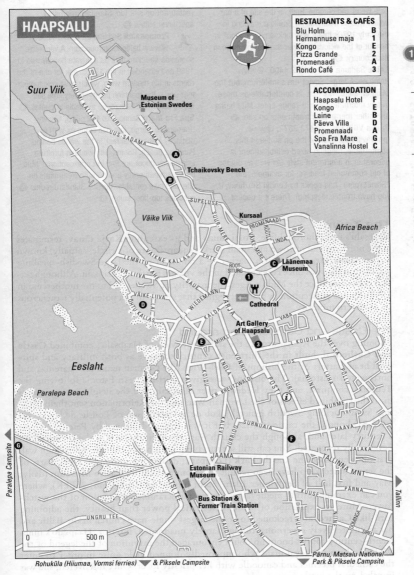

HAAPSALU

N

RESTAURANTS & CAFÉS

Blu Holm	B
Hermannuse maja	1
Kongo	E
Pizza Grande	2
Promenaadi	A
Rondo Café	3

ACCOMMODATION

Haapsalu Hotel	F
Kongo	E
Laine	B
Päeva Villa	D
Promenaadi	A
Spa Fra Mare	G
Vanalinna Hostel	C

Suur Viik

Museum of Estonian Swedes

Tchaikovsky Bench

Ⓐ

Ⓑ

Väike Viik

Kursaal

Africa Beach

Ⓒ Läänemaa Museum

Ⓞ

Ⓞ Cathedral

Art Gallery of Haapsalu

Eeslaht

Ⓔ

Ⓞ

Paralepa Beach

Ⓘ

Ⓕ

Estonian Railway Museum

Bus Station & Former Train Station

Ⓖ

0   500 m

Rohuküla (Hiiumaa, Vormsi ferries) ▼ & *Piksele Campsite*

Pärnu, Matsalu National Park & Piksele Campsite ▼

Paralepa Campsite ◄

Tallinn ►

Hotels

Haapsalu Hotel Posti 43 ☎ 473 3347, ⓦ www
.haapsaluhotel.ee. Despite an off-putting exterior
– an ugly concrete box on the busy main street
– you could do worse than the decent en suites

here, if the more characterful places in town are
booked up. ④

Kongo Kalda 19 ☎ 472 4800, ⓦ www.kongohotel
.ee. Modern en suites in what looks like a contemporary design showroom: lots of white surfaces,

99

pale wood and chrome. Built on the site of a bar which was so notorious for drunken brawling in the early 1970s that it was nicknamed "Congo" in honour of the vicious civil war then taking place in that country. ⑤

Laine Sadama 9/11 ℡ 472 4400, ⓦ www .laine.ee. A large, Soviet-era sanatorium, but the plain en suites are just as comfortable as those in any international, mid-range hotel. Mud baths and other therapeutic treatments on site. ⑤

Päeva Villa Lai 7 ℡ 473 3672, ⓦ www .paevavilla.ee. Each of the en suites in this comfortable, medium-sized establishment is decorated in a different style (as well as photos of old communist leaders, for example, the "Soviet room" has books by Leonid Brezhnev, if you have trouble sleeping). There's a decent

restaurant on site too. Standard rooms ④, split-level suites ⑤

🏃 **Promenaadi** Sadama 22 ℡ 473 7250, ⓦ www.baltichotelgroup.com. A venerable shoreside structure built as a private holiday villa in 1859 and extended in the 1990s. Ask for one of the rooms in the modern wing, which have chic furnishings and – the real high point – lovely little sea-facing balconies. Bike rental available to guests. ④

Spa Fra Mare Ranna 2 ℡ 472 4600, ⓦ www .framare.ee. Large, low-rise complex with a distinctly institutional feel, in the woods behind Paralepa Beach. Rooms with wooden furniture and dowdy decor are fine but unexceptional. Mud baths, aromatherapy and paraffin treatments on site, and bike rental for guests. Standard rooms ⑤, spacious top-floor suites ⑥

The Town

Haapsalu's main thoroughfare, **Posti tänav** and its extension **Karja tänav**, terminates at the northern end of town at a small market square (more of a circle, actually) known as the **Rootsiturg** – "Swedish market" – a reminder of the large Swedish-speaking population that was once concentrated in the villages north of Haapsalu. Although settled in the area since the Middle Ages, the majority of Swedes fled to the motherland in 1944 to avoid persecution by a Soviet regime that saw them as a potentially treacherous pro-Western minority.

The Castle and Cathedral and around

Looming over the Rootsiturg are the stark grey walls of Haapsalu's combined **Castle and Cathedral**, built in the thirteenth century to serve as both military and spiritual headquarters of the bishops of Ösel-Wiek (the German name for Saaremaa and northwestern Estonia). The bishops were given northwestern Estonia following the Teutonic conquest, and they lorded it over Haapsalu and the neighbouring islands until the combined effects of the Livonian Wars and the Reformation sent them packing. Swashbuckling Swedish general Jakob de la Gardie (son of Pontus de la Gardie; see p.81) bought the castle in 1628, but it was largely destroyed by Peter the Great a century later and, although the church was rebuilt in the 1880s, the fortifications never really recovered. You can still see surviving stretches of the ten-metre-high wall that once enclosed the **Castle Park** (Lossipark; daily 7am–midnight; free). Parts of the semi-ruined keep have been rebuilt to accommodate the **Castle Museum** (daily: May and first half of September 10am–5pm; June–Aug 10am–7pm; 25EEK), where you can examine rusting medieval weaponry and scramble up a section of the watchtower. More an expression of brute ecclesiastical power than beauty, the adjoining barn-like **Cathedral** is reckoned to be the largest single-nave church in the Baltic and has an impressively cavernous, though largely unadorned, interior. Haapsalu's nineteenth-century tourist boom no doubt encouraged the invention of the legend of the White Lady, a medieval maid who supposedly donned male guise in order to enter the cathedral precinct and canoodle with her priestly lover. Once discovered, she was impaled on the battlements (and/or immured in the walls, depending on which version of the tale you like the sound of best), bequeathing Haapsalu a lovelorn ghost that still puts in an appearance at one of the cathedral windows every August at full moon – although it might just be an illusion caused by moonbeams pouring through the window onto a wall behind. The apparition provides the perfect excuse for the good-natured ghoul-fest known as the **Days of the White Lady**, held in the castle park every summer (see p.59).

Just north of the castle, at the junction of Lossi plats and Kooli tänav, a pea-green, eighteenth-century Town Hall now houses the **Läänemaa Museum** (Wed–Sun: mid-May to mid-Sept 10am–6pm; mid-Sept to mid-May Wed–Sun 11am–4pm; 20EEK; ⑳www.muuseum.haapsalu.ee), where sepia photographs of crowded beaches reveal what a fun place pre-World War II Haapsalu must have been. There's passing mention of Ilon Wikland, the local-born Swede who went on to enjoy moderate renown as the illustrator of Astrid Lindgren's Pippi Longstocking books, and a shrine-like corner devoted to Tsarist-era mayor Gottfried von Krusenstern, who did much to promote the town's tourist profile before being shot on the main square by army deserters in 1917.

Back at the Rootsiturg, walk for five minutes south along Karja until it turns into Posti tänav; at number 3 is the **Art Gallery of Haapsalu** (Wed–Sun noon–6pm; free), which has small, frequently changing exhibitions of modern art from Estonia and abroad.

Africa beach and along Promenaadi

Head back to the Läänemaa Museum and then bear north to find one of the most attractive parts of Haapsalu, a web of quiet, cobbled streets lined with low-rise, nineteenth-century housing. Following these eastwards will bring you to **Africa Beach** (Aafrika rand), so named because bathers used to coat their bodies in the medicinal black mud found in the bay. Just back from the beach you can climb the birdwatching tower for sweeping views of nearby reed beds.

From here, Promenaadi winds west then north along the shore, passing the delicately carved eaves of the wooden **Kursaal** before arriving at the *Promenaadi* and *Laine* hotels, in front of which lies the stone seat known as the **Tchaikovsky Bench** (Tšaikovski pink). Placed here in 1940 to commemorate the 26-year-old composer's stay in 1867 (when he is said to have worked on parts of his first major opera, *Voyvod*), the memorial emits a light-activated blast of music whenever anyone approaches it.

The Museum of Estonian Swedes

Continuing north past the hotels eventually leads you to the **Museum of Estonian Swedes** at Sadama 32 (Rannarootsi muuseum; Wed–Sun: May to mid-Sept 10am–6pm; mid-Sept to April 11am–4pm; 20EEK; ⑳www.aiboland.ee; English-language leaflets available), which celebrates the heritage of this once-thriving community with a colourful display of richly embroidered costumes and household textiles. You can also see examples of Swedish-language newspapers once published in Haapsalu, including copies of the short-lived *Sovjet-Estland*, which appeared for a few months in 1940–41 and was so successful in selling the benefits of Soviet power that almost all of its target audience fled to Sweden when the Red Army returned in 1944. The highlight of the display is the twenty-metre-long tapestry recalling the history of the Estonian Swedes – from horn-helmeted Vikings onwards – in vivid, comic-strip style. It was made in 2002 by members of the local community who still claim Swedish ancestry and meet once a week at the museum to keep handicraft traditions alive. Outside the museum is a replica of a **jaala**, a traditional, three-sailed fishing boat from the island of Ruhnu.

The Estonian Railway Museum and Paralepa Beach

Built in 1904, Haapsalu's train station, in the southwest of town, carried out its last passenger service in 1996, but remains an enduring monument to the Tsarist Empire's *belle époque* – not least because of the elegant 214-metre-long canopy above the platform, built to shelter aristocratic arrivals from the unpredictable Baltic weather. Ensconced in the former imperial waiting room, the **Estonian Railway Museum** (Wed–Sun 10am–6pm; 20EEK) has a modest collection of tickets, uniforms and travel posters, and there are a couple of vintage locomotives parked out the back. A tenminute walk west of the station, the forest-fringed **Paralepa Beach** is the sandiest of Haapsalu's bathing areas.

Eating, drinking and entertainment

Haapsalu has a scattering of places to **eat and drink**, mostly concentrated on Posti tänav and Karja tänav. *Hermannuse maja*, Karja 1A (℡473 7131), is a reasonably smart, yet relaxed, pub-restaurant serving a mix of Estonian and international food. The nearby *Pizza Grande* at Karja 6 dishes out economical thin-crust pies. The hotel restaurants are less bland than you might expect: the *Blu Holm* in the *Hotel Laine* serves up excellent fish dishes in classy, starched-tablecloth surroundings; the café-restaurant at the *Hotel Promenaadi* is worth checking out for its glass-enclosed, waterfront position (mains 150–350EEK); and the restaurant of the *Kongo* hotel (see p.99) features ostrich fillet alongside more traditional Estonian standards; mains from 90EEK. *Rondo Café*, Posti 7, is the best place for pastries and cakes, while the café-bars underneath the *Haapsalu Hotel* are the liveliest spots for evening drinks.

The town offers a modest range of entertainment in summer and hosts a couple of worthwhile festivals. The **Kursaal** (open May to mid-Sept; ⊛www.kuursaal.ee) plays host to easy-listening crooners and (somewhat tame) discos in season, with outdoor concerts of light classics making use of the adjacent concert bowl in good weather. International ensembles take advantage of the cathedral's excellent acoustics during the **Haapsalu Early Music Festival** in July, while the decidedly more low-brow **Days of the White Lady** festival in mid-August involves live music, DJs and late-night partying in the castle park (see ⊛www.haapsalu.ee for more information).

Vormsi

Lying 3km off the mainland, **Vormsi** (⊛www.vormsi.ee) is a lush, green island, covered in forest, juniper heath and occasional patches of grazing land. Although there's not a great deal to see on Vormsi – about 10km by 20km in size – the general air of rustic calm and plentiful opportunities for walking and cycling make a visit here appealing. It was home to well over two thousand Estonian Swedes until 1944, when the vast majority left for the motherland. Although partially repopulated with Estonians during the Soviet period, humans are now outnumbered by elk, roe deer and wild boar.

Ferries from the mainland arrive at the small port of **SVIBY**, within easy walking distance of the main settlement, **HULLO**, 3km west. At the northern end of Hullo, the otherwise undistinguished **St Olav's Church** is worth a look for the thicket of wheel-shaped stone grave crosses in its cemetery. The remotest place on the island and the best spot for a swim is stubby **Rumpo peninsula**, 2km southeast of Hullo, a rock-strewn stretch of shoreline backed by juniper heath and peat bog.

Two daily **ferries** make their way to Sviby from **Rohuküla** (reached by bus #1, which runs roughly hourly from Haapsalu); check ferry timetable details at ⊛www .veeteed.com. One-way tickets are 15EEK per person, 55EEK for cars. Tanel Viks rents out **bikes** (130EEk per day) right on Sviby harbourfront, but they disappear fast on summer weekends, so it's best to reserve in advance (℡051 78722, ✉tanvx@neti.ee). Otherwise, rent one in Haapsalu and bring it with you.

Haapsalu tourist office (see p.98) is the best place to get information about Vormsi and may have a list of B&Bs on the island. Otherwise, *Mäe Farm*, Rumpo (April–Nov only; ℡472 9932, ⊛www.hot.ee/streng; ❸), offers charming rooms in two out-buildings (one of which is a traditionally built log cabin), as well as bike rental and camping space. Alternatively, try the *Elle-Malle Guesthouse*, Hullo (℡473 2072, ⊛www.vormsi .ee/ellemall; ❷), which has chalet-style accommodation, as well as a cosy double in a small windmill. Near here is the *Hullo Trahter*, a pleasant pub offering simple but decent light meals and snacks.

Matsalu

Thirty kilometres south of Haapsalu, **Matsalu Bay** is one of the biggest stop-off points for migrating birds in Europe, attracting thousands of ducks, barnacle geese, corncrakes, moorhens and mute swans every spring and autumn, as well as providing a year-round habitat for cormorants and gulls. All three sides of the bay have been under

the protection of the **Matsalu National Park** (Matsalu rahvuspark; ⓦwww.matsalu
.ee) since 1957, although it is the southern shore, with its dense reed beds and grassy
coastal heaths, which provides the best opportunities for getting up close to the birds.

The gateway to the area is the small provincial town of **LIHULA** (ⓦwww.lihula.ee),
served by Haapsalu–Virtsu and Tallinn–Kuressaare buses. Some 3km north of here is
the **Matsalu Nature Centre** in Penijõe Manor (Wed, Thurs, Sat and Sun 8am–5pm, Fri
8am–3.45pm; ⓣ472 4236, ⓦwww.matsalu.ee), where you can pick up maps, information on boat trips and contact details for guides. There's also a small museum (same
times; 10EEK) devoted to the local flora and fauna. From the centre, follow tracks
northwest to the birdwatching tower at **Suitsu**, 4km beyond Penijõe, for good views of
coastal wetlands edged by yellowy-gold reeds. Another tower can be found at **Keemu**,
6km west on the road to the village of Matsalu.

Should you wish **to stay**, staff at the Nature Centre can put you in touch with the
handful of B&Bs in the rustic communities near the reserve; otherwise *Luige Villa* in
Lihula (Tallinna mnt 23, ⓣ477 8872, ⓦwww.luigevilla.ee; ❸), has pleasant, well-
equipped doubles, as well as more frugal, four- and five-person rooms.

Hiiumaa

Shaped like a four-pointed star, **HIIUMAA** is the perfect place for anyone tired of
modern urban life and seeking a rural idyll. Estonia's second largest island – 75km east
to west, 50km north to south – is also one of its most sparsely populated, and while its
natural beauty is on a par with that of its more popular neighbour Saaremaa (see p.106),
it has had far less tourist development. Hiummaa's thin, sandy soil has never supported
much in the way of agriculture, so most of the island remains covered by virgin pine
forest, peat bogs and shrub-covered heathland – habitats favoured by elk, roe deer and
wild boar. The picturesque coastline meanwhile, dotted with isolated lighthouses,
deserted beaches and tranquil coves, encourages gentle exploration.

The island's main tourist office and most other facilities are in **Kärdla** to the north
of the island. For a taste of undiluted natural wilderness, head for the juniper-carpeted

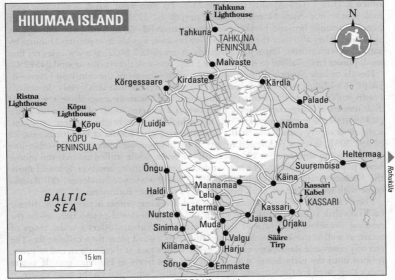

island of **Kassari**, linked to southern Hiiumaa by a causeway, or the wind-battered **Kõpu peninsula** at Hiiumaa's western end.

Laevakompanii (⊛www.laevakompanii.ee) runs four to six daily ferries from Rohuküla, just west of Haapsalu (see p.102), to the Heltermaa terminal on Hiiumaa's eastern coast, where there's a small **tourist information** office (☎463 1001; June–Aug daily 7.30am–7pm). A one-way ticket for the ninety-minute ferry journey costs 25EEK per person, plus 75EEK per car. Four daily Tallinn–Kärdla buses (calling at Haapsalu on the way) also make the crossing, with the ferry trip included in the ticket. There's also a ferry service from Sõru on Hiiumaa's southern tip to Triigi on Saaremaa, although it's operated by a small vessel that can take only a limited number of cars (expect queues at weekends) and it's not met by any buses. There are four daily ferries during the summer, two in winter. A one-way ticket costs 20EEK, plus 75EEK per car. Eomap's 1:50 000 **map** of Hiiumaa is the best aid to detailed exploration of the island.

Kärdla

Perched on the island's northeastern shoulder some 30km from Heltermaa, **KÄRDLA** is a wonderfully uneventful place with an infectiously laid-back atmosphere. Although it may not rank among the prettiest of rural capitals, it is Hiiumaa's only real service centre and transport hub – if you don't have your own vehicle it's the best place to base yourself. Timber houses and cottage gardens, most of which feature mounds of earth looking rather like air-raid shelters – but that (reassuringly) turn out to be potato cellars – are the main features of this low-rise town.

Kärdla was an important textile-producing town in the nineteenth century, and the factory manager's house at the northern end of the town – known as the Pikk Maja or "Long House" – now holds a branch of the **Hiiumaa Museum** (Mon–Fri 10am–5pm, Sat 11am–2pm; 15EEK). There's no permanent collection, but the sensitively restored rooms provide the perfect venue for seasonal art and photography displays. Five minutes northwest is Kärdla's most attractive feature, a grassy, boulder-strewn seaside park which fills up with bathers on summer weekends.

Practicalities

Buses stop on the fringes of the centre at Keskväljak, a few steps south of the **tourist office** at Hiiu 1 (mid-April to mid-Sept Mon–Fri 9am–6pm, Sat & Sun 10am–3pm; mid-Sept to mid-April Mon–Fri 10am–5pm; ☎462 2233, ⊛www.hiiumaa.ee); staff here can arrange bed-and-breakfast accommodation (❶–❷) in Kärdla and throughout the island. They also have the *Lighthouse Tour* booklet, a guide to exploring Hiiumaa by car, filled with stories, history and legends. Avies (☎605 8022, ⊛www.avies.ee) flies small **planes** from Tallinn to Kärdla twice a day; one-way tickets cost around 245EEK.

Hotels include *Sõnajala*, a fifteen-minute walk southwest of the centre on Leigri väljak (☎463 1220, ⊛www.sonajala.ee; ❷–❸). En suites are neat and freshly decorated; rooms with shared facilities are more timeworn. For a homely atmosphere, try *Kivijüri Külalistemaja* at Kõrgessaare mnt a little over a kilometre south of the tourist office (☎469 1002, ⊛www.hot.ee/kivijuri; ❷), which has four bright, modern en suites, some with comfy sofas. *Padu*, at the eastern entrance to Kärdla at Heltermaa mnt 22 (☎463 3037, ⊛www.paduhotell.ee; ❸), is more upmarket. Attractive log-cabin-like en suites come with satellite TV and small balconies, while stuffed animals and moose heads populate the lounge. The most stylish accommodation, however, is found above the *Nordtooder* café at Rookopli 20 (☎509 2054, ⊛www.nordtooder.ee; ❹). Rooms come with wooden floors, sleek black fittings and elegant bathrooms.

There's a handful of unassuming **eating and drinking** venues in town. *Café Arteesia* on Keskväljak is the best place for cheap and filling meat-and-potato fare, whilst the relaxing *Priiankru*, just north of the bus station on Sadama, offers a wider range of meals, as well as snacks. *Baar Espresso* at Hiiu 1A is a good place for a caffeine fix. The recently renovated *Rannapargu* café-bar, in the seaside park at the northern end of town, is open until the early hours at weekends and is as lively as Hiiumaa gets. If you're picnicking, head for the Konsum supermarket (daily 9am–9pm) on the main square.

Kassari and around

One of the main attractions in the southern part of the island is **KASSARI**, a separate land mass 8km long and 4km across, joined to the main body of Hiiumaa by a causeway. Containing some of the most unspoilt conifer-covered heathland in the region, it is compact enough to be explored on foot or by bike in a day. The main jumping-off point for exploring Kassari is **KÄINA**, a small town on the Hiiumaa side of the causeway. Built around the sombre ruins of a fifteenth-century church destroyed by World War II bombing, it's otherwise pretty forgettable. The nearby Käina Bay is home to a bird reserve, however, with over seventy different species; there's an observation tower close to the port of Orjaku.

Käina is one of the few places on Hiiumaa served by regular bus from Kärdla, and has some decent accommodation options to boot. *Liilia*, a family-run hotel just east of the bus stop at Hiiu mnt 22 (☏463 6146, ⓦwww.liiliahotell.ee; ⑤), has cosy en suites with TV, and a very good restaurant. One kilometre west of town in Lõokese, the *Lõokese Spa Hotel* (☏463 6146, ⓦwww.lookese.com; ⑤–④) is one of the swankiest places to stay on Hiiumaa, offering rooms with shower and TV, outdoor swimming and paddling pools, and spa facilities and treatments.

The road to Kassari leaves the Käina–Heltermaa road 3km east of Käina, crossing the causeway before passing after a further 3km a turn-off to the stocky, medieval **Kassari Kabel**, the only reed-roofed church in Estonia. A couple more kilometres beyond the turn-off is **Kassari** village itself, an appealing agglomeration of timber houses and tumbledown barns nestling among thickets of juniper. Just north of the village's main street is another branch of the **Hiiumaa Museum** (mid-May to mid-Sept Mon–Fri 10am–5pm; at other times contact in advance; 15EEK; ☏469 7121), offering a small but intriguing display of traditional agricultural implements and embroidered folk costumes. Beside the museum, the *Keldrimäe* guesthouse (☏518 2210, ⓦwww .keldrimae.ee; ②) has several simple rooms, as well as a pyramid-shaped lodge in the garden, the design of which is claimed to "raise levels of sexual energy".

At the western end of Kassari village a signpost points the way to **Sääre Tirp**, a pebbly promontory jutting out into the sea. After 2km, the track along the promontory terminates in a car park, and a path lined by juniper bushes leads to the foot of Sääre Tirp, ending in a desolate, otherworldly shingle spit that peters out into the sea.

Suuremõisa

The main settlement in the eastern corner of Hiiumaa is **SUUREMÕISA**, a frumpy little village 5km inland from the ferry terminal at Heltermaa and served by the Kärdla–Tallinn bus. The name literally means "Great Manor", a reference to the Baroque **manor house** built here in 1755 by Margarethe Stenbock, a descendant of the de la Gardie family (who owned most of Hiiumaa until dispossessed by the Russians in 1710). Nowadays an agricultural college, its interior is rarely accessible, although its rust-coloured exterior and extensive, unkempt grounds, open to the public, are sufficient excuse for a stop-off. In 1796, it was bought by Otto Reinhold Ludwig von Ungern-Sternberg (1744–1811), the shipping magnate and Hiiumaa landowner who became a by-word for arrogance and cruelty in nineteenth-century Estonia, when he faced accusations of piracy. In 1805, he shot one of his own captains in Suuremõisa's first-floor office, a crime for which he was deported to Siberia.

The Kõpu peninsula

Up to five buses a day wend their way west from Kärdla to the **Kõpu peninsula**, a rugged, rock-fringed tongue of heathland that juts out into the sea 45km or so west of town. Buses terminate at the village of Kalana, on the tip of the peninsula, although it's worth hopping off at the village of Kõpu, 35km out of Kärdla, to see the **Kõpu lighthouse** (Kõpu tuletorn), one of the oldest continuously operating lighthouses in the world. On the western side of the village, it dates back to 1531 and was built at the request of the Hanseatic League to warn ships away from the Hiiu Madal sandbank and the pirate-infested coastline. Strengthened by a quartet of bulky,

△ The Kõpu lighthouse

angular buttresses at its base, it looks at first sight more like a Maya temple than a piece of maritime architecture. Climb up it for a sea view (May to mid-Sept daily 9am–10pm; 20EEK). From July to mid-August a live classical and folk music evening is held at the lighthouse every Friday; Kärdla tourist office can provide more information about events at the lighthouse.

Some 12km west of Kõpu lies the equally striking maroon-coloured **Ristna lighthouse**, a rocket of a building that presides over a boulder-strewn stretch of shoreline. Like many nineteenth-century lighthouses in this part of Estonia, it was built abroad (in this case in France in 1874) and reassembled here on arrival.

The Tahkuna peninsula

Several daily buses run from Kärdla to the Tahkuna peninsula at the northern tip of Hiiumaa, home to the **Tahkuna lighthouse**, built in 1875 and the site of a fierce battle between German and Russian soldiers during World War II. Close to the lighthouse is a monument to the victims of the ferry *Estonia*, which sank during a storm on September 28, 1994, thirty miles north of Tahkuna. A cross and bell, which only rings when the wind is the same speed as it was on the night of the disaster, commemorate the 852 people who lost their lives.

Saaremaa

For Estonians, the island of **Saaremaa** epitomizes the nation's natural beauty more than any other place in the country. Cloaked with pine forest, juniper heath and grasslands, its coastline girdled with sandy beaches and tawny reed beds, it has long appealed to nature-loving, well-to-do Tallinners and now increasingly attracts Scandinavian and Western European tourists too. Estonia's largest island is also a fertile source of myths and legends, with local folklore centring on the adventures of Suur Töll, a friendly but short-tempered giant, and his wife Piret.

Back-to-nature instincts are catered for by a scattering of farmstead-based B&Bs across Saaremaa, although most accommodation is concentrated in the island's alluring capital, **Kuressaare**, site of the one must-see historic attraction on the island, the **Bishop's Castle**. North of Kuressaare lie some of Saaremaa's best-known sights, notably the strangely enchanting **Angla windmills** and the mysterious **Kaali meteorite crater**. On the western side of the island is the little-touristed coastal wilderness of the **Vilsandi National Park**, ideal for hiking. Historic churches crop up just about everywhere, with some especially fine ones at **Karja**, **Kaarma** and **Kihelkonna**.

Public transport on Saaremaa is limited, with services to most destinations leaving Kuressaare at different times on different days of the week, making timetable reading a bit of a nightmare – the Kuressaare tourist office is your best source of information. Thanks to its largely flat terrain, however, exploring the island by **bike** is a viable option; these can be rented in Kuressaare (see below).

Saaremaa is reached by taking the **ferry** (hourly in summer, every two hours in winter; ⓦwww.laevakompanii.ee) from Virtsu on the mainland to Kuivastu on **Muhu**, a small island, 8km across from which a causeway leads to Saaremaa itself. One-way tickets cost 20EEK per person, with an extra 85EEK per car. Numerous daily buses make the trip from Tallinn and Pärnu to Kuressaare – the price of the ferry crossing is included in the ticket. Approaching from Haapsalu is more awkward, although in summer there are three daily buses from Haapsalu to Virtsu, where you can change onto one of the Tallinn–Kuressaare or Pärnu–Kuressaare services. Ferries from Hiiumaa dock at Triigi near the village of Leisi on the northern coast; Leisi's tourist office (☎457 3073; June 4–Aug 31 noon–8pm) is on the main street.

If travelling by **car**, bear in mind that there are long queues for the ferries on summer weekends – leave it too late in the day and you may end up stranded. Avies (☎605 8022, ⓦwww.avies.ee) operates daily **flights** from Tallinn to Kuressaare; one-way tickets cost around 455EEK. It's also possible to fly from Pärnu and Rīga; contact Kuressaare Airport for more information (☎453 3793, ⓦwww.eeke.ee). Eomap's 1: 300 000 Saaremaa **map**, available from Kuressaare tourist office or bookshops in Tallinn, is useful if you intend to explore the island in any depth.

Muhu

The main launching point for Saaremaa, the island of **Muhu** is also worth visiting in its own right – with pine forests, juniper thickets, windmills and thatched cottages, it's just as attractive as its better-known island neighbour. Among its draws is the village of **LIIVA**, 6km inland from the Kuivastu ferry terminal and site of the thirteenth-century **St Catherine's Church** (Katariina kirik), an angular, whitewashed building, looking fashionably Modernist with its trio of steep-roofed sheds seemingly concertina-ed together.

Three kilometres beyond Liiva, a minor road branches right towards **KOGUVA**, a settlement on Muhu's west coast that has been declared a "museum-village" on account of its rich stock of stone-built, reed-thatched farmhouses. Far from being museum pieces, the majority of these houses are still inhabited by local farmers – wandering the village's grassy lanes leaves you thinking how nice it would be if more Estonian villages still looked like this.

If you want **to stay** on Muhu, head for ⚔ *Pädaste Mõis,* on the coast, 6km south of Liiva (☎454 8800, ⓦwww.padaste.ee; ⑤), one of the best hotels in Estonia, based in an old manor house. The decor in the luxurious doubles and split-level suites preserves a reassuringly rustic quality, while the attached **restaurant** is top class. It serves innovative – but, by Estonian standards, very expensive – dishes like fillet of hare with parsnip puree.

Kuressaare

Saremaa's "capital", **KURESSAARE**, is a captivating market town midway along the island's south coast that tempts you to stay longer than you'd planned. The town centre remains much as it was before World War II, with traditional houses, shady avenues and a spectacularly well-preserved castle, and only a scattering of Soviet-era buildings on the outskirts. This is not to say that Kuressaare is stuck in the past; it also boasts fashionable cafés, boutique hotels and innovative restaurants that make use of the enviable local produce. All of this combines to give the town a chic,

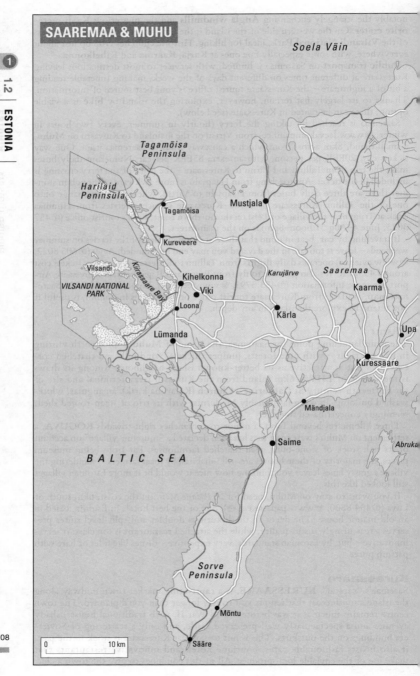

SAAREMAA & MUHU

Soela Väin

Tagamõisa
Peninsula

Harilaid
Peninsula

Tagamõisa

Mustjala

Kureveere

Vilsandi

VILSANDI NATIONAL
PARK

Kihelkonna

Karujärve

Saaremaa

Viki

Kaarma

Loona

Kärla

Upa

Lümanda

Kuressaare

Mändjala

Abruka

Saime

BALTIC SEA

Sorve
Peninsula

Mõntu

Sääre

0   10 km

▲ Sõru (Hiiumaa)

Nõmmküla

Koguva

Liiva *Muhu*

Kuivastu

▶ Virtsu

Leisi

Orissaare

Karja Church ✝

Padaste

Angla

Tagavere

Tornimäe

Karja

Laimjala

Kaali meteorite crater

Valjala

Kõljala

Püna

G u l f
o f R p g a

N

cosmopolitan air, which draws well-to-do Estonians and, increasingly, Western Europeans too. Although it's not much of a beach resort – the best beaches are some way out of town – Kuressaare has a health-tourism pedigree dating back to the 1840s, when the craze for mud baths first took off, and many of the local hotels do a brisk trade in rest cures and spa treatments. Kuressaare is the island's only real town and service centre, so wherever you're aiming for, you're likely to pass through here at least once.

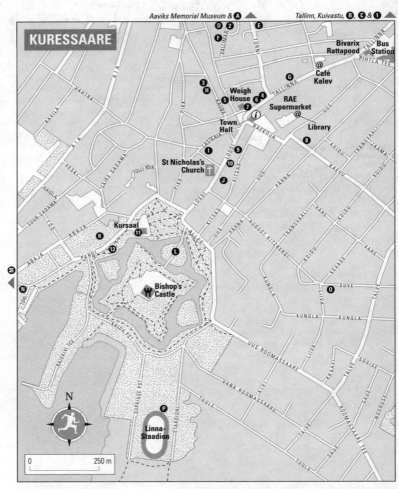

ACCOMMODATION			
Arabella	**E**	Lossi Hotel	**L**
Arensburg	**J**	Mardi	**D**
Georg Ots Spa Hotel	**N**	Ovelia B&B	**O**
Grand Rose Spa Hotel	**G**	Repo	**F**
Johan	**H**	Rüütli	**K**
Jurna turismitalu	**B**	Saaremaa Thalasso Spa	**M**
Kadri	**C**	Staadioni	**P**
Linnahotel	**I**	SÜG	**A**

RESTAURANTS, CAFÉS & BARS			
Classic Kohvik	**10**	Monus Villem	**1**
Georg Ots	**N**	Rose	**G**
John Bull Pub	**12**	Vaekoda	**6**
Kapiteni Körts	**3**	Vanalinna	**5**
Kass Kohvik	**2**	Veski	**8**
Kohvik Kuursaal	**11**	Wildenbergi Kohvik	**7**
La Perla	**9**		
Lokaal	**4**		

Arrival and information

Kuressaare's **bus station** is located just off Tallinna, the main street, five minutes' walk northwest of the **tourist office**, inside the Town Hall at Tallinna 2 (second half of May Mon–Sat 9am–5pm, Sun 10am–3pm; June–Aug Mon–Fri 9am–7pm, Sat 9am–5pm, Sun 10am–3pm; first half of Sept Mon–Sat 9am–5pm, Sun 10am–3pm; mid-Sept to mid-May Mon–Fri 9am–5pm; ☎453 3120, ⊛www.saaremaa.ee), where you can buy local maps and get info on walking and biking trails. The library at Tallinna 6 has free **Internet** access; otherwise try *Café Kalev* which has two terminals (20EEK per hour). You can rent a **car** at Hertz, Tallinna 9 (☎453 3660, ⊛www.hertz.ee), or a **bike** from Bivarix Rattapood, Tallinna 26.

Accommodation

There's a growing range of **hotels** in Kuressaare, although cheapies are outnumbered by a glut of places pitching three-star comforts and spa treatments to a mid-range market. Although it's a good idea to book ahead in summer, and on weekends throughout the year, prices tumble in the off-season (Oct–April) when it's relatively easy to pick up a bargain. The tourist office can book **bed-and-breakfast** accommodation (❶–❷) both in Kuressaare and on farmsteads across the island – the latter are an excellent way of savouring the local countryside, but you'll probably need your own transport to reach them. *SÜG* (also known as *SYG*) at Kingu 6, off Hariduse, ten minutes northwest of the centre (☎455 4388, ⊛www.syg.edu.ee) is a **hostel** for local high-school students, but usually has space for travellers in four-bed dorms (130–160EEK); simply furnished singles and doubles with shared facilities and no breakfast are also available (❶).

The nearest **campsite** is the *Mändjala*, 11km west of town just beyond the village of Nasva (May–Sept; ☎454 4193, ⊛www.mandjala.ee); it also has accommodation in cabins (❷). Kuressaare–Järve buses pass by.

Hotels

Arabella Torni 12 ☎455 5885, ⊛www.arabella
.ee. A spruced-up, Soviet-era, green and grey
residential block, *Arabella* has a fresh feel and
good-sized en suites, all with fridge and Ikea-style
furniture. ❹

Arensburg Lossi 15 ☎452 4700,
⊛www.sivainvest.ee. Through a castle-
like entrance lie compact, elegant and affordable
rooms, many with bathtubs rather than showers.
The restaurant, complete with cigar room, is
equally smart and there's a pleasant garden and
children's play area. ❹

Georg Ots Spa Hotel Tori 2 ☎455 0000, ⊛www
.gospa.ee. Don't let the concrete exterior put you
off – the hotel inside is first class. Chic rooms
come with king-sized beds, views of either the
sea or the castle, and vivid, stripy carpets. There's
a bewildering array of spa treatments on offer on
site, as well as one of the best restaurants in town
(see p.113). ❻

Grand Rose Spa Hotel Tallinna 15 ☎666 7012,
⊛www.grandrose.ee. Only open since December
2006, but already staking a claim to be Kuressaare's top hotel. No two rooms are the same,
but all are impeccably decorated, feature swanky
bathrooms and simply ooze class. Some have
chandeliers and rich carpets, others balconies and
polished wood floors. There's an indoor pool, a

spa and massage centre, and the attached *Rose
Restaurant* (see p.113) is a bonus. ❻

Johan Kauba 13 ☎453 3036, ⊛www.johan.ee.
A decent but slightly overpriced establishment,
with plain, pale-blue rooms with small TV and
shower. ❺

Jurna turismitalu Upa küla ☎452 1919,
⊛www.saaremaa.ee/jurna. This long, thatched-
roof farm building, dating back to the start of the
twentieth century, in a restful, rustic setting 6km
northeast of Kuressaare in the village of Upa, just
off the Leisi road, has a handful of snug rooms,
some en-suite. The owners can also arrange horse
riding, fishing trips and hunting excursions. ❸

Kadri Upa küla ☎452 4633, ⊛www
.hotelmardi.eu. Set amid juniper heath and forest,
5km northeast of town on the main road to Kuivastu, the *Kadri*, like the *Mardi* (see p.112), is run by
Kuressaare's Hotel and Restaurant School. Plain,
spick-and-span rooms in soothing colours. ❸

Linnahotel Lasteaia 7 ☎453 1888,
Ⓔlinnahotell@kontaktid.ee. A friendly hotel
tucked away in an appealing warren of alleyways.
Alongside the usual mid-range facilities, rooms
come with tea- and coffee-making facilities and
small balconies. ❺

Lossi Hotel Lossi 27, ☎453 3633, Ⓔlossihotel
@tt.ee. In the castle grounds, this lovely Art
Nouveau hotel has bright en suites, all with stylish

furnishings and many boasting striking views of the castle. Under renovation at the time of research, but due to reopen in summer 2007. ⑤

Mardi Vallimaa 5A ☎ 452 4633, ⓦ www .hotelmardi.eu. Renovated in 2006, the *Mardi* has bright twins, triples, suites and family rooms with pale-yellow walls, laminate flooring and big bathrooms. The hotel is spotless, the service is great and there's an excellent self-service café too (see opposite). ④

Ovelia B&B Suve 8 ☎ 518 5932. One of Kuressaare's few budget options, *Ovelia* is a red-panelled house on a quiet residential street 600m from the centre. Rooms are pretty basic but acceptable. ②

Repo Vallimaa 1A ☎ 453 3510, ⓦ www.saaremaa .ee/repo. Close to the *Mardi*, *Repo* is a friendly hotel with small but pristine rooms with showers and cable TV. ③

Rüütli Pargi 12 ☎ 454 8100, ⓦ www .saaremaaspahotels.eu. A big hotel with an uninspiring blue and grey exterior. Rooms are spacious and fully fitted but a little lacking in charm. There is, however, a full range of spa treatments available on site, as well as an indoor pool with water slide, a squash court and a children's playroom. ⑥

Saaremaa Thalasso Spa Mändjala ☎ 454 4100, ⓦ www.saarehotell.ee. A two-storey Art Deco pavilion 11km west of town boasting prim en suites with TV, plus views of either the surrounding pine forests or the nearby beach. A decent range of spa treatments is offered, and guests can rent bikes. ④–⑤

Staadioni Staadioni 4 ☎ 453 3556, ⓦ www .staadionihotell.ee. Open May to Sept, *Staadioni* is an unpretentious place, close to the sports stadium to the east of the castle, with good-sized, pastel-shaded en suites. ③

The Town

Most life in Kuressaare revolves around the elongated central square formed by the junction of Tallinna, Lossi and Raekoja streets. On the eastern side, an agreeable pair of stone lions guard the entrance to the seventeenth-century Town Hall (Raekoda), where a ground-floor **art gallery** (Tues–Sat 10am–5pm; free) hosts seasonally changing contemporary art exhibitions. One floor up, the main council chamber harbours an exuberant eighteenth-century ceiling painting in which flesh-flaunting Bacchantes enjoy an alfresco picnic. It was salvaged from a local house, but it's not known who painted it or for whom.

Opposite the Town Hall is one of Kuressaare's oldest surviving buildings, the step-gabled **Weigh House** (Vaekoda), dating from 1633 and now a pub (see p.114). Just to the west, cobbled alleys lead into an atmospheric quarter of low timber houses, many now occupied by shops and cafés.

A five-minute walk north of the Weigh House is the **Aaviks Memorial Museum** at Vallimaa 7 (Wed–Sun 11am–6pm; 10EEK). This small museum, in the former home of renowned Estonian linguist Johannes Aavik (1880–1973), gives an insight into his life, which was spent documenting the origins and development of the Estonian language. There are also displays on Aavik's cousin, Joosep Aavik (1889–1993), a noted conductor and organist.

Back to the square, heading southwest along Lossi takes you past a **monument** to the dead of the 1918–20 War of Independence, sculpted by Amandus Adamson, Estonia's leading inter-war sculptor and recently restored to pride of place after a lengthy Soviet-era absence. Just beyond, it's impossible to miss the jaunty green domes of **St Nicholas's Church** (Nikolai kirik), an eighteenth-century Orthodox foundation serving an Estonian rather than Russian congregation – a reminder of the fact that an estimated twenty percent of Estonia's population joined the Orthodox Church when the country belonged to the Tsarist Empire. A certain Estonian sobriety of character is retained in the interior decor – noticeably plainer than in Russian Orthodox churches.

Lossi continues south to the magnificent **Bishop's Castle** (Piiskopilinnus), a sturdy, sandy-coloured structure built from locally quarried dolomite. The original castle was built in 1261 by Bishop German of Ösel-Wiek in order to keep the restless natives of Saaremaa in check. The castle as it stands today, surrounded by a star-shaped system of earthworks and a deep-gouged moat, dates largely from the fourteenth century and is such a well-preserved quadrangle of smooth stone that – from a distance at least – it looks like a movie set. Surrounding it are bastions and ramparts thrown up by Danes and Swedes in the seventeenth century, now a grassy park. Used as a barracks by the Russians, the castle was restored by the Saaremaa nobility after 1904, to serve both as a symbol of provincial pride and to provide the local authorities with much-needed office space.

The labyrinthine keep now houses the **Saaremaa Regional Museum** (Saaremaa koduloomuuseum; May–Aug daily 10am–6pm; 50EEK; Sept–April Wed–Sun 11am–6pm; 40EEK), a didactic parade of artefacts covering the history of the island from prehistoric times to the present. Chunky chain jewellery worn by Iron Age Estonian chieftains and their molls helps to cheer up the proceedings, as do chalices and silverware once belonging to the Kuressaare bishops. There's plenty of material on Saaremaa-born worthies whom you might never have heard of otherwise, notably Tsarist-era explorers Richard Otto Mack (1825–86), who trekked off to eastern Siberia to study plant life; and Fabian Gottlieb von Bellingshausen (1778–1852), who saw himself as the successor to Captain Cook and led a major Russian expedition to the South Seas – he's credited with discovering Antarctica, although he thought it was a small island at the time. It's also possible to view the spartan living quarters of the bishops on the ground floor and climb the watchtowers. Pikk Hermann, the eastern (and thinner) corner tower is linked to the rest of the keep only by a wooden drawbridge. In the park surrounding the castle moat you'll find the wooden **Kursaal** building, dating from 1889 and now a genteel café.

Restaurants and cafés

There are plenty of places **to eat** in town, most of them offering a wide range of decent food at reasonable prices. You can pick up **picnic supplies** from the RAE supermarket on the main square (daily 9am–10pm). The establishments below are open daily from noon until 11pm or midnight, unless otherwise stated.

Classic Kohvik Lossi 9. A popular, modern café with blond wood tables and white suede chairs, serving up pancakes, salads, pastas and grills. Mon–Fri 8.30am–9pm, Sat & Sun 9am–10pm.

Georg Ots Tori 2. A big, bright dining room overlooking the harbour with appealing, if occasionally overcomplicated, dishes such as chicken fillet with mascarpone and sun-dried tomato, in a cream and fennel sauce. Mains start at 150EEK.

Kass Kohvik Vallimaa 5A. A self-service café offering dirt-cheap but excellent lunches. Part of the *Hotel Mardi* complex; the café entrance is round the side from the restaurant. Open daily 11.30am–3pm.

Kohvik Kuursaal in the Kursaal building in the castle park. An atmospheric place open during the summer offering soups and sandwiches for around 50EEK fish dishes for around 100EEK and terrace seating. Till 10pm.

La Perla Lossi 3. A smart Italian with good-value, thin-crust pizzas and pastas, a bargain weekday 45EEK lunch special and attentive service. Don't miss the free tomato and herb rolls.

Lokaal Tallinna 11. This subterranean bar-restaurant splices the old and the new: original stone roof and walls alongside red seats, black tables and tinted glass. The menu is filled with the usual Estonian standards. Fri & Sat till 6am, Sun–Thurs till 2am.

Rose Tallinna 15 ☏ 666 7000. The *Grand Rose Spa Hotel*'s cellar restaurant is the place to head to if you want a formal dining experience, first-class service and excellent food (try rack of Saaremaa lamb). Not cheap (mains 170–250EEK), but worth a splurge. Booking advised in the summer.

Vanalinna Kauba 8 ☏ 453 3689. One of the smartest restaurants in town, offering a mouth-watering range of steaks and fish, stupendous desserts and good wines. The attached café is cheaper and a good spot for pastries, cakes and salad. Booking advised in the summer. Daily 8am–7pm.

Veski Pärna 19. A café-restaurant in a unique setting: inside a (sadly motionless) windmill, with sails that light up at night. Sit round wooden tables or on vast millstones of polished granite and sample unusual dishes like chicken with pear or pork in beer sauce; mains from 120EEK. Daily Sun–Thurs till 10pm, Fri & Sat till 2am.

Bars and pubs

There's a good range of drinking venues in Kuressaare, mostly cosy, convivial places that become enjoyably raucous at weekends. Don't forget to try Saaremaa-brewed beer, which packs a bit more of a punch than Saku or A. Le Coq. Bars and pubs are usually open until 11pm or midnight during the week, later on Fridays and Saturdays.

John Bull Pub Pargi 4. A lively, pale-green wooden hut pub, with a great location overlooking the castle ramparts. You can perch at a bar made out of a discarded bus chassis, or lounge around in a Soviet corner overlooked by Lenin portraits. Open April–Sept daily 11am–2am.

Kapiteni Körts Kauba 13. This faux-rustic beer hall comes complete with wooden benches, fishing nets and snug alcoves. Daily 11am–3am.

Monus Villem Tallinna 63B. Few tourists make it up to this roomy bar, 500m northeast of the bus station – a shame because it has a strong local

following and a lively atmosphere. Daily 10am till at least 2am.

Vaekoda Tallinna 3. A rather staid drinking den in the seventeenth-century Weigh House, also offering rather stylish food featuring plenty of local fish. 10am–2am.

Wildenbergi Kohvik Tallinna 1. A civilized bar with an extensive drinks menu and tempting sweet snacks. The leather sofas by the window are great for lounging, whilst the outdoor seating area is a prime people-watching spot. Fri & Sat 9am–1am, Sun–Thurs 9am–midnight.

Entertainment

Despite the lack of a regular theatre or concert hall, a good deal of quality culture comes to Kuressaare in the summer. A canopy-covered podium next to the Kursaal becomes a bandstand-cum-concert bowl, hosting brass bands, classical performances and the occasional crooner. The castle courtyard is employed to dramatic effect during the **Kuressaare Opera Days** (Kuressaare Ooperipäevad; ⓦwww.festivals.ee/kuresoop_eng.html), when two major operas are performed over a long weekend at the end of July. The castle is also pressed into service during the **Kuressaare Chamber Music Days** (ⓦwww.kammerfest.ee) in August, featuring top performers from Estonia and further afield.

North of Kuressaare

There are several sights, notably the Kaali meteorite crater and the Angla windmills, strung out in the villages north of Kuressaare, many of which are on or near the Kuressaare–Leisi road and served by local buses. Just off this route, 10km north of Kuressaare and 5km west of the Leisi road, the small village of **KAARMA** is worth a detour for its venerable thirteenth-century **church** (Kaarma kirik), a large, red-roofed building unusual in having twin aisles. Inside is a christening stone from the same period and a pulpit supported by a wooden Joseph figure from 1450. The church's graveyard is littered with ancient stone crosses – the oldest are the so-called "sun crosses" – crosses set within a circle carved in stone.

The Kaali meteorite crater

Returning to the Kuressaare–Leisi road and heading north for 6km brings you to the turn-off for the village of **KAALI**, 2.5km further southeast, famous for its 4000-year-old **meteorite crater**. Signs at the entrance to the village direct you up onto the lip of the *kraater*, a 150-metre-wide pit surrounded by a huge embankment composed of the rubble thrown up on impact and now covered in mossy-trunked trees. At the base of the pit lies a murky, green pool. It's an eerily beautiful spot and one of the world's few easily accessible meteorite craters. The **Kaali Visitors' Centre** in the village (daily 9am–8pm; ☏514 4889, ⓦwww.kaali.kylastuskeskus.ee) has a small museum (25EEK) and simple accommodation (❸). On the opposite side of the car park from the crater, the *Kaali Trahter* **café-restaurant** is a good place for a breather, although it can get very busy at lunchtimes. One kilometre southeast of the crater in the village of **KÕLJALA**, the *Kõljala puhkeküla* (☏459 1255) offers **camping** and horse riding.

Getting to Kaali by public transport, it's a toss-up between catching the Kuressaare–Leisi bus (get off at the Liiva putla stop beside the Kaali turn-off and walk 2.5km southeast) and hopping aboard a Kuressaare–Kuivaste–Tallinn bus (get off at Kõnnu and walk 3km northwest) – either way, be sure to check return times first.

Angla and Karja

Around 15km north of Kaali is **ANGLA**, a village famed for its five wooden **windmills** (Angla tuulikud) standing in a much-photographed line by the roadside. The

△ Angla windmill

windmills aren't open to the public, but they're mesmerizing enough to merit a stop-off – like the stone heads on Easter Island, they exude an ageless dignity. Kuressaare–Leisi buses pick up and drop off at the northernmost of the mills.

A right turn just past the windmills leads after 2km to the thirteenth-century **Karja Church** (Karja kirik), a plain, white structure with an unusual Crucifixion carving above its side door. Inside the church are more stone-carvings, depicting religious figures and scenes from village life. The village of **KARJA** itself – actually 1km south of Angla back on the main road – is the site of an attractive graveyard.

Western Saaremaa

Western Saaremaa is arguably the most attractive part of the island: its rugged, deeply indented coastline is backed by a sparsely populated hinterland of grasslands, juniper heath, small lakes and bogs. Many of its more beautiful stretches fall under the aegis of the **Vilsandi National Park**, founded in 1993. Named after Vilsandi island, 3km off Saaremaa's western shore, the park covers much of the island's northwestern corner. Offshore islets and reed-shrouded shores provide a multitude of habitats for migrating birds, with hundreds of species – including mute swans, greylag geese, oystercatchers and Arctic terns – gathering in the area in the spring and autumn.

The main entrance point to the park is the visitors' centre at **Loona**, 2.5km south of the village of **Kihelkonna**, an easy bus ride from Kuressaare. The northwestern extremities of the park on the **Harilaid Peninsula** offer most in the way of desolate beauty, although you'll need your own transport to explore them.

Viki, Kihelkonna and Loona

The road west from Kuressaare forges through a landscape of arable land and forest before arriving after some 25km at the village of **VIKI**, home to the **Mihkli Farm Museum** (mid-April to Oct daily 10am–6pm; April and Sept closed Mon & Tues; 20EEK), a re-creation of a typical nineteenth-century Saaremaa farmstead. With a windmill in full working order and a small cluster of thatch-roofed farmhouses smothered in moss, it's as delightful a taste of traditional Saaremaa life as you'll get. From here it's only 5km further to **KIHELKONNA**, a bucolic village draped around a dazzlingly whitewashed **parish church**. Dating from the 1260s, it's one of the oldest on the island, although its dominant feature – a sky-rocketing steeple, for a time also a lighthouse – was only added in 1897. Crowning a hillock 200m south of the church is a squat, grey building that looks like a cross between a cow shed and a gun emplacement – it's actually the church's seventeenth-century belfry.

Thirty-five minutes' walk south of Kihelkonna on the Lümanda road, a signed right turn leads to Loona manor (Loona mõis), a nineteenth-century gentry farmstead housing the **Vilsandi National Park Visitors' Centre** (Mon–Fri 9am–5pm; ℡454 6880), where you can buy maps and get advice on where to walk. The park comprises over 150 uninhabited offshore islets favoured by local birdlife, as well as a narrow coastal belt criss-crossed by (largely unmarked) dirt roads. The quickest way to get a taste of the area is to follow forest paths due west of Loona, emerging after fifteen minutes onto the reed-fringed Kiirassaare Bay (Kiirassaare laht), which offers fleeting glimpses of rocky offshore islands. From here you can turn northeast back to Kihelkonna (20min), or improvise your own itinerary by following the coast southwest through a wonderfully tranquil region characterized by pine woods, grassland and swamp.

The best place **to stay** in the Kihelkonna–Loona region is the National Park Visitors' Centre itself, which has a handful of tastefully decorated en-suite rooms (May–Sept only; ℡454 6510, ⓦwww.loona.ee; ❸). Somewhat more frugal is the *Kihelkonna Parsonage* (Pastoraadi Oomaja; ℡454 6558, ⓔkihelkonna@eelk.ee; ❶) next to the church, offering four rooms with shared facilities. There's a well-stocked food shop in Kihelkonna diagonally across from the bus stop.

Towards the Harilaid peninsula

North of Kihelkonna the national park boundary continues to follow Saaremaa's west coast, ballooning out after some 20km to envelop the **Harilaid peninsula**, a compact thumb of land offering some of the island's most strikingly stark scenery, characterized by stony ground with a sparse covering of waist-high junipers. The easiest way to get here from Kihelkonna is to follow the northbound Tagamõisa road and take a left turn onto a dirt road 5km north of the village of Kureveere. This passes through the once-flourishing settlement of Kõruse, depopulated after World War II when the Soviets turned the area into a military zone and now a virtual ghost village. Carrying on, you arrive at a sandy neck of land that joins the main body of Saaremaa to the Harilaid peninsula – Harilaid was a separate island until the narrow channel between it and Saaremaa silted up in the seventeenth century. This is as far as cars can go; a national park information board bears details of hiking trails around the peninsula – the complete circuit is about 12km, but even a short walk will give you an idea of Harilaid's otherworldly beauty. The centre of the peninsula is thick with pines and junipers, ringed by a belt of steppe-like grassland, which in turn gives way to a part-sandy, part-pebbly shoreline supporting a stubborn covering of mosses and heathers. It takes about an hour to walk up the eastern side of the peninsula to the northern tip, just beyond which lies the slender, black-and-white-striped Kiipsaare lighthouse, built in 1933 and no longer in use – with its foundations battered by the sea, it's now listing dramatically to one side.

Pärnu

Estonia's premier seaside resort, **PÄRNU** is known as the country's "Summer Capital" – a fair description considering one in four Estonians visit at least once during the holiday season. The town's biggest asset is its seven-kilometre-long sandy beach, which is packed with sunbathers in July and August and a popular place for a walk all year round. While there are plenty of beach-side bars to keep the party-hard hedonists satisfied, Pärnu itself, spread around the estuary of the Pärnu River, preserves a small-town gentility, with shady parks, wide avenues lined with lime trees and an appealing mix of traditional wooden houses and Bauhaus-inspired inter-war villas. The town also enjoys a rich cultural life: its prestigious theatre and state-of-the-art concert hall mean that Pärnu is one of the few places outside Tallinn and Tartu where you can enjoy top-quality drama and music all year round.

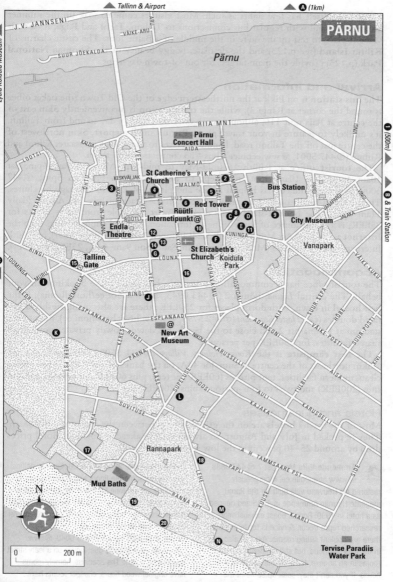

PÄRNU

Tallinn & Airport

A (1km)

Pärnu

Pärnu Concert Hall

St Catherine's Church

Red Tower

Rüütli Internetipunkt @

Endla Theatre

Tallinn Gate

St Elizabeth's Church

Koidula Park

Bus Station

City Museum

Vanapark

New Art Museum

Mud Baths

Rannapark

Tervise Paradiis Water Park

A & Train Station

N

0   200 m

ACCOMMODATION			
Ammende Villa	K	Laine	B
Bristol	D	Lõuna	G
Delfine	L	Rannahotel	N
Green Villa B&B	J	Vesiroos	I
Hommiku Hostel	C	Victoria	F
Hostel Staadioni	M	Villa Marleen	H
Koidulapark Hotell	E		
Konse Holiday Village	A		

RESTAURANTS & CAFÉS			
Asian Village	9	Steffani	16
Kohvik Georg	8		
Lahke Madjar	12	**BARS, PUBS & CLUBS**	
Mõnus Margarita	3	Bravo	2
Munga	4	Jazz Café	11
Paradiis	1	Kursaal	17
Postipoiss	14	Lehe	18
Seegi Maja	5	Mirage	7

Picadilly	10
Rannakohvik	19
Sunset	20
Tallinna Väravad	15
Veerev Õlu	6
Viies Villem	13

The town itself has few sights as such. Most visitors come to soak up the summer atmosphere, and with regular bus connections to Tallinn, Tartu and Rīga, it's a convenient place to rest up if you're in the middle of a Baltic tour. The rustic charms of **Kihnu Island** (see p.123) and the desolate, boggy beauty of the **Soomaa National Park** (p.123) provide the main targets for out-of-town day-trips.

Arrival and information

The **bus station** is on Pikk at the northeastern edge of the Old Town (the ticket office is round the corner at Ringi 3), while the **train station** is inconveniently 5km east of the centre at Riia mnt 116, although with only two trains a day to and from Tallinn, it's unlikely to feature in your travel plans. Pärnu's small **airport**, 5km northwest of the centre just off the Tallinn road, handles services to and from Kuressaare, Kihnu and Ruhnu (☎447 5001, ⓦww.eepu.ee); bus #23 connects it with town.

The **tourist office** at Rüütli 16 (mid-May to mid-Sept Mon–Fri 9am–6pm, Sat 10am–4pm, Sun 10am–3pm; mid-Sept to mid-May Mon–Fri 9am–5pm; ☎447 3000, ⓦwww.parnu.ee) has helpful advice and plenty of English-language brochures. There's also a small tourist information booth on the beach in July and August (daily 11am–5pm). The booklet-sized *Pärnu in Your Pocket*, available from news kiosks for 25EEK, is a useful source of local listings information, updated annually. Log onto the **Internet** at the New Art Museum, Esplanaadi 10 (open 24hr; 30EEK per hour), or Rüütli Internetipunkt, Rüütli 25 (Mon–Fri 9am–9pm, Sat & Sun 9am–6pm; 25EEK per hour).

Accommodation

The tourist office has accommodation price lists, but won't make bookings on your behalf. The central *Lõuna*, Lõuna 2 (☎443 0943, ⓦwww.hot.ee/hostellouna), is the best **hostel** in town, with dorm places for 250EEK; there are also small, freshly decorated doubles (②). *Hostel Staadioni* (☎442 5799, ⓦwww.hostelstaadioni.ee), next to the stadium at Ranna pst 2 and close to the beach, has dated, dowdy private rooms with shared facilities, for 250EEK per person.

The best **campsite** is the *Konse Holiday Village* (☎534 35092, ⓦwww.konse.ee), 1.5km northeast of the centre at Suur-Jõe 44A, on the banks of the Pärnu River; it has clean, modern facilities, tent pitches (60EEK per tent, plus 60EEK per person), caravan sites (200EEK) and two- to four-person cabins (200EEK per person).

Hotels and guesthouses

Most of the town's **hotels** are on the grid of streets between the centre and the beach. They're packed in July and August, so always reserve ahead if possible. Hotel prices drop by around 25–40 percent in the low season (Oct–April).

🏃 **Ammende Villa** Mere pst 7 ☎447 3888, ⓦwww.ammende.ee. A gorgeously restored Art Nouveau villa built for the Pärnu magnate Herman Ammende in 1905 and opened as a hotel in 1999. Rooms boast exhaustively researched repro decor, service is top-notch and there are opulent sitting rooms. You can also stay in the less luxurious, but still eminently comfy, rooms in an annexe, formerly the gardener's house. If you can't stay, soak up some of the atmosphere at the lovely – and suitably expensive – restaurant. ⑥–⑧

Bristol Rüütli 45 ☎443 1450, ⓦwww.victoriahotel.ee. Open June to Aug only, this downtown hotel on the main street offers pleasant en suites with TV, although the lime-green colour scheme takes a little getting used to. ⑤

Delfine Supeluse 22 ☎442 6900, ⓦwww.delfine.ee. The black marble floors and water feature in the lobby set the tone for this medium-sized hotel, on the road to the beach. Rooms are compact but immaculate, and come with swanky bathrooms. An excellent mid-range option. ④

Green Villa B&B Vee 21 ☎443 6040, ⓦwww.greenvilla.ee. A friendly guesthouse on a leafy street overlooking a park. The spacious, homely rooms have original wood floors; cheaper rooms have shared facilities, and there is a guest kitchen. ③

🏃 **Hommiku Hostel** Hommiku 17 ☎445 1122, ⓦwww.hommikuhostel.ee. A hostel in name and price only, *Hommiku* has a fantastic central location and tastefully decorated, modern en suites with big windows or skylights, TVs and mini-kitchens. ③

Koidulapark Hotell Kuninga 38 ☎ 447 7030, ⓦ www.koidulaparkhotell.ee. Open April to Nov, this lusciously restored wooden villa provides friendly service and swish, modern en suites, with wooden floors. Ask for one overlooking the park. ⑤

Laine Laine 6A ☎ 443 9111, ⓦ www.gh-laine.ee. The drab exterior and the location, 2km southwest of the centre, may be a little off-putting, but this hotel's decent but slightly cramped en suites are acceptable if the other cheapies are booked up. ②

Rannahotel Ranna pst 5 ☎ 443 2950, ⓦ www .scandic-hotels.com. A cool, Bauhaus-inspired structure dating from 1937, located right on the beach. Cream-coloured, smallish rooms boast neat black furnishings and small balconies, many with sea views. ⑥

Vesiroos Esplanaadi 42A ☎ 443 0940, ⓦ www.pina.ee. This modernist glass and concrete structure, recently redecorated, offers no-nonsense beige en suites overlooking a small outdoor pool. ④

Victoria Kuninga 25 ☎ 444 3412, ⓦ www .victoriahotel.ee. Slightly smarter than its sister hotel the *Bristol*, the *Victoria* has classy, traditional en suites with a salmon-pink colour scheme. The ground-floor *Café Grand* oozes olde-worlde charm and serves up delicious – if pricey – dishes. ⑥

Villa Marleen Seedri 15 ☎ 442 9288, ⓦ www .marleen.ee. Spread over two houses, a couple of minutes' walk from the beach, this welcoming guesthouse has simple but neat and spacious rooms, and a small café. ④

The Town

With most of Pärnu laid out in neat grids, it's a fairly easy place to navigate. The main thoroughfare is **Rüütli**, a pedestrianized shopping street running from east to west and featuring a fair sprinkling of attractive two-storey wooden houses. Occupying a rather more staid brick building near Rüütli's eastern end at no. 53, the **City Museum** (Linnamuuseum; Wed–Sun 10am–6pm; 30EEK; ⓦ www.pernau.ee) houses some of Estonia's oldest archeological finds, many of which originated in an 11,000-year-old Neolithic settlement unearthed near the village of Sindi just inland – among the pottery fragments, look out for a small human form carved from animal horn. After this promising start, the collection deteriorates into a rather colourless and badly labelled trot through local history.

Two blocks west of the museum, just off Rüütli on Hommiku, is the **Red Tower** (Punane torn), a fifteenth-century remnant of the medieval city walls and the town's oldest surviving building. Despite its name, this squat, unassuming cylinder is actually white – only the roof tiles are red.

Pühavaimu, a few blocks to the west, has a pair of seventeenth-century houses near the junction with Malmö, one lemon-yellow, the other washed-out green with a large gabled vestibule. Further west from Pühavaimu along Uus, you come to **St Catherine's Church** (Ekateriina kirik), built during the reign of Catherine the Great. Encrusted with sea-green domes and pinnacles topped by wrought-iron crosses, it's undoubtedly one of the most delicious Baroque buildings in Estonia and has an icon-rich interior. Immediately west of the church lies a flagstoned plaza dominated by the **Endla Theatre**, a functional piece of 1960s architecture built to replace the original theatre building, erected in 1911 and feted throughout northern Europe as an Art Nouveau masterpiece until bombed to smithereens in World War II – you'll see photographs of it in history museums both here and in Tallinn (notably at the Maarjamäe Palace. One of the most talked-about pieces of architecture in today's Estonia is the coquettishly curvy **Pärnu Concert Hall** (Pärnu kontserdimaja), between greying blocks just northeast of the Endla Theatre at Aida 4. Opened in 2002, this vast, glass-and-steel hatbox of a building accommodates a state-of-the-art thousand-seat auditorium for top-notch music and drama, and also finds room for the **City Art Gallery** (Linnagalerii; Tues–Fri noon–7pm, Sat noon–5pm; price depends on exhibition), where you can catch high-profile exhibitions by contemporary Estonian artists.

From the Tallinn Gate to the beach

South of the Endla Theatre, Vee runs down to Kuninga, the western end of which is marked by the seventeenth-century **Tallinn Gate** (Tallinna värav), a rather elegant relic of the Swedish occupation, set into the remains of the city ramparts and now home to

△ Pärnu beach

a quaint bar (see p.122). To see the gate at its best, head into the park on its outer side: from here, with its massive gable and decorative pillars, it looks more like a Baroque chapel. Head east along Kuninga to the eighteenth-century **St Elizabeth's Church** (Eliisabeti kirik; Mon–Sat noon–6pm, Sun 10am–1pm), which boasts a maroon and ochre Baroque exterior and plain, wood-panelled interior. As well as being the principal Protestant place of worship in the town, it's also home to a famously sonorous organ, put through its paces at weekend concerts. From here, Nikolai leads south to Esplanaadi, where a headless statue of Lenin stands watch over the entrance to an office block that once served as the headquarters of the Pärnu communist party. Taken over by local artists in the post-independence period, it was briefly renamed the Charlie Chaplin House (no longer its official moniker, but still very much in colloquial use) before becoming the **Pärnu New Art Museum** (Pärnu uue kunsti muuseum; daily 9am–9pm; 20EEK; Ⓦwww.chaplin.ee). Its collection of twentieth-century Estonian paintings is complemented by contemporary works donated by international artists, including Yoko Ono.

Beyond the art museum, Nikolai bends east to join Supeluse, which runs southwest through suburbia then parkland before arriving at the beach area after about ten minutes. Marking the southern end of Supeluse are the colonnaded **Pärnu Mud Baths** (Pärnu mudaravila), a bombastic piece of Neoclassicism that couldn't be more different from its contemporary, the inter-war **Rannahotel**, 400m to the east at Ranna 5, a cream-coloured ocean liner of a building that has become something of an icon of Estonian Modernism. Both buildings gaze out onto Pärnu's glorious white-sand **beach** and its new 500m promenade. To escape the summer crowds, make for the dunes east of the Mud Baths; in the opposite direction is a stretch of open sand backed by kiosks, bars, cafés and ice-cream stalls. There's also the Tervise Paradiis **Water Park** at Side 14 (daily: June–Aug 10am–10pm; day ticket 290EEK; Sept–April 11am–10pm; day ticket (Mon–Thurs) 240EEK, (Fri–Sun) 290EEK), which has four slides, various swimming pools, a Jacuzzi and a climbing wall.

The Lydia Koidula Museum

The grid of post-war suburban buildings stretching north of the Pärnu River is as unexciting as you would expect, and there's not much point in venturing out here unless you're keen to check out the **museum** honouring nineteenth-century poet

Lydia Koidula 1843–86

Estonia's leading nineteenth-century poet was born Lydia Emilie Florentine Jannsen in Vändra, where her father, Johann Voldemar Jannsen, was the village schoolteacher. The family moved to Pärnu in 1850, where Lydia was among the handful of Estonians admitted to the prestigious German-language Pärnu School for Girls.

In 1857, her father launched the first-ever Estonian-language weekly, *Perno Posti-mees* ("Pärnu Courier"), aiming to spread literacy among the local peasantry – it was just about the only non-religious reading material they had access to at the time. Koidula was roped in to help and ended up writing much of it herself, a role she continued when Jannsen moved to Tartu in 1863 to found the *Eesti Postimees* ("Estonian Courier") – a publication that bound together the nascent Estonian intelligentsia and transformed Jannsen into a pivotal figure in the national movement. A self-taught country boy of limited literary abilities, Jannsen was outshone as a writer and editor by his daughter, but her contribution to the paper had to remain in the background as nineteenth-century Estonia was not the kind of place where well-brought-up young women embarked on literary careers. When Koidula's first collections of lyric poems were published anonymously – *Vainolilled* ("Meadow Flowers") in 1866, *Emajõe Ööbik* ("Emajõgi Nightingale") in 1867 – Jannsen himself published reviews of them without knowing the identity of the author. Regular visitors to the family home were in no doubt about Lydia's literary potential, however. One, Karl Robert Jakobson (see p.126), gave her the pseudonym "Koidula" ("of the dawn") so that he could include some of her poems in an Estonian-language primer. Koidula's greatest admirer at this time was Friedrich Reinhold Kreuzwald, compiler of the Estonian folk epic *Kalevipoeg* (see p.161), with whom Koidula started to correspond in 1867. The epistolary relationship between the intelligent, witty Koidula and a man forty years her senior quickly became a mutual intellectual obsession. Kreuzwald finally invited Koidula to visit his home in Võru in June 1868, but the trip was cut short due to the hostility of Kreuzwald's wife.

Thanks to her father, Koidula remained at the centre of Estonian cultural life, helping him set up the Vanemuine Society (the first Estonian-language drama group), and organize the first All-Estonian Song Festival in Tartu in 1869. Her patriotic poem *Mu Isamaa* ("My Fatherland"), set to music by a Tartu choirmaster for the occasion, has been a prime ingredient of song festivals ever since – during the Soviet period, audiences insisted in closing festivals with a rousing rendition of the song.

The small size of the nineteenth-century Estonian reading public meant that it was nigh-on impossible for any writer to make a living without recourse to another profession. The only career options open to Koidula were marriage and domesticity, or a life of spinsterhood helping her father out behind the scenes. Koidula finally settled for marriage and set up home with a stolid Latvian doctor, Eduard Michelson, in 1873. The couple went to live in Russian-speaking Kronštadt, a Tsarist naval base in the Gulf of Finland, and had four children (two of whom died in infancy). Although Koidula continued to write poems, her contacts with Estonian literary circles were effectively severed, and her early death from cancer prevented her from fully enjoying the acclaim she deserved. Koidula exerted a huge influence over subsequent generations – she demonstrated that the Estonian language was versatile and lyrical enough to challenge the cultural predominance of German – and there's hardly an Estonian alive today who can't recite at least a few of her poems by heart.

Lydia Koidula (see box above), a ten-minute hop over the river from the city centre at J.V. Jannseni 37 (Wed–Sun 10am–6pm; 15EEK). Occupying the building where her father Johann Voldemar Jannsen ran a primary school from 1857 to 1863, Koidula is remembered through a modest collection of family photographs and rooms, including a re-creation of the bedroom (in the Russian town of Kronstadt) where Koidula breathed her last in 1886.

Eating and drinking

Pärnu has a respectable spread of cafés, restaurants and bars serving up a wide range of food and drink. While most cafés close by mid-evening, restaurants and bars are open daily from noon until 11pm or midnight. This is the case with the places listed below, unless stated otherwise.

Restaurants and cafés

Asian Village Rüütli 51A. This six-table restaurant has a strong local following for its huge range of (pretty authentic) Chinese, Thai and Indian favourites like Singapore noodles, satay and chicken tikka. Opens 11am.

Kohvik Georg Rüütli 43. A bustling self-service café that's popular with downtown shoppers for its low-priced and tasty meals and snacks. Mon–Fri 7.30am–7.30pm, Sat & Sun 9am–7.30pm.

Lahke Madjar Kuninga 18. Hidden away in a cosy cellar with wooden beams, a grandfather clock and cloves of garlic hanging from the walls, this Hungarian restaurant serves up hearty portions of interesting food; dishes include turkey with raisins and peanuts. Opens 11am.

Mõnus Margarita Akadeemia 5. A reasonably priced Tex-Mex joint, with Aztec-inspired paintings and decent – if not exactly explosively spicy – food. Lively at the weekend. Opens 11am, Fri & Sat till 1am.

Munga Munga 9. This refined and intimate café in a nineteenth-century wooden town house is decked out in rather posh period furnishings. A range of food is served, from soups to full meals, although expect to pay restaurant prices. Opens 11am.

Paradiis Riia mnt 57. Dark green tablecloths, frilly lace napkins and elegant lamps give this restaurant a reserved feel. But service is friendly and the food – pork, chicken and salmon dishes – is tasty and reasonably priced. Opens daily 8am, Fri & Sat till 2am.

Postipoiss Vee 12. A rustic Russian eatery with long wooden tables and waiting staff in an amateur dramatist's idea of folk costume. Excellent light meals like *pelmeni* or *blini* with caviar, as well as mainstream northern European meat dishes. Fills up with late-night drinkers at weekends, when you can expect live entertainment in crooner-meets-electronic-keyboard style. Sun–Thurs till 11pm, Fri & Sat till 2am.

Seegi Maja Hospidali 1. An atmospheric, impeccably restored seventeenth-century almshouse, with an inviting fireplace and waiters in traditional costume, *Seegi Maja* serves up expertly prepared meat and fish dishes. Those with more adventurous palates can order the baked bear with honey sauce. Mains from 130EEK.

Steffani Nikolai 24. Generous portions of pizzas, pastas and salads. Prices are slightly higher than in the other pizza joints in town, but probably justified. Opens daily 11am, Fri & Sat till 2am.

Bars and pubs

Jazz Café Ringi 11. A small, minimalist space just off Rüütli, with a good range of international cuisine and chilled-out background sounds. Daily till 2am.

Lehe Lehe 5. A funky café-bar decorated to look like an aquarium, within striking distance of the beach. Also does good lunchtime food. Sun–Thurs till 10pm, Fri & Sat till 11pm (June–Sept Fri & Sat till midnight).

Picadilly Pühavaimu 15. Café by day, wine bar by night, *Picadilly* is an intimate place, with orange walls, scores of cushions and subdued lighting. As well as a strong wine list, it has home-made chocolates, light meals and often live jazz in the evenings. Mon–Thurs till 11pm, Fri & Sat till midnight, Sun till 6pm.

Rannakohvik Ranna pst 1. This modern glass and steel structure, spread over three floors, right on the beach, is a great drinking spot – the sea views from the terrace and the relaxed ambience make it a very difficult place to leave. Sun–Thurs till midnight, Fri & Sat till 2am.

Tallinna Väravad Vana-Tallinna 1. An atmospheric, if surprisingly staid, bar in the top storey of the Tallinn Gate (see p.119) – a bit like having a drink in the converted attic of an old-fashioned neighbour. The outdoor terrace is more fun. Daily till 11pm.

Veerev Õlu Uus 3A. The "Rolling Beer" is an enjoyably unpretentious wooden-bench bar attracting an agreeable mixture of holidaymakers and garrulous locals. Daily till 1am.

Viies Villem Kuninga 11. A roomy basement pub that rounds up an enthusiastic cross-section of drinkers most nights of the week. Decent salads and meaty main courses. Till 2am at weekends.

Entertainment

Pärnu is a thriving cultural centre, with concerts and plays all year round. The Endla Theatre, Keskväljak 1 (☎442 0667, ⊛www.endla.ee), hosts top-quality **theatre and dance** performances, while the Pärnu Concert Hall, Aida 4 (Pärnu kontserdimaja;

☎445 5810, ✉pkm@concert.ee), provides the perfect venue for chamber **concerts** and major classical music events – the Estonian National Symphony Orchestra plays here a couple of times a month. Regular organ recitals are given at St Elizabeth's Church; ask at the tourist office for information.

Annual events attracting top-class international participants include the **Pärnu Days of Contemporary Music** (Pärnu Nüüdismuusika Päevad; ⊛www.schoenberg.ee) in mid-January; the **David Oistrakh Festival** (⊛www.oistfest.ee) in the first half of July, featuring plenty of star conductors and soloists; and the **Festival of Documentary and Anthropological Film** (⊛www.chaplin.ee), also in July.

For clubbers, *Mirage*, Rüütli 40, is a year-round, seven-days-a-week **disco** as well as a convenient late-night drinking joint, while the beachfront *Sunset*, Ranna pst 3 (⊛www.sunsetclub.ee) attracts a trendier, party-animal crowd. *Bravo* at Hommiku 3 (⊛www.bravoclub.ee), is home to a slightly older clubber. *Kursaal*, Mere 22 (⊛www.parnukuursaal.ee), hosts live music and club events, including DJs from Tartu's *Club Tallinn*, which sets up camp here in July and August, becoming the hottest spot in town.

Kihnu

Forty-five kilometres southwest of Pärnu, the mellow island of **KIHNU**, 7km long and 3.5km across, offers an enticing mixture of pine forest, juniper heath and pasture. The island supported a population of 1200 until the end of World War II, when a third fled to the West, and the seafaring activities of those who remained were severely curtailed by the security-conscious Soviet authorities. Nowadays, only around 600 souls live on Kihnu and many of the older female residents still wear traditional costume, especially the highly distinctive, red-tasseled headscarves and red, green and yellow-striped skirts.

The island is compact enough to explore on a day-trip from Pärnu, although you can stay in one of a handful of farmhouse **B&Bs** (booked through Kihnurand; ☎446 9924). Kihnu is served by **ferries** from the port of Munalaiu, 40km west of Pärnu (May to mid-Sept: Mon, Thurs and Sun one daily, Fri & Sat two daily; mid-Sept to Dec: Wed & Thurs two daily, Fri & Sun one daily; 70EEK one-way; ⊛www.veeteed .com). Pärnu–Tõstamaa **buses** pick up and drop off by the harbour. There are also daily **flights** from Pärnu, for around 150EEK one-way; contact Pärnu Airport for more information (☎447 5001, ⊛www.eepu.ee).

Two kilometres west of the ferry harbour, Kihnu's main settlement of **LINAKÜLA** huddles around a plain parish church that began as Lutheran when it was first built in the eighteenth century, but became Orthodox in 1858 after the mass conversion of most of the islanders – they switched faiths in order to take up an offer of free land promised by crafty Tsarist bureaucrats. The church graveyard is the final resting place of Kihnu Jõnn, a much-travelled merchant seaman who came to symbolize the sea-roving lifestyle of the average Kihnu male, for whom years of hard graft at sea – punctuated by intermittent bouts of drinking and fighting – was the norm. Jõnn drowned off the coast of Denmark, where he was buried in 1913, only to be reinterred here eight decades later. A small museum opposite the church contains several sprightly canvases by self-taught local painter Jaan Oad (1899–1984), whose pictures of pre-World War II fisherfolk exude a vitality that seems largely absent in the laid-back Kihnu of today.

Soomaa National Park

Extending across the flatlands some 20km due east of Pärnu, the **Soomaa National Park** (Soomaa rahvuspark; ☎435 7164, ⊛www.soomaa.ee) was established in 1994 to protect a patchwork of grassland, peat bog and riverine forest – home to elk, beavers, flying squirrels, brown bears, lynx and 160 bird species. The area is susceptible to flooding during the spring thaw, when roads in the centre of the park may become impassable – especially around the village of Riisa, where the Raudra, Lemmjõgi and Halliste rivers meet. Soomaa is the traditional home of the *haabja*, a canoe carved from a single trunk of aspen, and propelled by an enormous paddle, rather like a punt. *Haabjas* are still made in the area and a handful of local tour operators organize guided *haabja* excursions along Soomaa's waterways – although canoes and kayaks are more common. If you prefer to stick to dry land there are plenty of marked walking trails.

You'll need your own **transport** to reach the park, accessible by road from either Pärnu or Viljandi. Tourist offices in both places can provide **information**, although the one in Viljandi seems to be more clued up about accommodation and **canoe trips**. One of the best of the local canoe outfits is Soomaa.com (℡506 1896, Ⓦwww.soomaa .com), which has been operating in the area since 1994. As well as guided canoe trips (from 360EEK per person), it offers bog walks, cross-country skiing trips, log-boat building camps and snowshoe tours.

Regio's invaluable 1:100 000 *Soomaa jõed/Rivers of Soomaa* **map** can be obtained from Viljandi's tourist office or from bookshops in Tallinn, Tartu and Pärnu. A day-trip is enough to get a flavour of the park, although there's a smattering of accommodation around if you fancy a longer stay.

Into the park

The best way to reach the park from Pärnu is to head 35km northeast as far as the village of **JÕESUU**, where the River Navesti flows into the broader Pärnu. From here you can choose between the Kaansoo road, which follows the northern bank of the Navesti, or the Tipu road, which heads south through the centre of the park. The latter route provides a good first taste of Soomaa's archetypal bog-scape in the shape of the **Riisa Bog Trail**, signed off the road to the left after 7km. A boardwalk leads across the peaty soil, which supports a carpet of lichens, grasses and heathers punctuated by slender birches and stunted conifers. Three kilometres south, *Riisa Rantso* on the south side of **RIISA** village (℡510 0832, Ⓦwww.riisarantso.ee) organizes horse-riding trips and rents out simple rooms (❶).

Some 4km south of Riisa is **TÕRAMAA** (a road junction rather than a full-blown settlement) and the **National Park Visitors' Centre** (May–Sept Tues–Sun 10am–6pm; Oct–April Tues–Sat 10am–4pm; ℡435 7164, Ⓦwww.soomaa.ee), which has leaflets on what to see in the park, a small exhibition devoted to conservation issues and a handful of **rooms** (❷). The centre marks the start of the short **Beaver Trail** (Koprarada), which leads along the banks of the Tõramaa stream, passing enthusiastically gnawed tree trunks and branch-built dams. The minor road running east from the Visitors' Centre brings you after 3km to the **Lemmjõe Keelemets**, a short, but fascinating, marked trail through the riverine forest on the north side of the road.

South of the Visitors' Centre, the road runs along the western edge of the Öördi bog before veering east towards Viljandi. Twenty kilometres out from the Visitors' Centre, just beyond the village of **IIA**, a dirt road heads north towards Lake Öördi (Öördi järv), where there's a two-kilometre boardwalk path through a serene environment of squelchy mosses, speckled red with cranberries in the autumn. Back in Iia and heading east, it's only 5km to **KÕPU**, where you can pick up the main road to Viljandi.

Viljandi and around

Roughly midway between Pärnu and Tartu, **VILJANDI** is one of Estonia's more pleasant provincial centres – a pleasingly low-rise jumble of houses draped around the northwestern end of five-kilometre-long, boomerang-shaped Lake Viljandi. The grizzled ruins of a once-mighty castle bear witness to the town's erstwhile importance as a staging post on the Rīga–Novgorod trade route, although it's the handsome stock of early twentieth-century red-brick buildings and prim timber cottages that give the modern-day town centre its character. The town is at its busiest during July's **Viljandi Folk Festival** (Viljandi pärimuusika festival; Ⓦwww.folk.ee) in the castle grounds.

Arrival, information and accommodation

Viljandi's **bus station** is at the junction of Tallinna and Uus, ten minutes' walk north of the **tourist office** at Vabaduse plats 6 (May–Aug Mon–Fri 9am–6pm, Sat & Sun

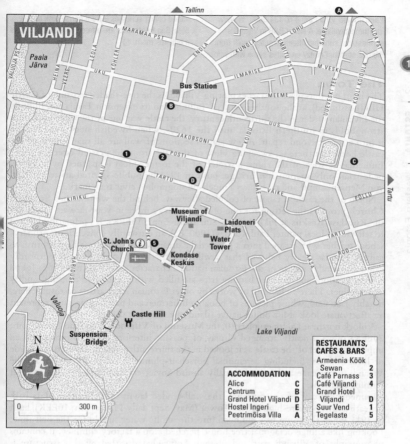

10am–3pm; Sept–April Mon–Fri 10am–5pm, Sat 10am–2pm; ☎ 433 0442, ⓦ www .viljandi.ee), which has free town plans and information about the Viljandi region – notably the Soomaa National Park (see p.123).

There's a handful of decent **hotels and B&Bs** in Viljandi, and the tourist office can provide details of rural accommodation in local villages – they're happy to call on your behalf if the owners don't speak English.

Alice Jakobsoni 55 ☎ 434 7616, ⓦ www.matti.ee/~alice. A seven-room B&B in a Bauhaus-influenced suburban building, a ten-minute walk east of the bus station. Small but bright en suites come with TV and parquet floors. ③

Centrum Tallinna 24 ☎ 435 1100, ⓦ www .centrum.ee. Opposite the bus station, the glass-fronted *Centrum* sits on top of a shopping centre-cum-office block and has spacious, sunny en suites aimed at business travellers. ③

Grand Hotel Viljandi Tartu 11/Lossi 29 ☎ 435 5800, ⓦ www.ghv.ee. The poshest place to stay in Viljandi, this Art Deco hotel's stylish and elegant en suites come with all the comforts you would expect from a four-star, but are let down slightly by an unimaginative grey-brown colour scheme. ⑤

Hostel Ingeri Pikk 2C ☎ 433 4414, ⓦ www .hostelingeri.ee. Across a wooden footbridge from the tourist office, this small hostel looks out onto the castle ruins. Spick-and-span rooms with shared facilities are good value for money. ②

Peetrimõisa Villa Pirni 4 ☎ 434 3000, 🖰 www
.peetrimoisavilla.ee. A smart B&B in Viljandi's
northeastern suburbs, fifteen minutes' walk from
the bus station. Chintzy en suites come with wildly
varied colour schemes – from garish pink to pale
blue. Spa treatments are offered on site and there's
a billiards room. ❹

The Town

The most obvious place to start exploring Viljandi is the tree-shaded expanse of **Castle
Hill** (Lossimäed), at the southern end of Tallinna and its extension Tasuja pst. Built by
the Livonian Order in the thirteenth century, the castle was one of the most important
strongholds in southern Estonia until the 1620s, when Swedish siege guns blasted
it into a state beyond repair. A few jagged sections of wall are all that remain of the
castle keep, but there's a sweeping view of the lake from the grassed-over ramparts.
Immediately west of the ruins, a stretch of the former moat is spanned by a dainty,
pedestrian-only **suspension bridge**, built in 1931 by public-spirited aristocrat Karl
von Mensenkampff and nowadays a much-photographed civic trademark.

North of the castle, a tangle of cobbled alleyways behind the whitewashed **St John's
Church** provides the setting for one of the country's more in-your-face art museums,
the **Kondase Keskus** at Pikk 8 (Wed–Sun 10am–5pm; 15EEK). It's primarily devoted
to self-taught local painter Paul Kondas (1900–85), an outwardly conventional primary-
school teacher who escaped into a psychedelic dream world whenever he put brush to
canvas. Kondas clearly believed that a wild zest for living lay behind the outwardly
calm, unexcitable nature of the Estonian national character and his pictures of St John's
Eve celebrations and summer bathing trips are filled with uninhibited dancing, nudity
and mischief. There's a handful of works by other Estonian naive artists on display here,
notably Jaan Oad, whose pictures of boozing fishermen and partying peasants represent
an affectionate look at life on his native island of Kihnu (see p.123).

A block north, at Laidoneri plats 10, the **Museum of Viljandi** (Wed–Sun 10am–5pm;
20EEK) offers a neatly arranged display of peasant interiors, local costumes and an
impressive model of the castle as it looked in the thirteenth century. Upstairs is a horde
of local oddities, including ceremonial horsehair-plumed helmets once worn by the
Viljandi fire brigade and unintentionally absurd Soviet-era dioramas showing socialist
farming methods.

Immediately east of the museum, the well-tended lawns of **Laidoneri plats** bask
beneath a thirty-metre-high **Water Tower** (May–Sept daily 11am–6pm; 10EEK), built
in 1911 when the town was plumbed into the public water supply for the first time.
Looking like a huge octagonal tree house perched atop a factory chimney, it contains
photographs of Viljandi past and present. Somewhat dwarfed by this structure is
the square's other main focus, a statue of locally born portrait painter **Johann Köler**
(1826–99), educated (and subsequently a teacher) at the St Petersburg Academy.
Passionately committed to the national cause, Köler was the most prominent of the
so-called "St Petersburg Patriots", ex-pat Estonians who lobbied the Tsarist authorities
for sweeping social reforms in their homeland.

North of Laidoneri plats, the junction of Lossi and Tartu provides downtown Viljandi with a sort of centre, a small plaza with a statue of schoolteacher and nationalist
firebrand **Karl Robert Jakobson** (1842–82). Overcoming years of obstruction by
the local Baltic barons, Jakobson founded the Estonian-language newspaper *Sakala* in
Viljandi in 1878. The paper's anti-clerical, anti-German stance represented a complete
break with the older generation of Estonian activists, grouped around Johann Voldemar
Jannsen's cautiously patriotic *Postimees* (see p.429), which Jakobson believed was funded
by German aristocrats. *Sakala* continues to be published in Viljandi, still bearing the
ornate masthead it had in Jakobson's time.

Heading east along Tartu brings you down to tranquil, sandy-shored Lake Viljandi
(Viljandi järv), where there's a beachside café and a place to rent pedalos. A round-trip
run, known as the **Lake Viljandi Race** (Viljandi järve jooks), has been held here on
May Day every year since 1928 and is one of the major events in the Estonian cross-
country calendar.

△ Viljandi suspension bridge

Eating and drinking

There are plenty of **eating** opportunities in and around the town centre. You'll get plush seating and a wide range of daytime eats at *Café Parnass*, inside the Kulturimaja ("House of Culture") at Tallinna 5, while the nearby *Armeenia Köök Sewan*, just off Tallinna, serves up expertly grilled kebabs in an outdoor yard. *Café Viljandi*, Lossi 31, is a popular local teahouse with simple meals, sweet and savoury pastries, and cream-filled cakes. *Tegelaste*, near the approach to the castle at Pikk 2B, offers a broad spread of Estonian meat dishes, with plenty of chicken and fish choices too. You can also eat at **drinking** venues like *Suur Vend*, which has a good range of hearty meals and bar snacks. For a more sedate experience, the *Grand Hotel Viljandi* has a suitably smart restaurant (mains 150–350EEK), an extensive wine cellar and a cigar lounge.

Travel details

Trains

Pärnu to: Tallinn (2 daily; 3–3hr 20min).

Buses

Haapsalu to: Kärdla (3–4 daily; 2hr); Tallinn (hourly; 1hr 50min); Virtsu (2–3 daily; 1hr 30min).
Kärdla to: Haapsalu (3–4 daily; 2hr); Tallinn (3–4 daily; 4hr 30min).
Kuressaare to: Karujärv (summer: Mon–Fri 1 daily; Sat & Sun 2 daily; winter: 1 daily; 25min); Kihelkonna (5 daily; 50min); Leisi (Mon–Fri 5 daily, Sat & Sun 4 daily; 1hr 10min); Tallinn (8 daily; 4hr 30min); Tartu (2–3 daily; 6hr); Undva (2 daily; 1hr).
Pärnu to: Kuressaare (3 daily; 3hr); Tallinn (hourly; 2hr); Tartu (hourly; 2hr 45min–3hr 45min).
Viljandi to: Kuressaare (2–3 daily; 4hr 45min); Tallinn (13 daily; 2hr 30m–4hr); Tartu (8 daily; 1–1hr 20min).

Ferries

Munalaiu to: Kihnu (summer: 2 daily; winter: 10 weekly; 2hr).
Rohuküla to: Heltermaa (Hiiumaa; 4–6 daily; 1hr 30min); Sviby (2 daily; 50min).
Triigi to: Sõru (2–4 daily).
Virtsu to: Kuivastu (for Muhu and Saaremaa; summer: hourly; winter: every two hours; 30min).

Flights

Kuressaare to: Rīga (2 weekly; 45min)
Pärnu to: Kihnu (daily; 15min); Ruhnu (2 weekly; 25min).
Tallinn to: Kärdla (1–2 daily; 40min); Kuressaare (1–2 daily; 55min).

International buses

Pärnu to: Rīga (5 daily; 3hr 20min); Vilnius (1 daily; 8hr 45min).

1.3

Eastern Estonia

astern Estonia may not attract as many visitors as the island-scattered west coast, but it offers just as much variety. Some of the countryside is typically Estonian – birch and pine forests alternating with arable land and patches of bog – but it also possesses landscapes less commonly found in the Baltics, notably the rippling hills of the southeast, the broad freshwater expanse of **Lake Peipsi** and the boulder-strewn beaches of the northeast coast. Long stretches of the last fall within the boundaries of the **Lahemaa National Park**, a vast area of primeval woodland, reed-shrouded coast and beautifully preserved fishing villages; just 50km east of Tallinn, it's one of the most accessible areas of natural wilderness in the country.

▼ Riga   ▼ Riga

The landscape east of Lahemaa is brutally different, characterized by the dour mining towns and cone-shaped slag heaps of Estonia's oil-shale industry, and there's little of interest until you arrive at **Narva**, a historical fortress town right on the border with Russia and inhabited, unsurprisingly, by a large number of Russian-speakers. Though somewhat blighted by post-war architecture, it's nevertheless an atmospheric base from which to explore the sweeping, sandy beaches at **Narva-Jõesuu** and the Stalinist-era, toy-town architecture of **Sillamäe**.

The southeast is dominated by **Tartu**, Estonia's second city and a university town that manages to combine nineteenth-century gentility with raw, student-fuelled energy. The one place outside Tallinn with a sufficient menu of urban sights to keep you going for several days, it's also a good base from which to explore the lakes and rolling hills of the far south, with **Suur-Munamägi**, the highest point in the Baltic, and the winter sports resort of **Otepää**, both within easy striking distance. Bearing witness to Estonia's cultural and racial diversity, Russian **Old Believers** continue to inhabit bucolic fishing settlements along the western shores of Lake Peipsi, while surviving communities of **Setu** – an Estonian people with a distinct folk culture – still live in the scattered villages of the extreme southeast.

Getting around the region is fairly straightforward, with buses from Tallinn and Tartu serving almost all the places mentioned in this chapter. In addition, the market town of **Rakvere** is a useful transport hub for the Lahemaa National Park, while calm, lakeside **Võru** serves many of the smaller places in the far southeast. There's a wide range of **accommodation** in Tartu and Otepää and a flourishing bed-and-breakfast trade in parts of the Lahemaa National Park – elsewhere in this part of the country, however, tourist facilities are less well-developed than in western Estonia, giving it much more of an off-the-beaten-track feel.

Lahemaa National Park and around

Extending over a deeply indented stretch of coastline an hour's drive east of Tallinn, the **LAHEMAA NATIONAL PARK** (Lahemaa rahvuspark; ⊛www.lahemaa.ee) embraces 725 square kilometres of the most varied and beautiful terrain in the country. Its most distinctive features are the four evenly spaced peninsulas sticking out into the Baltic Sea, each fringed with custard-coloured beaches and tawny reed beds and backed by a sandy coastal plain generously carpeted with mosses, lichens, pine and spruce. Five to ten kilometres inland is a limestone plateau covered with juniper heath, peat bog, forests of alder,

Fauna in the Lahemaa National Park

Given the park's array of unspoilt natural landscapes, it's not surprising that it supports a rich variety of wildlife. The four-legged denizens of Lahemaa you're most likely to catch sight of are roe deer, large numbers of which roam the forests and occasionally graze on farmland, especially early in the morning. Wild boar and moose are slightly less common and stick to the forests in winter, although you may see them foraging in open countryside in summer. The park's forests are also home to large populations of hares, martens and foxes and a small number (counted in the tens rather than the hundreds) of badgers, lynxes, wolves and brown bears. Beavers are extremely secretive, but signs of their industry are everywhere: dams can be seen beside the Beaver Trail at Oandu (see p.137) and elsewhere, and what look like clumsily felled tree trunks are a sure sign of their nocturnal gnawing activities.

As well as the resident songbirds thronging the forests, Lahemaa hosts several migrating bird species in spring and autumn. Eru Bay just west of Võsu is the best place to see migrating waterfowl, while Kahala Lake in the far west of the park is popular with ducks and grebes. White storks and cranes can be seen feeding in agricultural land from May onwards; black storks nest deep in the forest and are only sighted on rare occasions. The fields around Käsmu Bay are thick with corncrakes in June.

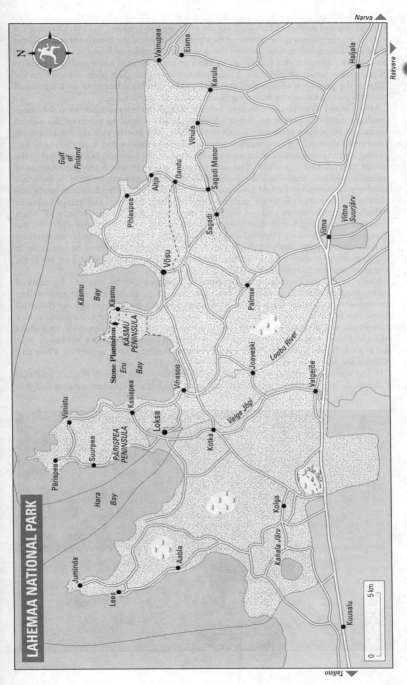

LAHEMAA NATIONAL PARK

ash and elm and patches of farmland mainly given over to potatoes and rye. Dividing the plain from the plateau is the limestone escarpment known as the **North Estonian Glint**, which runs from east to west through the middle of the park – although it's so smothered by soil and vegetation that it looks more like a gentle slope than a cliff and in some parts of the park is hardly visible at all. A more conspicuous geological phenomenon than the Glint is the profusion of so-called **erratic boulders**, isolated lumps of rock strewn all over this part of Estonia by retreating glaciers some 12,000 years ago.

After World War II the coastline became a high-security border area that non-residents needed a permit to enter, which ironically helped to preserve the natural landscape by stifling economic activity. However, the Soviet military establishment remained suspicious of Estonian environmentalists, which makes it all the more surprising that the authorities sanctioned the creation of the Lahemaa National Park – the Soviet Union's first – in 1971. The national park ethos, in which the preservation of nature was given a higher moral value than the furtherance of communism or any other ideology, immediately turned Lahemaa into a cult destination for Estonian intellectuals. Official permits to enter the park were still required, however, and strings had to be pulled in order to secure some of the park's meagre stock of accommodation. Foreign groups were admitted only after 1986 and were not allowed to stay overnight. Nowadays, tourist facilities are plentiful and Lahemaa is one of the most popular destinations in the country, particularly in the summer, when tour groups descend at weekends. It is an equally appealing place to visit in the winter, with tourists few and far between, and snow and ice to enhance the park's desolate beauty.

Many of the park's most exciting **natural features** can be accessed by marked paths, ranging from deep-forest hikes long enough to satisfy the seasoned walker to well-designed study trails (often with signboards en route detailing the flora and fauna you're likely to see), taking only an hour or two to complete. Restored palace complexes at **Palmse** and **Sagadi**, in the southeast of the park, provide an insight into the feudal manor-house culture of the German barons who once held sway over the region, while the charmingly under-commercialized beach resorts of **Võsu** and **Käsmu** are another attraction.

If you want to explore the park in depth, it's worth getting hold of Regio's 1:60 000 *Lahemaa Rahvuspark* **map**; it comes in Estonian, English and Russian versions and you

△ Lahemaa wildlife

can pick it up from bookshops in Tallinn and at the National Park Visitors' Centre in Palmse (see p.134).

Park practicalities

Most Lahemaa-bound tourist traffic approaches from the west along the Tallinn–Narva highway (which forms the park's southern boundary for a lengthy stretch) before arriving at Viitna, a major crossroads from which the road to Palmse, Võsu and Käsmu branches off to the north. The account below covers this main route first, before fanning out to explore outlying areas of the park – although any number of alternative itineraries are possible.

The main source of **information** is the National Park Visitors' Centre in the inland village of **Palmse** (see p.134), and if you're travelling by car then this should be one of your first ports of call. If you're dependent on public transport it makes more sense to aim instead for the seaside villages of Võsu and Käsmu, which offer much more in the way of accommodation and bus connections – you can always hike or hitch to Palmse once you get settled in.

Käsmu is the best base if you want a range of hiking possibilities on your doorstep, with a number of local trails ranging in duration from forty minutes to four hours. Staying in **Võsu** or elsewhere in the park, you'll still be able to see a great deal on foot, providing you don't mind tramping 20–30km a day. Otherwise, you'll need a car or bike to access all the main areas of interest. Võsu is the one settlement in the park that has a decent number of food and drink shops.

If you do come to Lahemaa by car, remember to leave nothing of value inside it wherever you park – it has been known for thieves from nearby towns to descend on the area in summer to rob vehicles while their owners are hiking in the woods.

Public transport to the park

There are around six daily services **from Tallinn bus station** to Võsu (some of which terminate at Altja, a useful name to look for on timetables and destination boards) and one to Käsmu. There are also four daily buses **from Tallinn train station** to Viinistu in the western part of the park, although this is less useful as a base from which to explore. Võsu and Viinistu are do-able as a **day-trip** from Tallinn.

If you're approaching Lahemaa **from Narva or Tartu**, make first for the town of **Rakvere** (see p.138), just outside the park, where you can catch connecting services to Võsu and Käsmu providing you don't arrive too late in the afternoon (aim to get there before 4pm). There's also a bus from Rakvere to Palmse, but only four days a week. See "Travel details" on p.166 for more detailed bus information.

Accommodation

Small **hotels and B&Bs** are scattered throughout the park, with the biggest concentration in and around Käsmu. Beware, however, that summer weekends are often booked up several months in advance. Most establishments claim to be open all year round, although in practice the smaller B&Bs turn away individuals or small groups of visitors in the October–April period – they can't afford to turn the heating on unless they have a houseful. In summer, **hostel**-style accommodation is available in Võsu, Käsmu, Palmse and Sagadi. There's also a network of free **campsites** (May–Sept) run by the National Park, in which firewood is provided (so that campers don't go around cutting their own), but little in the way of other facilities – although there may be a couple of dry toilets on hand. The sites are nicely spaced out so that hikers can feasibly walk from one to another in the course of a day.

Viru Bog

Approaching Lahemaa from the Tallinn direction, the first of the park's set-piece attractions you come across is **Viru Bog** (Viru raba), an area of peat bog, just over 2km square, created over a period of 10,000 years by decaying mosses, about 50km out from the capital. It's just north of the Tallinn–Narva highway – take the Loksa turn-off and look for a sign indicating the **Viru Bog Nature Trail** (Viru raba õpperada) on your right after about 1km. A 3.5-kilometre wooden walkway curves northeast across the bog, providing an excellent vantage point over this strange landscape of grey-brown lichens and stunted conifers, with pine-covered dunes just visible to the northwest. Late May to early June is the best time to visit, when stretches of the bog are covered in wild flowers.

Viitna

Twenty-two kilometres beyond the Loksa turn-off, **VIITNA** has served as an important rest-stop on the Tallinn–Narva road since medieval times, and is still the place where most people break for a breather before turning north towards Palmse and the central area of the park. Viitna's enduring popularity is in large part due to the presence of the *Viitna kõrts* **tavern**, built in imitation of an eighteenth-century coaching inn and boasting an atmospheric timbered interior – the perfect place to fill up on pork and freshwater fish dishes. Immediately south of the tavern, a 2.5-kilometre-long nature trail skirts **Great Viitna Lake** (Viitna suurjärv or Viitna pikkjärv), a glacier-gouged finger of water formed by retreating ice some 11,500 years ago. Fringed by pine forest, it's a supremely restful spot.Should you wish **to stay** in Viitna, head for the *Viitna Holiday Centre* (☎329 3651, Ⓔpartel.soidla@mail .ee; ❶), down a side road 500m east of the main crossroads, offering somewhat austere doubles – some en-suite – in pleasant wooded surroundings.

Palmse and around

Six kilometres north of Viitna, the village of **PALMSE**, home to the park's Visitors' Centre (see below), began life as a Cistercian convent before being bought in 1677 by the von Pahlens, a leading family of Baltic barons who stayed here until they were booted out by the land reform of 1919. The eighteenth-century complex of mano-rial buildings, bequeathed by the Pahlens, subsequently served as a barracks, then a children's holiday camp, before the Lahemaa National Park authorities set up their HQ here in 1972 and began painstakingly restoring the place. It's now an impressive ensemble of brightly painted cream and pale-blue buildings grouped around a central courtyard, bound by fruit orchards and landscaped parkland. Inside the courtyard, a balustraded staircase sweeps up to the doors of the Neoclassical **Manor House** (May–Sept daily 10am–7pm; Oct–April Mon–Fri 10am–3pm; 50EEK), filled with antique furniture from all over Estonia and sepia photographs of the estate as it was in the Pahlens' time. Outside, an old creamery (July & Aug only; same times as above) contains an exhibition of sleds and coaches, and beyond this lies a conservatory filled with palms and cacti. Lawns slope down towards a small lake, on the far side of which lies a wooded park criss-crossed by paths.

You'll find the **Lahemaa Visitors' Centre** (May–Aug daily 9am–7pm; Sept daily 9am–5pm; Oct–April Mon–Fri 9am–5pm; ☎329 5555, Ⓦwww.lahemaa.ee), in a former coach house at the entrance to the manor courtyard. It's well stocked with maps and English-language leaflets describing various trails. There's also a small museum with interesting displays on Estonia's national parks and conservation issues. One of the swishest **hotels** in the park is right next door to the Visitors' Centre. The *Park-Hotel Palmse* (☎322 3626, Ⓦwww.phpalmse.ee; ❹) is a converted vodka distillery with bright and airy wood-floored en suites, some with bathtubs. The hotel, which has a good **café-restaurant**, does not accept credit cards. At the other end of the scale, about 1.5km southeast of the manor, overlooking a lake just off the road to Sagadi, the *Ojaäärse Holi-day Home* (☎676 7532; Ⓔpuhkus@rmk.ee) has basic bunk accommodation in cramped, but clean, four- and eight-bed **dorms** (275EEK), with kitchen access and sauna.

Võsu

Strung out along the southern shores of Käsmu Bay (Käsmu laht), 8km north of Palmse, the village of **VÕSU** has been a holiday resort since the late nineteenth century, when its pine-fringed beach was discovered by the St Petersburg intelligentsia. This uneventful little place is a good base for further exploration of the area: within striking distance lie wood-shrouded Oandu (see p.137) and the appealing fishing village of Altja (p.137), both reached via a ten-kilometre-long forest trail starting at the southern entrance to Võsu, while the Käsmu peninsula, strewn with erratic boulders, is only 8km northwest.

Võsu is over 2km long from east to west, and **accommodation** in the settlement is scattered accordingly: beginning at the eastern end (where the road from Palmse enters the village), the *Võsu Viiking Guesthouse*, Karja 9 (☏323 8521; ❷), offers prim rooms with grey-brown decor, most of which come with en-suite shower and TV, while the *Männisalu Hostel*, signed off the main road at Lääne 13 (☏323 8320, ⓦwww.mannisalu.ee; ❷; May–Sept only), musters some sparsely furnished doubles with wooden floors and doors, more comfortable suites and dorm accommodation in quads (250EEK), with breakfast included. At the western end of the village, the smart *Rannaliiv*, Aia 5 (☏323 8456, ⓦwww.rannaliiv.ee; ❸), boasts slick en suites with wooden furnishings and TV; suites come with balconies. In the back streets just behind it, *Hostell Sinikorall*, Metsa 3 (☏323 8455, ⓦwww.sinikorall.ee; ❶; May–Sept only), has eight doubles with shared facilities and several family rooms. Breakfast costs extra. *Camping Lepispea*, 2km west of the centre on the Käsmu road (mid-May to mid-Sept; ☏324 4665, ⓦwww.hot.ee/lepispeale), is one of the best-equipped sites in the country (25EEK), with clean toilet blocks, sauna, barbecue area and electricity points for caravans (110EEK).

For **eating and drinking**, try the *Grillbaar*, a pub-restaurant midway through the village on the main street, where you can get a decent range of pork and chicken dishes. The *Võsu Pagariäri* bakery, near the eastern entrance to the village, is the place to stop off for cakes, pastries and pancakes.

Käsmu

People tend to speak in superlatives about **KÄSMU**, an appealing ensemble of pastel-coloured houses and neat gardens that seems to meet everyone's expectations of what a traditional Estonian village ought to look like. The place owes its prosperous, white-picket-fence appearance to a brief period in the seafaring limelight in the decades before World War I, when Käsmu Bay – not as prone to thick ice as some of the other spots along the northern coast – became a popular winter anchorage for sailing ships. A maritime school was opened here in 1884, many of whose graduates chose to settle down in the village once their ocean-going days were over, earning Käsmu the nickname of "Captains' Village". The development of deep-hulled steamships put paid to Käsmu's importance, however, and it's now a pleasant summer-holiday village, offering plenty of bed-and-breakfast accommodation and excellent walking opportunities in the forests of the Käsmu peninsula.

Käsmu's maritime heritage is remembered in a small, private **museum** (open whenever the owner's family is around – usually most days), signed off the main street midway through the village. There's an atmospheric, pre-World War I living room containing the furniture of the owner's grandfather, while elsewhere are displays of bits of old boats, fishing tackle and baskets made from birch-bark – some of them look more like modern art installations than historical artefacts. Just inland from the museum, the **parish church** is renowned for the charm of its graveyard, planted with a kaleidoscopic array of flowers every spring.

At the northern end of Käsmu village a path leads to the tip of the Käsmu peninsula, where you can gaze at a chain of erratic boulders stretching away towards the uninhabited island of Kuradisaare. From here a path leads along the rock-strewn northern and western coasts of the peninsula, before looping back to Käsmu village through dense forest – a scenic circuit of about 14km in all. For a shorter woodland walk – or simply to cut a huge corner off the main circuit – head west from the village along the track that starts roughly opposite the *Lainela Holiday Village* (see p.136). This soon lands you in the midst of the so-called **Stone Plantation** (Kivikülv), a vast, eerie expanse of moss-covered erratic boulders sheltered by pines.

Accommodation

Accommodation in Käsmu is provided by a string of B&Bs on the main street. It's always worth contacting them in advance to check room availability and make sure someone is there to meet you when you arrive. Most allow camping in their gardens for around 50EEK, although they'll turn campers away if things get too busy. A good fallback is the free national park **campsite** on the shores of Käsmu järv, a forest-shrouded lake about an hour's walk southwest of the village. The simple café at the *Lainela Puhkeküla* (see below), is the only place to eat around these parts.

Lainela Puhkeküla (Lainela Holiday Village)
Neeme 70 ☎ 323 8133, ✉ suved@hot.ee. A former children's holiday camp now open to everyone, with seven hostel-like halls offering sparsely furnished two- and three-bed rooms, with showers and WC on the corridors. Despite its hundred-bed capacity it's still likely to be packed with groups in the summer. Open May–Sept. ➊

Merekalda Neeme 2 ☎ 323 8451, ⊛ www .merekalda.ee. A plush B&B at the southern end of the village, right on the shore, with a range of en-suite rooms and apartments in the main family house, or in the annexe in the pleasant sea-facing garden. ➌

Rannamännid Neeme 31 ☎ 323 8329, ⊛ www .rannamannid.ee. On the main street, this smart B&B offers eight sunny rooms, some en-suite;

those on the top floor have sloping ceilings and are particularly atmospheric. There's also an attractive terrace, sauna and barbecue area. Half-board is well worth the extra fee. ➋

Uustalu Neeme 78A ☎ 325 2956, ✉ liina .laanemets.001@mail.ee. This cosy B&B in a beautiful position near the northern tip of the peninsula has simple but snug en suites, with wooden floors and furniture and pastel-coloured walls. There is kitchen access but breakfast costs an extra 50EEK per person. ➋

Vahtra Laane 9 ☎ 325 2917, ⊛ www.hot .ee/vahtraturismitalu. A friendly household just off the main street and close to the pretty parish church. Chalet-style structures harbour a family-sized apartment sleeping four (1000EEK), and four simple, cosy doubles. ➋

West of Käsmu Bay: the Pärispea peninsula

West of Käsmu Bay, roads from Võsu work their way along the southern shore of Eru Bay (Eru laht) before heading north onto the **Pärispea peninsula**, another inviting area of desolate, boulder-strewn beauty. You really need a car to explore this area, as public transport is negligible and settlements are far-flung.

As you head up the east coast you'll pass lots of reed beds, a paradise for migrating birds in late spring, especially mute swans, mallards and barnacle geese. The first village of any interest is **VIINISTU**, on the northeastern corner of the peninsula. During the inter-war years Viinistu was known throughout Estonia as the "Village of the Spirit Kings" (*Piiritusekuningate Küla*) on account of the huge profits made from smuggling vodka to Finland. After World War II, a sizeable fishing fleet was based here until that industry went into decline, and large parts of the portside canning factory have now been transformed into the **Viinistu Art Museum** (Viinistu kunstimuuseum; Wed–Sun 11am–6pm; 25EEK). Based on the private collection of Jan Manetski, a Viinistu native who made it big in Sweden, the gallery provides a definitive overview of Estonian art from the early twentieth century onwards, kicking off with one of the most frequently reproduced paintings in the country, Aleksander Vardi's impressionistic view of Paris's Boulevard Clichy. There are some inter-war graphics of North African tribesmen by the much-travelled, inter-war artist Eduard Viiralt, and a whole room devoted to the often unsettling conceptual creations of the post-1991 generation – look out for the pieces of cardboard daubed with paint on the afternoon of September 11, 2001 by Raul Kurvitz (who was staying in New York at the time). Two adjacent water towers provide the perfect place for temporary exhibitions, mostly devoted to new works by Estonian artists. The gallery also offers **accommodation**, with simple but pristine doubles with shower in an adjacent building (☎ 608 6422, ✉ viinistukunstimuuseum@hot.ee; ➋). On the landward side of the gallery, *Viinistu Kõrts*, in an old, whitewashed house, is a cheery place for fried fish and a cold beer.

The western side of the peninsula is characterized by a string of former Soviet military settlements, beginning with **PÄRISPEA** in the northwest, built to serve a radar installation on the headland, 2km to the northeast. A track runs past abandoned barracks to reach the headland, where an earthen mound (the erstwhile perch of the biggest of the eight radar dishes once sited here) provides a superb vantage point from which to survey a chain of sea-splashed erratic boulders strung out to the north. The free national park **campsite** just below the mound is very popular on summer weekends.

Three kilometres south of Pärispea, Suurpea once boasted an institute dedicated to making Soviet submarines invisible to sonar, but the sparsely inhabited concrete apartment blocks nowadays have a ghost-town look about them. More animated, but probably less interesting for the visitor, is Loksa 8km further south, a gritty shipbuilding town occupying an isolated pocket of non-national park territory.

East of Käsmu Bay

The road east out of Võsu skirts the northern fringes of Oandu forest and leads to **ALTJA**, a charming fishing village with timber buildings, 15km away. For walkers, there's a more direct, ten-kilometre path through the forest, starting at the southern end of Võsu and emerging near the Oandu nature trails described below. Altja's main landmark is an enormous **wooden swing** at the eastern end of the village. Before World War II, every Estonian village would have had one of these: they provided a summer-evening social focus where local youth would gather in the days before bus shelters were invented. Beyond the swing there's a short stretch of sandy beach and an ensemble of fishermen's cottages and net sheds, many sporting recently restored thatched roofs. If you want **to stay** in a traditional log-built building, head for *Toomarahva Turismitalu*, right by the village's main road (℡ 325 2511, Ⓦ www.zone .ee/toomarahva; ❷); it has small en-suite doubles, a converted barn that can house up to ten people and tent space in the garden (25EEK per person). Guests can also rent bikes. Built in the style of a nineteenth-century village tavern, *Altja Körts*, close to the swing, does a good line in local fish.

Oandu

Beyond Altja the road climbs uphill to the south, passing after 1.5km the start of the **Oandu Beaver Trail** (Koprarada) on the left side of the road, a 1.7-kilometre circuit which passes several beaver dams; no doubt you'll also see tree trunks bearing fresh gnaw marks. Just under 1km north of the Beaver Trail, **OANDU** itself is no more than a couple of scattered farmsteads in the forest. Signs on the right-hand side of the road mark the start of the **Oandu Forest Nature Trail** (Oandu loodusmetsa rada), a circular, 4.7-kilometre path designed to give you a taste of the park's varied forest landscape: a mixture of evergreen and deciduous trees drawing a dark-green canopy over a woodland floor covered in mosses and ferns. Here and there, scarred tree-trunks bear witness to the activities of itchy-scratchy moose and bark-nibbling bears. If you're camping, you could head for the free national park **campsite** just north of the Oandu Forest Nature Trail, right beside the road and overlooking a small lake.

Sagadi

Three kilometres beyond Oandu lies **Sagadi Manor** (Sagadi mõis), a handsome ensemble of cherry-and-cream buildings lying behind a low, brick wall. It was built for the von Fock family in the mid-eighteenth century and is now the regional HQ of the Estonian Forestry Commission. Presiding over a large, oblong courtyard, the Manor House (May–Sept daily 10am–6pm; combined ticket including Forestry Museum 35EEK) harbours an attractively arranged collection of period furniture and paintings, beginning in the central hall with a curious canvas by an unknown artist of a dog and cat fighting over a chicken. As in most Baltic aristocratic homes of the late eighteenth century, the lady of the house lived in one wing of the building, while the master lived in another – it's easy to see which wing is which in Sagadi, with businesslike green hues dominating the decor in one half of the house and shades of pink and purple holding sway elsewhere. Occupying outbuildings on one side of the courtyard, the **Forestry**

Museum (Metsamuuseum; same times) is mainly intended for schoolchildren, with a didactic display of stuffed woodland animals and a thorough run-down of all the types of tree found in Estonia.

Sharing the same building as the Forestry Museum, the *Sagadi Manor* **hotel** (⊕325 8888, ⊛www.sagadi.ee; ❹) offers comfortable en suites with Wi-Fi access and satellite TV; most also feature attic ceilings. The more expensive "Guest Rooms" have French windows that open onto an inner courtyard. Occupying the former bailiff's house on the opposite side of the courtyard, the impressively high-ceilinged quarters at *Sagadi Manor* **hostel** (same contact details as the hotel) are sparsely furnished but comfortable, with beds (200EEK) in a crowded dorm; breakfast isn't included, but you can buy it in the hotel café. Hostel and hotel guests can also rent **bikes**.

Rakvere

The laid-back, unindustrialized town of **RAKVERE** lies some 27km beyond the southeastern border of the park, just off the Tallinn–Narva highway. Its dominant feature is a long, grassy ridge topped by the sombre grey ruins of **Rakvere Castle** (Rakvere linnus; May–Sept daily 11am–7pm; 50EEK), built by the Danes in 1220 and expanded by the Livonian Order when they took over in 1346. A restored tower contains a display of archeological oddments, and you can walk a short section of the battlements. Just north of the castle is an enormous, golden-horned statue of an aurochs (a now-extinct breed of cattle) placed here in 2002 in honour of the beasts that long ago roamed the plains below.

Downhill from the aurochs, the high-profile temporary exhibitions on Estonian historical themes at the **Rakvere Exhibitions House Museum** at Tallinna 3 (Thurs–Sat 10am–5pm; 15EEK) are usually worthwhile. Heading from Tallinna along the eastern flanks of the castle hill, **Pikk** is the most atmospheric of Rakvere's streets, with a largely low-rise jumble of pre-World War I buildings. Occupying one of these at Pikk 50 is the **Rakvere Citizens' House Museum** (Rakvere linnakodaniku majamuuseum; Thurs–Sat 11am–5pm; 10EEK), which preserves a neat nineteenth-century interior, complete with a welcoming samovar on the sideboard, and all sorts of charming period crockery, including a butter dish in the form of a bundle of asparagus.

Rakvere's **bus station** is ten minutes' walk southeast of the centre on Laada, just beyond a brochure-stocked **tourist office** at Laada 14 (mid-Sept to mid-May Mon–Fri 9am–5pm; mid-May to mid-Sept Mon–Fri 9am–6pm, Sat & Sun 10am–3pm; ⊕324 2734, ⊛www.rakvere.ee). The *Wesenbergh* at Tallinna 25 (⊕322 3480, ⊛www .wesenbergh.ee; ❸) is the most upmarket **hotel** in town, with spacious, modern rooms aimed primarily at business travellers. More atmospheric is the 🎗*Katariina* guesthouse at Pikk 3 (⊕322 3943, ⊛www.katariina.ee; ❷), with its cosy, pastel-coloured rooms, the cheaper ones with shared facilities, in a building originally built in the 1840s for a Russian merchant. There's also a restaurant, often featuring live music, and a small art gallery. *Hostel Pansionaat* (⊕329 5420; ❶), beside the Rakvere Theatre at Kreutzwaldi 2A, was undergoing renovation at the time of writing, but will be offering simple, rustic rooms by autumn 2007. For **eating**, check out *Berliini Trahter*, occupying an old brick building at Lai 15, which does a wide range of pork-and-potato staples. A few doors along is the classy *Art Café*, Lai 13, an excellent spot for an evening drink, also serving up tasty omelettes, burgers, salads and pancakes. The *Inglise Pubi Old Victoria*, Tallinna 27, has a charming **beer garden**.

Narva and around

"For sheer romantic medievalism, **NARVA** ranks even above Tallinn," wrote author Ronald Seth in 1939, unaware that this atmospheric city of cobbled streets was about to be pummelled into oblivion by German-Soviet artillery battles. On the country's far eastern border, with a population that is over ninety percent Russian-speaking, Narva is closer – geographically, socially and culturally – to St Petersburg than to Tallinn. Economic activity has slumped since the collapse of communism, however, and while

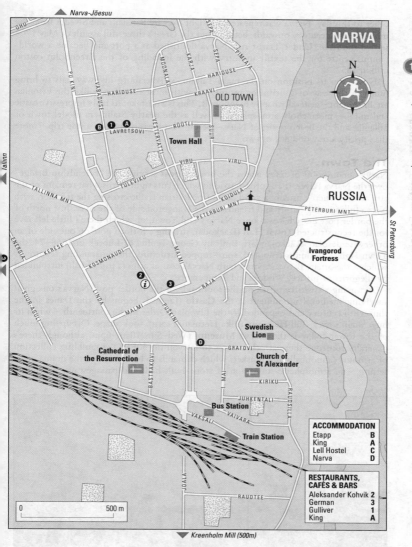

Narva-Jõesuu

NARVA

N

OLD TOWN

Town Hall

RUSSIA

St Petersburg

Ivangorod Fortress

Tallinn

Swedish Lion

Cathedral of the Resurrection

Church of St Alexander

Bus Station

Train Station

0   500 m

Kreenholm Mill (500m)

ACCOMMODATION	
Etapp	B
King	A
Lell Hostel	C
Narva	D

RESTAURANTS, CAFÉS & BARS	
Aleksander Kohvik	2
German	3
Gulliver	1
King	A

the city remains an important manufacturing centre, it is more famous for its high levels of unemployment and drug abuse. As Estonia as a whole looks to the future, its third-largest city appears trapped in limbo.

It's hardly surprising that this oft-disputed border town has ended up this way. Founded by the Danes in 1229 and bequeathed to the Livonian Order a century later, the city, on the Narva River, marked for centuries the frontier between the Teutonic-ruled western Baltic and the emerging Russian state. The building of Narva Castle on the western side of the river was soon followed by the construction of Ivangorod on the opposite bank; the two strongholds continue to glower across the water at each other to this day. Narva was repeatedly fought over by Russians and Swedes from the mid-sixteenth century onwards, before Peter the Great's successful assault of May 1704 settled the issue. Under Tsarist rule Narva flourished as a port and became a world-famous centre for the textile industry with the founding of the Kreenholm cotton mill in 1857.

Now even its position on the main Tallinn–St Petersburg highway fails to bring much in the way of tourism or prosperity, with most travellers – like the Estonian establishment – generally happy to ignore it. This is a mistake: its truly impressive castle and unique, melancholy atmosphere, as well as the nearby Stalin-era model town of Sillamäe and the beach resort of Narva-Jõesuu – both easily seen on a side trip – more than justify a stay of a day or two.

The Town

Narva's main point of reference is the **border post** serving the "Friendship Bridge" over the Narva River, the approach road to which cuts right across what remains of the city centre. There's usually a good deal of pedestrian traffic crossing the frontier, with Narva folk visiting family and friends on the Ivangorod side of the river. Just north of the border post lies what was once Narva's Old Town, of which there's little left save for the reconstructed **Town Hall** (Raekoda), striking a forlorn pose on one side of an otherwise desolate Raekoja plats. Built by Georg Teuffel of Lübeck in 1668–74, the Town Hall is a salmon-coloured, spire-topped structure, the outstanding feature of which is the ornate Baroque portal with Narva's coat of arms (a pair of fish) surrounded by allegories of Justice, Wisdom and Temperance.

Occupying a riverfront park on the south side of the border post, Narva's one great surviving medieval monument is the **Castle** (Linnus), begun by the Danes in the thirteenth century and expanded by the Livonian Order in the fourteenth – when its huge main tower, Tall Hermann (Pika Hermanni torn), took shape. Occupying much of the tower today is the **Narva Museum** (Wed–Sun 10am–6pm, although there's generally someone there at other times to let you in; 30EEK), a rambling collection of armour, cannonballs and muskets which demands to be visited for the drama of its setting – an atmospheric succession of stone-built halls and passageways. Ascending

△ Narva Castle and Ivangorod Fortress, Narva

through exhibition galleries inside Tall Hermann ultimately brings you out onto an enclosed walkway just below the top of the tower, affording majestic views of Ivan-gorod fortress on the opposite side of the river.

The main focus of the riverside park stretching south of the castle is the so-called **Swedish Lion**, a modern replica of a 1936 memorial commemorating Charles XII's victory over Narva's Russian besiegers in 1701, when the Swedes audaciously used a driving snowstorm as cover for their attack. As an implicitly anti-Russian monument, the Lion, its tail dismissively turned to the east, is just about tolerated by the locals. Fur-ther south lie a handful of architectural oddities, beginning with the Lutheran **Church of St Alexander** (Aleksandrikirik) between Grafovi and Kiriku, a curious rotunda built for Kreenholm cotton-mill workers in 1884 and largely gutted in 1944 – resto-ration is ongoing. About 200m due west, the roughly contemporaneous **Orthodox Cathedral of the Resurrection** (Õigeusu Ülestõusmise kirik) is in much better shape, an impressive barrel of red brick bursting with Byzantine domes.

Southeast of here, a footbridge crosses the railway tracks towards the southbound Joala tänav, lined with moderately well-preserved Stalin-era apartment buildings rich in Neoclassical mouldings. Further down Joala lie some impressive workers' housing projects of the pre-Soviet era, huge slabs of red brick encrusted with neo-Gothic detail, built to house workers at the **Kreenholm Mill**. The mill itself sprawls at the southern end of Joala, the three vast towers of its facade mounting a confi-dent nineteenth-century challenge to the medieval battlements of Narva Castle and Ivangorod just downstream.

Practicalities

Narva's **train and bus stations** are just off the southern end of Puškini, the boulevard that runs roughly north–south through the city centre, with the friendly and helpful **tourist office** at Puškini 13 (mid-Sept to mid-May Mon–Fri 10am–5pm; mid-May to mid-Sept Mon–Fri 9am–6pm, Sat & Sun 10am–3pm; ☏356 0184, ⓦwww.narva.ee) on the way.

Most budget travellers head to the *Lell* **hostel** at Partisani 7, a twenty-minute walk west of the centre (☏354 9009, ✉lell@narvahotel.ee; ❶). Straightforward singles, doubles and quads are housed in a somewhat depressing, grey concrete block. Much more upmarket is the brand-new *Narva* **hotel**, at Puškini 6, close to the bus station (☏359 9600, ⓦwww.narvahotell.ee; ❹), which has slightly overpriced, business-style rooms, some with views of the castle. *Etapp*, a lemon-yellow town house on Lavretsovi 5 (☏359 1333, ⓦwww.hot.ee/etapp; ❸), offers large, comfortable en suites. A few doors along from *Etapp*, and just outdoing it in the style and comfort stakes, is ⚥ *Hotel King*, Lavretsovi 9 (☏357 2404, ⓦwww.hotelking.ee; ❸), which has bright, modern rooms with faux wrought-iron fittings and smart orange- and terracotta-coloured bathrooms. As well as an atmospheric cellar-style restaurant, the hotel also provides free Internet access.

Narva isn't exactly overflowing with decent places to **eat and drink**. One of the best bets is *Aleksander Kohvik*, Puškini 13, a cheap and restful place in which to relax over coffee and cakes or more substantial snacks; try the delicious *pelmeni*, served with sour cream and paprika. Alternatively, *German*, Puškini 10 (entrance round the corner on Malmi), is a pub-like subterranean space with a full menu of satisfying meat-and-two-veg main courses. The restaurant of the *Hotel King* has a wider range of dishes and a slightly smarter clientele. For drinks, head for *Gulliver*, Lavretsovi 7, a cosy café-bar serving up cheap Wiru beer in a mock-Tudor building.

Narva-Jõesuu

The road leading northwest out of Narva runs along the left bank of the Narva River, passing a string of German and Soviet military cemeteries – a reminder of just how fiercely the region was fought over in 1944. After some 13km, the road winds up in the beachside settlement of **NARVA-JÕESUU**, a four-kilometre-long line of holiday homes and concrete hotels sheltered by pines. One of the most glamorous watering holes in the Baltic during its pre-World War I heyday, Narva-Jõesuu now has the half-abandoned air of so many post-Soviet resorts. A central spa park, complete with swan-patrolled lake and bandstand, serves as a reminder of past glories, as does the neighbouring *Kursaal* public hall, now falling into ruin, where the cream of St Petersburg high society used to congregate for concerts and balls. The sandy beach is as good as they come, however, and the general peacefulness of the place makes Narva-Jõesuu a more restful place to stay than Narva.

Narva-Jõesuu is easily reached from central Narva by catching municipal **bus** #31 or #31R from outside the post office on Puškini (every 20–30min). Privately operated minibuses run the same route, but don't keep to a regular timetable. Of the high-rise **hotels**, one of the most basic is the beachside *Hostel Mereranna* (⊕357 2826; ❷) which has no-frills, economical rooms; you'll get more in the way of creature comforts at the *Liivarand* at the western end of the resort (⊕357 7391, ⓦwww.liivarand .ee; ❷), where you can choose between plain, standard en-suite doubles, and slightly plusher "business class" and "de luxe" rooms. Hidden away in the back streets near the *Liivarand*, the more intimate *Pansionaat Valentina* (⊕357 7468, ⓦwww.zur.ee; ❸) offers cosy bed-and-breakfast accommodation.

Sillamäe

Some twenty-five kilometres west of Narva and served by hourly buses, the seaside town of **SILLAMÄE** is a living memorial to the showpiece architecture of the late Stalinist period, its elegantly proportioned apartment blocks combining neo-Egyptian pilasters and scallop-shell lunettes with hammers, sickles and facade-topping, five-pointed stars. The model town's inhabitants were almost all employed in the local uranium mine, built by prison labour in 1948. The mine fed the USSR's nuclear energy programme before being closed down by the Estonian government in 1991. The mine's environmental legacy constitutes a considerable headache for the authorities, with a waste pond just west of town bleeding radioactive material into both sea and soil – an EU-funded clean-up operation is under way. Neat-and-tidy Sillamäe itself is an enchanting urban relic and well worth a trip from Narva.

From the bus station on the edge of town a tree-lined boulevard takes you past manicured parks to the set-piece main square, where a statue of a bare-torsoed miner juggles a confusion of hoops and balls – signifying, presumably, molecules orbiting the nucleus of an atom. Opposite the statue, the mock-medieval Town Hall sprouts an incongruous-looking church spire, while the nearby House of Culture, a notable example of Stalinist-era architecture, flaunts the kinds of colonnades and pediments you'd expect to see on a Greco-Roman temple. From the House of Culture, a mauve-and-turquoise staircase leads down to the stately apartment buildings of Mere pst, at the far end of which you'll find a shingle seashore – the brown-coloured headland over to the west is where most of the mining took place.

For somewhere **to stay**, try *Krunk* on the main square (⊕392 9030, ⓦwww.krunk .ee; ❸). The hotel dates back to 1949 but was renovated in 2003 and has comfortable en suites with satellite TV and a decent restaurant.

Tartu

Set across the banks of the River Emajõgi, the tranquil, leafy city of **TARTU** is the undisputed intellectual centre of the country and home to a 370-year-old university that, during its nineteenth-century heyday, was the most prestigious seat of learning in the Baltics. The academic world remains absolutely central to the character of Estonia's second-largest city: one fifth of the population of 100,000 is reckoned to be made up of students, researchers, lecturers and professors, while many of the city centre's Neoclassical buildings date back to the university's greatest period of expansion in the early 1800s.

Tartu has long been considered the home of the nation's educated elite (ambitious Estonians still tend to choose to study here in preference to the capital), and as such has a suitably diverse choice of cultural attractions. The city's tangible sense of superiority over Tallinn is bolstered by the fact that it's one of the most truly Estonian urban centres in the country – it was spared mass immigration from other parts of the Soviet Union and less than a quarter of today's population count Russian as their first language. While it may be flushed with self-importance, Tartu has an engaging small-town feel – and as a student capital it's naturally also overflowing with cafés suitable for discussing the meaning of life, raucous drinking venues and vibrant nightclubs that stay open till the sun comes up.

A couple of days are enough to take in Tartu's sights, although the relaxed atmosphere of its parks, cafés and pubs will tempt you to stay longer. It's certainly an excellent base from which to explore the south of the country, with Lake Peipsi, Võrumaa, Setumaa and even Viljandi (see p.124) within easy day-trip range.

Some history

An Estonian hilltop stronghold conquered by the Livonian Order in the thirteenth century, then fought over by Russians, Poles and Swedes in the sixteenth – the history of Tartu (or Dorpat as it was known until 1918) would be much the same as that of any other Estonian provincial city were it not for the decision of the Swedish king, Gustav Adolphus, to found a university here in 1632. With government jobs in Swedish Livonia open only to those who had a degree from Tartu, it soon became the only academic institution in the region worth attending. The early history of the university was somewhat chequered, largely owing to Tartu's proximity to a zone of almost constant Swedish–Russian warfare: it was evacuated to Tallinn in 1656, didn't function at all between 1665 and 1690, and spent ten years in Pärnu after 1699.

When Peter the Great captured Tartu in 1708, he deported its leading citizens and had the city walls demolished. The townsfolk were allowed back in 1714, but the university had to wait until 1802 before it could resume its activities. Energized by the prospect of having a prestigious seat of learning in their own backyard, the Baltic nobility poured money into the university's wholesale reconstruction, the resulting rash of assembly halls, libraries and lecture theatres lending Tartu a distinguished, Neoclassical appearance, still very much the city's hallmark today.

Despite being an almost wholly German-speaking institution, the university became an important centre for research into indigenous Estonian culture. The Gelehrte Estnische Gesellschaft (Estonian Learned Society), founded by Tartu professors in 1837, was one of the first organizations to treat the local language as a serious object of study. Those Estonians lucky enough to be admitted to the university still had to Germanize their names in order to be socially accepted, but as the nineteenth century progressed Tartu nevertheless established itself as a major centre of Estonian – and not just German or Russian – learning. It's no coincidence that cultural activist Johann Voldemar Jannsen chose Tartu as the place to publish *Eesti Postimees* ("Estonian Courier"), the nation's first genuinely influential newspaper, in 1863. Jannsen also founded the Vanemuine cultural society here in 1868 (an institution that is still going strong), and organized the first-ever All-Estonian Song Festival a year later.

This upsurge in Estonian consciousness coincided with a period of creeping Russification throughout the empire. Russian superseded German to become the sole language of instruction at Tartu University in 1889, and the town itself was renamed Yuryev four years later. In other respects the university remained a relatively progressive institution by Tsarist standards: women were allowed to follow courses (but not sit exams) from 1905 and were admitted as full students in 1915. Jews were not discriminated against as they were elsewhere – on the eve of World War I they made up 23 percent of the student body.

During World War I, the university was evacuated to Voronezh – where many of its Russian-speaking professors stayed and later founded a new university, still thriving today. Back in Tartu, a university largely cleansed of Russian and German influences was reopened in December 1919, the city strengthening its position as the nation's intellectual capital. Appropriately, Tartu was at the centre of opposition to Soviet rule

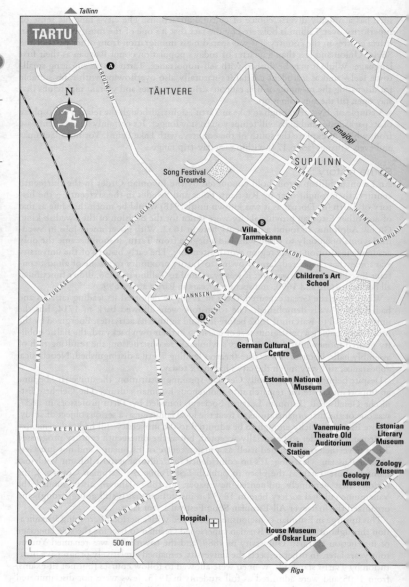

after June 1940, with medical students turning the university's Health Care Society into a front for subversive activities. On July 10, 1941, the society's members led a citywide revolt against the Soviets, aiming to establish an independent Estonian administration prior to the arrival of the Germans. The latter were unimpressed, closing the university down and planning its rebirth as an elite academy serving the Nazi province of Estland.

▲ Narva & Kallaste

ACCOMMODATION
Aleksandri	F
Carolina	G
Hansa	A
Hiie Kodumajutus	C
Hostel Tähtvere	B
Pallas	E
Vikerkaare külalistemaja	D

Song Festival Monument

PUIESTEE

Church of St George

NARVA MNT

FR. R. KREUTZWALDI

Botanical Garden

PIKK · KIVI

RAATUSE

UUS

Illusiooni Cinema

Virtuaal

PÄRNA

UUS

ANNE

PAJU

PIKK

SOPRUSE PST

See 'Central Tartu' map for detail

Sadamateater

Anne Kanal

Emajõgi

Anne Kanal

KALDA TEE

TURU

Vanemuine Theatre

RIIA

Aura Swimming Centre

KGB Cells Museum

Ekraan Cinema

KALEV

St Paul's Church

VÕRU

TÄHE

KARLOVA

KALEV

TOLSTOI

TURU

RESTAURANTS, CAFÉS, BARS & CLUBS
Bagua	4
Club Tallinn	1
Illusion	3
Pattaya	6
Shakespeare	5
Zavood	2

▼ Võru & Otepää

After 1945, a revitalized university preserved its pre-eminence in Estonian academic life, but found it difficult to retain international contacts – the presence of a Soviet bomber squadron at Tartu airport rendered the city virtually off-limits to foreigners. Since the regaining of independence, however, the university has lost no time in rejoining the international academic mainstream, with increasing numbers of foreign students and visiting lecturers turning it into a more cosmopolitan place than its founder ever imagined.

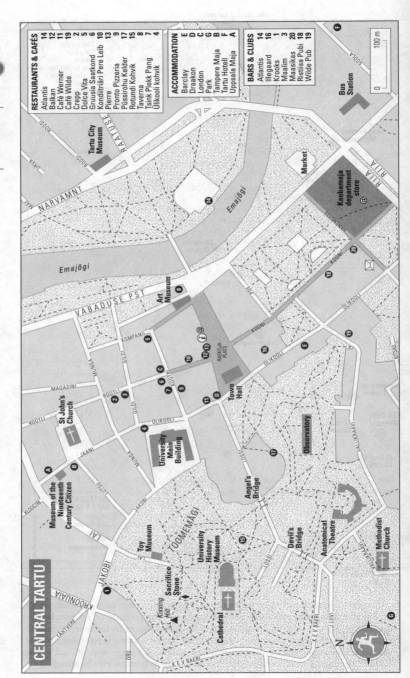

CENTRAL TARTU

RESTAURANTS & CAFÉS
Atlantis	14
Balkan	12
Café Werner	11
Café Wilde	19
Crepp	2
Dolce Vita	5
Gruusia Saatkond	6
Konditriäri Pere Leib	10
Pierre	13
Pronto Pizzeria	9
Püssirohu Kelder	17
Rotundi Kohvik	15
Taverna	8
Tsink Plekk Pang	7
Ülikooli kohvik	4

ACCOMMODATION
Barclay	E
Draakon	D
London	C
Park	G
Tampere Maja	B
Tartu Hotell	F
Uppsala Maja	A

BARS & CLUBS
Atlantis	14
Illegaard	16
Krooks	1
Maalim	3
Maasikas	20
Ristisa Pubi	18
Wilde Pub	19

0   100 m

Arrival, information and getting around

Major points of arrival are conveniently located on the western side of the river. Tartu's **bus station** is ten minutes' walk east of the centre at Turu 2. The dilapidated **train station** 1.5km west of the centre looks more like a haunted house than a transport terminal – the ticket office opens about thirty minutes prior to each departure, but there are no other facilities.

Tartu's **tourist office** at Raekoja plats 14 (mid-May to mid-Sept Mon–Fri 9am–6pm, Sat 10am–5pm, Sun 10am–3pm; mid-Sept to mid-May Mon–Fri 9am–5pm, Sat 10am–3pm; ☎744 2111; ⓦwww.visittartu.com) is an extraordinarily efficient source of information on just about everything in Tartu and the surrounding region, and also offers free **Internet** access.

With almost everything of sightseeing interest within walking distance of the city centre, you're unlikely to make use of Tartu's municipal **bus** network unless you're staying in the suburbs. Flat-fare tickets cost 10EEK from kiosks (or 12EEK from the driver) and must be inserted into the ticket-punch machines on board. **Taxi** ranks can be found at the bus station and at the junction of Raekoja plats and Turu; otherwise call Tartu Taksopark (☎730 0200) or Linna Takso (☎736 6366).

Accommodation

There's no shortage of good-quality accommodation in the city centre, although most of it is geared towards foreign businessmen and prices are creeping up. There are a few mid-range choices in the centre and a scattering of cheaper **hotels** and family-run **guesthouses** in the suburbs, although you're well advised to reserve in advance if you're looking for a bargain.

In addition to the hotels and guesthouses listed below, a number of private households in Tartu's suburbs offer **bed-and-breakfast** accommodation in the 400–500EEK range, although few of the hosts speak English: you're best off asking the tourist office (see above) about these and getting them to book for you.

Central Tartu

Barclay Ülikooli 8 ☎744 7100, ⓦwww.barclay .ee. It's hard to imagine that this handsome Art Nouveau building once served as the regional HQ of the Soviet army. The *Barclay* now has high-quality en suites and is well worth the money if you get one of the east-facing rooms overlooking a leafy square. If you're prepared to hand over the readies go for one of the suites with private sauna. ⑥–⑦

Draakon Raekoja plats 2 ☎744 2045, ⓦwww .draakon.ee. *Draakon* has a prime position on the main square and boasts thick carpets and quality furniture. Standard doubles come with simple showers instead of bathtubs – if you want one of those, you'll have to pay a little extra for a "de luxe" room or a suite. ⑥–⑦

London Rüütli 9 ☎730 5555, ⓦwww.londonhotel .ee. The only hotel in Tartu with a water feature in the lobby offers compact but snazzy en suites with satellite TV, decorated in contemporary style. De luxe doubles are slightly bigger than regular rooms and have bathtubs, while suites come with private sauna. The (nowadays disappointingly well-behaved) café-restaurant was a prime hangout of drunkard-intellectuals in the inter-war years. ⑥–⑦

Pallas Riia 4 ☎730 1200, ⓦwww.pallas.ee; see map p.144 The three-star *Pallas*, above a glass and concrete shopping mall, maintains the heritage of the influential Pallas School of Fine Arts, which stood here until being destroyed in 1944: standard en suites are decorated with Pallas School-inspired paintings, whilst the suites are covered with breathtaking reproductions of inter-war works of art. All rooms are refreshingly modern and those on the northern side have floor-to-ceiling windows with great city views. ⑤–⑥

Park Vallikraavi 23 ☎742 7000, ⓦwww .parkhotell.ee. Set amid trees on the western side of Toomemägi, this white-cube Modernist building dating from the 1930s is beginning to show its age, but the parquet floors and pastel decor are soothing enough. The simply decorated en suites are slightly overpriced. ④

Tampere Maja Jaani 4 ☎738 6300, ⓦwww .tamperemaja.ee. A historic town house refurbished with money from the Finnish city of Tampere to serve as a cultural centre, art gallery and guesthouse. Along with two four-bed family rooms with kitchens, there is a handful of en-suite doubles. All are kitted out with wooden floors, muted colours and tasteful fabrics. ④

Tartu Hotell Soola 3 ☎731 4300, ⓦwww .tartuhotell.ee. A Soviet-era concrete slab opposite the bus station offering functional grey-and-yellow, business-style en suites. There are also cheaper "youth rooms": simple triples with shared facilities. ❸–❹

🏃 **Uppsala Maja** Jaani 7 ☎736 1535, ⓦwww.uppsalamaja.ee. Located in a wonderfully restored eighteenth-century house – one of the oldest surviving dwellings in Tartu – this small and super-friendly guesthouse is nicely decorated in clean, Swedish style. Only five rooms, some with shared bathroom, so book ahead. ❹

The suburbs
Aleksandri Aleksandri 42 ☎736 6659, ⓦwww.aleksandri.ee. A red-brick building on the fringes of the Karlova district, fifteen minutes' walk southeast of the centre. Unfussy, clean and bright rooms come with TV; the vast majority are also en-suite. There are several good-value triples and quads – some with kitchens – for families or small groups. ❷–❸

Carolina Kreuzwaldi 15 ☎742 2070, ⓦwww.carolina.ee. A comfy guesthouse 4km north of the centre (you'll see it on the left as you enter town from the Tallinn direction), harbouring a homely warren of odd-shaped rooms, all with en-suite shower and TV. All rooms are non-smoking. To get there from the centre, take bus #6 from opposite the Kaubamaja department store to the Teemeistri stop. ❸

Hansa Aleksandri 46 ☎737 1800, ⓦwww.hansahotell.ee. A couple of buildings down from the *Aleksandri*, *Hansa* has large and comfortable, if somewhat chintzy, rooms set around a courtyard with a bar, a tavern-style restaurant and even a model windmill. Some of the suites come with their own bar areas. ❺

Hiie Kodumajutus Hiie 10 ☎742 1236, ⓦwww.bed.ee. This cheapie in the peaceful Tähtvere suburb, fifteen to twenty minutes' walk northwest of the centre, has four simply decorated rooms, as well as space in the garden for pitching tents (60EEK per person). ❶

Hostel Tähtvere Laulupeo 19 ☎742 1708 or 421 364, ⓔsktahtvere@hot.ee. This basic guesthouse, 1km northwest of the centre, has six timeworn rooms – one to try if your funds are running low. No breakfast, but staff will provide morning tea or coffee if you ask nicely. ❶

🏃 **Vikerkaare külalistemaja** Vikerkaare 40 ☎742 1190, ⓦwww.hot.ee/tdc. A welcoming B&B, close to *Hiie Kodumajutus*, with exceedingly comfy rooms, all with wooden furniture, shower and TV. Breakfast costs an extra 50EEK. Standard doubles ❷, with private sauna ❸

The City
Tartu's main point of reference is the Emajõgi River, which winds lazily through the city from northwest to southeast. The largely pedestrianized historic centre, arranged around the attractive **Raekoja plats**, lies on the west bank of the Emajõgi, while many of the set-piece **university** buildings are just uphill from here on **Toomemägi** ("Cathedral Hill"), a wonderfully leafy area that is bordered by atmospheric nineteenth-century suburbs.

The Raekoja plats
Tartu's focal point is the **Raekoja plats** (Town Hall Square), paved with lumpy cobblestones and surrounded by prim Neoclassical buildings, the most eye-catching of which is the lilac-and-orange **Town Hall** (Raekoda). It was designed in the 1780s by Rostock builder J.H.B. Walter, whose brief was to give the town a European flavour; he duly obliged with this Dutch-influenced edifice. The bell tower emits a shrill, music-box-like ditty on the hour – until about 10pm, after which it reverts to discreet bonging sounds.

Directly in front of the Town Hall stands a fountain topped by a three-metre-high statue of a young couple kissing under an umbrella. Unveiled in 1998 to provide Tartu with a millennial marker, it was immediately criticized for spoiling the eighteenth-century character of the square – pictures of the statue have nevertheless found their way onto most of the mugs and T-shirts sold by nearby souvenir shops.

At the eastern end of the square, the house at no. 18, leaning crookedly to one side (owing to a shifting of the water table), was originally the *pied-à-terre* of **Mikhail Barclay de Tolly** (1761–1818), a Livonian baron of Scottish descent and one of Tsar Alexander I's top generals during the Napoleonic Wars. Roundly criticized by St Petersburg society for his strategy of retreating before Napoleon's advance in 1812, de Tolly was vindicated when the French ran out of steam, fleeing homewards with the

△ The Raekoja plats, Tartu

onset of winter. His country estate was some 70km southwest of Tartu in Jõegeveste – where his mausoleum can still be seen. De Tolly's house in Tartu now accommodates the **Tartu Art Museum** (Tartu kunstimuuseum; Wed–Sun 11am–6pm; 25EEK; Ⓦwww.tartmus.ee), a vast collection embracing works by just about any Estonian ever to pick up a paintbrush. The collection is regularly shifted around in order to accommodate temporary themed exhibitions and it's impossible to predict what will be on display at any given time.

South of Raekoja plats

South of Raekoja plats, pedestrianized Küüni heads past an area of modern shops, passing first through a garden graced with a bust of Mikhail Barclay de Tolly. Behind him loom the Gothic-looking gables of an Art Nouveau office block, now occupied by the *Barclay* hotel (see p.147). Immediately south of the hotel on the corner of Vallikraavi (just outside the *Wilde Pub*; see p.156) is one of the most popular sculptures in Tartu, showing **Oscar Wilde** and his Estonian near-contemporary **Eduard Vilde** (see p.84) in earnest conversation – although one wonders what the straight-laced Vilde would have made of the high priest of camp had the pair ever met in real life. As well as being a rather obvious play on the similarity of the two writers' names, the ensemble also points up the fact that Vilde – who led a bohemian existence in Paris and Berlin in the years before World War I – is the only Estonian cultural figure who can compete with the aura of celebrity decadence cultivated by Wilde.

North of Raekoja plats

North of Raekoja plats, Ülikooli runs past the colonnaded facade of **Tartu University Main Building** (Tartu ülikooli peahoone), a cool, lemon meringue-coloured confection designed by J.W. Krause, the architect who presided over the expansion of the university once the Tsarist authorities permitted its reopening in 1802. Pass through the unassuming main doorway and head left towards the south wing to find the **Tartu University Art Museum** (Tartu ülikooli kunstmuuseum; Mon–Fri 11am–5pm; 8EEK), where plaster replicas of ancient artworks throng a suite of galleries decked out in imperial Roman style. Familiar Classical-era friends like the *Discus Thrower*, the *Belvedere Apollo* and the *Venus de Milo* are joined by comparatively less well-known characters such as the *Suicidal Celt*, here portrayed plunging a dagger into his throat.

The art museum sells tickets for two remaining public attractions in the university building: the first, the **Assembly Hall** (Aula; Mon–Fri 11am–5pm; 10EEK), is just a big, grey-white function room – the decision to open it up to the public seems more like a statement of the university's preening self-regard than anything else. Considerably more interesting is the **Lock-up** (Kartster; Mon–Fri 11am–5pm; 5EEK), in the attic of the south wing, where badly behaved students had to endure a few days of solitary confinement. According to the exhaustive list of offences pinned to the wall, you could get three days here for being rowdy in the streets – were such punishments still in force today, half the university would be cooped up here.

North of the University Main Building, the corner of Ülikooli and Gildi is graced by a modern **statue of Jan Tõnisson** (1869–1942), who was Estonia's prime minister for a brief spell, and long-serving editor of the Tartu newspaper *Postimees*. As the most respected organ in the country, *Postimees* traditionally symbolized Tartu's pre-eminence over Tallinn in the field of journalism as well as in that of academia – until the paper's head office finally moved to the capital in the mid-1990s.

Along Ülikooli and Jaani

Continuing along **Ülikooli** and its extension, **Jaani**, you soon come to the red-brick bulk of the Gothic **St John's Church** (Jaani kirik), founded in 1330, bombed out in 1944 and left half-ruined until 1989, when the restorers moved in and added a new spire. The building is still inaccessible, but from the street you can admire the gallery of terracotta heads arranged in niches around the main entrance. Placed here some time in the fourteenth century, they portray mostly medieval archetypes – nobles, tradesmen, peasants and so on – and were no doubt modelled on Tartu folk of the time.

Diagonally opposite the church, the **Museum of the Nineteenth-Century Citizen** at Jaani 16 (19. sajandi Tartu linnakodaniku muuseum; Wed–Sun 10am–3pm; 10EEK) features the kind of furnishings and textiles that would have graced the dwelling of a middle-ranking merchant family. With a kitchen lit by candlelight and a grandfather clock ticking away in the background, it's a charming period piece.

The Botanical Garden

Following Jaani to the end and turning right into Lai soon brings you to the **Botanical Garden** at no. 38 (Botanikaaed; daily: May–Sept 7am–9pm; Oct–April 7am–7pm; free). Tropical and subtropical plants are packed into the central Palm House (Palmimaja; daily 10am–5pm; 20EEK), behind which lies a small, but enormously varied, display of outdoor plants, occupying what's left of a defensive earthwork built to protect the northeastern corner of the (now disappeared) town wall. The most striking of the sculptures littering the garden is an imperious-looking Lithuanian fertility spirit carved from a tree trunk, presented to Tartu by Vilnius University in 1982.

Toomemägi

From behind the Town Hall, Lossi tänav climbs **Toomemägi** ("Cathedral Hill"), site of a fortress and a cathedral during the Middle Ages, subsequently abandoned after damage in the Livonian Wars. The area was derelict until the refounding of the university in 1802, when it was chosen as the site of several key academic buildings and generously planted with the trees that make it such a marvellously relaxing spot today.

Presiding over the bottom end of Lossi is a bust of Russian medical hero **Nikolai Pirogov**, who taught at Tartu in the 1840s and went on to become a pioneer in modern surgical technique. A kind of Florence Nightingale with hairy whiskers, Pirogov introduced new standards of cleanliness and organization to Tsarist military hospitals during the Crimean War, and hordes of high-born Russian ladies thronged to Sevastopol to join his nursing staff. The steeply banked park behind the bust is a favourite place for lounging around in summer – especially with students who, suitably armed with take-out beers, turn the area into a vast outdoor bar.

From here, Lossi heads uphill beneath Angel's Bridge (Inglisild), a brightly painted wooden structure dating from the nineteenth century; carry on over the brow of the hill and you'll pass under its counterpart on the other side, the Devil's Bridge. Heading right at the brow will bring you face to face with the stark, skeletal remains of the red-brick **Cathedral** (Toomkirik), built by the Knights of the Sword during the thirteenth century. Although Tartu became a thoroughly Protestant city in the 1520s, the Poles returned the cathedral to the Catholic fold when they took control of Tartu in 1582, and the building's destruction by fire in 1624 – the result of sparks flying from a Midsummer Night's bonfire – was seen by many contemporaries as a sign of divine displeasure. It was J.W. Krause, the architect in charge of the redevelopment of Toomemägi at the beginning of the nineteenth century, who hit on the idea of leaving the bulk of the cathedral as a romantic ruin, while rebuilding the choir to serve as the university library – the charmingly lopsided results of which can be seen today.

Since 1979, the library has served as the **University History Museum** (Wed–Sun 11am–5pm; 20EEK), a three-floor collection beginning (at the top) with portraits of the university's first rectors and a diorama of a seventeenth-century anatomical theatre, in which intestines hang from the table like a string of butcher's sausages. On the floor below, a stuffy display of professors through the ages is enlivened by the re-created physics lab of Rector Georg Friedrich Parrot (1765–1852), where a host of beautifully crafted instruments includes an electrostatic generator constructed from Karelian birchwood and turquoise glass tubes. On the same floor, one hall is preserved as it was in the nineteenth century, with rows of musty books and an unlabelled dummy of what looks suspiciously like the library's founder, Professor J.K.S. Morgenstern, who also established the University Art Museum (see opposite). Nearby are the sabres and flags brandished by nineteenth-century student fraternities – predominantly German-speaking affairs until 1870, when the first Estonian student association emerged. All the fraternities had tricolour banners, and in 1884 the Estonians chose a blue, black and white colour scheme (by this time it was the only combination left), subsequently adopted as Estonia's national flag. Despite being banned during the Soviet period, fraternities are once again a central feature of university life, not least because of the networking opportunities that membership (by invitation only) affords.

Toomemägi's main landmark north of the museum is a monument to one of Tartu University's most famous alumni, **Karl Ernst von Baer** (1792–1876), whose pioneering work in the field of embryology was credited by Charles Darwin as being a major step towards the development of evolutionary theory. West from here, it's easy to miss the so-called **Sacrifice Stone** (Ohvrikivi), an unobtrusive lump of rock where pre-Christian Estonians would place offerings to the departed – and where present-day students come to burn their exam papers. Behind it rises a knoll known as **Musumägi**, or "Kissing Hill", possibly because the path leading up it is barely wide enough to allow two people to walk side by side without rubbing up against each other.

Just east of here, paths descend towards the **Tartu Toy Museum** at Lai 1 (Mänguasjamuuseum; Wed–Sun 11am–6pm; 20EEK, children 15EEK; @www.mm.ee), an entertaining jumble of playthings through the ages, including the inevitable display of dolls from around the world and a model train set. There is also a new film and animation display, as well as a playroom (an extra 5EEK).

From the Anatomical Theatre to the Methodist Church

Returning to Angel's Bridge and heading for the southern end of Toomemägi brings you face to face with the impressive, barrel-shaped **Anatomical Theatre**, designed by J.W. Krause in 1803. In many ways the university's trademark – medicine was always one of the most prestigious subjects taught here (and still is) – the building was in use as an anatomical theatre right up until 1999. Pondering the parkscape just in front of the theatre is a bust of **Friedrich Robert Faehlmann** (1798–1850), the Germanized Estonian who played a leading role in the founding of the Estonian Learned Society (see p.429), and whose enthusiasm for collecting old folk tales inspired F.R. Kreuzwald (see p.161) to compile Estonia's epic, *Kalevipoeg*. A short distance further south, a building that looks like a decapitated windmill turns out to be the **University Observatory**, also designed by the ubiquitous Krause. Best known among the astronomers who came to ogle celestial bodies here was F.W. Struve (1793–1864), one of the first scientists to accurately measure the distances of various stars from the earth – he's celebrated by an angular concrete monument out front.

The sunken street of **Vallikraavi** coils its way around the southern end of Toomemägi, presenting a choice of itineraries: either back towards the *Wilde Pub* (see p.156), or uphill and west past a brand-new **Methodist Church** (Metodisti kirik). With its angular belfry clad in copper-coloured strips and minimalist interior decor (the altar would do quite nicely as a desk in an ultra-cool office), the church is as popular with devotees of modern design as it is with the Christian faithful.

South of Toomemägi

Beyond the Methodist Church, Vallikraavi curves south and comes out on Kuperjanovi. Here, at no. 9, is the **Estonian National Museum** (Eesti rahva muuseum; Wed–Sun 11am–6pm; 20EEK; @www.erm.ee), offering an exemplary overview of the nation's ethnography, with some imaginatively re-created farmhouse interiors, good English labelling and a comprehensive display of folk costume from all over the country. Rakes the size of small trees serve as a reminder of how haymaking and preparation of winter fodder was a matter of life and death to the average Estonian farmstead, while a sizeable collection of carved wooden beer tankards introduces a section on village feasts and holidays. There's an astounding array of other handicrafts, including hand-woven textiles that look far more exotic than the bland linen tablecloths sold in the Estonian souvenir shops of today. As if in deliberate counterpoint to the natural creativity of the Estonian peasant, a re-created living room from 1978 is filled with the dull-brown furniture that was standard issue in the Soviet Union.

A short detour north of the museum along Kastani will take you past some evocatively shabby nineteenth-century buildings, including a palatial-looking wooden apartment house at no. 17, with intricately carved door and window frames. Part

The great outdoors

Once you get beyond the capital cities, the Baltic States are predominantly rural in character, with isolated farmsteads and rustic market towns scattered across a landscape of grazing land, forest and bog-filled wilderness. The region's most dramatic natural feature is its coastline, however, with long sandy beaches stretching the length of Lithuania and Latvia, and on into southern Estonia. Occupying a prime position on north–south migration routes, the Baltic States are visited by hundreds of bird species every year, and its forests harbour a wide variety of fauna, from deer to wild boar to elk.

▲ Lake Pühajärv, Estonia

Lakes and forests

Glaciers carved out a series of ruts and hollows in the Baltic interior, allowing the formation of the **lakes** which splash bright blue across any map of the region.

Lake tourism is a large part of outdoor life in the Baltics: large lakes at Trakai in Lithuania (see p.342) or Pühajärv in Estonia (see p.159) are places to head for the beach, hire a boat or dine at a shoreside restaurant, while the smaller, quieter lakes strewn across eastern Latvia and southern Estonia are the perfect places to get lost in solitary contemplation. The chance to commune with nature is also offered by the region's huge tracts of dense **forest**, predominantly made up of pine, spruce and silver birch, and providing protective cover to a large population of deer, elk, wild boar and other mammals. Forest-based activities such as mushroom-picking and berry-gathering still form an important part of village life, while the otherworldly stillness of the deep forest exerts a powerful hold over the nature-worshipping side of the Baltic character.

Bogs

Created by the gradual accumulation of moisture-bearing mosses, **bogs** can be starkly beautiful places. The archetypal Baltic bog-scape comprises a spongy green carpet of sphagnum moss, frequently punctuated by shimmering blue ponds and supporting a sprinkling of heathers, stunted conifers and spindly birches. Plants which relish the soggy conditions include cloudberries and cranberries, making the bog a popular feeding ground for birds and insects. Several Baltic bogs have been rendered accessible to visitors by wooden boardwalk trails, notably the Great Ķemeri Bog in Latvia (see p.236) and the Viru Bog in Estonia (see p.133).

Dunes

Arguably the most memorable landscape in the Baltics is provided by Lithuania's Curonian Spit, a four-kilometre-wide strip of land composed almost entirely of **sand dunes**, formed over several millennia by the prevailing winds. Most of these dunes

▼ Dunes at Nida, Lithuania

now have a sparse coverage of grasses or pine forest, producing a rhythmically undulating landscape in varying shades of green. Just south of the fishing village of **Nida**, however, significant stretches of dune remain beautifully bare. Rising up to 50m in height, and still classified as "live dunes" due to their wind-driven tendency to change shape from one generation to the next, the Nida dunes exude an almost Saharan majesty.

▲ Saaremaa Island, Estonia

Birds

The relatively unspoilt Baltic countryside supports a year-round profusion of **bird life**. Dense forests provide a habitat for woodpeckers, eagles and buzzards, while bogs and heaths offer inviting hunting grounds for sandpipers, grouse and cranes. The Baltic coastline forms part of one of the main north–south avian migration routes, and the skies are filled with birds on the move in spring and autumn. The marshes and lagoons of Matsalu Bay in Estonia (see p.102) are an important seasonal feeding ground for migrating geese and ducks, with mute swans, moorhens and corncrakes foraging among the coastal reeds. Slightly further northwest, the Vilsandi National Park on the island of Saaremaa (see p.107) is a major stopping-off point for greylag geese and arctic terns.

▼ A juvenile eagle

Islands

Estonians regard their cluster of offshore **islands** as the purest embodiment of everything that is beautiful about the country. The island communities were pretty much left to their own devices during the Soviet period, thereby preserving a patchwork of farmsteads, fishing villages and market towns that has changed little in the last fifty years. The two largest islands, Saaremaa (see see p.106) and Hiiumaa (p.103), boast an extraordinary variety of landscapes, with cow-grazed meadows giving way to bleak stretches of bog, thick coastal reedbeds, dense woodland and – most characteristically of all – open heath covered in grey-green juniper. The squall-battered shores of both islands are made even more compelling by the historic lighthouses that jut from many a rocky headland – head for Kõpu (see p.105) or Ristna (see p.106) on Hiiumaa to enjoy these landscape-defining structures at first hand.

▲ Roe deer

Mammals

The **wild animals** you are most likely to see during
your travels are deer (either roe or red), which
live pretty much everywhere in the Baltic States
and can often be seen foraging in open farmland,
especially in the early morning or late evening. Wild
boar rarely emerge from their woodland habitats,
although you may well catch sight of them in areas
where they are concentrated, such as the densely
forested Curonian Spit in Lithuania. The other
principal forest-dwelling animals of the Baltics
– moose, elk, martens and lynx – are much more
secretive, and sightings are correspondingly rare.
Small numbers of bears live in the national park
areas of Estonia and occasionally make it as far
south as Latvia, although the only ones you're
likely to encounter are the captive examples held in
enclosures at the Līgatne Nature Trail (see p.264).
Freshly gnawed tree-trunks and log-built dams –
evidence of beavers – are a frequent sight in Baltic
national parks. The Oandu Beaver Trail in Lahemaa
(see p.137) is specifically designed so you can
learn more about these industrious creatures.

One wild animal you don't need to leave the
city to find is the bat – for whom the high-walled
tenement buildings and church belfries of Vilnius'
Old Town provide the perfect habitat.

fairytale cottage and part medieval fortress, the building on the corner of Kastani and Näituse once served as the headquarters of the Neobaltia student fraternity (dissolved when the Baltic Germans were repatriated in 1940) and now houses the **German Cultural Centre**, which holds a small gallery (Mon–Fri 9am–5pm; free).

Heading south and west from the National Museum along Kastani, then Tiigi brings you out onto a leafy square centred on a smooth granite statue of **Jakob Hurt** (1839–1907), whose mania for transcribing village songs and collecting traditional artefacts inspired a new appreciation of folk culture among educated nineteenth-century Estonians – and provided the impetus for the establishment of the National Museum in 1905. A trio of less-than-gripping museums lurks in the university buildings along Vanemuise tänav on the southern side of the square: the **Estonian Literary Museum** at no. 44 (Eesti kirjandus muuseum; Mon–Thurs 9am–5pm; Fri 9am–4.30pm; free), whose changing exhibitions on great writers and their works are usually labelled in Estonian only; the **Zoology Museum** at no. 46 (Wed–Sun 10am–4pm; 20EEK); and the **Geology Museum** in the same building (same times; 8EEK).

The KGB Cells Museum

Considerably more compelling is the **KGB Cells Museum** one block south, at Riia 15B (KGB kongid; Tues–Sat 11am–4pm; 5EEK), where the so-called "Grey House" (Hallis majas) served as the regional headquarters of the Soviet secret police. As well as preserving the basement cells in their original state, the museum offers a history lesson in Soviet methods of control. Any lack of English-language labelling is more than made up for by the narrative power of the grainy photographs on display, recalling the deportations of 1941 and 1949, as well as the gruelling conditions of life in Siberia experienced by the victims. Most poignant of all are the pictures of idealistic schoolchildren who joined secret patriotic organizations like the Tartu-based Blue-Black-and-White (named after the colours of the Estonian flag), only to be confined in the cells here before being sent to work camps in the east.

Riia mnt and Karlova

Another 400m southwest along Riia, the red-brick **St Paul's Church** (Paulusekirik) is a highly individual piece of Estonian inter-war architecture, its central tower resembling a bloated Egyptian obelisk thrust skywards by rocket boosters. Continuing along Riia for another five minutes brings you to the **House Museum of Oskar Luts**, Riia 38 (Oskar Lutsu majamuuseum; Wed–Sat 11am–5pm, Sun 1pm–5pm; 8EEK), celebrating the Tartu-trained pharmacist and author (1887–1953), best known for the semi-autobiographical *Kevade* ("Spring"), a classic account of growing up in the Estonian countryside. The house where he lived from 1918 until his death is packed with inter-war furnishings, old photographs of Tartu and the hideous-looking puppets used in animated films based on Luts's children's story "Forest Fairytale". Luts was one of the pillars of the inter-war literary establishment, and a 1937 newsreel shows the great and the good flocking to his fiftieth birthday party.

Returning back to town along Riia, it's worth making a southward detour along streets like Tähe or Kalevi into the suburb of **Karlova**, famous for the handsome array of nineteenth-century wooden houses that still line its streets. Some of the best are to be found 750m southeast of Riia along Tolstoi.

Northwest of the centre

There's enough interesting architecture in the northwestern suburbs of Tartu to justify a brief stroll up **Jakobi**, the street which connects the city centre with a plateau of residential streets above. The **Children's Art School** at Jakobi is a wonderful example of a pre-World War I timber mansion, with a fanciful, medieval-style central tower, and lovingly carved door and window frames. Jakobi's extension, Kreuzwaldi, enters **Tähtvere**, an elite suburb built for university professors in the 1920s and packed with the kind of Bauhaus-influenced houses that were all the rage with the inter-war Estonian middle class. The best known of these is the white-cube **Villa Tammekann** at Kreuzwaldi 6, designed by Alvar Aalto in 1932 and now occupied by a university research institute. From here it's only a ten-minute walk to the **Song Festival Grounds** (Laululava), on the very edge of Tartu, where a stage capable of accommodating 10,000 singers shelters under a boldly contemporary sea-shell canopy. Built in 1994 to symbolize Tartu's place in Estonian choral culture (it was here that the first ever national song festival was held), it's nowadays the venue for pop concerts, musicals and folk-singing performances. From here, you can either dally in the adjacent amusement park, or return to the centre via the streets of **Supilinn** immediately to the east, a ramshackle residential area of old wooden houses and vegetable plots. Thoroughfares such as Oa ("Bean Street"), Kartuli ("Potato Street") and Herne ("Pea Street") help explain how the suburb got its name – "Soup Town".

Across the river

At the eastern end of Raekoja plats, pedestrian traffic bustles across the River Emajõgi on a small bridge built in modest commemoration of the so-called Stone Bridge, an elegant eighteenth-century structure and a symbol of the city until the retreating Red Army destroyed it in 1941. A five-minute walk through parkland on the opposite bank takes you to the **Tartu City Museum** at Narva mnt 23 (Tartu linnamuuseum; Tues–Sun 11am–6pm; 20EEK; ⊛www.linnamuuseum.tartu.ee), an easy-on-the-eye display of furniture, prints and porcelain in a lusciously restored eighteenth-century mansion. Highlights include a round table of truly Arthurian proportions, around which the Estonian–Soviet Peace Treaty was signed on February 2, 1920, and a fascinating model of Tartu as it was in 1940 – free of the Soviet-era tower blocks that now clutter the suburbs.

A ten-minute walk northeast along Narva mnt is the **Church of St George** (Jüri kirik), the most delightful of Tartu's Orthodox places of worship. Like Mikhail Barclay de Tolly's house, it has a slightly crooked appearance owing to shifting foundations and, resplendent in a bright-pink paint job, it looks rather like a wobbly cake. Just beyond, at the junction of Narva mnt and Puiestee, a monument marks the spot where the very first **All-Estonian Song Festival** took place in 1869. Featuring a row of disembodied heads squashed beneath a hunk of granite, it looks less celebratory than its creators intended. The festival, largely put together by newspaper editor Johann Voldemar Jannsen and his daughter, the poet Lydia Koidula (see box, p.121), was a huge undertaking, bringing together 46 choirs, five brass bands, 800 singers and an audience of 15,000. Koidula wrote the patriotic hymn *Mu Isamaa* ("My Fatherland", closely based on the Finnish patriotic song *Maame*) especially for the festival and it subsequently became Estonia's national anthem.

Eating and drinking

Tartu has the widest range of **cafés and restaurants** outside Tallinn, and it's a tribute to the cosmopolitan nature of the place that plenty of ethnic and vegetarian fare exists alongside the usual north European favourites. As you would expect from a university town, there are plenty of **pubs and bars**, many of which offer a full menu of main-course food. Restaurants are usually **open** daily from noon until 11pm/midnight, bars and pubs from 11am/noon till midnight Sunday to Thursday and till 2/3am on Friday and Saturday. Unless stated otherwise, the places listed below follow these opening hours.

You can pick up **picnic supplies** from the covered market at Vabaduse pst 1 or the big supermarket inside the Kaubamaja department store, Riia 2 (Mon–Sat 9am–9pm, Sun 9am–6pm).

Cafés

Café Werner Ülikooli 11. Dating back to 1895, this used to be a hangout for quarrelsome intellectuals during the Soviet period. A recent modernization, however, has brought it firmly into the twenty-first century; fortunately it still has superior coffee and cakes. There's an upstairs restaurant if you want something more substantial. Café: Mon–Thurs 7.30am–11pm, Fri & Sat 8am–1am, Sun 9am–9pm; restaurant: Mon–Thurs 11am–11pm, Fri & Sat 11am–1am, Sun 11am–9pm.

Café Wilde Vallikraavi 4. In a former print works – some of the old presses are still on display – this relaxing café serves up some of the best coffee in town and some toothsome cakes; try the *tarte tatin*. It also has a good bookshop. Mon–Sat 9am–7pm, Sun 10am–6pm.

Crepp Rüütli 16. As its name suggests, this spartanly furnished French café does a good line in filling, sweet and savoury crepes, as well as quiches, baguettes and salads. Daily 11am–midnight.

Kondiitriäri Pere Leib Rüütli 5. A pervading smell of coffee and freshly baked nibbles makes this bakery one of the best places in the centre to sit down for a day time breather. Croissants and pastries for breakfast, scrumptious cakes for later. Mon–Fri 8am–7pm, Sat 9am–6pm, Sun 10am–4pm.

Pierre Raekoja 12. This new café has a distinct 1930s air, with extravagant silk tablecloths and elegant table lamps. Its delicious range of handmade chocolate truffles makes it a must for anyone with a sweet tooth. Mon–Thurs 8am–12am, Fri 8am–1am, Sat 10am–1am, Sun 10am–11pm.

Rotundi Kohvik Toomemägi. A summer-only café in a cosy, octagonal pavilion, with outdoor seating beneath the trees of Toomemägi. Daily 10am–8pm.

Shakespeare Vanemuise 6. A roomy establishment inside the Vanemuine theatre and concert hall offering a full range of drinks, reasonably cheap salads and meat-and-potatoes main courses. There's often live music in the evenings. Sun–Thurs 10am–midnight, Fri & Sat 10am–2am.

Ülikooli Kohvik Ülikooli 20. A student café with cheap and tasty canteen food, and a good-value, all-day buffet. Located in a suite of lovingly restored rooms in a historic house, next door to the main university building. Mon–Thurs 7.30am–11pm, Fri & Sat 11am–1am, Sun 11am–10pm.

Restaurants

Atlantis Narva mnt 2. Civilized but not overexpensive dining in a curved, glass-fronted building overlooking the river. You'll get the same pork, chicken and beef as elsewhere, but with more stylish service and presentation. Sun–Thurs noon–midnight, Fri & Sat noon–1am.

Bagua Pikk 40. An informal eatery with Chinese menu in one half, Thai in the other. Sufficiently spicy to make a trip over the river worthwhile. Sun–Thurs 11am–11pm, Fri & Sat 11am–1am.

Balkan Rüütli 5. A friendly, understated restaurant with a mainly Bulgarian menu. Alongside good – and cheap – kebabs and meat dishes, there are more unusual options like grilled halloumi cheese and cold cucumber soup.

Dolce Vita Kompanii 10. This chilled-out Italian, its whitewashed walls decorated with Federico Fellini movie posters, dishes up good thin-crust pizzas, soups and salads. Mon–Thurs 11.30am–10pm, Fri & Sat 11.30am–midnight, Sun noon–10pm.

Gruusia Saatkond Rüütli 8. Refined and relaxing, the "Georgian Embassy" is justifiably popular with both locals and tourists. Waiters in traditional dress serve up appetizing dishes like beef in walnut sauce, lamb shish kebabs and beef and aubergine stew. The freshly baked bread is delicious, and there is a good range of reasonably priced lunch options.

Pronto Pizzeria Küütri 3. Serving up thin-crust pies – many with unusual toppings, such as hamburger or peach – this is a conveniently central, cost-effective stomach filler rather than one for the cognoscenti. Take-out service is also available.

Püssirohu Kelder Lossi 28. Housed in a cavernous, red-brick armoury built under Peter the Great, *Püssirohu Kelder* is a suitably atmospheric place in which to swig beer at big wooden tables and tuck into platefuls of pork and sauerkraut. A wide choice of traditional Estonian dishes, and none too expensive. Mon–Thurs noon–2am, Fri & Sat noon–3am, Sun noon–midnight.

Taverna Raekoja 20. A cosy basement restaurant with an Italian flavour – the regular repertoire of porky Estonian fare augmented by a good range of filling pizzas, and several pasta choices too. Service, however, can be sluggish. Mon–Thurs 11.30am–midnight, Fri & Sat 11.30am–1am, Sun 11.30am–11pm.

Tsink Plekk Pang Küütri 6. This popular local haunt – whose name, somewhat bizarrely, is Estonian for "zinc-plated bucket" – serves up tasty Chinese-influenced food, milkshakes and beer in wonderfully relaxed, loungey surroundings. A good venue for an evening drink, with DJs at the weekends.

Bars and pubs

Illegaard Ülikooli 5. This subterranean hideaway – formerly a private members' club – has managed to preserve an intimate feel. Jazzy background music and regular live gigs. Closed Sun.

Krooks Jakobi 34. A laid-back, red-brick bar popular with local rockers. The interior is decked out in an engaging clutter of album covers and beer-related bric-a-brac. Usually open later than the other bars in the centre. Till 4.30am.

Maalim Rüütli 12. A bar-restaurant with an eccentric twist – you can sit on an indoor swing and read the newspaper and magazine clippings that decorate the walls – and a wide range of international dishes. Mon–Sat noon–1am, Sun noon–10pm.

Ristiisa Pubi Küüni 7. The "Godfather" is a city-centre boozer with a mafia/1920s speakeasy theme that attracts a cross-section of Tartu society. There's also a full menu of food.

Wilde Pub Vallikraavi 4. This (fairly) authentic Irish pub, above the café of the same name attracts a

mix of tourists, students, academics and expats. The pub serves up Irish and Estonian fare, and often has live music.

Zavood Lai 30. A studenty bar near the Botanical Garden with post-industrial decor, late opening hours, a billiards table and eccentric indie sounds. Till 4am.

Nightlife and entertainment

Tartu's main **theatre** and **concert** venue, the Vanemuine, Vanemuise 6 (box office Mon–Sat 10am–7pm; ☎744 0165, ⊛www.vanemuine.ee), is one of the most prestigious in the country, presenting top-quality drama, classical music, opera and dance performed by top acts from Tallinn or abroad – either in the comfortable modern main building, or in the smaller but equally stylish nineteenth-century auditorium just uphill at Vanemuise 45A. A range of broadly contemporary theatre and dance performances also takes take place in the modern auditorium of the riverside Sadamateater, Soola 5B (box office Mon–Sat noon–5pm & 1hr before performance; ☎734 4248, ⊛www.vanemuine .ee/sadamateater). Big productions of an operatic or musical nature are staged at the Song Festival Grounds in summer. Posters with details of upcoming events are put up around town; otherwise check out ⊛www.visittartu.com.

Tartu is poorly served with **cinemas**, with the two-screen Ekraan, Riia 14 (⊛www .superkinod.ee), currently the only really central option.

Clubs

The venues listed below are usually open from Wednesday to Saturday. Themed club nights and DJ evenings also take place at *Shakespeare* (see "Cafés", p.155), *Tsink Plekk Pang* (see "Restaurants", p.155), and the Sadamateater (see above).

Atlantis Narva mnt 2 ⊛www.atlantis.ee. A riverside disco of many years' standing that packs in a youngish, hedonistic crowd. Tues & Wed till 3am, Thurs–Sat till 4am, closed Mon & Sun.

Club Tallinn Narva mnt 27 ⊛www.clubtallinn .ee. One of Estonia's best clubs, this is the main gathering point for the more style-conscious music freaks, offering a variety of cutting-edge sounds and the best in the way of big-name DJs. Open Wed–Sat till 3am.

Illusion Raatuse 97 ⊛www.illusion.ee. Housed in an old cinema, and a former underground dance venue in the 1990s, *Illusion* is now among the most popular – and the priciest – clubs in Tartu, with a good range of hip-hop, house, drum & bass and disco. Open Wed–Sat till 6am.

Maasikas Küüni 7 ⊛www.maasikas .com. *Maasikas* – "strawberry" in Estonian – attracts a slightly older (mid-20s) crowd than the other clubs in town. Cool and kitsch, it plays an

---

The University Spring Days and other annual events

The best-known and probably most enjoyable of Tartu's annual events is the University Spring Days (Ülikooli kevadpaevad), a five-day fiesta straddling May 1, when the town is transformed into a vast open-air student party. Highlights include a fund-raising rubber-boat regatta on the Emajõgi River, and the night of May 1 itself, when the town's pubs are allowed (nay, expected) to stay open all night.

Other festivals include the Soup City Days (Supilinna päevad), when open-air concerts are organized in the suburb of Supilinn (see p.154) over the last weekend of April; the International Dance Festival (Rahvusvaheslisel tantsufestival) in late May/early June; and the medieval-themed Hansa Days festival on the last weekend in June. Rather than a specific event, the Tartu Summer Music Festival is the general banner under which a broad range of classical and jazz concerts take place from early June through to late August. ⊛www.visittartu.com has further information on all events.

eclectic mix of music – from live jazz to DJ sets. Wed & Thurs till 3.30am, Fri & Sat till 4.30am, closed Sun–Tues.

Pattaya Turu 21 ⓦ www.pattaya.ee. Enjoyable mish-mash of top-40, techno and retro in this swish club just south of the bus station. Wed till 3am, Thurs–Sat till 4am, closed Sun–Tues.

Listings

Bicycle rental Jalgratas, Laulupeo 19 ⓣ 742 1731; Velospets, Riia 130 ⓣ 738 0406, ⓦ www .velospets.ee.

Books For the biggest range of maps, local guidebooks and English-language paperbacks, head for Apollo, Küüni 1; Tartu Ülikooli Raamatupood (Tartu University Bookshop), Ülikooli 11; or the *Café Wilde*, Vallikraavi 4.

Car rental Avis, Vallikraavi 2, ⓣ 744 0360, ⓦ www.avis.ee; Hertz, Jõe 9A, ⓣ 611 6333, ⓦ www.hertz.ee.

Ferry trips Tartu Sadam, Soola 5 (ⓣ 734 0026, ⓦ www.transcom.ee/tartusadam) organizes short cruises on the Emajõgi, as well as longer excursions to the island of Piirissaar in Lake Peipsi.

Hospital The main city hospital is at Puusepa tee, 2km southwest of the centre (for an ambulance call ⓣ 112).

Internet Tourist Office, Raekoja plats; Kaubamaja Digimaalim, Riia; Virtuaal, Pikk 40.

Left luggage At the bus station (daily 7.30am–9pm; 6–20EEK per day).

Pharmacy Raekoja Apteek, Town Hall, Raekoja plats (24hr).

Police Raekoja plats 7. In emergencies call ⓣ 112.

Post office Vanemuise 7 (Mon–Fri 7am–7pm, Sat 9am–4pm).

Ski equipment rental To get kitted out before heading for the slopes of Otepää (see below), try Surfar, Baeri 1 ⓣ 744 1359.

Swimming Aura, just beyond the bus station at Turu 14, is a massively popular indoor complex with fifty-metre pool, paddling sections and water slides. For outdoor bathing, the beach at the Anne Canal, just across the river from the city centre at the southeastern end of Pikk, is nowhere near as nice as the stretch of the River Emajõgi northwest of town, reached by walking along Ujula from the Kroonuaia bridge.

Travel agents Baltic Tours, Ülikooli 10 (ⓣ 740 0000, ⓦ www.baltictours.ee) deals in tours, hotel reservations and plane tickets; Estravel, Vallikraavi 2 (ⓣ 744 0300, ⓦ www.estravel.ee), is the official American Express agent.

South of Tartu

South of Tartu is the one genuinely hilly region in Estonia, a glacier-sculpted landscape of smooth, dome-shaped heights and lake-filled depressions that stretches all the way to the Latvian border. With few summits exceeding 300m above sea level, there's little for ambitious hillwalkers to get excited about, but it's a visually arresting area all the same, with swathes of pine forest, deciduous woodland, arable land and pasture combining to produce a crowded palette of greens. The principal destination in this part of the country is **Otepää**, an endearing small town set among rippling hills that becomes an important centre for both downhill and cross-country skiing in winter. Further south, the larger, but equally laid-back, town of **Võru** has a lakeside beach, but is really a staging-post en route to attractive villages like Haanja and Rõuge.

Otepää

Although known as Estonia's "winter capital", **OTEPÄÄ** is a great place to enjoy the region's landscape of lakes and hillocks all year round. Forty-five kilometres southwest of Tartu and reached by regular bus, this country town has been a favourite holiday retreat for urban Estonians ever since the inter-war years. As the only place in the country with a sufficient number of slopes to make downhill skiing worthwhile, it is much frequented on winter weekends, when the town's pubs and hotel bars take on a new lease of life. The mellow beauty of the surrounding area – and the presence of Lake Pühajärv 3km south of town – has also helped turn Otepää into one of Estonia's most popular inland summer resorts, and there's a correspondingly wide choice of accommodation in and around town.

The town is full to bursting for the **Tartu Marathon** (Ⓦwww.tartumaraton.ee), a cross-country skiing race that takes place on the first or second Sunday in February, starting at the Otepää ski stadium and winding up 63km later in the town of Elva, southwest of Tartu. The same course is pressed into service for the Tartu Cycle Marathon in mid-September.

Otepää's **bus station** is right behind the Town Hall, inside which you'll find a helpful **tourist office** (mid-May to mid-Sept Mon–Fri 9am–6pm, Sat & Sun 10am–3pm; mid-Sept to mid-May Mon–Fri 9am–5pm, Sat 10am–3pm; Ⓣ766 1200, Ⓦwww .otepaa.ee), well stocked with local maps and brochures.

Accommodation

There's a handsome choice of **hotels** in Otepää and the surrounding region, and the tourist office can book you into local **B&Bs** (❶–❷), either in town or in the neighbouring countryside. The price codes listed below refer to the room rates charged during Otepää's two high seasons (Jan–Feb and July–Aug). Some hotels officially drop their prices outside these periods, and others may well be open to bargaining, especially midweek.

Bernhard Kolga 22A Ⓣ766 9600, Ⓦwww .bernhard.ee. *Bernhard* is a classy place 3km southeast of town and a short walk from Lake Pühajärv. It offers balconied en-suite rooms decked out in warm reds and browns, an indoor pool, spa facilities and bike rental. ❺

Karupesa Hotell Tehvandi 1A Ⓣ766 1500, Ⓦwww.karupesa.ee. A medium-sized hotel with all the creature comforts, a five-minute walk south of the town centre. Carpeted en suites come with satellite TV and slightly chintzy decor; some also have views towards Linnamägi and the parish church. As well as restaurant and bar, the hotel also has a tennis court that is turned into an ice-skating rink during the winter. ❹

Kuutsemäe Puhkekeskus Arula village Ⓣ766 9007, Ⓦwww.kuutsemae.ee. A holiday centre 11km southwest of Otepää, close to several downhill runs. Four- to six-person self-catering cottages (from 2500EEK/night) and a range of simple rooms in the main guesthouse. May–Oct ❶; Nov–April ❸

Lille Lille 6B Ⓣ766 3999, Ⓦwww.lillehotel.ee. This small B&B, in a quiet residential area just off the main street, has plain but homely rooms with en-suite facilities and TV. ❸

Nuustaku Nüpli Ⓣ766 8208, Ⓦwww.nuustaku.ee. Formerly known as *Setanta*, this B&B is attached to the popular pub of the same name, perched above the Pühajärv shore – perfect if you want a lakeside location and don't mind staying up as late as the pub's patrons downstairs. En-suite rooms come with woody furnishings; those with lake views cost a little more. ❸

Pühajärve Pühajärve Ⓣ766 5500, Ⓦwww .pyhajarve.com. A fourteenth-century manor house with modern annexes tacked on either side, offering a superb lakeshore position and a variety of on-site spa facilities. Rooms are done out in pleasant pastel colours with chic, Nordic-style furnishings. Standard en suites ❸, doubles with private sauna ❹

Tehvandi Nüpli Ⓣ766 9500, Ⓦwww.tehvandi.ee. A vast concrete horseshoe bearing a distinct resemblance to a bomb shelter, this winter-sports training centre nevertheless has no-frills, en-suite rooms and is right beside the cross-country skiing tracks. ❷

The Town

Otepää's ridge-top town centre looks out towards a series of pudding-shaped hills. The first of these to the east is crowned by the **parish church**, a dainty Baroque edifice whose exterior is decorated with plaques recalling the one historical event for which Otepää is famous: on June 4, 1884, members of Tartu University's Estonian student fraternity came here to consecrate the blue-black-and-white tricolour they had chosen as their banner. Obligingly stitched together by fraternity members' wives and girlfriends, the tricolor was subsequently adopted as the Estonian state flag and Otepää has been enshrined as a low-key patriotic pilgrimage centre ever since. Opposite the church's main door, a memorial honouring those who fell in the 1918–20 War of Independence shares the history of many similar monuments up and down the country – erected in 1928, it was removed by the Soviets in 1950, only to be restored to its rightful place in 1989.

Five hundred metres due south of the parish church, paths curl their way towards the summit of **Linnamägi**, a low wooded hill which served Iron Age Estonian chieftains as a natural stronghold until German crusading knights expelled them from it in the thirteenth century. Apart from a few stretches of reconstructed wall there's nothing much to see here now, but the bare hilltop offers excellent views back towards the church and the rippling hills to the south, where you'll see the summit of Otepää's ski-jump ramp poking up above the trees.

Lake Pühajärv

From the centre of Otepää it's an easy thirty-minute walk to the northern shore of **Lake Pühajärv** – the journey is also made by about twelve daily buses (destination Kariku or Valga), which drop off beside the *Pühajärve* hotel. About 3km from north to south and 1km across, this serene stretch of water occupies an important place in Estonian folklore – according to legend, it was formed by the tears of a mother grieving for five sons killed in battle and its waters have had healing powers ever since – especially if drunk on Midsummer's Eve. Most visitors only get as far as the northern end of the lake, where there's a sizeable sandy beach, pedalos for rent and a couple of waterfront cafés. To get away from the throng it's well worth exploring the thirteen-kilometre-long hiking route that follows the lake's heavily indented shoreline (partly on asphalt road, partly off-road), passing through an enthralling landscape of coastal meadows and golden-brown reed beds. You'll probably catch sight of plenty of grebes and ducks on the way, with sandpipers, kingfishers and herons occasionally making an appearance towards the quieter, southern end of the lake.

For one weekend in mid-July the northern shores of Pühajärv play host to the **Beach Party** (ⓦwww.beachparty.ee), Estonia's biggest pop/rock festival, when bands and DJs perform to up to 20,000 revellers, many of whom pitch tents in the lakeside camp grounds specially set aside for the occasion.

Skiing around Otepää

The main **downhill skiing** areas around Otepää are at Väike Munamägi, 3km southeast of the town centre, and Kuutsemäe, 11km southwest. At both places you'll find an undemanding range of 150- to 250-metre-long slopes served by simple draglifts, and kiosks renting out gear. In addition, there's an impressive network of **cross-country skiing** routes in the area, many of them fanning out from the Winter Sports Stadium on the southeastern outskirts of town. You can rent ski gear here, and from most of the bigger hotels in and around Otepää; ski and snowboard rental costs around 250–450EEK per day.

Eating and drinking

The most central place for an inexpensive meal is *Raekohvik*, behind the Town Hall, dishing out pastries, salads and simple main meals. *Oti Pubi*, occupying a glass-fronted cylinder right by the bus station, does reliable, cheap set lunches as well as more substantial main meals, while *Hermanni*, diagonally opposite the Town Hall on Lipuväljak, offers more of the same in an enjoyable pub-like interior plastered with ski memorabilia. Further afield, *Nuustaku*, on the eastern shore of Pühajärv, is a roomy wooden-floor pub with a big verandah overlooking the lake and serves a good choice of meaty main courses, while the *Karupesa Hotell* (see opposite) and *Bernhard* (see opposite) have more upmarket restaurants.

Võru

Ranged along the eastern edge of Lake Tamula, **Võru** is a quiet provincial town with leafy parks and a stretch of sandy shoreline. Although the town is of relatively recent origin – it was founded by decree of Catherine the Great in 1784, which helps explain the neat, grid-plan appearance – Võru folk are known for their distinct dialect, and consider themselves more outspoken, but also better-tempered, than their compatriots.

The long, straight strip of Jüri tänav runs through the centre, separating the modern, concrete parts of town to the northeast from an altogether more charming neighbourhood of timber houses to the southwest. Heading into the latter along Katariina brings you to the **Võrumaa County Museum** at no. 11 (Võrumaa muuseum; Wed–Sun 11am–6pm; 10EEK), a fairly traditional display with little English-language labelling. The most venerable item in the collection is the skull of a Stone Age woman, thought to date from the fourth millennium BC, making it the oldest human remains to be found in Estonia. There's also a history of the Võru region as told through old photographs, domestic knick-knacks and an at times eccentric choice of artefacts: a display case devoted to the political confusion that followed World War I contains the visiting card of local Bolshevik leader Oskar Leegen and the noose used by German occupying forces to hang him. Inter-war agricultural life is illustrated by the inclusion of a machine that looks like an enormous meat grinder – it's actually a hand-operated contraption for separating the milk from the cream.

At the bottom of Katariina, turn left onto Kreuzwaldi and after ten minutes you come to the **F.R. Kreuzwald Memorial Museum** at no. 31 (F.R. Kreuzwaldi memoriaalmuuseum; Wed–Sun 11am–6pm; 10EEK), occupying the property where the author of Estonia's national epic, *Kalevipoeg* ("Son of Kalev"), practised as a doctor from 1833 until his retirement in 1877. The exhibition opens with a stolid, text-based survey of Kreuzwald's life, and it's something of a relief to move on to the barn in the courtyard, where works of art inspired by his writings are displayed – look out for Kristjan Raud's celebrated illustrations for the inter-war editions of *Kalevipoeg*. Finally, visitors are ushered into the house that also contained Kreuzwald's waiting room, surgery and library. An inkpot in the form of a dragon is the only artefact on display that Kreuzwald actually owned, but the period furnishings convey a strong flavour of nineteenth-century small-town life.

Southwest of here, streets slope down to the sandy shores of **Tamula järv (Lake)** a popular year-round strolling area, with a sandy beach and good views of the low green hills to the southwest. Built to celebrate the millennium, the ultra-modern footbridge at the beach's northern end leads over towards a reed-shrouded park.

Practicalities

Võru's **bus station** is on the northeastern side of town, about five minutes' walk downhill from the main Jüri tänav. The **tourist office**, on the southwestern side of Jüri at Tartu 31 (mid-May to mid-Sept Mon–Fri 9am–6pm, Sat & Sun 10am–3pm; mid-Sept to mid-May Mon–Fri 9am–5pm, Sat 10am–3pm; ℡782 1881, ⊛www.voru.ee), has plenty of local brochures and can help find **bed-and-breakfast accommodation** in the villages south of town. The best of the town's **hotels** is the *Tamula*, right on the beach at Vee 4 (℡783 0430, ⊛www.tamula.ee; ❹), offering swish en suites in a stylish, modern building; ask for one facing the lake. The central *Randuri* guesthouse, above the pub of the same name at Jüri 36 (℡786 8050, ⊛www.randur.ee; ❹), also has comfortable en suites, each – not always authentically – decorated in the style of a different country, including England, Japan, Russia and Egypt. A less central, but very pleasant, option is the pine-shrouded *Kubija*, 5km southeast of town at Männiku 43A (℡782 2341, ⊛www.kubija.ee; ❹), which has appealing rooms with en-suite shower, and a good restaurant. It also allows **camping** in the grounds.

As far as **eating and drinking** are concerned, *Paula*, Jüri 20, may have an underwhelming exterior, but it's one of the best places in town for pastries and cakes. *Katariina*, diagonally opposite the Võrumaa Country Museum at Katariina 4, is a cheap but basic pizzeria; for a filling sit-down meal, head for *Õlle Nr. 17*, Jüri 17, a wonderfully relaxed pub with a wide choice of cheap meat and fish dishes. *Hundijalg*, Jüri 18B, isn't nearly as atmospheric, but serves up decent salads and economical dishes of the day.

The **Võru Folklore Festival** (⊛www.werro.ee/folkloor) attracts a variety of Estonian and international ensembles for three days of parades, dancing and concerts in mid-July.

F. R. Kreuzwald 1803–82

"And what is wrong if an Estonian learns the German language and becomes a learned man, as long as he remains true to his people in his heart… I have been fortunate because it has been so with me and I am really proud that I can call myself an Estonian."

F.R. Kreuzwald

Throughout the nineteenth century, many ambitious Estonians turned their backs on their native heritage, regarding it as a mark of peasant backwardness from which they had been lucky to escape. By providing Estonians with a literary heritage they could be proud of, Friedrich Reinhold Kreuzwald was one of the first to buck this trend.

Kreuzwald was born to a family of Estonian serfs in Jõepere near Rakvere. After doing well at school he was groomed to become one of the first instructors at an Estonian-language teacher-training college. The college never got off the ground, however, and Kreuzwald became a private tutor in Tallinn, then in St Petersburg, saving enough money to enter Tartu University as a student of medicine in 1826. Receiving a Third Class Physician's Licence (insufficient to become a doctor to gentlefolk) he set up a modest practice in Võru in 1833.

Kreuzwald's enthusiasm for indigenous folklore had been nurtured through contact with other young intellectuals at Tartu University, notably Friedrich Robert Faehlmann, who set up the Estonian Learned Society in 1838. Inspired by the example of Elias Lönnrot, who had created a Finnish national epic in the 1830s by bundling together traditional folk tales to form the heroic tale known as the *Kalevala*, Faehlmann came up with the idea of collecting indigenous Estonian material to the same end. The project was enthusiastically taken up by Kreuzwald, and *Kalevipoeg* ("Son of Kalev") was the result.

Published as a series of booklets in Tartu between 1857 and 1859, *Kalevipoeg* immediately made Kreuzwald's reputation and has enjoyed an almost sacred position in Estonian culture ever since. It was initially believed that *Kalevipoeg* was a compilation of genuine folk tales – it only emerged later that Kreuzwald had made most of the story up, by which time Estonian intellectuals had already embraced the epic and were unwilling to question its value.

Despite the success of *Kalevipoeg* among educated Estonians, Kreuzwald never earned much from writing it and came to resent contemporaries like Johann Woldemar Jannsen (editor of *Postimees*; see p.143), who managed to make a living from journalism, while the great intellectual Kreutzwald continued to languish as a country doctor in Võru. Despite remaining aloof from the emerging cultural scene in Tartu and Tallinn, Kreuzwald exerted a strong influence over young, educated Estonians – not least Jannsen's poetry-writing daughter Lydia Koidula. Koidula saw the author of *Kalevipoeg* as her mentor, while Kreuzwald regarded Koidula as an intriguing prodigy who looked set to continue the literary upsurge his own work had started. The pair exchanged over ninety letters from 1867 onwards, a touchingly intimate correspondence full of mutual intellectual admiration. When Koidula married Eduard Michelson – a Latvian doctor who didn't speak Estonian – in 1873, Kreuzwald regarded it as a betrayal of her cultural mission, and never wrote to her again.

Suur-Munamägi and around

Twelve kilometres south of Võru, the wooded dome of **Suur-Munamägi** ("Great Egg Hill") would barely register as a bump in most other European countries, but at 318m above sea level it's the highest point in the Baltic States – and a popular focus for Estonian day-trippers. The surrounding landscape of farmsteads, hump-backed hills and forests is as attractive as any in the region, and the country lanes are perfect for cycle rides and undemanding hikes. There's a lot of off-the-beaten-track **bed-and-breakfast accommodation** in the area if you want to stay – it's best to ask the tourist offices in Võru (see p.159) or Rõuge (see below) to reserve a place for you, as knowledge of English is patchy. Regular **buses** make their way from Võru to **HAANJA**, an uneventful village, 1km north of the hill. There's also one daily bus to Haanja from Tallinn (passing through Tartu on the way), which arrives in the early afternoon and heads back again after about ninety minutes – giving you ample time to clamber up Suur-Munamägi and down again.

The path to Suur-Munamägi's summit heads uphill about 1km south of Haanja, starting from a roadside monument recording an episode from the War of Independence, when a clash with Bolsheviks on March 20, 1919, left seven Estonians dead. It takes only five minutes to reach the fir-tree-carpeted hilltop, where a 1939 **Art Deco Viewing Tower** (Vaatetorn; mid-April to Sept daily 10am–8pm; Oct Sat & Sun 10am–5pm; mid-Nov to mid-April Sat & Sun noon–3pm; 60EEK to take the elevator, 30EEK to walk up the steps) offers a superb panorama of the surrounding countryside.

Rõuge

Nine kilometres west of Haanja, **RÕUGE** is famous for being one of Estonia's most picturesque villages, its buildings scattered haphazardly around the shores of Rõuge Suurjärv Lake – which, at 38m, is the deepest in the country. Behind the whitewashed, eighteenth-century church stretches the 300-metre-long Ööbikuorg ("Valley of Nightingales", so-called because it's a favourite nesting area of the birds in spring), an eerily self-contained, steep-sided vale that seems a world away from the flatlands that make up most of Estonia.

The **tourist office**, occupying a timber hut at Haanja mnt 1 (☏785 9245, ⊛www .rauge.ee), can fix you up with farmhouse **accommodation**; otherwise try *Suurjärve Külalistemaja*, a tastefully renovated farmstead at Metsa 5 (☏785 9273, ⊛www.hot .ee/maremajutus; ➋), which has numerous simply decorated rooms with shared facilities, more modern en suites and a log-built smoke sauna in the garden (150EEK/ hour). If you've got your own transport, you can choose from plenty of **B&Bs** within a short drive of Rõuge, including the *Lätte Turismitalu*, 5km northwest near Nursi village (☏786 0706, ⊛www.hot.ee/lattetalu; ➋), with rustic wood-panelled rooms in the main house or its two annexes, right beside Kahvila Lake; and the *Kanarbiku Tourist Farm* (☏785 9373, ⊛www.hot.ee/aretalu; ➊), 4km west, offering rooms in a snug farmhouse and camping in the garden (50EEK per person).

Lake Peipsi

Thirty kilometres east of Tartu, **Lake Peipsi**, measuring 3555 square kilometres, forms a large stretch of Estonia's border with Russia. Despite ranking as the fifth-biggest lake in Europe, Lake Peipsi is a low-key area of sleepy fishing settlements, thick reed beds and quiet, sandy beaches, offering little in the way of tourist facilities. If you have a taste for simple rusticity, however, you'll find a visit here rewarding, not least because of Lake Peipsi's ethnographic peculiarities. Many of the shoreline villages are home to members of the Russian Orthodox sect of **Old Believers**, who came here in the early eighteenth century to escape persecution at home and settled down to catch fish and grow onions. Renowned for their surviving stock of wooden houses and timber churches, Old Believer settlements like Nina, Kasepää, Varnja, and most of all **Kolkja**, exude an untroubled tranquillity that probably hasn't changed much since the community first arrived.

Lake Peipsi is easy to access **from Tartu**: the main road passes through **Kallaste**, the chief settlement and service centre on the central part of the lake, before wheeling north towards Narva (see p.138). The principal Old Believer villages are a short detour away from this route, but a handful of Kallaste-bound buses pass through Kolkja en route.

About 35km from Tartu, the Kallaste-bound road passes through the village of **KOOSA**, where an eastbound turn-off leads to a string of Old Believer villages occupying a reedy stretch of the Lake Peipsi shoreline. The first of these is **VARNJA**, a

The Old Believers

The origins of the Old Believers – or *Staroviertsii* as they are known in Russian – lie in the liturgical reforms introduced into the Russian Orthodox Church by Nikon, the mid-seventeenth-century patriarch of Moscow. Faced with the task of systematizing the divergent liturgical texts and practices then in use in the national church, Nikon opted to comply with the dominant Greek practices of the time, such as the use of three fingers instead of two when making the sign of the cross and the use of Greek ecclesiastical dress. Priests who opposed the reforms were removed from office, but many of their congregations persisted with the old practices and were dubbed "Old Believers" by a church hierarchy eager to see them marginalized. Peter the Great was particularly keen to get rid of them and it was under his rule that groups of Old Believers moved to Lake Peipsi – and other areas on the western fringes of the empire – in the hope that here at least they would be left alone to practise their religion as they wished. In liturgical matters, the Old Believers are egalitarian, rejecting the ecclesiastical hierarchy of conventional Orthodoxy, choosing clergy from among the local community rather than relying on a priesthood. Services are conducted in Old Church Slavonic – the medieval tongue into which the Scriptures were originally translated – rather than in modern Russian.

An estimated 15,000 Old Believers still live in Estonia, most of whom remain in the Lake Peipsi region. Strict adherence to their beliefs has traditionally prevented them from being assimilated by post-World War II Russian migrants, although their numbers are now in decline – largely owing to the migration of the young to the towns and their intermarriage with other groups.

largely nondescript huddle of houses grouped around a church with a tower shaped like a spear. **KASEPÄÄ**, 3km up the shore to the north, is more picturesque, its jauntily pea-green church surrounded by a thicket of graveyard crosses. The northern end of Kasepää runs imperceptibly into **KOLKJA**, a four-kilometre shoreline stretch of brightly painted wooden houses, most of which are surrounded by neat onion plots. Set back from the shore in the modern part of the village, the **Museum of Old Believers** (☎745 3431; donation requested) occupies a back room of the village school. Unfortunately, it's only open if you phone in advance, and the curator doesn't speak English, though staff at Tartu tourist office (see p.147) will arrange things for you if you ask. Inside lies an incandescent display of beautifully embroidered traditional costumes, including some especially attractive pink caftans – which turn out to be burial shrouds. There's a cabinet full of liturgical books in Old Church Slavonic – a handful of local schoolchildren still receive lessons in the language.

There's nowhere **to stay** in Kolkja, but the *Kala-ja Sibula* **restaurant**, midway between the museum and the lakeshore, serves up *sudak* (pike-perch) and other local fish, often garnished with sauces featuring the local onions.

Towards Kallaste

Back on the main Tartu–Kallaste road, 4km northeast of Koosa, the village of **RUPSI**, provides an attractive setting for the **Juhan Liiv Museum** (May–Sept Tues–Sat 9am–7pm; Oct–April Tues–Sat 9am–4pm; 20EEK), in a timber farmstead just beside the main road. The author of some notoriously dour and depressing verse, Liiv (1864–1913) eventually died of pneumonia after being turfed off a train to Warsaw for travelling without a ticket – he was suffering from the delusion that he was descended from the Polish royal family at the time. As well as facsimile manuscripts and first editions, there's a pleasing array of rustic nineteenth-century furnishings inside. Some five kilometres up the road from Rupsi, the village of **ALATSKIVI**, served by Tartu–Kallaste buses, is worth a brief stop on account of its dreamily neo-medieval **Manor House**, built by Baron Arved von Nolckens in the 1880s and said to be modelled on Balmoral – hence the pointy-headed turrets. The interior is currently being restored and will be open to visitors at some point in the future. For restful **bed-and-breakfast accommodation**, try *Hirveaia*, near the Manor House at Hirveaia 4 (ⓣ745 3837, ⓔhirveaia@hot.ee; ❷) – they also have a few rooms in the village of Nina, 4km east on the shores of the lake.

Kallaste

Beyond Alatskivi, the road runs parallel to the lakeshore, passing through the western suburbs of **KALLASTE** before speeding north towards Narva. The main fishing port on this part of the lake, Kallaste looks disconcertingly like a grey, industrial settlement at first sight, although there's something of an old quarter on the south side of town, where you'll find a knot of cobbled alleyways edged with one-storey timber houses and a hilltop cemetery overlooking the lake. Kallaste's main attraction for local holiday-makers, though, is its superb sandy **beach**, backed by brooding sandstone cliffs. There's a pair of supermarkets in the town centre, and a couple of beachside bars open up in summer to cater for trippers.

Piirisaar

Lying off the shores of Lake Peipsi, some 40km due east of Tartu, **Piirisaar** is a small, marshy island (only 3.5km across at its widest), whose inhabitants, like those of Kolkja, earn a living from fishing and growing onions. A mixture of Estonian Lutherans and Russian Old Believers, they're scattered among three small villages, Piiri, Tooni and Saare – each characterized by oblong timber houses and quiet, grassed-over streets. It's a marvellous place for a rustic ramble and draws its fair share of birdwatchers in spring as the island is an important staging-post for migrating birds, especially mute swans and white-tailed eagles.

From mid-May to mid-September there are a number of ways of reaching Piirissaar: by hydrofoil from Tartu (Fri, Sat & Sun; note that the Friday service comes straight back without giving you time to look around) and from Värska Sanatorium outside Värska (see opposite; Sat only). Details of these services can be obtained from Tartu Sadam, Soola 5 (ⓣ734 0026, ⓦwww.transcom.ee/tartusadam).

Setumaa

East of Võru, rolling hills give way to a more gently undulating landscape, with broad pastures and arable land broken up by occasional wedges of forest. This southeastern corner of the country is known as **Setumaa** or "land of the Setu" – a branch of the Estonian nation that has preserved distinctive ethnographical features and an archaic dialect. The historic isolation of the **Setu** from the rest of the country owes much to the fact that the region was under the jurisdiction of the Russian principalities of Pskov and Novgorod during the Middle Ages and, unlike the rest of Estonia, was Christianized by the eastern Orthodox Church.

The grammar and pronunciation of the Setu dialect is sufficiently close to that of the nearby Võru region for local linguists to group the two together, claiming the existence of a Võro-Seto language which is distinct from modern Estonian. Although Võro-Seto is yet to be officially recognized, Estonian society is much more tolerant towards this kind of regional particularism than it was during the Soviet period – when cultural and linguistic unity was considered essential to the nation's survival. Indeed, the Setu region is increasingly seen as a source of ethnographic riches, not least because of the survival of archaic **folk-singing** techniques that have died out elsewhere. Often featuring partly improvised epic narratives, Setu songs or *leelos* are usually sung by a group of five or six women, one of whom sings a semitone higher than the others – producing a discordant polyphony which once heard is never forgotten. Traditional Setu dress is also distinctive, with dark red the dominant colour, augmented by plenty of heavy, metal jewellery – notably the vast metal breastplates worn by unmarried women.

What makes the Setu heritage particularly precious to present-day Estonia is the fact that of the twelve *nulks*, or tribal units, into which Setumaa is divided, four lie across the border in the Russian Federation – a division made all the more galling by the knowledge that they were all part of Estonia until the Soviets arbitrarily re-drew the frontier in 1940. Setumaa's main market centre, **Petchory** (Petseri in Estonian), now lies 3km on the wrong side of the border, leaving the Estonian Setu without an urban focus. Nowadays, the main centres of Setu culture are the villages of **Obinitsa** (served by regular buses from Võru) and **Värska** (reached by bus from Tartu) – if only because both places possess museums and singing groups, keeping the local folklore alive.

Värska

Ninety kilometres southeast of Tartu, **VÄRSKA** is a pleasant, forest-shrouded village on the southwestern shores of Lake Pihkva, a southern extension of Lake Peipsi. Set in an attractive, reedy landscape frequented by herons and other waterfowl, it's a relatively undramatic place, its only real sight being the rather charming **Setu Farm Museum** at Pikk 40 (May–Sept daily 10am–5pm; Oct–April Tues–Sat 10am–4pm; ☎505 4673, ⓦwww.hot.ee/setomuuseum; 10EEK). It has a collection of old tools, farm machinery, textiles and traditional handicrafts from the end of the nineteenth century, housed in original reed-thatched buildings around a common yard. It also offers a number of traditional cookery or handicraft workshops.

Värska's **tourist office**, on the main street at Pikk 12 (mid-May to mid-Sept daily 10am–6pm; mid-Sept to mid-May Mon–Fri 8.30am–4.30pm; ☎796 4782, ⓦwww .verska.ee), can advise on local **B&B** possibilities. Other options include the *Hirvemäe Holiday Centre*, Silla 2A (☎797 6105, ⓦwww.hirvemae.ee; ❷), offering modern en suites with pine furnishings and attic ceilings. You can **camp** in the grounds for 50EEK per tent, plus 25EEK per vehicle. Three kilometres north of town, the Värska Sanatorium (☎799 3901, ⓦwww.spavarska.ee; ❸) offers prim en suites and a range of spa treatments good for respiratory complaints, arthritis and gastric ulcers. The café of the *Hirvemäe Holiday Centre* is the best place to **eat**, although it closes at 4 or 5pm out of season. The quay outside Värska Sanatorium is the departure point for weekend hydrofoil **trips to the island of Piirisaar** (see opposite).

Obinitsa

The quiet agricultural settlement of **OBINITSA** lies 20km southwest of Värska and 25km east of Võru. Buses from Võru pick up and drop off just south of the staggered central crossroads, where a signed alley leads east to the **Setu Museum House** (Seto muuseumitare; mid-May to mid-Sept Mon–Fri 10am–5pm, Sat & Sun 11am–5pm; mid-Sept to mid-May Mon–Fri 10am–5pm; 10EEK). Housed in a traditional timber building, the museum gives an insight into Setu family life in the 1920s–40s, with beautiful embroidered folk costumes, religious icons and intricate handicrafts. To sample a traditional Setu meal, contact the Obinitsa tourist office inside the museum in advance (same times; ☎785 4190, ⓦwww.setomaa.ee).

If you continue east from here, you'll arrive after five minutes at an artificial lake with a beach. Overlooking the lake from its unmissable hillside position is the granite statue of the **Setu Song-Mother** (Setu Lauluimä), a stylized tribute to the female singers who have kept the tradition of epic narrative songs alive. Scattered in the grass around the statue are boulders engraved with the names of individual performers who were bestowed with the honorific title of Lauluimä during their lifetime, notably Miko Ode, Irõ Matrina and Hilane Taarka, who did more than most to preserve Setu traditions into the modern age. About 500m north of the central crossroads is Obinitsa's wooden **church**, built in 1905 and largely destroyed after World War II, but returned to use in the early 1950s, when the communist authorities turned a blind eye to its reconstruction. **Transfiguration Day** (Paasapäev) on August 6 is one of the biggest feast days in Setumaa: thousands of Orthodox descend on Obinitsa church to commemorate the dead, and local families tuck into picnics on top of their ancestors' graves in the adjoining cemetery.

Piusa Sand Caves

The **Piusa Sand Caves**, one of the country's more offbeat tourist attractions, lie 5km north of Obinitsa. They're relatively easy to find: the road north from Obinitsa church forges through an entrancing landscape of farmland, forest and farmsteads before passing over the Piusa River and under the rail tracks, just beyond which a sign on the right reading "Piusa koopad" directs you to the caves themselves. The caves (really a single chamber rather than a network of caverns) were excavated between 1922 and 1970 to extract sand for use in the glassmaking industry. The area became a protected nature reserve in 1999, largely owing to the caves' importance as a habitat for bats – the creatures have flourished since the end of mining activities, and Piusa now harbours one of the biggest colonies in the Baltics. You're free to enter the excavations at any time, although some sections are boarded off for fear of cave-ins. Inside, there's not a great deal to see or explore, but it's a marvellously atmos-

△ Piusa Sand Caves

pheric place, its rows of sand-carved arches bringing to mind some kind of abandoned subterranean cathedral. The section nearest the entrance is hauntingly illuminated by the daylight leaking in from outside; if you want to venture further in you'll need to bring a torch. Round the back of the caves, paths lead around the edges of the Piusa Sandpit (Piusa liivakarjäär), a Sahara-like expanse of sand edged by rare grasses and shrubs.

Travel details

Trains

Narva to: St Petersburg (3 weekly; 3hr 30min).
Tallinn to: Narva (2 daily; 3hr 30min); Tartu (4 daily; 3hr 30min).

Buses

Narva to: Narva-Jõesuu (every 20–30min; 20min); Otepää (2 daily; 4hr 30min); Rakvere (7 daily; 2hr 20min); Sillamäe (hourly; 30–40min); Tartu (11 daily; 2hr 50min–3hr 35min).
Otepää to: Narva (2 daily; 4hr 30min); Põlva (1 daily; 1hr 10min); Tallinn (2 daily; 3hr 30min); Tartu (10 daily; 1hr 10min–2hr); Võru (3 daily; 1hr 10min).
Rakvere to: Käsmu (Mon–Fri 4 daily, Sat 3 daily, Sun 2 daily; 1hr 15min); Narva (7 daily; 2hr 20min); Palmse (Mon, Wed, Fri & Sun 1 daily; 40min); Võsu (Mon–Fri 4 daily, Sat 3 daily, Sun 2 daily; 1hr).
Tallinn to: Altja (2 daily; 1hr 35min); Haanja (1 daily; 4hr); Käsmu (1 daily; 1hr 30min); Narva (hourly; 3hr 40min); Tartu (every 30min; 2hr 20min–3hr); Võsu (Mon–Thurs & Sat 3 daily, Fri & Sun 4 daily; 1hr 15min).

Tartu to: Haanja (2 daily; 1hr 30min); Kallaste (Mon–Fri 5 daily, Sat & Sun 3 daily; 1hr 20min–1hr 50min); Käsmu (mid-May to mid-Sept 1 daily, 2hr 50min); Kolkja (Mon–Fri 4 daily, Sat 1 daily; Sun 2 daily; 1hr 20min); Kuressaare (2–3 daily; 6hr); Narva-Jõesuu (2 daily; 3hr 30min); Otepää (10 daily; 1hr 10min–2hr); Põlva (10 daily; 1hr 10min–2hr); Rakvere (8 daily; 2hr 10min–3hr); Rapina (4 daily; 1hr 15min); Rõuge (2 daily; 2hr); Sillamäe (3 daily; 2hr 30min); Värska (3 daily; 2hr); Viljandi (8 daily; 1hr–1hr 20min); Võsu (mid-May to mid-Sept 1 daily; 2hr 40min).
Võru to: Haanja (5 daily; 25min); Obinitsa (Mon–Sat 4 daily, Sun 3 daily; 40min–1hr 30min); Põlva (10 daily; 40min); Rõuge (Mon–Fri 8 daily, Sat & Sun 5 daily; 25min); Tallinn (12 daily; 3hr 45min); Tartu (every 30min–1hr; 1hr 20min).

International buses

Narva to: St Petersburg (7 daily; 3hr).
Tartu to: Moscow (4 weekly; 14hr); St Petersburg (1 daily; 6hr).

2

Latvia

Latvia highlights

※ Rīga Old Town A nest of narrow streets lined with an engaging ensemble of buildings reflecting eight centuries of history. See p.190

※ Art Nouveau Architecture, Rīga Nymphs, caryatids and a host of other creatures peer down from the richly ornamented facades of Rīga's nineteenth-century centre. See p.204

※ Rundāle A veritable Versailles of the north, this stupendous eighteenth-century palace is filled to the rafters with sumptuous Baroque and Rococo furnishings. See p.226

※ Cape Kolka A hauntingly beautiful horn of land extending into the Baltic Sea and flanked by semi-deserted sandy beaches. See p.232

※ Kuldīga An attractive huddle of half-timbered houses set beside the foaming River Venta, Kuldīga represents small-town Latvia at its most picturesque. See p.239

※ Gauja National Park The River Gauja cuts its way through pine-carpeted sandstone hills to create this paradise for hikers, canoeists and nature lovers. See p.257

※ Latgale A sparsely populated area of rustic villages and rolling hills, this is one of the most delightful rural landscapes in the region. See p.273

△ The River Gauja

Introduction and basics

Contemporary Latvia presents two very contrasting faces to visitors. The first is provided by the bustling, million-strong capital city of Rīga, where several centuries of fine architecture rub shoulders with a brash, rapidly developing commercial culture. Outside Rīga, however, Latvia comes across rather differently, as a restful country of market towns, farmsteads, forests and bogs. The Latvian landscape also offers stately homes, ruined castles and historic churches aplenty, although most of these bear witness to the waves of foreign occupiers who put down roots in Latvian soil. A Baltic tribe closely related to their Lithuanian neighbours, the Latvians were overwhelmed at the start of the thirteenth century by German crusading knights, who massacred and enslaved them in the name of Christianity. The Germans continued to dominate both land and trade even after political control passed to the Polish-Lithuanian Commonwealth, then Sweden and finally Russia. Despite a brief period of independence between 1918 and 1940, Russian power returned in 1940 when all three Baltic republics were annexed by the Soviet Union. Latvian language and culture have re-established themselves in the years following the regaining of independence in 1991, although certain aspects of the Soviet legacy still remain. Most obvious of these is the presence of a large Russian minority on Latvian soil: encouraged to settle here as industrial workers in the 1950s and 1960s, their descendants now make up an estimated thirty percent of the population.

Where to go

The most obvious destination in Latvia is its capital, **Rīga**, a boisterous, mercantile city whose Gothic red-brick heart is girdled by one of the richest collections of Art Nouveau apartment blocks anywhere in Europe. The Latvian capital is also known for its varied and often wild nightlife, and offers easy access to the sands of **Jūrmala**, a seaside suburb northwest of the city.

One of the most scenic stretches of the Latvian countryside can be found just east of Rīga, where the **River Gauja** winds its way through wooded sandstone hills, passing medieval castles at **Sigulda** and **Cēsis** en route.

Further southeast, Latvia's gritty second city **Daugavpils** is very much an acquired taste, but it does possess an enchanting rustic hinterland in the shape of **Latgale**, a region of rippling hills and beguiling villages, of which **Aglona** – Latvia's most popular Catholic pilgrimage centre – is the most obvious target.

South of Rīga lies a flat-as-a-pancake region of rich farmland, dotted with the country palaces of the eighteenth-century Baltic aristocracy, with the Rococo finery of **Rundāle Palace** making a rewarding daytrip from the capital. On the west coast, the port city of **Ventspils** offers museum attractions and sandy beaches, although **Liepāja** offers more in terms of historical heritage and night-time diversions. Just inland, the riverside settlement of **Kuldīga** can't be beaten for countryside charm. For the best in deserted beaches, dunes and sea views, head for **Cape Kolka** in the far northwest.

Getting around

Latvia's public transport network is, on the whole, efficient and comprehensive. Travelling by **bus** is generally slightly quicker, but also a little more expensive, than by **train**. For details of travelling between Latvia and the other Baltic States, see p.36.

Buses

Latvia is covered by a comprehensive bus network; frequent services run between the

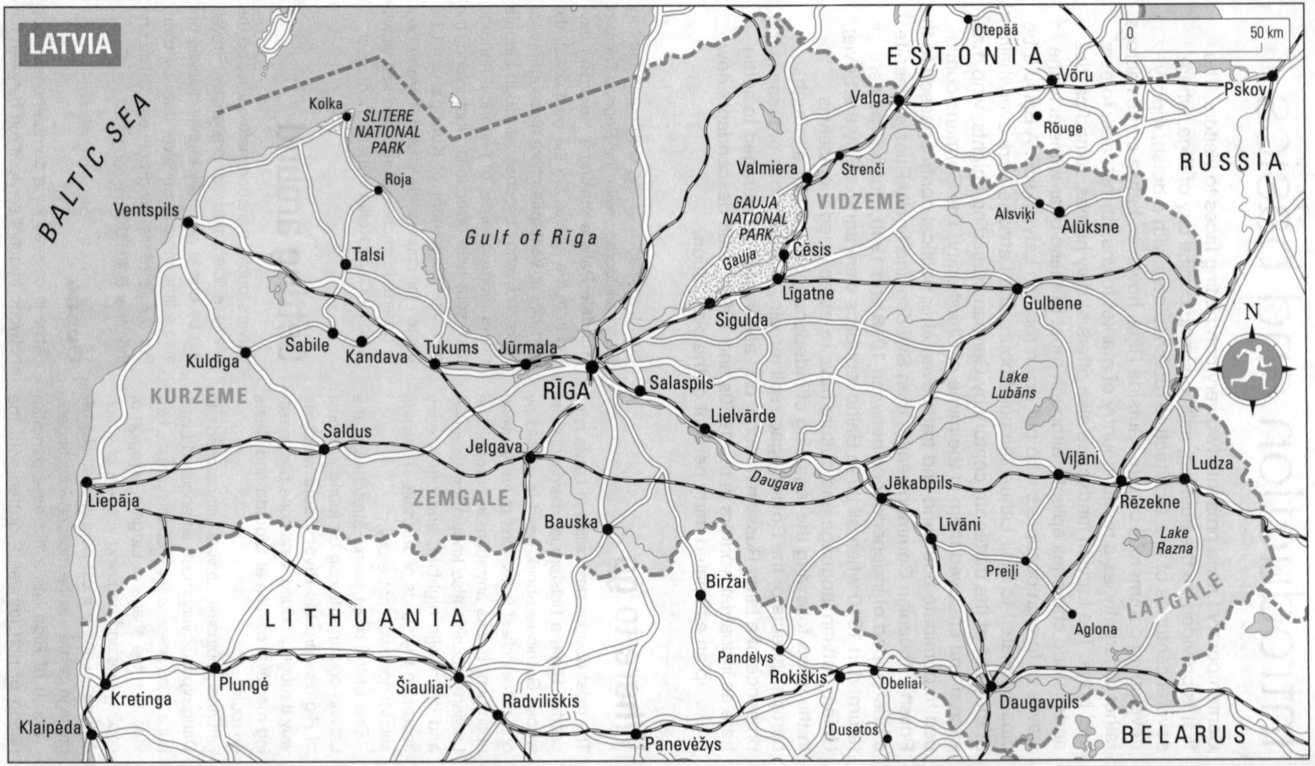
LATVIA
BALTIC SEA
Gulf of Rīga
ESTONIA
RUSSIA
BELARUS
LITHUANIA
KURZEME
ZEMGALE
VIDZEME
LATGALE
0
50 km
N
Otepää
Võru
Pskov
Valga
Rõuge
Valmiera
Strenči
GAUJA NATIONAL PARK
Gauja
Cēsis
Alsviķi
Alūksne
Līgatne
Gulbene
Sigulda
Kolka
SLITERE NATIONAL PARK
Roja
Ventspils
Talsi
Sabile
Kandava
Kuldīga
Tukums
Jūrmala
RĪGA
Salaspils
Lake Lubāns
Lielvārde
Saldus
Jelgava
Viļāni
Ludza
Daugava
Jēkabpils
Rēzekne
Liepāja
Bauska
Līvāni
Lake Razna
Preiļi
Biržai
Aglona
Pandėlys
Plungė
Šiauliai
Rokiškis
Obeliai
Kretinga
Radviliškis
Daugavpils
Klaipėda
Panevėžys
Dusetos

main cities and even the smallest villages are served by at least one bus a day. Buses on the intercity routes are reasonably comfortable; those plying rural routes may well be ancient contraptions with sagging seats. At the bigger bus stations **tickets** should be bought in advance wherever possible; if you're catching the bus from an intermediate stop-off rather than its point of origin, you'll have to pay the driver. Normally **luggage** is taken on board, though if you have a particularly large bag you may have to pay extra to have it stowed in the luggage compartment.

Departure boards at bus stations are fairly easy to understand, with most of the terminology the same as that used in train stations (see below). **Express buses** are usually shown on timetables with the letter "E"; buses that only travel on a certain day of the week are marked with an initial denoting the day in question ("P" means *pirmdiena* or Monday, for example; see p.471 for a full list of days in Latvian).

Information provided in bus stations rarely covers the times of return buses from the particular place you're heading for, making it difficult to plan day-trips with any certainty – a problem made worse by the fact that station staff outside Rīga rarely speak any English. If in doubt, telephone the tourist office of the place you're aiming for and ask them for advice on how to get there and back – they're usually quite happy to help. Timetable information is available on Ⓦwww.118.lv – although it's in Latvian only for the time being.

Trains

Latvia's train network is exceedingly useful if you're making short trips in and around the Rīga region: there are regular services to Jūrmala, the Gauja National Park and the Daugava Valley towns, putting lots of destinations within comfortable day-trip range. Most carriages feature hard, wooden seating, so bring a cushion if you're accustomed to travelling in comfort. Long-distance journeys are in any case better attempted by bus: trains from Rīga to the western Latvian cities of Liepāja and Ventspils have been discontinued, and services to the southeastern urban centres of Daugavpils and Rēzekne take three to four hours to arrive and don't

have a buffet car – so you'll need to bring your own food and drink.

Train **tickets** (*biļete*) should be bought in advance if the ticket office is open – if not, pay the conductor. All but the smallest of train stations will have the **timetable** (*kustības saraksts*) written up on a board – departures are listed under *atiešana* or *atiet*, arrivals under *pienākšana* or *pienāk*. *Darbdienās* means on working days, *brīvdienās* or *svētdienās* means on Sundays and public holidays; the words *nepietur stacijās* mean "doesn't stop at". Trains with four-digit route numbers stop at virtually every halt; those with three-digit route numbers are "fast" trains that miss some of the smaller stations out – although even these are unlikely to travel at speeds exceeding 60km/hr.

Driving

Road conditions in Latvia can vary dramatically. There are no two-lane highways, apart from a brief stretch between Rīga and Jūrmala. Roads linking major towns are usually in a reasonable state, but off the beaten track, conditions deteriorate rapidly. The biggest hazard is reckless drivers – Latvia's road casualty rate is shocking.

To bring a car into Latvia you need a valid Green Card or third-party insurance policy. **Speed limits** are 50kph in built-up areas, 90kph on the open road and 100kph on highways. In towns it's forbidden to overtake stationary trams. The wearing of seatbelts is compulsory, and headlights should be switched on at all times. It's illegal to drive with more than 0.05 milligrams of alcohol in the blood (which is roughly equivalent to one and a half pints of beer).

Though most towns and major highways are well provided with round-the-clock **petrol stations** (*degvielas stacija*), there are few in rural areas – carry a spare can. Petrol costs around €1/£0.70/$1.40 for a litre.

Accommodation

The last decade has seen a hotel-building boom in Rīga, ensuring that the mid-range and business ends of the market are increasingly well catered for. There's a shortage of budget hotels, but plenty of B&Bs and

Accommodation price codes

The hotels and guesthouses listed in the Latvian chapters of this guide have been graded according to the following price bands, based on the cost of the least expensive double room in summer.

❶ Under 18Ls
❷ 18–24 Ls
❸ 24–32 Ls
❹ 32–44 Ls
❺ 44–60 Ls
❻ 60–80 Ls
❼ 80–120 Ls
❽ Over 120 Ls

backpacker-oriented hostels have emerged to fill the gap. Outside the capital things are less predictable, although the number of affordable B&Bs and rural homestays is on the increase, and there are plenty of idyllic camping opportunities if you don't mind roughing it a bit.

Hotels

Latvian hotels (*viesnīcas*) are yet to be graded according to the international five-star system, and room prices are not always an accurate indication of the quality of accommodation you're going to get – if you want extras like satellite TV and full-size bathtubs, it always pays to ask before making a reservation.

In general, the **cheapest hotels** tend to be Soviet-era establishments that haven't been refurbished for a couple of decades; usually these come with gloomy furnishings and en-suite shower and WC, although a few places have a handful of cheaper rooms with shared toilet facilities in the hallway. For a double in this type of hotel you'd expect to pay 25–35Ls in Rīga, 15–20Ls in the provinces.

In the capital at least, there's a broad range of **mid-price hotels** – either reconditioned Soviet-era places or new establishments built in the last ten years – offering plush carpets, TV and a modern bathroom. There's a growing number of such establishments in provincial cities and popular areas like Jūrmala and the Gauja Valley. A double will cost 60–80Ls in the capital, 30–40Ls elsewhere.

Latvia can also claim a good choice of **upmarket hotels** that would merit four or more stars in any other European country, and charge room rates to match; for the time being, these are all limited to the capital. Some hotels in Rīga offer cut-price rates at weekends and in off-season periods,

such as autumn and early spring – it always pays to ask.

Guesthouses and rural homestays

Outside the big cities there's an increasing number of family-run places calling themselves a **guesthouse**, or *viesu nams*. Standards vary widely from place to place – some guesthouses are small hotels in all but name, while others are simply suburban houses or rural farmsteads that rent out rooms and are similar to B&Bs. They're usually a good deal cheaper than mid-range hotels and offer a friendlier, more intimate atmosphere to boot.

Most tourist offices outside Rīga will have a list of local households offering **bed-and-breakfast** accommodation, and in most cases will make reservations on your behalf – the hosts themselves rarely speak much English. Many of these B&Bs are in rural areas and may indeed be run by a farming family – as such they represent a great way to experience the countryside, but you'll probably need your own transport to make full use of them. One agency that deals exclusively with **rural homestays** and can fix up your whole holiday in advance is Lauku ceļotajs, Kuģu 11, Rīga (①6761 7600, ⓦwww.celotajs.lv).

Hostels and private rooms

There's an impressive array of backpacker-friendly **hostels** in Rīga, although they are less easy to find outside the capital. Conditions can be cramped in summer, but prices – at 9–10Ls a bed – are reasonable.

In Rīga, **private rooms** rented out by locals with flat-space to spare are another budget option. Most of these are located in ageing apartment blocks and you'll probably be sharing your host's bathroom – but at 15–20Ls per person they're better value than many of the city's hotels. See the Rīga chapter for further information.

Campsites

The most basic form of campsite in Latvia is a **tent site** (telšu vieta), which, as its name suggests, is basically a meadow where you're allowed to pitch a tent – additional facilities such as earth toilets or a water tap may or may not be provided. A nominal fee of 0.50–1Ls is charged for using these places. Several national parks (notably the Gauja National Park; see p.257) provide tent sites free of charge, and even supply free wood for bonfires – the idea being that this prevents campers from illegally chopping timber themselves.

One step up from a telšu vieta is a **kempings** (campsite), where – alongside tent and caravan space – accommodation consists of two- or four-person cabins, with shared toilets and washing facilities. On average, a two-person cabin costs 15–20Ls.

Food and drink

Traditionally, Latvian cuisine is rich in meat and dairy products, with pork, cheese and sour cream forming the mainstay of most main courses. In recent years, however, chicken, fish and fresh salads have started appearing on menus, providing some respite for those who haven't just come to the Baltics to bulk up on fatty food. As you'd expect, Rīga boasts the best range of restaurants, cafés, bars and pubs, and can also lay claim to a growing stable of ethnic-influenced eateries; the further away you travel from the capital, the narrower the choice, with most establishments concentrating on a tried-and-tested repertoire of traditional Latvian fare.

Where to eat

The word restorāns (restaurant) usually denotes a smartish, starched-tablecloth establishment – and although there are plenty of these in Rīga, many Latvians prefer to eat in the more informal (and cheaper) surroundings of a krogs or krodziņš (pub-like

taverns often decked out in folksy wooden furnishings), or in a kafejnīca (a catch-all term covering anything from a greasy spoon to an elegant coffee-and-cakes café). Many kafejnīcas are in fact sizeable, self-service restaurants in which a handsome selection of traditional eats is displayed at the counter and you simply point to what you want – an excellent way to fill up at an affordable price.

Snacks and starters

Certain Latvian staples crop up on most menus, and function rather well as snacks, starters, quick lunches – or simply an accompaniment to a round of drinks. An ever-present staple in just about all kafejnīcas, restaurants and supermarket deli counters is rasols, a salad containing diced meat, herring, potatoes, peas, carrots and gherkin – all drenched in a mixture of sour cream and mayonnaise. Other ubiquitous snacks include pīrāgi or pīradziņi (parcels of dough with various stuffings, usually cabbage and/or bacon bits), and pelmeņi (meat-filled pockets of pastry akin to ravioli). Also common are savoury pancakes (pankūkas), usually filled with cheese or ham – kartupeļu pankūkas are potato pancakes.

One typically Latvian dish that is frequently ordered alongside a round of beers but works perfectly well as a snack in its own right is pelēkie zirņi (mushy grey peas cooked in smoky-bacon fat). Zirņu pikas, in which peas and bacon bits are mashed and moulded into balls, is a posher variation on the same theme. Other indigenous specialities include pork in aspic (cūkas galerts) and smoked sausage (žāvēta desa). Some Baltic Sea fish dishes likely to find their way onto starter menus include sprats with onions (šprotes ar sēpoliem), herring (siļķe) and fried, smoked or salted eel (zutis). Popular soups (zupas) include kāpostu zupa or cabbage soup, and soļanka, a meat, vegetable and gherkin broth of Russian origin.

Whatever you order it will come with several slices of bread (maize), including some of the delicious, dark rye bread (rupjmaize) for which the Baltic region is famed.

Main courses

A main course based on **meat** (gaļa) usually comes in the form either of a fileja (fillet) or *karbonāde* (chop, often a lightly battered schnitzel). *Cūkas fileja* is a pork fillet, *teļa* veal, *liellopu* beef and *cālīšu* chicken. Cuts of pork and other meats usually come edged with fatty rind – giving people only lean meat was traditionally considered rather rude.

Common varieties of **fish** (*zivs*) include *lasis* (salmon), *forele* (trout) and *zandarts* (pikeperch). Main courses are usually served with boiled potatoes or french fries, accompanied by a coleslaw-style salad or a pile of pickled vegetables. Popular garnishes include lashings of sour cream (*krējums*), or a ladleful of mushroom sauce (*sēņu merce*).

Desserts

One traditional Latvian dessert that crops up almost everywhere is *ķīselis*, an oat porridge sweetened with seasonal fruit and forest berries. Otherwise, dessert menus tend to concentrate on more familiar items such as ice cream (*saldējums*), gateau (*torte*) and all manner of cakes (*kūkas*). Pancakes (*pankūkas*) come with a variety of fillings, notably *biezpiens* or curd cheese, which is slightly sweetened to achieve a cheesecake-ish taste. Tasty little chocolate-coated cubes of *biezpiens* (Kārums is the best-known make) can be picked up from supermarket chiller cabinets.

Drinking

Traditionally Latvian drinking culture revolves around the **kafejnīca** or café, which serves non-alcoholic drinks and closes early in the evening, and the **krogs** or tavern, where serious evening boozing sessions take place. Nowadays, the range of internationally styled bars and pubs in Rīga and other big cities has massively broadened the range of venues available – and the global choice of drinks you can consume in them.

The main alcoholic drink in Latvia is *alus* (beer), which comes either as *gaišs alus* (the regular, lager-like brew) or as *tumšs alus* (a strong dark porter). The biggest of the breweries are Aldaris from Rīga, and Cēsu from Cēsis, although there are plenty of regional brewers producing ales of considerable individuality: Bauskas, Užavas and Tervetes are among those worth trying.

One Latvian spirit you should definitely try at least once is **Rīgas melnais balzāms**, or Rīga black balsam, a bitter-tasting potion brewed according to a two-and-a-half-centuries-old recipe that combines various roots, grasses and herbs. It's a bit of an acquired taste when drunk neat, but combines rather well with cola and other mixers. Decent **vodka** is easy to get hold of in Latvia – world-renowned brands such as Stolichnaya and Moskovskaya are made under licence in the same distillery as melnais balzāms. The local **sparkling wine**, Rīgas šampanietis, is both potent and cheap.

One traditional non-alcoholic beverage that is making something of a comeback is *kvass*, a drink made from malt extract, resembling cola in colour and just as popular locally. **Coffee** (*kafija*) and **tea** (*tēja*) are usually served black – if you want milk (*piens*), you'll have to ask. *Ar cukuru* means with sugar, *bez cukura* means without.

The media

For a country containing little over 1.5 million native speakers, Latvia can boast an astonishing array of **newspapers** and magazines. Best by far of the national dailies is *Diena* ("The Day"; ⓦwww.diena.lv), a well-designed and -written broadsheet. Latvia's Russian-speaking inhabitants have a handful of tabloid-style dailies of their own, and at least one influential business daily in the shape of *Biznes & Baltija*.

As far as **magazines** are concerned, *Rīgas laiks* is a good-looking but intellectually obscure cultural monthly; it's more a fashion accessory than something you would ever dream of reading. More down-to-earth, but impeccably stylish with it, *Pastaiga* and *Ieva* are the most broad-based of the women's interest titles. If you're interested in architecture and interior design, *Latvijas Architektūra* is worth getting just for the photos, while *Studija* (ⓦ www.studija.lv) is a highly recommended fine arts magazine with English-language summaries.

As for **television**, most people tune in to state-owned terrestrial channels LTV1 and LTV7 for serious news and culture, and to privately owned LNT and TV3 for game shows and imported dramas. English-language films are shown in the original language with

Remembrance days

A number of dates in the Latvian calendar are set aside for remembering specific events or particular groups of people who made some contribution to the nation. Commemorative events are organized, and wreaths are laid at monuments.

March 16 Latvian Legion
March 25 Deportations of 1949
May 8 Victims of World War II
June 14 Victims of Communist Terror
July 4 Holocaust Day
November 11 Lāčplēsis Day (Marking the defence of Rīga from the Baltic Germans; 1919)

Latvian subtitles on LTV7 only – all other Latvian channels show them dubbed. Many hotels and households are equipped with a multitude of cable channels, offering a broad range of English-, German- and Russian-language programming.

Festivals

In pagan times, Latvian festivals were closely related to the position of the sun, with solstices and equinoxes providing the main occasions for ritual celebration. Many of these practices still exist, although they dovetail so neatly with the Christian calendar that they're no longer recognizable as the pagan holidays they originally were.

The run-up to **Easter** (*Lieldiena*) is marked by street hawkers selling bunches of catkins (*pūpoli*), which, as well as serving as a symbol of the coming spring, are also used to thrash your nearest and dearest on the morning of Palm Sunday (*Pūpolsvētdiena*). In days gone by, rural communities celebrated Easter itself by gathering beside the village swing – a huge wooden platform capable of bearing whole families – and taking it in turns

Arts festivals

International Bach Festival Rīga, March; ⓦwww.music.lv/bach.
Baltic Ballet Festival Rīga, March or April; ⓦwww.ballet-festival.lv.
Skaņu mežs (Forest of Sound); Rīga, May; experimental music and film; ⓦwww.skanumezs.lv.
Opera Festival Rīga, June; ⓦwww.opera.lv.
Early Music Festival Rīga, Bauska & Rundale, June; ⓦwww.latvijaskoncerti.lv.
Kremerata Baltica Festival Rīga & Sigulda, June & July; ⓦwww.kremerata-baltica.com.
All-Latvian Song and Dance Festival Rīga and locations countrywide; held every five years (the next in July 2008) and featuring as many as 30,000 singers; ⓦwww.dziesmusvetki2008.lv.
Organ Music Festival Rīga, July.
Saulkrasti Jazz Festival Saulkrasti, July; ⓦwww.saulkrastijazz.lv.
Sigulda Opera Festival Sigulda, July; ⓦwww.sigulda.lv.
Sacred Music Festival Rīga, August; ⓦwww.koris.lv.
Liepājas dzintars Rock Festival Liepāja, August.
International Chamber Choir Festival (Rīga dimd) Rīga, September; ⓦwww.culture.lv/choirfestival.
International Chamber Music Festival Rīga, September; ⓦwww.music.lv/bachfestival.
Arēna New Music Festival Rīga, October; ⓦwww.arenafest.lv.

to swoop up and down to the accompaniment of suitably rhythmic chants. A fertility ritual of ancient, pre-Christian origins, the practice is kept alive by folklore societies.

The one big ritual event which is still celebrated en masse is *Jāņi*, or **Midsummer's Eve**, when urban Latvians head for the countryside to spend the whole night drinking beer around a bonfire and singing sun-worshipping songs known as *līgotne* – named after the swaying "*līgo, līgo*" refrain that almost all of them feature. Traditionally, *Jāņi* represented the last chance for a booze-up before the hard work of the harvest season began, and it's the hedonistic aspect of the occasion that has made it enduringly popular – and also explains why there are so many drunk drivers careering around Latvia's roads on midsummer morning.

At some stage in summer or autumn, each town and village has a **graveyard festival** (*kapu svētki*), when family plots are tidied up and picnics are eaten beside the graves – urban dwellers often go back to their home village to take part.

Latvian **Christmas** (*Ziemassvētki*) is nowadays the commercialized occasion that it is in the rest of Europe, and few families still celebrate Christmas Eve by tucking into the traditional fare of boiled pig's head and peas. A couple of practices connected to the winter solstice are still enacted by folklore societies, especially at the open-air museum in Rīga (see p.212), where you can see mummers masked as bears, horses, cranes, goats or the grim reaper going from house to house to drive away evil, and a yule log (*bļuks*), symbolizing the misfortunes of the previous year, is dragged around by celebrants before being ritually burned. **New Year** (*Jaungads*) is marked by the familiar round of boozing, partying and firework displays.

Entertainment

Although most Latvian cities can muster a theatre, a cinema and the odd music venue, the bulk of the country's entertainment options are concentrated in Rīga, a culture-saturated metropolis with something to satisfy most tastes. Details of where to catch opera, ballet, orchestral music and theatre in the capital can be found on p.217.

Choral and classical music

Choral singing has played a central role in Latvian culture ever since 1868, when 150 singers attended the first-ever national song festival in Valka. The nurturing of an indigenous folk-song tradition was seen as an important way of opposing the domination of German-language culture and it helped to keep Latvian traditions alive during the Soviet period. Nowadays, there's hardly a village, factory or government department without a choir, most of them performing material which is deeply rooted in Latvia's rich folk tradition (for more on folk music, see p.447). The nation's choirs get together every five years to participate in the **All-Latvian Song and Dance Festival**, when the sound of thousands of massed voices issuing forth from the open-air song bowl in Rīga's Mežaparks can be a truly visceral experience. If you can't make it to the festival (the next is due in July 2008; ⓦ www.dziesmusvetki2008.lv), there are plenty of opportunities to hear top-quality choirs in Rīga. Prominent among these are the all-female **Dzintars**, and the mixed choir, **Ave Sol**, both of whom perform startlingly modern arrangements of archaic Latvian songs, as well as specially commissioned contemporary compositions.

One outstanding modern composer known for his choral as well as orchestral works is **Pēteris Vasks** (b.1946), whose journeys into contemplative, deeply spiritual territory have earned him comparisons with the likes of Gorecki, Tavener and Pärt. His works are regularly performed in Rīga, and the city's record shops are full of his CDs. One of the best-known interpreters of Vasks's work is the Rīga-born violin virtuoso **Gidon Kremer** (b.1947), whose multinational chamber ensemble Kremerata Baltica has garnered an international reputation for its performances of contemporary classical music. Tickets for Kremer performances sell out fast in Rīga – again, there are plenty of CDs in the shops if you miss out.

Club culture and pop music

Rīga's club scene offers a bit of everything, from cavernous mega-clubs pumping out frenetic techno to thousand-strong herds, to more intimate alternative spaces where you can hear anything from hip-hop and reggae to post-industrial noise. A lot of the latter places offer a regular programme of live music, with the result that the underground gig scene is slightly more vibrant here than in Tallinn or Vilnius. There's also a respectable range of mid-sized venues hosting performances by Latvia's sizeable stable of homegrown, pop-rock acts.

Ever since the 1960s, Latvia has developed a strain of melodic, lyrical pop that has gone against the grain of both Soviet showbiz culture and Western rock, and has been embraced as an important element in national identity as a consequence. Central to its evolution has been **Imants Kalniņš**, a classically trained composer (his symphony no. 4 is widely held to be on a par with most contemporary classical production), who has written songs for just about every Latvian pop performer of consequence from the late 1960s onwards. His 1967 song *Dziesma par četriem baltiem krekliem* ("Song About Four White Shirts") – recorded by the group Menuets for the cult film *Elpojiet Dziļi* ("Breathe Deeply") – was banned by the authorities because the shirts in question were taken as a metaphor for Latvian dignity in the face of Soviet oppression, and Kalniņš has been a symbol of national integrity ever since. His wide-ranging oeuvre is difficult to pin down, but if you crossed Paul McCartney with Leonard Cohen and Burt Bacharach, something resembling Kalniņš would probably come out the other end. Your best bet is to get hold of best-of compilation *Dziesmu izlase* and make up your own mind.

Few subsequent songwriters have enjoyed similar stature, save perhaps for **Ainars Mielavs**, originally lead singer with rousing folk-pop practitioners **Jauns Mēness** – their early 1990s albums represent the high point of Latvian rock. Mielavs is now a solo performer of adult-oriented, mellow songs and also heads leading folk label Upe records. Latvian pop's current international standard bearers are **Brainstorm**, one of the few groups to appear in the Eurovision Song Contest (they came third in 2000) and survive with their career unscathed. They have recorded numerous albums of bright, infectious, indie-influenced melodies, some of which come in both Latvian and English versions, and they have a sizeable fan base in central Europe and Scandinavia.

No discussion of Latvian music would be complete without a mention of composer, impresario and all-round national institution **Raimonds Pauls**. His recently re-released album *Tik Dzintars Vien* – recorded in 1970 but recalling European popular songs of the 1950s – is a landmark in Latvian easy-listening. He went on to become a big star in the Soviet Union, penning albums for astronomically popular, variety-show warblers like (Latvian) Laima Vaikule and (Russian) Alla Pugacheva. You might want to give his latter-day work a wide berth, though, ranging as it does from Eurovision-style pop-pap to cocktail-bar piano-tinkling of the queasiest kind.

Cinema

Latvian cinemas show feature films in the original language – with subtitles in both

Latvian and Russian blotting out the bottom third of the screen. During the Soviet period, Rīga's film studio turned out an average of eight features a year, but with the collapse of state funding after 1990 the tally has shrunk to one or two low-budget affairs. Ask locals to name their favourite Latvian film of all time and they'd probably plump for 1973's "Blow, Wind!" (*Pūt Vējiņi!*), a lavishly costumed tale of love and death set in pre-Christian Latvia, and featuring a rousing score by Imants Kalniņš – the soundtrack CD is worth having on its own.

Internationally, Latvia is more famous for its documentaries than its feature films. This is almost entirely due to the career of **Juris Podnieks**, whose 1986 work *Is it Easy to be Young?* – an unflinching investigation into the lives of directionless, delinquent youth in Rīga – eloquently stripped bare the inner psychoses of a disintegrating society and attracted massive audiences throughout the Soviet Union as a result. He subsequently devoted his efforts to documenting the death throes of Soviet communism – his TV series *Hello, Can you Hear Us?* (1989) was a disturbing portrait of a multinational empire on the skids, while *Homeland* (1992) dealt movingly with the drive to independence in the Baltic States. Production of the latter was marred by the deaths of two of Podnieks's cameramen – shot while filming the Soviet attack on the Latvian Interior Ministry in January 1991 (see p.437). Podnieks himself died in a freak scuba-diving accident in 1992.

A major showcase for new Latvian films (whether dramas or documentaries) is the **Lielais Kristaps festival** (organized by the Latvian National Film Centre; ⊛www.nfc.lv), a not-quite-annual affair that's held whenever enough films are produced to justify it.

Sport

Most international team games enjoy moderate popularity in Latvia, although it's **ice hockey** that generates most in the way of mass enthusiasm. The sport's big breakthrough in the public consciousness came during the world championships of 2000, when an unfancied Latvian team defeated title favourites Russia in the group stages,

sending thousands of Latvians out onto the streets of Rīga in celebration. The Latvians have remained in or around the world's top ten ever since, but are yet to break through to the medal-winning stages of a major competition. League games in Latvia itself are lacklustre affairs (the best Latvian players ply their trade in North America), and the best way to enjoy the sport is to catch a major international encounter on the big screen in a crowded pub. The distinctive maroon Latvian hockey jerseys make highly desirable souvenirs, and can be bought from some of the Rīga souvenir shops listed on p.219. Still on the subject of winter sports, Latvia has a couple of decent **bobsleigh** crews, and the national track at Sigulda is used annually for international world cup meetings.

After a decade of under-achievement, the Latvian **football** team astonished everybody (not least themselves) by qualifying for the 2004 European Championships, but have failed to build on this success. International matches are played in Rīga in front of sizeable crowds (see p.219), but domestic league games are poorly attended. Owing to Latvia's harsh winters, the football season runs from April to October.

Culture and etiquette

Tipping is only expected in restaurants or in the smarter cafés with waited tables, in which case you add ten percent to the bill or round it up to the nearest convenient figure.

Public toilets can be found at most bus stations. Ladies are *dāmas*; gents are *kungi*.

The best place to look for condoms (*prezervatīvi*) is near the checkout of big supermarkets.

Smoking is banned from all public places, including hotels, restaurants, cafés and bars. Some eating, drinking and nightlife venues provide a smoking zone in a separate room, although this is the exception rather than the rule.

Travel essentials

Emergencies **Police** ☏02; ambulance ☏03; fire ☏01.

Costs

The Latvian capital, Rīga, has the highest cost of living of any city in the Baltics, and your daily spend here will be greater than in Vilnius or Tallinn. Things are different outside Rīga, where you can live exceedingly well on very little.

Wherever you stay in Latvia, **accommodation** will take a major chunk out of your daily budget. In Rīga, hostel beds start at around €15/£10/$19, while B&Bs and the cheapest hotels cost €45–60/£30–40/$57–76 for a double. Comfortable, mid-range hotels start at around the €90/£60/$115 mark for a double; anything more stylish costs considerably more than this. Out in the provinces you won't find much in the way of hostels, but the price of a double room can fall to €22/£15/$29 in a rustic B&B, €45/£30/$57 in a hotel.

Public transport costs are comparatively low: short journeys by bus or train (Rīga–Jūrmala or Rīga–Sigulda, for example) are unlikely to break the €1.50/£1/$1.90 barrier; inter-city journeys from Rīga to Daugavpils rarely exceed €6/£4/$7.50.

If you're shopping in markets for picnic ingredients during the daytime and sticking to the cheaper cafés and bars in the evening, then €22/£15/$29 per person per day will suffice for **food and drink**. For a sit-down lunch and a decent dinner followed by a couple of evening drinks, you'll need at least €50/£35/$66 per person per day in Rīga, €36/£25/$48 outside the capital. Visits to museums and galleries – costing anything from €0.75/£0.50/$0.95 for the smaller attractions to €3.70/£2.50/$4.75 for the major sites – will considerably increase your daily spend.

Internet

Rīga and other cities are well served by **Internet cafés** (*interneta kafejnīca* or *interneta klubs*), although they're not very common in smaller towns. Internet access is also available in public libraries, although you may have to wait to use a terminal. Thirty minutes of surfing time rarely costs more than 1Ls.

If your computer is equipped with Wi-Fi-compatible software you can access the Internet in any hotel lobby, restaurant or bar where an orange Wi-Fi sticker is displayed in the window. It is not a free service, however: prepaid cards can be bought from participating establishments.

Left luggage

Most bus stations have a left-luggage counter (*Bagāžas novietne* or *Rokas bagažas glabātava*), with a daily charge of about 0.50–1Ls per item, depending on size.

Mail

The **Latvian postal service** (*Latvijas pasts*) is reasonably reliable, even if post offices themselves tend to be gloomy and disorganized places, with a confusing array of different counters. **Opening times** are generally Mon–Fri 8am–7/8pm, Sat 8am–4pm. City-centre post offices may also be open Saturdays 8am–6pm and Sundays 8am–4pm. Cards (0.40Ls) and letters (0.50Ls) to Europe take about seven days to arrive; cards (0.450Ls) and letters (0.60Ls) to North America or Australasia take fourteen days. Most post offices have a fax (*fakss*) counter where you can send documents for a few santimi.

Money

Latvia's unit of currency is the **lats** (plural **lati**), abbreviated to Ls and divided into 100 **santimi**. Coins come in denominations of 0.01, 0.02, 0.05, 0.10, 0.20, 0.50, 1 and 2Ls, and notes in 5, 10, 20, 50, 100 and 500Ls. At the time of writing €1 was worth 1.45Ls, £1 was worth 1Ls and $1 was worth 1.90Ls.

Major **banks** (*banka*) like Hansabanka, Latvijas Krājbanka and Unibanka will change money and cash traveller's cheques (Thomas Cook and American Express preferred), and some give advances on major credit cards. **Opening times** are usually Mon–Fri 9/10am–5/6pm, with some banks in big cities opening 10am–3pm on Saturday. Outside these hours you can change cash in **currency exchange offices** (*valūtas maiņa*), many of which are little more than kiosks found in unlikely locations like food shops or gambling arcades. These are often open until around 10pm at night, and one or two in Rīga are open 24 hours. You'll find **ATM cash machines** (*automāts*) liberally dotted around most town centres.

Credit cards can be used in a growing number of bars, restaurants and shops in Rīga and other cities, as well as in most petrol stations, but are not widely accepted in small towns and villages.

Opening hours and public holidays

Shops are usually open Mon–Fri 10am–7/8pm, Sat 10am–4/5pm, though some close for an hour around lunchtime. Supermarkets and food shops often stay open until 10pm and also open on Sunday.

Museums and galleries are usually open Tues–Sun or Wed–Sun 10am–5pm, with the addition of the odd extra hour or two in summer. Latvia's Lutheran **churches** can be very hard to get into outside Sunday service times, unless – like those in central Rīga for example – they're of particular cultural and historic importance, in which case they'll be open on a nine-to-five basis every day of the week. Orthodox churches, in contrast, are

Public holidays

All banks and offices, as well as most shops, are closed on the following public holidays. Big supermarkets and food stores in Rīga may well stay open, apart from on January 1, when there is a genuine national shutdown.

Jan 1 New Year's Day

Good Friday

Easter Sunday

Easter Monday

May 1 Labour Day

May 4 Declaration of Independence (1990)

Mothers' Day (second Sunday in May)

June 23–24 Midsummer celebrations

Nov 18 Declaration of Independence (1918)

Dec 24–26 Christmas

Dec 31 New Year's Eve

much more accessible, and there's usually an attendant selling candles and icon-bearing postcards during the daylight hours.

For post office and bank opening hours, see "Mail" (p.179) and "Money" (p.179) respectively.

Phones

During the course of 2008 all Latvian **telephone numbers** will change from 7-digit to 8-digit numbers. The new numbers will be formed by tacking a new digit onto the beginning of the existing number (all mobile numbers will begin with a 2, while all fixed-line numbers will begin with a 6). There will be a period of transition when both the old 7-digit numbers and the new 8-digit numbers will remain valid. We have quoted the new 8-digit numbers throughout the guide.

The Latvian telephone system is generally hitch-free and easy to use: there are no separate area codes. Direct international calls are possible from all phones – dial 00 followed by the country code, area code and number.

Town centres are well supplied with public **telephone boxes**, operated using magnetic cards (*telekarte* or *zvaņu karte*). These come in 2, 3 and 5Ls denominations and can be bought at the post office or from newspaper kiosks. A 2Ls card should just about stretch to a three-minute call to Europe, the US or Australasia.

For general information on using mobile phones in the Baltic States, see p.44. If you have a **GSM mobile phone** it's possible to avoid heavy call costs by purchasing a pre-paid SIM card from one of the local operators such as Amigo, Okarte or Zelta Zivtiņa. This will provide you with a Latvian telephone number and allow you to make local calls at the local rate. In each case it costs 5–6Ls for the SIM card and your first few minutes of airtime, after which you can buy top-ups in increments of 2, 3, 5Ls and above. Starter packs and top-up cards can be bought from newspaper kiosks and supermarket checkouts just about everywhere in the country.

2.1

Rīga and around

With just over 725,000 inhabitants, almost one third of the country's population, **RĪGA** is the biggest city in the Baltics, offering a degree of cosmopolitan bustle, sophistication and sheer urban chaos that neither Tallinn nor Vilnius can really compete with. It's also one of the best-looking Baltic cities, its rich history as a military, ecclesiastical and, above all, mercantile powerhouse having bequeathed the city a legacy of fine architecture: medieval red-brick churches and gabled merchants' houses rise above the alleyways of the Old Town, while the surrounding nineteenth-century streets hold some remarkable examples of Art Nouveau, as well as buildings in National Romantic style, a local offshoot of Art Nouveau, in which architects drew on Latvian folk symbols for ornamental inspiration. And you don't need to wander far from the centre to find neighbourhoods full of tumbledown wooden houses and cobbled back streets.

Almost totally absent from the capital are the national characteristics that many Latvians ascribe to themselves – an enduring attachment to wholesome peasant values and a love of nature, to name but two. Since its very inception, Rīga has dedicated itself to commerce and wheeler-dealing. Hard-headed mercantile instincts have always served to bond together Rīga's ethnically diverse population: currently, half of the city's inhabitants are Latvian, while the other half are either Russian or Russian-speaking, giving the city a strangely schizophrenic character – the two communities get on peaceably enough, but tend to lead separate lives, reading their own newspapers and

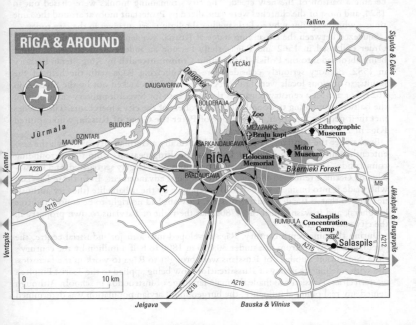

watching their own TV stations, and often displaying a staggering indifference to each others' language and culture.

Boasting historic buildings on almost every corner and a strong hand of set-piece museums, **downtown Rīga** can easily fill two or three days of your holiday time-longer if you're drawn towards the more offbeat attractions of the city's **suburbs**, such as the impressive Open-air Ethnographic Museum. Also within easy reach are the beguiling beach resort of **Jūrmala**, 20km to the northwest, and the Holocaust memorial sites at **Rumbula** and **Salaspils**, just outside the city to the southeast. You could even use the city as a base for exploring sizeable chunks of north and central Latvia, much of it no more than a couple of hours' journey away.

Some history

Rīga was founded by **Albert von Buxhoeveden**, a priest from Bremen who arrived in 1201 with twenty shiploads of crusaders to convert the Baltic tribes to Christianity. Taking over a site previously occupied by Liv fishermen, Albert lost no time in building a fortified settlement strong enough to withstand the frequent raids made by Livs and Latvians, and civilians from northern Europe flocked to the new town to take advantage of the new opportunities for business and trade. As the headquarters of the crusading effort in the Baltics, Rīga was home to three often quarrelsome groups – the church, the knights of the Livonian Order and the increasingly assertive citizenry. With the last refusing to put up with the dictates of the other two, Rīga became a self-governing municipality owing symbolic fealty to the Order, whose Grand Master continued to base himself in Rīga's castle. Eager to exploit this new freedom of manoeuvre, the city joined the **Hanseatic League**, a loose alliance of north German trading cities, in 1282 (see box on p.66 for more on this). Civic life was to remain in the hands of a German-speaking mercantile elite for the next six hundred years.

Rīga grew rich on the trade of timber, furs and flax, which were floated down the Daugava River on enormous rafts before being loaded onto ships and exported west. Perennially suspicious of the grasping Baltic clergy, the citizenry provided fertile ground for the spread of **Protestantism** in the early sixteenth century, and Rīga became a bastion of the new creed. The city's remaining monks were chased out in 1524, and most of the churches were vandalized by Protestant mobs at around the same time – which explains why so little medieval religious art survives in the city today.

Squeezed between the expanding states of Russia, Sweden and Poland, the Livonian Order collapsed in 1562 and Rīga briefly became an independent city-state before being absorbed into the **Polish–Lithuanian Commonwealth** by King Stefan Bathory in 1582. Bathory seriously considered re-Catholicizing Rīga with the help of the Jesuits, so anxious locals were not sorry to see the Poles kicked out by the **Swedes** in 1621. For almost a century Rīga was the main base for Swedish military campaigns in the Baltics, stimulating trade and filling the coffers of the city's merchants. The Swedes met their nemesis, however, in the shape of **Peter the Great of Russia**, who captured Rīga in 1709 after a nine-month siege.

Even under the Russians, Rīga remained culturally a German city, although the seventeenth century saw an influx of **Latvian-speaking** peasants from the surrounding countryside. The German and Latvian populations were largely segregated, and knowledge of German remained the only route to social advancement. Even those Latvians who made it into business were denied acceptance by the urban elite (the city authorities argued that as the descendants of serfs, Latvians had no right to be considered free burghers), and it wasn't until the 1780s that the right of Latvians to own property in the city was recognized.

During the nineteenth century, Rīga developed into a major industrial centre, the population growing from just under 30,000 in 1800 to half a million by the century's close. Significant numbers of Russians were brought to Rīga to work in the factories, and with a deliberate policy of **Russification** now being applied to the Tsarist Empire's western cities, Russian was made the main language of instruction in schools. Although denied any real political influence, the burgeoning Latvian population was determined to make its presence felt, with events like the first all-Latvian song festival (held in the city in June 1873) signalling their increasing cultural self-confidence. On the eve of World War I the Latvians were the biggest ethnic group in the city – the Germans had in the meantime been pushed into third place behind the Russians.

Having spent much of World War I as a front-line city, Rīga was abandoned by the Russians in September 1917 and German Kaiser Wilhelm II arrived in person to take possession of the city. The collapse of Germany just over a year later ushered in a period of extreme chaos. Latvian independence was proclaimed in the National Theatre on November 18, but with no army at their disposal, the new government surrendered the city to the **Bolsheviks** on January 3, 1919. Home-grown Latvian revolutionary Pēteris Stučka presided over four months of communist terror – during which the bourgeoisie were made to perform demeaning tasks (or were simply taken away to be shot) – before being chased out by a combined force of Latvians, White Russians and Germans. This marriage of convenience didn't last long, however, and the White Russians and Germans were finally seen off by the Latvians in November, 1919, with the assistance of a British naval bombardment.

Now the capital of an independent Latvia, Rīga entered the new era a massively changed city. Industry was in ruins, and the population had fallen by half since 1914. The city recovered quickly, however, and for much of the 1920s and 1930s Rīga enjoyed something of a *belle époque*, earning the city the sobriquet of "Little Paris". The city's cosmopolitan mix was boosted by an influx of anti-Bolshevik refugees from Russia, whose taste for old-world etiquette and lavish entertaining led American diplomat George Kennan to remark that Rīga was "the only place where one could still live in Tsarist Russia".

World War II – during which Rīga was occupied by the Soviets, then by the Germans – once again left the city impoverished, a situation that didn't radically improve when the Soviets returned to stay in October 1944. The communists dedicated themselves to the development of heavy industry in Rīga and radically changed the ethnic profile of the city by importing a (largely Russian-speaking) workforce from all over the Soviet Union. By the late 1980s the influx of Russian immigrants had reduced the Latvians to a minority in their own capital.

Most of Rīga's non-Latvians were unenthusiastic about leaving the Soviet Union when the independence drive took off in the late 1980s, but few supported the use of OMON troops and tanks to seize control of key buildings in January 1991, an action which cost five innocent lives and destroyed any shred of credibility communist rule still had.

Nowadays, with memories of the Soviet period beginning to fade and EU membership attracting huge levels of foreign investment, Rīga has become something of a boom town, with gleaming office blocks sprouting up on vacant lots everywhere and real estate prices going through the roof. New wealth has been slow to trickle down to the majority, however, and while there's no shortage of flashy, fuel-guzzling four-wheel drives bouncing their way around Rīga's cobbled streets, many denizens of the capital continue to eke out a living on meagre wages.

Arrival, information and city transport

Rīga's smart, modern **airport** (Rīgas lidosta) is 8km southwest of the Old Town. Head straight out of the arrivals hall and cross the car park to find the bus stop, from where bus #22 (2–3 every hour; 0.30Ls; pay the conductor) runs to Abrenes iela on the south-eastern fringes of the centre, passing the bus and train stations on the way; bus #22A (1–2 every hour; 0.40Ls; pay the driver) runs to "Katedrāle" – the Russian Orthodox cathedral just east of the Old Town. A taxi to the centre will cost around 8–10Ls.

Rīga's main **train station** (Centrālā stacija) and **bus station** (Autoosta) are within 200m of each other, five minutes' walk south of the Old Town. Taxi drivers outside both stations aren't keen on ferrying passengers short distances, and will demand a minimum of 5–6Ls to take you anywhere in the city centre.

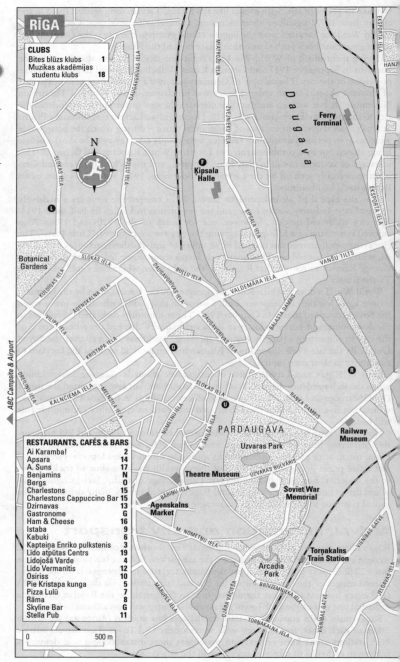

ABC Campsite & Airport

184

RĪGA

CLUBS

| Bites blūzs klubs | 1 |
| Muzikas akadēmijas studentu klubs | 18 |

N

Daugava

Ferry Terminal

Kipsala Halle

Botanical Gardens

PARDAUGAVA

Uzvaras Park

Railway Museum

Theatre Museum

Soviet War Memorial

Agenskalns Market

Tornakalns Train Station

Arcadia Park

RESTAURANTS, CAFÉS & BARS

Ai Karamba!	2
Apsara	14
A. Suns	17
Benjamins	N
Bergs	O
Charlestons	15
Charlestons Cappuccino Bar	15
Dzirnavas	13
Gastronome	G
Ham & Cheese	16
Istaba	9
Kabuki	6
Kapteiņa Enriko pulkstenis	3
Lido atpūtas Centrs	19
Lidojošā Varde	4
Lido Vermanītis	12
Osiriss	10
Pie Kristapa kunga	5
Pizza Lulū	7
Rāma	8
Skyline Bar	G
Stella Pub	11

0   500 m

O & Dauderi

B, Braļu kapi & Mežaparks

Cinema Museum, Motor Museum, Holocaust Memorial & Ethnographic Museum

Jewish Cemetery ▶

Jewish Cemetery ▶

ⓐ Sporta Manēža, Rumbula & Salaspils

Hospital

Skonto Stadium

Daile Theatre

Rozentāls & Blaumanis Museum

St Gertrude's Church

Corner House

See Riga Old Town map

Kronvalds Park

Jewish Museum

City Park

A. Keniņš Highschool

Cathedral of the Nativity

Esplanāde

CENTRS

VECRĪGA

A. Čaks Museum

Vērmane's Garden

K. Barons Museum

Natural History Museum

Patricia Agency

Train Station

Bus Station

MARIJAS SATEKLES IELA

Central Market

Church of the Annunciation

Academy of Sciences

Former Synagogue

Jesus Church

MOSCOW SUBURB

D a u g a v a

Grebenshchikov Church

ACCOMMODATION

Alberts	**C**	Laine	**E**
B&B Rīga	**K**	Maritim	**U**
Backpackers Planet	**S**	NB	**L**
Barons B&B	**M**	O.K.	**Q**
Bergs	**O**	Posh hostel	**T**
City Hostel	**P**	Radisson-SAS	
Elizabeth's Hostel		Daugava	**R**
Europa Royale	**N**	Reval Hotel Latvia	**G**
Homestay	**B**	Riga City Camping	**F**
Jūrnieks	**A**	Valdemārs	**D**
KB	**J**	Viktorija	**I**
Krišjānis & Ģertrūde	**H**		

185

TV Tower ▼

Moving on from Rīga

Rīga is a major transport hub, with a multitude of **bus** routes fanning out across the Baltic region and beyond. There are several daily buses to Vilnius and Tallinn and plenty of direct services to Germany, France, the Netherlands and Great Britain. There are also overnight **trains** to Russia, the Ukraine and Belarus, as well as **car ferries** to Scandinavia and Germany.

By bus

Rīga's **bus station** (ⓦwww.autoosta.lv) is relatively user-friendly, with easy-to-read departure listings and an English-speaking information office in the main ticket hall. Domestic tickets are sold from the ticket counters immediately opposite the main entrance; international services are handled by a cluster of offices just around the corner on the right. The main **agents** for international tickets are Eurolines (ⓣ6721 4080, ⓦwww.eurolines.lv) and Ecolines (ⓣ6721 4512, ⓦwww.ecolines.net); both have outlets at the station, and Ecolines also has an office at Čaka iela 45 (ⓣ6727 4444). Facilities in the station are limited to a coffee shop and a couple of newsagents in the ticket hall.

By train

Rīga's recently renovated **central station** feels more like a vast shopping mall than somewhere to get a train. With all the cafés and bakeries around, you'll certainly have no trouble stocking up on supplies for the trip. There are daily or thrice-weekly services to Moscow, St Petersburg, Minsk, Vitebsk, Lvov and beyond – all of which require at least one night on the train. **Tickets** for international services are bought from the "Starptautiskie vilcieni" counters; those for journeys within Latvia are purchased from windows marked "*Iekšzemes vilcienu biļešu kases*".

By ferry

The **ferry terminal** at Eksporta iela 3A (tram #7 from the bus station or National Opera to Ausekla iela) is a pretty joyless place, with ticket counters, an exchange office and a duty-free shop – but not much else. Last-minute food or souvenir shopping should be done before you get here. The thrice-weekly ferry **to Stockholm** is operated by Rīgas Jūras Līnija, which has a ticket office at the terminal (ⓣ6720 5460, ⓦwww.rigasealine .lv). DFDS, Zivju iela 1 (ⓣ6735 3523, ⓦwww.lisco.lt), sells tickets for the twice-weekly ferry **to Lübeck**.

The **ferry terminal** (Jūras pasažieru stacija) is 1500m north of the Old Town at the end of Eksporta iela. Trams #5, #7 or #9 run from the stop 100m east of the terminal on Ausekļa iela to the edge of the Old Town (two stops; 0.30Ls pay the conductor).

Information

The main **tourist office** is on the Old Town's main square, Rātslaukums (daily 10am–7pm; ⓣ6703 7900, ⓦwww.rigatourism.com). In addition, there are tourist information booths at the airport (just outside the arrivals hall; Mon–Sat 10am–6pm; ⓣ6720 7800), the bus station (Mon–Fri 9am–6pm, Sat & Sun 10am–5pm; ⓣ6722 0555) and the train station (daily 8am–8pm; ⓣ6723 3815). All three offices are a mine of information, and can provide accommodation lists, although they don't book hotels on your behalf. They also sell the **Rīga Card** (8Ls for 24hr, 12Ls for 48hr, 16Ls for 72hr; ⓦwww.rigacard.lv), which allows unlimited use of public transport, entry to the major museums, a guided tour of the city and discounts in some restaurants – worth buying if you intend to do a fair amount of sightseeing. For information on travel throughout Latvia, the **Latvian Tourist Information Centre** at Smilšu 4

(Mon–Fri 9am–5pm; ☎6722 4664; ⓦwww.latviatourism.lv) offers brochures and advice on every conceivable destination.

There's a plethora of locally published English-language guides to the city, of which *Rīga in Your Pocket* (from news kiosks; 1.20Ls; ⓦwww.inyourpocket.com) is the most reliable source of well-written and up-to-date information on eating, drinking and shopping.

City transport

The centre of Rīga is easily walkable and outlying attractions are served by **bus**, **tram** or **trolleybus**. All run from around 5am until 11pm. Night buses run on a small number of routes connecting the city centre to key suburbs. Useful stops are Stacijas laukums (the square immediately in front of the train station) and Katedrāle, the part of Brīvības iela adjacent to the Orthodox cathedral. Flat-fare, single-journey **tickets** cost 0.30Ls. Tickets for one form of transport are not valid on any other. Tram tickets should be purchased in advance from newspaper kiosks. Trolleybus and bus tickets are bought on board from the conductor or driver. Some bus routes are operated by express buses, which only stop at selected points; tickets for these cost 0.40Ls and can be bought from the driver. Speedier still are the minibuses (*taksobuss* or *mikroautobuss*; 0.35–0.50Ls; pay the driver), which run along the main boulevards joining the centre to the suburbs, in many cases duplicating the routes operated by trams and buses.

Taxis are generally cheap: the basic fare is around 0.50Ls plus an additional charge of 0.50Ls per kilometre during the day and 0.60Ls between 10pm and 6am. Although rip-off merchants are the exception rather than the rule, some drivers will take advantage of foreigners by switching the meter off and demanding a set price. You'll find taxi ranks at all the main entry points to the Old Town, although it's usually cheaper to phone for a taxi in advance rather than picking one up from a rank. See "Directory", p.220, for recommended taxi firms.

Accommodation

Rīga has undergone a hotel-building boom in the years since independence, and there's no shortage of middle- to upper-bracket establishments to choose from. There's a modest sprinkling of mid-price **hotels**, and budget travellers are catered for by an ever-expanding range of backpacker-friendly **hostels**.

The most conveniently located **campsite** is *Riga City Camping*, behind the Ķipsala exhibition hall at Ķipsalas 8 (☎6706 7519, ⓦwww.bt1.lv/camping). Not much more than a field with views of factories, it is nevertheless a convenient twenty-minute walk from the Old Town. The seaside site of *Nemo* in Vaivari, Jurmāla (see p.221) is also worth considering, although it is a forty-minute drive or train ride from central Rīga.

Hostels

Argonaut Kalēju 50 ☎2614 7214, ⓦwww .argonauthostel.com. The pine-bunk dorms are no different from those on offer elsewhere but you can count on the added advantages of back-packer-friendly staff and a home-from-home living room to relax in. Free coffee and tea in a small kitchen area. A handful of cosy quads and doubles available. Rooms ❸, dorms 8–14Ls
Backpackers Planet Neģu 17 ☎6722 6232, ⓦwww.backpackersplanet.lv. Located in a char-acterful former warehouse behind Rīga's central market. Accommodation mostly consists of four- or six-bed rooms (each with their own WC/shower), although there are some snug top-floor doubles.

Breakfast is available for an extra cost. Doubles ❹, dorm beds 12–14Ls
City Hostel Elizabetes 101 ☎6728 0124, ⓦwww.cityhostel.lv. Located one floor above *Elizabeth's Hostel* (see below), *City Hostel* offers beds in six- to ten-bed dorms, and a common room with free Internet access and tea and coffee. The double rooms share facilities and are a bit pokey. Doubles ❹, dorm beds from 8Ls
Elizabeth's Hostel Elizabetes 101 ☎6721 7890, ⓦwww.youthhostel.lv. Pine bunks in sparsely furnished dorms. Though a bit stuffy in summer, the hostel is laid-back and friendly. There's a social

area with TV, tea, coffee and free Internet. Doubles ❹, dorm beds 8–12Ls

Old Town Hostel Valņu 43 ☎6722 3406, ⓦwww .rigaoldtownhostel.lv. Offering airy, bright, clean dorms in an ideal location, and with a lively ground-floor bar, this place is perfect if you've always dreamed of living above a pub. There's a kitchen and a sauna for guests in the basement. Doubles ❷, dorms from 8Ls

Posh Pupolu iela 5 ☎6721 0917, ⓦwww .poshbackpackers.lv. Right behind the central market, the *Posh* offers functional, eight-bed dorms, along with a few quads, doubles and singles; decor ranges from grey lino to colour-clash carpets. No breakfast but plenty of nearby cafés. Doubles ❸, dorms from 10Ls

Profitcamp Teatra 12 ☎6721 6361, ⓦwww .hotelprofitcamp.lv. Welcoming warren of dorm rooms, doubles and triples, with shared toilets and showers in the hallway. Very popular due to its heart-of-the-Old-Town location, so reserve well in advance. Breakfast included. Doubles ❸, dorms from 8Ls

Riga Backpackers Marstaļu 6 ☎6722 9922, ⓦwww.riga-backpackers.com. A choice of dorms, doubles and triples in an impressively high-ceilinged Old Town apartment, all done up in attractive peachy colours. Doubles ❹, dorms from 10Ls

Riga Hostel Marstaļu 12 ☎6722 4520, ⓦwww .riga-hostel.com. Conveniently central hostel on the upper floors of a nineteenth-century apartment block. Bunk-beds in 10- to 15-person dorms, and some attractive doubles and quads in the attic. Doubles ❸, dorms from 8Ls

Hotels

There's no shortage of hotels in and around the Old Town, though the range is somewhat limited, with a glut of mid-price establishments offering neat but rather bland rooms, with little to distinguish them. Places of charm and character do exist, though – typically in the more expensive categories.

Generally speaking, you'll be hard-pushed to find a double room in the Old Town for less than 50Ls. Cheaper deals do exist in the grid of streets that make up the Centre, although many of the hotels in this part of Rīga haven't renovated their rooms since the communist period and can be slightly gloomy. Providing you don't mind being a ten-minute tram ride away from the sights, there's a growing choice of accommodation in Pārdaugava, just across the river from the Old Town, and there are a couple of choice picks elsewhere in the city – notably in the northern suburbs of Mežaparks and Sarkandaugava. Another alternative is to stay at the beachside suburb of Majori (see p.221), a 35-minute commute from central Rīga by train.

Some hotels cut their prices in winter (typically October–March), while others offer weekend **discounts** – it always pays to ask. **Breakfast** is included in the price in the listings below unless otherwise stated.

The Old Town

Ainavas Peldu 23 ☎6781 4316, ⓦwww.ainavas.lv. A small, intimate and characterful hotel in a restored medieval house, offering attractive en-suite rooms, each decorated in different pastel colours – hence the place's name, which means "Landscapes". ❼

🏃 **Centra** Audēju 1 ☎6722 6441, ⓦwww .centra.lv. Spacious, smart rooms, decorated in modern, minimalist style, with shower and TV, each offering good views of the Audēju iela street scene below. Good value for the location. ❼

Grand Palace Pils 12 ☎6704 4000, ⓦwww .grandpalaceriga.com. A luxury hotel in a wonderful old building, stuffed full of antique-effect furniture, just off Doma laukums. Rooms from 160Ls. ❽

Gutenbergs Doma laukums 1 ☎6781 4090, ⓦwww.gutenbergs.lv. Affordable and superbly situated, this comfy, medium-sized place fills up fast. Faux-rustic rooms in one wing, more chintzy affairs in the other. The restaurant's summer terrace, with views of the Old Town's roofscape, is a major plus point. ❼

Konventa Sēta Kalēju iela 9/11 ☎6708 7501, ⓦwww.konventa.lv. A charming, 140-room hotel in the heart of the Old Town, with modern en-suite rooms surrounding the beautifully restored courtyard of a former convent. Some of the doubles are apartment-style, with kitchenettes. ❻

Metropole Aspazijas 36/38 ☎6722 5411, ⓦwww .metropole.lv. Between the Opera House and the train station, this stately old hotel has been going since 1872 and was given a complete facelift in the 1990s. Rooms are fully equipped, but something seems to have gone wrong in the interior design department – Scandinavian minimalism meets overpowering chintz. ❻

Monte Kristo Kalēju 56 ☏ 6735 9100, ⓦ www
.hotelmontekristo.lv. This medium-sized hotel on
the fringes of the Old Town is a reliable source of
three-star comforts – offering en suites in warm
colours – and couldn't be better placed for the bus
and train stations. ❺

⛷ **Radi un Draugi** Mārstaļu iela 1/3 ☏ 6782
0200, ⓦ www.draugi.lv. Neat and cosy
en-suite rooms in an excellent downtown location.
Decor is on the bland side, but it's superb value for
the location. Advance reservations essential. ❺

Vecrīga Gleznotāju iela 12/14 ☏ 6721 6037,
ⓦ www.vecriga.lv. This ten-room hotel occupying
a historic building on a quiet Old Town street offers
standard en suites, most with bathtubs rather than
showers. ❻

Viesturs Mucenieku 5 ☏ 6735 6060, ⓦ www
.hotelviesturs.lv. Sensitively renovated medieval
house on a cobbled Old Town street, containing
thirteen rooms that mix folksy furnishings with
snazzy modern bathrooms. Buffet breakfast in
served the stone-lined cellar. ❼

The Centre

Alberts Dzirnavu 33 ☏ 6733 1717, ⓦ www
.alberthotel.lv. Modern ten-storey slab popular with
both tourist groups and business conferences, and
close to the Art Nouveau buildings of Alberta iela.
Rooms have an amusing Albert Einstein theme
(quotes from the great man are strewn around
the place, and textiles are decorated with quirky
molecular patterns). The top-floor lounge bar offers
excellent views of the city. ❻

B&B Riga Ģertrudes 43 ☏ 6526 400, ⓦ www
.bb-riga.lv. Eighteen en-suite rooms in a nineteenth-century apartment block, all decorated
in different styles – from funky split-level studio
apartments to cosy doubles with wooden floors
and bold fabrics. Breakfast is in the café across the
road. ❹–❺

Barons B&B Barona 25 ☏ 2910 5939, ⓦ www
.baronsbb.com. Converted fifth-floor apartment
offering sparsely furnished but pleasant rooms with
shared facilities, each of which can be used as
a double or adapted to sleep three, four or more.
There's also a multi-bed dorm, giving the place a
hostelly feel, as well as a relaxing sitting room. No
breakfast, but plenty of cafés on the street outside.
Doubles ❹, dorm beds 10Ls

⛷ **Bergs** Elizabetes 83/85 ☏ 6777 0900,
ⓦ www.hotelbergs.lv. Rooms in this
unabashedly contemporary hotel are either studio
apartments or multi-room suites, each featuring
matt-black floorboards, swish bathroom, kitchenette and an arty mix of ethnic fabrics and designer
fittings. African sculptures and portraits lend the

lobby areas an art-gallery feel. Free use of the top-
floor sauna and gym, and Wi-Fi throughout. Studios
from 120Ls, apartments from 160Ls. ❽

⛷ **Europa Royale** Barona 12 ☏ 6707
9444, ⓦ www.europaroyale.com. Classy
accommodation in an opulent nineteenth-century
mansion. Rooms are spacious and regally
furnished, providing you steer clear of the modern
annexe tacked onto the back, where low ceilings
and small windows conspire to spoil the four-star
ambience. Breakfast is served in the eye-popping,
neo-Baroque restaurant on the first floor. ❼

KB Barona 37 ☏ 6731 2323, ⓦ www.kbhotel.lv.
This eight-room B&B on the fifth floor of an apartment block is reached via a wonderfully ornate
stairwell. Rooms – on the plain side with functional
furnishings – are mostly en-suite, although a
couple share facilities. There's a pleasant breakfast
room, and guests are free to use the kitchen. ❹

Krišjānis & Ģertrūde Barona 39/1 ☏ 6750 6603,
ⓦ www.kg.lv. Altogether charming B&B featuring a
handful of chinzy en suites. Cosy breakfast room,
free Internet access and friendly hosts. ❺

Laine Skolas iela 11 ☏ 6728 8816, ⓦ www.laine
.lv. Entered via the courtyard of an anonymous-
looking apartment block, the mid-sized *Laine*
is much more welcoming than its surroundings
suggest, with simply furnished but spacious rooms
(many with bathtubs), plants in the corridors and
obliging staff. Only ten minutes' walk northeast of
the Old Town. ❺

Reval Hotel Latvia Elizabetes 55 ☏ 6777 2222,
ⓦ www.revalhotels.com. A twenty-seven-floor
block, once part of the Soviet state-run Intourist
organization, now privatized and fully refurbished.
Neat en suites, great views from the upper floors.
Disabled rooms available. ❼

Valdemārs Valdemāra iela 23 ☏ 6733 4462,
ⓦ www.valdemars.lv. A venerable Art Nouveau
building totally renovated in 2006, and providing
simple, clean en suites. Some of the better rooms
have elegant 1920s–30s furnishings, while the
main stairwell boasts Art Nouveau stained glass. ❺

Viktorija Čaka iela 55 ☏ 6701 4111, ⓦ www
.hotel-viktorija.lv. Historic pre-World War I structure
ten minutes west of the train station along the
grimy but animated Čaka iela. Renovated rooms
are simple, neat, carpeted affairs with modern
bathrooms. Cheaper, unrenovated rooms have
creaky parquet floors and shared facilities. ❸–❺

Pārdaugava

Maritim Slokas 1 ☏ 6706 9000, ⓦ www.maritim
.lv. This 239-room cruise liner of a hotel, with all
creature comforts, would be overpriced for this
part of Rīga were it not for its position overlooking

the savannah-like expanses of Uzvaras Park. A nice place to stay in summer when the park is at its lushest – at other times of year this area can be miserable. Tram #2, #4 or #10 from the Central Market. **⑥–⑦**

NB Slokas 49 ☎6781 5333, ⓦwww.nb.lv. Mid-sized modern place offering trim en suites, 4km northwest of the city centre and just round the corner from the Botanical Gardens (see p.209). The ground floor doubles as a pool club. Tram #5 from 13. Janvāra iela to Konsula iela. **⑥**

O.K. Slokas 12 ☎6786 0050, ⓦwww.okhotel.lv. *O.K.*, on a drab Pārdaugava street but within walking distance of most of the area's green spaces, offers nicely refurbished rooms with en-suite shower, although the green and red colour scheme can take a bit of getting used to. Tram #4 from the Central Market or #5 from 13. Janvāra iela to the Kalnciema stop. **⑤**

Radisson SAS Daugava Kuģu 24 ☎6706 1111, ⓦwww.riga.radissonsas.com. Comfort can be taken for granted in this 350-room monster offering good-quality business-class rooms. Great views of the Old Town skyline. There's a covered pool, and a couple of rooms equipped for wheelchair-users. **⑦**

Mežaparks and Sarkandaugava

Homestay Stockholmas iela 1 ☎6755 3016 and 2646 4113, ⓦwww.homestay.lv. A welcoming B&B set in the leafy garden suburb of Mežaparks, offering four comfortable rooms and a home-from-home atmosphere. Tea- and coffee-making facilities, free Internet access and use of fridge and washing machine if you ask nicely. Reserve well in advance. Tram #11 from Radio iela to Visbijas prospekts. **③**

Jūrnieks Sofijas 8 ☎6739 2350, ⓦwww .hoteljurnieks.lv. Recently refurbished cheapie with small, neat en-suite rooms. "Lux" rooms come with a lounge and only cost a few lati extra. A 25-minute tram ride from the centre, this place can feel a bit isolated, but it's handy for Mežaparks (see p.210). English-language skills are not the staff's strong point, and breakfast costs extra. Tram #5 or #9 from 13. Janvāra or the National Opera to Allažu iela. **②**

The City

The majority of Rīga's historical buildings are concentrated in the **Old Town** (Vecrīga), a compact web of narrow, cobbled streets, medieval merchant houses and brick-built churches squatting on the eastern bank of the broad **River Daugava**. To the east, the spacious belt of **parkland**, with its sedate nineteenth-century buildings sheltering beneath beech, elm and lime trees, couldn't be more different. Beyond here, streets radiate outwards through the so-called **Centre** (Centrs), the nineteenth- and early twentieth-century extension of the city and its commercial and administrative heart – a gritty, grey area redeemed by the innumerable gems of Art Nouveau architecture lining its streets. Further afield, Rīga's suburban sprawl harbours a number of quirky sights, such as the engaging Open-air Ethnographic Museum and the fascinating Motor Museum, while sizeable stretches of park in **Pārdaugava** and **Mežaparks**, and woodland around **Biķernieki**, present plenty of opportunities for strolling. Just to the southeast of the city lie the sombre Holocaust memorial sites at **Rumbula** and **Salaspils**.

The Old Town

World War II bombardment and insensitive post-war restoration notwithstanding, Rīga's **Old Town** still looks and feels like the warren it was in the Middle Ages. Nineteenth-century German guidebook writer, J.G. Kohl, could easily have been addressing today's tourists when he compared it to a "huge mass of rock, bored through, with holes for houses", adding that "the temperature of the town is that of a cavern, and there are parts of it which the sun has not seen for centuries."

The main thoroughfare is the dead-straight **Kaļķu iela**, which cuts through the Old Town from northeast to southwest. Many of the Old Town's attractions are located away from this strip in a maze of crooked alleyways – which explains the zigzagging itinerary described below.

Doma laukums

At the core of the Old Town, just off Kaļķu iela to the north, **Doma laukums** (Cathedral Square) is dominated by the red-brick bulk of Rīga's Romanesque **Cathedral**

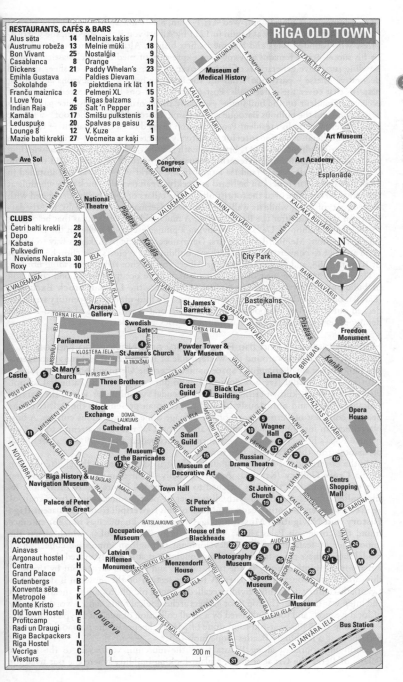

RĪGA OLD TOWN

RESTAURANTS, CAFÉS & BARS

Alus sēta	14	Melnais kaķis	7
Austrumu robeža	13	Melnie mūki	18
Bon Vivant	25	Nostalģia	9
Casablanca	8	Orange	19
Dickens	21	Paddy Whelan's	23
Emihla Gustava		Paldies Dievam	
Šokolahde	16	piektdiena irk lāt	11
Frančū maiznīca	2	Pelmeņi XL	15
I Love You	4	Rīgas balzams	3
Indian Raja	26	Salt 'n Pepper	31
Kamāla	17	Smilšu pulkstenis	6
Leduspuķe	20	Spalvas pa gaisu	22
Lounge 8	12	V. Ķuze	1
Mazie balti krekli	27	Vecmeita ar kaķi	5

CLUBS

Četri balti krekli	28
Depo	24
Kabata	29
Pulkvedim	
Neviens Neraksta	30
Roxy	10

ACCOMMODATION

Ainavas	O
Argonaut hostel	J
Centra	H
Grand Palace	A
Gutenbergs	B
Konventa sēta	F
Metropole	K
Monte Kristo	L
Old Town Hostel	M
Profitcamp	E
Radi un Draugi	G
Rīga Backpackers	I
Rīga Hostel	N
Vecrīga	C
Viesturs	D

0   200 m

(Rīgas dome; Tues 11am–6pm, Wed–Fri 1–6pm, Sat 10am–2pm; 1.50Ls). The biggest cathedral in the Baltics, it was begun in 1211 by Albert von Buxhoeveden, the warrior-priest who founded Rīga and became its first bishop. Although much tinkered with by his successors, it remains an exuberant expression of medieval ecclesiastical power, bowling successive generations of visitors over with its combination of sheer size and decorative finesse – particularly fine are the intricate brickwork chevrons and zigzag patterns that cover the outer walls. Post-medieval add-ons have bestowed a degree of eccentric grandeur on the building – especially the enormous Renaissance gable at its eastern end and the bulbous Baroque belfry rising improbably from the roof – a feature which inter-war English resident Peggie Benton likened to "a Georgian silver teapot".

In true Lutheran style, the **interior** is relatively austere, its most eye-catching features being a florid pulpit from 1641, bristling with statues of saints and trumpet-wielding angels, and a magnificent nineteenth-century organ with 6768 pipes – said to be the fourth largest in the world (and *the* largest in the world when it was first installed in 1884); its stentorian tones can be heard at weekly organ recitals – pick up a schedule at the cathedral entrance or at the tourist office. The pillars of the nave are decorated with carved coats of arms, while its walls are lined with German memorial slabs, mostly dating from the period after the Reformation. A much older gravestone is that belonging to Meinhard, Bishop of Uexküll, occupying a pinnacle-capped niche on the left-hand side of the choir. Meinhard was the first German ecclesiastic to make his way to Latvia in an attempt to convert the local heathens, building the region's first church southeast of Rīga in 1188, and paving the way for Albert von Buxhoeveden's crusading hordes.

The remaining three sides of the Doma laukums are occupied by an odd collection of buildings from various eras, grandest of which is the **Latvian Stock Exchange** (Latvijas birža), on the corner with Pils iela, a stately mid-nineteenth-century structure decked out in hues of maroon and green and decorated with reliefs of Greco-Roman demigods serving as allegories of various industries and trades.

Herdera laukums and the Rīga History and Navigation Museum

Doma laukums extends around the western side of the cathedral and runs into **Herdera laukums**, a small triangular space named after the German philosopher Johann Gottfried von Herder (see box opposite), who once taught in the cathedral school. Herder was a well-known critic of the harsh feudal system under which the Latvian peasantry lived, and notoriously likened the German presence in the Baltics to the Spanish conquest of Peru in terms of the damage done to indigenous culture. A bust placed here in his honour was removed after World War II in an attempt to de-Germanize Rīga's history – only to be returned to its pedestal in 1959 when a fraternal delegation from the GDR flew into town.

On the eastern side of Herdera laukums is the grilled entrance to the cloister known as the **Cross Gallery** (Krusteja; April–Oct daily 10am–5pm; 0.50Ls), a surviving part of the monastery that was attached to the cathedral before the Reformation. Its rib-vaulted arcades are stuffed with all manner of post-medieval junk, from coats of arms to seventeenth-century cannons. Much of this is overspill from the adjacent **Rīga History and Navigation Museum** (Rīgas vestures un kuģniecības muzejs; entrance round the corner on Palasta iela; Wed–Sun 11am–5pm; 1.50Ls), which charts the importance of seafaring in Rīga's development through an impressive collection of model ships. These range from the Viking longboats that regularly visited the Daugava estuary in the ninth century to the tugs, tankers and trawlers turned out by the local shipyards some thousand years later. A further section of the museum is devoted to twentieth-century urban life, vividly recalled through old photographs, theatre posters and inter-war fashions. The top floor gathers archeological finds, with a worthy display of local weapons and tools enlivened by a small collection of ancient Egyptian artefacts – including the 3400-year-old tombstone of Merire, keeper of the pharaoh's seal, seen here sporting a fetchingly Beatles-esque mop-top.

Continuing southeast along Palasta from the museum, you come to the former **Palace of Peter the Great** at no. 9, a plain-looking building where the tsar lived for all of three months in 1711. Peter first visited Rīga in 1697 during the so-called Grand Embassy, when he traversed northern and western Europe accumulating the kind of technological and military knowledge that would help Russia become a great power. He was prevented from studying Rīga's fortifications by local officials, an incident (subsequently dubbed the "insult at Rīga") which so rankled that Peter is said to have hurled the first grenade at the city himself when besieging it twelve years later. When Princess Sophie von Anhalt-Zerbst (the future Catherine the Great) stayed in the palace in 1744, her guard of honour was commanded by a certain Hieronymus Karl Friedrich von Munchhausen (1720–97), the bogus baron who went on to regale European society with improbable tales of his adventures while in imperial service.

Turning left into Jauniela takes you back towards Doma laukums, passing on the way the haughty female head that presides over the arched doorway of **Jauniela 25**. One of the most striking Art Nouveau buildings in the Old Town, it used to be the home of *Pie Kristapa*, Rīga's most famous restaurant during the Soviet period, now standing empty.

Just before you rejoin Doma laukums, a brief detour down the narrow Krāmu iela will bring you to the **Museum of the Barricades** at no. 3 (Mon–Fri 10am–5pm, Sat 11am–5pm; donation requested), displaying pictures and diagrams recalling the tension-filled days of January 1991, when it was feared that Soviet military action would crush the Latvian independence movement. Photographs of crowds brandishing Estonian and Lithuanian flags alongside the Latvians' own show the level of pan-Baltic solidarity at the time – a sentiment that has now all but evaporated.

Johann Gottfried von Herder (1744–1803)

Although ruled by a German-speaking aristocracy for seven hundred years, the Latvians retained a rich national culture, including a vast repertoire of folk songs that were passed down orally from one generation to the next. Ironically, the first person systematically to put these songs down in writing was a German, **Johann Gottfried von Herder**.

Born in the small East Prussian town of Mohrungen (now Morąg in Poland), Herder studied medicine and theology in Königsberg before arriving in Rīga to teach at the cathedral school in 1764. Herder's interest in folklore was initially focused on Germany, a country then divided into petty principalities, each ruled by an aristocratic elite that preferred French manners and culture to their own. Herder maintained that the rediscovery and propagation of authentic folklore would provide the German people with the cultural confidence that they lacked. The five years Herder spent in Rīga were enough to persuade him that the folk cultures of other nations – including the Latvians and Estonians – deserved to be taken just as seriously.

Believing that the very soul of a nation resided in its folk poetry, Herder spent the rest of his life collating traditional songs of peasant cultures, from the Baltics to the Balkans. Many of these were collected together in his *Stimmen der Völker in Liedern* ("Voices of the Peoples in Song"). A large number of these songs were of an epic nature, recalling heroic struggles against powerful enemies or foreign occupiers, and they went down a storm with a Europe-wide public hungry for an exotic, romantic read.

When an ethnic Latvian intelligentsia began to emerge in the late nineteenth century, Herder's work provided the foundations upon which a modern national culture could be built. The poet and journalist Andrējs Pumpurs (see p.271) came up with just the kind of national epic that Herder had been so enthusiastic about and concocted the tale of superhuman warrior *Lāčplēsis* (published in 1888) by weaving several folk tales into a single narrative and adding his own material. His near-contemporary Krišjānis Barons (see p.434) carried out the more painstaking task of systematically collecting over one million folk songs, thereby bequeathing a vast library of indigenous literature to the nation. The songs collected by Barons still form the staple diet of Latvia's choral societies, and remain central to the country's self-image to this day.

Pils laukums

From Doma laukums, Pils iela runs west to leafy **Pils laukums** (Castle Square), the site of Rīga's **Castle** (Rīgas pils). The castle began life as the headquarters of the Livonian Order, and now serves as the official residence of the Latvian president and also accommodates three museums. It has had a somewhat chequered history: the original thirteenth-century construction was demolished in 1484 by Rīga's municipal authorities, who were eager to celebrate the Livonian Order's declining influence over life in the city, and even sent individual bricks to other Hanseatic cities as a mark of their success. In 1491, the Order forced the townsfolk to rebuild it, and after numerous later additions, the castle ended up looking like the rather nondescript office block it is today. Beyond the discreet front door lies the first of the three museums, the **Foreign Art Museum** (Ārzemju mākslas muzejs; Tues–Sun 11am–5pm; 1Ls); its occasional visiting exhibitions are usually more interesting than its permanent collection – which comprises plaster copies of Greek and Roman sculptures plus a smattering of minor Flemish and Dutch paintings. A couple of floors above is the considerably more colourful **Latvian History Museum** (Latvijas vēstures muzejs; Wed–Sun 11am–5pm; ⓦwww.history-museum.lv; 1Ls), containing a well-presented display of Neolithic pots, early Latvian weaponry and medieval jewellery – the necklaces and headbands made from coil-like strips of metal look surprisingly contemporary. A room full of ploughs, rakes and wicker baskets evokes the back-breaking toil endured by nineteenth-century villagers, although the traditional Latvian taste for the fine things in life is evident in the display of folk costumes from all over the country – exquisitely embroidered belts and bonnets for the ladies, sober grey or blue tunics for the blokes. Still on the same floor, the **Museum of Writing, Theatre and Music** (Rakstniecības, teātra un mūzikas muzejs; Wed–Sun 11am–5pm; 0.50Ls) isn't as exciting as it sounds, consisting as it does of a stuffily didactic display devoted to the big names of Latvian literature – useful if you're writing a thesis but not much fun otherwise.

From the Three Brothers to the Swedish Gate

Heading back east from Pils laukums along Mazā Pils iela takes you past the trio of venerable houses known as the **Three Brothers** (Trīs brāli). The first of the three, at no. 17, which looks like a Cubist painter's nightmare and appears to be toppling into its neighbours, is also the oldest, dating from the early 1400s. While the slight, green brother at no. 21 is a little on the unassuming side, the middle sibling at no. 19 is a handsome, yellow-ochre structure with an elegant Renaissance portal and wood-beamed interior that now harbours the **Latvian Architecture Museum** (Latvijas architektūras muzejs; Mon–Fri 9am–5pm; donation requested), hosting small but worthwhile temporary exhibitions.

A left turn into Jēkaba iela at the end of Mazā Pils iela leads to the thirteenth-century red-brick **St James's Church** (Jēkaba baznīca), the seat of Rīga's Roman Catholic archbishop. As the centre of efforts to re-Catholicize Rīga in the late sixteenth century, St James's was trashed by the townsfolk on Christmas Day, 1584, and its rich inventory of Renaissance artworks destroyed. In a totally unconnected piece of urban lore, the church was famous for possessing bells which would supposedly peal of their own accord whenever a two-timing woman walked past. Those who wish to test the veracity of this belief should be warned that the bells were melted down to provide Russia with munitions in World War I and the church has been chime-free ever since.

Next door, at Jēkaba 11, is Latvia's **Parliament** (Saeima), a rather workmanlike neo-Renaissance building that you wouldn't normally notice were it not for the discreet purr of ministerial motorcars on the cobbled street outside. Built in 1867 as an assembly hall for the Barons of Vidzeme (a region in eastern Latvia), and accordingly dubbed the Ritterhaus, or "Knights' House", it became the headquarters of Peteris Stučka's Bolsheviks during their brief reign over Rīga in spring 1919, only to be taken over by the British Mission to the Baltic States when the Reds retreated. Stučka's headed notepaper was still on the desks when the mission moved in, and its members immediately used it to write jokey letters home. Attendance at the mission's not infrequent parties was considered de rigueur by any party animal still left standing in the war-scarred city. When mission head Stephen Tallents held a reception for Latvian parliamentarians in May 1920, he commented drily that "the drinks were vodka, port and beer. Some of our guests drank them separately, others preferred them mixed."

At its northern end, Jēkaba iela opens out onto Torņa iela, where a left turn brings you to the **Arsenal Gallery** (Arsenāls; Tues–Sun 11am–5pm; 1.50Ls), the place to catch high-profile contemporary art shows. Heading in the opposite direction along Torņa iela takes you past **St James's Barracks** (Jēkaba kazarmas), a two-hundred-metre-long block built in the seventeenth century by the Swedes and now occupied by a string of upmarket shops and offices. Fired by cultural patriotism and revolutionary fervour, Latvian units of the Russian army invited Rīga's artists to establish a commune in the barracks in 1917. It was soon closed down by the city authorities, but its members went on to dominate the Latvian cultural scene during the inter-war years.

Over the road from the barracks is another legacy of Swedish rule, the **Swedish Gate** (Zviedru vārti), a simple archway beneath a three-storey town house. The only surviving city gate, it no longer leads anywhere in particular, although the alleyways on the other side – Aldaru iela and Trokšņu iela – are as picturesque as any in this part of town.

The Powder Tower and the Latvian War Museum

At the end of Torņa iela is the **Powder Tower** (Pulvertornis), a portly fourteenth-century bastion whose red-brick walls are still embedded with cannonballs from various sieges. In the years before World War I the tower served as the headquarters of the German-dominated Rubonia student fraternity, one of whose leaders was Alfred Rosenberg, future ideological mentor to Adolf Hitler and leading exponent of the idea of German superiority over the peasant races of Eastern Europe – Latvians included. Somewhat appropriately, the tower now forms part of the adjacent **Latvian War Museum** (Latvijas kara muzejs; Wed–Sun: May–Sept 10am–6pm; Oct–April 10am–5pm; free), a well-presented, four-storey array of guns, uniforms and photographs that provides a thorough introduction to modern Latvian history. The narrative kicks off with World War I and the Latvian Riflemen – local units who fought with the Tsarist armies before defecting to the Bolsheviks (see box, p.435). The establishment of the inter-war state (when both Germans and Bolsheviks had to be beaten off) gets equally thorough coverage: it comes as a bit of a surprise to see Latvian aeroplanes of the 1920s sporting swastikas until you learn that this common folk symbol was politically neutral at the time. Space is also devoted to the Latvian Legion – volunteers who served with the German Waffen SS during World War II. Most poignant of all is the room devoted to the anti-Soviet partisans of the 1944–56 period: cheery black-and-white portraits of optimistic young fighters are juxtaposed with Russian intelligence photographs of those who were later captured and summarily shot.

The Great and Small Guilds

From the Powder Tower, Meistaru iela runs down to the **Great Guild** (Lielā Ģilde) on the corner of Meistaru and Amatu, once the centre of commercial life in Hanseatic Rīga. The building owes its present neo-Gothic appearance to a nineteenth-century facelift, its main hall now pressed into service as the major venue for concerts by the Latvian National Symphony Orchestra. Immediately next door is the smaller but infinitely more arresting **Small Guild** (Mazā Ģilde), a playfully asymmetrical building featuring a castellated turret on one side and a jaunty spire on the other. A statue of the guild's patron, St John, occupies a niche beneath the spire. Rīga's business class had been divided into these two guilds since the fourteenth century, when the richer traders organized the Great Guild in order to differentiate themselves from shopkeepers and artisans, who quickly formed themselves into the Small Guild. Both guilds were exclusively German institutions – Latvian-speaking Rīgans had to make do with the significantly less prestigious Guild of Fishermen and Boatmen, which collected together all those who worked on and around the Daugava River. Between them, the guilds regulated almost all commercial activity in the city until the mid-nineteenth century, after which they survived as social clubs until dying out completely in the 1930s, largely owing to lack of interest.

Opposite the Great and Small Guilds stands a yellow building known as the **Black Cat** (Melnais Kaķis), a wonderfully fluid piece of late Art Nouveau named after the lithe feline forms that ornament its two fanciful turrets. According to urban legend, the building's owner had been black-balled by the Great Guild, and so arranged for a cat statuette to be placed on his rooftop, proffering its behind in the guild's general direction. After a successful legal action by the guild, the beast had to be repositioned with its cheeks pointing the opposite way.

Kalķu iela and Skārņu iela

South of the guilds, Meistaru joins up with **Kalķu iela**, the Old Town's main thoroughfare and its most popular evening promenading ground. Numerous narrow streets lead off the southern side of Kalķu; the most graceful is **Skārņu iela**, which curves past a row of medieval buildings, their pastel-painted facades providing the photogenic backdrop to a clutch of souvenir stalls.

At Skārņu 10, the austere stone interior of the thirteenth-century chapel of St George provides a suitably atmospheric home to the **Museum of Decorative and Applied Arts** (Dekoratīvi lietišķās mākslas muzejs; Tues, Thurs–Sun 11am–5pm, Weds 11am–7pm; ⓦwww.dlmm.lv; 1.50Ls), which showcases crafts as diverse as textile-weaving, glassware and book-binding. During the inter-war years, Rīga's crockery factories employed some of the country's best artists to design their tableware, and plates by the likes of Aleksandra Beļcova, Romans Suta and Sigismund Vindbergs – imaginatively mixing folksy Latvian motifs with more modern abstract forms – deservedly occupy centre stage here. Next door to the museum is the thirteenth-century **St John's Church** (Jāṇa baznīca; Tues–Sat 10am–5pm; donation requested), the red and green brickwork of its stepped gable catching the late afternoon sun to spectacular effect. Legend has it that two monks chose to be immured in the southern facade during the church's construction, where they lived on food delivered through a hole in the wall – an extreme act of ascetic piety not unknown in the Middle Ages. The Gothic interior, whose rib-vaulted ceiling has recently been repainted in jolly primary colours, is a popular venue for chamber concerts.

St Peter's Church

Looming up on the western side of Skārņu iela is **St Peter's Church** (Pētera baznīca; Tues–Sun 10am–5pm; 0.50Ls), an imposing red-brick structure whose graceful three-tiered spire is very much the city's trademark symbol. Although of thirteenth-century origins, the main body of the church acquired its present shape in the early 1400s and, notwithstanding the addition of some Baroque statues on either side of the main door, has remained pretty much the same ever since. The history of the spire is another story, however, beginning in 1491 with the construction of a 137-metre wooden spire – the highest in Europe at the time. It collapsed just under two hundred years later and was rebuilt twice in Baroque style before being destroyed by German shelling in 1941. Today's 123-metre spire is a steel replica of the eighteenth-century version, its three slender tiers seeming to sprout from a succession of onion domes. A lift (same times as the church; 2Ls) takes visitors to a gallery in its upper reaches, where you can enjoy a panoramic view of the city from the observation platform. After this, the impressively lofty church interior is a bit of a come-down, rioting Protestants having destroyed its original medieval furnishings in the 1520s.

Rātslaukums and the House of the Blackheads

From the main door of St Peter's you look directly across Kungu iela towards **Rātslaukums** (Town Hall Square), whose buildings were largely destroyed in World War II and subsequently replaced by ponderous, Soviet-style blocks. Since independence, however, the square has been the focus of an ambitious rebuilding effort centred on the late-Gothic **House of the Blackheads** (Melngalvju nams), shelled by the Germans in 1941 and totally demolished by the Soviets at the war's end. Work began in 1995 to rebuild the house from scratch and was completed in time for Rīga's eight-hundredth birthday celebrations in 2001. It's a wackily asymmetrical affair, comprising two joined buildings, one set back slightly from the other, both of which boast enormous stepped gables studded with ornate windows and statue-bearing niches. Although you wouldn't know from the present-day replicas, the building on the right was originally the older of the two, begun in the fourteenth century and progressively tinkered with over the next two hundred years; the one on the left was tacked on in 1891, in conscious imitation of the original.

The house was initially used as a meeting place by several of Rīga's guilds, but gradually became associated with just one of them – the group of unmarried merchants that took the name "Blackheads" in honour of their patron, the Roman warrior-saint of North African origin, Maurice. A rowdy bachelors' drinking club, and the scene of grandiose feasts such as the Fasnachtsdrunken ("Carnival Drinking Bout"), celebrated on the Saturday before Shrove Tuesday, the house was both a focus of civic life and a symbol of Rīga's cosmopolitan, mercantile identity. For centuries it was a magnet for tourists and foreign conquerors alike – both Peter the Great of Russia (in 1709) and Kaiser Wilhelm of Germany (in 1917) made it their first port of call in order to stamp their authority on the city. Since it was the smartest auditorium in Rīga, the House was also a major concert venue – as musical director of the City Theatre in the late 1830s, Richard Wagner frequently brandished his baton here, sometimes conducting his composition *Nikolai: Hymn of the People* (written in honour of Tsar Nicholas I) as a show-stopping finale. The Blackheads as an organization survived until 1940, when the last of its members were repatriated along with the rest of Latvia's Germans. Today, the house is resuming something of its former social role, with its main hall serving as the venue for chamber concerts, and the ground floor shared between the Rīga tourist office and an upmarket café, pretentiously decked out in reproduction nineteenth-century furnishings.

On the other side of the square, the similarly war-ravaged **Town Hall** was also rebuilt in 2001, although without the same commitment to accuracy – it's essentially a twenty-first-century office block with a Neoclassical portal tacked on for good measure. Presiding over the flagstoned square between the Town Hall and the House of the Blackheads

△ The House of the Blackheads

is a **statue of Roland**, the legendary eighth-century knight who died defending a Pyrenean mountain pass against invading Arabs – an act immortalized in the epic medieval romance *The Song of Roland*. The cult of Roland was immensely popular in northern Europe, and Rīga honoured him with a statue on this spot in the fourteenth century – although the current version is a modern replica of a nineteenth-century incarnation.

The Occupation Museum

The western end of Rātslaukums is dominated by a squat, forbidding structure built to house the now-defunct Museum of the Latvian Riflemen, local troops who fought with the Bolsheviks during the Russian Civil War (see box opposite). After independence, donations from Latvians abroad paid for its transformation into the **Museum of Latvia's Occupation** (Latvijas okupācijas muzejs; Ⓦ www.occupationmuseum .lv; daily 11am–5pm; donation requested), a moving and in parts disturbing display devoted to Latvia's occupation by the Nazis and the Soviets respectively. Portraits of Hitler and Stalin hover, demon-like, above the entrance to the exhibition – it was their decision to parcel up Eastern Europe into mutually agreed spheres of influence in 1939 that condemned Latvia (along with Estonia and Lithuania) to the first period of Soviet occupation, which began in June 1940. Germany's declaration of war on the Soviet Union a year later ushered in four years of Nazi control (a photograph on display here shows Latvian girls in national costume welcoming the German troops with flowers), after which the Soviets returned in 1944 – and stayed for another 45 years. Contemporary photographs, propaganda posters and political proclamations recall these events in punchily effective style. The Soviets tried to rob Latvia of its ethnic identity by deporting a large proportion of its citizens to Siberia, implementing a first wave of mass arrests in June 1941, and a second in March 1949. The victims were often chosen arbitrarily – one of the Soviet warrants on display here gives the reason for arrest as simply "belonging to the Latvian nationality". Most of the deportees lived in log-cabin work camps that they had to build themselves – the interior of a typical barrack block has been reconstructed here to give an idea of the harshness of camp life. Display cases contain examples of the artefacts made by deportees to make the experience of exile bearable – beautiful hand-drawn Christmas cards, carved wooden chess sets and, most poignantly of all, the bizarre, balaclava-like face masks fashioned from scraps of material in a desperate attempt to ward off the Siberian winter.

Latvian Riflemen's Square and 11 Novembra Krastmala

A further echo of Soviet culture can be found in the windswept car park immediately west of the museum, which still bears the heroically communist name of **Latvian Riflemen's Square** (Latviešu strēlnieku laukums), and where the riflemen themselves are commemorated with a suitably red, granite monument. Depicting three stern figures buried in enormous greatcoats, it is one of the last examples of ideological sculpture left in the city. The natural gathering point for pro-communist, anti-independence protesters in 1991, the square is nowadays just a bus stop.

Northwest of the Riflemen's Square, along the right bank of the Daugava extends the traffic-choked strip of **11 Novembra Krastmala**, named in commemoration of the defeat of von der Goltz's Germans outside Rīga in November 1919, rather than the end of World War I in November 1918. The pleasant riverside walkway on the far side of the road is punctuated with steps leading down to the water's edge and provides a good vantage point from which to observe the traffic pulsing across Rīga's bridges – with the futuristic Vanšu tilts suspension bridge to the north and the elegant five-arched span of the railway bridge to the south. Until the building of the latter in 1872, the only Daugava crossing was a pontoon affair, laid out every spring and packed up again in the autumn. In winter, people simply drove their carts across the ice.

Heading along 11. Novembra towards Vanšu tilts, you'll come across a glass-covered shrine holding a wooden statue of St Christopher bearing the Christ Child on his broad shoulders. Known as **Lielais Kristaps**, or "Big Christopher", it's very much a symbol of the city.

The Latvian Riflemen

Considered heroes by Latvian patriots and Soviet loyalists alike, the **Latvian Riflemen** (*Latviešu strēlnieki*) continue to occupy a paradoxical place in the nation's heritage. Made up of local recruits, the unit was created by the Russians in 1915 and charged with the task of defending central Latvia against the advancing Germans. The Russian military authorities considered the creation of ethnic Latvian infantry units an effective way of harnessing local patriotism to the Tsarist cause and, initially at least, were not disappointed. The riflemen often bore the brunt of the heaviest fighting and soon became a symbol of military pride to the folks back home. Increasingly aware that they were being used as cannon-fodder by their Tsarist commanders, however, the riflemen came under the sway of revolutionary propaganda as the war dragged on. Radicalized by Bolshevik agitators, Latvian Riflemen played a key role in Lenin's seizure of power in November 1917.

Many of the riflemen simply drifted back to Latvia as World War I drew to an end, but those who remained loyal to the new Soviet state soon became a byword for Bolshevik discipline and were regarded by Lenin as the only revolutionary troops he could really trust. When anti-Bolshevik socialists attempted a coup in June 1918, the Latvians under General Vacetis were charged with defending the Kremlin – and saved the regime in the process.

The importance of the Latvian Riflemen to the Soviet regime was not lost on the Western powers, and in summer 1918 the British representative in Moscow, Robert Bruce Lockhart, aided by Sidney "Ace of Spies" Riley, briefly entertained the idea of bribing the Latvians into deserting the Bolsheviks. Agents of the Soviet security services, or Cheka (which counted numerous Latvians among its leaders), soon infiltrated the Lockhart plot and it was quickly abandoned.

The Menzendorff House and Grēcinieku iela

Immediately east of Rātslaukums, on the corner of Grēcinieku and Kungu, is the so-called **Menzendorff House** (Mencendorfa nams; Wed–Sun 10am–5pm; 1.20Ls), an impeccably restored merchant's house decorated in grand style and adorned with period furniture and artefacts. Built by alderman Jürgen Helm in 1695, the house got its name from the Menzendorff delicatessen, which occupied the ground floor of the building in the years before World War I and kept Rīga society supplied with Swiss chocolates and other luxury nibbles. The four-storey interior was turned into flats after World War II and allowed to decay, but was completely renovated in the 1980s and pretty much restored to its eighteenth-century self – complete with creaky pine floors, mullioned windows and chunky Baroque wardrobes. It provides a charming insight into the world of Rīga's mercantile elite – and with house plants adding that homely touch, it will probably give you a few interior design ideas into the bargain.

East of the Menzendorff House, **Grēcinieku iela** threads its way past a clutch of shops and bars. With a name that translates as "Sinners' Street", Grēcinieku was for a long time Rīga's pleasure quarter, a tradition that still holds true today if excessive alcohol consumption counts among the major vices – several of the Old Town's most popular bars are located here. Grēcinieku gives way to Audēju iela, where swarms of shoppers are daily sucked up into the city's main multistorey shopping mall **Centrs**. Nowadays much expanded, Centrs's central feature is a distinctive wedge of grey concrete that was considered a bold piece of modern architecture when it first opened as a department store in the 1920s.

From Grēcinieku iela to the Central Market

On the southern side of Grēcinieku and Audēju lies a warren of narrow streets lined with ancient, mostly unrestored, merchants' houses. Turning off Grēcinieku into Marstaļu and taking a sharp left into Alksnāja iela brings you to the **Photography**

Museum (Fotogrāfijas muzejs; Tue, Fri & Sat 10am–5pm, Wed & Thurs noon–7pm; 0.70Ls), which offers an entertaining jaunt through the history of photography in Latvia. Things get under way with Tsarist-era family portraits and an early photo-journalist's record of President Ulmanis's arrival in Rīga in 1919, greeted by head of the British Mission (and temporarily governor of Rīga) Steven Tallents. Moving on to the 1920s and 1930s, glamour photos and publicity shots of Latvian actresses reveal what an exciting place inter-war Rīga must have been. There's surprisingly little in the display relating to Eižens Finks, the 1930s clairvoyant and celebrity photographer of Romany origin who became the subject of a Latvian musical (*Sfinks*) in 2002. However, there is a small section devoted to the desirably sleek and silvery Minox, a miniature camera developed by Rīga's VEF factory in the 1930s and displayed – with understandable pride – as a shining example of how technologically advanced the Latvian republic was before the Soviets took over.

A little further along Alksnāja, the **Sports Museum** (Sporta muzejs; Tues–Fri 10am–5pm, Sat 11am–5pm; 0.50Ls) at no. 9 is largely given over to changing exhibitions, although there's bound to be something on display recalling the phenomenal line of Latvian-trained javelin throwers who won Olympic medals for the Soviet Union – as well as the country's only post-independence gold medallist, gymnast Igors Vihrovs, granted his gong for floor exercises in Sydney in 2000.

Hidden in an unassuming courtyard off the southeastern end of Alksnāja iela, the **Rīga Film Museum**, Māza Peitavas iela (Tues–Sat 11am–6pm; 2Ls), mounts temporary exhibitions devoted to different aspects of Latvian cinema history – they're usually highly colourful and entertaining affairs, accompanied by screenings of historic films.

Emerging from Alksnāja and crossing the busy 13. Janvāra iela, you come to the **Central Market** (Centrāltirgus), an animated, seven-days-a-week affair housed in five hulking pavilions, each the size of a small football pitch. The pavilions are recondi-tioned World War I zeppelin hangars, built near Liepāja by the Germans and re-erected here in the 1920s, with ochre Art Deco facades tacked on at each end lending an air of architectural extravagance. Inside, stallholders sell top-quality farm produce from all over Latvia; as well as excellent honey and cheeses, you'll come across rows of animal carcasses waiting to be carved into cutlets in the meat hall (gaļu pavilions), and gurgling tanks full of eels and carp in the fish hall (zivu pavilions). Outside the hangars, Rīgans who can't afford supermarket prices throng around the fruit, veg and flower stalls, or peer into the jumbled window displays of kiosks selling everything from alarm clocks to zebra-print underwear.

East of the Old Town: the park belt

From the eastern edge of the Old Town, the broad asphalt stripe of **Brīvības bulvaris** (Freedom Boulevard) and its extension, Brīvības iela, forge a path out to the suburbs and beyond, cutting through a sequence of parks marking the boundary between medieval Rīga and the nineteenth-century parts of town to the east. The parks come in two parallel strips running roughly northwest to southeast: the first, comprising **City Park** and **Kronvalds Park**, is bordered to the east by **Raiņa bulvaris**, a busy street lined with imposing nineteenth-century mansions – mostly occupied by banks, foreign embassies and Rīga University. Beyond Raiņa lies the second strip of parkland, made up of **Esplanāde** and **Vērmane's Garden**. Landscaped when the city walls were demolished in the 1850s, the whole area is now a much-loved green belt, characterized by well-tended lawns, stately rows of trees and the odd formal flowerbed. It's packed with promenaders whatever the season – although it may no longer offer the kind of nocturnal thrills that Graham Greene encountered in the early 1930s, when he noted with excitement that "all the lights in Rīga were dimmed by ten: the public parks were quite dark and full of whispers. Giggles from hidden seats, excited rustles in the bushes. One had the sensation of a whole town on the tiles."

Marking the start of Brīvības on the corner of Aspazijas bulvaris is the **Laima Clock**, an unassuming four-metre-high pillar erected in the 1930s to advertise the Laima chocolate factory, and still sporting its original Art Deco logo. It's a much-loved monument to inter-war Rīga and is also the place at which half the city agrees to meet in the evening.

The Freedom Monument

Dominating the view as you head east along Brīvības iela is the defiantly Modernist **Freedom Monument** (Brīvības piemineklis). Unveiled on November 18, 1935, it's a soaring allegory of Latvian independence and has occupied an important place in the national psyche ever since. A red granite pedestal bearing reliefs of Latvian heroes and inscribed with the words *Tevzemei un brīvībai* ("for fatherland and freedom") provides the base for a slender fifty-metre-high column, crowned by a stylized female figure affectionately known as "Milda" – the most popular female first name in the country between the wars, Milda became emblematic of Latvia as a whole. She holds aloft three stars symbolizing the three regions of Latvia – Kurzeme, Vidzeme and Latgale – a constant source of puzzlement to Latvian schoolchildren who have always been taught that the country is made up of four regions, not three. (The reason for this confusion lies in the fact that the fourth region, Zemgale, fell within the administrative boundaries of Kurzeme for much of its history and is therefore overlooked in Milda's case.)

Oddly, the Soviets never attempted to demolish this rallying point for Latvian patriotism – unsurprisingly, it was the scene of the first pro-independence demonstrations in August 1987. During the 1990s it became the focus for gatherings of former SS Latvian volunteers on **March 16** – the official day of remembrance for World War II veterans. A government keen to ingratiate itself with both NATO and the EU banned the event after 2001, although the general public still gravitate towards the Freedom Monument for a bout of flower-laying on the same date.

The City Park and Bastejkalns

On either side of Brīvības, paths dive into the **City Park** (Pilsētas parks), the first of the wedges of greenery that extend along the eastern boundaries of the Old Town. A ribbon of well-tended lawns patrolled by ducks, it's split by the serpentine form of a rather stagnant-looking **City Canal** (Pilsētas kanāls) – what's left of Rīga's moat. The main feature of the park on the southeastern side of Brīvības is the coolly imperious Rīga **Opera House**, built in 1887 and recently restored to something approaching its *belle époque* splendour.

Northwest of Brīvības, paths wind their way around **Bastejkalns** (Bastion Hill), a low knoll which began life as a pile of left-over rubble after the city defences were dismantled and was subsequently grassed over. It is also a reminder of Rīga's more recent history: on January 20, 1991, five people were killed here by sniper fire as Soviet OMON troops stormed the Latvian Ministry of the Interior on nearby Raiņa bulvaris during an attempted crackdown on Latvia's independence drive. Stones on the northern side of the hill mark the spots where they fell – the victims were Gvido Zvaigzne and Andris Slapiņš (cameramen attached to the film crew of acclaimed documentarist Jūris Podnieks), teenage schoolboy Edijs Riekstiņš and militiamen Sergejs Kononenko and Vladimirs Gomanovics.

Further over to the northwest, progress through the park is briefly broken by the busy thoroughfare of **Valdemāra iela**, the far side of which is overlooked by the **National Theatre** (Nacionālais teātris), a pair of muscular Titans bearing the weight of its newly renovated, neo-Baroque facade. It was here that Latvian independence was proclaimed on November 18, 1918, although the nation's new leaders had hastily to evacuate a city that was soon overrun by the Bolsheviks. The resolutely modern **Rīga Congress Centre** (Rīgas kongresu nams), which stands at the corner of Kronvalds Park (Kronvalda parks) 200m further north, played host to another generation of Latvian leaders in 1988, when it served as the venue for the first-ever congress of the Latvian Popular Front.

Museum of Medical History

Heading northeast across Kronvalds Park from the Congress Centre and crossing over Kalpaka bulvaris takes you to one of Rīga's most compelling museums, the **Stradiņš**

Museum of Medical History (Stradiņa medicīnas muzejs; Tues–Sat 10am–4pm; closed on last Fri of month; 0.50Ls), on the corner of Kalpaka and Antonijas iela. Based on the collection of the Latvian physician Pauls Stradiņš (1896–1958), it's packed with eccentric oddities, beginning with a series of dioramas illustrating man's first forays into medicine; in one of them, a witch-doctor is trepanning a patient by hammering a pointed stick into his skull with a rock. A re-creation of a medieval street scene has plague victims grimacing from upstairs windows, and a man having his leg sawn off with the aid of a prayer book rather than an anaesthetic. Upstairs, a re-created dental surgery of the 1930s will probably have you vowing never to visit the dentist's again, while a nearby section on the Soviet space programme includes a cabin built to accommodate space dog Veterok ("Breeze"), who flew on Kosmos 110 together with fellow four-legged cosmonaut Ugolek – both returned safely to earth. The canine theme concludes with the museum's most notorious exhibit, the (stuffed) **two-headed dog** of Dr Demihov, the eccentric Soviet scientist who pioneered a range of organ transplants in animals, few of which lived to tell the tale. Looking more like a creature from the novels of Mikhail Bulgakov than a monument to scientific progress, this particular specimen was produced by grafting the head and torso of a small dog onto the back of a larger one, ostensibly in order to see whether the vital functions of a weakened animal could be sustained by attaching it to a stronger host (apparently the dogs were so enraged they almost bit each other to death before being put down).

The State Art Museum

Heading back southeast along Kalpaka brings you face to face with the stern, red-brick bulk of the **Art Academy** (Mākslas akademija), a building so perfectly neo-Gothic that it was used to represent London locations in Soviet-made Sherlock Holmes adventures. Immediately northeast, the junction of Valdemāra and Elizabetes is dominated by the **State Art Museum** (Valsts mākslas muzejs; Wed–Mon 11am–5pm; ⊛ www.lnmm .lv; 1.50Ls), a grandiose Neoclassical edifice with an imperious-looking Athena gazing down from above the entrance. A staircase ascends from an ostentatious Second-Empire-style lobby to the galleries, where you'll find an exhaustive overview of Latvian painting and sculpture, although the collection stops short in the 1950s (artists have to be dead before they're allowed in here, as the local wags have it).

Prime among the past masters is the St Petersburg-educated **Jānis Rozentāls** (1866–1916), who employed a lively Impressionistic style in documenting the Latvian landscape and its people – although the most famous of his works on show here (and one that most Latvians would instantly recognize) is the comparatively dour *Coming from Church after the Service* (1894), depicting sober village folk togged up in their Sunday best. Others who sought to capture the character of the Latvian countryside were **Jānis Valters** (1869–1932) and **Vilhelms Purvītis** (1872–1945), both represented here by a number of Post-Impressionistic canvases featuring, for the most part, forests. The diversity of Latvian inter-war art on display owes a lot to the activities of the Rīga Artists' Group, an organization that brought together most of the painters who had been involved in the St James's Barracks commune (see p.195) – look out for the brooding expressionist works of **Jēkabs Kazaks** (1895–1920) and the angular, cubist pictures of **Niklāvs Strunke** (1894–1966). The most revolutionary artist of the period was **Gustavs Klucis** (1895–1938), an enthusiastic Bolshevik who chose a career in the Soviet Union rather than life in inter-war Latvia – constructivist collages like *Lenin and Socialist Reconstruction* (1927) and *More Coal and Metal* (1932) are masterpieces of the agitprop genre. The leading Latvian female artist of the twentieth century, **Aleksandra Beļcova** (1892–1981), is represented by a striking series of female portraits, combining the glamour of glossy magazine covers with a palpable atmosphere of listlessness and boredom.

Esplanāde

Stretching southeast of the State Art Museum is the **Esplanāde**, a park planted with rows of lime trees at the close of the nineteenth century and popular with strollers and pram-wielding parents ever since. Rising above the trees at its southeastern end are the neo-Byzantine domes of the **Cathedral of the Nativity** (Kristus dzimsanas katedrāle), built for the city's expanding Russian community in 1884 and turned into a planetarium during the Soviet period, when the planetarium's café was a popular hangout for the city's bohemian intelligentsia. Restored and repainted since being returned to the church in 1990, the cathedral boasts some wonderfully expressive Byzantine-style frescoes.

A little way west of the cathedral is a pink granite statue of **Jānis Rainis** (1865–1929), the poet and playwright whose dour, socially engaged works form the staple diet of Latvian schoolchildren. Gracing a pedestal on the eastern side of the cathedral is a statue of **General Barclay de Tolly**, the Livonian baron of Scottish descent who was commander-in-chief of the Russian armies during the Napoleonic Wars. The statue itself was evacuated – along with other Tsarist-era public sculptures – by the retreating Russian army in World War I, only to enjoy something of a second coming in 2001, when local businessman Yevgeny Gomberg commissioned a replica of the work and began to campaign for its reinstatement. Gomberg previously financed the restoration of an equestrian statue of **Peter the Great**, which once stood on the site now occupied by the Freedom Monument, and briefly displayed it in the Esplanāde in 2001 before returning it to storage. He then offered it as a gift to the city of St Petersburg, but the Rīga city authorities stymied the move; the Russians, however, commissioned a copy of the statue, which now stands outside St Petersburg's Constantine Palace, where it is affectionately known as "the Rīga Peter".

Vērmane's Garden and the Natural History Museum

Continuing southeast along Elizabetes iela, you soon come to the next park, **Vērmane's Garden** (Vērmanes dārzs), occupied by residential houses until 1812, when the Tsarist authorities burnt them down to provide the army with a field of fire from which to defend the city against the advancing French. This may have been a huge miscalculation – it's said that one of the Russian scouts saw dust rising from a herd of cattle just south of the city and mistook it for Napoleon's cavalry; the cavalry however weren't actually anywhere near Rīga and decided to give it a miss. Five years later, the wasteland was redeveloped as a park by the wife of Rīga merchant, A. Wöhrmann (transliterated as "Vērmane" in Latvian, hence the park's name), although for decades it was reserved for Rīga's elite – the plebs had to content themselves with observing the Sunday promenade from behind the railings. Nowadays, the park is a favoured meeting point for elderly chess-players, who hog the benches of a little-used outdoor theatre in the park's northwestern corner.

Leaving Vērmane's Garden at the southernmost corner and crossing Barona iela brings you to the **Latvian Natural History Museum** at Baroņa 4 (Latvijas dabas muzejs; ⓦ www.dabasmuzejs.gov.lv; Wed, Fri & Sat 10am–5pm, Thurs 10am–6pm, Sun 10am–4pm; 1Ls), which has three floors of exhibits covering everything from moths to mammoth tusks, all exhaustively labelled in Russian and Latvian. If you head southwest from here along Baroņa and cross the canal you end up back in the Old Town.

The Centre (Centrs)

East of the Vērmane's Garden and Esplanāde parks is the district known as the **Centre** (Centrs) – a name that never fails to confuse first-time visitors, who, not unreasonably, assume that Rīga's centre is somewhere in the Old Town. Although it's a largely residential area, the reason it's called "the Centre" is because it also contains the city's most important shopping and commercial district – concentrated in the region enclosed by **Valdemāra iela** to the northwest and **Čaka iela** to the southeast. The boulevards that characterize the Centre bear witness to a period of rapid urban expansion that began in the mid-1800s and lasted right up until World War I. With Rīga growing into a major industrial city, rows of four- and five-storey apartment buildings were erected to house the expanding middle class, and the single-storey wooden houses which then predominated were gradually cleared.

Sergei Mikhailevich Eisenstein (1898–1948)

Cinema pioneer Sergei Eisenstein was born in Rīga in 1898. He grew up at Valdemāra 6 (a plaque outside the Zvaigzne bookshop marks the spot), and was educated at the gymnasium just down the road at Valdemāra 1 (which still serves as a high school). His report cards gave little indication of his future calling – he only ever got average marks for art and, appropriately for someone who went on to become a master of propaganda, his best subject was theology. However, the development of Eisenstein's visual imagination is apparent in the letters he wrote to his mother, who had moved to St Petersburg in 1909 – in these, Eisenstein recounts the events of the week in vivid film-storyboard style, with cartoon strips and caricatures.

During World War I, the Eisensteins were evacuated to Russia, Sergei going on to study art in Moscow after the war, before specializing in film. Many observers have interpreted his choice of the new and revolutionary form of cinema as a rebellion against the florid style of his architect father. His cinematic trademark – the employment of a vigorous, jump-cut editing style–he called "the montage of attractions".

Cinema was regarded as the most politically effective art form of all by Soviet Russia's new rulers, and Eisenstein quickly established himself as its greatest practitioner. His first feature film, *Strike* (1924), was an attack on the evils of capitalism, while *October* (1928) offered up an over-dramatized reconstruction of the Bolshevik seizure of power – it's said that more people were injured during the making of the film than during the event itself.

During the inter-war years Eisenstein's films were rarely seen in the city of his birth. Playwright and socialist MP, Jānis Rainis (see p.221), campaigned successfully to have Eisenstein's greatest masterpiece *Battleship Potemkin* (1925) shown in Rīga, despite the hostility of government censors towards such outright Soviet propaganda. Things changed when Latvia was sucked into the Soviet sphere of influence in 1939, and Eisenstein's epic of medieval Russia's struggle against the Germans, *Alexander Nevsky*, arrived in local cinemas at a time of growing anti-German feeling. "At each reverse suffered by the Teutonic Knights," wrote British diplomat's wife Peggie Benton, "the Latvian audience stamped their feet and clapped until the management had to silence them by turning on the lights."

These long lines of apartment blocks look a little grey and unwelcoming on first sight, but as you get up close a wealth of **Art Nouveau** embellishments comes to light: florid stucco swirls adorning doorways, stylized human faces incorporated into facades and towers fancifully placed on top of buildings. It always pays to look up to catch details that might otherwise pass unnoticed – and if the number of scantily clad nymphs gazing down from the Centre's facades is anything to go by, Sigmund Freud would have had a field day analyzing the architectural tastes of Rīga's bourgeoisie.

Along Elizabetes iela to Alberta iela

The biggest concentration of Art Nouveau buildings lies in the northwestern corner of the Centre, the majority of them designed by **Mikhail Eisenstein**, the architect father of cinema pioneer Sergei (see box above). One of Eisenstein *père*'s most famous creations lies just north of the Esplanāde park at **Elizabetes 10A and 10B**, an apartment building adorned with plaster flourishes and gargoyles and topped by two vast, impassive faces. Eisenstein was also responsible for just about everything on the even-numbered side of **Alberta iela**, one block north of here, a uniquely exotic terrace of town houses, each of which is stylistically different from the next. The most extrovert of the lot is the florid neo-Egyptian affair at no. 2A, although the fact that the facade is slightly higher than the building itself makes it look more like a film set than a real building. At ground level things are more reassuring, with a brace of contented-looking sphynxes standing guard on either side of the entrance.

△ Art Nouveau facade on Elizabetes iela

The most striking of the buildings on the opposite side of the street is the dark-grey apartment block at no. 11 designed by Eižens Laube, the prime exponent of **National Romanticism**. Following hard on the heels of Art Nouveau in Rīga, this new style sought to establish a truly Latvian form of architecture through the inclusion of folksy touches like shingled roofs, irregular window frames and pointy gables – all of which are employed here to monumental effect.

The Rozentāls and Blaumanis Museum

Laube also helped to design the neo-Gothic building looming over the corner of Alberta iela and Strēlnieku iela. Prominent among the pre-World War I yuppies and arty types who were attracted to such real-estate developments was painter Jānis Rozentāls (1866–1916) – his top-floor apartment is now open to the public as the **Jānis Rozentāls and Rudolfs Blaumanis Museum** (Jāņa Rozentāla un Rudolfa Blaumaņa memoriālais muzejs; Wed–Sun 11am–6pm; 0.70Ls). The museum is packed with period furnishings and evocative pictures of Rīga at the beginning of the twentieth century. In many ways the father of Latvian painting, Rozentāls (1866–1916) is primarily known for his large-format landscapes, although the smaller canvases gathered together here are full of intimacy and warmth – especially the portraits of his friends, children and Finnish mezzo-soprano wife. The family spent their summers in Finland, and pictures of the Rozentāls lolling around lakeshores fill the light-flooded attic studio where Rozentāls received students. The guest room next door was set aside by Rozentāls for his friend Rudolfs Blaumanis (1863–1908), the journalist, playwright and master of the Latvian realistic novel, who, despite enjoying a towering reputation among the local intelligentsia, never earned enough money to rent his own big-city pad. The room is largely bare save for a few facsimile manuscripts and a glass case containing a huge bearskin coat – donated by Rozentāls to help the tubercular Blaumanis ward off the winter chill.

The Museum of Latvia's Jews

A five-minute walk east of Alberta iela is the small but compelling **Museum of Latvia's Jews** (Muzejs Ebreji Latvijā; Mon–Thurs and Sun noon–5pm; donation requested), located on the third floor of the Jewish community's cultural centre at

Skolas 6. Built around documents amassed over many years by two Rīga-based Holocaust survivors, Zalman Elelson and Margers Vestermanis, the display commemorates a community that on the eve of World War II made up eleven percent of Rīga's population – the second-largest ethnic group in the city after the Latvians themselves – before being all but wiped out by the Nazis.

Until the twentieth century there was little evidence of anti-Semitism in Latvia, a point pressed home by the following quote from the 1881 article, *A Word on the Baltic Jews*, by nineteenth-century national ideologue Krišjanis Valdemārs: "Not one Latvian, neither wise nor fool, in the townlet or on the land, neither thought nor spoke about Jews being injurious to them. I myself perceived that Jews do somewhat to the benefit of Christians but nothing to the detriment." As photographs in the exhibition show, Jewish volunteer batallions fought on the Latvian side in the 1918–20 War of Independence and numerous Jewish politicians stood for mainstream Latvian parties in the years that followed. Although many Jews spoke German or Latvian (and frequently both), Rīga was also an important centre of Yiddish culture in the inter-war period, known above all as the home town of the quality colour magazine *Yidishe Bilde*, the Jewish *National Geographic* of its time. All of this was snuffed out when the Germans moved into Latvia in 1941: most of the city's Jews were herded into ghettos southeast of the Old Town, then taken to forests outside the city and shot. Viewed against this background, the museum's photographs of Jewish life in the 1930s – banal pictures of football teams, trips to the beach and family picnics – assume a tragic and profoundly moving significance. There are also some deeply disturbing pictures of the Holocaust itself, including images of a massacre of Jews on Liepāja beach in July 1941, filmed dispassionately by an amateur German cameraman.

St Gertrude's Church to Čaka iela

Running parallel to Skolas is Baznīcas iela, sloping gently uphill towards the red-brick, neo-Gothic **St Gertrude's Church** (Sv Ģertrūdes baznīca), its green-capped spire encrusted with nobbly quatrefoil shapes. Immediately opposite, an Art Nouveau apartment block on the corner of Ģertrūdes iela and Baznīcas iela looks like something out of the Brothers Grimm, with sprites and gargoyles sprouting from its upper storeys.

A few steps southeast is the Centre's main artery, **Brīvības iela**, along which trolleybuses trundle laboriously towards distant suburbs. There's a sprinkling of National Romantic buildings along its length, although few have more historical significance for the Latvians than the so-called **"Corner House"** at no. 61, a gaudily balustraded building used by the Soviet secret police during the 1940–41 occupation and still in use as the headquarters of the Latvian police. Locals come to lay flowers at a memorial to KGB victims on the Stabu iela side of the building.

Jollier by half is the **A. Ķeniņš Highschool** (A. Ķeniņa ģimnāzija), another block southeast at Tērbatas 15. Built in 1905 by Laube and Pēkšēns, it combines bold modernism (as seen in the irregular hexagonal window frames) with fanciful folkloric touches, including ground-floor archways so low that they look as if they've been made with a race of urban elves in mind.

Parallel to Tērbatas iela to the southeast is **Barona iela**, home to some of the Centre's smarter shops. Hogging most of the architectural limelight is the deliciously gaudy Art Nouveau office block at the junction of Barona and Blaumaņa, a veritable bestiary in vertical form, the facade of which features bat-like demons just above ground level, lions and hogs further up and dragons crowning the battlements at the top. Providing an escape from the daytime bustle is the **Krišjānis Barons Memorial Museum** (Krišjāņa Barona memoriālais muzejs; Wed–Sun 11am–6pm; ⓦ www.baronamuzejs.lv; 0.70Ls) at no. 3, the flat where the eponymous writer and ethnographer lived for four years following World War I. Barons' great service to Latvian culture was the cataloguing of over one million traditional Latvian *dainas* – four-line folk poems that country people knew by heart but had never been systematically recorded before. Barons wrote each *daina* on a tiny piece of paper, bundles of which were then placed in specially made chests of drawers – a pair of them are preserved here. Elsewhere there are pictures of people and places associated with Barons, although it's the chance to see the flat's well-preserved 1920s interiors that make a visit here worthwhile.

Moving a block to the southeast, you come to the last of the Centre's big lateral boulevards, **Čaka iela** and its extension, Marijas iela. Čaka takes its name from the poet Aleksandrs Čaks (1901–50), who broke with Latvian literature's traditional obsession with the countryside to pen eulogies to the edgy urban landscape of inter-war Rīga. He was particularly enthralled by the low-life atmosphere of the street that now bears his name, calling it "forever the merchant...buying and selling anything from a piece of junk to human flesh". From 1937 until his death, Čaks lived in a flat at the junction of Čaka iela and Lāčplēša iela, now the **Aleksandrs Čaks Memorial Museum** (A. Čaka memoriālais muzejs; entrance at Lāčplēša 48/50; Tues–Sat 11am–5pm; 0.60Ls). The poet's cosy sitting room, stuffed with prints, paintings and other objets d'art, is a charming period piece.

Southeast of the Old Town

Immediately southeast of the Old Town, the bustling area around the Central Market gives way to a quiet, run-down district seemingly untouched by the post-Soviet economic changes so evident in other parts of the centre. Many of the disparate sights in this part of town have a deep historical resonance – the prime reason for venturing here.

The principal landmark in this area of greying, nineteenth-century apartment blocks is the **Academy of Sciences** (Latvijas zinātņu akademija) at the junction of Turgeņeva and Gogoļa, built during the early 1960s and nicknamed "Stalin's Birthday Cake" because of its resemblance to the monumental, pseudo-Baroque structures that sprang up all over Moscow in the 1940s and 1950s. Constructed from enormous, gingerbread-coloured chunks of stone, this unloved communist heirloom radiates a melancholy beauty.

Standing in the academy's shadow on the opposite side of Gogoļa is the green-domed Orthodox **Church of the Annunciation** (Tserkva blagoveshtenya), one of the city's more atmospheric places of worship, largely because it's so dark inside – you can't see much apart from the gilded icon frames glittering in the candlelight. Round the other side of the academy on Elijas iela is the ochre-painted **Jesus Church** (Jēzus baznīca), surrounded by a horseshoe of grubby flats. Dating back to 1635, this is Rīga's oldest wooden church, though it's been rebuilt following fires a couple of times since then. The interior is unusual, with a circular central hall supported by wooden pillars.

The Great Synagogue and the Moscow Suburb

A block northeast of the Jesus Church, at the intersection of Gogoļa and Dzirnavu, stand the remains of Rīga's **Great Synagogue**, deliberately set alight on the night of July 4, 1941 (just three days after the Germans entered the city) with, it is thought, about a hundred worshippers still inside. The attack was thought to be the work of Viktors Arājs, leader of the Latvian security team that worked in tandem with the German SS and played a major role in murdering Rīga's Jews. Living in Germany under an assumed name after the war, Arājs was unmasked in 1979, extradited to Latvia and sentenced to life imprisonment (he died in 1988). The walls of the synagogue have been reconstructed to a height of a few metres to serve as a memorial and there's a lone boulder in the adjoining park inscribed with the simple legend "1941. 4/VII".

East of here stretches the so-called **Moscow Suburb** (Maskavas forštate), so named because the main road to Moscow ran through it. The area was inhabited by many of Rīga's Jews and is the site of the wartime ghetto to which they were confined by the Nazis. The erstwhile core of the ghetto is a good 400m east of the Great Synagogue, in the area now bounded by Lāčplēša, Maskavas, Lauvas and Kalna ielas. The Nazis started clearing the ghetto almost immediately after its establishment in September 1941 and by December of the same year almost all of its 25,000 inhabitants had met their deaths in the Rumbula and Biķernieki forests, just east of the city. The ghetto was then repopulated by Jews from Western Europe, brought here to work as slave labourers, until they, too, were considered surplus to Nazi requirements and murdered. It's now an area of gritty apartment blocks and warehouses, and there's a dearth of memorials to those who lived and suffered here, save for a lone inscription at the entrance to the former **Jewish cemetery** (Ebreju kapi; tram #3, #7 and #9 from the Central Market to the Balvu iela stop) at the corner of Maskavas iela and Ebreju iela. Shorn of its gravestones in World War II, it's now a grassy park.

The Grebenshchikov Church and Rabbit Island

On the southern edge of the former ghetto at Krasta 73 is the gold-domed **Grebenshchikov Church** (Grebenščikova baznīca), built in 1814 for the Old Believers, a dissenting sect which broke away from the Orthodox Church during the seventeenth century and many of whose members fled Russia to escape persecution (see box, p.163). There are still enough Old Believers around in Rīga to maintain a small congregation, although the church is rarely open outside prayer times – 7/9am and 5pm seem to be your best bet.

Immediately south of the Moscow Suburb, the main road to Vilnius bridges the Daugava, crossing a long thin landmass known as **Rabbit Island** (Zaķu sala) on the way. You can't walk across the bridge, but there's a bus stop halfway along it (served by trolleybus #20 from Raiņa bulvaris, or buses #40 or #40A from Gogoļa iela) from which you can descend to the island and walk south to **Rīga's TV Tower**, a 368-metre concrete tripod with a viewing platform halfway up – come prepared for stunning views across the Daugava River towards the pitched roofs and belfries of the Old Town skyline.

Pārdaugava

Immediately west of the Old Town, trams #2, #4, #5 and #10 rattle across the Akmens tilts ("Stone Bridge") towards the downbeat suburb of **Pārdaugava** (literally "Across the Daugava"), characterized by rickety old wooden houses and 1950s-era apartment blocks. It's well worth making the trip, however – there's a handful of quirky museums and some beautiful **Botanical Gardens**; furthermore, the Pārdaugava riverbank affords majestic **views** back towards the city centre – revealing a spire-studded skyline that appeared to Laurens van der Post in the early 1960s "as tranquil and translucent as any of Vermeer's views of Delft".

The Railway Museum, Uzvaras Park and the Latvian Theatre Museum

Four hundred metres beyond the western end of Akmens tilts, an unassuming brick warehouse at Uzvaras 2/4 accommodates the **Latvian Railway Museum** (Latvijas dzelzceļa muzejs; Tues–Sat 10am–5pm; Ⓦwww.railwaymuseum.lv; 1Ls), a small collection of old train tickets and timetables, enlivened by a model railway of which the curator is extremely proud – it features a faithful reconstruction of Līvberže station (on the Rīga–Ventspils line) that he made himself.

Five hundred metres southwest of the railway museum, Bāriņu iela forges west across the grassy expanse of **Uzvaras Park** ("Victory Park"), passing the most overstated of Rīga's Soviet-era monuments, erected in honour of the Red Army's victory in World War II. Its giant concrete needle spangled with shiny five-pointed stars might at first glance be taken for some outsize advertisement for a nightclub – though at ground level there's no mistaking the political message hinted at by the statue of Victory being saluted by machine-gun-toting Soviet soldiers. Just beyond the western corner of the park, at the junction of Bāriņu and Smiļģa, the **Latvian Theatre Museum** (Latvijas teatra muzejs; Wed–Sun 11am–6pm; 0.50Ls) occupies the former home of actor and theatre director Eduards Smiļģis (1886–1966), whose book-lined study is preserved in its original state – complete with a shrine to Italian poet Gabriele d'Annunzio, the high-priest of decadence and egoism who exerted such a big influence over early-twentieth-century arty folk. Elsewhere there's a well-presented history of Latvian stagecraft, including set designs, opera costumes and fanciful fairy tale creatures from Rīga's puppet theatre. It's worth taking a peek at some of the nearby streets before moving on: **Smiļģa iela** is rich with examples of pre-World War I wooden architecture, while Bāriņu iela leads to **Agenskalns covered market** (Agenskalņa tirgus), a deliciously doom-laden, red-brick pavilion that looks like something out of a horror movie.

Arcadia Park and Torņakalnis

At its southern end, Uzvaras parks runs into **Arcadia Park** (Arkādijas parks), a smaller but prettier stretch of greenery arranged around a winding waterway popular with ducks. Just across the rail tracks to the east, **Torņakalns train station** was a key embarkation point in the deportations of 1941 and 1949, when thousands of Latvians were loaded into cattle trucks and shipped to Siberia. A cluster of knobbly granite shapes, erected behind the station by sculptor Pauls Jaunzems, serves as their memorial.

The Botanical Gardens

Some 2km northwest of Akmens tilts, and best reached by riding tram #5 to the Konsula iela stop, Rīga's **Botanical Gardens** (Botāniskais dārzs; daily: May–Sept 9am–8pm; Oct–April 9am–5pm; 0.50Ls) make a beautifully laid-out park which receives only a fraction of the visitors it deserves. The outdoor parts of the garden can be a bit dull until mid-May, when magnolias and rhododendrons presage the explosion of colour that lasts right through the summer. The central Palm House makes for a worthwhile excursion whatever the time of year, with halls filled with cacti and subtropicals and a central chamber housing a soaring pair of South American araucaria.

North and east of the city centre

North and east of the city centre sprawl industrial estates and concrete residential zones, softened here and there by sizeable patches of woodland. A great deal of interest is hidden away in these suburban areas. To the north lie the monumental inter-war sculptures of the **Braļu kapi cemetery** and the dense woodland of the **Mežaparks** recreation area; both are on the same tram route, making a combined outing feasible. To the east are a small but rewarding **Cinema Museum**, an engaging **Motor Museum** and a moving **Holocaust Memorial**, all grouped in or near the deep-green swathe of Biķernieku forest – and close enough together to be do-able as one trip if you're prepared to wait around for buses and do a bit of walking. Further out are the former presidential summer house, now a quirky museum of inter-war life, at Dauderi, and the enthralling collection of village architecture at the **Open-air Ethnographic Museum** near Lake Jugla.

Braļu Kapi and around

Some 4km northeast of the centre, **Braļu kapi** ("Brothers' cemetery"; tram #11 from Radio iela) was planned in 1915 as a shrine to the Latvian soldiers then serving in the Tsarist army; by the time it was finished a decade later, it had become a powerful symbol of the newly independent Latvian state and the price in blood that had been required to build it. It remains a strongly evocative spot, its rows of graves guarded by the hulking, muscular creations of sculptor Kārlis Zāle, who blended folkloric traditions with Modernism to produce a heroic national style. His monumental *Mother Latvia* (Māte Latvijā) towers over one end of the cemetery, with accompanying pieces *Divi Braļi* ("Two Brothers") and *Ievainotais Jatnieks* ("Wounded Horseman") driving home the message of comradeship and sacrifice.

On either side of Braļu kapi lie larger, rambling civilian cemeteries set in pleasant, park-like woodland. On the northern side, **Meža kapi** (Woodland cemetery) is full of wooden benches, provided so that Latvians can sit and commune with their ancestors – indeed certain days of the year are set aside as cemetery holidays (each town or region will pick a different date), when entire graveyards can be full of families cleaning up the tombs, tending shrubs or munching picnic fare. Immediately south of Braļu kapi, many of Latvia's leading writers, artists and stage performers are buried in **Raiņa kapi**, so named because it centres on the granite tomb of Latvia's most respected man of letters, Jānis Rainis (see p.204). When Colin Thubron came to pay his respects here in the early 1980s, his Latvian companion complained that Rainis "would be a Goethe or a Shakespeare if he'd been born anywhere else. But he wrote in Latvian... and who reads that?".

Mežaparks and the zoo

From Braļu kapi, tram #11 meanders through northeastern Rīga for another 3km before terminating at **Mežaparks**, a prosperous garden suburb that has been popular with the city's upper crust for well over a century. Mežaparks means "Forest Park", although it was originally known as Kaiserwald in honour of Swedish King Gustavus Adolphus, who landed his invasion force here in 1621. Occupying a wooded, hilly site right beside the tram stop is Rīga's **zoo** (Rīgas zooloģiskais dārzs; daily: mid-April to mid-Oct 10am–6pm; rest of year 10am–4pm; 2Ls), with a pleasant if predictable collection of elephants, camels and zebras enlivened by a pair of Amur tigers, their cage sponsored by a well-known brand of cat food. Beyond the zoo, you can follow paths into a sizeable expanse of woodland and park, somewhere in the middle of which sit both a funfair and the **Song Stadium**, built to accommodate the mind-bogglingly enormous choirs that perform at the National Song Festivals held every five years (the next one is due in 2008) – when over 10,000 people might be singing their hearts out on stage at any one time.

The Motor Museum

Some 6km east of the centre, a sleek brick-and-glass pavilion on the edge of Bikernieki forest holds the **Motor Museum** (Rīgas motormuzejs; Tues–Sun 10am–6pm; 0.50Ls) at Eizensteina 6, an eye-opening round-up of Latvian – and Soviet – transport history. The easiest way to get there is to catch bus #21 from Stacijas laukums or opposite Katedrāle to Pansionāts, then bear right down the broad sweep of Eizenšteina iela. The wide-ranging collection's most venerable exhibit is the fire engine made by Rīga's Russko-Baltiiski engineering factory in 1912. The Ford family cars made under licence by the Latvian Vairogs ("Shield") firm in the 1930s look frumpily utilitarian in comparison with the luxury motors favoured by fat cats in Bolshevik Russia during the same period: note the sleek 1934 Lincoln used by writer Maxim Gorky and the 1939 Rolls Royce Wraith used by Stalin's foreign minister, Molotov. Eloquently summing up the Kremlin's love affair with big cars is the somewhat crumpled 1966 Rolls Royce Silver Shadow owned by notorious speed freak Leonid Brezhnev, who pranged it himself during one of his customary nocturnal drives around Moscow. Upstairs, bikes and sports cars round off a wonderful display.

Bikernieku forest and the Holocaust Memorial

Behind the Motor Museum, paths lead into the deep evergreen cover of the **Bikernieku forest** (Bikernieku mežs), site of the winding racetrack where Soviet motorcycling championships were once held.

The southwestern end of Bikernieku forest, traversed by the dead-straight Bikernieku iela, was used by the Nazis as a mass murder and burial ground in World War II – thousands of Jews from all over Europe were shot here between 1941 and 1944. The sixtieth anniversary of the first wave of exterminations (which actually began not here but in Rumbula forest; see p.212) was marked on November 30, 2001, by the unveiling of an impressive new **Holocaust Memorial**, just off the southwestern side of Bikernieku iela. A profoundly beautiful piece of *plein-air* sculpture, it's well worth a trip from central Rīga to see. The memorial's central feature is an angular concrete canopy covering a black slab, on which an inscription in Latvian, German, Hebrew and Russian quotes Job 16.18: "Oh earth, cover not my blood, and let my cry have no peace." Radiating out from the slab is a garden of jagged stones marked out into plots – each inscribed with the name of the European city the victims came from. Some visitors place small pebbles on or around individual stones in a personal act of

△ The Motor Museum

remembrance. In the forest around the memorial, mass graves are marked by raised beds of grass, each with a rough-hewn rock planted in the middle.

Trolleybus #14 (from opposite Katedrāle) goes past the memorial, but there's no stop beside the site itself – you need to get off at the Keguma iela stop and continue east along Biķernieku iela on foot (1km), or stay on the bus until the Eisenšteina iela stop and walk back along the same road (1.5km). If you've just been to the Motor Museum, you can walk to the memorial by following forest paths from the former racetrack, although you'll probably need a decent Rīga city map to navigate your way through the woods – there aren't any signs.

The Ethnographic Museum

The **Latvian Open-air Ethnographic Museum** (Latvijas etnogrāfiskais brīvdabas muzejs; daily 10am–5pm; 1Ls), 12km east of the centre on the Tallinn road but easily reached by public transport, brings together over a hundred traditional buildings from all over Latvia, reassembled in a partly forested setting by the shores of Lake Jugla. It's a big site, and you'll need a couple of hours and an appetite for woodland strolling to get the best out of it. Consider buying the English-language plan (0.70Ls) at the entrance – you could quite easily get lost in the eastern reaches of the museum without it. The display captures perfectly the atmosphere of nineteenth-century rural life, when the majority of Latvians lived in isolated farmsteads rather than villages or towns. Although most of the timber-built houses look comfortably large, much of the space was devoted to storing grain or keeping animals, and families lived in cramped, spartan quarters at one end of the building, their tiny beds crammed into corners. Open hearths were used for smoking meats and drying hay, which was then stored in the loft. Farmsteads had to be self-sufficient in everything – and the re-created kitchen gardens here are full of every manner of vegetable, fruit tree and medicinal herb. The oldest of the buildings in the museum is a sixteenth-century church from Vecborne near Daugavpils, its interior featuring a painted, wooden ceiling filled with jovial-looking angels.

On **summer** weekends, blacksmiths and other craftsmen demonstrate their work, while around **Christmas** time, folk groups from all over Latvia converge on the museum to perform Yuletide songs and dances. There's a traditional-style **inn** just up from the entrance serving Latvian specialities such as *zirņi* (grey peas with bacon), alongside regular coffee-and-cake fare. To get to the museum, take **bus** #1 from Brīvības iela, and get off at the first stop after passing the shores of Lake Jugla on your right.

Rumbula and Salaspils

Thick woodland southeast of Rīga provided Latvia's Nazi occupiers with the cover they needed to murder tens of thousands of Jews; they were either shot at **Rumbula forest**, 11km southeast from the city centre, or crowded into **Salaspils** concentration camp, 3km further on. Both sites are now home to dignified memorials, with the serenity of the surrounding pines helping to concentrate the mind on themes of remembrance.

Located on or near the highway to Daugavpils, Rumbula and Salaspils are easy to reach **by car** from central Rīga. They're also just one stop apart on the Rīga–Ogre–Lielvārde **train** route, so it's not hard to combine them in a single trip, providing you swot up on timetable information before setting out – not all trains stop at Rumbula and Dārziņi and there's no information on arrivals or departures at the stops themselves. You can also get to Rumbula by a combination of **tram and bus** from central Rīga (see below).

Rumbula forest

Some 11km from the city centre, **Rumbula forest**, a once dense area of woodland, is now broken up by a patchwork of post-war factories, housing projects and vegetable plots. As many as 28,000 Latvian and Lithuanian Jews were brought in to be shot in Rumbula on November 30, 1941, and mass killings continued here throughout the war. A **memorial site** now occupies a wooded knoll beside the road, the entrance to the access path marked by a striking modern stone-and-steel sculpture that looks like a swooning tree. A restful place surrounded by birches, the site consists of a central plaza, the main focus for the laying of wreaths, and a surrounding area of park where several raised beds planted with grass (each with rough-hewn rocks sprouting out of them) mark individual massacre sites.

To get here **by car**, head southeast from central Rīga along Maskavas iela (the main highway to Daugavpils) for 11km and you'll find the site right at the city limits, just past a used car lot and opposite a petrol station. The easiest way to get here **by public transport** is to take trams #7 and #9 from the Central Market to the Kvadrāts terminus, followed by bus #15 to the Rumbula terminus (from where you walk back the way you came for 100m and cross the road). Be warned that Rumbula train station, just east of the memorial, is no more than an unmarked wayside halt in the middle of a meadow and you may well miss it altogether.

Salaspils

Between October 1941 and October 1944 an estimated 100,000 people met their deaths in **Salaspils concentration camp**, hidden in dense woodland 14km southeast of Rīga and 3km short of the town of Salaspils itself. Although originally intended as a transitional camp in which Jews from Germany, Austria and Czechoslovakia could be held before their deportation to work camps and extermination sites elsewhere, Salaspils was increasingly used as a killing zone as the war went on.

At the centre of the site is a long, concrete hall, mounted on pillars and slightly tilted to form a gently ascending processional way, intended to concentrate the visitor's mind on the journey from life to death. At the end of the hall a staircase drops down into a small museum space, containing a series of gripping illustrations evoking the harshness of camp life by K. Būss, a Latvian political prisoner interned here. Outside, a long, black concrete slab containing a slowly ticking metronome is the main focus for wreath-laying, remembrance and prayer. The surrounding terrain is peppered with concrete tablets marking the locations of the barrack buildings where the prisoners were held. An ensemble of heroic statues intended to depict the uncrushable human spirit comes across as tastelessly Soviet – one angular-jawed example is entitled "Red Front", as if to suggest that resistance to Nazi barbarity was entirely the preserve of the communists.

You can get to the memorial by taking a suburban **train** to the Dārziņi stop – there's currently no station signboard in evidence, but you'll recognize it from the fact that it's the first station out of Rīga that is completely surrounded by pine forest. From here a signed path leads to the memorial site – a fifteen-minute walk through peaceful woodland. Approaching the site **by car** along the Daugavpils-bound highway, you'll see a long concrete slab 15km out on the northern side of the road pointing the way to the site – assuming you're in the eastbound lane, however, you'll have to carry on for another couple of kilometres and do a U-turn.

Eating

The majority of Rīga's **restaurants** serve international cuisine. Establishments offering indigenous meat-and-potatoes fare do exist, but most of these are self-service cafeterias rather than restaurants in the traditional sense – they're good sources of filling and cheap food nevertheless. Restaurant **prices** are on the whole higher than in Vilnius or Tallinn, but still significantly lower than in Western European capitals, unless you're eating in a particularly upmarket establishment. On average, main courses cost around 3–4Ls in the self-service places, 6–10Ls in full-blown restaurants; a three-course meal with drinks will be somewhere in the 20–30Ls range – more if you're ordering bottles of wine. We've included telephone numbers for those restaurants where reservations are recommended at weekends.

For livelier eating options check out the **bars** listed under "Drinking" below – many offer substantial eats at reasonable prices. Most of Rīga's **cafés** also offer a range of hot meals, which can often be just as good as anything available in a restaurant, and cheaper to boot. If you're **self-catering**, you can pick up fruit, veg and other basics at the Central Market just beyond the bus station, or at supermarkets like Rimi, at Audēju 16 and Matīsa 27. Gastronome Konditoreja underneath the *Reval Hotel Latvia* (Mon–Sat 9am–9pm, Sun 10am–6pm) is the place to go for fresh seafood, fancy French cheeses and Mediterranean treats.

Cafés and self-service cafeterias

Old Town

The places listed below are marked on the Rīga Old Town map on p.191.

Alus Sēta Tirgotu iela 6. A justifiably popular pub with huge meals served from the grill. A good place to sample good, cheap Latvian ales accompanied by the national beer-snack – *zirņi* (grey peas garnished with bacon). Outdoor seating in warm weather. Daily 11am–1am.

Emihla Gustava Shokolahde Aspazijas 24. Coffee, cakes and gourmet chocolates in restful, waitress-service surroundings. In the same building as the Valters un Rapa bookshop (see p.219). Mon–Sat 9am–11pm, Sun 11am–11pm.

Franču Maiznīca Basteja 8. A French patisserie right opposite Bastejkalns hill. The perfect place to pig out on melt-in-the-mouth croissants and brie-filled baguettes. Mon–Sat till 10pm, Sun till 9pm.

I Love You Aldaru 9. Old Town café-bar with a nice mixture of old and new furnishings: chose one of the wooden tables in the medieval brick cellar or perch in a plush armchair upstairs. Salads, sandwiches and pastas make this a good spot for lunch. *I Love You* also serves as a mildly bohemian drinking den at night. Daily 11am–midnight.

Leduspuķe Vaļņu 28. One of Rīga's most popular coffee-and-ice-cream destinations for decades, *Leduspuķe* ("Ice Flower") consistently draws in city-centre shoppers of all ages and types. A recent lounge-bar makeover has failed to dent its down-to-earth charm. Mon–Sat 8am–9pm, Sun 10am–8pm.

Nostalģia Kaļķu 22. Ironic, Soviet-styled café occupying extravagantly stuccoed rooms, complete with monumental Socialist-Realist frescoes. Full range of drinks, and substantial meals. Daily 10am–2am.

Pelmeņi XL Kaļķu 7. A popular self-service joint on the Old Town's main street offering *pelmeņi* (Russian ravioli) filled with meat or cheese, alongside *soļanka* (Russian meat-and-vegetable soup), borscht and other Eastern-European staples. Daily 9am–4am.

Smilšu pulkstenis Corner of Meistaru iela and Mazā smilsu iela. A cosy café conveniently located just off Livu laukums, serving decent tea and coffee, delightful pastries and an impressive array of cakes. Daily 10am–9pm.

V. Kuze Jēkaba 20/22. Sumptuous choice of coffees and cakes in an atmospheric recreation of an inter-war coffee shop. Furniture and staff uniforms all look some seventy years behind the times; unfortunately the prices are bang up to date and still rising. Daily 10am–10pm.

The Centre

The places listed below are marked on the Rīga map on p.184.

Ai Karamba! Pulkveža Brieža 2. A cross between a funky London café and an American diner, with tables tightly packed into a cosy interior, serving up toasted sandwiches, pasta and salads. Popular with a younger crowd, it's also a good place for a drink. Mon–Sat 8am–midnight, Sun 10am–midnight.

Apsara Elizabetes iela. Quaint wooden pavilion on the eastern side of Vērmane's Garden, with a big range of speciality teas, and comfy cushions to sit on. Popular with school-age teenagers in the late afternoon, but quiet at other times of day. Daily 10am–10pm.

Charlestons Cappuccino Bar Blaumaņa 38/40. Great coffee, some excellent salads and dangerously delicious cakes and sweets straight from the kitchens of the *Charlestons* restaurant next door (see opposite). Mon–Fri 8am–midnight, Sat & Sun 10am–midnight.

Dzirnavas Dzirnavu 76. Solid repertoire of Latvian fish-, pork- and potato-based meals, in a self-service restaurant decorated in enjoyably over-the-top folk style. Mon–Sat 8am–11pm, Sun 9am–10pm.

Ham & Cheese Arhitektu 1 ⓦ www.ham-cheese .com. Friendly, informal sandwich bar that also doles out filling bowls of chilli con carne and other quick-lunch fare. Mon–Fri noon–8pm, Sat & Sun noon–6pm.

Istaba Barona 31A. Cosy, chic and quirky café tucked into the second-floor gallery of an enjoyably odd art gallery-cum-gift shop. Coffee, tea and cakes are tip-top, and there's also a range of full meals – the menu is not written down and you'll be asked what kind of food you like by a waiter-cum-chef. Mon–Sat noon–midnight.

Līdo Atpūtas Centrs Krasta 76. A vast self-service restaurant complex 3km southeast of the centre on the Daugavpils road. Huge choice of belly-filling Latvian cuisine, local draught beers, a children's play area and a real-size reproduction windmill. The kind of place you have to visit at least once. Daily 10am–11pm.

Līdo Vērmanītis Elizabetes 65. Cafeteria serving all manner of tasty Latvian meat-and-potato dishes, pancakes and salads, with an interior decked out in country-cottage style. Mon–Sat 8am–11pm, Sun 8am–10pm.

Osīriss Barona 31. A stylish, intimate café in the Centre, with coffee, cakes, breakfasts, salads and a full menu of mouth-watering international main courses. Candlelit at night, it has always been a popular place for an intimate tête-à-tête. Mon–Fri 8am–midnight, Sat & Sun 10am–midnight.

Rāma Barona 56. A vegetarian bistro run by Hare Krishna devotees. The food is a bit unexciting sometimes, but it's wholesome, filling and cheap. Can get crowded at lunchtimes. Mon–Sat 10am–7pm, Sun 11am–7pm.

Restaurants

Old Town and around

The places listed below are marked on the Rīga Old Town map on p.191.

Austrumu robeža Vagnera 8 ☎6781 4202. Subterranean eatery which looks like a cross between one of the Kremlin's dining rooms and a Red Army training camp. Moderately priced Latvian and international food, and live music or cabaret a couple of nights a week (entrance charge) – a programme of events is posted on the door. Sun–Thurs 11am–11pm, Fri & Sat 11am–1am.

Indian Raja Vecpilsētas 3 ☎6722 1617. Authentic Indian food, good service and an atmospheric warren of rooms. Daily noon–11pm.

Kamāla Jauniela 14. Smart, but not overpriced, vegetarian restaurant just round the corner from Doma laukums, serving Indian and Middle Eastern dishes in a room stuffed with cushions and exotic textiles. Mon–Sat noon–11pm, Sun 2–10pm.

Mazie balti krekli Kalēju 54. Relaxing bar-restaurant with wooden tables and whitewashed walls covered in Latvian pop-rock memorabilia. Dishes are named after hit songs but don't veer too wildly from the tried-and-tested Baltic pork-and-chips repertoire. Good quality and moderate prices. Mon–Sat 11am–11pm.

Melnie mūki Jāņa sēta 1 ☎6721 5006. An elegantly converted medieval building offering an imaginative range of top-notch, moderately inexpensive international fare. Daily noon–midnight.

Salt 'n Pepper 13. Janvāra 33. Laid-back bar-restaurant with a bit of everything, from hearty breakfasts through lunchtime soups to international mains. Situated in a corner by the river, it's the perfect vantage point from which to observe trams and trains rattling their way across the Daugava bridges. Daily 9am–midnight.

Vecmeita ar kaķi Mazā pils 1. An informal cellar restaurant just off Doma laukums, the "Grandma with Cat" offers up pork-based Latvian favourites alongside healthy salads and pasta dishes. Nicely priced for the area. Daily 11am–11pm.

The Centre

The places listed below are marked on the Rīga map on p.184.

Benjamins in the *Europa Royale* hotel (see p.189). Stuccoed gryphons, chandeliers and stained glass set the scene for one of Rīga's most atmospheric restaurants, with a menu that runs the gamut of international cuisine from octopus salad to roast lamb. With mains at 15–25Ls, it's classy without being wallet-emptying – although the impressive list of vintage French wines could have you running for the ATM. Daily noon–11pm.

Bergs in the *Bergs* hotel (see p.189) ☎6777 0957. Inside the ultra-chic hotel of the same name, this ultra-chic restaurant has a calming modern interior and a terrace overlooking the comings and goings in the Berga bazārs upmarket shopping precinct. Constantly changing menu of imaginative, modern European dishes. Prices high but not stratospheric. Daily noon–11pm.

Charlestons Blaumaņa 38 ☎6777 0573. Quality food in relaxingly informal surroundings, with a menu that offers a range of global eats, from steak through ribs to pasta. Consistently reliable quality, good service and desserts to die for. Noon–midnight.

Gastronome Brīvības 31, ☎6777 2391, ⓦ www.mc2.lv. Located in a mall beneath the *Reval Hotel Latvia*, *Gastronome* makes up for what it lacks in atmosphere with some of the best fish and seafood in the city. Mains in the region of 15–20Ls; inexpensive lunchtime specials are chalked up on a board at the door. Daily 11am–11pm.

Kabuki Tērbatas 46 (entrance from Mārtas). A rash of sushi restaurants has opened in Rīga in recent years but this remains one of the most pleasant and reliable, with a functional but chic interior, a big choice of sushi and noodle dishes, generous pots of Far-Eastern tea and reasonable prices. Daily 11am–10.30pm.

Lidojošā Varde Elizabetes 31A ☎6732 1184. A bright basement restaurant with a profusion of frog motifs, and a terrace on the street outside. The eclectic international menu features salads, pastas and vegetarian choices, alongside more substantial steak and fish dishes. Long popular with the ex-pat community but remains moderately priced, with mains in the 6–8Ls region. Daily 10am–1am.

Pie Kristapa Kunga Baznīcas 27/29, ⓦ www .piekristapa.lv. This roomy restaurant with a vaguely medieval theme has a pair of ground-floor dining rooms and several stone-lined chambers below. A good place to tuck into hearty meat and fish dishes swilled down with good local beer on tap. Daily 11am–11pm.

Pizza Lulū Ģertrūdes 27. A fashionable little American-style pizzeria where you can eat well at a reasonable price. Deep-pan pies, good choice of salads. Can get crowded. Open 24hr.

Drinking

Rīga offers innumerable opportunities for bar-hopping, with the Old Town in particular offering a multiplicity of supping venues that fill up with fun-seeking locals seven nights a week. There's a healthy scattering of characterful bars in the Centre, although they're somewhat more spread out – so it makes sense to aim for one in particular rather than expect to crawl your way through several. Most places are open until midnight or later on weekdays, with closing times of 2am or later being the norm on Fridays and Saturdays. Drinks are affordable even in the most stylish of places and there's usually a food menu of some sort. Bars regularly featuring live music or DJs have been included under "Clubs and live music" (see opposite).

Old Town

The places listed below are marked on the Rīga Old Town map on p.191.

Bon Vivant Belgian Beer Café Mārstaļu 8 ⓦ www.bon-vivant.lv. Wood-panelled interior decorated with vintage beer adverts and sepia photographs of nineteenth-century Belgians sets the tone for this bar which also serves a decent choice of hearty main meals. A couple of Belgian beers on draught and plenty more in bottled form. Expensive, but marginally more classy than the average pub. Daily 11am–1am or later.

Casablanca Smilšu 1 ⓦ www.casablanca.lv. A bar, restaurant and club all in one, *Casablanca* has a roomy dining area featuring live jazz on the ground floor, and a fuggier DJ bar down below. Mildly North African design touches, mainstream international food. Daily 11am–2am or later.

Dickens Grēcinieku 11. Brit-pub with wide range of international beers. It heaves with ex-pats and locals at weekends, but can seem like a characterless city-centre boozer at other times – although the nostalgic adverts for train sets hanging on the walls might cheer you up. Pricey pub grub in the businessmen-oriented restaurant at the back. Sun–Thurs till midnight, Fri & Sat till 2pm.

Lounge 8 corner of Vaļņu and Gleznotāju. In a city chock-full of lounge bars, this is one of the leaders of the genre, with elegant if pricey cocktails, groovy decor and equally groovy DJ-driven sounds. The food menu offers some rather dainty mains, but there are also some tasty Thai and vegetarian options. Daily noon–midnight.

Melnais kaķis Meistaru 10/12. Worth knowing about due to its late opening hours, the "Black Cat" serves alcohol all night long without ever descending into being a dive. Daily 9am–7am.

Orange Jāņa sēta 5 ⓦ www.orangebar.lv. Hidden away in a cobbled courtyard, this minimalist bar regularly fills up with boisterous local revellers, its alternative music policy helping to make it something of a cult destination. Daily noon–1am or later.

Paddy Whelan's Grēcinieku 4. A big, lively Irish pub occupying lovely stucco-ceilinged rooms, popular with young locals and ex-pats alike. Head upstairs to the laid-back *Paddy Go Easy* bar for a quiet pint. Sun–Thurs till midnight, Fri till 2am, Sat till 1am.

Paldies Dievam piektdiena ir klāt ("Thank God it's Friday") 11. Novembra krastmala 9. Brash cocktail bar with kaleidoscope-coloured interior and Caribbean-themed food. Sun–Thurs till 2am, Fri & Sat till 4am.

Rīgas balzams Torņa 4. A chic, roomy cellar bar serving up Rīga's favourite firewater – the black, syrupy *balzams* – either on its own or in a mind-boggling number of mixer combinations. Daily 11am–midnight.

Spalvas pa gaisu Grēcinieku 2. A snazzy café-bar with loungey corners, loud music and good cocktails. Full menu of food, including some delicious desserts. Sun–Tues 11am–midnight, Wed & Thurs 11am–2am, Fri & Sat 11am–5am.

The Centre

The places listed below are marked on the Rīga map on p.184.

A. Suns Elizabetes 83–85. Named after *Un Chien Andalou*, the Surrealist film made by Salvador Dalí and Luis Buñuel, this roomy café-bar is equally suited to an evening meal or a beery night out. The menu lists some eclectic dishes, with main courses from around 3Ls and some good vegetarian options. Sun–Wed till 1am, Thurs–Sat till 3am.

Kapteiņa Enriko pulkstenis Antonijas 13. Comfy café-bar boasting distressed wooden tables, a good choice of Latvian beers on draught, and a tempting menu of soups, salads and omelettes. Named after *Captain Enrico's Watch*, a much-loved Latvian comedy film made in 1967. Daily 9am–midnight.

Skyline Bar in the *Reval Hotel Latvia* (see p.189). Up on the twenty-sixth floor of central Rīga's tallest hotel, and offering mesmerizing views of the Old Town skyline. Retro 1960s and '70s furnishings and a long list of cocktails add an air of camp luxuriance to the proceedings, although none of it comes cheap. Daily 3pm–2am.

Stella Pub Lāčplēša 35. Long, thin, subterranean space with a good choice of beer on tap and a solid selection of meals. A good place to watch Champions League soccer and other televised sporting events. A second, more tourist-oriented branch of *Stella* is in the Old Town, at Šķūņu 19. Mon–Sat 10am–midnight, Sun 2–8pm.

Nightlife and entertainment

With an ever-increasing number of **nightclubs** and **music bars** in the city, you can go out partying in Rīga every night of the week. More refined cultural tastes are catered for, too, with a wealth of top-notch **classical music**, a spread of good **cinemas** and some enjoyable **theatre**.

Rīga in Your Pocket carries advance **information** on classical music and theatre events, although the *Baltic Times* is better for week-by-week listings. If you can read Latvian, you'll find a comprehensive run-down of concerts, plays and club nights hidden away in the *Diena* newspaper's TV supplement, which appears on Friday.

Clubs and live music

Most **dance venues** concentrate on a commercial diet of techno, Euro-hits and golden oldies, although more specialized styles of music might receive an airing in the smaller clubs, especially on week nights. **Live music** is largely limited to the middle-of-the-road pop-rock groups that Latvia seems to churn out in ever greater numbers, with gigs taking place in a wide range of music bars and clubs. International touring acts perform at the Sapņu Fabrika, a post-industrial venue for alternative music, theatre and dance at Lāčplēša 101 (Ⓦ www.sapnufabrika.lv), or Arena Rīga, a much bigger auditorium for mega-bands at Skanstes 13 (Ⓦ www.arenariga.com) – check posters and press for details. Clubs and music venues charge an entry fee of anything from 1–5Ls depending on what's on; once inside, drinks shouldn't be too much more expensive than in regular bars.

Bites blūzs klubs Dzirnavu 34A. Relaxed music pub with live acts most nights – performed by visiting bluesmen or by the house band. Fri & Sat till 2am. Sun–Thurs till 1am.

Četri Balti Krekli Vecpilsētas 12. Large, upmarket cellar bar, restaurant and disco known for its Latvian-only music policy (the better-known domestic bands perform here) and correspondingly popular with an older crowd keen to escape the techno on offer elsewhere. Strictly no trainers. Daily 8pm–3am.

Depo Valnu 32 Ⓦ www.klubsdepo.lv. Post-industrial cellar space with alternative DJ nights and live bands. Functions as a laid-back café during the day. Daily 8pm–3am.

Kabata Peldu 19. A basement club in the Old Town, with a small dance floor and live bands, popular with late teens and early twentysomethings. Daily 8pm–3am.

Muzikas akadēmijas studentu klubs Raiņa 23 Ⓦ www.studentuklubs.lv. Riotous student discos once a week (usually Fri) and occasional gigs in the basement of Rīga's Music Academy. Friendly crowd and cheap drinks. Days and times vary.

Pulkvedim Neviens Neraksta Peldu 26/28 Ⓦ www.pulkvedis.lv. Taking its name from the Gabriel García Márquez novel *Nobody Writes to the Colonel*, this hip bar with industrial-chic decor hosts different breeds of DJ on different nights of the week, as well as occasional live bands, attracting a laid-back artsy crowd. Mon–Thurs 8pm–3am, Fri & Sat 8pm–5am.

Roxy Kaļķu 24. Vast city-centre place blasting out Euro-pop and Russian techno to an undiscerning, fun-seeking crowd of ex-pats and beautiful young things. Bar, billiards and erotic dancers. Daily 9pm–6am.

Classical music and theatre

Classical music in Rīga is of an exceptionally high standard. Performances are reasonably accessible – tickets are unlikely to cost more than 5–6Ls (unless you're visiting the opera and you rarely need to book weeks in advance. The Latvian National Symphony Orchestra and the Latvian National Opera are the biggest shows in town, but be sure to look out for performances by Kremerata Baltica, a chamber ensemble put together by the Rīga-born violinist Gidon Kremer, and the world-famous choral group, Ave Sol.

The box office in the Great Guild (see below) handles information and **tickets** for most – but not all – classical music events in town; otherwise you'll have to contact the venues themselves. One major festival worth noting is the **Riga Opera Festival** (middle two weeks of July; ⓦ www.lmuza.lv), when the best of the previous season's productions are reprised. Rīga can offer a rich and varied diet of **theatre**, although you'll probably need a working knowledge of Latvian or Russian to appreciate it to the full.

Concert and opera venues

Ave Sol Concert Hall (Koncertzāle Ave Sol) Citadeles 7 ⓣ 6702 7570. Home of Ave Sol, one of the best choral ensembles in the Baltic States. Also hosts concerts by other choirs and chamber musicians.

Great Guild (Lielā Ģilde) Amatu 6 ⓣ 6722 4850, ⓦ www.music.lv/orchestra. Main venue for the Latvian National Symphony Orchestra, who usually play here on Saturday evenings unless they're away on tour. Frequent Saturday- or Sunday-lunchtime concerts aimed at children and families, featuring popular classics. Box office Tues–Fri noon–7pm, Sat noon–6pm, Sun 2hr before performance.

House of the Blackheads (Melngalvju nams) Rātslaukumā 7 ⓣ 6704 4300. Solo recitals and chamber music.

Latvian National Opera (Latvijas Nacionālā Opera) Aspazijas bulvaris 3 ⓣ 6707 3777, ⓦ www.opera.lv. The main auditorium – lavishly refurbished in late-nineteenth-century style – stages classic operatic productions and is also home to the Rīga Ballet (Rīgas Balets). The New Hall (Jaunajā zāle) hosts anything from chamber music to civilized, sit-down pop-rock. Opera tickets range from 8Ls in the stalls to 30Ls for the best boxes. Box office daily 10am–7pm.

Rīga Cathedral (Rīgas Doms) Doma laukums ⓣ 6721 3498. Recitals given on the sonorous cathedral organ every Friday, sometimes midweek as well. Box office Mon–Sat 10am–5pm and 1hr before performance.

Wagner Hall (Vāgnera zāle) Vāgnera 4 ⓣ 6722 7105. Orchestral music and chamber concerts.

Theatres

Daile Theatre (Dailes Teātris) Brīvības 75 ⓣ 6729 4444, ⓦ www.dailesteatris.lv. Big, modern auditorium hosting a mixture of classical drama, musicals and comedy. Small-scale productions in the adjoining Mazā zāle, or "small hall". Box office Mon–Fri 10am–6.30pm, Sat & Sun 11am–6pm.

Kabata Peldu 19 ⓣ 6722 3334. Contemporary fringe productions in small, intimate venue.

National Theatre (Nacionālais Teātris) Kronvalda bulvaris 2 ⓣ 6700 6337. Elegant pre-World War I building with mainstream classical drama on the main stage, and more experiemental stuff in the Aktieru zāle studio theatre.

New Theatre (Jaunais Teātris) Lāčplēša 25 ⓣ 6728 0765, ⓦ www.jrt.lv. Generally considered the best place to see contemporary plays by international playwrights.

Puppet Theate (Leļļu teātris) Barona 16/18 ⓣ 6728 5355. Great puppets, great stage designs, great fun for children of all ages. Productions usually kick off at 11am or 3pm.

Russian Drama Theatre (Krievu drāmas teātris) Kaļķu 16 ⓣ 6722 4660, ⓦ www.trd.lv. Varied Russian-language programme featuring everything from Chekhov to musical cabaret. Box office Mon–Fri 9.30am–6pm, Sat 10am–3pm.

Cinema

Big-name movies arrive in Rīga almost immediately after their release in Western Europe. **Films** are usually shown in the original language with Latvian and Russian subtitles, unless they're art-house movies that are in Rīga for a short run only – in which case they'll have Latvian-language voice-over.

Tickets cost somewhere in the 2Ls–3.50Ls range, although most cinemas reduce their rates by thirty to fifty percent on at least one day a week – usually Mondays or Tuesdays.

Daile Barona 31 ⓣ 6728 3854, ⓦ www.forumcinemas.lv. Reasonably modern cinema with first-run Hollywood movies on two screens.

K. Suns. Elizabetes 83/85 ⓣ 6728 5411. Mix of mainstream films and art-house flicks.

Rīga Elizabetes 61 ⓣ 6728 1105, ⓦ www.cinema-riga.lv. The oldest of Rīga's surviving cinemas (formerly the Splendid Palace), and still a plush, atmospheric place. Commercial films and the occasional art-house offering.

Sport

International **football** matches, as well as those featuring leading club side Skonto Rīga (ⓦ www.skontofc.lv), are held at the Skonto stadium, fifteen minutes' walk north of the Old Town at Melngaiļa iela. Tickets for internationals should be bought at the stadium box office in advance; those for league matches can be picked up on the day.

Big **ice hockey** and **basketball** matches take place in the Arena Rīga, Skanstes iela 13 (ⓦ www.arenariga.com), 2km northeast of the centre.

Shopping

Rīga's Old Town possesses a reasonable selection of fashion boutiques, souvenir **shops** and bookshops. The more mainstream high-street clothes, shoe and toiletries shops are concentrated in the streets east of here – Čaka, Barona, Tērbatas and Brīvības ielas. Great for browsing for cheap clothes, fake designer watches and Russian fur hats is the vast **Central Market** (Centraltirgus; see p.200), though you're unlikely to turn up anything of quality.

Rīga is an excellent place in which to stock up on traditional, **hand-knitted woollens** (mostly hats, gloves, socks and scarves, plus sweaters). Many are decorated with traditional Latvian geometric patterns – often sun, star and fir-tree shapes, symbolizing nature's bounty. The same designs crop up on tablecloths, linen garments and other textiles, many of which are hand-embroidered. You'll find all of the above in souvenir shops and on the occasional street stall, alongside pendants, necklaces and bracelets made from the ubiquitous Baltic amber, and handmade ceramics – including candle-lit lanterns in the form of tiny clay houses.

Souvenirs

Art Nouveau Rīga Strēlnieku 9 ⓦ www
.artnouveauriga.lv. Textiles, ceramics and other knick-knacks made to traditional Art Nouveau designs. Daily 8am–7pm.

Istaba Barona 31A. Funky gallery-shop selling T-shirts, prints, artist-designed greetings cards and off-the-wall gifts. Also worth visiting for the upstairs café. Mon–Fri noon–8pm.

Laipa Laipu 2/4. Reasonable across-the-board selection of linenwear, woollens, amber jewellery and wooden toys. Mon–Fri 10am–6pm, Sat 10am–3pm.

Senā Klēts Merķeļa 13. A treasure trove of Latvian ethnography, with traditional folk costumes, tablecloths, bedspreads and more. Quality handiwork, high prices. Located inside the Latviešu biedrības nams (Latvian Society House), so not immediately visible from the street. Mon–Fri 10am–6pm, Sat 10am–5pm.

Tīne Vaļņu 2. Large store selling ceramics, amber trinkets, linen goods and plenty of woolly mittens and socks. Mon–Sat 9am–7pm, Sun 10am–5pm.

Upe Vāgnera 5 ⓦ www.upe.parks.lv. Wooden craft toys and traditional folk instruments, plus Latvian folk CDs. Mon–Fri 11am–7pm, Sat 11am–4pm.

Books

Jāņa Rozes Barona 5. Good choice of tourist-oriented guidebooks and photo albums, and a decent range of English-language paperbacks. Mon–Fri 10am–8pm, Sat 10am–7pm.

Jāņa Sēta Elizabetes 83/85. The best place in the Baltics for maps and travel guidebooks. Mon–Fri 10am–7pm, Sat 10am–5pm.

Valters un Rapa Aspazijas 24 ⓦ www
.valtersunrapa.lv. Big bookstore selling stationery, calendars and coffee-table books about Rīga. Mon–Fri 9am–9pm, Sat 10am–9pm, Sun 10am–4pm.

Zvaigzne ABC Valdemāra 6. Educational literature specialist: a good place to find dictionaries and Latvian language textbooks. Mon–Fri 10am–6pm, Sat 10am–4pm.

Music

Randoms Kaļķu 4. Large mainstream music store, where you'll find most Latvian classical, folk and pop titles, as well as familiar international stuff. Mon–Fri 10am–7pm, Sat 11am–6pm.

Upe Vāgnera 5 ⓦ www.upe.parks.lv. Folk and world music store run by the Upe record label, and the best place to seek out many of the CDs recommended in our "Baltic Folk Music" section (see Contexts p.450). The branches at Vaļņu 26 and Barona 37 are good for rock, classical and jazz. Mon–Fri 11am–7pm, Sat 11am–4pm.

Listings

Airlines Aeroflot, Skolas 9 ☎6778 0770, ⓦwww
.aeroflot.lv; AirBaltic, Elizabetes 85A ☎900 6006
and 6720 7777, ⓦwww.airbaltic.lv; ČSA, at the
airport ☎6720 7636, ⓦwww.czech-airlines.com;
Finnair, at the airport ☎6720 7069, ⓦwww
.finnair.lv; LOT, at the airport ☎6720 7113,
ⓦwww.lot.com; Lufthansa, at the airport ☎6750
7711, ⓦwww.lufthansa.lv; SAS, see AirBaltic.

Airport 8km southwest of the centre at the end of
bus routes #22 and #22A. Airport information on
☎6720 7009, ⓦwww.riga-airport.com.

Car rental Avis, at the airport ☎6720 7353,
ⓦwww.avis.com; Europcar, Tērbatas 10/12
☎6722 2637, ⓦwww.europcar.lv, and at the
airport ☎6720 7825; Hertz, at the airport ☎6720
7980, ⓦwww.hertz.com; Sixt/Baltic Car Lease, at
the airport ☎6720 7121, ⓦwww.sixt.lv.

Embassies and consulates Belarus,
Jēzusbaznīcas 12 ☎6722 2560, ⓦwww
.belembassy.org; Canada, Baznīcas 20/22 ☎6781
3945, ⓔcanembr@bkc.lv; Estonia, Skolas
13 ☎6781 2020, ⓦwww.estemb.lv; Ireland,
Valdemāra 21 ☎6703 5286, ⓔirijas
.vestnieciba@gmail.com; Lithuania, Rūpniecības
24 ☎6732 1519, ⓔlithemb@ltemb.vip.lv; Russia,
Antonijas 2 ☎6733 2151, ⓦwww.latvia.mid.ru;
UK, Alunāna 5 ☎6777 4700, ⓦwww.britain.lv; US,
Raiņa 7 ☎6703 6200, ⓦwww.usembassy.lv.

Exchange Round-the-clock service at Marika,
Basteja 14, Brīvības 30.

Hospital The main emergency department is
at Hospital No. 1 (Rīgas pirmaja slimnīca) on
Bruņinieku iela, although for all but the most
urgent complaints you'd do far better to book an
appointment with one of the English-speaking
doctors at Diplomatic Service Medical Centre,
Elizabetes 57 (☎6722 9942); or Ars, Skolas 5
(☎6720 1007).

Internet access Dualnet Café, Peldu 17 (24hr);
Interneta Kafejnīca, Elizabetes 75 (Mon–Fri
10am–10pm, Sat & Sun 10am–9pm).

Laundry Vienmēr Tirs, Barona 52 (Mon–Fri
8am–8pm, Sat 10am–4pm).

Left luggage in the basement of the train station
(daily 4.30am–midnight) and at the bus station
(24hr).

Libraries British Council, Blaumaņa 5A (Tues,
Thurs & Fri 11am–5pm, Wed 11am–6pm, Sat
10am–3pm, ⓦwww.britishcouncil.lv).

Parking 24hr guarded car parks at Prāgas 2,
Basteja bul. 8, Republikas laukums 2.

Pharmacies 24hr service at Rīgas Vecpilsētas
Aptieka, Audēju 20.

Photographic developing and supplies Kodak
Laboratorija, Audēju 1.

Police Emergency number ☎02.

Post office Main office at Stacijas laukums 1
(Mon–Fri 7am–8pm, Sat 8am–6pm, Sun 8am–
4pm); also at Brīvības 19 (Mon–Fri 7am–10pm, Sat
& Sun 8am–8pm).

Taxis Ranks can be found at the junction of Kaļķu
and Aspazias, and at the junction of Audēju and
Aspazijas. Otherwise call Rīga Taxi (☎800 1010);
or Rīgas taksometru parks (☎800 1313).

Travel agents Latvia Tours, Kaļķu 8 (☎6708 5001,
ⓦwww.latviatours.lv), and Via Rīga, Barona 7/9
(☎6728 5901, ⓦwww.viariga.lv), for international
airline and ferry tickets, car rental and excursions
within Latvia. Country Holidays/Lauku ceļotājs, Kuģu
11 (☎6761 7600, ⓦwww.celotajs.lv), arranges
accommodation in country cottages and rural hotels
throughout Latvia and the Baltics. Skaisto skatu
aģentūra, Maza Jaunavu 8 (☎6722 1767, ⓦwww
.skaistieskati.lv) organizes excursions to places of
interest throughout Latvia – tours will probably be in
Latvian only but the sights themselves will be pretty
self-explanatory. Insane Tours, Argonaut hostel,
Kalēju 50 (☎2611 3680, ⓦwww.insanetours
.com) organizes activity trips to the bobsled track in
Sīgulda (from 40Ls per person) and shooting ranges
in Rīga (from 25Ls per person), as well as karting,
paintballing and other activities.

Jūrmala

JŪRMALA, or "Seashore", is the collective name for a string of small seaside resorts
that begins just beyond the estuary of the River Lielupe, 15km northwest of Rīga, and
straggles along the Baltic coast for a further 20km. Originally favoured by the Tsarist
nobility, Jūrmala had become a virtual suburb of Rīga by the 1920s and 1930s, when
anyone who could afford it would rent a holiday house here for the duration of the
summer. Jūrmala's seasonal citizens would commute to Rīga by train every morning,
returning late in the afternoon to change into sanatorium-style pyjama suits in which
they would then promenade down to the beach. The resorts' simple, timber-built
holiday villas appealed to the "back-to-nature" instincts of the local elite – indeed the

lack of modern plumbing ensured that most of them had to perform their morning ablutions in the sea. After World War II, Jūrmala became popular with Soviet citizens from all over the USSR, not least because it was considered more Westernized and sophisticated than resorts elsewhere in the Union. Today, its sandy beaches backed by dunes and pine woods seethe with people at weekends and on public holidays. Despite the presence of a few decaying Soviet-era hotels, it's a delightfully low-rise area on the whole, with brightly painted wooden houses and tasteful modern holiday homes nestling beneath the trees. The main centre is the small town of **Majori**, 20km west of Rīga, where a handful of outdoor cafés cater for a constant stream of summertime visitors; elsewhere, Jūrmala is wonderfully underdeveloped and laid-back.

Arrival, information and accommodation

Trains to Jūrmala leave from platforms 3 and 4 of Rīga's central station (every 30min, 5am–11pm). The **tourist office**, just off Majori's main street at Lienes 5 (Mon–Fri 9am–7pm, Sat 10am–5pm, Sun 10am–3pm; ☏6714 7900, ⓦ www.jurmala.lv), can arrange **private rooms** (❷) and give advice on **hotels** throughout the Jūrmala region. Some 4km west of Majori, *Camping Nemo*, Atbalss iela 1, Vaivari (☏6773 2350, ⓦ www.nemo.lv), is a spacious and pleasant **campsite** with forest on one side and coastal dunes on the other. There's also a small swimming pool and waterslide on site. *Nemo* is well signed from the main east–west road through Jūrmala; by train, get off at Vaivari station and walk 1.5km west from the ziggurat-like Vaivari Sanatorium.

Hotels

The price codes below refer to the (pretty extortionate) rates charged during the July–August peak season. Prices can fall by 20–30 percent in May, June and September, and by as much as 50 percent in winter.

Baltic Beach Hotel Juras 23/25, Majori ☏6777 1400, ⓦ www.balticbeach.lv. Gargantuan concrete resort complex amid the dunes just north of Majori, with various different room options: the sparsely furnished en suites in the three-star "Bismuth" section are perfectly adequate, although rooms in the five-star "Amber" wing are somewhat more plush. Indoor pool, massage facilities and beauty treatments on site. ❺–❽

Hotel Jūrmala Spa Jomas 47/49, Majori ☏6778 4415, ⓦ www.hoteljurmala.com. Nine-storey hotel on the main strip offering comfortable en suites, some with deep-pile carpets, others with laminate floors. A wide range of spa facilities is available, and there's also an indoor pool (free to guests till 4pm). Two rooms are wheelchair-accessible. ❼

Jūras banga Jūras iela 30 ☏6776 2391, ⓦ www.jurasbanga.lv. Trad-style semi-timber house a short distance from the beach, with tastefully decorated – if small – en suites with laminate floors. ❻

Pegasa Pils Jūras 60, Majori ☏6776 1149, ⓦ www.pegasapils.lv. Much-restored nineteenth-century villa complete with fanciful turrets and spindly balconies, offering fully equipped en suites with rich-coloured fabrics and deep-pile carpets. Right by the main entrance to the beach. ❼

Villa Joma Jomas 90, Majori ☏6777 1999, ⓦ www.villajoma.lv. Timber building of pre-World War I vintage, nicely modernized inside. The en-suite rooms are small but comfortable, decorated in cheerful colours. ❼

Majori, the beach and beyond

Standing at the centre of Jūrmala's string of beachside settlements, **MAJORI** is the area's most urbanized resort and main service centre. Cafés and boutiques line Jomas iela, the pedestrianized main street that conveys new arrivals from the station square northeast towards the beach. Just off Jomas to the south on Tirgoņu iela, the **Jūrmala City Museum** (Wed–Sun 11am–5pm; 0.50Ls) hosts some excellent contemporary art exhibitions in the light-filled space upstairs, although the ground-floor permanent collection of nautical bric-a-brac is a bit of a let-down. About 800m further down Jomas, a left turn into Pliekšāna iela brings you to the **Rainis and Aspazija Memorial Summer House** (Raiņa un Aspazijas memoriālā vasarnica; Wed–Sun 11am–6pm; 0.70Ls), in which Latvia's leading literary couple, Jānis Rainis (1865–1929) and Elza "Aspazija" Rozenberga (1865–1943), spent three summers in the late 1920s. Rainis was an anti-Tsarist newspaper editor before World War I, who suffered exile in Siberia as a result of his support for the 1905 Revolution, before going on to write poetry, novels and plays, becoming Latvia's "national" writer in the process. His wife Elza was his equal as a playwright, her allegorical drama *Sidabra Šķidrauts* ("The Silver Veil") causing riots in 1905 because of its perceived anti-Tsarist message. She earned the nickname Aspazija (after the brainy and beautiful wife of Pericles) because her hidebound male contemporaries considered it unusual for Latvian women to be both good-looking and intelligent at the same time. There's an absorbing collection of heirlooms, photographs and manuscripts relating to the pair, and a chance to peruse the relaxing, sun-lit verandah where Rainis scribbled his verse.

Another five minutes' walk down Jomas brings you to **DZINTARI** – allegedly a separate town from Majori, although there's no appreciable boundary between the two – a locality rich in pre-World War I holiday villas, many adorned with mock-medieval spires and towers. Running parallel to Jomas to the north is Jūras iela, from where paths lead over the dunes to the **beach**, a pale grey ribbon of sand stretching as far as the eye can see in either direction. Despite being prone to strong winds, it's packed with people sunbathing, playing beach volleyball or drinking in alfresco cafés in July and August, and is a popular – if bracing – place for a stroll throughout the year. During the inter-war years the beach was given over to naturist bathing every morning, with different time slots reserved for each sex. Patrolling policemen (considered neuter for the occasion) ensured that segregation was maintained, although American travel writer E. Alexander Powell observed that during women's hour on Sundays the dunes behind the beach were full of "gentlemen equipped with telescopes, binoculars and opera glasses".

Some of the most beautiful, least crowded parts of the beach are at the eastern end of Jūrmala, near the point at which the Lielūpe River curves round to meet the sea. You can get there by alighting from the train at **BULDURI**, 4km east of Majori, and walking northeast through the pines. Bulduri itself was once named "Edinburg" after Prince Alfred, Duke of Edinburgh and second son of Queen Victoria (he married Marie, daughter of Tsar Alexander II of Russia, in 1874); always considered to be Jūrmala's upmarket end, it's currently home to some of the most expensive real estate in Latvia.

On the southern side of Bulduri, right beside the Lielupe River at Viestura iela 24, **Livu Akvaparks** (ⓦwww.akvaparks.lv; Mon–Fri noon–10pm, Sat & Sun 10am–10pm; 2hrs 7Ls, day pass 13Ls) is Latvia's biggest swimming complex, providing a year-round opportunity to splash around in a variety of indoor pools and plummet down waterslides. Wave pools, palm trees and a replica pirate ship provide plenty of fun for the kids. The Akvaparks is a fifteen-minute walk from either Bulduri or Lielupe train stations.

Eating, drinking and entertainment

The eating and drinking scene are at full throttle in peak season, when Jomas iela in particular is lined with establishments serving up Caucasian-style *šašliki* kebabs to the accompaniment of blaring Russian pop music. Many places work limited hours in spring and autumn and may close altogether in winter.

Kafejnīca Kazbeks, Jomas iela 39, is a good place for *šašliki* alongside other Caucasian dishes such as *harcho* (spicy rice-and-vegetable soup). Moving upscale, the restaurant of the *Hotel Jūrmala Spa* (see p.221) serves up seafood, steak, duck and lamb dishes in a modern, minimalist setting. *Sue's Indian Asia*, Jomas 74, offers satisfyingly spicy Thai and Indian dishes, although it can't compete in terms of location with the dune-top *Al Thome* (ⓣ6775 5755), just north of Jomas at Pilsoņu iela 2, where you can enjoy excellent Lebanese cuisine on a terrace overlooking the beach.

The open-air stage next to the concert hall at Dzintari hosts perfomances over the summer ranging from Russian-language crooners to the Latvian Symphony Orchestra – consult the tourist offices or street posters to find out what's on.

Travel details

Trains

Rīga to: Cēsis (5 daily; 1hr 50min); Daugavpils (4 daily; 4hr); Majori (every 20–30min; 45min); Rēzekne (3 daily; 4hr); Salaspils (every 30min–1hr; 30min); Sigulda (10 daily; 1hr).

Buses

Rīga to: Aglona (3 weekly; 4hr 30min); Bauska (every 30–40min; 1hr 10min); Cēsis (hourly; 1hr 50min–2hr 5min); Daugavpils (8 daily; 3hr 30min–4hr); Kolka (3 daily; 3hr 30min–4hr 30min); Kuldīga (Mon–Sat 9 daily, Sun 6 daily; 2hr 30min–3hr 45min); Liepāja (hourly; 4hr); Rēzekne (4 daily; 4hr); Sigulda (hourly; 1hr 10min); Ventspils (hourly; 4hr).

International trains

Rīga to: Moscow (2 daily; 16–17hr); St Petersburg (1 daily; 13hr).

International buses

Rīga to: Berlin (1 daily; 20hr); Hamburg (4 weekly; 24hr); Kaliningrad (2 daily; 10hr); Kaunas (3 daily; 4hr 30min–5hr 20min); Klaipēda (2 daily; 5hr 30min–6hr); Köln (1 daily; 32hr); Minsk (1 daily; 12–14hr); Moscow (2 daily; 12hr); Paris (2 weekly; 40hr); Pärnu (4 daily; 3hr 30min); St Petersburg (2 daily; 12hr); Šiauliai (4 daily; 3hr 15min); Stuttgart (2 weekly; 32hr); Tallinn (6 daily; 5–6hr); Tartu (2 daily; 5hr); Vilnius (4 daily; 5hr–5hr 30min); Warsaw (4 weekly; 12hr).

International flights

Rīga to: Amsterdam (2 daily; 2hr 30min); Berlin (1 daily; 1hr 45min); Brussels (1 daily; 2hr 30min); Copenhagen (4 daily; 1hr 30min); Dublin (3 daily; 3hr); Frankfurt (2 daily; 2hr 20min); Hamburg (1 daily; 1hr 45min); Helsinki (4 daily; 1hr 10min); Kiev (1 daily; 4hr); Liverpool (1 daily; 3hr); London (3 daily; 3hr); Milan (1 daily; 3hr); Moscow (2 daily; 1hr 45min); Oslo (1 daily; 1hr 45min); Prague (2 daily; 2hr); Stockholm (4 daily; 1hr 30min); Tallinn (2 daily; 50min); Vienna (1 daily; 2hr); Warsaw (1 daily; 1hr 30min).

International ferries

Rīga to: Lübeck (2 weekly; 36hr); Stockholm (daily; 16hr).

2.2

Western Latvia

Western Latvia has a rich variety of attractions, ranging from vibrant port cities to historic palaces and plenty of quirky market towns, not to mention long, sandy beaches – the region's 320-kilometre-long coastline amounts to virtually one long, continuous strand. Inland, there are innumerable areas of genuine wilderness, especially in the slightly hillier north, where squelchy bogs and deep forest break up fields of crops and stretches of grazing land. The southwest is made up of Latvia's most fertile arable land, its farms producing bountiful harvests of grain, potatoes and sugar beet.

The region consists of two ethnographically distinct areas. **Zemgale**, extending south from Rīga to the Lithuanian border, is named after the Zemgaļi (Semgallians), one of the original Baltic tribes that subsequently coalesced to form the Latvian nation. Over to the west, **Kurzeme** – usually rendered into English as **Courland** – gets its name from the Kurši (Cours), a tribe that once held sway over the western seaboard of both Lithuania and Latvia and established the area's enduring reputation for fishing, seamanship and trade. From the 1560s onwards, Zemgale and Kurzeme were united to form the **Duchy of Courland**, which exploited Polish, Swedish and Russian rivalries to ensure over two centuries of semi-independence.

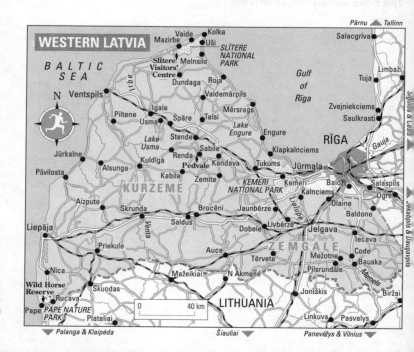

Much of western Latvia is within day-trip distance of Rīga. Easily reached are the Baroque palaces at **Rundāle** and **Jelgava** south of Rīga, providing some insight into the lavish tastes of Courland's eighteenth-century dukes. Nearby, the aristocratic seat of **Mežotne** provides a cool Neoclassical riposte. West of the capital, the green, rolling countryside of Kurzeme enfolds attractive rural centres like **Tukums**, **Talsi**, **Kandava** and, best of all, **Kuldīga**, a taste of small-town Latvia. All this contrasts with the hurly-burly of western Kurzeme's great port cities, **Ventspils** and **Liepāja**. The best of the region's wild, unspoiled nature is to be found in the beaches and forests of the **Slītere National Park** around Kurzeme's northernmost point; the desolate beauty of **Cape Kolka**; the bogs of the **Ķemeri National Park** just west of Rīga; and the reedy environs of the **Lake Pape Nature Reserve** south of Liepāja.

Zemgale

The region of **Zemgale** occupies central Latvia, cut through by the busy Rīga–Vilnius road. The landscape is largely flat and unremarkable, made up of arable farmland, but whatever Zemgale lacks in terms of natural beauty is more than made up for by the presence of two sumptuous palaces: park-girdled, Neoclassical **Mežotne** and the splendid Baroque–Rococo confection that is **Rundāle**. Both lie just outside the small town of **Bauska**, the major transport hub for the area. All three places can be visited as a day-trip from Rīga, providing you make an early start.

Zemgale's only real city – and a more exciting urban prospect than Bauska – is **Jelgava**, 55km southwest of Rīga. One-time capital of the Duchy of Courland, it's home to a fine ducal palace, though sadly many of its other venerable buildings were destroyed in World War II. A short hop from here is **Tērvete Nature Park**, offering some particularly rewarding woodland walks.

Bauska

The main road to Vilnius ploughs right through the bland market town of **BAUSKA**, 75km south of Rīga. As well as offering public transport links to both Rundāle and Mežotne, Bauska can also boast a substantial aristocratic seat of its own. Looming over parkland fifteen minutes' walk west of the town's main T-junction, **Bauska Castle** (Bauskas pils; May–Oct daily 10am–6pm; 1Ls) began life as a Livonian-order strongpoint commanding the confluence of the Mēmele and Mūsa rivers. Subsequently used by the dukes of Courland as a temporary residence, it was destroyed by order of Peter the Great in 1706. The newer, fifteenth-century parts of the castle are currently undergoing reconstruction – several restored halls are already accessible and have a modest museum display devoted to the history of Courland. The older, thirteenth-century wing of the castle is largely a ruin save for one reconstructed tower, which affords sweeping views of the Mēmele and Mūsa; they converge just upstream to become the Lielupe ("Great River"), which flows into the Baltic Sea just west of Rīga.

If you've got a bit of time to kill, check out the **Museum of Regional Studies and Art** (Bauskas novadpētniecības un mākslas muzejs; Tues–Fri 10am–5pm, Sat & Sun 10am–4pm; 0.50Ls), just off the flagstoned main square at Kalna 6. Its old sepia photographs of firemen, brass bands and schoolchildren eloquently sum up Bauska's small-town sense of community.

Practicalities

Bauska's **bus station** is at the southeastern end of town, ten minutes' walk away from the **tourist office** on the main square, Rātslaukums 1 (Mon–Fri 9am–6pm, Sat & Sun 9am–2pm; ☏6392 3797, ✆www.bauska.lv), stocked with information on sights and accommodation throughout Zemgale. The *Bauska* **hotel**, beside the bus station at Slimnīcas 7 (☏6784 7411, ✆www.hoteldayandnight.lv; ④), is equipped with recently refurbished en suites. *Kafejnīca pie Rātslaukuma*, on the main square at Plūdoņa 38, is a good place for a cheap, filling **meal**.

The Duchy of Courland: a brief history

The original inhabitants of Courland were the **Livs** (see p.233), a Finno-Ugric tribe related to the Estonians who arrived in the wake of the last Ice Age and are still around – albeit on the verge of extinction – in the isolated fishing villages of the extreme north. Very much in the majority until the early Middle Ages, the Livs were gradually forced out by the **Kurši**, one of the bedrock Baltic tribes that make up the modern Latvian and Lithuanian nations. Despite giving Courland its name, the Kurši succumbed to the Livonian Order in 1267, and power passed to a new class of German-speaking landlords. Courland emerged as a distinct political entity in 1562, when the last Grand Master of the Livonian Order, **Gottfried Kettler**, faced with the prospect of Livonia's collapse under pressure from the Swedes and the Russians, dissolved the Order and created the **Duchy of Courland** to serve as a new power base. In need of a strong ally, Kettler made Courland a vassal of the Polish-Lithuanian Commonwealth, while retaining internal autonomy for himself and his successors.

Extending from the Baltic coast in the west to the River Daugava in the east, Courland under the Kettlers was a generally peaceful and prosperous place, with towns like Jelgava, Ventspils and Kuldīga growing fat on the profits of expanding trade. The duchy even enjoyed a brief spell as a transatlantic trading power when ambitious **Duke Jakob** (ruled 1642–82) received an unusual gift from his godfather, King Charles I of England, in the shape of the Caribbean island of **Tobago**. Merchantmen bearing Courland's standard – a black crayfish on a red background – were seen in ports all over northern Europe. Jakob's dreams of empire soon faded, however: the Swedes, unwilling to tolerate the existence of a rival maritime power in the Baltic, forced Jakob to disband his fleet in 1658. The overseas colonies were abandoned – although the waters around the Tobagan town of Plymouth are still known as Great Courland Bay.

Eventually, the rise of Russia and the decline of Poland seriously compromised Courland's independence. Peter the Great married his niece, **Anna Ioannovna**, to Duke Frederick Wilhelm in 1710 and sent his troops to take control of the region when the duke died childless two months later. Anna herself became Empress of Russia in 1730 and presented the dukedom to court favourite **Ernst Johann von Bühren** (1690–1772) – better known by his Russified name of **Biron** – marrying him off to one

Rundāle Palace

Rising above rich farmland 13km west of Bauska, **Rundāle Palace** (Rundāles pils; daily: June–Aug 10am–7pm; May & Sept 10am–6pm; Oct–April 10am–5pm; ⓦ www.rpm.apollo.lv; 2.50Ls) is one of the architectural wonders of Latvia, a haughty slab of Baroque masonry filled to the gills with Rococo furnishings. This monument to eighteenth-century aristocratic excess is all the more impressive for its situation – plonked incongruously among the more modestly proportioned farmhouses and cottages of the Latvian countryside. The site was bought in 1735 by Empress Anna's fancy-man, Duke of Courland **Ernst Johann von Biron**, who named it *Ruhetal* (German for "Vale of Peace") and engaged Francesco Bartolomeo Rastrelli, architect of the Winter Palace in St Petersburg, to build the 138-room summer hideaway that you see today. Most of the construction work was completed by 1740, but Biron was exiled to Siberia in the same year, and it wasn't until his return in the 1760s that the interiors were finally decorated in the opulent Rococo style that was all the rage at the time. On the abolition of the duchy in 1795, Biron's son Peter was thrown out of Rundāle (he took most of the moveable furnishings to Żagań in Silesia, where they were destroyed in World War II), and the palace was given to Catherine the Great's favourite, Platon Zubov. It remained in private hands until 1920 and thereafter fell into disrepair, but meticulous restoration, begun in 1972, has returned large chunks of the palace to their former glory. With approximately a third of the palace open to the public, Rundāle is very much a work in of her ladies-in-waiting, Benigna Gottlieb von Trotta-Treyden. Flush with wealth and success, Biron commissioned Italian architect Rastrelli to design sumptuous palaces at **Rundāle** and **Jelgava**. With the death of Anna Ioannovna in 1740, Biron fell from grace and was exiled to Siberia by new Empress Elizabeth. Finding favour again under Catherine the Great and resuming his ducal office in 1764, he went on to supervise the completion of Rundāle Palace and presided over a glittering court at Jelgava. Before long, Jelgava's palace had become a popular stop-off for society folk travelling from Western Europe to St Petersburg. One house guest was Casanova, whose ability to sound off on subjects he knew nothing about tricked Biron into believing he was an internationally recognized authority on mining techniques – somewhat improbably, Biron paid the Venetian charmer 200 ducats to write a report on the minerals of Courland. Biron's son and successor Peter was no less gullible a host, giving board, lodging and lavish gifts to bogus faith-healer Cagliostro.

With Courland's formal incorporation into the Russian Empire in 1795, the duchy was finally extinguished. Shifts in sovereignty made little difference to local society, with the Latvian-speaking majority remaining subject to a Germanized landowning elite. Life continued to be centred on the great manor houses, and the nobles themselves overcame isolation by devising a busy round of social events, attending society gatherings in provincial towns like Jelgava and Aizpute (where balls usually lasted three days in order to justify the travelling involved) and decamping to the seaside in July. Their easy-going, hospitable nature was much appreciated by German guidebook writer J.G. Kohl, who summed up a visit to Courland in the 1840s by asking, "What gentleman or lady values time? The whole day is made up of leisure. No one looks at the clock, except to know when it will be dinner time, or whether tea may soon be ordered."

The duchy was briefly resurrected in March 1918 by Kaiser Wilhelm, who believed that a chain of German-dominated states could be established along the Baltic seaboard prior to their outright incorporation into the Reich. Even after the defeat of Germany in November 1918, this dream was kept alive by a Baltic German army of General von der Goltz, who based themselves at Liepāja, then Jelgava, before finally being beaten off by the Latvians in November 1919.

progress. Judging by the fanatical dedication to detail deployed thus far, completion of the rest of the palace will probably take decades.

The grandeur of Rundāle unfolds gradually: after you've passed through a belt of orchards and crossed a small moat, a wine-red gatehouse heralds the entrance to an oval-shaped outer courtyard. At the far end of this, a brace of regal-looking lions guard the entrance to the inner courtyard, closed off on three sides by the ochre wings of the palace itself. Once inside, you ascend to the **staterooms of the east wing,** where the original decorations – wall and ceiling paintings by St Petersburg-based Italians Francesco Martini and Carlo Zucchi, stucco work by Johann Michael Graff – have been faithfully re-created by modern-day restorers.

First up is the **Gilded Hall**, a long, showpiece chamber intended for ceremonial receptions, with exuberant ceiling frescoes swirling above a row of mirrors, each topped by a relief of birds fighting over berries. A sequence of smaller chambers lead on to the **White Hall**, a ballroom the size of a basketball court, with a stucco frieze depicting cherubs in a range of rather unlikely pastoral situations – tootling away on flutes, riding goats or warding off big-tusked boars. Side chambers are devoted to displays of fancy porcelain, the asymmetrical Rococo shelving so ornate that it upstages the vases themselves.

Return the way you came and proceed to the south wing and you will come to the **Rose Room**, with its fanciful ceiling painting of Flora (goddess of spring) surrounded by fleshy attendants, and the **Lord's Bedchamber**, whose gargantuan pair of tiled

△ Rundāle Palace

stoves give some idea of how difficult it must have been to keep the palace warm during the dark Baltic nights. Passing through the **Shuvalov Room**, filled with portraits of the Russian family who inherited the palace after the death of Platon Zubov, you arrive in the west wing, where the **Lady's Boudoir**, **Bedchamber** and **Washroom** display a frivolous combination of floral wall decorations and cherub-encrusted stucco work.

Practicalities

Getting to the palace is easy enough: it's a well-signed thirteen-kilometre drive west of Bauska on the Eleja road. There are five daily buses (four on Sundays) from Bauska – make sure you catch a service that's going to Pilsrundāle or Rundāles pils ("Rundāle Palace") rather than simply the village of Rundāle, which is 3km further west. Get off the bus when you see a big hedge: the palace gates are hidden just behind it. You can eat well at the rather formal **restaurant** in the palace basement, which serves up superb cuts of veal and steak in the former kitchen – where spits big enough to skewer an entire family of buffalo are lined up in front of gaping fire grates. A more modest **café**, also in the palace basement, serves simpler food at half the price.

Next to the palace car park, the *Baltā Māja* has a folksy café-restaurant and is also a characterful place **to stay** (℡6392 3172 and 2912 1374, ⊛www.kalpumaja.lv; ❷–❸), offering rooms in a lovingly restored nineteenth-century house full of trad furnishings – most come with shared facilities although there is one en-suite double with Jacuzzi-style bathtub.

Mežotne Palace

Some 10km northwest of Bauska and another easy jaunt by local bus, the cool, lemon-yellow bulk of **Mežotne Palace** (Mežotnes pils; daily 9am–5pm; 1Ls) could almost be seen as a restrained Neoclassical response to the lavish ostentation of Rundāle. It began life as the country estate of Princess Charlotte von Lieven, who was given the land by Catherine the Great in 1795 in recognition of her services as governess to the imperial children. The princess visited Mežotne only once, but the palace stayed with the Lieven family until the Land Reform of 1920 (when most Baltic German aristocrats were kicked off their lands), after which it became an agricultural college. It was badly damaged in World War II and subsequently various parts of the building served as a library, post office and residential flats. Now lavishly restored, it functions primarily as a hotel and conference centre, although several staterooms are open to the public. Decked out in pastel shades of ochre, pink and eau-de-nil, the interiors exude an easygoing elegance, with decoration limited to stuccoed floral motifs and friezes of personable gryphons, their paws raised as if in friendly greeting. There's a small display of engravings showing how the estate looked at the time of the Lievens and a forest-green ballroom framed at each end by ionic columns. One space you'll want to return to again and again is the so-called **Cupola Room**, a light-filled chamber said to be modelled on the Pantheon in Rome and featuring a dome held up by Titans – it also offers panoramic views of the palace park from its windows. The park itself is a terrific place for a stroll, stretching away along the bank of the River Lielupe and densely wooded at its far end.

The palace **hotel** (℡6392 8984 and 6392 8796, ✉mezotnpils@apollo.lv; ◐) is one of the most charming in Latvia, offering eight double rooms and five three- to four-person apartments (70–80Ls), each decorated in olde-worlde style – expect things like cast-iron bedsteads, Thonet furniture and your great-grandmother's wallpaper.

Jelgava and around

Straddling the road between Rīga and Kaliningrad, **JELGAVA** is a predominantly postwar, concrete city, although a reconstructed ducal palace and a smattering of other old buildings make a short stop-off here worthwhile. Jelgava was founded by the Livonian Order in 1265. The Livonians named it Mitau and used it as a base from which to mount successive campaigns against the pagans of Zemgale just to the south. In the seventeenth and eighteenth centuries, it was the capital of the Duchy of Courland and became an important social centre: Duke Jakob resided here for at least part of the year, and his successor Friedrich Casimir founded an (albeit short-lived) opera house. By the nineteenth century, most of Courland's German barons owned town houses in Jelgava and spent the coldest months here rather than on their country estates, turning winter into one long round of parties and balls – young Tsarist officers considered Jelgava a dream posting owing to its seemingly endless supply of charming debutantes. Sadly, little architectural evidence of Jelgava's golden age survives today: Baltic German forces under General von der Goltz put much of the town to the torch in November 1919 and World War II bombing raids largely put paid to what was left.

The City

Twice rebuilt almost from scratch following devastation in both world wars, the Baroque **Jelgava Palace**, with its dignified, maroon-and-cream facade, graces the riverbank just east of the city centre, next to the main Rīga road. The palace was built by Rastrelli for Count Ernst Johann von Biron in 1738 and was intended as an urban equivalent to the edifice then taking shape at Rundāle. Now part of the Latvian University of Agriculture, its student-tramped corridors and lecture rooms retain little in the way of original features. For some idea of what the palace looked like before World War I, visit the small **palace museum** (9am–4pm: May–Oct daily; Nov–April Mon–Sat; 0.50Ls), displaying photographs and prints recalling the days when Jelgava was a popular stop-off for society folk travelling from Western Europe to St Petersburg. To gain access to the museum, go into the main courtyard and through the doors on the right.

If asked, the museum curator will open up the **Burial Vault of the Dukes of Courland**, beneath the east wing of the palace, where all the duchy's rulers, from Gottfried Kettler to Peter Biron, are lined up in a series of richly decorated caskets. Hogging the limelight is the burnished copper affair belonging to Ernst Johann von Biron, adorned with a dull-grey death's head and mounted on feet in the form of snarling lions. The adjoining anteroom displays the richly embroidered burial shrouds in which seventeenth-century dukes were originally laid to rest, and a fetching pair of felt pantaloons once worn by Ernst Johann von Biron.

Over on the west bank of the River Lielupe lies Jelgava's modern centre. Its principal landmark is a grizzled, seventeenth-century tower, the last surviving remnant of the war-ravaged **Church of the Holy Trinity** (Sv Trīsvienības baznīca). In front of it stands a modern statue of **Janis Čakste**, the first president of independent Latvia during the inter-war years. Just round the corner, at Akadēmijas 10, is the **Museum of History and Art** (Vēstures un Mākslas Muzejs; Wed–Sun 10am–5pm; ⓦwww.jvmm .lv; 0.50Ls), a Neoclassical building, pinstriped with cream pilasters and topped by a thrusting clock tower. It was built in 1775 to house Duke Peter von Biron's Academia Petrina, an ambitious attempt at turning Jelgava into an internationally renowned university town that never quite caught on. The museum recalls the glory days of the Duchy of Courland through a display of old furniture mutely presided over by Duke Jakob in dummy form.

A few steps to the south, the corner of Akadēmijas and Raiņa is dominated by the bright-blue domes of the **Orthodox Cathedral of SS Simeon and Anna** (Sv Simeona un Sv Annas pareizticīgo katedrāle), built on the site of a wooden chapel originally used by Anna Ioannovna and her Russian entourage. Dating from the 1890s, the current structure was used as a warehouse during the Soviet period, and after extensive restoration in the 1990s the interior is now decked out once more in vibrant greens and blues.

Practicalities

Jelgava is easily reached from Rīga; trains leave every hour from the central station and minibuses every fifteen to thirty minutes from the bus station. Jelgava's **bus station** is right in the city centre, about 400m west of the tower of the Church of the Holy Trinity. The **train station** is about 1km to the south: bear left down Zemgales prospekts to reach the centre. The **tourist office** in the municipal council building at Pasta 37 (Mon 8am–6pm, Tues–Thurs 8am–5pm, Fri 8am–3.30pm; ☎6302 2751, ⓦwww .jelgava.lv, ⓦwww.jrp.lv) hands out free town maps and gives advice on accommodation throughout the region.

The city's most central **hotel** is the *Jelgava*, near the bridge at Lielā 6 (☎6302 6193, ⓦwww.hoteljelgava.lv; ②–③); staff tend to direct you towards the more expensive, renovated doubles with en-suite bathroom and TV, although the cheaper rooms with older furnishings and shared facilities are perfectly habitable. Twenty minutes' walk east of the centre, the *Zemgale Complex* at Rīgas 11 (☎6300 7707, ⓦwww.zemgale .info; ④) offers unfussy doubles and quads with en-suite facilities next to a sports centre – the hotel is often booked solid by visiting sports teams.

Good for a relaxing sit-down **meal**, *Tobago*, just beyond the tourist office at Čakstes bul. 7, has all manner of steak and fish, and an attractive riverside position. More informal is *Silva*, opposite the bus station on the pedestrianized Driksas iela, a stylish order-at-the-counter canteen with the added advantage of a drinks bar and an outdoor terrace. A block west of the bus station, *Jelgavas baltie krekli*, Lielā 19A (ⓦwww.krekli .lv), is a café-restaurant by day and club at night, featuring live performances by some of Latvia's top rock-pop performers.

Tērvete

Some 30km southwest of Jelgava, **Tērvete Nature Park** (Tērvetes dabas parks; daily: April–Aug 9am–6pm; Sept–Nov 9am–5pm), just outside the town of **TĒRVETE**, is one of Latvia's most popular rural attractions. Measuring little more than 3km across in any direction, the park is made up of riverside meadow and woodland, criss-crossed by well-marked trails. If Tērvete holds a cherished place in the hearts of Latvians, it's largely due to the children's stories of **Anna Brigadere** (1861–1933), who lived in the nearby hamlet of Plavnieki and evoked the beauty of the region in her writings. The park is dotted with wooden statues of dwarves, goblins and other characters from Brigadere's stories, making it a popular outing with young families.

Buses from Jelgava drop you at the northeastern end of the village; bear right down the gently sloping lane, then right again at the T-junction to reach the **tourist office** (Mon–Fri 8am–5pm; ☎6372 6212, ⓔtervete@lvm.lv) and, a little way beyond, a kiosk marking the **park entrance** – either place will sell you a ticket (1Ls) and a map detailing the main trails (0.30Ls).

Opposite the park entrance, a traditional-style log cabin with shingle roof accommodates the **Tērvete History Museum** (Tērvetes Vēstures muzejs; May–Sept Wed–Sun 10am–5pm; 0.50Ls), containing an absorbing collection of handmade, wooden farm utensils and traditional textiles. The same ticket allows you to climb the adjacent **viewing tower** for a 25-metre-high panorama of the surrounding treetops. On the other side of the park entrance a path leads down to the **Anna Brigadere House Museum** (Anna Brigaderes māja muzejs Sprīdīši; May–Sept Tues–Sun 10am–5pm; 0.50Ls), a cottage presented to the writer in 1922 to mark 25 years of literary work and subsequently used by Brigadere as a summer house. Decorated in flowery period wallpaper, embroidered cushions and furnishings that exude rustic chic, it looks like the ideal place to spend the holidays. Displays of first editions and their accompanying artwork recall the best-known of Brigadere's creations, a Tom Thumb-sized character named Sprīdītis (*sprīdis* means the span of one hand in Latvian) who wins the hand of a beautiful maiden by overcoming a series of seemingly impossible tasks set by the girl's father. As well as making great bedtime story material, Sprīdītis's exploits (including plenty of David-meets-Goliath encounters with giants and bears) have since become an enduring metaphor for Latvia's struggles against more powerful neighbours. Older kids move on to Brigadere's autobiographical *Dievs, Daba, Darbs* ("God, Nature, Work"), which is a much more lyrical read than its dour title suggests and remains a staple of the Latvian school curriculum.

Once you've digested the museums you can start exploring the **trails**, which fan out from the entrance kiosk in all directions, crossing horse-grazed pastures and bridging gurgling streams. Immediately north of the entrance, chunks of ruddy masonry crowning the **Tērvete Castle Mound** (Tērvetes pilskalns) bear witness to the presence of the Livonian Order, which fortified the spot after their thirteenth-century defeat of the indigenous Zemgaļi; there's a replica of the kind of stockade fort favoured by the latter in the woods ten minutes' further north. Twenty minutes' walk west of the entrance, **Rūķīšu mežs** ("Dwarf Forest") features paths lined with wooden sculptures of mushrooms and dwarves, as well as a dwarf village with little timber houses and a windmill – a popular children's play area. Marking the extreme northeastern extent of the park, a good fifty minutes away from the entrance, **Gulbju ezers** ("Swan Lake") is a favourite springtime stop-off for migrating bitterns, whose distinctive call is similar to the sound produced by blowing across the top of a bottle.

A couple of **cafés** just outside the park open on summer weekends; otherwise the shop next to the tourist office will pour you a coffee and sell you basic foodstuffs. The nearest **place to stay** is the welcoming, six-room *Kliņģeri* guesthouse (℡6376 8567; ❶), 6km northwest of Tērvete – head along the Dobele road and look for a right turn after about 3km. You can **camp** beside Gulbju ezers for less than 1Ls.

Northern Kurzeme:
Cape Kolka, Talsi and around

Separating the Gulf of Rīga from the open Baltic Sea, the horn-shaped land mass of **northern Kurzeme** is endowed with one of the most captivating stretches of coast in the country: an almost uninterrupted ribbon of white sand backed by pines and spruce trees. The main focus for visitors is **Cape Kolka**, at the northernmost tip, a short, sandy spit jutting out into the Baltic Sea, backed by an enchanting hinterland of dunes, bogs and forests. A ten-kilometre belt of territory around the cape is protected by the **Slītere National Park**, the well-maintained walking trails of which provide access to the best of the local landscape. Although a good 70km south of Kolka, the attractive lakeside town of **Talsi** is the main service centre and transport hub for this part of Kurzeme.

Despite the presence of a few thriving fishing ports, such as Mērsrags and Roja, most of the settlements in Latvia's far northwest have an eerie, semi-abandoned air – the result of decades of rural depopulation. During the Soviet period, the whole of this shore was a sensitive border area, and resources like schools and hospitals were deliberately concentrated inland in order to dissuade people from moving to the coast.

The best way to get to northern Kurzeme from Rīga **by car** is to head for Jūrmala (see p.220) and simply keep going – the scenic coastal road goes all the way to Cape Kolka. You could easily see Cape Kolka and be back in Rīga by nightfall, though it's well worth sticking around for a day or so to appreciate the beauty of the area in full. If you're reliant on public transport you'll have no choice but to stay overnight – the three daily **buses** from Rīga all set off in the afternoon (and a couple of them seem to travel all over Kurzeme before arriving). It's advisable to book accommodation in advance, especially at weekends, as places to stay are thin on the ground – Talsi tourist office can help make bookings. Jāņa Sēta's 1:100 000 **map** of the Talsi region (Talsu rajons) covers the whole of northern Kurzeme and is essential if you're exploring the area in any depth.

The Gulf of Rīga

The road from Rīga to Cape Kolka sticks to the coast for most of its 150-kilometre length, providing plenty of opportunities for scenic stop-offs. After leaving the urbanized sprawl of Jūrmala, the Kolka road passes through a series of small settlements whose beaches are popular with day-trippers keen to escape the more crowded stretches of sand further east. The first of these, some 10km out of Jūrmala, is **Lapmežciems**, a fishing village renowned for its smoked fish – which can be sampled at a string of roadside cafés. The village also abuts the eastern corner of Lake Kanieris, a brackish stretch of water separated from the Gulf of Rīga by a one-kilometre-long, thick bar of sand. The marshy shores of the lake attract white-tailed eagles, ospreys and bitterns, and are particularly popular with migrating cranes in the autumn. Further on, the stretch of coast between **Ragaciems** and **Klapkalnciems** is particularly beautiful, with a wonderful beach backed by pines – there are a couple of secure car parks along the road if you want to rest up for a while. The next settlement up the coast, **Apšuciems**, is likewise bordered by huge, pine-covered dunes.

Forty-five kilometres beyond Apšuciems, the working port of **MĒRSRAGS** marks the turn-off for **Lake Engure** (Engures ezers) just inland. The lake, 20km long and 4km wide, is one of the most important nesting sites for migratory birds in this part of Latvia: the reedy northern and eastern shores are particularly popular with grebes, bitterns, mute swans and 23 different species of goose. There are no paths, however – your best bet is to head for the birdwatching tower on the northern shoulder of the lake, 5km west of Mērsrags.

Some forty kilometres further north, **ROJA** has the gruff feel of a working fishing port, but is surrounded by sand-and-forest scenery as inviting as any along this coast – it's also near enough to Kolka to serve as a base from which to explore the region. The *Roja* **hotel**, Jūras iela 6 (☎6323 2226, ✉rojahotel@inbox.lv; ❶–❷), offers simply furnished, bright en suites with TV, plus a handful of cheaper rooms with shared facilities in an adjoining cottage; while the *Dana* **guesthouse**, Raudu iela 3 (☎ 2992 7556; ❶) is a cosy, intimate B&B. The **bus station**, in the town centre, has good connections with Talsi (see p.235).

Cape Kolka and around

Buses from Rīga stop 2km short of **Cape Kolka** in **KOLKA** village, which, like most settlements in these parts, consists of a single street running parallel to the coast. To reach the cape, head to the northern end of the street and turn right. Apart from a pile of rubble left over from an old lighthouse, there's nothing much here, but it's a uniquely beautiful spot nevertheless, with a desolate, end-of-the-world feel about it. Looking out to sea, you'll catch sight of the Kolka lighthouse rising up from a small island 6km to the northeast. In certain conditions, currents from the Gulf of Rīga meet countercurrents from the Baltic Sea to produce a chevron pattern of wavelets. In spring, the cape is an important collection point for migrating birds, with thousands of geese and ducks joined by herons, buzzards and eagles.

There's also a lot more in the vicinity to enjoy, whether it's the fishing villages west of the cape, **Vaide**, **Košrags** and **Mazirbe** (see p.234), where time seems to have stopped,

The Livs

The **Livs** (Lībi in Latvian; Livod in their own language), despite being the longest-established of Latvia's indigenous peoples, are the closest to extinction. A Finno-Ugric people closely related to the Estonians, the Livs settled in Latvia just after the last Ice Age, several millennia before the Latvians, who have only been here a mere 4000 years. The Livs remained in possession of northern Latvia and its coastline right up until the Middle Ages – the fact that the thirteenth-century German crusaders named one of their Baltic provinces "Livonia" suggests that the Livs were still in the majority at the time. Gradually, however, the Livs were assimilated by the Kurši and other Latvian tribes, and by the eighteenth century the fishing villages of northern Kurzeme were the only parts of Latvia where their culture survived. With the advent of mass schooling in the nineteenth and twentieth centuries, the Liv language suffered a severe blow. German and then Latvian were the only languages of educational and career advancement, and the Livs increasingly regarded their own tongue as a social hindrance and resigned themselves to assimilation by the Latvian-speaking majority. During the Soviet period, when the coast was militarized and fishing discouraged, most young Livs left the Kolka region for the big cities, intermarried with Latvians and left their culture behind.

Estimates differ as to how many Livs still exist. The number of native speakers can be counted on the fingers of one hand, although a couple of hundred urbanized Latvians of Liv descent declare themselves as Livs in official documents and actively study the language in an attempt to revive it. The main Liv cultural organization, Livod it (Union of Livs), has a membership of around 250. The Liv House in Mazirbe teaches Liv language and songs to anyone of Liv descent who's interested, and also organizes the annual Liv Festival in Mazirbe at the beginning of August. However, the long-term outlook for the language's survival is bleak in the extreme and it looks set to become the object of academic curiosity rather than a living tongue.

or the distinctive landscape inland, shaped over millions of years: at the end of the last Ice Age, the sea extended all the way to the Zilie Kalni (Blue Hills), a seventy-metre-high escarpment that lies about 10km inland from the present-day coast. Since then the sea has been in slow retreat, leaving behind the rippling succession of duney ridges that characterize the landscape today. Many of these ridges are covered in forest, but there are also large tracts of heath and bog – notably Bažu bog (Bažu purvs), just off the main Rīga–Kolka road, though it's a protected reserve and is closed to the public. The whole area falls under the protection of the **Slītere National Park** (Slīteres nacionlais parks; Ⓦwww.slitere.gov.lv), which maintains a modest visitors centre at Slītere lighthouse. The park is also a haven for roe deer, elk, wild boar and lynx.

One of the best sea views to be had in the area is from **Ēvaži cliff** (Ēvažu stāvkrasts), a bank of moss- and tree-covered dunes that rises above the seashore 5km south of Kolka, just off the Rīga road, and is reached by a short trail just opposite the Novakari bus stop. From the top, you get a great view of the coast all the way down to Roja. Walking back to Kolka along the beach is a great way of taking in the pines-and-sands landscape.

Accommodation in Kolka is limited to the *Zītari*, next to a supermarket of the same name at the southern entrance to town (℡6327 7145; ❷), with acceptable en suites but indifferent service; and the more basic but much friendlier *Ūši*, well signed at the northern end of the main street (℡6327 7350, Ⓦwww.kolka.info.lv; ❶), offering two sparsely furnished rooms, a communal kitchen and tent space in the garden. There's a **café** serving meat-and-two-veg main courses at the *Zītari*.

West of Kolka

West of Kolka, the main Ventspils-bound road runs a couple of kilometres inland to a string of sleepy fishing villages, connected to the outside world by a dirt road. The first

△ Mazirbe parish church

you come to is **VAIDE**, a dune-encircled collection of fishermen's cottages and holiday houses about 7.5km west of Kolka. Aside from another glorious stretch of white sand, Vaide's main attraction is the **Horn Museum** (Ragu kolekcija; daily 9am–8pm; 0.40Ls), a forest ranger's large collection of elk and stag antlers, gleaned from the forest and artfully arranged in an attic. You can pitch a tent in the meadow behind the museum for 0.50Ls.

From Vaide you can continue westwards via a dirt road – a great ride through coastal heath and forest (if your suspension's up to it) – or return to the main road, turning off again after 6km for the village of **KOŠRAGS**, where wooden fishermen's houses huddle around sand-paved streets. There's a highly attractive **B&B** here, *Jauntilmači viesu nams* (☎2941 2974, ⓦwww .kolka.lv; ❸), offering smart, fully equipped rooms and an on-site sauna. A further 3km beyond Košrags lies the village of **MAZIRBE**, set back from a beautiful stretch of dune-backed beach.

Like all the villages along this part of the coast, Mazirbe is inhabited by descendents of the Livs (see box, p.233), although you're unlikely to find anyone here who still speaks the language. The study of Liv culture is kept alive by the **Liv House** (Lībiešu Tautas Nams/Līvlist Roukuoda), a Modernist white cube built in 1939 with financial support from other Finno-Ugric nations – as a polyglot inscription in Estonian, Finnish and Hungarian attests. Towards the southern end of the village, the **Rāndali Ethnographic Collection** (Etnogrāfiska kolekcija Rāndali) has a small display of Liv costumes, while a little further on, on the far side of the Kolka–Ventspils road, Mazirbe **parish church** sports a highly personable pebble-dashed exterior and a lovely wooded cemetery. Back in the village, there's a cosy **B&B**, *Kalēji* (☎6324 8374; ❷), with tent space in the grounds, and a **food shop** opposite the Liv House.

After Mazirbe the main road continues southwest towards Ventspils, while another route forks south towards Talsi, climbing up the Zilie Kalni escarpment. Taking the latter route, you'll pass a sign to the **Pēterezers Nature Trail** (Pēterezera dabas taka) on your right after about 4km. This enjoyable boardwalk trail takes you up and down some of the region's trademark dune ridges and across heath before arriving at Pēterezers, a shallow lake edged by dark pines. Returning to the road and continuing up the hill for another 5km brings you to **Slītere lighthouse** (Slīteres bāka; Wed–Sun 10am–6pm; 0.30Ls), a stocky cylinder dating from 1849 and now containing a display of photographs of lighthouses throughout the world. You aren't allowed all the way to the top of the lighthouse, but you get a good view of the surrounding countryside from the penultimate floor, with a lush plateau of farmland to the south and wooded wilderness stretching seawards to the north. On the ground floor is the **Slītere National Park Visitors' Centre** (same times), where you can buy brochures and rudimentary maps. Immediately behind the lighthouse, a wooden stairway leads down the escarpment towards the start of the **Slītere Nature Trail** (Slīteres dabas taka), which winds through a lush expanse of mixed forest with occasional stretches of semi-bog, the undergrowth thick with bird's-eye primrose and all manner of ferns. The trail's only drawback is its short length, taking barely thirty minutes to complete.

Talsi

Some seventy kilometres south of Kolka and 5km north of the Rīga–Ventspils high-way, **TALSI** is the administrative capital and transport hub of northern Kurzeme – you'll probably change buses here if you're travelling between the Kolka area and the west coast. It's in any case a rewardingly pretty market town, ranged across a series of low hills. The town's cobbled streets slope down towards a neck of land separating two small lakes, Lake Talsi (Talsu ezers) to the south and Lake Vilkmuiža (Vilkmuižas ezers) to the north.

Squatting on a ridge to the northeast, the stocky white **Lutheran Church** (Luteranu baznīca) is famous for being the workplace of pastor Karl Amenda (1774–1836); a friend of both Beethoven and Mozart, he assisted in the care of the latter's children after the composer's early demise. Rising above the east bank of Lake Talsi, **Talsi Castle Mound** (Talsu pilskalns) was the site of a Liv fortress before falling in the tenth century to the Kurši, for whom Talsi was a key strategic stronghold until the arrival of the Livonian Order in 1263. Occupying a restored nineteenth-century manor house just east of the Castle Mound, the **Talsi District Museum**, K. Mīlenbaha 19 (Tues–Sun: April–Oct 11am–5pm; Nov–March 11am–4pm; 0.50Ls), harbours an enjoyable collection of local crafts, and the surrounding manor park is the perfect place for a relaxing stroll.

Practicalities

Talsi's **bus station** is ten minutes' walk northwest of the centre on Dundagas iela: walk downhill and bear left to reach the main street, Lielā iela, where you'll find the **tourist office** at no. 19/21 (June–Sept Mon–Fri 9am–6pm, Sat 10am–2pm; Oct–May Mon–Fri 9.30am–5.30pm; ☏6322 4165, ⓦwww.talsi.lv), a good source of informa-tion on **accommodation** throughout northern Kurzeme, especially in the Kolka region. There's not much to choose from in town itself: *Hotel Talsi*, just east of the bus station at Kareivju 16 (☏6323 2020, ⓦwww.hoteltalsi.lv; ❸), offers basic en suites in a frumpy building, while *Mikus*, 5km south of town (☏2924 3392; ❸–❹) is marginally more comfortable but in a less appealing location – it's right behind the Talsi exit of the Rīga–Ventspils highway.

Campers should push on to the popular **camping** spot at sandy-shored, forest-shrouded **Lake Usma**, 30km west of Talsi on the Rīga–Ventspils highway and served by plenty of Talsi–Ventspils buses. Several well-equipped sites are dotted around the lake's serene, heavily indented shoreline: there's tent space and cabins for rent at *Mežmalas* (☏2934 1582; cabins ❶), *Usmas kempings* (☏6367 3654 or 2936 4154, ⓦwww.usma.lv; cabins ❷) and *Dzītari* (☏6367 3759; cabins ❸). You can rent boats at all three, and *Usmas kempings* also has a small stock of bikes.

The best place for **eating and drinking** in Talsi is *Mara*, at Lielā 16, with a coffee shop and cafeteria-style eatery at ground level, and below, a beer cellar, complete with full menu of grilled meats and salads. *Kafejnīca Depo*, tucked away below the church at Ezera iela 1, offers hearty meat-and-potato stodge in a cosy, wooden-bench interior, while nearby *Kai*, Lielā 30, has a full menu of hot food, as well as a billiards room and late-night disco.

West of Rīga: Ķemeri and Tukums

The commuter rail line which loops northwest out of Rīga via Jūrmala puts a couple of worthwhile destinations within day-trip range of the capital. Around fifty kilome-tres out of Rīga, **Ķemeri** was one of the show-pieces of the inter-war Latvian state – a high-society spa resort, which, despite several decades of decay – still retains some-thing of its former elegance. More importantly, the town is the centre of the **Ķemeri National Park** and provides access to one of the most captivating wetland landscapes in the country in the shape of the **Great Ķemeri Bog**. The line's terminus is at **Tuku-ms**, a quiet country town with a modest clutch of museums.

Drivers should note that although very much a town in its own right, Ķemeri is in administrative terms part of Jūrmala – this accounts for the rather confusing signs reading "Jūrmala" which you'll see if you enter Ķemeri by road.

Kemeri

An upmarket resort in the inter-war years and a popular health spa during the Soviet era, **ĶEMERI** has fallen off the tourist map since Latvia regained independence and nowadays has a rather abandoned air. However, a tangible sense of grandeur still lingers in the **spa park** (a fifteen-minute walk northeast across town from the train station), where manicured lawns and flowerbeds and elegant, tree-lined avenues seem tailor-made for hours of recuperative walks. At its centre stands the **Ķemeri Hotel**, a stately ocean liner of a building whose combination of smooth curves and castellated towers brings to mind some sort of Art Deco Camelot. Designed in the early 1930s by leading National Romantic architect Eižens Laube, it seems a world away from the Gotham City-style apartment blocks he built in central Rīga. The hotel is currently being restored and looks set to resume its role as playground of the Rīga elite when it reopens.

Northeast of the hotel, a path leads off through densely forested parkland, arriving after 1km at the Meža Māja, or Forest House, where the **Ķemeri National Park Visitors' Centre** (Mon–Fri 9am–5pm; ☏6773 0078 and 6773 0200, ⓦwww.kemeri .gov.lv) sells maps and advises on walks. Immediately north of here lies the start of the **Black Alder Wetland Path** (Melnalkšņu dumbrāja taka), an 800-metre-long boardwalk trail through dense and leafy woodland and over soggy (and sometimes rather smelly) soil, fed by the same sulphurous springs that provide the Ķemeri spa with its restorative waters.

Great Ķemeri Bog

Lovers of bleak wilderness landscapes will want to make the trip to **Great Ķemeri Bog** (Lielais Ķemeru tīrelis), a 6000-hectare expanse of bog covered in springy sphagnum moss and punctuated by stunted birch trees and conifers. Leading out into the bog is a three-kilometre-long boardwalk trail, which starts a good 4km south of Ķemeri itself. To get there, head south from Ķemeri train station to the main Rīga–Ventspils road, turn right and follow it for 800m before turning left down a dirt road that leads past Ķemeri cemetery. Curving through the forest, the road eventually arrives at a national park signboard, where you veer right and follow the "laipa" sign to find the start of the trail.

The boardwalk leads out onto a patchwork of greens and tawny browns, and, further along, a glinting archipelago of ponds. Local flora worth looking out for include cranberries (picking them is strictly forbidden) and sundews, which use the sticky red hairs on their lower leaves to trap insects – that's if the creepy crawlies haven't already been gobbled up by the bog's community of wood sandpipers.

Tukums

Occupying a low hill above the River Slocene, **TUKUMS** is a tranquil country town whose transport links with the capital have made it something of a dormitory settlement for Rīga-based commuters. It's not a hugely exciting place by any means, but it's a useful stop-off if you're heading west from Ķemeri towards central Kurzeme, and a handful of moderately appealing museums make it worth a couple of hours of your time. Just off the southern end of Brīvības laukums, Tukums' sleepy central square, a rather undistinguished **Castle Tower** (Livonijas ordeņa pils tornis; Tues–Sat 10am–5pm, Sun 11am–4pm; ⓦwww.tukumamuzejs.lv; 0.50Ls) is the last surviving remnant of a Livonian Order fortress, once a favoured residence of sixteenth-century Grand Master Walter von Plettenburg. Inside is a modest museum display, the highlight of which is a room full of exquisitely modelled dioramas illustrating different periods in the town's history.

North of here, behind a whitewashed **parish church**, quiet cobbled streets like Harmonijas, Darza and Zirgu, lined with wooden houses, look as if they haven't changed much since the inter-war years. The **Art Museum**, Harmonijas 7 (Mākslas muzejs; same times as the Castle Tower; 0.40Ls), is worth visiting for its themed seasonal exhibitions, although the permanent collection of canvases by local painters is somewhat lacklustre.

Three kilometres southeast of the town centre and reached by heading along Rīgas iela and turning right into Durbes iela, **Durbe Palace** (Durbes pils; Tues–Sat 10am–5pm, Sun 11am–4pm; 1Ls), set in landscaped parkland, is a Neoclassical manor house graced with a wedding-cake portico and Ionic columns (grafted on in the 1820s). The interior contains nineteenth-century furnishings and photographs of Tukums through the ages – look out for sepia portraits of the Durbe-owning von Recke family, many of whom were shot by Bolsheviks in 1919. Behind the palace, a stone footbridge leads to the trees and meadows of the landscaped palace park.

Perched on a hillock overlooking the Rīga–Ventspils highway 8km west of town, the soaring red-brick towers and pinnacles of **Jaunmoku Palace** (Jaunmoku pils; Mon–Fri 9am–6pm, Sat 9am–4pm, Sun 10am–6pm; 1Ls) look like something out of a Gothic horror story. Built as a country retreat for third-generation Baltic Scot, bone-meal magnate and mayor of Rīga, George Armistead (1847–1912), it now belongs to the Latvian Forestry Authority and has been converted into a hotel and conference centre. The interior still preserves some of its late-nineteenth-century decorations – look out for an august pair of ceramic stoves adorned with landscape scenes of Jūrmala and Rīga. Also on site is a museum of hunting and forestry, but it's of rather minor interest, featuring antlers of long-departed stags and cabinets filled with stuffed woodland creatures.

Practicalities

Situated at the end of the rail line that runs through Jūrmala and Ķemeri, Tukums is served by regular commuter trains from Rīga. The town has two **train stations**, Tukums I just east of town, and Tukums II just to the west: the former is much nearer the centre and next door to the **bus station**, which has regular connections to Rīga, Talsi and Ventspils. The **tourist office**, Pils iela 3 (May–Oct Mon–Fri 9am–7pm, Sat 9am–4pm, Sun 10.30am–3pm; Nov–April Mon–Fri 9am–5pm; ☎6312 4451, ⊛www .tukums.lv), has brochures on the whole region and can fix you up in bed-and-break-fast accommodation, either in Tukums or nearby villages (①–②).

Centrally located **hotels** include *Arka*, Pils iela 9 (☎6312 5747, ⊛www.hotelarka .lv; ③), which has a handful of pastel-coloured en suites and hosts weekend discos in its beer-cellar-style restaurant; and *Harmonija*, a fitness centre just north of the main square at Jāņa iela 3A (☎6312 5775, ⊛www.harmonija.lv; ②), which has neat en suites, with sauna and small indoor pool on site. Offering more in the way of atmosphere, *Jaunmoku Palace* (see above; ☎6310 7126, ⊛www.lvm.lv, ⊛www.jaunmokupils.lv; ②–④) har-bours a strange mixture of rooms, ranging from sparsely furnished affairs with shared facilities to opulent en suites with stately decor. Back in central Tukums, the *Margo* **café**, Lielā 1, will sort you out with a cheap and tasty *karbonāde* (pork chop) or a salad.

The Abava Valley

Northwest of Tukums, the glacier-carved, U-shaped **Abava Valley** is one of the most picturesque spots in western Latvia – not least because it offers a welcome change from the flat arable landscape that dominates elsewhere. Quaint country towns like **Kandava** and **Sabile** provide reason to pause – the latter is conveniently placed for the most attractive stretches of the Abava River and also a short hike away from the open-air art museum at **Pedvāle**. Further west lies **Kuldīga**, arguably Latvia's most appealing provincial town.

Five daily Rīga–Kuldīga **buses** run through the Abava Valley, and a handful of addi-tional Rīga–Sabile and Sabile–Kuldīga services increase the range of options. If you're coming from the north, there are buses from Talsi to Sabile.

Kandava

Some thirty kilometres northwest of Tukums, **KANDAVA** drapes itself between a trio of hillocks just above the main Kuldīga-bound road. Boasting a handsome col-lection of two-storey houses, and with central streets still paved with their original nineteenth-century cobblestones, it's the ideal place for a mid-journey stop-off. The hillock nearest to the road is **Bruņinieku pilskalns**, the easily scaled site of a Livonian Order castle which still preserves the remnants of its thirteenth-century fortifications. Behind Bruņinieku pilskalns lies a neat town square overlooked by a curious nineteenth-century fire station with fortress-like lookout tower. A little way further up the main Lielā iela, at no. 51, a whitewashed former **synagogue** (and subsequently town cinema) stands in mute commemoration of the fact that fifty percent of Kandava's population was Jewish prior to World War I – after which mass emigration in the 1920s and 30s, followed by the murder by Nazis of those that remained, put paid to their presence in the town. A few steps north along Talsu iela, the **Town Museum** at no. 11 (Tues–Fri 9am–4pm, Sat 10am–2pm; ⓦwww.kandavasmuzejs.viss.lv; 0.50Ls) displays photographs documenting Courland's tragic role in World War II's closing stages, when Latvian volunteers were used as cannon fodder by Germans desperate to stem the Soviet advance. There's also a "red corner" filled with objects – Soviet flag, bust of Lenin – that date back to the building's former role as a branch of the Soviet state bank.

East of the centre, on the far side of the main Tukums–Kuldiga road, a dainty four-arched **bridge** spans the Abava River – built in 1873, it has been a much-loved local landmark ever since.

Practicalities

Kandava's **tourist office**, right behind the main bus stop at Kūrortu iela 1B (☎6318 1150, ⓦwww.kandava.lv), will provide a free town map and sheaves of regional information. The *Pils* **guesthouse**, on the site of a former *mikva* (Jewish bathhouse) at Pils iela 7 (☎6312 4919 and 2643 8887, ⓦwww.pils.viss.lv; ❸), contains six simply decorated en suites above a café. There's more accommodation 10km east of town on the road to Sabile (see below), where *Plosti*, ☎2631 0303, ⓦwww.hotelplosti.lv; ❸) offers motel-style, self-catering apartments, tent and caravan space, plus boat and bike hire. Just beyond, the *Imulas* guesthouse (☎6312 3647 and 2919 6494, ⓦwww.imulas.lv, ❸) is an attractive timber roadside building containing cosy, wood-panelled en suites.

The *Pils* **café** (see above) has an inexpensive range of salads, savoury pancakes and meaty mains. The charming *Tējas bode* teahouse, Lielā 30 (Mon–Fri till 8pm, Sat till 10pm, Sun till 6pm), is the place to go for a refreshing brew.

Sabile

Sheltering beneath a south-facing escarpment 16km west of Kandava, **SABILE** is famous for being the northernmost location at which vines are cultivated. On the hill just north of town, **Sabile vineyard** (Sabiles vīnakalns) was founded in the seventeenth century by Duke Jakob of Courland, one of many pet schemes designed to lessen the duchy's dependence on foreign imports. It never produced much in the way of wine and soon fell into disuse, but was re-established in 1936 in order to carry out research into hardy strains of vine – the hundred or so bottles of plonk produced here annually are unlikely to make it as far as the supermarket shelves. If you want to inspect the wine terraces at close hand, you need to buy a ticket from the tourist office (0.15Ls) – worth doing if you want to stretch your legs and enjoy the view across Sabile's rooftops. Back on the main street, it's hard to miss the stately apricot-coloured form of Sabile's nineteenth-century **synagogue**, recently restored and pressed into service as a contemporary-art exhibition space managed by the Open-air Museum at nearby Pedvāle (opening hours vary according to what's on). At the western end of town, the seventeenth-century **Lutheran Church** (Luteranu baznīca), so white that it looks as if it's been carved out of a big lump of chalk, harbours a striking Baroque pulpit held up by a quartet of gryphon-headed snakes. Behind the church, a brisk five-minute ascent brings you to the summit of the pudding-shaped **Castle Hill** (Sabiles pilskalns), site of an ancient Latvian fortress and affording excellent views across the valley.

The **tourist office** in the town council building at Pilskalna 6 (Mon–Fri 10am–noon & 12.30–5.30pm; ☎6325 2344, ⓦwww.sabile.lv) will put you in contact with local

bed-and-breakfast hosts (①–②), few of whom speak English. For something to eat, try one of the couple of decent **cafés** along the main street: *Sabiles vīnakalns*, at Rīgas 11, does a good line in pork and chicken standards, while *Kafejnīca Zane*, Rīgas 8, has more in the way of salads and soups.

Pedvāle

Up on the ridge on the opposite side of the valley to Sabile lies Pedvāle Manor, an abandoned estate entrusted to sculptor Ojārs Feldbergs in the early 1990s on condition that he restore the buildings and open them up as a cultural centre. The result of his labours is the **Pedvāle Open-air Art Museum** (Pedvāles brīvdabas mākslas muzejs; May–Oct daily 9am–6pm; 1Ls; ⊛www.pedvale.lv), a sculpture park set in part-agricultural, part-virgin countryside. The park functions wonderfully well as a nature trail, too, whether you're interested in sculptures or not, with paths taking you down beside densely wooded streams and up over wildflower-carpeted hills, with several storks' nests scattered around for good measure.

To get to Pedvāle, cross the river from Sabile and head uphill – a left turn takes you to the **main entrance** at Firkspedvāle manor house, where there's a window selling tickets. Spread over 2km are well over a hundred works, ranging from the profound to the pretentious, donated by abstract and conceptual sculptors from all over the world – including some throwaway pieces that you wouldn't allow within a ten-mile radius of your own garden. Many of the more memorable works are by **Ojārs Feldbergs** himself – an ever-expanding collection of brooding, deeply mysterious granite lumps. The collection of rocks dangling from poles that make up his *51 Heartstones* (51 sirdsakmens) is the most impressive work in the whole park, although the quietly enigmatic stone hut that is Ryan Hoover's and Kerin Rozycki's *Fire Inside* (Iekšējā uguns) comes a close second.

If you want **to stay**, the restored manor house at Firkspedvāle (☎6325 2249) has a handful of doubles, triples and quads, all at 5Ls per person – all rooms are atmospheric affairs with wooden floors and beams, although showers/WCs are in the hallway. The nearby *Krodziņš Dāre* **pub-restaurant** serves up everything from simple salads to substantial steak and trout dishes.

Carrying on southeast from Firkspedvāle and turning left after 3km will bring you to **Zviedru cepure** (⊛www.zviedrucepure.lv), a hill overlooking the Abava which boasts a dry toboggan run in summer and a 250-metre-long ski piste served by drag lift in winter (Dec–April daily Mon–Sat noon–1am, Sun 10am–11pm). You can rent ski and snowboard gear on site.

Along the Abava to Renda

There are a couple of much-frequented local beauty spots just west of Sabile, beginning with the **Abava Falls** (Abavas rumba), 4km west of town and 500m from the road, a series of frothing rapids where the river descends what looks like a stairway of stratified rock. Back on the main road, another 15km brings you to the turn-off (near the Kaleši bus stop) for **Māra's Chambers** (Māras kambari), a series of sandstone hollows 2km away on the banks of the Abava, where it's thought that ancient Latvians made sacrifices to Māra the Earth Mother. Some 5km beyond, the main road traverses the river at the village of **Renda** and leaves the Abava Valley, crossing low hills before dropping down towards Kuldīga.

Kuldīga

If you only have time to visit one provincial town in Latvia then it really ought to be **KULDĪGA**, 155km west of Rīga, a pretty little town of cobbled streets and half-timbered houses on the banks of the Venta. Kuldīga can also boast one of the natural wonders of Latvia right on its doorstep – a set of rapids known as the Venta Falls. Thanks to the navigability of the Venta River, Kuldīga was once one of most important trading towns in Kurzeme and a member of the Hanseatic League. The birthplace of Duke Jakob, Kuldīga's castle was a favourite residence of the dukes of Courland until

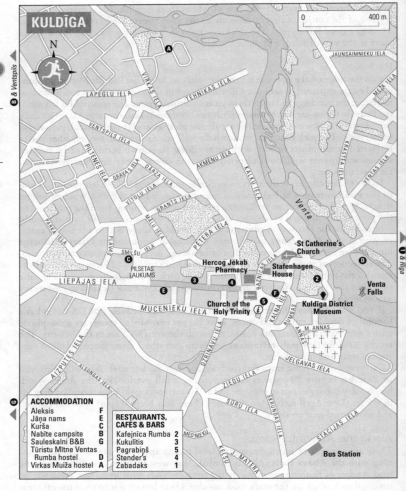

KULDĪGA

N

0   400 m

JAUNSAIMNIEKU IELA

A

LAPEGLU IELA

VIRKAS IELA

TEHNIKAS IELA

VENTSPILS IELA

MEŽA IELA

KRASTA IELA

PILTENES IELA

GRAVAS IELA

DARZA IELA

AKMENU IELA

KALKU IELA

VENIAS IELA

PARKA IELA

VĪTOLU IELA

GRANTS IELA

Venta

SMILŠU IELA

MALU IELA

PĒTERA IELA

▶ **D** & Riga

PLAVAS

C

PILSETAS
LAUKUMS

**St Catherine's
Church**

LIEPĀJAS IELA

E

**Hercog Jēkab
Pharmacy**

3

4

BAZNICAS IELA

**Stafenhagen
House**

2

**Venta
Falls**

**Church of the
Holy Trinity**

5

F

KALNA IELA

**Kuldīga District
Museum**

MUCENIEKU IELA

RUMBAS

AIZPUTES IELA

DZIRNAVU IELA

M. ANNAS

ALSUNGAS IELA

ANNAS

+ + +
+ + +
+

◀ **G**

JELGAVAS IELA

ZIEDU IELA

SORU IELA

SARUNDAS IELA

ACCOMMODATION
Aleksis   **F**
Jāņa nams   **E**
Kurša   **C**
Nabīte campsite   **B**
Sauleskalni B&B   **G**
Tūristu Mītne Ventas
   Rumba hostel   **D**
Virkas Muiža hostel **A**

**RESTAURANTS,
CAFÉS & BARS**
Kafejnīca Rumba   **2**
Kukulītis   **3**
Pagrabiņš   **5**
Stender's   **4**
Zabadaks   **1**

MED NIEKU

STACIJAS IELA

Bus Station

J. MATERA

KELSU

its destruction by the Russians in the Great Northern War, after which Kuldīga settled back into the state of small-town tranquillity that still characterizes the place today.

The Town

Central Kuldīga is such a compact place that you can probably see all its sights in half an hour and still have time for a coffee, although the relaxing effect of its quiet streets and gingerbread-house buildings will make you want to stay longer. The most attractive of its jumble of well-preserved houses are concentrated on or around the junction of Baznīcas iela, Liepājas iela and Pasta iela. The creamy-yellow house on the corner of Baznīcas and Pasta is supposedly the oldest surviving wooden building in Kurzeme, dating from 1632, although it has been much rebuilt since. Of similar vintage is the single-storey timber building just opposite, at Baznīcas 5, formerly the town hall and now the tourist office. Heading east along Liepājas and taking the first left down Raiņa

△ Kuldīga

iela brings you to the seventeenth-century Catholic **Church of the Holy Trinity** (Sv Trīsvienības baznīca; Mon 3–7pm, Tues, Wed & Fri 11am–7pm, Thurs & Sat 11am–4pm, Sun 9.30am–4pm), a delightful stone building, sheltering in a neat garden square. The main focus of attention inside is a nineteenth-century altar rich with Neoclassical detail, with urn-topped pillars and smooth-skinned angels framing a much older statue of the Virgin. On the right side of the nave, look out for a seventeenth-century confessional booth decorated with jolly floral squiggles.

Returning to Baznīcas iela and heading north, you'll pass a string of old stone houses, including the building at no. 17 which played host to King Charles XII of Swedish in 1701; when not preoccupied with planning military campaigns against Peter the Great, he enjoyed hunting in the local forests. At its northern end, Baznīcas curves its way around **St Catherine's Church** (Sv Katrīnas baznīca), an oft-rebuilt structure where Duke Jakob of Courland was baptized and later married to Princess Louisa Charlotte of Brandenburg. Unfortunately, the church doesn't have regular opening times – if you do manage to find it open, look out for an exquisitely carved wooden altar by Nicholas Soffrens, the seventeenth-century Ventspils-based sculptor who created works for churches throughout the duchy.

A right turn at the end of Baznīcas takes you down to the bridge across the Venta, affording a superb view of the **Venta Falls** (Ventas rumba) immediately upstream. At less than 2m in height, they're not exactly Niagara, but provide a memorable spectacle nevertheless, curving across the 250-metre-wide river in an elegant S-bend. If the mid-nineteenth-century guidebooks of J.G. Kohl are to be believed, locals used to hang nets and traps from the top of the falls in order to catch fish attempting to jump their way upriver.

Occupying high ground on the south side of the bridge is a grassy park covering the site of the (now demolished) castle. In the middle stands the **Kuldīga District Museum** (Kuldīgas novada muzejs; Tues–Sun 11am–5pm; 0.40Ls), occupying a wooden house built in 1900 to serve as the Russian pavilion at the Exposition Universelle in Paris. Intended to show off prefabricated house-building techniques, it was successfully dismantled and re-erected here by a Liepāja businessman eager to impress his Kuldīga-born fiancée. The creaky-floored interior harbours a scale model of Kuldīga castle as it looked in its sixteenth-century heyday, and a colourful display of playing cards through the ages.

Practicalities

The **tourist office** at Baznīcas 5 (Mon–Fri 9am–5pm; July & Aug also Sat 10am–4pm & Sun 10am–2pm; ☎6332 2259, ⓦwww.kuldiga.lv) is a good source of information on Kurzeme as a whole. Bikes can be rented from the tourist office or from *Tūristu Mītne Ventas Rumba* (see below).

Accommodation options in Kuldīga include a handful of **hotels**: one of the nicest is *Aleksis*, Pasta iela 5 (☎6332 2153; ❸), offering sweet little doubles with modern furniture and jazzy colour schemes, all with shower, some with TV too. Also a good bet is *Jāņa Nams*, Liepājas 36 (☎6332 3456, ⓦwww.jananams.lv; ❸), with neat, simply-furnished en suites in a quiet courtyard. Alternatively, snuggle down in one of the en suites at the ⅔ *Sauleskalni B&B* (☎2680 6054 and 6332 2850, ⓦwww.sauleskalni .com; ❸), with wooden floors and furnishings and set in idyllic countryside south of Kuldīga – it's signed off the bypass that carries through traffic on the Rīga–Ventspils route. A cheaper, but less attractive, option is the central *Kurša*, Pilsētas laukums 6 (☎6332 2430; ❶–❷), a Soviet-era block on the main square featuring frumpy furnishings and unrenovated bathrooms; the more expensive rooms come with TV.

Hostel beds are available at *Virkas Muiža*, twenty minutes' walk northwest of the centre at Virkas iela 27 (☎6332 3480; 4–10Ls per person depending on room size), and at *Tūristu Mītne Ventas Rumba*, across the river from town right beside the Venta Falls (☎6332 4168 or 2643 8250, ⓦwww.ventasrumba.lv) – an attractive, shingle-roofed old house offering doubles with shared facilities (❷), en suites (❸) and some quads (35Ls) – and you can pitch tents on the lawn outside. Breakfast (extra) is in the nearby Pīlādzītis café. Otherwise, the nearest **campsite** is the *Nabīte*, about 12km northwest of town (signed off the Ventspils road; ☎2945 8904, ⓦwww.nabite.viss.lv), offering four-person cabins (15Ls) on the wooded shores of Nabes lake.

There are plenty of places **to eat** in town. For a relaxing drink and a great view, try *Kafejnīca Rumba*, a kiosk near the museum with an outdoor terrace overlooking the Venta Falls. *Kukulitis*, Liepājas 35, is the best place for take-away pastries. *Stender's*, a two-tier wooden pavilion at Liepājas 3, has the full range of meat-and-potato fare and is an enjoyable place for an evening **drink**, as is *Pagrabiņš*, occupying a cellar behind the tourist office at Baznīcas 5 and featuring steaks, salmon and trout on its menu.

Check posters to see if anything is happening at alternative **club** *Zabadaks*, on the western side of the Venta at Vijolīšu 24, one of the few places outside Rīga or Liepāja to host live bands.

Ventspils and around

Once the most hard-edged of port cities, **VENTSPILS** has spent the last decade reinventing itself as a tourist-friendly city, and now enjoys the enviable status of being the number-one day-trip destination in Latvia – which is why you'll see more crocodiles of schoolchildren winding their way through the streets here than anywhere else in the country. While a stark industrial landscape of warehouses and cranes still dominates the north bank of the River Venta, the southern bank is characterized by cutely cobbled pavements, neat flowerbeds and sculpture-scattered parks. A recently restored medieval castle, a white-sand beach, an open-air ethnographic museum and the "Children's City" adventure playground are the keynote attractions that Latvians come here to see.

Traditionally, Ventspils' main source of municipal wealth was the oil transit business, although this dried up totally in 2003, when Russian producers started shipping their crude elsewhere. With the port no longer as busy as it once was, Ventspils' reinvention as a tourist destination has not come a moment too soon.

Arrival, information and accommodation

Ventspils **bus station** is conveniently located on the southeastern fringes of the centre on Kuldīgas iela. **Ferries** from Västervik and Lübeck dock some 400m from the centre, at the eastern end of Ostas iela. The **tourist office** at Tirgus 7 (May–Sept Mon–Fri 8am–7pm, Sat 9am–5pm, Sun 10am–3pm; Oct–April Mon–Fri 8am–5pm,

VENTSPILS

RESTAURANTS, CAFÉS & BARS

Don Basil	2
Kafejnīca Buģiņš	3
Kafejnīca	4
Jaunpilsēta	1
Melnais Sīvens	5
Pankoki	

ACCOMMODATION

Dzintarjūra	B
Jūras brīze	D
Olympic Centre	C
Piejūras kempings campsite	E
Raibie logi	A

▲ Riga

N

DURBES IELA

LĀČPLĒŠA IELA

SARKANMUIŽAS DAMBIS

LIELAIS PROSPEKTS

BRĪVĪBAS IELA

Venta

Orthodox Church

St Nicholas's Church

Bus Station

BRĪVĪBAS IELA

LAUKU IELA

ALEKSANDRA IELA

STRĒLNIEKU

SPORTA IELA

Olympic Centre Sports Hall

KULDĪGAS IELA

VAIGZNU IELA

Hercogs Jēkabs

LIELA IELA

PILS IELA

KULDĪGAS IELA

RAIŅA IELA

JŪRAS IELA

GANĪBU IELA

PLAVAS IELA

VĪTOLU IELA

BĒRZU IELA

PUTNU IELA

Livonian Order Castle

Former Synagogue

OSTAS IELA

PILS IELA

PLATĀ

LIELA DZIRNAVU IELA

SAULES IELA

GANĪBU IELA

PRIEZU IELA

PUĶU IELA

DZIRNAVU IELA

PAVILA IELA

MEŅĢESS

DZINTARU IELA

Venta

LIEPU IELA

JŪRAS IELA

MEŽA IELA

KATOLU IELA

LIEPĀJAS IELA

LIELAIS PROSPEKTS

MEŽA IELA

PĒTERA IELA

SAULES IELA

BĒRZU IELA

INŽENIERU IELA

RĪGAS IELA

ANOTU IELA

KATOLU IELA

JŪRKALNES IELA

TĒRANDES

DZINZAJU IELA

Venta

K VALDEMĀRA

LĪVU

KĀRLINES

OSTGALS

Children's City

PĒTERA IELA

J PORUKA

INŽENIERU IELA

STRADU

AIZPUTES

LĪDUMS

South Pier

Town Beach

LOČU IELA

ŪDENS IELA

VIĻŅU IELA

MEDŅU IELA

VASKARNICU IELA

PARKA IELA

TĀRGALE

LAIMAS

RIŅĶA IELA

Aquapark

Seaside Open-Air Museum

0   500 m

Sat 10am–3pm; ☏6362 2263, 🌐www.tourism.ventspils.lv) sells town maps. Although good-value, quality **accommodation** in Ventspils is on the rise, there's still not enough of it to go round in a city of this size – always book ahead if you can.

Hotels

Dzintarjūra Ganību 26 ☏6362 2719, 🌐www
.dzintarjura.lv. A seventy-room Soviet-era hotel
offering perfectly habitable rooms with TV and
small-sized bathrooms. The colour-clash decor will
appeal to Seventies retro freaks but will induce
headaches in just about everyone else. The fifteen-
metre ground-floor swimming pool (free to guests
mornings only) is a major plus. ❸

Jūras brīze Vasarnīcu 34 ☏6362 2524, 🌐www
.hoteljurasbrize.lv. Small hotel in a traditional-style
house close to the Aquapark and the beach, offering en suites with laminate floors and citrus-col-
oured fabrics. There are some family-sized suites
sleeping three or four, and room #14 (reached
by a wobbly spiral staircase) offers cosy quarters
beneath a steeply sloping attic ceiling. Standard
doubles ❸, suites 36–40Ls

Olympic Centre (Olimpiskā centra viesnīca)
Lielais prospekts 33 ☏6362 8032,
🌐www.ocventspils.lv. A former housing block converted into a bright, modern hotel in 2003, offering
functional, grey-carpet-meets-plain-furniture en
suites. A ten-minute walk south of the bus station.
No breakfast, but there's a small café on site. ❷

Raibie logi Lielais prospects 61 ☏2914
2327 and 2912 3903, 🌐www.raibielogi
.lv. Charming timber house offering a handful of
traditionally decorated en suites with TV. Plenty
of triples and quads make this a good choice for
families. ❸

Campsite

Piejūras kempings Vasarnīcu 56 ☏6362 7925,
🌐www.camping.ventspils.lv. A large, well-
tended campsite with tent and trailer pitches
(1.50–3Ls respectively) and smart timber cottages sleeping four people – 20Ls per cottage
with en-suite facilities, 10Ls per cottage without.
Open all year.

The City

Most of Ventspils' sights are spread out over 2km along the south side of the Venta estuary. Starting at the eastern end of this strip, there's a handsome collection of nine-teenth-century buildings around **Rātslaukums**, the historic centre of the city. From here your best bet is to proceed westwards along the waterfront, taking in views of the bustling container port before arriving at the superbly restored **Livonian Order Castle**, now home to an absorbing history museum. Strolling west through the picturesque nineteenth-century suburb of **Ostgals** brings you eventually to the vast, green, open spaces of the **Children's City** play area, **Seaside Open-Air Museum** and **Seashore Park**, which together provide much of the focus of Ventspils' blossoming tourist industry.

Rātslaukums and the waterfront

At the centre of Ventspils lies a tangle of narrow streets zeroing in on an unassuming **Town Hall Square** (Rātslaukums). On the square's eastern edge is the nineteenth-century **St Nicholas's Church** (Sv Nikolaja baznīca), the principal Lutheran place of worship in the city. It looks rather like a Greek temple with an observatory growing out of its roof, and has a beautifully proportioned balustraded interior. From here, Tirgus iela leads north to a market square thronging with shoppers on weekday mornings.

Beyond the market square lies **Ostas iela**, a waterfront promenade running along the southern bank of the River Venta and dotted with an impressive array of public sculpture. The eastern end starts with the *Sea Stone* (Jūras akmens), a rough-hewn lump of grey rock mounted on granite supports, and continues with several similarly inscru-table abstract pieces by local artists. You'll also come across two ends of a cow joined by a section of oil pipeline – one of a whole herd of bovine-related artworks placed throughout the city during 2002's "Cow Parade", a project designed to highlight the links between industrial Ventspils and its dairy-farming hinterland. Looking equally sculptural are the immense loading chutes and cranes of the cargo port on the opposite bank of the river. For a closer look at the port facilities, including the oil terminal just north of town, take a 45-minute trip with the **Hercogs Jēkabs excursion boat**

(May–Sept sailings roughly hourly between 10am & 6pm; Oct 5 times daily; 0.80Ls), which departs from a mooring just to the east of the cow.

The Livonian Order Castle

At the western end of Ostas iela, lanes lead back inland towards the egg-yolk-coloured bulk of the **Livonian Order Castle** (Livonijas ordeṇa pils; daily: May–Sept 9am–6pm; Oct–April 10am–5pm; 1Ls), a medieval fortress and, later, Tsarist prison, that has become something of a Ventspils landmark in the wake of its much-publicized restoration in 2001. Inside is an exceedingly well-designed **museum of the city's history**, which makes up for a lack of genuinely dramatic artefacts through imaginative use of diagrams and touch-screen computers. The castle's renovated halls and galleries are a major attraction in themselves, especially the beautifully lit central courtyard overlooked by arched, red-brick galleries. Seasonal arts and crafts exhibitions are held in the main tower, where you'll also chance upon a clumsily painted fresco featuring weightlifters – a reminder that this part of the castle was used as a Soviet army gym in the 1960s.

West of the castle

Ten minutes' walk west of the castle lies a grid of cobbled streets and wooden single-storey houses known as **Ostgals** ("Port's End"), an attractively sleepy suburb dating from the mid-nineteenth century, when the Tsarist authorities encouraged local fishermen and farmers to build homes in the area, in order to prevent the Sahara-like encroachment of nearby dunes. Head south from here and you'll find it hard to avoid the hordes of little ones making a bee-line for **Children's City** (Bērnu pilsētiṇa; free), a kiddies' playpark featuring all manner of slides, climbing frames and sandpits. The parkside café, *Pepija*, is appropriately furnished with toddler-sized chairs and tables.

From here it's a five-minute walk southwest along Vasarnīcu iela, lined with Tsarist-era summer houses, to the **Seaside Open-Air Museum** (Piejūras brīvdabas muzejs; May–Sept daily 11am–6pm; Oct–April Wed–Sun 11am–5pm; 0.50Ls). Alongside a display of beached fishing boats of all eras and sizes, there's a street of fishermen's cottages (each with a pair of crotch-high wading boots hung up in the hallway) and a nineteenth-century windmill whose mechanism is driven by wood-carved cogs. One of the museum's most popular attractions is the **narrow-gauge railway** (Mazbānītis), on which a steam-hauled train (0.50Ls extra) takes passengers on a brief circuit of the lawns and trees of the adjacent **Seashore Park** (Jūrmalas parks), its shrill whistle audible all over the western side of the city.

Immediately north of the museum lie the swimming pools and waterslides of the **Aquapark** (Akvaparks; May–Sept daily 10am–10pm; 1.50Ls), while over to the west lies a glorious stretch of white-sand **beach**, with yet more swings and climbing frames for the kids. If it's not the right weather for sunbathing, consider strolling as far as the lighthouse at the end of the 800-metre-long **South Pier** (Dienvidu mols), which, together with the North Pier (Ziemeḷu mols), just across the water, forms the so-called "Sea Gates" through which tankers and cargo ships lumber their way towards Ventspils' port.

Eating and drinking

Although culinary culture in Ventspils has yet to catch up with the visible signs of modernization elsewhere in the city, the generous sprinkling of cafés and restaurants in the centre is perfectly adequate if you're after a functional meal accompanied by a relaxing drink rather than fine dining.

Don Basil Annas iela 5 ☏ 2680 9086. Cosy bistro-style eatery with wooden tables and earthy colours. As usual, there are plenty of pork, chicken and freshwater fish dishes on the menu, although a fair selection of pastas and risottos help to broaden out the menu. Main courses in the 8–10Ls bracket.

Small but varied wine list. Daily 11am–11pm.

Kafejnīca Bugiņš Lielā iela 1/3. A cosy café-bar decked out in the style of a log cabin. A good place to tuck into inexpensive pork-based favourites or snuggle down for an evening drinking session. Daily 10am–11pm.

Kafejnīca Jaunpilsēta Saules 48. Of all the self-service cafeterias in town, this is probably the best in terms of food quality and sit-down comfort. Good choice of salads and fresh fruit as well as the customary pork-chop mains. Mon–Sat 10am–10pm, Sun 11am–7pm.

Melnais Sīvens Jāņa 17 ☏ 6362 2396. In the basement of Ventspils Castle (entered from the river-facing side), this restaurant has a vaguely medieval feel, with wood floors, stone walls and candlelight. Mains – slabs of pork, chicken or salmon – are in the 10Ls range. Sun–Thurs 11am–11pm, Fri & Sat 11am–midnight.

Pankoki Vasarnīcu 17. An old-fashioned and rather basic order-at-the-counter café in a timber-built villa, specializing in sweet and savoury pancakes. Handy for the Open-Air Museum. Daily 10am–7pm.

Liepāja

Squeezed between a sandy seashore and the marshy Lake Liepāja (Liepājas ezers), the port city of **LIEPĀJA** has undergone several shifts in identity over the last century or so: bustling mercantile centre, then genteel bathing resort, Soviet garrison town and now cultural and commercial capital of Latvia's southwest. Its history is reflected in the city's engaging hodge-podge of architectural styles: wooden seaside villas rub shoulders with red-brick industrial buildings, crumbling barrack blocks and dockside cranes. Although tourism hasn't received as much investment here as in its west-coast rival Ventspils, there's still much to enjoy, including an attractive stretch of seaside gardens and long sandy beaches, a handful of worthwhile museums and churches and the grimly fascinating northern suburb of **Karosta**, once a Tsarist naval fortress and then a Soviet submarine base – virtually a walk-through history lesson.

Locals will tell you that Liepāja was the birthplace of Latvian rock music in the 1970s and '80s – although the rather staid **Liepājas Dzintars Festival** ("Liepāja's Amber"), held annually in mid-August, is about the only sign of this heritage you're likely to come across. The city is also famous for its **lingerie**, being the home city of Latvian textile giants Lauma – you'll see posters of young ladies clad (somewhat scantily) in the company's products all over the country.

Although served by regular **buses** from Rīga, Liepāja is too far away from the capital (220km) to make a comfortable day-trip. Luckily, there's enough to see and do here to make a stay of a couple of days an enjoyable option. Above all, the city is a good base from which to explore Latvia's south coast, notably the nature reserve at **Lake Pape**, 45km to the south.

Some history

Liepāja grew out of the village of Līva, a medieval fishing settlement subsequently taken over by the Livonian Order in the thirteenth century; they re-named it Libau and used it as a base from which to extend their rule over the Curonian coast. As one of the region's few ice-free ports, the city was developed by Tsarist Russia as a naval base in the late nineteenth century and was also one of the main departure points for passenger liners heading for the US, taking thousands of Latvian, Estonian and Lithuanian migrants with them.

In 1919, with Rīga in the hands of the Bolsheviks, Liepāja became the seat of the Latvian Provisional Government. Unfortunately, it had to share the town with an army of Baltic Germans under General von der Goltz, who still entertained the dream of turning Latvia (or a large part of it at least) into a German-dominated statelet dependent on the Reich. The British, who needed both the Latvians and the Germans to stave off the westward advance of Bolshevism, sent the Royal Navy to Liepāja to keep the peace. When von der Goltz tried to have the Latvian government arrested, however, Ulmanis and his ministers were offered protection by the British, who installed them on a former Tsarist battle cruiser, the *Saratov*, anchored in Liepāja's port. A period of uneasy cohabitation unfolded, with British and German troops patrolling different parts of the city. Eager to offer Ulmanis a modicum of moral support, the British, French and Americans established diplomatic missions in Liepāja and were soon joined by representatives of international aid agencies. The situation changed when von der

Goltz marched off to kick the Bolsheviks out of Rīga in May 1919. After a couple of months of confused diplomacy, the British persuaded the Germans to hand Rīga over to the Latvian government – who promptly sailed away in the *Saratov* to take up office in their newly liberated capital. Liepāja's brief period in the political limelight was over.

The Soviet navy established itself here after World War II and Liepāja was virtually closed to foreigners until 1990 – which goes some way to explaining why the tourist potential of its long, sandy beaches has waited until now to be exploited.

Arrival, information and accommodation

Liepāja's **bus and train stations** occupy the same building at the northern end of Rīgas iela, some 1500m from the town centre. Catch any tram heading down Rīgas iela to reach the centre (tickets 0.10Ls from kiosks or 0.12Ls from the driver) – get off when you see the grey spire of the Church of the Holy Trinity on your left. **Ferries** from Rostock and Karlshamn arrive at the Brīvosta terminal on Siļķu iela, 2km north of the centre and buses #3, #6, #10 and #15 run into town from Kalpaka iela, just inland.

The South Kurzeme **tourist information centre** (Lejaskurzemes tūrisma informācijas birojs; Mon–Fri 9am–5pm; ☎6348 0808, ⓦwww.liepaja.lv/turisms), Rožu laukums 5/6, is a mine of information on the whole region and sells city maps. There's a rapidly improving collection of **hotels and hostels** in the city, and the tourist office can book **bed–and–breakfast** accommodation in the villages scattered along the coast from here to the Lithuanian border.

Hotels

Amrita Rīgas iela 7/9 ☎6340 3434, ⓦwww .hotelamrita.lv. Smart en suites measuring up to international business standard, housed in a newish building ten minutes' walk north of the Old Town. ⑥

Bura Jūras iela 22 ☎6340 4858, ⓔbura@arcus .lv. A bold, contemporary building on the northern side of the centre, offering tidy en suites with pale-wood furniture and pastel colour schemes. ④–⑤

Fontaine Jūras iela 24 ☎6342 0956, ⓦwww.fontaine.lv. Lovingly restored nineteenth-century villa with lots of original timber features and rooms decorated in pretty much any interior design style the owners could think of – some display folksy Latvian touches while others come with Middle Eastern fabrics or brash pop-art (notably the much in-demand "Elvis Room", which should be booked well in advance). ②–③

Fontaine Royal Stūrmaņu iela 1 ☎6348 9777, ⓦwww.fontaine.lv. Partner hotel to the *Fontaine* (see above) and displaying the same devotion to eccentricity, with a handful of spacious rooms filled with gilt fittings, shiny surfaces and rich fabrics. Wannabe rock-star types with an appetite for camp will feel right at home. ⑤

Kalēja māja Kalēju iela 8 ☎2648 8200, ⓦwww .kalejamaja.et.lv. Charming nineteenth-century house on a residential street, with three snug rooms in the attic, each decorated with traditional furniture and fabrics. Toilet, shower, kitchenette and fridge are shared. You can rent the whole house if travelling as a family or group. ②

Līva Lielā iela 11 ☎6342 0102, ⓦwww.liva.lv. A conveniently central block offering a mixed bag of en suites – the recently refurbished "business class" rooms feature new carpets, warm colours and satellite TV, while "economy" rooms still proudly display their grey-brown, Soviet-era colour schemes. ②–⑥

Poriņš Palmu iela 5 ☎2915 0596, ⓦwww.porins .lv. A renovated nineteenth-century town house on a cobbled street, with nine comfy rooms, each with en-suite shower. The homely atmosphere makes this very popular with the foreign business community, so it's best to book in advance. ③–④

Promenade Vecā ostmala 40 ☎2200 7332, ⓦwww.promenadehotel.lv. Attractively restored grain warehouse on a nineteenth-century quayside currently being redeveloped as a yachting marina. Expect stylish en suites with hardwood floors, exposed brickwork and flat-screen TVs. ⑥

Roze Rožu 37 ☎6342 1155, ⓦwww .parkhotel-roze.lv. A pair of renovated villas beside the Seafront Park offering repro furniture, roomy doubles with spacious bathrooms and a handful of swish self-catering apartments. Standard doubles ④, apartments ⑦

Hostels

Brīze Oskara Kalpaka 68/70 ☎6344 1566, ⓦwww.brizehostel.lv. A large concrete building midway between the city centre and Karosta, offering dorm-style accommodation in sparsely furnished triples and quads, although there are also some simple doubles with shared bathroom

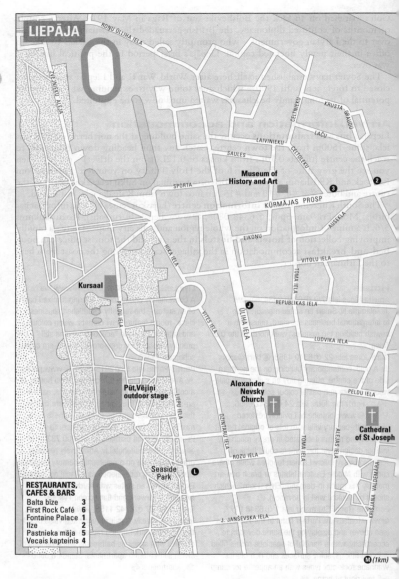

LIEPĀJA

RONU ULIHA IELA

ZVEJNIEKU ALEJA

KRUSTA

GRAUDU

CETNIEKU

LAIVINIEKU

CEĻTVEKU

LAČU

SAULES

Museum of History and Art ❸ ❷

SPORTA

KŪRMĀJAS PROSP

AUSEKLA

EIKONU

HIKA IELA

VITOLU IELA

TOMA IELA

Kursaal

PELDU IELA

VITES IELA

ULIHA IELA

REPUBLIKAS IELA ❶

LUDVIKA IELA

Pūt,Vējiņi outdoor stage

LIEPU IELA

DZINTARU IELA

Alexander Nevsky Church ✝

PELDU IELA

TOMA IELA

ALEJAS IELA

Cathedral of St Joseph ✝

ROZU IELA

Seaside Park ❶

KRIŠJĀNA VALDEMĀRA

J. JANŠEVSKA IELA

Ⓜ (1km) ▶

RESTAURANTS, CAFÉS & BARS

Balta bīze	3
First Rock Café	6
Fontaine Palace	1
Ilze	2
Pastnieka māja	5
Vecais kapteinis	4

and a handful of bright en-suite rooms with TV. Breakfast isn't included in the price but there is a ground-floor café. Bus #10 or #11 from Lielā iela to the Siļķu iela stop. Standard doubles ❶, en-suite doubles ❸, triples from 18Ls, quads from 24Ls **K@2 Hostel** Katedrāles iela 2, Karosta ☏2627 0850, ⓦwww.karosta.lv/hostel. Informal

hostel run by the K@2 cultural organization located in a former Tsarist naval building in the highly individual Karosta suburb (see p.251) a fifteen-minute bus ride from the centre. Accommodation consists of bunk-beds in a warren of high-ceilinged rooms, many of which are stuffed with eccentric bits of sculpture left behind by

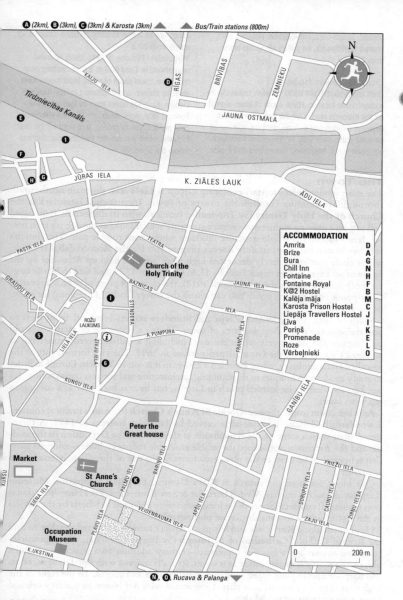

A (2km), **B** (3km), **C** (3km) & Karosta (3km) ▲ ▲ Bus/Train stations (800m)

KAIJU IELA

RĪGAS

BRĪVĪBAS

ZEMNIEKU

D

Tirdzniecības Kanāls

JAUNĀ OSTMALA

E

0

F

H **G**

JŪRAS IELA

K. ZIĀLES LAUK

ĀDU IELA

PASTA IELA

TEATRA

Church of the
Holy Trinity

BAZNICAS

JAUNĀ IELA

GRAUDU IELA

STENDERA

IELA

FRANČU IELA

ROŽU
LAUKUMS

i

LIELĀ IELA

ZIVJU IELA

A PUMPURA

5

6

KUNGU IELA

GANĪBU IELA

Peter the
Great house

PRIEŽU IELA

BARIŅU IELA

Market

St Anne's
Church

K

DĀRUPES IELA

CĀUNU IELA

ZIRNU IELSA

KURSU

SIENA IELA

PLAVU IELA

VEIDENBAUMA IELA

APŠU IELA

ZAJU IELA

**Occupation
Museum**

K.UKSTINA

0   200 m

N, **O**, Rucava & Palanga ▼

ACCOMMODATION

Amrita	**D**
Brīze	**A**
Bura	**G**
Chill Inn	**N**
Fontaine	**H**
Fontaine Royal	**F**
K@2 Hostel	**B**
Kalēja māja	**M**
Karosta Prison Hostel	**C**
Liepāja Travellers Hostel	**J**
Līva	**I**
Poriņš	**K**
Promenade	**E**
Roze	**L**
Vērbeļnieki	**O**

visiting artists. Bus #7 or #8 from Lielā iela. Open
May–Sept. Beds from 7Ls.
Karosta Prison Hostel Invalidu iela 4 ☎ 2636
9470, ⊛ www.karostascietums.lv. Bus #7 or #8
from Lielā iela. Another unusual Karosta hostel,
occupying the former cells of a naval prison. The
mattresses are comfortable but the surroundings

are somewhat bare – which should suit travellers
of an ascetic disposition. Open May–Sept. Beds
from 8Ls.
Liepāja Travellers Hostel Republikas iela 25
☎ 2869 0106, ⊛ liepajahostel.lv. Run by the
same team as *Argonaut* in Rīga, this is a relaxing
and comfortable backpacker-oriented place in a

central, beach-adjacent location. Doubles with shared facilities ②, en suites ③, dorm beds from 7Ls.

Out-of-town hotels

Chill Inn Arāji ☏ 6346 0896, ⓦ www.chillinn.lv. In a countryside location 10km south of town, signed off the Klaipēda road, *Chill Inn* looks like a cross between a ranch and a motel, with a single line of en-suite units, each with TV, fridge and hammock-equipped porch. Meadows, forests and shore-side dunes are all within strolling distance. Doubles ③, quads from 30Ls

Vērbeļnieki Pērkone ☏ 2913 8565, ⓦ www .verbelnieki.lv. Cosy B&B in a rustic setting near the shore 15km south of town. Most rooms have en-suite shower and fireplace. Liepāja–Nica and Liepāja–Klaipēda buses pass by (get off at the Pērkone stop, walk down into Pērkone village and bear right). If you're driving, turn right off the main highway when you see the Pērkone bus stop and follow the signs. ②

The Town

The most obvious place to start exploring Liepāja is **Lielā iela**, the main north–south thoroughfare running through the centre of town. Its principal landmark is the **Church of the Holy Trinity** (Sv Trīsvienības baznīca), with its distinctive, four-tiered bell tower, a greying eighteenth-century structure which looks as though it's seen better days – indeed the whole structure shudders when trams rumble past. The church's weather-beaten exterior certainly doesn't prepare you for the Rococo delights inside, where there's an exuberantly decorated high altar, a pulpit held up Atlas-like by the figure of an angel and an organ built by H.A. Contius in 1779 (and said to be the largest mechanical organ in the world until 1912), the clustered pipes of which appear to be dripping with molten gold. You can climb the **tower** (daily 11am–5pm) for views of the town.

South of here, the pedestrian **Zivju** and **Stendera streets** break off from Lielā to pass through the main shopping area of town. There's a scattering of picturesque old buildings in the side streets off to the east, including a half-timbered former inn at Kungu 24 where Peter the Great allegedly stayed in 1697. The visit formed part of the so-called Great Embassy, when Peter led a 250-man mission to Western Europe in order to study modern techniques in shipbuilding, architecture and fortress construction. It's not known whether he learned much in Liepāja, but he was back here as a conqueror ten years later.

Another 200m south, the neo-Gothic **St Anne's Church** (Sv Annas baznīca) contains a wonderfully delicate Baroque altar carved by Nicholas Soffrens in 1697. A three-tiered affair with a scene of the Crucifixion at the bottom, the Deposition in the middle and the Ascension at the top, the whole ensemble radiates a honey-coloured glow that is in marked contrast to the plain grey tones of the rest of the – largely unadorned – interior.

One block south of the church at Kļava Ukstiņa, **Liepāja Occupation Museum** (Liepājas okupacijas muzejs; Wed, Thurs, Sat & Sun 10am–6pm, Fri 11am–7pm; donation requested) commemorates those locals who were deported to Siberia by the Soviets in the 1940s, with a moving display of photographs.

Head north along Kuršu iela and left past Liepāja's animated covered **market** to find the Roman Catholic **Cathedral of St Joseph** (Sv Jāzepa katedrāle), whose pinnacle-encrusted towers are a fanciful nineteenth-century addition to a structure of much older vintage. It's as ornate inside as it is out, its walls covered with floral designs, saints and harp-strumming angels, all rendered in bright reds and greens. To the right of the high altar there's a stunning side chapel, decorated with Art Nouveau stucco work and hung with an intricate model ship.

From here Peldu iela heads west towards the beach, passing through a residential zone of timber villas where nineteenth-century industrialists spent their summers – some have been lovingly restored, others are slowly crumbling into the ground. At the junction with Ūliha iela you'll catch sight of the brittle spire of the Russian **Orthodox Church of St Alexander Nevsky** on your right; it's rarely open, but the turquoise exterior is pure eye-candy. Continuing west along Peldu and turning right into Hika iela brings you face to face with some of the best preserved of Liepāja's *belle époque* villas, their filigree wooden window frames giving them the appearance of festive doily-trimmed cakes. Down an alley from a swan-stocked pond lies Liepāja's derelict **Kursaal** (Kūrmāja), a colonnaded, Neoclassical facade hinting at its former grandeur. Extending south of the Kursaal is the **Seaside Park** (Jūrmalas parks), a well-tended area of lawns and leafy promenades separated by a line of dunes from the beach itself – as pristine a stretch of sand as you're likely to find on Latvia's west coast and a good spot for amber-hunting after storms.

Returning towards the town centre via the lime-tree-shaded Kūrmājas prospekts will take you past the **Museum of History and Art** at no. 9 (Vestures un mākslas muzejs; Wed, Thurs, Sat & Sun 10am–6pm, Fri 11am–7pm; ⊛www.liepajasmuzejs.lv; 0.50Ls), a didactically arranged assemblage of local artefacts occupying a villa built in 1901 for the Katzenelson family. The inlaid wooden floors and stuccoed ceilings of the interior provide an attractive setting for models of the Neolithic villages and fortresses that were once scattered along this stretch of coast, and a rather magnificent display of the eighteenth-century pewter tankards that were made for the town's guilds – encrusted with heraldic emblems and topped with statuettes of mermaids, they look like trophies awarded for some long-forgotten exotic sport. A words-and-pictures romp through Liepāja's history includes family snapshots of generations of Liepājans at work and play, and chilling photographs of Latvians shot dead by Stalin's NKVD in 1941. There's also a colourful display of traditional Kurzeme costumes and a gallery that hosts seasonal exhibitions by some of Latvia's best contemporary artists.

Karosta

Some 4km north of the Old Town lies **Karosta** (a contraction of "kara osta", which means simply "naval port"), a military suburb developed by Tsarist Russia in the late nineteenth century in order to guard against the growing threat of German sea power. Paradoxically, Karosta's expensively fortified port facilities and gun batteries were never put to the test – on the outbreak of war in 1914 the Russians withdrew their Baltic fleet to Tallinn and Helsinki and sank blockships in Karosta harbour in order to dissuade the Germans from bothering to capture it. Subsequently adopted by the Soviets as a submarine base, Karosta grew into a self-contained, Russian-speaking city inhabited by naval ratings, ancillary workers and their families. Many of the civilians are still here, left stranded by the pull-out of the military machine they served.

Today Karosta is a curious place, with stately, semi-abandoned boulevards bisecting a landscape of imposing Tsarist-era buildings (the best of which have been bagged by the Latvian armed forces), skeletal remains of ruined barracks and depressing lines of run-down housing blocks.

The best way to **get there** is to take bus #7 or #8 from Lielā iela to Baloža iela in the heart of Karosta. From here you can't miss the yellow domes of Karosta's finest Tsarist-era heirloom, the **Orthodox Cathedral of St Nicholas** (Sv Nikolaja pareizticīgo katedrāle). With a facade of ochre-coloured bricks speckled with turquoise, blue and green tiles, it looks as though it might be a shiny toy made for giants. The main object of veneration in the sparsely furnished interior is an icon depicting a placid Madonna and Child flanked by angelic beings bearing gifts. West of here on Atmodas bulvaris, the red-brick building at no. 6 holds the **K-Maksla Gallery** (daily 2–7pm; ⊛www.karosta.lv; free), home to a regular programme of contemporary art exhibitions organized by the K@2 organization – formed to breathe new life into the culture of Karosta.

About 1km east at Invalīdu 4 lies the forbidding red-brick **Karosta Prison** (Karostas cietums; May–Sept daily 10am–6pm; Oct–April on request: call ☎2636 9470; 2Ls), a punishment block for unruly sailors used successively by Tsarist, inter-war Latvian, then Soviet navies. Visitors are given an atmospheric tour of the grim-looking cells, as well as the red-flag-draped offices once occupied by Soviet administrators. One prison experience you'll have to book in advance is the increasingly popular interactive show **"Behind Bars"** (Aiz restem; ☎2636 9470, ⊛www.karostascietums.lv; 2Ls), which involves actors dressed up as Soviet prison guards herding groups of visitors into the

△ Cathedral of St Nicholas

cells at gunpoint, bellowing orders and initiating rounds of repeat-after-me Leninist sloganeering. The show is normally conducted in Latvian or Russian, but if you book well in advance someone will be on hand to translate for you. Special night performances (5Ls) involve bedding down for a night in the cells.

At the northern end of Karosta, lanes lead west to the seashore, where the **Northern Pier** (Ziemeļu mols) extends into the Baltic, providing amateur fishermen with a 1.5km-long perch. Beyond the pier, paths lead north along a sandy shore overlooked by gun emplacements built by the Russians between 1894 and 1908. Long abandoned, they're now collapsing slowly into the Baltic Sea.

Eating and drinking

Liepāja can boast a decent variety of places to eat and drink, mostly concentrated on or around Lielā iela and Graudu iela. Additionally, in summer, a handful of relaxing outdoor cafés open up in the Seaside Park, near the western end of Peldu iela.

Balta bize Kūrmājas prospects 8/10. Bright, self-service café in the daytime, restaurant with table service in the evening. The menu is dominated by meaty Latvian staples, although there's plenty in the salad and fried-fish line too. Daily 9am–midnight.

First Rock Café Stendera 18/20. The social hub around which much of Liepāja's day- and nightlife revolve, with an enjoyable pub-restaurant at ground level, decorated with memorabilia donated by local rock performers. There's a café with roof terrace upstairs and a basement nightclub by the name of *Pablo* (ⓦ www.pablo.lv), which regularly features live bands. Daily 9am–4am.

Fontaine Palace Dzirnavu 4. The restaurant section of this converted canal-side warehouse serves up fantastic and none-too-expensive grill-steaks and kebabs, while the roomy, ground-floor bar hosts regular DJ nights and concerts by alternative rock bands. There's a 24-hour burger bar outside should you still be hungry in the small hours.

Ilze Graudu 23. Solid if unadventurous choice of inexpensive Latvian pork and fish dishes, in an atmospherically arched red-brick cellar, decorated with vintage adverts and old sewing machines. Sun–Wed 11am–11pm, Thurs–Sat 11am–2am.

Pastnieka māja Brīvzemnieka 53 Ⓣ 6340 7521. A reconditioned red-brick and timber building harbouring a snazzy pub-restaurant with a large outdoor terrace. Alongside good-quality pork and fish there are always several vegetarian main courses on the menu, and the extravagant puddings are worth leaving room for. Daily noon–midnight.

Vecais Kapteinis Dubelšteina iela 14. Tastefully restored timber house with a mouth-watering menu of steak, duck, trout and salmon dishes, as well as the usual pork-based staples. It's atmospheric too, with wooden beams, an open fireplace and a metre-long model ship hanging from the ceiling. More expensive than other places in town but still reasonable. Daily 11am–11pm.

Entertainment

Liepāja is the only Latvian city outside Rīga to have a **symphony orchestra** – it performs regularly at the Filharmonija, Graudu iela 50 (Ⓣ 6342 5538, ⓦ http://lso.apollo .lv). You can also hear music – mostly musicals and rock opera – at Liepāja's **theatre**, Teātra 4 (Ⓣ 342 0145, ⓦ www.liepajasteatris.lv). Balle, Rozu laukums 5/6 (Ⓣ 6348 0638), is a comfortable, modern and central **cinema** showing mainstream films. In summer, all kinds of concerts take place at the Pūt vējiņi outdoor stage in the Seaside Park – most importantly it's the venue for Liepājas Dzintars (early to mid-August), which, although unlikely to set the pulse racing, is traditionally Latvia's biggest **rock festival**.

Lake Pape

Beyond Liepāja, a sandy sliver of beach backed by forest and coastal heath continues all the way to the Lithuanian border, some 60km to the south. There are any number of picturesque spots where you could stop off along the way, although it's the World Wildlife Fund-sponsored nature reserve at **Lake Pape** (ⓦ www.wwf.lv), just short of the border, that shows this part of the coast at its unspoilt, desolate best. Cut off from the sea by a bar of sand, the lake is surrounded by reeds, wetland forest and grassy meadow, grazed by a herd of wild horses, the only such herd in the country and one of the reserve's main attractions. The area also offers some rewarding walks; the best start from the lake's main settlement, **Pape village**, and wend along the seashore.

Lake Pape is best explored with your own transport, though getting to the lake by bus is just about possible. The main entry point to the region is the village of **Rucava**, on the main Liepāja–Klaipēda highway, 7km east of Lake Pape. International **buses** operating the Rīga–Liepāja–Klaipēda–Kaliningrad route all stop in Rucava, but beware that the timetable information displayed at Rucava's tiny bus station is only approximate – allow thirty minutes either side when moving on. From Rucava you could just about walk to the lake's main sights in the space of a day, though it's a hard slog.

The lake's eastern shore

Since 1999, the eastern shore of Lake Pape has been the centre of a project to reintroduce **wild horses** to Latvia. Wild horses died out in the area in the eighteenth century and the aim of the project is to re-create the kind of naturally grazed landscape that would have existed all over the Baltic States before the Middle Ages. Eighteen stocky, grey *konnik polski* (a type of horse with wild traits selectively bred in Poland in the 1930s) were imported initially and there are now over fifty horses living in five or six so-called "harems" or social units – with new groups being formed every time older males drive younger ones away to form harems of their own.

The best way to reach them if you're coming by car is from **Kalnišķi** on the main southbound highway. Take the signed dirt road that branches off from Kalnišķi, and after ploughing through forest for about 5km the road arrives at a ticket barrier (May–Sept daily 9am–5pm; 0.50Ls), where a warden will either guide you through the lakeside meadows, or simply give you advice on where you can walk and leave you to get on with it. Although they're far from tame, the horses are relatively unfazed by humans and are unlikely to scamper off on your arrival – they're certainly a delight to watch. The rush-shrouded shores of the lake itself lie about 1km west of the ticket barrier and are favoured by all kinds of **migrating birds** in spring. The arrival of the horses has helped to increase the numbers of visiting greylag geese, who favour the short-grass habitat created by grazing animals.

Pape village

Located on the low sandy ridge that separates the lake from the sea, the wind-battered village of **PAPE** was a thriving fishing port until the communist period (when the Soviet military sank ships in the narrow coastal waters and used the wrecks for target practice), and is now a sleepy, dune-enclosed settlement, with a largely Lithuanian-speaking population. You can walk from the horse reserve to Pape in about two hours by following paths running southwestwards beside the irrigation dykes. If you're driving, you'll have to return to the main road and head south to Rucava and the Pape turn-off. Just before arriving at the village from the Rucava direction, you'll pass a wooden observation tower offering panoramic views of the lake's reedy south shore – although don't be surprised if the bulk of Pape's birdlife is away at the quieter, northern end of the lake.

Pape itself is the starting point for wonderful seashore walks in either direction, particularly to the south, where the signed **Path of Natural Processes** (Dabas procesu taka) takes you through landscape of meadow, forest and dunes before returning to Pape along the beach – a circuit of 9km in all. About 1.5km into the trail (and just about accessible by car), a delightful **Vītolnieki Fishermen's Homestead Museum** ("Vītolnieki" zvejnieku sēta; May–Oct daily except Mon & Thurs; 0.30Ls) occupies the private house of a woman who has kept everything pretty much as it was in her grandfather's time. It somehow makes a difference to know that the simple wooden furnishings, cast-iron kitchenware and trunk-sized bedstead are still in use. There's more of a museum-style display in the outbuildings, with a collection of traps and baskets in the net-mending shed and a thousand-year-old, carved tree-trunk canoe in the granary.

Practicalities

The **tourist offices** in both Liepāja (see p.246) and the Rucava public library (Mon–Fri 9am–5pm; ℡6349 4766) can book you into local **B&Bs** (●). You can also stay in the WWF Nature House in Pape (Dabas māja; ☎ 2947 5734; ❶), at the entrance to the village; it offers a handful of plain rooms and a kitchen, and you can pitch a tent in the grounds.

There are a couple of **food and drink** shops on Rucava's main square and a rudimentary daytime café in the nearby town hall. If you're planning on doing a lot of walking in the area, consider buying **map** no. 3113 in the 1:50,000 Latvias satelitkarte series, available from the Jāņa Sēta shop in Rīga (see p.219).

Travel details

Trains

Jelgava to: Rīga (hourly; 50min).
Rīga to: Jelgava (hourly; 50min); Ķemeri (every 40–50min; 1hr 5min); Tukums (every 40–50min; 1hr 25min).

Buses

Bauska to: Jelgava (6 daily; 1hr 20min); Mežotne (Mon–Fri 6 daily, Sat & Sun 4 daily; 25min); Rundāles pils (Mon–Fri 12 daily, Sat 10 daily, Sun 5 daily; 25min).
Jelgava to: Bauska (6 daily; 1hr 20min); Rīga (every 20min; 50min); Tērvete (6 daily; 30min).
Kuldīga to: Liepāja (Mon–Sat 5 daily, Sun 3 daily; 1hr 20min); Rīga (5 daily; 2hr 30min–3hr 30min); Sabile (Mon–Sat 11 daily, Sun 7 daily; 1hr); Ventspils (Mon–Sat 5 daily, Sun 3 daily; 1hr 20min).
Liepāja to: Pavilosta (1 daily; 1hr); Rīga (14 daily; 3hr 30min–4hr); Rucava (5 daily; 40–50min); Sabile (4 daily; 3hr); Ventspils (Mon–Sat 6 daily, Sun 4 daily; 3hr).
Rīga to: Bauska (every 30min; 1hr 10min–1hr 30min); Jelgava (every 30min; 50min); Kolka (3 daily; 3hr 15min–4hr 30min); Kuldīga (5 daily;

2hr 30min–3hr 30min); Liepāja (14 daily; 3hr 30min–4hr); Mazirbe (2 daily; 4hr); Rucava (4 daily; 4hr 30min); Sabile (Mon–Sat 13 daily, Sun 6 daily; 2hr); Talsi (12 daily; 2hr 30min); Tukums (12 daily; 1hr 40min); Ventspils (14 daily; 3–4hr).
Sabile to: Kuldīga (Mon–Sat 11 daily, Sun 7 daily; 1hr); Liepāja (4 daily; 3hr); Talsi (Mon–Sat 9 daily, Sun 5 daily; 40min); Rīga (Mon–Sat 13 daily, Sun 6 daily; 2hr).
Talsi to: Kolka (3 daily; 1hr 15min); Rīga (12 daily; 2hr 30min); Roja (Mon–Sat 7 daily, Sun 5 daily; 1hr); Sabile (Mon–Sat 9 daily, Sun 5 daily; 40min); Ventspils (Mon–Sat 6 daily, Sun 4 daily; 1hr 40min).
Ventspils to: Kuldīga (Mon–Sat 4 daily, Sun 2 daily; 1hr 20min); Liepāja (Mon–Sat 6 daily, Sun 4 daily; 3hr); Rīga (14 daily; 3–4hr); Talsi (Mon–Sat 6 daily, Sun 4 daily; 1hr 40min).

International buses

Bauska to: Panevēžys (2 daily; 2hr 30min).
Jelgava to: Šiauliai (4 daily; 2hr 30min).
Liepāja to: Kaliningrad (1 daily; 8hr); Klaipēda (4 daily; 3hr 30min); Moscow (2 daily; 18hr); Palanga (4 daily; 3hr).

2.3

Eastern Latvia

astern Latvia is made up of two distinct regions with very different histories. **Vidzeme** (literally "the land in the middle"), was conquered by the Knights of the Sword – and then taken over by their successor organization, the Livonian Order – in the thirteenth century, and is dotted with the crumbling relics of their hilltop castles. The Livonian Order had much more difficulty imposing its authority on **Latgale**, the region to the southeast, a disputed borderland prone to frequent incursions from the Russians to the east and Poles and Lithuanians to the west. When the Livonian Order collapsed in the mid-sixteenth century, Vidzeme went to the Protestant Swedes, while Latgale was taken over by the solidly Catholic Polish-Lithuanian Commonwealth – and although the foreign overlords have long since departed, the spiritual divide remains to this day. Political and religious borders also aided the survival of Latgale's archaic dialect, which – unlike the speech

of Vidzeme, more or less indistinguishable from mainstream Latvian – is even now almost unintelligible to fellow Latvians.

The dominant geographical features of eastern Latvia are its two main river valleys: the gloriously unspoilt **Gauja**, northeast of Rīga, and the broad **Daugava**, to the southeast, the main transport corridor to Latgale and beyond. The combination of cliff-lined riverscapes and forest-clad hills make the **Gauja National Park** the one must-see natural attraction in the country, with the relaxing resort of **Sigulda** and the historic market town of **Cēsis** providing the ideal entry points. The settlements along the Daugava are as a rule much more industrialized, although there's a wealth of historical attractions along its banks – the ancient Latvian stockade fort of **Lielvārde** and the handsome provincial town of **Jēkabpils** being stand-out sights. The last big settlement on the Latvian stretch of the Daugava before the Belorussian border, the brooding industrial city of **Daugavpils** is very much an acquired taste, and a totally misleading introduction to the surrounding province of **Latgale** – a rustic paradise of forests and lakes which counts the Catholic pilgrimage centre of **Aglona** and the tranquil country town of **Ludza** among its highlights.

The Gauja Valley

Rising in an area of rolling uplands 90km due east of Rīga, the River Gauja winds its way through most of northeastern Latvia before emptying into the Baltic Sea a short distance north of the capital. The most exciting stretch of the valley is between the towns of Sigulda and Cēsis, where the river carves its way through hills of Devonian sandstone, leaving ruddy cliffs and steep, forest-covered banks in its wake. Even though

---

Canoeing down the Gauja Valley

To experience the Gauja landscape at its best, you really have to see it from the river itself. The favoured craft is a canoe and in fact, **canoeing down the Gauja** has become one of Latvia's most popular outdoor holiday activities. True aficionados start at Strenči, northeast of Valmiera, and spend four to five days paddling their way downstream to Sigulda – a total distance of 95km. However, it's the 35-kilometre stretch between Cēsis and Sigulda that is the most scenic and correspondingly the busiest, especially on summer weekends. Most people do the Cēsis–Sigulda trip in two to three days, overnighting at designated national park campsites spaced at convenient intervals along the way. The easiest way to start is simply to rent a canoe (and a tent if you don't have one) and set off, or if you prefer, you can opt for a guided canoe trip organized by one of the adventure tourism agencies listed below. The season lasts from early June to the end of August.

A number of agencies that rent out gear and organize trips are listed below; the tourist offices in Sigulda and Cēsis can advise on others. It's best to organize canoe rental and trips a few days in advance if possible – things get booked up quickly at summer weekends. Expect to pay 15Ls a day for canoe rental, 20Ls per person per day for a guided canoe tour.

Canoe rental contacts

Campo Kroņu iela 25D, Rīga ☏6750 5322, ⓦwww.laivas.lv, ⓦwww.campo.lv. Canoe rental, advice and guided canoe trips on the Gauja. They can also organize the transport of your canoe to and from the Gauja – at a cost of 0.25Ls per kilometre.

Cēsu Tūrisma Inventāra Noma Jaunstilbi, Cēsis ☏2942 3270. Canoe (3–10Ls/day) and tent rental (1–2.50Ls/day).

Eži Raiņa iela 26/28, Cēsis ☏6410 7022, ⓦwww.ezi.lv. Canoe rental and guided one-to three-day tours.

Makars Peldu 2, Sigulda ☏2924 4948, ⓦwww.makars.lv. Canoes (15–20Ls/day), rowing boats (1Ls/hr) and tents (1.50Ls/day) for rent. Guided one- to seven-day tours.

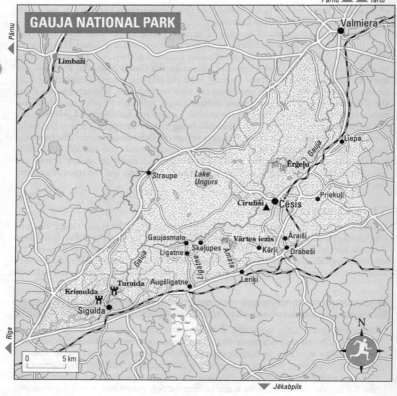

the highest peaks in the region barely scrape altitudes of 100m above sea level, it's a spectacularly lumpy region by local standards – so much so that the Baltic Germans were moved to call it the "Livonian Switzerland".

Much of the Sigulda–Cēsis stretch falls within the boundaries of the **Gauja National Park** (Gaujas nacionālais parks; ⓦwww.gnp.gov.lv), founded in 1973 to protect the region's diverse flora and fauna and establish a well-maintained network of walking routes. Given the park's proximity to Rīga, it's relatively easy to access, with regular trains and buses heading for **Sigulda** and the next major town upriver, **Cēsis**, either of which serves as a handy and attractive base for further exploration. Midway between the two, the **Ligatne Nature Trail** offers the opportunity to examine the park's flora and fauna at close quarters, while the reconstructed lake-village at **Āraiši**, just south of Cēsis, provides a fascinating insight into the lives of the Latvians' ancient forebears.

Throughout the park you'll find a multitude of **forest and riverbank trails** suitable for exploration on foot or by bike, while **canoeing** down the Gauja itself is a particularly invigorating way of enjoying the scenery. Although the pistes at Sigulda and Cēsis are puny by alpine standards, the potential of the area as a low-level, laid-back **skiing** centre shouldn't be overlooked – given the rigours of the Baltic winter, at least snow cover is guaranteed. Jāņa sēta's 1:100 000 *Gaujas nacionālais parks* **map**, on sale in local tourist offices, covers the whole region, and comes with smaller-scale inset maps of Ligatne, Āraiši and other key localities.

△ Ērgeļu Cliff, Gauja National Park

Sigulda and around

Sprawled across a plateau on the south bank of the River Gauja, **SIGULDA** is not so much a town as a vast leafy park with a few houses and apartment blocks tastefully scattered across it. Close to some of the most beautiful stretches of the Gauja Valley, it has been Latvia's most popular inland resort ever since the mid-nineteenth century, when the construction of the Rīga–Valka railway line put it within reach of vacationing St Petersburg folk. It's a great base for short- and mid-range walking, with a variety of woodland and riverbank trails within easy striking distance of the town centre. It's also the obvious starting point for visits to the reconstructed castle at **Turaida** and the nineteenth-century aristocratic seat of **Krimulda**, both of which adorn hilltops on the opposite side of the valley. In the colder months, **winter-sports** enthusiasts flock here to experience the thrills of the country's only Olympic-standard bobsleigh track and its downhill ski runs.

Arrival and information

Sigulda is an easy day-trip from Rīga, with **buses** and **trains** running almost hourly. If you're approaching from the east, catch a Cēsis–Rīga bus – these don't actually pass through Sigulda's town centre, but pick up and drop off on the main highway 1km south.

Sigulda's centrally located **tourist office**, Valdemāra iela 1A (May–Oct daily 10am–7pm, Nov–April Mon–Fri 10am–5pm; ☏6797 1335, ⊛www.sigulda.lv) is a good source of advice on local sights, accommodation and activities, while the **Gauja National Park Visitors' Centre**, Baznīcas 3 (daily: April–Oct 9.30am–6pm, Nov–March 10am–4pm; ☏6780 0388, ⊛www.gnp.gov.lv), has information about hiking trails and sells a wide range of maps.

You can rent **bikes** from Buru sports, 1km south of the centre at the junction of Gāles iela and the main Rīga–Cēsis highway (☏6797 2051, ⊛www.burusports.lv) and Tridens, Cēsu 15 (☏2964 4800). For **canoe** and rowing boat rentals see the box on p.257.

One other good way to experience the riverside landscape is to sign up for a **rafting trip** (8–12Ls per person) organized by Makars at the *Siguldas pludmale* campsite (see below). Gently drifting affairs rather than high-adrenalin white-water thrills, these usually involve one- or two-hour trips in scenic stretches of the valley upstream from Sigulda.

Accommodation

There is a small but good-quality selection of hotels in and around town. The tourist office (see above) can book you into **bed-and-breakfast** accommodation in private houses from 8Ls per person.

Campers are well catered for by the *Siguldas pludmale* **campsite**, Peldu 1 (☏2924 4948, ⊛www.makars.lv), which occupies an attractive, tree-shaded stretch of riverbank and is equipped with toilet blocks but no other facilities.

Aparjods Ventas 1B ☎ 6797 2230, ⓦwww
.aparjods.lv. Hotel, restaurant and nightclub
complex at the southwestern end of town right
beside the Rīga–Cēsis highway. Built in folksy style
(complete with shingle roof), but the rooms inside
are modern, with shower and TV. ④

Līvkalns Pēteralas 3 ☎ 6797 0916,
ⓦwww.livkalns.lv. Traditional-style, reed-
thatched house with a lovely lakeside garden,
offering eight pine-furnished en suites with
soothingly-coloured fabrics. Within easy striking

distance of Satzele Castle Mound and numerous
forest trails. ③

Melnais kaķis Pils iela 8 ☎ 6787 0272 and 2915
0104, ⓦwww.cathouse.lv. Medium-sized hotel on
the main street offering en-suite rooms decorated
in warm colours with contemporary furnishings. ④

Sigulda Pils iela 6 ☎ 6797 2263, ⓦwww
.hotelsigulda.lv. Centrally located, nineteenth
-century building with modern add-ons, including a
tiny indoor pool. The en-suite rooms are smart but
not particularly spacious. ④

The Town

From the train station, **Raiņa iela** runs north through the centre of town, passing the
bus station before forging through a swathe of parkland shaded by limes, oaks and
maples. After about 800m, a right turn into **Baznīcas iela** takes you past the bril-
liant-white spire of the **Lutheran church** (Luterānu baznīca) and on to **Sigulda New
Castle** (Siguldas Jaunā Pils), a nineteenth-century manor house with medieval preten-
sions, sporting an ostentatiously crenellated turret and now used as offices by the town
council. Out in front, regimented flowerbeds lie in the shade of a monument to Atis
Kronvalds (1837–75), a prominent nineteenth-century publicist who energetically
promoted Latvian-language education at a time when knowledge of German was seen
as the only passport to a successful career.

Immediately north of the New Castle, a path leads across a long-dried-up moat
to the ruins of **Sigulda Castle** (Siguldas Pilsdrupas), a thirteenth-century Livonian
Order stronghold built from rough-hewn blocks of honey-coloured stone. Behind
it lies an outdoor stage which is put to good use during the summer opera festival,
and beyond that is a knobbly hillock which affords sweeping views of the Gauja
Valley, with the fat red tower of Turaida Castle (see below) spearing up out of the
forest to the north.

More fine views across the valley can be savoured by following footpaths east from
the castle ruins to Miera iela, through the enchantingly shrubby town cemetery, then
northeast along the ridge known as **Artist's Hill** (Gleznotāju kalns). The viewpoint
at the end of the ridge offers an expansive panorama of Turaida, Krimulda and the
surrounding woodland – unsurprisingly, it was a favourite spot with early-twentieth-
century landscape painters Jānis Rozentāls and Vilhelms Purvītis. Southeast of here,
paths descend steeply to meet the Vējupite stream, which flows into the Gauja a few
hundred metres to the north. Sticking to the high ground and heading south will
bring you to the **Satezele Castle Mound** (Satezeles pilskalns), a Liv stronghold associated with semi-legendary chieftain Dabrelis, who fought unsuccessfully to stem the
Teutonic advance in the early thirteenth century.

Over on the western side of Sigulda, a five-minute walk from Raiņa iela along Cēsu
iela, the ferris-style **Panoramic Wheel** (Panorāmas rats; May–Oct daily 9am–5pm;
0.50Ls) provides another way of getting to grips with the Gauja landscape, affording
views across the valley to Krimulda and Turaida. South of the wheel, a steep, west-fac-
ing escarpment becomes a ski piste in winter and is the site of the town's state-of-the-
art **toboggan and bobsleigh track** (Kamaniņu un bobsleja trase). As well as hosting
World Cup luge and bobsleigh events in winter, the track is put to good use from May
to October when you can descend the course in a "summer bob" – a thick-tyred, futur-
istic-looking silver kart – for 3Ls per person.

From Sigulda to Turaida

From central Sigulda, Gaujas iela descends towards the bridge over the Gauja, and then
heads north along the northern bank of the river before climbing up to **Turaida Castle**,
some 3km distant. Sigulda–Krimulda buses pass along this route roughly every hour,

△ Turaida Castle

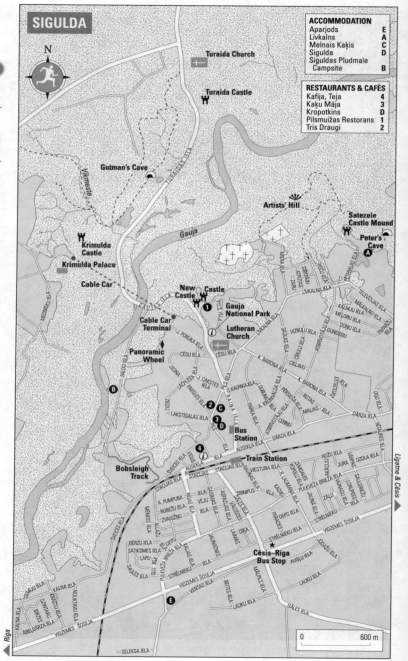

SIGULDA

N

ACCOMMODATION

Aparjods	E
Līvkalns	A
Melnais Kaķis	C
Sigulda	D
Siguldas Pludmale	
Campsite	B

RESTAURANTS & CAFÉS

Kafija, Teja	4
Kaķu Māja	3
Kropotkins	D
Pilsmuižas Restorans	1
Tris Draugi	2

Turaida Church

Turaida Castle

Gutman's Cave

Artists' Hill

Satezele Castle Mound

Peter's Cave
A

Krimulda Castle

Krimulda Palace

Gauja

Cable Car

New Castle

Castle
1

Gauja National Park

Cable Car Terminal

Lutheran Church

Panoramic Wheel

2
C

3
D

Bus Station

4

Train Station

Bobsleigh Track

Cēsis–Riga Bus Stop

E

0   600 m

Līgatne & Cēsis

Riga

but you're unlikely to take in much of the scenery through the window – walking at least part of the way seems a good idea.

Starting on the far side of the bridge from Sigulda, paths lead away from the main road and into the shadow of the densely forested escarpment that overlooks the valley from the northwest. Here, all kinds of alternative trails and interesting detours present themselves: you can head due west up to Krimulda (see below), or follow the path (built by American-Latvian youth in 1990, as the signboard proudly proclaims) that winds its way up the enchanting, wooded gully of the Vikmeste stream before emerging at the top of the ridge midway between Turaida and Krimulda. Alternatively, you can stick to the valley floor, following a level trail that runs past a sequence of small lakes and several sandstone caves. Despite its small, unexciting proportions, **Gūtman's Cave** (Gūtmaņa ala) is the most famous of these fissures, not least because of the key role it plays in the story of *Turaida Rose* – a heady tale of love, death and Latvian virtue. National poet Jānis Rainis based his play *Love is Stronger than Death* (Mīla stiprāka pār nāvi) on the story and most Latvian schoolchildren know the plot by heart. The rose in question was a seventeenth-century local maiden named Maija, who fell in love with the Turaida castle gardener Viktor, while at the same time being subject to the unwanted advances of Polish army deserter, Adam Jakubovsky (the suitor is a Swedish officer in some versions of the tale). When Jakubovsky trapped her in Gutman's Cave, she wound a scarf given to her by Viktor around her neck in the hope that it would shield her from evil. When the Pole struck out with his sword, however, the scarf unsurprisingly failed to provide the degree of protection expected. Maija's murder was initially pinned on Viktor, but he was released when a guilt-tormented Jakubovsky committed suicide.

Beyond the cave, the path rejoins the main road for the final 800-metre climb to the **Turaida Museum Reserve** (Turaidas muzejrezervāts; daily: May–Oct 10am–6pm; Nov–April 10am–5pm; ⑳www.turaida-muzejs.lv; 2Ls), which comprises a partially reconstructed castle and extensive grounds scattered with outbuildings. Built on the site of a Liv stockade fort, Turaida was one of the bishop of Rīga's key strongholds from 1214 onwards, surviving numerous wars until finally reduced to rubble when lightning hit its gunpowder magazine in the early eighteenth century. The castle was popular with tourists as a romantically crumbling ruin until the 1950s, when a heritage-conscious Latvian government decided to restore parts of the structure. With a handful of towers and halls now open to the public, the castle's museum spaces are short on actual exhibits but strong on atmosphere. Outside the castle, the eighteenth-century **Turaida Church** (Turaidas baznīca), an appealing shingle-roofed building with a Baroque tower, contains a small but alluring display of thirteenth-century Latvian jewellery. Just outside the church, a plaque honouring the Turaida Rose is one of the most popular venues in the country for the post-wedding photo shoot. From here, grassy parkland scattered with modern sculptures stretches east along the ridge-top overlooking the Gauja valley. South of the church, a restored nineteenth-century **manorial complex** (Muižas saimnieciskais centrs), comprising stables, fishpond, smithy and bath house (the latter filled with fragrant dried herbs) recalls life on the agricultural estates of yore.

Krimulda

Commanding superb views of the Gauja Valley 2.5km southwest of Turaida is the custard-coloured, Neoclassical **Krimulda Palace** (Krimuldas pils), seat of the Baltic German Lieven family in the nineteenth century and now a sanatorium. Though the palace is closed to visitors, the wooded ridge-top setting provides reason enough to visit. There's a neat park with flowerbeds on the western side of the building, while over to the east lie the fragmentary remains of **Krimulda Castle** (Krimuldas pilsdrupas), a thirteenth-century stronghold perched dramatically on a rocky bluff overlooking over the valley.

As well as being served by Sigulda–Krimulda buses, the sanatorium can also be reached by paths from the Gauja Valley (notably from the Vikmeste stream path. The most stylish way to arrive, though, is by **cable car** (Gaisa trosu ceļš; May–Sept weekends only 10am–6pm; 1.50Ls; ⑳www.lgk.lv), which sets off from the terminal on Poruka iela in Sigulda every hour.

Eating and drinking

The *Kropotkins* **restaurant** (closed Mon) inside the *Sigulda* hotel (see p.260) is an elegant but not over-posh place to enjoy a relaxing sit-down meal, with freshwater fish dishes enjoying pride of place on the menu. *Kafija Teja*, near the tourist office at Valdemara 3, is a comfortable coffee-and-cake stop and has a small but well-chosen menu of quality main courses too. For fans of faded charm, *Pilsmuizas Restorans* in the New Castle (see p.260) offers staid meat-and-potatoes fare in a slightly tatty, old-fashioned interior. For a quicker, on-your-feet meal, try *Tris Draugi*, Pils 9, a glass-fronted pavilion with a canteen-style food counter at one end and a bar open till 2am at the other. Just over the road at Pils 8, *Kaķu Māja* offers similar canteen fare in a slightly funkier interior.

Līgatne Nature Trail and around

Twelve kilometres northeast of Sigulda, the **Līgatne Nature Trail** (Līgatnes dabas takas) provides one of the best ways to sample the sheer variety of the Gauja Valley landscape. Located on the south bank of the river, the trail meanders through a changing landscape of dense pine woods, evergreen forest and meadow clearings, and also gives access to some cliff-lined stretches of the riverbank itself. Entrance to the trail is 2km west of the village of **Gaujasmala** and 3km northwest of the village of **Līgatne**, which in turn is 5.5km north of its sister settlement on the main Rīga–Cēsis highway – variously called Augšlīgatne ("Upper Līgatne"), Līgatnes stacija ("Līgatne Station") or simply "Līgatne", depending on which map you look at. It's this place that Rīga–Cēsis **trains and buses** serve: once here, you can either walk to Līgatne proper (1hr), or wait for one of the six daily buses (three at weekends) which start at the train station, then call at Augšligatne's main bus stop before continuing to Līgatne proper, terminating at Gaujasmala. If you're approaching from the Cēsis direction, you can take one of the three daily Cēsis–Līgatne–Gaujasmala buses (weekdays only).

Līgatne and Gaujasmala

LĪGATNE village is a pretty little place hugging the banks of the Līgatne stream, a tributary of the Gauja, here overlooked by a handsome set of the region's trademark red sandstone cliffs. Līgatne is also the site of one of Latvia's oldest paper mills, which explains the attractive complex of nineteenth-century industrial buildings just east of the village centre and the red-brick workers' houses that cluster around it. The village possesses a modest **café** and a couple of food shops for stocking up on picnic fare. From the main crossroads, Dārza iela winds west then north before coming to a T-junction after 2km: a left turn takes you to the Līgatne Nature Trail (see below), while a right turn leads directly into grubby **GAUJASMALA**, a village of Soviet-era apartment blocks, worth visiting on account of its **ferry** (pārceltuve; May–Sept: shuttle service 6am–11pm; 0.20Ls per person; 1Ls per vehicle). Basically a small open-topped raft, guided across the river by a fixed chain, it's one of the last such contraptions still in use in the Baltics. There's a free **campsite** next to the riverbank, supplied with a couple of rudimentary earth toilets.

Līgatne Nature Trail

Established in 1975, **Līgatne Nature Trail** (May–Sept Mon 9.30am–5pm, Tues–Sun 9.30am–6.30pm; 1Ls) is basically an open-plan zoo of indigenous fauna, including brown bears and bobcats, with several large enclosures scattered, safari-park-style, over a wide area. The animals spend the summer roaming their spacious quarters at Līgatne, returning to Rīga zoo for the winter. Getting from one enclosure to another involves passing through undulating terrain carpeted in sweet-smelling forest, and it's this that constitutes the trail's main appeal. There are two circular routes about 6km long – one for cars, one for pedestrians – both of which pass the principal enclosures; the information desk at the entrance will provide you with a map. Things are in any case well signposted along the trail and it's easy to find the most popular way-stations: a field full of aurochs (European bison) on the eastern side of the circuit, and a wooded hillside over to the west populated by brown bears – although extinct in Latvia by the late nineteenth century, the creatures began migrating back from Estonia in the 1970s. Elsewhere you'll see wild boar, roe deer, red deer and (if you're very lucky) lynx. A couple of subsidiary footpaths lead off the main trail and are well worth exploring: one track (the Gaujmalas taka, or "Gauja bank trail") heads west from the information kiosk towards the riverbank, where you can admire the **Gūdu iezis** sandstone outcrop on the opposite bank, while another (the Neskartās dabas taka, or "wild nature trail") branches off just south of the brown-bear enclosure and heads down **Paparžu grava**, a leafy gully whose name – "fern glen" – gives you some idea of what kind of undergrowth to expect.

Some 2km northwest of Līgatne on the way to the nature trail, the *Lāču Miga* **hotel** at Gaujas iela 22 (℡ 2913 3713, ⊛ www.lacumiga.lv; ❸), an attractive guesthouse built in rustic style, offers thirteen en suites, and also has a **café-restaurant**. There's a free riverside **campsite** at Katrīnas iezis, 500m north of the trail entrance.

The Rehabilitation Centre and the underground bunkers

Some 3km northeast of Līgatne village on the road to Zvārtes iezis (see below), the **Vidzeme Regional Rehabilitation Centre** (Rehabilitācijas centrs) at Skalupes once served as the holiday retreat of high-ranking members of the communist regime. It was also the cover for a top-secret complex of **underground bunkers** (*pazemes bunkuri*), to which Soviet Latvia's civilian and military leadership would be evacuated in the event of nuclear war. Entered via an anonymous-looking staircase in the Rehabilitation Centre's lobby, the bunker complex (guided tours only; English-language tours available if booked 24hrs in advance; reserve by calling ℡ 6413 1321; 20Ls per person; discounts for groups of ten and over) was begun in 1968 and consists of 89 rooms, 9m below ground level. Furnished with lino flooring and plywood furniture, the complex looks like a sinister underground high school. The tour takes in military command rooms hung with maps and flags, and equipped with some of the earliest computers produced in the Soviet Union (data was stored on cumbersome reel-to-reel tape). Visitors will also see a pumping system designed to keep the complex supplied with air for three months – how the Soviet top brass aimed to stay alive beyond this period remains unclear.

The Rehabilitation Centre itself (℡ 6413 1321 and 6413 1119, ⊛ www.rehcentrsligatne .lv; ❸) is now open to the public as a sanatorium and spa **hotel** offering massages, mineral-water baths and beauty treatments. With the sandy banks of the Gauja River only a five-minute walk through the forest, it's an undeniably restful spot.

The Amata Valley

Providing you have your own transport, it's easy to combine a trip to the Līgatne nature trail with a visit to the winding, steep-sided valley of the Amata River, a fast-flowing tributary which joins the Gauja 7km northeast of Gaujasmala. The most picturesque part of the valley is the rocky outcrop known as **Zvārtes iezis**, reached by following the Skalupes–Kārļi road out of Līgatne village, heading straight on for 10km, then taking a (signed) turn-off to the right that leads after another 2km to a car park and a national park information board. Overlooking the car park from the west bank of the river, Zvārtes iezis is on the edge of the Roču meža woodland reserve, an area of dense coniferous cover, most of which is closed to the public. However, you can gain a flavour of the landscape by following a footpath from the car park that crosses the Amata and works its way up onto the cliff-top before looping back down again. An equally attractive trail heads north from the car park and hugs the east bank of the river, which zigzags its way between a further stretch of forest-shrouded cliffs. Each of the trails takes under an hour to complete.

Cēsis and around

The well-preserved, laid-back market town of **CĒSIS**, on a hillside 35km northeast of Sigulda, is reckoned by many Latvians to come as close as you'll get to pre-war, small-town Latvia. The knot of narrow streets at its heart, characterized by sturdy stone houses and one-storey timber dwellings, was largely undamaged in World War II and spared any significant modernization in the years that followed. The town's other main draws are its moody **castle ruins**, fine **museum** and convenience as a touring base for the rest of the Gauja Valley; particularly close at hand are Līgatne, the Iron Age settlement at **Āraiši** and **Ērģeļu Cliff**. The Gauja riverbank 3km west of town is one of the main starting points for canoe trips heading downstream (see p.257), while the steep escarpment above it is the raison d'être of the popular downhill skiing resort of **Cīrulīši**.

Cēsis was one of the Livonian Order's key power centres, serving as the official seat of their grand master, as well as being an important trading post on the route to the Russian towns of Pskov and Novgorod. By World War I it had also garnered a reputation as a minor spa resort, encouraging the locals – no doubt carried away by the Gauja Valley's "Livonian Switzerland" tag – to dub it the "Davos of the Baltic", though rest cures are now largely a thing of the past.

Arrival and information

Both **buses** and trains use the **train station** building 500m east of the main square, Vienības laukums: bus timetables and ticket windows are on the left-hand side as you enter from the street; train timetables and tickets are on the other. The helpful **tourist office** lies five minutes west of the square at Pils laukums 1 (June–Sept Mon–Fri 9am–6pm, Sat & Sun 10am–5pm; Oct–May Mon–Fri 9am–5pm; ℡ 6412 1815, Ⓦ www.turisms.cesis.lv). You can rent **bikes** from Eži, Raiņa iela 26/28 (℡ 6410 7022, Ⓦ www.ezi.lv).

Accommodation

Cēsis has a decent range of **hotels**, with a handful of stylishly modern establishments in the centre of town and a scattering of cheap-and-simple options in the suburbs. The nearest **campsite** is *Zagarkalns* (℡ 6412 5225, Ⓦ www.zagarkalns.lv), pleasantly sited on the shores of Lake Ungurs (Ungura ezers), 15km northeast on the Limbaži road; as well as space for tents, there are four-person cabins for 20Ls.

Cīrulīši Kovārņu 22 ℡ 6412 5476, Ⓦ www
.atputa-cirulisi.lv. A Soviet-era hotel and
sanatorium near the ski slopes southwest of
town. It looks pretty grim from the outside, but
the rooms are all en-suite, clean and have new
furniture. ❷
Katrīna Maza Katrīnas iela 8 ℡ 6410 7700, Ⓦ www
.hotelkatrina.lv. A modern but cosy eight-room place
on a quiet street in the heart of historic Cēsis. Rooms
are smallish with shower and TV, each decorated in
a different colour. ❹
Kolonna Cēsis Vienības laukums 1 ℡ 6412 0122,
Ⓦ www.hotel.kolonna.com. A recently modernized
inter-war hotel right on the main square, offering
thick-carpeted en suites with bathtubs and high
standards of service. ❹

Mārtiņš Rīta 9 ℡ 6412 3678, Ⓦ www.cesis
.lv/martins. Bed-and-breakfast-style accommodation, twenty minutes' walk north of the centre,
featuring neat en suites with satellite TV, friendly
hosts and a decent buffet breakfast. ❷
Province Niniera iela 6 ℡ 6412 0849,
Ⓔ province@inbox.lv. This five-room hotel has a
conveniently central location and smart en suites
with soothing decor. ❸
Putniņkrogs Saules 23 ℡ 6412 0290. Located
in a housing estate fifteen minutes' walk east of
the centre, this hotel offers simple rooms with
battered furniture and weird scraps of carpet, with
WC/shower in the hallway – but it's basically clean
and secure. Breakfast isn't included, though there's
a café next door. ❶

The Town

Marking the eastern entrance to the town centre of Cēsis's is the broad square **Vienības laukums**, dominated by the quirky, impressive **Victory Monument**, an obelisk licked by concrete flames and topped by what looks like a golden ping-pong ball. Erected in the 1920s, demolished by the Soviets in the 1950s (presumably for political rather than aesthetic reasons) and reconstructed in the 1990s, it commemorates June 1919's **Battle of Cēsis**, an impressive display of pan-Baltic cooperation in which an Estonian army, backed up by Latvian volunteers, defeated the Iron Division of German General von

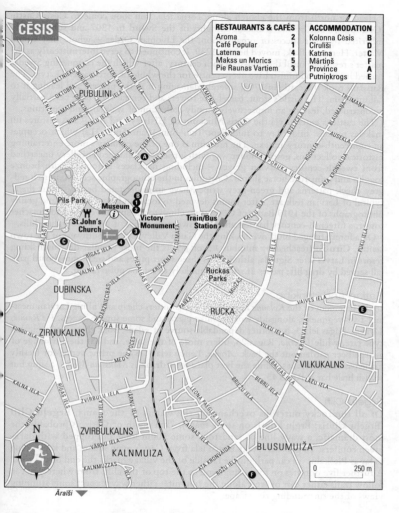

CĒSIS

RESTAURANTS & CAFÉS	
Aroma	2
Café Popular	1
Laterna	4
Makss un Morics	5
Pie Raunas Vartiem	3

ACCOMMODATION	
Kolonna Cēsis	B
Cirulīši	D
Katrīna	C
Mārtiņš	F
Province	A
Putniņkrogs	E

Āraiši ▼

der Goltz. The Estonians chased von der Goltz's men all the way back to Rīga, only to be dissuaded from finishing them off entirely by the British, who argued that German troops might still come in useful in helping to fight off the Bolsheviks, proving difficult to dislodge from Latvia's southeastern corner.

Southwest of the square, Skolas iela descends towards the thirteenth-century **St John's Church** (Sv Jāņa Baznīca), a heavily buttressed structure containing the tombs of several masters of the Livonian Order, most notably Walter von Plettenberg (1494–1535). Something of a national hero among Baltic Germans, Plettenberg pushed back seemingly unstoppable Russian offensives at the beginning of the sixteenth century, winning a brief but significant respite for the Livonian Order – which struggled on for another fifty years before bequeathing its territories to the Poles and the Swedes. The narrow streets just west of the church are among Cēsis's most atmospheric, with one-storey wooden dwellings huddled over the cobbles.

Heading north from the church along Torņa iela, you soon come to **Cēsis Castle** (Cēsu pils), built by the crusading Knights of the Sword in 1207 and subsequently inherited by their successor organization, the Livonian Order – whose first Grand Master, Hermann Balk, moved here in 1239. It continued to serve intermittently as the master's residence until the mid-sixteenth century, after which the conquering Swedes turned it into an administrative nerve centre for the whole of northeastern Latvia. The Russians took the castle in 1703, severely damaging it in the process and leaving it to fall into ruin. The castle's stout, barrel-like towers and central keep have been partially reconstructed, leaving an impressively moody collection of walk-around grey ruins.

The castle is entered via the **Cēsis Museum of History and Art** (Cēsu vēstures un mākslas muzejs; mid–May to mid–Sept Tues–Sun 10am–5pm; 1Ls) which occupies an eighteenth-century annexe. The museum is one of the country's more entertaining historical collections, getting under way with intricately fashioned jewellery unearthed from twelfth-century Latvian graves – including necklaces festooned with bronze toggles and miniature horse shapes. Costumes in the ethnographic section, in rich red-grey check patterns and green-grey stripes, have an understated beauty about them, typical of Latvian folk art. After rooms devoted to local landscape painters and grainy photographs of the 1919 Battle of Cēsis, steps climb to the summit of the Ladermacher tower, a fifteenth-century bastion affording sweeping views of the surrounding hills.

On a forest-fringed bluff overlooking the Gauja Valley, 2.5km southwest of the town centre, **Cīrulīši** (reached by minibus #5 or #9) is the most popular downhill skiing resort in Latvia after Sigulda, although its three short pistes and small snowboard park (all served by drag lift; passes 2Ls/hr) are unlikely to set the pulse racing.

Eating and drinking

In the basement of the *Kolonna* hotel, *Café Popular* offers cheap and filling Latvian meat-and-two-veg meals, alongside workmanlike pizzas and some superb sweets. *Pie Raunas Vārtiem*, Rigas iela 3, is another dependable source of salad-, pork chop- and pancake-type fare, while *Laterna*, Rīgas 25, offers more of the same, and has the advantage of a large beer garden out the back. *Aroma*, Lenču iela 4, is the prime venue for freshly made pastries and cakes, while the best place for a **drink** is *Makss un Morics*, a snug but stylish little bar at Rīgas 43.

Ērģeļu Cliff

Of all the rocky outcrops overhanging the waters of the Gauja, **Ērģeļu Cliff** (Ērģeļu klintis; Ergļu klintis on some maps), 7km north of Cēsis, is probably the most dramatic, a wavy line of sandstone some 500m long and topped with dark-green conifers. To get there, take Lenču iela from Cēsis's main square and keep going as far as Pieškalni – a car park on the far side of the village marks the end of the road. A further five minutes on foot brings you to the top of the cliff, from where you can follow trails either east or west along the summit – either way, expect some stunning views of the surrounding riverscape.

Āraiši

Some 7km south of Cēsis, the rustic lakeside village of **ĀRAIŠI** would be a charming enough spot for a stroll even without the added attraction of the **Āraiši Lake Fortress** (Āraišu ezerpils; May to mid-Oct daily 10am–6pm; 1Ls), a modern-day reconstruction of an Iron Age settlement. Built on a man-made island and joined to the lakeshore by a causeway, it's an exact replica of the ninth-century original that once stood on this very site. It's not really a "fortress", rather a compact village with fifteen dwellings, rendered defensible by its watery location. Shrouded by reeds and with the ruddy roof of Āraiši village church in the background, it couldn't be more picturesque. Locally available trees provided the raw material for almost everything in the lake dwelling, with the tiny log-built houses with bark roofs huddled together on wooden decking. The houses are currently bare inside, although sleeping benches, domestic artefacts and authentically attired mannequins are planned for the future.

△ Āraiši Lake Fortress

Once you've had a look at the lake dwelling, there's plenty in the way of minor attractions to justify lingering a little while, beginning with the ruins of **Āraiši Castle** (Āraišu pilsdrupas), sitting on a hillock immediately to the southeast. Built by the Livonian Order in the thirteenth century, it was abandoned after Ivan the Terrible's Russians sacked it in 1577.

Heading northwards around the lake, you come to **Āraiši village** and its slender-spired parish church, erected in the thirteenth century and rebuilt in the eighteenth – when a human skeleton was found bricked up in the wall. The discovery soon entered local folklore, with villagers claiming that the church's original architect had pledged to ensure the structure's longevity by immuring the next human being he saw, unaware that his own daughter was at that moment advancing up the street with his lunch.

Finally, for a great view back towards lake, fortress and village, it's worth walking as far as the **windmill** on the low hill to the west, its overhanging wooden canopy looking like an upturned boat.

At least one daily Rīga–Cēsis **bus** passes through Āraiši itself; most other Rīga–Cēsis services use the main road 1km west of the site – get off at the Betes stop and walk via the windmill, clearly visible on the brow of the hill above the road. In addition, four daily Rīga–Cēsis **trains** call at the Āraiši stop, although it's 2.5km southeast of the village.

The Daugava Valley

Rising in the same part of western Russia as the Volga and the Dniepr, the 1020-kilo-metre-long **Daugava** is the longest and most majestic waterway in the country, flowing through Belarus and Latvia before emptying into the Gulf of Rīga. The Daugava Valley has been Latvia's main northwest–southeast **transport corridor** since time imme-morial and until the twentieth century was busy with rafts and barges carrying timber, hemp, flax and hides downriver to the export markets of Rīga. Nowadays, goods travel via the main road and rail routes on the right bank of the Daugava, the river itself having been rendered unnavigable by the construction of a series of **hydroeletric projects**, that together provide for the bulk of the country's energy needs. The first of these, damming the river at Ķegums, was built by the Ulmanis regime in 1937 and was a symbol of Latvian technological progress at the time, although subsequent, Soviet-era projects have proved much more controversial. Upriver at Aizkraukle, the Pļaviņas Reservoir (Pļaviņu ūdenskrātuve) project involved flooding the most picturesque part of the Daugava Valley and only went ahead after patriotic-minded politicians had been purged from the Latvian Communist Party in the late 1950s. A project planned (but never completed) further upstream near Daugavpils provoked one of the first environmentalist protests in the Soviet Union in 1986, when Latvian intellectuals successfully called for its cancellation.

Such ecological concerns are understandable given the importance of the Daugava landscape in Latvian culture. As the country's longest river, it has inspired more mythic tales and folk songs than any other inland geographical feature. Nineteenth-century writer **Andrējs Pumpurs** (see box opposite) set much of the action of his epic poem *Lāčplēsis* on the Daugava riverbank. Upriver from Rīga, the writer's home town, **Lielvārde**, with its Pumpurs museum and reconstructed Iron Age stockade fort, is the first of the riverside settlements worth a stop. Further upstream, the ruined castle at **Koknese** is an evocative place to ponder the river's history, although it's the prosperous market town of **Jēkabpils** that offers most in terms of sightseeing potential.

Getting up and down the valley is easy enough, with Rīga–Daugavpils **buses** passing through the main settlements on the right bank. Using the Daugava Valley rail route (served by Rīga–Daugavpils, Rīga–Rēzekne and some commuter trains), you can quite feasibly train-hop your way up the valley, visit a few sights, and still get back to Rīga before nightfall – although bear in mind that most of the train stations are some way away from the town centres they serve, so you'll need to employ a certain amount of leg power to get around.

Lielvārde

The first town upstream from Rīga worth spending some time in is **LIELVĀRDE**, situated midway along a broad stretch of the Daugava – the Ķegums dam upstream causes the river to widen here. It's an uneventful little place with a rather nondescript town centre, but has a brace of intriguing sights on its riverside outskirts. The first of these, the reconstructed **ancient Latvian castle** (Senlatviešu pils; April–Nov daily 10am–6pm; 0.50Ls), is right beside the Rīga–Daugavpils highway at the western entrance to town. Its outer perimeter bristling with sharpened stakes, this timber-built stockade fort is a reasonably authentic approximation of what twelfth-century strongholds would have looked like in general rather than the exact replica of one in particular. Quite small in scale, such forts supported only a small population of warriors in peacetime, filling up with civilians from the surrounding farmsteads in times of war. The simple log dwellings crowding the courtyard are all chimneyless – it's thought that the inhabitants only lit fires for the length of time it took to warm their heat-radiating hearthstones. With its dinky wooden ramparts, the whole scene looks more like an adventure playground for adults than a military installation, and it's not difficult to see why the log-based civilization of the Latvian chieftains was so quickly brushed aside by the crusading Knights of the Sword.

About 2.5km southeast of the fortress, on the far side of the town centre, a tree-lined lane leads from the main road to the **Andrējs Pumpurs Museum** (Tues–Sat 10am–5pm; 0.50Ls), honouring the locally born author (see box opposite) of the epic tale of *Lāčplēsis*, bear-slaying hero and symbol of Latvia's resistance to outside rule. The display of photographs, facsimile manuscripts and first editions is less exciting than the museum's park-like setting, with a riverside path leading past wooden sculptures inspired by Pumpurs' poem to the cliff-top ruins of **Lielvārde Castle**, a crusader stronghold built on the site of an earlier Latvian stockade fort.

Practicalities

Served by frequent commuter services from Rīga, Lielvārde **train station** is at the northwestern end of town, a five-minute walk from the ancient Latvian castle. **Buses** working the Rīga–Jēkabpils–Daugavpils route pick up and drop off at stops at the

Andrējs Pumpurs (1841–1902)

A versatile journalist and poet, **Andrējs Pumpurs** is primarily remembered for *Lāčplēsis*, a composition in verse that weaves numerous Latvian folk tales into a harmonious, epic whole. Born at Birzgale, near Lielvārde, and receiving only an elementary education, Pumpurs worked as an agricultural worker and assistant land surveyor before heading for Moscow in 1876 to join the Slav Volunteer Regiment, a unit formed by idealistic young Russians to aid Serbia in its struggles against the Ottoman Empire. With combat experience in the Balkans under his belt, Pumpurs made easy work of an officer training course in Odessa and spent the rest of his years occupying a succession of administrative posts in the Russian army.

Despite unswerving loyalty to the Russian Empire, Pumpurs was a keen champion of Latvian culture and had been writing for the burgeoning Latvian-language press since his twenties. Pumpurs saw Latvian folklore in particular as a profound source of cultural and spiritual wealth, the study of which he believed would help the Latvians – a politically powerless people ruled over by Russian bureaucrats and German-speaking landowners – to regain a sense of self-respect. Enthused by the work of Elias Lönnrot in Finland and Friedrich Reinhold Kreuzwald (see p.161) in Estonia – both of whom had used traditional folk material to compose chest-beating epic poems – Pumpurs set out to produce a Latvian equivalent.

Like Kreuzwald, Pumpurs was prepared to invent the narrative himself if the folk fragments available to him didn't add up to the kind of epic story he was looking for. He chose an archetypal character from Latvian myth, born of man and female bear (and, in original folk versions, blessed with a pair of bear's ears), and transformed him into Lāčplēsis, the "Bear Slayer", a virtuous youth bestowed with almost superhuman strengths – including the ability to tear wild beasts apart with his bare hands.

Pumpurs then put Lāčplēsis through all manner of adventures – battling sorceresses, helping out good chieftains in their struggles against the bad – in order to showcase the richness and diversity of Latvian lore. Many of Pumpurs' protagonists were either his own inventions or composite figures drawn from numerous traditional sources, but they soon entered the national consciousness and are nowadays treated as authentic characters from national mythology – two of the most popular being Staburadze, the water nymph who lives in a crystal palace beneath the waters of the Daugava, and Laimdota, the sugar-and-spice Latvian girl who tends Lāčplēsis's wounds. However, Pumpurs' overriding aim was to provide the Latvians with an action hero with whom they could identify in what he saw as their coming struggle with the Baltic German aristocracy. The world of fairies, witches and forest sprites that Lāčplēsis inhabits is a clear metaphor for an idealized, pre-conquest Latvia that existed before German-speaking crusaders arrived on their shores, and it's no accident that the bear-bashing protagonist fights his last battle against the unmistakably Teuton Black Knight. The story ends with Lāčplēsis making the ultimate sacrifice, dragging his adversary with him over a cliff and into the murky waters of the Daugava.

northeastern end of town near the castle and at the southeastern end, near the lane to the Pumpurs Museum.

To **stay**, you can choose between *Oši*, a homely B&B just opposite the train station at Pils iela 2 (℡6507 1855; ❷), and *Lielvārdes osta*, a cosy, eight-room hotel with **café–restaurant** near the replica fort at Krasta iela 2 (℡6505 3041, ⓦwww.lielvardesosta .lv; ❸). The best place to pick up supplies is the Olvi supermarket, midway between castle and museum at Lielvārde's central crossroads; it also has a café attached.

From Lielvārde to Koknese

Beyond Lielvārde there's little to slow your progress until you get to **SKRĪVERI**, a further 30km upriver, where the roadside **Dendrological Park** (Dendroloģiskais parks) gathers together more than 380 tree species from all over the world. First planted by lord of the local manor, Max von Sivers, in 1891, it remains surprisingly little visited, and the expanse of parkland criss-crossed by trails has an appealingly wild and untamed feel.

Some 10km beyond Skrīveri, **AIZKRAUKLE** was built from scratch in the 1960s to house workers at the nearby Pļaviņas hydroelectric project and has been burdened ever since with the unofficial title of ugliest town in Latvia. It's a good 4km west of the main road and rail lines – savouring the blur of housing blocks that appears on your right as you speed past is probably the best way to experience it.

Rather more interesting is the smaller town of **KOKNESE**, 20km further on, where a single street leads down from the train station and main road to the remains of a **riverside fortress** built by the German crusaders in 1209. The castle was robbed of its romantic cliff-top position by the rising water level resulting from the construction of the Pļaviņas dam, but the Daugava-lapped ruin still possesses undeniable charm. The dam also dwarfed the erstwhile majesty of **Staburags cliff**, which used to tower above the river just upstream from Koknese on the opposite bank. As the rock from which the eponymous hero of Andrējs Pumpurs's *Lāčplēsis* (see box, p.271) hurls both himself and the Black Knight, Staburags occupies an important place in the Latvian psyche – and its near-disappearance under the Pļaviņas reservoir was enough to persuade many Latvian patriots that the Soviet-era project was a deliberate attack on their national culture.

If you want to break your journey near Koknese, the **tourist office**, Blaumaņa 3 (Mon–Fri 9am–5pm; ☎6516 1296, ✉tic@koknese.apollo.lv), can direct you to one of a handful of **B&Bs** in the surrounding villages, or you could head for *Kalnavoti*, on the main road just southeast of Koknese (☎2911 7795; ❷), an eight-room guesthouse set in riverside meadows and serving up traditional fare in its **pub-restaurant**.

Jēkabpils

The main settlement on the middle stretch of the Daugava, **JĒKABPILS** managed to escape the kind of wartime destruction and post-war industrialization visited on most other places in the region and preserves the laid-back charm of a Latvian country town. With its one-storey wooden houses complete with neat cottage gardens, it exudes a palpable nice-place-to-bring-up-the-kids vibe.

Jēkabpils is made up of what were originally two separate towns – **Krustpils** on the northern bank of the river, and **Jēkabpils** immediately opposite on the south. While Krustpils dates back to the establishment of a castle here by the Archbishop of Rīga in the thirteenth century, Jēkabpils originated as a seventeenth-century sanctuary for Old Believers – schismatic Orthodox Christians fleeing persecution in Tsarist Russia (see box, p.163). Eager to take trade away from Krustpils, the ambitious Duke Jakob of Courland (whose territory then extended as far as the Daugava) bestowed free-town status on the new settlement in 1670 and also gave it its name – Jēkabpils being the Latvianized form of the original Jakobstadt, or "Jacob's town". Before long, the place had become the main stop-off point for rafters taking logs and furs downstream to Rīga, and a cosmopolitan community of Latvians, Jews, Poles and Russians (both orthodox and schismatic) sprung up to rake in the proceeds. These groups bequeathed the town a fine set of religious buildings in a variety of architectural styles, which – along with a pair of worthwhile museums – constitute the town's main sights.

Buses pick up and drop off on the main square in Jēkabpils, and the **train station** is on the Krustpils side of the river, 3.5km from the centre – consequently Krustpils (and not Jēkabpils) is the name used on train timetables and destination boards.

The Town

The town's prim main square is **Vecpilsētas laukums**; heading west of here, Brīvības iela passes a semi-derelict **Uniate church** (Uniātu baznīca) before arriving at the nineteenth-century **Orthodox Church of St Nicholas** (Sv Nikolaja baznīca), which presides over a walled enclosure at Brīvības 202. The church is rarely open, but its exterior is worth a brief once-over, especially its delicately carved wooden porch and cluster of domes resembling a huddle of bulbous-hatted priests. Five minutes' walk southeast of Vecpilsētas laukums is the equally personable **Old Believers' Church** (Vecticībnieku baznīca) at Viestura 15, a bright-blue timber building, topped off by a trio of tiny cupolas. East of the main square, the comparatively sober **Lutheran Church** (Luterāņu baznīca) marks the turn-off to the **Sēlian Farmstead Museum** (Sēļu sēta; May–Oct Mon–Fri 9am–5pm, Sat & Sun 10am–3pm; 0.50Ls) on the corner of Dambja and Filozofu, displaying buildings rescued from the villages of Sēlia – the rural region extending south from Jēkabpils as far as the Lithuanian border. The nineteenth-century reed-thatched farmhouses are almost upstaged by a functional grey slab of a windmill, that looks as if it could have been designed by Mies van der Rohe's country cousin and has a long pole attached to it so it can be pulled round on its axis to face the wind.

The chief attraction on the opposite side of the river is **Krustpils Castle** (Krustpils pils), reached by crossing the bridge from Jēkabpils and turning left up Rīgas iela (a ride on bus #1, #4, #5 or #9 will save you a twenty-minute walk). Built shortly after the Teutonic conquest in 1237, it was extensively remodelled in the sixteenth century, and received repeated batterings in wars between Swedes and Poles. However, its interior has been elegantly restored and now houses the **Jēkabpils History Museum** (Jēkabpils vēstures muzejs; Mon–Fri 9am–5pm, Sat 10am–3pm; 0.50Ls), harbouring the usual hodge-podge of archeological and ethnographic trinkets and a wealth of old furniture culled from the region's manor houses.

Practicalities

The **tourist office** in the town library, at Vecpilsētas laukuma 3 (Mon–Fri 10am–6pm; ☎6523 3822, ⓦwww.jekabpils.lv), is short-staffed and doesn't always abide by its advertised opening times. The best **hotel** is the six-room *Hercogs Jēkabs*, Brīvības 182 (despite the three-figure street number, it's only five minutes' walk west of the main square; ☎6523 3433, ⓔsaule@niko.lv; ❸), offering parquet-floored, pastel-coloured en suites, some with river views. Next best is the riverside *Daugavkrasti*, 1.5km east of the centre at Mežrūpnieku 2 (☎6523 1232, ⓦwww.daugavkrasti.lv; ❸); the rooms come with shower and TV, but the furnishings are beginning to show wear and tear. For **eating** and **drinking**, *Kafejnīca Uguntiņa*, at the top of the main square, is a good daytime source of no-nonsense pork-and-potatoes staples, while *Kafejnīca Atpūta*, Viestura 5, has a wider-ranging menu and is snazzier all round, attracting a coffee-and-cake crowd in the daytime and cool young drinkers in the evening.

Latgale

Extending east from Jēkabpils to the Russian border, the region of **Latgale** (ⓦwww .latgale.lv) offers some of the most enchanting landscapes in the country: pleasantly rolling upland studded with lakes, girdled with a mixture of reed beds, pine trees and birch. Along with Vidzeme, Kurzeme and Zemgale, it's one of the four main historical regions of Latvia and, although it no longer exists as an administrative unit, preserves a stronger sense of local identity than any other part of the country. The region's name comes from the Latgalians, one of the original Baltic tribes who settled in Latvia four millennia ago. Latgale still preserves an archaic dialect that differs sufficiently from standard Latvian for some to consider it a separate language (it's not officially recognized as such, but publication of Latgalian poetry and prose is an increasing preoccupation of the local literati).

Latgale's uniqueness is largely due to the fact that it was cut off from the rest of Latvia for large chunks of its history, thereby missing out on the process of cultural and linguistic unification that bound the other three regions together as a nation. Most significantly, it was part of the Polish-Lithuanian state from 1561 until the first partition of Poland in 1772. During this period the tribes living in northern and western Latvia gradually standardized their languages into a mutually intelligible national tongue, while the isolated Latgalians stuck to their own archaic dialect. Latgale was also cut off from the Protestant culture then developing in the rest of Latvia, remaining under the sway of the **Catholic Church** – a faith to which the Latgalians are still passionately devoted to this day. Under Russian rule from 1772, Latgale was attached to the Vitebsk Gubernia (covering what is now most of eastern Belarus), distancing it even further from the main currents of Latvian culture. The Latgalian intelligentsia always regarded themselves as a legitimate branch of the Latvian national family, however, and in April 1917 the **Latvian-Latgalian Congress** convened in Rēzekne to declare Latgale's "independence" from Vitebsk and its unification with Latvian territories governed by Rīga. For the next three years Latgale was the scene of fierce battles between pro-Latvian forces and Bolsheviks invading from the east and it wasn't until 1920 that real political unity was achieved.

Latgale was always an ethnically mixed area, with Latgalian Latvians dominating the countryside and Russians and Poles congregating in the towns. Jews made up forty to fifty percent of the population in urban areas like Daugavpils, Ludza and Krāslava, though Nazi terror in World War II destroyed this centuries-old presence at a stroke. After the war, Latgale's cities were earmarked for industrialization, encouraging mass immigration from other parts of the Soviet Union – with the result that Russians are now the largest ethnic group in the region, making up some 43.5 percent of the population.

The cities of **Daugavpils** and **Rēzekne** are the region's main transport hubs and service centres, although neither is likely to hold your attention for long. Rural Latgale is another matter, however, with the Catholic pilgrimage site of **Aglona** and the drowsy market town of **Ludza** providing access to the best of the lakeland scenery.

Daugavpils

Despite being Latvia's second city, **DAUGAVPILS** is usually dismissed by the rest of the country as an economically depressed backwater with few redeeming features. It's true that this erstwhile industrial powerhouse has fallen on hard times, but it remains – in parts at least – a ruggedly handsome city whose historical resonances run deep. If there is so much prejudice against Daugavpils it's probably because so few Latvian-speakers actually live there: over ninety percent of the population is Russian-speaking and although the street signs are in Latvian, you'll hardly ever hear the language used in everyday conversation.

Perhaps appropriately for a town with such a large Russian population, Daugavpils appears to have been founded by marauding Muscovite Ivan the Terrible, who sacked the Livonian Order fortress of Dünaburg, 19km upstream, and ordered its reconstruction on the site of the present-day city. An important garrison town under successive rulers, Daugavpils experienced its most rapid period of growth in the years before World War I, when a developing manufacturing industry sucked in migrant workers from all over the Russian Empire. The process repeated itself after 1945, when the Soviet authorities deliberately imported a non-Latvian workforce to feed the city's expanding factories, which produced everything from landmines to lawn mowers. Daugavpils took an economic battering in the immediate post-independence years, with mass unemployment engendering an atmosphere of despondency that is only now beginning to lift. However, it's by no means the unremittingly ugly city that many Latvians claim it to be, and with a downtown area full of robust nineteenth-century buildings, it has enough in the way of gruff charm to reward even the briefest of visits.

Arrival, information and accommodation

Daugavpils' **train station** lies at the northeastern end of the main street, Rīgas iela, while the **bus station** is two blocks southeast of this thoroughfare; both are within easy reach of the helpful **tourist office** at Rīgas 22A – the entrance is round the back of the building (Mon–Fri 9am–6pm, Sat 10am–4pm; ☎6542 2818, ©tourinfo @daugavpils.apollo.lv).

With a gradually improving stock of **hotels** in Daugavpils, you shouldn't have any problems finding a central place to stay.

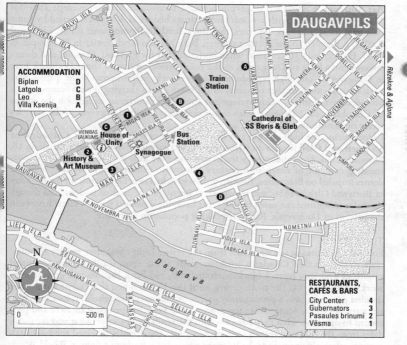

Hotels

Biplan 18. Novembra iela 50 ☏ 6544 0596, ✉ biplan.hotel@apollo.lv. Unassuming red-brick building with two floors of tastefully decorated en suites. Within handy walking distance of pretty much everything you need. ④

Latgola Ģimnazijas 46 ☏ 6540 4900, ⓦ www .hoteldaugavpils.lv. Ten-storey slab right in the centre, offering comfortable if cramped en suites with camel-coloured fabrics and fittings. Views from the upper floors are excellent, and breakfast is eaten in the pop-art, panoramic top-floor café-restaurant. Standard doubles ⑤, "business-class" doubles ⑥

Leo Krāslavas 58 ☏ 6542 6565, ⓕ 6542 5325. Unpretentious B&B in a residential courtyard midway between the bus and train stations. Homely en suites come with chintzy fittings; there are only five rooms, so call in advance. ④

Villa Ksenija Varšavas 17 ☏ 6543 4317, ⓦ www .villaks.lv. Pre-World War I mansion twenty minutes' walk uphill from the centre, just behind the Orthodox cathedral, offering slightly cramped but otherwise comfy and stylish en suites. ⑤

The Town

Slicing straight through the middle of Daugavpils' grid-iron city centre is **Rīgas iela**, a stately, pedestrianized strip lined with tastefully restored nineteenth-century apartment blocks. Midway along the street's 1.5-kilometre length, the tree-fringed open spaces of **Vienības laukums** provide downtown Daugavpils with some kind of focus. It's overlooked by the ten-storey bulk of the **Hotel Latgola**, long considered one of the most graceless buildings in the country until much improved by its 2003 facelift. Squatting immediately opposite is the grey-brown **House of Unity** (Vienības nams), a combined theatre and administrative building which holds the dubious distinction of being the largest construction project undertaken by the inter-war Latvian state. From here it's a short hop southwest to the **Daugavpils Regional History and**

Art Museum at Rīgas 8 (Daugavpils novadpētniecības un makslas muzejs; Tues–Sat 11am–6pm; 0.80Ls), with a words-and-pictures historical display enlivened by some colourful local costumes. Upstairs, the **Mark Rothko Room** (same times; additional 0.80Ls) is devoted to the abstract painter, born Markus Rothkowitz in Daugavpils in 1903. He was only 10 years old when his family left for Portland, Oregon, and there's consequently little of Daugavpils in the man's work, or indeed the man's work here in Daugavpils – although reproductions of his works help to provide the display here with some focus. A further reminder of the town's once-thriving Jewish community is provided by the smart, ochre **synagogue** four blocks northeast of here on the corner of Cietokšņa and Lāčplēša – with fewer than four hundred Jews left in the city, it's rarely open outside prayer times.

Dominating the high ground east of the city centre is the **Orthodox Cathedral of SS Boris and Gleb** (Borisa un Gļeba pareizticīgo katedrāle) – head northeast along 18. Novembra iela, cross the railway tracks and you can't miss it. The cathedral is an out-standing example of nineteenth-century Muscovite exuberance, its shiny bauble-like domes impaled on lilac spires. Russian armies marched into Daugavpils on the feast day of Boris and Gleb in 1656, and re-named it "Borisoglebsk" in their honour, and though the Poles recaptured the town twelve years later, the medieval warrior saints have been the patrons of Daugavpils' Russian-speaking population ever since.

The Citadel

Following Cietokšņa iela northeast from the centre brings you after twenty minutes' walk to the so-called **Citadel** (Cietoksnis; daily 10am–8pm; 0.20Ls), a self-contained suburb of grid-iron barrack blocks surrounded by red-brick bastions and grassy earth-works. This area was the town centre until the 1770s, when the Tsarist authorities decided to turn it into a permanently garrisoned military stronghold, relocating civil-ian activities to the southeast in the process. The French captured it in 1812 and pro-ceeded to demolish what they found – with the result that most of what you see today dates from the mid-nineteenth century and after. The Citadel survived the twentieth century relatively unscathed: the Russians evacuated it without a fight in World War I, and having failed to do much damage to it in World War II, the Soviet Air Force turned it into an Aviation High School – which it remained until 1990. Nowadays it's one of the most bizarre places in the whole of Latvia (topped only by Karosta in Liepāja; see p.251), its long, grey lines of peeling buildings enlivened by the odd patch of greenery or ornamental artillery piece. Most of the blocks are now derelict and boarded up, although some have been pressed into use to provide cheap housing for locals – as if to complete the experience of alienation, these sections are surrounded by security fences in order to ward off intruders.

Eating and drinking

There are plenty of **cafés** along the length of Rīgas iela, especially at the train-station end. *Vēsma*, Rīgas 49, has an order-at-the-counter canteen with a good salad bar, a cakes-and-ice cream café section and a summer-only roof terrace with grill-restaurant. *Pasaules brinumi*, just off the main square at Vienības 17, does a good line in salads, pork chops and pancakes. The attractive, cellar-bound *Gubernators*, Lāčplēša 10, offers the best in the way of traditional Latvian pork-chop cuisine, and is also a lively place to **drink**. The *City Center* bowling alley, just east of the bus station at Viestura 8 (ⓦwww.citycenter.lv) boasts a smart café-bar with snack-food menu and a nightclub open on Fridays and Saturdays.

Aglona

Nestling picturesquely between a pair of lakes 45km northeast of Daugavpils and 10km east of the Daugavpils–Rēzekne highway, the one-horse village of **AGLONA** is dwarfed by the twin-towered, late-Baroque basilica that stands on its outskirts. The most important Catholic shrine in Latvia, it can draw anything from 100,000 to 150,000 celebrants for the Feast of the Assumption on August 15, and remains popular with pilgrims throughout the year – Easter, Pentecost and September 8 (Birth of the Virgin) being the other key dates. Aglona's importance as a religious centre dates back to 1699, when Dominicans chose to settle in this tranquil spot, bringing with them a seventeenth-century image of the Virgin that soon developed a reputation for miraculous healing powers. The first (wooden) monastery burnt down in 1766 and Aglona's burgeoning popularity with the Baltic Catholic faithful was considered sufficient reason to justify construction of the impressive basilica which dominates the landscape today. Aglona's holy aura was boosted further when a local woman claimed to have seen a vision of the Virgin on the hillock beside the basilica in 1798. During the Soviet period the monastery was closed down and pilgrimages discouraged, although the basilica was allowed to publicly celebrate its two-hundredth anniversary in 1980. Thoroughgoing restoration was carried out in time for Pope John Paul II's visit in September 1993, when a massive paved area was laid down for outdoor Masses.

The **basilica** has the severe appearance of a freshly iced, but otherwise undecorated, cake. Its distinguishing feature is the pair of chunky sixty-metre-high towers rising on either side of the main door – the basilica was by far the highest man-made object for miles around until the erection of the next-door TV transmission mast, a clear indication of where spiritual power in contemporary Latvia really lies. With the population of Latgale presumably far too busy watching soap operas and game shows actually to visit the basilica, it's no surprise to discover that it doesn't keep regular opening hours, and unless you arrive on Sundays, gaining admittance is rather a matter of luck. Inside, the icon-like image of the Virgin which graces the high altar is hidden behind a curtain – and only unveiled on holy days. If all this is a bit of a let-down, you can always enjoy the scenery by following the paths around Lake Aglona immediately east of the basilica, or the larger, reed-fringed expanse of Cirīšs to the west.

Getting to Aglona

If you're travelling to Aglona by public transport **from Rīga**, it's best to aim first for the market town of **Preiļi**, 25km northwest of Aglona, and pick up a local bus from there – you should be able to see Aglona as a day-trip from the capital providing you set off early in the day and double-check return times at each stage of the journey. Preiļi's bus station is right on the central square, just across from a **tourist office** at Tirgus laukums 1 (Mon–Fri 9am–5pm; ☎6532 2041, ⊛www.preili.lv).

Approaching Aglona **from Daugavpils or Rēzekne**, note that Daugavpils–Rēzekne buses don't pass through Aglona itself, however much staff in local bus stations may persuade you otherwise; they stop off instead in the similarly named Aglonas stacija ("Aglona Station") on the main highway, a hamlet huddled around a barely used railway halt and not the kind of place you want to get stranded in. A handful of Daugavpils–Aglona and Rēzekne–Aglona services do exist, although they may set off too late in the day to allow sufficient time to look around and get back to town.

Driving to Aglona is much less complicated all round: the main turn-off from the Daugavpils–Rēzekne highway at Aglonas stacija is marked by a huge, unmissable white cross. For a more picturesque approach, turn off the highway at **Spoģi**, 30km out of Daugavpils, and head east via the tiny lake resort of **Višķi** – not all of this road is tarmacked, but it's a lovely up-hill-and-down-dale ride through rolling, partly forested countryside.

Buses stop on what passes for a main square, 500m uphill from the basilica. There is a helpful **tourist office** in the local government building roughly opposite at Somersētas 34 (☎2911 8597, ⊜tic@aglona.lv). The **café** immediately opposite the bus stop serves up soups, salads and pork cutlets; and the *Aglonas maize* **bakery** at Daugavpils iela 7 (Mon–Fri 8am–6pm, Sat & Sun 9am–4pm) sells freshly made rye bread – including speciality loaf *Veistuklis* which contains tasty chunks of bacon fat.

Accommodation

Campers will find tent and caravan space at *Pussala*, a lakeside site 2km northwest of the village off the Preiļi road (☎2644 7747), and at *Aglonas Alpi*, 4km south on the shores of the Ciriša reservoir (☎2919 4362 and 6532 1465, ⓦwww.aglonasalpi.viss.lv) – the latter also has en-suite cottages (four-person cottages from 37Ls, two-person ❹).

There's a handful of welcoming **B&Bs** in and around Aglona – hosts may speak Russian or German but not much English, so contact Aglona tourist office (see p.277) if you need an intermediary. Most B&Bs offer half- or full-board arrangements for a few extra lati – well worth considering as the quality of cooking is generally excellent and other eating and drinking opportunities are few and far between.

B&Bs

Aglonas Cakuli Ezera 4 ☎6537 5465 and 2919 4362, ⓦwww.aglonascakuli.lv. Lakeside house in the centre of Aglona with small, simply furnished rooms, some equipped with tiny bathrooms. There's usually locally caught fish on the menu for those that choose the half-board option. Doubles with shared facilities ❷, en suites ❸

Aglonas maize Daugavpils iela 7 ☎2928 7044 and 6532 1905, ⓔaglonas-maize@visitaglona.lv. Five rooms above the *Aglonas maize* bakery, each featuring attic ceilings, original timber features, bright cake-icing colours and bread-baking smells wafting up from below. Shared WC & shower in the hallway. ❷

 Mežinieku mājas Gūteņi ☎2923 4425 and 2632 4038, ⓔmeziniekumajas@inbox.lv.

Secluded farmstead 7km west of Aglona, at the end of a well-signed forest track just off the Viški road, with neat and simple wood-panelled rooms spread over a couple of buildings, and a communal kitchen and sauna. Idyllic surroundings include birch groves, woodland trails and a "druidic zodiac park" planted with the talismanic trees associated with each group of birthdates (no, we didn't understand it either). ❸

Upenīte Tartakas 7 ☎2631 2456, ⓔa.upenite@inbox.lv. Farmstead 2km west of town on the Viški road, offering snug rooms (one double and one quad) with painted-plank floorboards, wooden ceilings and textiles that granny probably made. Lake Ciriss is a few metres downhill. Ponies, a traditional smoke sauna and tasty home cooking provide additional incentives to stay. ❸

Rēzekne

Despite being fortified by both Latgalian chieftains and the Livonian Order, **RĒZEKNE**, 90km northeast of Daugavpils, didn't really take shape until the nineteenth century, when it was laid out in the grid pattern beloved of the Tsarist Empire's town planners. Unfortunately, few historic buildings survive from any era: Rēzekne found itself among the most artillery-pummelled towns in Latvia in World War II, which helps to explain why it's unremittingly grey and modern today. That said, it's a relatively relaxing, leafy city, and with a decent museum and a couple of other cultural oddities to its name, it's worth a brief stop before moving on.

The City

Rēzekne's main point of reference is **Atbrīvošanas aleja** ("Liberation Alley"), the long, straight street which runs north–south through the centre of the city. Marking its midpoint is a roundabout, the central reservation of which is occupied by the region's most famous resident, **Māra of Latgale** (Latgales Māra), a statue of a woman brandishing a cross in celebration of victory over the godless Bolsheviks in 1920 and Latgale's subsequent absorption into the infant state of Latvia. The inscription on the statue's pedestal reads *Vienoti Latvijai* ("For Latvian Unity!"), just to drive the point home.

Photographs of the local woman who modelled for the original sculpture are on display at the **Latgale Museum of History and Culture** (Latgales kultūrvēstures muzejs; Tues–Fri 10am–5pm, Sat 10am–4pm; 0.80Ls), just north of the roundabout at Atbrīvošanas 102. The museum's collection is something of a nostalgic evocation of the Rēzekne of old: you can see sepia photographs of the handsome brick buildings that used to line Rēzekne's main street in pre–World War I days and re-creations of shop interiors – including the dressing table of a 1930s beauty parlour. Upstairs, a thorough chronology of arts and crafts in Latgale kicks off with Bronze and Iron Age necklaces and continues with several rooms devoted to contemporary ceramics – a traditional Latgale craft still alive and well. Among the glossily glazed pots and plates look out for the many-branched candlesticks, very much a local trademark.

Heading south from the roundabout and turning left into Pils iela brings you face to face with the stark ruins of Rēzekne's **medieval fortress**, crowning a hillock. It's a good spot from which to admire the red-brick **Catholic cathedral** on the far side of the river; not that interesting a building to merit a close-up encounter, but it has a certain nobility when viewed from here.

Practicalities

Rēzekne has two **train stations**: Rēzekne II, just off the northern end of Atbrīvošanas aleja and about twenty minutes' walk north of the central roundabout, handles trains to and from Rīga and Ludza, while Rēzekne I, fifteen minutes southwest of the roundabout, is currently served by the Vilnius–St Petersburg express only, which passes through three times a week in each direction. The **bus station** is ten minutes' walk south of the roundabout. Overlooking the roundabout, and offering some good views of the city from its upper floors, the tower-block *Latgale* **hotel** (℡ 6462 2180; ❶–❷), Atbrīvošanas aleja 98, doesn't offer much in the way of modern furnishings, but the en-suite rooms are habitable enough – cheaper rooms come with shower/WC in the hallway. The best place for a quick bite is *Mols*, near the bus station at Latgales 22/24, a combined **café**, art gallery and craft shop which serves the usual repertoire of salads, soups and pork chops on traditional Latgalian ceramic plates. *Little Italy*, beside the roundabout at Atbrīvošanas aleja 100, serves up pizza, pasta and mainstream pork and chicken dishes in an elegant but not-too-formal environment.

Ludza

A short 25-kilometre ride from Rēzekne across a pleasing landscape of low hills and lakes, **LUDZA** is reckoned to be one of the most attractive small towns in Latvia, with neat rows of wooden houses draped across a neck of land separating three lakes. Overlooking the scene from a small hill are a pert, twin-towered Catholic church that – from a distance at least – looks like a souvenir-sized copy of the basilica at Aglona, and a ruined red-brick fortress, built by the Livonian Order to keep Russian invaders at bay. Head to the rugged shell of the three-storey keep to enjoy a sweeping panorama of the lakes, with Mazais Ludzas ezers ("Little Ludza Lake") over to the west, Lielais Ludzas ezers ("Great Ludza Lake") to the northeast and Dunakļu ezers further away to the north.

North of the fortress, on the far side of a bridge, the **Ludza District Museum** (Ludzas novadpētniecības muzejs; Mon–Sat 10am–5pm; 0.50Ls), at Kuļņeva 2, occupies the former villa of Yakov Petrovich Kulnev (1763–1812), a dashing cavalry officer who was the first Russian general to be killed in defence of the homeland during Napoleon's invasion of Russia of 1812 and became something of a national hero as a result. Alongside more Latgale ceramics, the display includes a fine collection of spiral headbands, necklaces and bracelets found in locally excavated tenth-century graves.

Behind the museum, Soikāna iela leads uphill onto a ridge running along the north side of the lake, arriving after ten minutes at an atmospheric, tree-canopied **Jewish cemetery**, with hundreds of Hebrew-engraved tombstones amid the long grass. Back in the eighteenth century, an estimated 59 percent of the town's population was Jewish, earning Ludza the title of "Latvian Jerusalem" – although the community thinned out in the 1930s owing to emigration to Rīga or America, and was annihilated completely by the Nazis in summer 1941. Back in town, there's a (currently unused) synagogue on the lakeside Ezerkrasta iela, just behind the tourist office, although there's nothing to indicate its former function.

Practicalities

Ludza can be reached by two daily trains and two daily buses from Rīga; otherwise public transport comes from Rēzekne. The **bus station** is right in the town centre, while the **train station** is a good twenty-minute walk south, at the top of Stacijas iela. The enthusiastic **tourist office**, Baznīcas 42/11 (Mon–Fri 8am–5pm; ℡ 6570 7202, ❾ www .ludza.lv), supplies brochures and town plans and can book you into bed-and-breakfast accommodation in villages throughout the district. **Accommodation** in Ludza itself is limited to the *Ezerzeme* hotel (℡6572 2490; ❶), Stacijas 44, a Seventies-era grey block offering frumpy doubles with shared bathrooms and no breakfast; and *Motelis Pie kamīna* (℡6572 5498; ❶), 2km south on the Zilupe road at Latgales 238, which, despite the motel tag, is a friendly five-room guesthouse. *Kafejnīca Kristīne*, a **restaurant** near the tourist office at Baznīcas 25, serves up the usual pork-and-potatoes fare.

Travel details

Trains

Rīga to: Cēsis (4 daily; 2hr); Daugavpils (4 daily; 3hr 20min–4hr); Jēkabpils (6 daily; 2hr 30min); Lielvārde (10 daily; 1hr); Līgatne (4 daily; 1hr 15min); Rēzekne (2 daily; 4hr); Sigulda (10 daily; 1hr 5min–1hr 20min).

Buses

Cēsis to: Erģeļu klintis (Mon–Fri 2 daily, Sat 5 daily, Sun 4 daily; 30min); Līgatne (Mon–Fri 3 daily; 40min).
Daugavpils to: Aglona (3 daily; 1hr 20min); Ludza (Mon–Sat 2 daily; 2hr 30min); Rēzekne (7 daily; 2hr 10min).
Līgatne train station to: Līgatne village (Mon–Fri 6 daily, Sat 3 daily, Sun 5 daily; 15min).

Preiļi to: Aglona (6 daily; 55min).
Rēzekne to: Aglona (2 daily; 1hr 30min); Daugavpils (7 daily; 2hr 10min); Ludza (5 daily; 30–50min); Rīga (8 daily; 5hr).
Rīga to: Cēsis (hourly; 2hr); Preiļi (6 daily; 3hr 30min); Sigulda (Mon–Sat 15 daily, Sun 7 daily; 1hr 10min).
Sigulda to: Krīmulda (9 daily; 20min); Rīga (Mon–Sat 15 daily, Sun 7 daily; 1hr 10min); Saulkrasti (4 daily; 1hr); Turaida (10 daily; 15min).

International trains

Daugavpils to: Vilnius (3 weekly; 3hr 30min).

International buses

Daugavpils to: Vilnius (2–3 daily; 3hr).

Lithuania

Lithuania highlights

✳ **St Casimir's Fair, Vilnius** A colourful craft fair attracting just about every woodcarver, ironmonger and basket-weaver in the country. See p.307

✳ **Vilnius Old Town** An inviting warren of alleyways overlooked by a handsome collection of Baroque and neoclassical churches. See p.309

✳ **Trakai** This beautifully restored fourteenth-century fortress, set in serene lakeland, is one of the finest in the Baltics. See p.342

✳ **M.K. Čiurlionis Art Museum, Kaunas** A huge collection of haunting, hallucinatory pictures by Lithuania's finest artist. See p.366

✳ **Museum of Lithuanian Life at Rumšiškės** A rambling, enormously enjoyable collection of nineteenth-century wooden homes from all over the country. See p.375

✳ **Dzūkija National Park** Rural Lithuania at its most unspoiled, with tumbledown villages, and sandy-soiled pine forests teeming with mushrooms and berries. See p.380

✳ **Hill of Crosses** Set amid the green pasturelands of the northwest, this is a compelling memorial to faith, national suffering and hope. See p.393

✳ **Nida** A relaxing village of fishermen's cottages at the foot of towering, tawny dunes. See p.408

✳ **Palanga** A something-for-all-the-family resort with bucket-and-spade beach culture and dance-till-dawn nightlife. See p.413

△ Trakai Castle

Introduction and basics

Boasting the best rye-based black bread in the world, a unique range of herb-infused alcoholic spirits and a distinctive cuisine in which the humble potato is elevated to sacred status, Lithuania possesses plenty in the way of individual identity.

Such character owes a lot to the fact that Lithuania, unlike its Baltic neighbours, once enjoyed a period of sustained international greatness, building a medieval empire which stretched south and east across modern Belarus, Russia and the Ukraine. Such strength allowed Lithuania to remain a nature-worshipping pagan state until well into the fourteenth century, and a mystical relationship with the landscape's lakes and forests marks out the Lithuanian character to this day. Christianity came to Lithuania after dynastic union with the Kingdom of Poland in 1386, and Polish Catholic culture went on to exert an increasing influence over the country, especially after the creation of the so-called Polish-Lithuanian Commonwealth in 1569. After 1795, Tsarist Russia became the dominant power. Despite successive waves of Polonization and Russification, however, Lithuanian culture was preserved in villages and farmsteads, and the country remains extraordinarily rich in folk art, rural festivals and traditional song.

Lithuania can also claim to be the first Baltic State to declare its independence from Moscow, breaking free in 1990 and forcing the pace of change which led to the collapse of the Soviet Union, the spread of civil society and free-market economics – and, ultimately, the accession of all three Baltic States to the European Union in 2004.

Where to go

The Lithuanian capital **Vilnius**, with its cobbled alleys and Baroque churches, is arguably the most architecturally beautiful of the Baltic capitals, with an easy-going charm all of its own. Easily reached from the capital is the imposing island fortress of **Trakai**, perhaps the country's best-known landmark and something of a national symbol. The rest of eastern Lithuania is characterized by deep forest, sandy-soiled pine woods and lakes, the most scenic stretches of which fall within the **Aukštaitija National Park** and **Dzūkija National Park**. Close to the latter are the relaxing spa resorts of **Druskininkai** and **Birštonas**, each of which offers the opportunity to splash around in invigorating spring water or embark on long woodland walks.

Set amid the green farmland of central Lithuania is its second city, **Kaunas**, which boasts an attractive old town and several set-piece museums. The main city in the northwest is **Šiauliai**, a rather workaday place, but a convenient base from which to visit the **Hill of Crosses**, a remarkable monument to Catholic piety and native Lithuanian mysticism.

On the coast, the busy port city of **Klaipėda** has something of an old quarter and a handful of lively bars and clubs. It's also the gateway to the **Curonian Spit**, a uniquely beautiful offshore strip of sand dune and forest that shields Lithuania from the open Baltic Sea.

Up the coast from Klaipėda, **Palanga** is an inviting cross between family beach resort and bar crawler's paradise, while the **Žemaitija National Park**, just inland, offers an engaging mixture of pretty rural villages and forested wilderness.

Getting around

Lithuania's cheap and comprehensive **public transport system** somehow continues to function efficiently, despite being reliant on

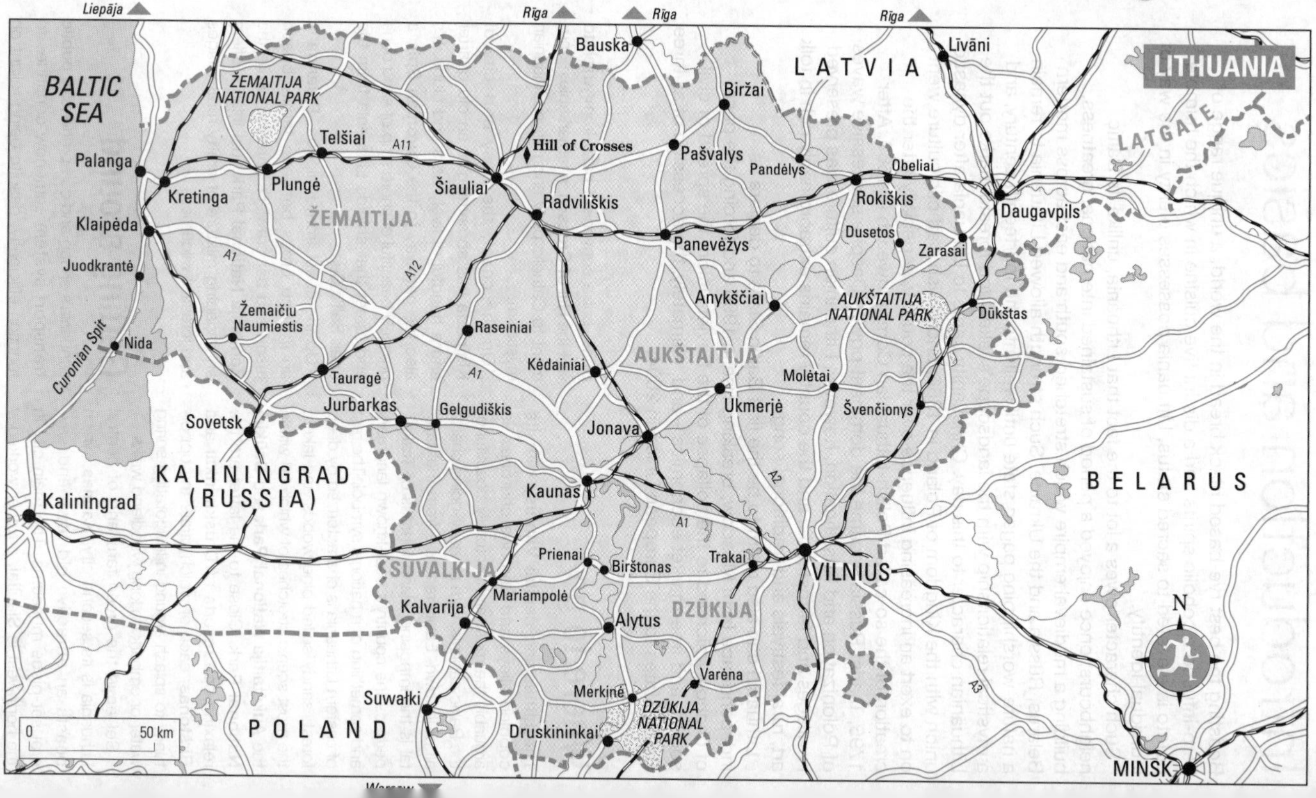
LITHUANIA
BALTIC SEA
LATVIA
BELARUS
POLAND
KALININGRAD (RUSSIA)
LATGALE
ŽEMAITIJA
AUKŠTAITIJA
SUVALKIJA
DZŪKIJA
ŽEMAITIJA NATIONAL PARK
AUKŠTAITIJA NATIONAL PARK
DZŪKIJA NATIONAL PARK
Curonian Spit
Liepāja
Rīga
Rīga
Rīga
Warsaw
Bauska
Līvāni
Biržai
Pašvalys
Pandėlys
Obeliai
Rokiškis
Daugavpils
Dusetos
Zarasai
Dūkštas
Hill of Crosses
Telšiai
Palanga
Kretinga
Plungė
Šiauliai
Radviliškis
Panevėžys
Anykščiai
Klaipėda
Juodkrantė
Nida
Žemaičiu Naumiestis
Raseiniai
Tauragė
Kėdainiai
Molėtai
Švenčionys
Ukmerjė
Jurbarkas
Gelgudiškis
Sovetsk
Jonava
Kaunas
Kaliningrad
Prienai
Birštonas
Trakai
VILNIUS
Mariampolė
Kalvarija
Alytus
Varėna
Merkinė
Druskininkai
Suwałki
MINSK
A1
A1
A1
A2
A3
A11
A12
N
0
50 km

clapped-out vehicles and decaying station buildings. Buses provide the most convenient way of getting around: there are frequent services between the main cities and departures to the remotest of villages at least once or twice a day. Trains are slightly cheaper, but although they connect the major towns, departures are infrequent and journey times painfully slow. For details of travel from one Baltic State to another, see p.36.

Buses

Lithuania's **bus network** is run by an at times confusing array of local companies – Toks (Ⓦwww.toks.lt) in Vilnius and Kautra (Ⓦwww.kautra.lt) in Kaunas being two of the biggest – but services are well integrated and bus stations (*autobusų stotis*) are generally well organized, with clearly marked departure boards and ticket counters allowing you to book your seats in advance. Smaller towns and villages will have a simple bus stop (*stotelė*) with no timetable information, so it's best to enquire about timings at one of the bigger bus stations before heading out into rural areas.

On inter-city routes you might have a choice between **regular buses**, which stop at innumerable places en route, and **expresses** (*ekspresas*, usually marked on timetables by the letter E), which travel more or less directly to their destination and cost a few litai extra. An express bus from Vilnius to Klaipėda, for example, will cost around 60Lt. Short routes (such as Vilnius to Kaunas, Klaipėda to Nida, and Klaipėda to Palanga) are often operated by minibuses (*mikroautobusas*) – timetable information for these services is usually displayed in bus stations.

At big-city bus stations, you usually buy your **ticket** from ticket windows before boarding the bus. Tickets show the departure time (*laikas*), platform number (*aikštė*) and seat number (*vieta*). It will also probably carry the name of the bus company you're travelling with – useful to know if two companies are running services to the same destination at round about the same time. If you're catching a bus from some intermediate point on the route, it's often impossible to buy tickets in advance – pay the driver or conductor instead. Small items of **luggage** are taken on board; large bags are stowed in the luggage compartment, for which you might have to pay an extra 3–5Lt.

Buses on the major inter-city routes can get busy on summer weekends, so it's well worth **reserving seats** a day or two in advance.

Trains

Services run by **Lithuanian Railways** have been cut back considerably since the fall of communism. Commuter lines running in and out of Vilnius and to Kaunas are still served by frequent trains, but longer routes (Vilnius to Šiauliai, or Vilnius to Klaipėda, for example) only see a couple of departures a day – they're also slower than the much more frequent buses.

Tickets (*bilietas*) have to be bought before you board. Train stations (*geležinkelio stotis*) often have separate windows for long-distance (*priemiestinis*) and suburban (*vietinis*) trains. **Long-distance services** are divided into two categories: passenger (*keleivinis traukinys*) and fast (*greitas*). Both are in fact painfully slow, but the latter at least won't stop at every second village. Most international trains (*tarptautinis*) travel overnight and offer couchette or sleeping-car accommodation.

Printed **timetables** (*tvarkaraštis*) are few and far between, so you'll have to rely on train-station departure boards for information, or consult the Lithuanian railway's website Ⓦwww.litrail.lt. "Departure" is written *išvyksta*, *išvykimas* or *išvykimo laikas*; and "arrival" *atvyksta*, *atvykimas* or *atvykimo laikas*. Trains that operate on working days (ie Mon–Sat) are marked with the words *darbų dienomis*; those running on Sundays and public holidays are marked *švenčių dienomis*. Otherwise, numbers 1–7 are used to denote the days of the week on which a particular service operates (1 is Monday, 2 is Tuesday, and so on), often accompanied by the word *kursuoja* ("it is running") or *nekursuoja* ("it isn't running").

Driving

Driving in Lithuania throws up an assortment of hazards. Besides a number of high-powered Western cars and four-wheel drives, you'll also see some spectacularly decrepit cars on the roads, and in country areas you may have to contend with slow-moving tractors, horses and carts, stray farm animals and the odd drunk wandering onto the road.

The **roads** from Vilnius to Panevėžys, and from Vilnius to Klaipėda via Kaunas, are fairly respectable two-lane highways for much of their length. Most other main roads are in reasonable repair, but many minor roads are little more than dirt tracks.

How much of the road network is passable depends very much on the time of year. From April through to November you can go pretty much where you like, but in winter you may well need a four-wheel drive to access country areas. **Snow** is the main problem here; although the main routes are regularly ploughed and only become impassable during the heaviest blizzards, secondary roads are often left with a covering of snow throughout the winter season.

Petrol (*degalinė*) is reasonably cheap by European standards, costing roughly €0.75/£0.50/$0.90 per litre. Though most towns and highways are well provided with 24hr petrol stations, there are few in rural areas – so carry a spare can if you're spending time in the sticks.

The use of **seatbelts** is compulsory, and **headlights** must be switched on at all times. It is against the law to drive after drinking any alcohol – even the tiniest drop. **Speed limits** are 60kph in built-up areas and 90kph on the open road. The limit on two-lane highways is 130kph (April–Sept) and 100kph (Oct–March). The police are extremely vigilant, and will spot-fine you for any transgressions.

Car rental costs around €60–80/£40–55/$75–105 per day from one of the big companies, slightly less from some local firms – bear in mind though that with the latter, insurance coverage may be sketchy and the cars may not be well maintained. Addresses of major car rental firms are given on p.36.

Accommodation

There's a growing range and diversity of accommodation in Lithuania, especially at the top end of the scale, with new, business-oriented hotels opening up and international franchises moving in; in addition, many old, state-run establishments are being privatized and refurbished. The overall effect of these developments has been to push prices up. That said, however, bargains are still easy to come by – especially if you're staying in hotels and guesthouses on the coast or in the provinces. If you don't mind having a bit less privacy, there's also plenty of inexpensive, good-value accommodation in the form of rooms in private houses and on rural farmstays. At the budget end of the scale, a handful of backpacker-oriented hostels exist in Vilnius, though they're few and far between in the rest of the country. Most campsites tend to be rather basic, but on the plus side, are usually set in idyllic rural surroundings.

Hotels

There's a good variety of hotel accommodation in Lithuania, although standards of service and value for money vary widely from place to place. Most hotels have been graded according to the international five-star system, although ratings tend to be on the optimistic side and may not be an accurate indication of quality.

Many towns and cities still retain one or two **budget hotels** dating from the Soviet period, offering dowdy but perfectly habitable rooms with shared bathrooms – often for under 100Lt for a double room (breakfast not included). However, there's a natural tendency to modernize and upgrade these establishments (or simply sell them off and put them to some other use), so these bargain deals may be disappearing soon.

Accommodation price codes

The hotels and guesthouses listed in the Lithuanian chapters of this guide have been graded according to the following price bands, based on the cost of the least expensive double room in summer.

❶ Under 90Lt
❷ 90–120Lt
❸ 120–160Lt
❹ 160–220Lt

❺ 220–300Lt
❻ 300–400Lt
❼ 400–600Lt
❽ Over 600Lt

You'll find plenty of competitively priced **mid-range hotels** offering en-suite showers, TV and breakfast – establishments that would fit comfortably into the international two- and three-star brackets. Prices and quality vary considerably in this category: the majority are of post-1991 vintage, often occupying renovated town houses and featuring new furniture. Expect to pay 250–300Lt for a mid-range double in Vilnius, slightly less in Kaunas. Elsewhere, doubles are more likely to fall somewhere in the 150–200Lt range.

International business-class hotels are sprouting up all over Vilnius and are increasingly common in other cities as well. For 400–500Lt you'll get a standard range of familiar comforts: satellite TV, air conditioning, minibar and a lavish buffet breakfast.

Private rooms

Private rooms (*kambariai*) with local families are available in Vilnius, Kaunas, Klaipėda and Palanga, and in the resorts of the Curonian Spit. Conditions vary significantly from place to place: some hosts have refurbished their flats and installed new furniture with guests in mind; others will plonk you in a bedroom recently vacated by their grown-up offspring. In most cases you'll be sharing your host's bathroom and whether or not you'll be allowed access to tea/coffee-making facilities is a matter of pot luck. Staying in private rooms doesn't necessarily constitute a great way of meeting the locals: some hosts will brew you a welcome glass of tea and show a willingness to talk; others will simply give you a set of house keys and leave you to get on with it.

Local tourist offices can sometimes help you secure a room, but the only nationwide booking agency is **Litinterp**, with offices in Vilnius,

Kaunas and Klaipėda (the latter also deals with Palanga and Nida) – see the relevant sections of the guide for contact details. Rooms arranged through Litinterp cost 70–90Lt per person and an additional 10–15Lt gets you breakfast. Cheaper rooms are available in Palanga and Nida if you're prepared to tramp the streets looking for vacancies – signs advertising *kambarių nuoma* ("rooms for rent") and *laisvos vietos* ("vacancies") are posted outside individual houses.

Rural homestays

In an attempt to stimulate the provincial economy, authorities are encouraging the development of **rural homestays** (*poilsis kaime*), where you have the chance to stay on working farms or in village houses and eat locally produced food and drink.

Room quality varies from place to place, although most are neat little en suites, often with a rustic feel. Some hosts offer self-contained apartments with catering facilities.

Prices start from as little as 50Lt per person, rising to about 100Lt if the property has been swankily modernized. Half- or full-board featuring tasty, home-cooked food is often available for an extra cost (20–30Lt per person). While offering a wonderful taste of rural life, bear in mind that most of these homestays are a long way from regular bus routes – so you'll really need your own transport to get around.

Local tourist offices are extremely keen to push this form of tourism and will always help you secure a room in their region, although it pays to contact them a few days in advance. The **Lithuanian Rural Tourism Association** (Lietuvos kaimo turizmo asociacija; Lietuvos respublikos žemės ūkio rūmai, Donelaičio 2, LT-3000 Kaunas, ☎37/400

354, ⓦ www.atostogos.lt) publishes a cata-
logue of properties throughout the country
and also handles advance reservations.

Hostels and camping

Backpacker-oriented hostels can be found in
Vilnius and Klaipėda, offering dorm accommodation for as little as 40Lt a night, although
they're oversubscribed in summer, so it's a
good idea to reserve in advance. Vilnius also
has a couple of students' and teachers' hostels that rent out rooms throughout the year
when there's space – expect to pay around
40Lt for a bed in a double or triple room.

The Lithuanian Youth Hostelling Association's website, ⓦ www.lithuanianhostels.org,
provides contact details for individual hostels
in Vilnius, Šiauliai, Klaipėda and Zverynos (in
the Dzūkija National Park).

Lithuania can boast a handful of well-
appointed **campsites** (*kempingas*) with toilet
blocks, washing facilities and electric power
points for caravans, the main locations
being Trakai, Druskininkai and Nida. Expect
to pay 10Lt per pitch, 10Lt per person and
10Lt per vehicle in these places. Elsewhere
in the country, camping can be a wonderfully idyllic experience if you're prepared to
rough it; in many cases campsites are nothing more than grassy areas supplied with
picnic benches and (if you're lucky) simple
outhouse toilets, which will probably just be
a hole in the ground. National park areas are
particularly well supplied with these sites,
charging as little as 5Lt for a tent space.

Food and drink

Lithuanian cuisine is based around a traditional repertoire of hearty peasant dishes,
in which potatoes and pork play the starring roles. **Main meals** tend to be heavy and
calorie-laden – perfect for the long winters.
International and ethnic cuisine is beginning
to appear in the cities, and pizzerias are
popping up almost everywhere. Although
vegetarianism has yet to establish itself, it's
possible to find meat-free options on most
menus – mushroom- or cheese-filled pancakes being the most common.

Lithuanian **restaurants** (*restoranas*)
range from swanky city-centre places, with
starched napkins and pan-European menus,
to unpretentious eateries offering a cheap
range of Lithuanian standards and not much
else – a quick glance through the window
will tell you which market they're aiming for.
Most Lithuanians like to combine eating
and drinking in the same venue. Many cafés
(*kavinė*), for example, are restaurants in all
but name, serving up inexpensive and simple
Lithuanian standards at low prices alongside
the usual coffee and cakes, and most places
that describe themselves as **bars and pubs**
(see "Drinking", p.290) also offer a full menu
of hot food. In addition, there's a growing
number of homely establishments featuring
folksy wooden furnishings and a big choice
of drinks and local specialities at mid-range
prices – these places often go under names
such as *užeiga* ("inn") or *smuklė* ("tavern"),
underlining the cosy, bucolic theme.

Even in a fairly upmarket restaurant, a meal
shouldn't work out much more expensive
than in a mid-range establishment in Western
Europe, and it's possible to eat really well for
much less if you head for the inns and cafés,
where a main course often costs less than
15Lt. Wherever you eat, though, be prepared
for **slow service**. You'll find a **glossary** of
food and drink terms on p.475.

What to eat

Most Lithuanians tuck straight into a main
course (usually listed under *karšti patiekalai*
or "hot meals"), although menus invariably
include a short list of starters that would also
do as light snacks (*šalti užkandžiai* are cold
starters; *karšti užkandžiai* are hot starters)
– typical choices are marinated mushrooms
(*marinuoti grybai*), herring (*silkė*) and smoked
sausage (*rūkyta dešra*). Soup (*sriuba*) is
sometimes offered as a starter, although
it's more commonly treated as a quick and
cheap lunchtime meal in its own right. Cold
beetroot soup (*šaltibarščiai*) is a Lithuanian
speciality, and can be deliciously refreshing
in summer.

Typical Lithuanian staples

The mainstay of the nation's cuisine is the
potato, which not only serves as the staple accompaniment to most main courses,
but also forms the central ingredient in a
series of typical Lithuanian specialities. Raw

potatoes are passed through the fine end of a grater, mixed with egg and then dropped in hot oil to form *bulviniai blynai* (potato pancakes) – they're delicious on their own, or are sometimes filled with meat. The same grated-potato mixture forms the basis of *cepelinai*, Zeppelin-shaped parcels stuffed with minced meat, mushrooms or cheese and then boiled, while *kugelis* (also known as *bulvių plokštainis* or "potato slab") is a brick-shaped helping of grated or mashed potato baked in the oven. Another favourite is *žemaičių blynai* (*Žemaitija* pancakes) – mashed potato moulded into heart shapes, stuffed with minced meat and then fried. One dish that is definitely tastier than it sounds is *vedarai*: sausage made from pig's intestine and filled with potato pieces.

Common potato-free dishes include *koldūnai* (ravioli-like pasta stuffed with minced pork), *balandeliai* (cabbage leaves stuffed with meat and rice) and all manner of crepe-style pancakes (for which *blynai*, *blyneliai* or *lietiniai* are synonyms for more or less the same thing), containing ham, cheese, mushrooms and other savoury fillings.

All of the above are usually served without accompanying vegetables or bread, but can be enormously filling in their own right – not least because they're invariably garnished with pieces of fried bacon fat, lashings of sour cream (*grietinė*), or a tasty mixture of both.

Meat and fish dishes

Meat (*mėsa*) in Lithuanian restaurants usually comes in the form of *kepsnys*, a chop or cutlet that is either roasted or pan-fried (menus find it difficult to specify which, because the expressions "to fry" and "to roast" are covered by the same verb: *kepti*). A *kepsnys* traditionally consists of a fat slice of pork (*kiauliena*), although cuts of beef (*jautiena*), veal (*veršiena*), chicken (*vištiena*) and turkey (*kalakutiena*) are increasingly common. A *kepsnys* might come garnished with a sauce (*su padažu*), mushroom sauce (*grybų padažas*) being the most common.

Other common meat dishes include **sausages** (*dešrelės*), usually made from spicy, heavily seasoned pork rather than the bland, boiled variety. **Stew** (*troškinys*) may come in the form of a satisfying meat-and-vegetable

meal, but might equally be a thin soup with a few bits of beef floating around in it. **Lamb** (*aviena*) rarely figures on menus, except in recipes borrowed from other republics of the former Soviet Union – notably in the form of *šašlykai* (grilled kebabs) from the Caucasus.

The commonest kinds of **fish** (*žuvi*) are trout (*upėtakis*), pike-perch (*sterkas*), cod (*menkė*) and salmon (*lašiša*); all are usually pan-fried or baked, although salmon steaks are sometimes prepared *ant grotelių* ("grilled"). A speciality of the Nida region is smoked eel (*rukytas unguris*), sliced and eaten cold.

Meat and fish main courses are usually accompanied by (often quite small) portions of potatoes and seasonal **vegetables**, alongside generous amounts of bread.

Desserts and cakes

Typical restaurant desserts include ice cream (*ledai*), cakes (*pyragai*), cottage cheese (*varškė*) with fruit, and innumerable fruit-filled varieties of pancake (*blyneliai* or *lietiniai*). One of the most popular pastries you'll come across in cafés and bakeries are Lithuanian doughnuts (*spurgos*), which look like deep-fried tennis balls and have neither a hole nor jam in the middle – but they're delightfully fluffy when fresh. More spectacular are *šakotis*, a large, honey-coloured cake in the shape of a spiky fir tree; and *skruzdėlynas* (literally "ant-hill"), a pyramid of pastry pieces covered in syrup. These two creations are usually consumed at family feasts and birthday parties and hardly ever appear on café or restaurant menus – though you can always buy a small one from a supermarket or a bakery and scoff it in your room.

Breakfasts and snacks

Unless you're staying in a budget hotel, hostel or private room, **breakfast** will almost always be included in the cost of your accommodation. At its simplest, it will consist of bread, cheese, ham and a choice of tea or coffee. Mid- and top-range hotels will offer a buffet breakfast, complete with a range of cereals, scrambled eggs and bacon. Pastries (*bandelės*) can be picked up from bakeries, cafés and street kiosks.

Basic self-catering and **picnic ingredients** like cheese, vegetables and fruit can be bought at a food store (*maisto prekés*), supermarket (*prekybos centras*) or open-air market (*turgus*). **Bread** (*duona*) can be bought from any of the above places or from a bakery (*kepykla*). Most Lithuanian bread is of the brown, rye-flour variety found across the Baltics. It's often baked in big square blocks, and you're more likely to buy a quarter (*ketvirtas*) or half (*pusé*) than a whole loaf (*kepalas*). White bread is much less common, and is usually produced in French-style, baton form (*batonas*).

Lithuanian **street-food culture** revolves around kiosks (often located near markets or bus stations), selling *čeburekai* or *kibinai* (pies stuffed with spicy minced meat).

Drinking

Cafés (*kaviné*) come in all shapes and sizes: some are trendy and modern in style and have a varied food menu, others are chintzy places serving pastries and cakes. Most serve a full range of alcoholic as well as soft drinks. **Coffee** (*kava*) and **tea** (*arbata*) are usually served black, unless you specify *su grietinele* ("with cream") or *su pienu* ("with milk"). *Su cukrumi* is with sugar, *be cukraus* is without.

City centres and resort areas feature a growing range of lively **bars** – many aping American or Irish models, although there are also plenty of folksy Lithuanian places featuring wooden bench seating and rustic decor.

Beer (*alus*) is the most popular alcoholic drink. The biggest local brewers – Utenos, Švyturys and Kalnapilis – all produce eminently drinkable, light, lager-type beer (*šviesus alus*), as well as a dark porter (*tamsus alus*). It's well worth seeking out the more characterful brews produced by Lithuania's many small regional breweries – Biržų alus, Rinkuškiai and Ponoras (all from the Biržai region) being among the best. It's common to nibble bar-snacks (*užkandžiai prie alaus*) alongside your drinks – *kepta duona* (fingers of brown bread fried with garlic) being the standard order.

An increasingly impressive range of imported **wines** (*vynas*) is available in bars and shops. Alita, the locally produced brand of sparkling, champagne-style wine (*šampanas*) is both extremely palatable and very cheap – a bottle of the stuff costs around €6/£4/$7 in supermarkets.

Vodka (*degtiné*) is widely consumed, alongside more traditional firewaters like Starka, Trejos devynerios and Medžiotojū – invigorating, amber-coloured **spirits** flavoured with a variety of herbs and leaves. Lithuanian mead (*midus*) is particularly potent. Strongest of all the spirits is *samané*, a clear, grain-based spirit which is often brewed illicitly in the countryside and speedily incapacitates the brains of all who drink it; a weaker version is available in shops.

The media

The biggest-selling and most influential of Lithuania's daily **newspapers** is *Lietuvos Rytas* ("Lithuanian Morning"; ⓦ www.lrytas .lt), a self-consciously serious publication famous for stodgy reporting and tortuously long sentences. The lifestyle supplements that come with the weekend editions provide light relief, and Friday's entertainment listings are pretty thorough if you can understand the language. Tabloid-sized *Respublika* is a bright and breezy alternative, while evening paper *Vakaro Žinios* is an entertainingly downmarket scandal rag.

News **magazines** and special-interest periodicals are pretty uninspiring, and it's in the women's market that you'll find most in the way of good design and visual style: avoid the Lithuanian-language versions of well-known international titles like *Cosmopolitan* and take a look instead at home-grown monthlies like *Laima* ("Fortune") and *Moterys* ("Woman") to get an idea of how contemporary Lithuanians really see themselves. Interior-design magazines like *Naujas Namas* and *Namas ir Aš* convey a Scandinavian sense of contemporary cool and may well provide you with a few make-over ideas into the bargain. For details of **English-language publications** common to all three Baltic States, see p.37.

Most hotel-room **televisions** will probably offer a handful of German- and English-language channels in addition to national networks like state-owned LRT and private stations LNK and TV3. All the national TV channels feature a surfeit of quiz programmes and reality shows, and almost all of their drama output is imported from

North or South America. The schedules include lots of English-language films invariably dubbed into Lithuanian, usually with a single actor reading all the parts.

For details of pan-Baltic media in the English language, see p.37.

Festivals

The Lithuanian year is peppered with traditional events and celebrations that mix ancient pagan tradition, Catholic ritual and the simple, pragmatic need for a knees-up. Falling into the last category are the **Sartai horse races** on the first weekend of February, a contest of nineteenth-century origins involving horse-and-trap teams racing each other on the frozen surface of Lake Sartai, 150km north of Vilnius. It's one of the most important social events of the winter, attracting top politicians from Vilnius. If the ice isn't thick enough, the races are moved to the hippodrome in the nearby village of Dusetos.

The promise of approaching spring brings people out onto the streets of Vilnius on the weekend nearest March 4, St Casimir's Day, to take part in **Kaziuko Mugė** (St Casimir's Fair), an enormous handicrafts market at which artisans from all over Lithuania come to display and sell their wares. At around the

Cultural festivals

Vilnius will be **European Capital of Culture** in 2009 (along with Linz in Austria). A packed programme of cultural events and exhibitions will run throughout the year; for more information, see ⓦwww.vilnius2009.lt.

The following festivals take place annually.

Kino Pavasaris Film Festival Vilnius, late March.

Birštonas Jazz Festival Birštonas, last weekend in March (even-numbered years only).

Kaunas Jazz Kaunas, late April.

City Festival Kaunas, third weekend in May.

Skamba Skamba Kankliai Vilnius, late May. *Folk music festival.*

Kunigunda Lunaria Goth Festival Vilnius, late May; ⓦwww.dangus.net. *Music festival (metal and goth) with strong neo-pagan undertones.*

LIFE International Theatre Festival Vilnius, late May to early June.

Klaipėda Jazz Klaipėda, early June.

Vilnius Festival Vilnius, late May to early July. *Classical music festival.*

St Christopher Summer Music Festival Vilnius, July. *Chamber music performed in St Casimir's Church and in Old Town courtyards.*

Experimental Archeology Festival Vilnius and Kernavė, early July. *Enthusiasts in Iron Age dress demonstrate ancient Lithuanian music, dancing and traditional crafts.*

Thomas Mann Festival Nida, second half of July. *Chamber music festival.*

Sea Festival Klaipėda, late July. *Carnival floats, folk dancing and pop music.*

Pažaislis Music Festival Pažaislis and other venues in and around Kaunas, July and August. *Classical music festival.*

Trakai Festival Trakai, August. *Orchestral music and opera.*

Mėnuo Juodaragis Late August. ⓦwww.dangus.net. *Weekend-long neo-pagan festival of folk, metal and electronica, held in a different countryside location each year.*

Sirens Theatre Festival Vilnius, late Sept–early Oct. ⓦwww.sirenos.lt. *New work from big-name directors from Lithuania and Europe.*

Modern Dance Festival Kaunas, early October.

Gaida Festival of Contemporary Classical Music Vilnius, October.

Vilnius Jazz Festival Vilnius, October.

Autumn Poetry Festival Druskininkai, October.

same time, **Užgavėnės** (Shrove Tuesday) marks the beginning of the Lenten fast – as in the rest of Europe, it's celebrated by the over-consumption of pancakes. However, Užgavėnės in Lithuania bears characteristics that are clearly pre-Christian in origin – children in animal masks pass from house to house bringing good luck for the coming agricultural year (they're given sweets or small gifts in return), and the symbolic ending of winter is marked by burning an effigy of the Morė – an archetypal scapegoat figure – on a bonfire. Užgavėnės celebrations are organized in Vilnius on Shrove Tuesday, and the Museum of Lithuanian Life at Rumšiškės (see p.375) also organizes a full day of Užgavėnės-related events, but these usually fall on the nearest Sunday rather than on the Tuesday itself.

Most Lithuanians mark the coming of spring by purchasing a sprig of catkins (*kačiukai*) with which to decorate the home. This practice is closely related to **Verbų sekmadienis** (Palm Sunday), when *verbos* (colourful wands bound from dried grasses, corn stalks and flowers) are bought from street vendors – they're usually on sale from St Casimir's Day onwards – and are proudly displayed in the home for the remainder of the year. *Verbos* would make the perfect Lithuanian souvenir were it not for the fact that the dried flowers disintegrate as soon as you put them in your luggage. **Velykos** (Easter Day) is marked with a large family meal – usually ham accompanied by a sharp-tasting purée made from horseradish (*krienas*).

The biggest event of the year for many is the night of June 23–24, which in origin is a pagan summer solstice celebration, despite being known by its Christian name of **Joninės** – after St John's Day, June 24. The festival is also known in some quarters as Rasos ("Dew") on account of the magical healing properties attached to the dew collected at sunrise on June 24. Most people celebrate Joninės by heading for the countryside, where they either sing songs around a bonfire until dawn or head off into the woods with a loved one – deities attached to fertility are supposedly particularly powerful on this night.

As in the rest of Catholic Europe, November 1 and 2 (**All Saints'** and **All Souls'** days

respectively) are marked by mass visits to cemeteries to honour the dead. Full of flowers and lit up by innumerable candles, they can be atmospheric places to visit at dusk.

The central event of **Kalėdos** (Christmas) is the Christmas Eve meal (*kučios*), when the whole family gathers to eat twelve courses (symbolizing the twelve apostles), none of which should contain meat or dairy products – pies stuffed with mushrooms, and top-quality fish (notably carp) feature heavily. Also gracing the Christmas table are *kučiukai*, tiny, hard biscuits which are sold in shops in the weeks before Christmas, and dipped into poppy-seed milk before eating.

Sport

The country's most popular spectator sport by far is **basketball** (*krepšinis*). Lithuania has been a basketball superpower ever since the 1930s, when the national team won the first-ever European championships in Rīga in 1937, and retained the title on their home turf two years later. During the communist period, Lithuania's leading club team, Žalgiris Kaunas, was a major force in the Soviet league and served as an important symbol of national pride at a time when outright manifestations of Lithuanian patriotism were officially discouraged. With the restoration of independence in 1991, Lithuania bounced back onto the international basketball scene, winning the Olympic bronze in 1992, 1996 and 2000. Victory in the European championships in Sweden in 2003 confirmed Lithuania's international standing.

In domestic competition, Žalgiris Kaunas remains the top side, although Lietuvos Rytas Vilnius has offered stiff competition in recent years – matches between the two can be intensely heated affairs. The season runs from October through to April, with a regular diet of Lithuanian league matches (on Saturdays or Sundays) augmented by midweek games featuring Lithuanian representatives in one of two international leagues – the Euroleague, which is the continent's premier club competition, and the North European Basketball League (NEBL), which features teams from the Ukraine to the UK.

No other team sports can compete with basketball in terms of popularity. Lithuanian **football** (*futbolas*) is in a comparatively sorry state, with top-league matches frequently attracting crowds of under a hundred and most fans contenting themselves instead with TV broadcasts of top European games.

Of the individual **sporting heroes** to have made an impact on Lithuanian society, most prominent is discus-thrower Virgilijus Alėkna, gold-medal winner in both the 2000 and 2004 Olympics.

Entertainment and the arts

Lithuania offers a broad spectrum of entertainment, including a lot of serious music and drama. It's all very accessible too: tickets for even the most prestigious events are rarely impossible to come by, and prices are cheap by European standards. Almost every branch of culture is marked by at least one major festival – see the "Cultural festivals" box on p.291 and the "Nightlife and entertainment" section of the Vilnius chapter (see p.337) for a thorough run-down.

Classical music and opera

Between them, Vilnius and Kaunas ensure a rich programme of music year-round. Vilnius boasts two symphony orchestras, an opera and a ballet company, while Kaunas has a chamber orchestra and highly rated choir. The capital attracts a large number of top international conductors and soloists during the regular concert season, while the **Vilnius Festival** in June and **Trakai Festival** in August bring the top performers out into the open air.

The one "national" composer who features regularly in the repertoire is **Mikalojus Konstantinis Čiurlionis** (1875–1911), whose tone poems *Jūra* ("The Sea") and *Miške* ("In the Forest") were the first full-length symphonic pieces to be composed by a Lithuanian and the first to attempt a symbolic evocation of the country's unspoiled landscapes.

Less regularly performed, but creating big waves internationally, are works by an impressive stable of **contemporary composers** led by Bronius Kutavičius, Mindaugas Urbaitis and Ona Narbutienė, who mix the mystical sounds of Lithuanian folklore with minimalism and contemporary instrumentation. The **Gaida Festival of Contemporary Classical Music** (see p.338) is one occasion when you can bank on hearing a wide selection of their music. Ⓦ www.mic.lt is a site devoted to Lithuanian contemporary composers, with biogs, scores and downloads.

Pop music and clubbing

Lithuanians love dancing and are much less self-conscious about what they strut their stuff to than their modish north European counterparts. Mainstream **discos** are hugely enjoyable affairs featuring everything from Eminem to Boney-M – but you're unlikely to chance upon niche dance music outside a handful of specialist clubs in Vilnius.

Plenty of bars host **live bands** who play rock-pop covers in order to keep people moving and grooving, but there's little in the way of a serious gig circuit, and many local groups restrict themselves to ad hoc performances in unofficial spaces. Unsurprisingly then, there's little in the way of a local rock scene (and any scene that does exist will be so far underground that you probably won't find it), although several semi-legendary names still mean a great deal to local fans. In the late 1980s and early 1990s, the angular, experimental band **Bix** seemed to personify Lithuania's break-out from the Soviet cultural straightjacket – their CDs are still available even though the band no longer performs. At around the same time, **Fojė** imported a stylish new-wave sensibility to Lithuanian pop – since going solo, its lead singer **Andrijus Mamantovas** has proved to be the country's most enduring rock-pop performer.

Jazz

A handful of venues stage regular **jazz** gigs in Vilnius and Klaipėda, and there are worthwhile festivals involving international guests in Vilnius, Birštonas and Kaunas (see p.291). In the 1970s and 80s, Vilnius was home to the **Ganelin-Chekasin-Tarasov Trio**, the greatest – and perhaps the only – avant-garde jazz ensemble in the Soviet Union, still enjoying legendary status. Keyboardist Ganelin emigrated years ago, but saxophone-bellower **Vladimir Chekasin** and drummer **Vladimir Tarasov** are still around, working on a variety of (no longer connected) musical projects. Other contemporary performers to look out for are sax-player **Petras Vyšniauskas**, a pioneer in the field of jazz–folk crossover, and younger-generation vocalist **Neda**, a far more stirring live performer than her bland MOR albums would suggest.

Drama

The Lithuanian capital is currently home to some of the most critically acclaimed directors in Europe – their works are regularly staged in Vilnius and if you're at all interested in theatre it's well worth making the effort to find out what's on in the city during your stay. English-language earphone commentary is sometimes provided in the bigger theatres, although there's usually enough happening on stage to make a visit worthwhile whether there's a translation or not.

Godfather of the Vilnius drama scene is **Eimuntas Nekrošius**, who spent most of the 1980s as director of the Vilnius Youth Theatre (see p.339) and now heads a production company of his own, Meno Fortas ("Art Fortress"). His lengthy performances (4–5 hours being typical) feature minimal stage props and repetitive, ritualistic movement.

A generation younger, **Oskaras Koršunovas** is something of an antidote to this, combining an experimental approach (strongly influenced by Russian avantgardists Daniil Kharms and Aleksandar Vvedensky) with a thoroughly contemporary taste for bright lights, big noises and visual jokes – he's probably one of the few directors who could stage a version of Oedipus Rex in which the inclusion of a giant talking teddy bear fails to detract from the tragic sense of the original. Koršunovas has turned his hand to everything from intense studio performances to musicals, and has latterly become something of a one-man national industry, with numerous productions on the go at any one time.

One other name worth looking out for is **Rimas Tuminas**, founder of Vilnius Little Theatre (see p.339); his understated but innovative productions of contemporary pieces and Shakespearean classics have earned him Europe-wide critical acclaim.

Cinema

Lithuanian cinemas show **English-language films** soon after their release in Western Europe – in the original language with Lithuanian subtitles. During the Soviet period, Lithuania's film studios churned out a respectable handful of local-language movies a year, and their facilities are currently very much in demand with Western production companies seeking to employ skilled technicians on the cheap; domestic film production, meanwhile, has shrivelled to nothing.

One hugely popular Lithuanian cinema classic which you'll see in video stores – and might be tempted to buy if you have a taste for the bizarre – is Arūnas Žebriūnas's 1973 film *Velnio Nuotaka* ("Devil's Bride"), a lavish musical based on Lithuanian folk tales and featuring the cream of theatrical and artistic talent of the time. Featuring an overblown screenplay by poet Sigitas Geda (see "Books", p.460) and a prog-rock-meets-Europap score courtesy of keyboard-bashing groovster Vyacheslav Ganelin (see "Jazz", p.293), it's a one-of-its-kind experience.

Culture and etiquette

Smoking is forbidden in public places, including all bars, restaurants and clubs. An increasing number of small and medium-sized hotels are strictly non-smoking throughout, although some larger establishments may still allow nicotine addicts to puff away in the privacy of their rooms.

Public **toilets** (*tualetas*) are rare outside bus and train stations (where a small fee, normally no more than 1Lt, is charged), although almost every café, restaurant and bar will have one. Gents are marked with a letter V or a ▼ symbol; ladies with an M or an ▲ symbol.

Tipping is not always expected in Lithuania, especially if you've only had a cup of coffee or a snack. After a round of drinks or a full meal, however, it's polite to leave roughly ten percent or to round up the bill to a convenient figure.

Travel essentials

Costs

Most of life's **essentials** – including food, drink and travel – are relatively cheap in Lithuania, and even if you're on a strict budget you shouldn't have too much trouble enjoying yourself here. The only real exception is the price of **accommodation**, which is slowly creeping up towards Western European levels. Prices vary considerably, though, depending on which parts of Lithuania you stay in. In Vilnius and Klaipėda, a bed in a hostel will cost €15/£10/$19, while private rooms and the cheapest hotels work out at around €40/£28/$53 for a double, with the price of the same in a comfortable, medium-range hotel rising to €90/£60/$115. Out in the provinces you won't find much in the way of hostels or private rooms, but you can stay in a cheap hotel for as little as €24/£16.50/$25 per double room.

Once you've got accommodation out of the way, things are reasonably inexpensive: short journeys by **bus** are unlikely to make a serious dent in your budget: travelling from Vilnius to Trakai will cost you just over €1/£0.70/$1.30, while a ticket from Vilnius to Kaunas weighs in at around €5/£3.50/$6.60. Moving across country from Vilnius to Klaipėda costs in the region of €17/£12/$23.

About €15/£10/$19 per person per day will suffice for **food and drink** if you're shopping in markets for picnic ingredients, maybe allowing yourself a meal out in a cheap café or restaurant and limiting yourself to a couple of drinks; €30/£20/$38 a day should be enough for a sit-down lunch and a decent dinner followed by a couple of night-time drinks.

Lithuania's unit of currency is the **litas** (usually abbreviated to Lt), which is divided into 100 **centai**. Coins come in denominations of 0.01, 0.02, 0.05, 0.10, 0.20, 0.50, 1, 2 and 5Lt and bank notes in 1, 10, 20, 50, 100 and 200Lt denominations.

Currently the exchange rate is 5Lt to the pound sterling, 3.45Lt to the euro and 2.60Lt

to the dollar, and looks set to remain reasonably stable.

Internet

There's a good choice of **Internet cafés** in Vilnius, Kaunas and Klaipėda, but they're still pretty rare elsewhere; expect to pay around 5–6Lt for an hour of surfing time. Wireless Internet coverage is widespread in Vilnius's hotels, restaurants and cafés, and is increasingly common in other cities too.

Laundry

Dry-cleaners (*cheminis valymas*) are reasonably common, but self-service launderettes are almost non-existent in Lithuania – you may have to resort to washing your smalls in the hotel sink.

Left luggage

Most train and bus stations have a left-luggage office (*bagažinė*). The daily charge per item deposited is rarely more than 3–4Lt.

Mail

Lithuanian postal and telephone services are generally well organized and easy to use. In major towns, **post offices** (*paštas*) are usually open Monday to Friday 8am to 6/7pm, Saturday 8am to 3pm; in smaller places hours are more restricted. Larger post offices often have a confusing array of counters: if you just want to buy a stamp, head for the counter marked *laiškai* ("letters"). Airmail takes about four days to reach Britain, eight to reach North America; surface mail takes twice as long.

Money

The main high-street **banks** (*bankas*) are Vilniaus bankas, Lietuvos taupomasis bankas, Lietuvos žemes ukio bankas, Hansabankas and Snoras bankas – this last, despite operating out of a chain of pre-fabricated blue kiosks, is a perfectly respectable outfit. Branches of all the above can change money, give cash advances on Visa, MasterCard or American Express cards, and cash traveller's cheques (for a commission of 2–3 percent). **Opening hours** vary, with most branches operating Monday to Friday 8am to 5/7pm. Big-city branches may well open on

---

Emergencies

Police ☎02; ambulance ☎03; fire ☎01.

Saturday (typically 8am–3pm or 10am–5pm), and in rare cases for a few hours on Sunday too. **ATM cash dispensers** are scattered liberally throughout central Vilnius, Kaunas and Klaipėda, and you'll find one or two in most other town centres.

If you want to exchange cash outside banking hours, head for an **exchange office** (*valiutos keitykla*), often just a counter in a corner of a high-street department store. They only deal in cash transactions, but they're usually open in the evenings and at weekends.

Credit cards are widely accepted in hotels, restaurants, big shops and petrol stations in Vilnius and other major urban centres. In small towns and villages, you're unlikely to have much luck.

Opening hours and public holidays

Typical **opening times of shops** are Monday to Friday from 10/11am to 6/7pm, and Saturdays from 10/11am to 3/4pm. Food stores and supermarkets in the cities usually keep longer hours, opening as early as 7am and working right through to 8 or 10pm, even at weekends. In rural areas, shops may take a break for lunch and close earlier in the evenings.

The opening times of **museums**, galleries and other tourist attractions vary widely from one place to the next. Generally speaking, they're open from Tuesday to Sunday (in some cases Wed to Sun) from around 11am to 5/6pm – although be warned that some museums work on a Monday-to-Friday basis.

Churches in city centres may well be open seven days a week from 7am until around 7pm, but in most other cases they only open their doors for holy Mass (times of which are posted outside).

Phones

Public telephones use phonecards (*telefono kortelė*; 9Lt, 13Lt, 16Lt and 30Lt) available from post offices and newspaper kiosks – a 9Lt card will suffice for a handful of local calls; a 13Lt card should cover a short international call.

For all local calls from landlines, you just dial the subscriber number. To make a long-distance call within Lithuania, first dial 8, before dialling the area code and phone number. If you're using a mobile phone inside Lithuania, all numbers have to be preceded by 8 and the area code, even if you're in the same city as the recipient. When calling Lithuania from abroad on any phone, the initial 8 is omitted. For international calls from Lithuania, dial 8, wait for the tone, then dial 10, then the country code, area code and subscriber number.

For general information on using **mobile phones** in the Baltic States, see p.44. Lithuania's three **mobile phone operators**, Bitė, Omnitel and Tele2, run schemes that allow you to make calls within the country at local rates and receive calls without the caller incurring international charges. To get on one of these schemes, you need to buy a local SIM card for your GSM phone – this costs as little as 13Lt – after which you can purchase pre-payment top-ups from newspaper kiosks in increments of 10Lt and upwards. Tele2 allows you to go roaming in Latvia and Estonia, too, where your calls will cost only slightly more than the local Lithuanian rate. Starter packs including SIM card and subsequent top-up cards, can be purchased from newspaper kiosks.

Public holidays

Most shops and museums and all banks are closed on the following public holidays:

Jan 1 New Year's Day
Feb 16 Independence Day
March 11 Restoration of Independence Day
Easter Sunday
Easter Monday
May 1 May Day
June 24 Midsummer
July 6 Coronation of King Mindaugas
August 15 Assumption
Nov 1 All Saints' Day
Dec 25 and 26 Christmas

3.1

Vilnius and around

"Narrow cobblestone streets and an orgy of Baroque: almost like a Jesuit city somewhere in the middle of Latin America," wrote the author Czesław Miłosz of pre-war **VILNIUS** – a description that in many ways still holds true. Laid out in a bowl carved by the winding River Neris and surrounded by pine-covered hills, central Vilnius remains largely untainted by the high-rise development that characterizes the post-war suburbs and boasts perhaps the most impressive concentration of Baroque architecture in northern Europe, its skyline of domes and belfries making a lasting impression on visitors to the city. At ground level, the centre is a maze of atmospheric alleyways lined with solid, eighteenth-century town houses, punctuated by archways leading through to cobbled backyards.

Despite the impression of continuity given by its well-preserved architecture, Vilnius's history is as fragmented as any in Eastern Europe. Since the city's emergence as capital of the Lithuanian dukes in the Middle Ages, Russians, Belarussians, Jews and Poles have all left their mark, and Vilnius has been an important cultural centre to each in turn. The city is particularly cherished in Polish hearts: as well as Nobel prize-winner Miłosz, literary figures as diverse as Adam Mickiewicz, Juliusz Słowacki and Tadeusz Konwicki all spent their formative years here. Vilnius is still a cosmopolitan place – around twenty percent of its population is Polish and another twenty percent is Russian – though with just under 600,000 inhabitants it has an almost village-like atmosphere, making it an easy place to get to know.

Vilnius's single most important attraction is the **Old Town**, an ensemble of winding, narrow streets and stately churches. An engaging clutch of museums (including some gripping displays recounting both the Nazi and Soviet occupations) ensure that sightseeing here can easily be spun out to fill several days. Vilnius is also a good base from which to explore much of eastern Lithuania; the medieval fortress at lake-bound **Trakai**, the Iron Age hill-forts of **Kernavė** and the grandly named **Museum of the Centre of Europe**, are easy day-trips from here, and Lithuania's second city **Kaunas** (see Chapter 1.2) can also be reached in a couple of hours.

Some history

The city of Vilnius was born some time in the eleventh century when the sandy hills overlooking the confluence of the Vilija and Neris rivers became key strongholds for Lithuanian chieftains seeking to secure a rapidly expanding tribal state. Mindaugas, the thirteenth-century chieftain who first united the Lithuanian tribes into a centralized state, probably based his court here for a time, although it was his grandson, Gedimi-nas, who made it a permanent power base. Although still a pagan, Gediminas encouraged the settlement of **Christian peoples** – notably German traders from Rīga and Russian-speaking nobles from the east – and many of Vilnius's churches pre-date the Lithuanian state's official acceptance of Christianity in 1386.

After the dynastic union between Lithuania and Poland in 1387, real power shifted towards Kraków (and subsequently Warsaw), where the kings of the new **Polish-Lithuanian state** spent most of their time – although Vilnius remained the capital of the Grand Duchy of Lithuania. However, the nobility of the Grand Duchy increasingly adopted the language and manners of their more sophisticated Polish neighbours, turning Vilnius into a culturally (if not necessarily ethnically) Polish city.

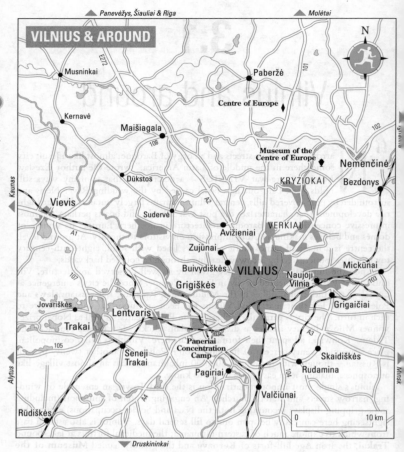

The close relationship with Poland ensured that Vilnius remained in touch with many of the key developments in central European culture. Sigismund August (Grand Duke of Lithuania 1544–72 and King of Poland 1548–72) maintained a magnificent court in the city, encouraging learned minds from the rest of Europe to settle here. In addition, his successor-but-one, Stefan Bathory, presided over the creation of Vilnius University in 1579, and it has been one of the most prestigious seats of learning in northeastern Europe ever since.

When the creation of the **Polish-Lithuanian Commonwealth** in 1569 effectively ended the autonomy of the Grand Duchy, Vilnius lost some of its pre-eminence and increasingly became a peripheral, provincial city. Nevertheless, the Grand Duchy's leading magnates – drawn from powerful families such as the Radvilas, Sapiehas and Pacs – continued to build palaces in Vilnius and fund the building of churches, often in the exuberant Baroque style that soon became the town's architectural trademark.

The incorporation of Vilnius into the **Russian Empire** in 1795 led to an influx of Russians, a renewed wave of Orthodox-church building and the expansion of the city beyond its Old Town boundaries. The key Russian legacy was the construction of Gedimino prospektas, the showpiece boulevard around which the principal administrative and business districts subsequently developed. If anything, Tsarist rule only reinforced Vilnius's role as a centre of Polish patriotism and culture, however, and the university was closed down in 1831 (and remained closed for over eighty years) in order to prevent the nurturing of a seditious anti-Russian elite.

By the end of the **nineteenth century**, Vilnius was an amazingly diverse city, with the Jews making up 40 percent of the population, followed by Poles at 31 percent and Russians at 20 percent; Lithuanians had been reduced to a tiny minority. Notwithstanding their numerically weak position in the city, the Lithuanians still regarded Vilnius as their historical capital, and accordingly based most of their social and cultural institutions here. The opportunity for the Lithuanians to flex their political muscle came with the withdrawal of the Russian authorities in **World War I**. Vilnius's new German masters encouraged Lithuanian sentiment as a counterbalance to the other nations competing for the city, and on February 16, 1918, community leaders declared Lithuania's **independence** from a second-floor flat on Pilies gatvė in the Old Town. World War I was followed by two years of confused three-way fighting, with Lithuanian and Polish armies fighting both against each other and the Bolsheviks, who were advancing into Central Europe in an attempt to export the Russian Revolution. In 1920, the Polish leader Marshal Piłsudski – himself a native of the countryside outside Vilnius – encouraged the maverick General Lucjan Ǽeligowski to seize the city once and for all.

World War II saw Vilnius occupied by the Soviets, the Germans and then the Soviets again; the Polish resistance played a major part in the liberation of Vilnius from the Germans, only to see their leaders arrested by the victorious Red Army and deported to Siberia.

With Vilnius becoming the capital of the Soviet Republic of Lithuania after 1945, the majority of Vilnius's Poles left for Poland, although in many cases their place was taken by immigrant Polish-speakers from the surrounding villages – with the paradoxical result that the Polish population of Vilnius today is just as numerous as it was in 1939.

Despite the straitjacket of Soviet rule, Vilnius soon became the focus of Lithuanian political and cultural activity, and it was inevitable that the struggle for **independence from the Soviet Union** was concentrated here at the close of the 1980s. The attempt by Soviet forces to gain control of strategic buildings in the city on January 13, 1991, was met by mass unarmed resistance from Vilnius's citizens – twelve of them died under the wheels of Soviet tanks in an attempt to defend the TV Tower (see p.443), provoking a flood of international sympathy and paving the way for full Lithuanian independence.

While many of the outlying high-rise suburbs still bear the imprint of post-Soviet decay, parts of the city centre can easily bear comparison with some of the more prosperous central European capitals. Filled with banks and snazzy shops, and spruced up by a succession of ambitious mayors, the heart of old Vilnius is now an island of wealth in a country which, taken as a whole, is still to reap the benefits of post-communist change.

Arrival, information and city transport

Vilnius **airport** (Oro Uostas) is around 5km south of the city centre on Rodūnios kelias and is connected by regular buses. From outside the main entrance, bus #2 runs a couple of times an hour to Lukiškių aikštė, handy for the downtown area around Gedimino prospektas, while bus #1 (roughly hourly) will take you to the train and bus station area, from where you can walk into the Old Town. Both journeys take approximately 25 minutes and **tickets** cost 1.40Lt from the driver. **Taxis** should cost no more than 30–40Lt for the journey to the Old Town, though some will try to get away with charging more.

The main **train station** (Geležinkelio stotis) is just south of the Old Town, and the main **bus station** (Autobusų stotis) is just across the road. You could walk into the Old Town from here or catch trolleybus #2 from the square in front of the train station to Katedros aikštė, the main square. Station-based taxi drivers don't like picking up short-distance fares and may overcharge as a result.

Information

Branches of the municipal **tourist office** can be found at the train station (Mon–Fri 9am–6pm, Sat & Sun 10am–4pm), the Town Hall on Rotušės aikštė (May–Sept daily 10am–6pm; Oct–April Mon–Fri 10am–6pm; ☎8-5/262 6470), and at Vilniaus 22 (May–Sept Mon–Fri 9am–7pm, Sat noon–6pm; Oct–April Mon–Fri 9am–6pm; ☎8-5/262 9660, ⊛www.vilnius-tourism.lt). All offer information on hotels and museums, sell maps, guidebooks and concert tickets, and can make accommodation bookings for a 6Lt fee. It's also worth buying a copy of the *Vilnius in Your Pocket* city guide (5Lt from newspaper kiosks and bookshops; ⊛www.inyourpocket.com), which provides entertaining and insightful restaurant and bar listings, as well as addresses of all kinds of useful services.

The best **maps** of Vilnius (sold in the tourist offices and bigger bookstores) are produced by the Rīga-based cartographers Jāņa Sēta; their 1:25 000 plan includes public transport routes and a street index, and is available either as a foldout map or a spiral-bound street atlas. Local firm Briedis's 1:18 000 foldout map of the city is also pretty serviceable.

City transport

Central Vilnius is easily explored on foot, while the more far-flung sights can be reached by **bus** or trolleybus. **Tickets**, costing a flat fare of 1.10Lt, are best bought in advance from newspaper kiosks (*kioskas*), or you can get them from the driver for 1.40Lt. Validate your ticket by punching it in the machine on board. Ticketless travellers face a spot-fine if caught by an inspector. Some routes are also served by minibuses (*maršrutinis taxi*), which halt at the same stops as buses, but tend to be faster; there's a fare of 2–3Lt (depending on distance travelled), and you pay the driver.

Taxi prices are very reasonable, providing you stick to companies using newer cars and functioning meters (see "Listings" on p.342 for reputable taxi firms), and fares should cost no more than around 1.50–2Lt per kilometre in the daytime, double that at night.

Moving on from Vilnius

There are several **bus** departures a day from Vilnius to Rīga, Tallinn, Warsaw, Minsk and Kaliningrad, as well as a fair number of buses to Western Europe, including direct services to Berlin, London, Paris and Amsterdam. Numerous other destinations can be reached by changing in Warsaw – tickets covering the whole journey can be purchased in Vilnius from either the Eurolines or Toks counters in the bus station. See Travel details on p.347 for frequency of departures and journey times.

There's less in the way of international **trains**, and services are usually slower than buses. There are daily trains to Warsaw, Kaliningrad, Minsk, Moscow and St Petersburg; the latter two destinations both entail an overnight journey.

Accommodation

Vilnius is reasonably well served with **hotels**, although budget choices are relatively thin on the ground and should be booked well in advance, especially in summer. Other inexpensive options include an increasing number of **hostels** and **bed-and-breakfast** accommodation with local families – the cheapest way of staying in or close to the Old Town. The best bed-and-breakfast agency is Litinterp, Bernardinų 7-2 (Mon–Fri 8.30am–5pm, Sat 9am–3pm; ☎8-5/212 3850, ⓦwww.litinterp.lt), which charges from 80Lt for a single room, 140Lt for a double, and also has its own guesthouse (see p.304 under "Hotels"). The three Vilnius tourist offices (see "Information", opposite) also have lists of local families offering homestays at similar prices.

There is a summer-only **campsite** 3km west of the city centre, in the grounds of the Litexpo exhibition centre at Laisvės prospektas 5 (June to mid-Sept; ☎8-680 32 452, ⓦwww.camping.lt/vilniuscity). To get there catch trolleybus #16 from the train and bus stations and get off at the Parodų rumai stop. The nearest all-year campsite is the lakeside *Kempingas Slėnyje*, near Trakai (see p.343), 25km southwest of Vilnius – you'll need your own transport to get there.

Hotels

There are plenty of moderate-to-expensive hotels in Vilnius, with new ones opening up all the time. Many are modern, business-oriented affairs, but there's also a good choice of characterful, cosy establishments occupying stylishly restored old buildings. A number of budget and mid-range hotels are concentrated **near the train and bus stations**, a generally safe area despite grubby appearances and within easy walking distance of the sights. There's an increasingly good range of places immediately west of the Old Town around **Gedimino prospektas**, the city's main commercial boulevard, and in the **Naujamiestis**, the nineteenth-century residential area on the high ground above it. Another concentration of moderately priced hotels can be found **north of the River Neris**, a rapidly developing area of office blocks and shopping centres, still within walking distance of the centre. All hotels reviewed below include **breakfast** in the price unless otherwise stated.

Near the train and bus stations

City Gate Bazilijonū 3 ☎8-5/210 7306, ⓦwww.citygate.lt. A newish place in a peaceful, courtyard location, offering simply furnished but comfortable rooms with pristine bathrooms. The cosy top-floor doubles come with sloping attic ceilings. Staff are attentive and the breakfast is substantial. ⑥

Comfort Gelių 5 ☎8-5/264 8833, ⓦwww.comfort.lt. Halfway between the stations and the Old Town, the *Comfort* offers a minimum of frills. Decorated in inoffensive ochres, greens and reds, the standard rooms aren't exactly huge but you do get a desk, a TV and a simple bathroom. Fourth-floor deluxe rooms are more spacious, have bigger TVs and come with attic ceilings and skylight windows. Standard ⑤, deluxe ⑥

Mikotel Pylimo 63 ☎8-5/260 9626, ⓦwww.mikotel.lt. A medium-sized budget hotel situated at the downmarket, bus-station end of Pylimo, but within easy strolling distance of the Old Town. Rooms are simple and neat with TV, WC and shower, and quirky paintings in the common areas help to cheer the place up. ⑤

Panorama Sodų 14 ☎8-5/273 8011, ⓦwww.hotelpanorama.lt. Directly opposite the train and bus stations, the *Panorama* (formerly the *Gintaras*) was a notoriously grotty place until recent renovations started to get rid of the Soviet-era decor. The en-suite rooms still have a few rough edges but the furnishings are for the most part new, and the ground-floor breakfast room and bar area is invitingly chic. Rooms on the north side have great views of the Old Town – ask for one on the top floor to enjoy the *Panorama* experience in full. ⑤

The Old Town

🏃 **Apia** Šv. Ignoto 12 ☎8-5/212 3426, ⓦwww.apia.lt. Cosy and intimate place in the heart of the Old Town offering eleven differently furnished but equally charming rooms. Most come with hardwood floors and pastel colour schemes; rooms on the top floor have the added cuteness of sloping ceilings and skylight windows. Breakfast is in the *Briusly* café next door. ⑥

Bernardinu Guest House Bernardinų 5 ☎8-5/260 8410, ⓦwww.avevita.lt/guesthouse. Converted town house on a quiet Old Town street

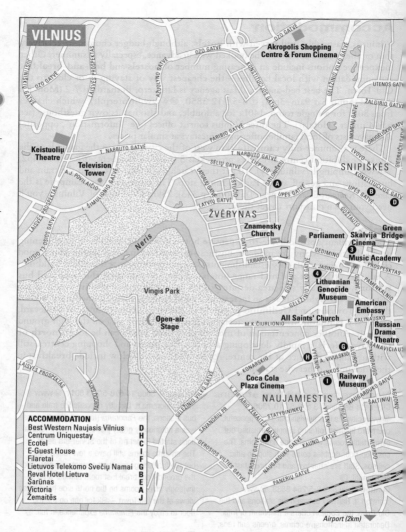

VILNIUS

Akropolis Shopping
Centre & Forum Cinema

OZO GATVĖ

OZO GATVĖ

UTENOS GATV

ŽALGIRIO GATVĖ

KONSTITUCIJOS GATVĖ

GELEŽINIO VILKO GATVĖ

LINKMENŲ GATVĖ

DAUGĖLIŠKIO GATVĖ

LVOVO

LAISVĖS PROSPEKTAS

OZO GATVĖ

AŽUOLYNO GATVĖ

DŪŠILENUSIS

SNIPIŠKĖS

Keistuolių
Theatre

Television
Tower

T. NARBUTO GATVĖ

T. NARBUTO GATVĖ

SĖLIŲ GATVĖ

TIĖPYNO G.

SATONISKIU

A.J. POVILAIČIO

ŠIMULIONIO GATVĖ

LAISVĖS PROSPEKTAS

LATVIŲ GATVĖ

LARBAUGATVE

KĘSTUČIO

UPĖS GATVĖ

A

UPĖS GATVĖ

B

KONSTITUCIJOS GATV

D

A. GOŠTAUTO

ŽVĖRYNAS

PARIBIO GATVĖ

Znamensky
Church

Parliament

Skalvija
Cinema

Green
Bridge

Neris

GEDIMINO

LIUBARTO G.

Music Academy

PROSPESKTAS

SAUSIO 13-OSIOS GATVĖ

J. JASINSKIO

PAMENKALNIO

GELEŽINIO VILKO GATVĖ

A. GOŠTAUTO

Lithuanian
Genocide
Museum

American
Embassy

Vingis Park

Open-air
Stage

All Saints' Church

M.K. ČIURLIONIO

K. KALINAUSKO

Russian
Drama
Theatre

J. BASANAVIČIAUS

LAISVĖS PROSPEKTAS

A. VIVULSKIO

VYTENIO

G

H

ALGIRDO

PARODŲ GATVĖ

S. KONARSKIO

T. ŠEVČENKOS

Railway
Museum

Coca Cola
Plaza Cinema

GELEŽINIO VILKO GATVĖ

V. PIETARIO ŽEMAITĖS GATVĖ

I

NAUGARDUKO GATVĖ

MINDAUGO

NAUJAMIESTIS

STATYBININKŲ

VYTENIO

ŠVITRIGAILOS GATVĖ

AGUONŲ

ALGIRDO

SAVANORIŲ PR.

GEROSIOS VILTIES GATVĖ

SKROBLŲ GATVĖ

J

KAUNO GATVĖ

NAUGARDUKO GATVĖ

PANERIŲ GATVĖ

SALTINIU

Airport (2km) ▼

ACCOMMODATION

Best Western Naujasis Vilnius	D
Centrum Uniquestay	H
Ecotel	C
E-Guest House	I
Filaretai	F
Lietuvos Telekomo Svečių Namai	G
Reval Hotel Lietuva	B
Šarūnas	E
Victoria	A
Žemaitės	J

offering a range of rooms, most of which come with en-suite facilities, TV, hardwood floors and snazzy fabrics. A couple of rooms with foldout sofa beds can be adapted to sleep 3 or 4. Continental breakfast is available for a few extra litas. En suites ④, doubles with shared WC/shower ③

Domus Maria Aušros vartų 12 ☎8-5/264 4880, Ⓦwww.domusmaria.lt. Friendly hotel occupying one large wing of the Vilnius Archbishopric, and offering roomy en suites complete with TV and smart, Scandinavian-style

furnishings. There are some good-value triples and quads too. Long, high-ceilinged corridors and views of the Archbishopric courtyard add to the atmosphere. ⑤

Europa Royale Vilnius Aušros vartų 6 ☎8-5/266 0770, Ⓦwww.europaroyale.com. A medium-sized hotel in an attractive building. En-suite doubles come equipped with TV and desk, and some boast small, street-facing balconies. The top-floor suites, with barrel-vaulted ceilings and lunette windows, ooze with character. For something out of the

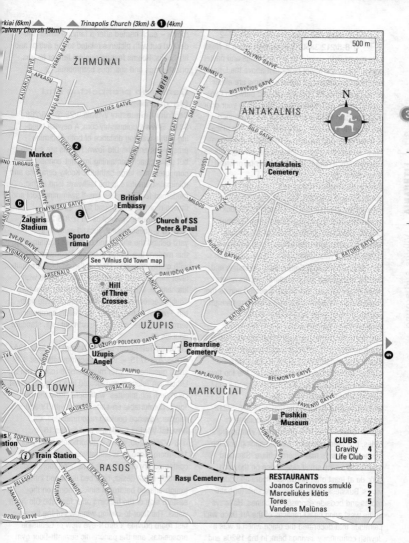

Trinapolis Church (3km) & ❶ (4km)

ŽIRMŪNAI

ANTAKALNIS

Antakalnis
Cemetery

Market

British
Embassy

Church of SS
Peter & Paul

Žalgiris
Stadium

Sporto
rūmai

See 'Vilnius Old Town' map

Hill
of Three
Crosses

UŽUPIS

Bernardine
Cemetery

Užupis
Angel

OLD TOWN

MARKUČIAI

Pushkin
Museum

Train Station

RASOS

Rasų Cemetery

CLUBS
Gravity 4
Life Club 3

RESTAURANTS
Joanos Carinovos smuklė 6
Marceliukės klėtis 2
Tores 5
Vandens Malūnas 1

ordinary look no further than cylinder-shaped room no. 401, which has a round bed and panoramic, floor-to-ceiling windows. Standard doubles ⑥, suites ⑧

Grotthuss Ligoninės 7 ☏8-5/266 0322, ⓦwww.grotthusshotel.com. Intimate and luxurious hotel in an attractively restored town house, featuring stuccoed ceilings, rich fabrics and dark-wood furniture. Contemporary Lithuanian artwork adds a touch of class to the hallways, and excellent international food can be had in the hotel's *La Pergola*

restaurant. Standard doubles ⑦, business-class doubles ⑧

Grybas House Aušros Vartų 3a ☏8-5/261 9695, ⓦwww.grybashouse.com. A congenial, family-run place occupying an attractive old house in the heart of the Old Town. Rooms are decked out in soothing colours, each featuring TV, Wi-Fi and well-equipped bathroom. The breakfast room in the cellar has plenty in the way of quirky interior-design details. Only ten rooms and four suites, so reservations essential. Standard doubles ⑥, suites ⑧

Litinterp Guest House Bernardinų 7–2
☎8-5/212 3850, ✉vilnius@litinterp.lt. Neat
little rooms with simple, pine furnishings and pastel
decor, in the apartment block just above the Litinterp bed-and-breakfast agency. Rooms are either
en suite or have WC/shower (shared between two
rooms) in the hall. Breakfast is brought to your door
on a tray, and fridges and kettles are positioned
strategically between every few rooms. The place
is deservedly popular, and reservations are essential in summer. If you're going to be arriving outside
Litinterp office hours, you'll have to ring or email
in advance. ❸

Mabre Residence Maironio 13 ☎8-5/212
2087, ⓦwww.mabre.lt. Elegant quarters in the
colonnaded courtyard of a converted Orthodox
monastery, just round the corner from St Anne's
Church. Standard doubles boast plush carpets
and rich colour schemes. There's also a range of
suites (one of which features a kitchenette); the
presidential suite with timber-beamed ceiling and
palatial lounge will suit megalomaniac travellers
down to the ground. Breakfast is served across the
courtyard in the brick-vaulted *Hazienda* restaurant.
Standard doubles ❼, suites from 950Lt

Narutis Pilies 24 ☎8-5/212 2894, ⓦwww
.narutis.lt. A central, intimate hotel housed in a
much-modernized sixteenth-century building, with
rooms grouped around a glass-roofed courtyard.
Rooms are plain but elegant; those on the top floor
have low attic ceilings. Breakfast is served in an
atmospheric medieval cellar. ❼

Radisson SAS Astoria Didžioji 35/2 ☎8-5/212
0110, ⓦwww.radissonsas.com. Popular with
businessmen, large tour groups and visiting dignitaries, this hotel occupies a commanding position
on the Old Town's main thoroughfare. Standard
rooms are on the small side; those on the sixth
floor do at least offer hardwood floors and good
views. Business-class rooms have smarter bathrooms and bedside espresso machines. Hallways
in the west wing boast replicas of the Art Deco wall
paintings that decorated the place when it was a
Jewish community savings bank in the 1920s and
1930s. ❽

Rinno Vingrių 25 ☎8-5/262 2828, ⓦwww.rinno
.lt. A clean and cosy place on a quiet side street,
offering a mixture of "standard" rooms with TV and
en-suite shower, and more spacious "superior"
rooms equipped with minibars and bathtubs.
Strictly speaking, this isn't really in the Old Town,
but it's close enough – just across the road – not to
make much difference. ❹–❺

Shakespeare Bernardinų 8 ☎8-5/266 5885,
ⓦwww.shakespeare.lt. On a narrow alley, this is
an attractively renovated town house with fifteen

rooms – each named after a famous writer and
decked out with pictures related to the author and
his books. Rooms feature original timber beams,
oriental rugs and spacious bathrooms. ❼

Gedimino prospektas and Naujamiestis

Centrum Uniquestay Vytenio 9/25 ☎8-5/268
3310, ⓦwww.uniquestay.com. A newish building within walking distance of both Gedimino
prospektas and the Old Town. Rooms are simple,
but stylish, each containing Internet-connected
computers and large bathtubs. Kooky ceramics and
minimalist furniture in the hallways lend a chic,
modernist feel. There's a small swimming pool and
fitness room on the ground floor. ❼

E-Guest House Ševčenkos 16 ☎8-5/266 0730,
ⓦwww.e-guesthouse.lt. Tucked away in a
yard behind the shops and offices of Naujamiestis,
this modern five-storey building decorated with
with quirky artworks. Most of the doubles are split-
level mini-studios, while "lux" rooms come with
kitchenette. Top-floor "VIP" apartments have two
double bedrooms, lounge and Jacuzzi-style bathtub. Free Wi-Fi throughout, as well as computer
terminals in the corridors. Apartments ❼, standard
doubles ❺

Lietuvos Telekomo Svečių Namai Vivulskio 13A
☎8-5/260 3715, ⓦwww.telecomguesthouse.lt. A
small guesthouse, with mostly single rooms, run by
Lithuanian Telecom and located in a quiet off-street
courtyard, ten minutes' walk uphill from the Old
Town. Comfortable en-suite rooms with TV and
minibar. Advance booking recommended. ❻

Novotel Vilnius Gedimino prospektas 16
☎8-5/266 6200, ⓦwww.accorhotels.com. This
150-room monolith is something of a temple to
contemporary design, with light-filled rooms boasting matt-black desks, bold bed linen and intriguing,
trough-shaped bathroom sinks. Rooms on the
eastern side of the building offer fantastic Old Town
vistas. The floor-to-ceiling windows of the breakfast room provide a bird's-eye view of Gedimino
prospektas, and the panoramic seventh-floor gym
is a great place to exercise. Wi-fi throughout. ❼

Scandic Neringa Vilnius Gedimino 23
☎8-5/268 1910, ⓦwww.scandic-hotels.com.
One of the better downtown business choices,
offering relatively spacious rooms decked out in
warm colours. Top-floor "superior" rooms have
hardwood floors and bigger bathrooms. The
hotel restaurant – long famous for its chicken
Kiev – was the birthplace of Soviet jazz in the
late 1960s (see p.324), although the polo-neck-
wearing crowd moved on years ago. Ask about
weekend reductions. ❻–❼

Žemaitės Žemaitės 15 ⊤ 8-5/213 3193, ⓦ www
.hotelzemaites.lt. A modern block in an uninspiring
area 2km west of the Old Town, but fairly handy
for the stations; take trolleybus #15 or #16 or bus
#23 or #54 from the train and bus stations. Comfy
en-suite doubles with TV and Scandinavian-style,
pale-wood furniture. ⑤

North of the River Neris

Best Western Naujasis Vilnius Konstitucijos14
⊤ 8-5/273 9595, ⓦ www.hotelnv.lt. Reliable and
long-established business-class hotel, with professional service and comfortable rooms. Facilities
include on-site gym and sauna and a dinky swimming pool. Handily placed for the Baltasis Tiltas
footbridge, which leads across the Neris towards
Gedimino prospektas. ⑦

Ecotel Slucko 8 ⊤ 8-5/210 2700, ⓦ www.ecotel.lt.
In a mixed area of residential apartments and office
blocks, but still within walking distance of the Old
Town, *Ecotel* offers minimally furnished but smart
en suites in unobtrusive pale colours. Most have
shower cabins; some come with bathtub. Triples
available. Ask about weekend reductions. ④

Reval Hotel Lietuva Konstitucijos 20 ⊤ 8-5/272
6272, ⓦ www.revalhotels.com. Right in the middle
of the sparkly new buildings of Vilnius's emergent
business district, this smart tower block offers four-
star comforts and expansive views. The panoramic
top-floor *SkyBar* provides added inducement to
stay. ⑥

Šarūnas Raitininkų 4 ⊤ 8-5/272 3888,
ⓦ www.hotelsarunas.lt. A modern hotel on
the north bank of the river, owned by former
Sacramento Kings basketball player Šarūnas
Marčiulionis. Far enough from the main road to
be peaceful, and set around a quiet courtyard, the
hotel offers comfy rooms, a fully equipped gym and
a bar stuffed with NBA memorabilia. ⑦

Victoria Saltoniškių 56 ⊤ 8-5/272 4013,
ⓦ www.victoria.lt. Despite its unprepossessing
blockhouse exterior, this hotel in the residential
Žvėrynas district offers friendly service and pleasant en suites. Within walking distance of Gedimino
prospektas and 2km away from the Old Town; from
the train and bus stations take trolleybus #5 to
Žaliasis Tiltas followed by trolleybus #8, #9 or #19
to Pedagoginis universitetas. ⑤

Hostels

Hostels in Vilnius are basic compared to their counterparts in Western Europe: rooms
are often cramped and very simply furnished, though invariably clean, and the staff
usually enthusiastic and friendly.

A Hostel Sodų 17 ⊤ 8-5/213 9994, ⓦ www
.ahostel.lt. Newish hostel just down the road from the
train and bus stations, offering dorm accommodation (40Lt per person) in the form of Japanese-style
sleeping capsules. With an annexe a few metres
away, it has more capacity than the other hostels in
town and may have peak-season vacancies when
others are full. A bit lacking in atmosphere and the
on-duty staff don't always speak English.

Filaretai (HI) Filaretų 17 ⊤ 8-5/215 4627 ⓦ www
.filaretaihostel.lt. A simple but clean and well-run
hostel about a 15min walk from the Old Town in
the atmospherically shabby Užupis district; take
bus #34 from bus/train stations to the Filaretų
stop. Accommodation ranges from two-bed rooms
(②) to eight-bed dorms (30Lt per person), with
a swanky self-catering family apartment in the
house across the yard. 2Lt surcharge for non-HI
members. Breakfast is sometimes available in
summer for an extra charge. Facilities include a
well-equipped kitchen, a common room with TV,
and washing machines (10Lt per load).

Old Town Hostel (HI) Aušros Vartų 20-15A
⊤ 8-5/262 5357, ⓦ www.lithuanianhostels.org.
A small, friendly place which fills up quickly
owing to its prime location, midway between
the train station and the Old Town. Most accommodation comes in the form of functional, clean,
six- and eight-bed dorms, although a double and
a triple are available if you book far enough in
advance. There's also a cosy kitchen. A good place
to stay if you want to meet other travellers and
don't mind co-hostellers rolling home in the early
hours after a night on the town. Double room (②),
dorms 35Lt per person; 2Lt surcharge for non-HI
members.

Sleep Inn Šv. Mikalojaus 3, ⊤ 8-638/32 818
ⓦ www.vb-sleep-inn.lt. Comprising a pair of neat,
bright bunk-bed dorms, and one spacious double
room, this hostel combines a central location with a
relaxing, laid-back vibe. There's a spacious kitchen
with cooking facilities and free hot drinks, and you
can do your laundry for a few extra litas. Double
rooms ②, dorms 42Lt per person.

The City

Most of Vilnius's sights are concentrated in a reasonably compact area on the south
bank of the River Neris. At the centre of the city is the main square, **Katedros aikštė**,

site of the **cathedral**. South of here extends the atmospheric **Old Town**, with its impressive collection of Baroque churches and venerable university, while to the west stretches the long, straight boulevard of **Gedimino prospektas**, the focus of the city's commercial and administrative life. On the high ground above it lies the nineteenth-century residential area of **Naujamiestis** (New Town). Running towards Gedimino prospektas along the eastern side of the Old Town is **Pylimo gatvė**, bearing just a few traces of the sizeable Jewish community that once lived here. Beyond the centre, there's only a handful of sights – mostly in the western, southern and eastern suburbs – for which you'll need recourse to public transport or taxi.

Katedros aikštė and around

Lording it over the broad, flagstoned expanse of **Cathedral Square** (Katedros aikštė) is the off-white, colonnaded **Cathedral** (Arkikatedros bazilika; daily 7am–7pm), rather accurately described as "a cross between a Greek temple and a Polish civic theatre" by the German Expressionist writer Alfred Döblin, who passed through town in the early 1920s. The site was originally a shrine to Perkūnas, the Lithuanian god of thunder, and Mindaugas the Great chose to build a simple brick church here in the thirteenth century – a move which didn't go down well with the resolutely pagan Lithuanian nobles, who had him murdered in 1263. The spot wasn't associated with Christianity again until the conversion of Lithuania to Catholicism under Grand Duke Jogaila after 1387. The church Jogaila built was constantly added to and reconstructed over the next four hundred years, and the building you see today is

△ Vilnius Cathedral

largely the result of a late-eighteenth-century facelift carried out by Laurynas Stuoka-Gucevičius. Turned into a museum by the Soviets, it was restored to the Catholic Church by a reform-minded local communist leadership in 1988, and reconsecrated the following year. As the symbolic heart of Lithuanian Christianity, the cathedral was the natural focus of mass rallies in the run-up to independence. The most moving of these took place in January 1991, when the coffins of those killed by Soviet troops at the TV Tower (see p.443) were laid on the flagstones of the square, draped in Lithuanian tricolours, for an outdoor memorial service that united tens of thousands in grief and defiance.

The pediment of the cathedral's main **facade** is crowned by a trio of monumental statues, with St Helena brandishing a huge cross at the apex, accompanied by Casimir, patron saint of Lithuania, on the right, and Stanislas, patron saint of Poland, on the left. All are modern replicas of early nineteenth-century originals, destroyed by the Soviets after World War II. Running round the sides of the building are statues of past rulers of Poland-Lithuania, caught in stiff mid-gesture, often to unintentionally comic effect. To the right of the main entrance looms the freestanding, three-tiered **belfry** (Arkikatedros varpinė), a coffee-and-cream-coloured cylinder which looks like a stranded Baroque lighthouse.

Inside (head for the side door on the northern side if the main doors are shut), devotional paintings crowd the walls and pillars, and locals kneel deep in prayer, reinforcing the aura of devotion and spirituality found in so many Lithuanian churches. The most dramatic of the canvases on display are the scenes of the life of Christ running right round the ambulatory, a cycle painted by Franciszek Smugliewicz, Vilnius's leading Neoclassicist and professor at the local art academy in the early nineteenth century.

A constant stream of pilgrims heads down the right-hand ambulatory towards the cathedral's main attraction, the **Chapel of St Casimir** (Kazimiero koplyčia), commissioned by King Sigismund Wasa III in 1623 in a propagandistic attempt to associate the Wasas (a dynasty which was relatively new to the throne of Poland-Lithuania) with their rather more illustrious Jagiellonian predecessors – the family to which fifteenth-century royal Prince Casimir (see box above) belonged. A riot of marble, stucco and silver statuary, the chapel is Vilnius's most complete Baroque statement

– and was one of the few parts of the cathedral untouched by Stuoka-Gucevičius's refurbishments. Designed by Italian architect Costante Tencalla, the chapel consists of a black, marble-lined square chamber, with a second octagonal tier on top supporting a richly decorated cupola. On the south-facing wall is the ornate, silver-plated casket containing the bones of St Casimir, a relic that was returned to the cathedral with much pomp in 1989 after being exiled to the Church of SS Peter and Paul during the Soviet period. The icon-like image of the saint directly below depicts Casimir with three hands, probably because the artist over-painted his first attempt at rendering the saint's right arm with a second version – when the painting was subsequently cleaned, the first arm miraculously re-emerged. Occupying niches in the walls of the chapel are eight silver-plated statues of Jagiellonian and Wasa rulers, while frescoes on the ceilings and side walls show episodes from the saint's life. Two of the larger scenes, painted by Michelangelo Palloni in 1692, portray the miracle cures experienced by those praying at St Casimir's grave.

Leaving the cathedral and moving round towards the square's eastern end, you'll come across a tall, grey plinth bearing a statue of the Grand Duke of Lithuania and legendary founder of Vilnius, **Gediminas** (1271–1341), depicted here as a lean, martial figure gesturing towards the city with an outstretched sword. Below the duke and his horse crouches a wolf – a reference to the popular folk tale that seeks to explain Vilnius's origins. Gediminas, so the story goes, was taking a rest while hunting in the hills above the Vilnia River when he dreamt of an iron wolf howling in the night. Asked to explain this dream, the duke's head priest suggested that the wolf's howling represented the fame of a great city built on this site that would one day reverberate around the world. Suitably impressed, Gediminas ordered the construction of a new capital here without delay.

The Lower Castle

Immediately behind the cathedral rises the cool grey bulk of the so-called **Lower Castle** (Žemutinės pilis), where the Grand Dukes of Lithuania once held court. Demolished by the Russians in the eighteenth century, the castle was reconstructed at great expense at the beginning of the twenty-first, using archeological evidence and period engravings as a guide to what the original must have looked like. The castle's most famous resident was Sigismund Augustus (1520–72), King of Poland and Grand Duke of Lithuania, who maintained a glittering ducal court complete with an orchestra, an art collection and a library of over four thousand books, enhancing Vilnius's reputation as an important cultural centre. A **museum** in the castle (slated to open some time in 2009) will display a sequence of historic interiors containing the kind of furnishings, fabrics and paintings that a monarch of Sigismund's stature would have owned; with the castle's original contents lost, the Lithuanian government is currently procuring period pieces from elsewhere in Europe to ensure as authentic a re-creation as possible.

The Upper Castle

The tree-clad hill immediately behind the Lower Castle was originally crowned by the **Upper Castle** (Aukštutinės pilis), a tenth-century stockade fort subsequently strengthened in stone by Gediminas and his successors. An easy ten-minute stroll up from the park behind the cathedral, the Upper Castle can also be reached by a **funicular** (keltuvas; Tues–Sun 10am–6pm; 2Lt both ways), which shuttles up and down from behind the Prehistoric Lithuania exhibition (see opposite). The only bit of the Upper Castle left standing – and one of the city's best-known landmarks – is the **Gediminas Tower** (Gedimino bokštas), an appealing, red-brick octagon that rises sand-castle-like from the brow of the hill. It retains little original stonework from Gediminas's time, having been rebuilt in the nineteenth century to provide recreational strollers with a viewing platform. You can get an idea, though, of what the castle looked like in medieval times by examining the impressive array of scale models in the **Upper Castle Museum** (Aukštutinės pilies muziejus; Wed–Sun 11am–5pm;

4Lt; free on Wed in winter) inside the tower. There's a superb panorama of the Old Town's church spires and towers from the top.

The Lithuanian National Museum

A hundred metres or so north of the cathedral lie the arsenal buildings, a pair of creamy-yellow barrack blocks built in the sixteenth century and given a touch of neo-classical grandeur by the Russians some three hundred years later. The first of these, at Arsenalo 1, is now home to the **Lithuanian National Museum** (Lietuvos Nacionalinis muziejus; Wed–Sun: May–Sept 11am–6pm; Oct–April 11am–5pm; 6Lt; free Wed in winter), containing an engaging jumble of artefacts ranging from old prints of Vilnius to re-created farmhouse interiors from the eighteenth and nineteenth centuries. Traditional Lithuanian crafts are represented with an assortment of wicker baskets, chequered bedspreads and the wood-carved figures of saints used to decorate wayside shrines in the countryside.

A separate annexe of the museum (entrance a little further north on Arsenalo) houses the **Prehistoric Lithuania exhibition** (same times; 6Lt), an extremely well-presented display, with explanations in English, on the history of Lithuania up to the twelfth century. It begins with the flint and bone tools and distinctive boat-shaped battle-axes used by the Baltic region's earliest inhabitants – the ancestors of today's Lithuanians and Latvians arrived in the area sometime on the cusp of the second and third millennia BC. In the museum's upstairs gallery, you can see models of the stockaded hill-forts, dating from the tenth to the twelfth centuries, in which tribal leaders held sway. Isolated from the rest of Europe by thick forests, the Lithuanians were slow to develop unified state structures, and lived in loosely bound tribal units until well into the Middle Ages. Also on display are reproductions of sumptuous Iron Age Lithuanian costumes and some delicate silver jewellery.

The Applied Art Museum

A hundred metres further east along Arsenalo at no. 3 is the **Applied Art Museum** (Taikomosios Dailės muziejus; Tues–Sat 11am–6pm, Sun 11am–4pm; 6Lt), displaying chalices, reliquaries and Baroque paintings – including a fleshy *Lot and his Daughters* by the Austrian master Johann-Michael Rottmayr – taken from the region's churches. There's also a wide-ranging display of folk art, with several examples of the wooden wayside crosses (still a common feature of rural Lithuania) that typically combine Christian imagery with much older pagan sun motifs, as well as bunches of colourful *verbos* – the bundles of dried grasses and flowers traditionally prepared in the run-up to Palm Sunday.

The Old Town

Just south of Cathedral Square lies the **Old Town** (Senamiestis), a dense network of narrow, largely pedestrianized streets that forms the heart of Vilnius and invites aimless wandering. The following account starts in the north and proceeds roughly southwards, although any tour of the area will inevitably involve numerous detours down side streets or into inviting corners. The main reference points are **Pilies gatvė** (Castle Street), which ascends gently from Cathedral Square, and its extensions **Didžioji** and **Aušros Vartų**, which cut south through the heart of historic Vilnius. Almost everything you'll want to see in the Old Town lies on or just off this artery.

Bernardinų gatvė

Leading off Pilies to the east is **Bernardinų gatvė**, one of the Old Town's most appealing back streets, a narrow lane lined with seventeenth- and eighteenth-century houses. Occupying no. 11 is the **Adam Mickiewicz Memorial Apartment** (Adomo Mickevičiaus Memorialinis butas; Tues–Fri 10am–5pm, Sat & Sun 10am–2pm; free), where the Polish poet (see box, p.312) lived for a few short months in 1822. The rather

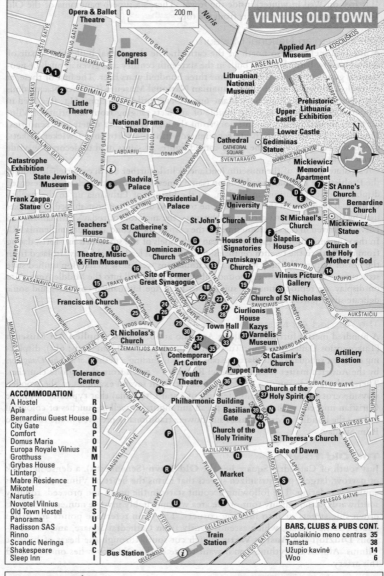

VILNIUS OLD TOWN

0 — 200 m

ACCOMMODATION

A Hostel	R
Apia	G
Bernardinu Guest House	D
City Gate	Q
Comfort	P
Domus Maria	O
Europa Royale Vilnius	N
Grotthuss	M
Grybas House	L
Litinterp	E
Mabre Residence	H
Mikotel	T
Narutis	F
Novotel Vilnius	B
Old Town Hostel	S
Panorama	U
Radisson SAS	J
Rinno	K
Scandic Neringa	A
Shakespeare	C
Sleep Inn	I

RESTAURANTS & CAFÉS

Balti drambliai	10	Lokys	23	Skonis ir kvapas	15
Čili kaimas	29	Mano kavinė	20	Sorena	5
Čili pica	1 & 19	Markus ir Ko	22	Steak House Helios	31
Delano	2	Pieno baras	28	Stikliai	13
Freskos	33	Pilies menė	4	Žemaičiai	24
Gabi	8	Poniu Laimė	18		
Gusto blyninė	37	La Provence	26		
Keisti ženklai	16	Šauni vietelė	25		

BARS, CLUBS & PUBS

Absento fėjos	41	Helios	31
Amatininkų Užeiga	27	Ibish Lounge	40
Avilys	3	In Vino	39
Bix	36	Intro	7
Brodvėjus	34	Neringa	A
Café de Paris	17	Pabo Latino	21
Cozy	11	The Pub	12
Grasas	30	Savas kampas	32
		Sole Luna	9

BARS, CLUBS & PUBS CONT.

Suolaikinio meno centras	35
Tamsta	38
Užupio kavinė	14
Woo	6

paltry collection of exhibits includes a couple of period chairs, a desk once owned by Mickiewicz and a number of Polish and Lithuanian first editions of his works.

St Michael's Church

At the far end of Bernardinų, the stately ochre bulk of **St Michael's Church** (Šv Mykolo bažnyčia) peeks out from its walled enclosure. The twin towers of its seventeenth-century facade are complemented by a freestanding belfry, the main gateway into the church courtyard. The church was founded by **Leo Sapieha** (1557–1633), who envisaged St Michael's as his own family mausoleum. A typical product of the Grand Duchy of Lithuania's cosmopolitan elite, Sapieha was a nobleman of Belorussian origin who converted from the Orthodox faith to Protestantism and then to Catholicism in an attempt to retain his political influence in the shifting religious landscape of sixteenth-century Europe. Sapieha's own granite-coloured memorial is located in the southeastern corner of the church: his reclining figure is clad in impressively voluminous pantaloons and ruff, while his two wives lie obediently on either side.

St Anne's Church

Opposite St Michael's Church soar the fairytale, pinnacle-encrusted towers of **St Anne's** (Šv Onos bažnyčia; daily 10am–3pm), the church that so impressed Napoleon Bonaparte that he's said to have wanted to take it back to Paris in the palm of his hand. Intricate, red-brick traceries weave like intertwined thorn branches across its tall, narrow facade. The most outstanding Gothic building in Lithuania, it's nevertheless a relatively late example of the style: the facade is thought to have been completed only in 1582, by which time the Baroque was already beginning to make its presence felt in Vilnius. Inside, spindly lines of red-brick rib vaulting extend across a white ceiling, sheltering a relatively undistinguished ensemble of altars bunched up at the end of the small nave.

The Bernardine Church

Rising directly behind St Anne's is the considerably more restrained facade of the much larger **Bernardine Church** (Bernardinų vienuolyno bažnyčia), built at around the same time as its neighbour, together with the adjoining Bernardine **monastery** (now occupied by the Vilnius Art Academy). According to communist folklore, the church cellar was where Vilnius high-school student and future founder of the KGB Felix Dzerzhinsky (see p.327) established an underground printing press, confident that the Tsarist police would never think of looking for it here. The church's **interior**, rich in Baroque furnishings and medieval frescoes, was neglected during the Soviet era and is currently undergoing restoration. Among the few things that have escaped damage are the two fine seventeenth-century funerary monuments (that of Stanislaus Radziwiłł on the north side, Petras Veselovskis on the south) that face each other across the nave – their incumbents are depicted in relief form, reclining contentedly as if on a country picnic.

The Mickiewicz statue and the Church of the Holy Mother of God

Just south of the Bernardine Church is a modern **statue** of Adam Mickiewicz (see box, p.312), leaning authoritatively on a lectern as if about to launch into a reading of his verse. The statue was the site of one of the first Glasnost-era demonstrations against Soviet power in Lithuania, when on August 23, 1987, a few hundred people gathered to demand the publication of the **Molotov–Ribbentrop Pact**, the secret agreement in which the Soviets and Germans carved out spheres of influence in the Baltics and Poland in 1939.

South of here, Mairono gatvė swings around the **Church of the Holy Mother of God** (Skaisčiausios dievo motinos cerkvė; daily 8am–6pm), Vilnius's largest Orthodox place of worship, an off-white nineteenth-century cube topped by a fat central cupola and four fortress-like towers. Beside the church a small bridge leads across the River Vilnia to the inner-city suburb of Užupis. West of Mairono, the network of crooked

Adam Mickiewicz (1798–1855)

Litwo! Ojczyzno moja! ty jesteś jak zdrowie;
Ile cié trzeba cenić, ten tylko się dowie,
Kto się stracił
(O Lithuania, my homeland, thou art like health itself;
I never knew till now, how precious,
Till I lost thee)

The opening lines of Adam Mickiewicz's *Pan Tadeusz* (1834)

It's paradoxical that the most famous lines ever written about Lithuania were the work of a Polish poet, yet **Adam Mickiewicz** (or Adomas Mickevičius, as he is known in Lithuania) is one of the few literary figures whose words have been adopted as rallying cries by both nations. Above all, Mickiewicz embodies the nostalgia shared by both Lithuanians and Poles for the **Grand Duchy of Lithuania**, the multi-ethnic and multilingual territory carved out by Lithuanian rulers in the Middle Ages, and subsequently a key component (some would say equal partner) in the Polish-Lithuanian Commonwealth.

Mickiewicz himself was a typical product of the Grand Duchy, born to an impoverished Polish gentry family in the countryside near Novogrudok (now in Belarus). In 1815, Mickiewicz went to study at **Vilnius University**, and was a founder member of the Philomaths, a pseudo-masonic organization dedicated to fighting Tsarist rule through the promotion of local culture. In November 1823, he was arrested along with fellow members on suspicion of "spreading Polish nationalism", and imprisoned in the Basilian monastery (see p.318) before being deported to Russia where he remained, mostly in **Moscow**, for the rest of the decade.

Mickiewicz already had a local literary reputation, but it was in Russia that his talents blossomed. Notable works of this period include *Konrad Wallenrod*, a popular epic poem depicting the medieval struggle between the Teutonic Knights and the Grand Duchy of Lithuania, in reality a thinly disguised allegory of the age-old conflict between Germany on one side and Poles and Lithuanians on the other.

Following the failure of the **November 1830 Polish Uprising**, Mickiewicz, like many Polish intellectuals, went into exile in **Paris** and quickly immersed himself in émigré

alleys made up of Rusų, Volano, Literatų and Šv Mykolo provides numerous opportunities for zipping back towards Pilies.

The House of Signatories

The middle reaches of Pilies boast a handsome ensemble of balconied town houses, most dating from the eighteenth and nineteenth centuries, and now occupied by a brash collection of cafés and upmarket jewellery and shoe shops. One of the most impressive edifices along this stretch is the lovingly restored **House of Signatories** (Signatarų namai; Tues–Sat 10am–5pm; 4Lt) at no. 26, where the Lithuanian National Council declared the country's independence on February 16, 1918. The Germans, whose army was in control of Vilnius at the time, initially encouraged the National Council to make such a move, but soon withdrew their support when it became clear that the Lithuanian government-in-waiting was unwilling to act as Germany's puppet. Lithuania had to wait until Germany's defeat in November the same year before it could begin setting up state institutions of its own, yet February 16 is still considered a hallowed date in the country's history, officially celebrated as one of Lithuania's two independence days. The second-floor suite of apartments occupied by the National Council in 1918 is today the site of a small **museum**, worth visiting for its beautifully restored *belle époque* interiors. The room where the declaration was signed has been left bare save for a baize-topped writing desk, although the council and its members – sober politics. It was here too that Mickiewicz wrote *Pan Tadeusz* (1834), his greatest epic poem; modelled on the novels of Walter Scott, it is a masterful, richly lyrical depiction of traditional gentry life in the multi-ethnic borderlands east of Vilnius. As in all of Mickiewicz's works, Lithuania is represented as a wild, mythic land of dark forests – a seductive contrast to the ordered, urban world of Warsaw or Kraków.

Banned from re-entering the Tsarist Empire, Mickiewicz never returned to either Poland or Lithuania. For the next two decades he taught Slavonic literature at both Lausanne and Paris, at the same time canvassing the courts of Europe for support in Poland's struggle against the Russians. The writer's life came abruptly to an end in 1855 when Prince Adam Czartoryski, a leader of the Paris exile community, sent Mickiewicz on a mission to Turkey to organize Polish volunteer forces in the approaching Crimean War: having contracted typhus soon after his arrival, Mickiewicz died in November 1855 in **Istanbul**. Already a national hero of almost mythic proportions, his remains were eventually brought back to Poland and placed, along with other Polish "greats", in the crypt of Kraków's Wawel Cathedral.

Although Mickiewicz was never a Lithuanian patriot in the modern sense (he believed that the country's destiny was inextricably bound up with that of Poland), his heritage was readily appropriated by the Lithuanian national movement. His fascination with the history and traditions of the Grand Duchy helped to provide Lithuanians with a sense of their own past greatness, and his lyrical descriptions of the Lithuanian countryside inspired hordes of local imitators. When priest and poet Antanas Baranauskas wrote the seminal *Forest of Anykščiai* in 1861, he was essentially trying to prove that the Lithuanian language was versatile enough to evoke the Lithuanian landscape in the manner of Mickiewicz. Translations of Mickiewicz's works were very popular in late nineteenth-century Lithuania, and nationalist ideologue Vincas Kudirka adapted the opening words of *Pan Tadeusz* to form the first line of a patriotic hymn – which is still in use as the Lithuanian National Anthem. However *Pan Tadeusz* was always treated with suspicion by a Lithuanian elite who felt that it over-romanticized the Polish-speaking gentry. It wasn't translated in its entirety until 1927, and even then most of the references to "Poland" were left out – sparking the inevitable protests from Warsaw.

men in stiff collars and with even stiffer beards – are celebrated in a modest display of photographs in the adjoining halls.

Rearing up immediately opposite the house is the back end of St John's Church (entered via the main entrance to the university; see below), beside which Šv Jono gatvė veers west towards the university district.

The University

Occupying a jumble of buildings constructed between the sixteenth and eighteenth centuries around nine linked courtyards, **Vilnius University** (Vilniaus Universitetas; access to the courtyards Mon–Fri 9am–5pm, Sat 9am–noon) squeezes into a neat quadrant of land between Pilies and Universiteto gatvė. In response to the spread of Calvinism in Vilnius, a college was established here by Bishop Walerijan Protasewicz in 1569 to serve as a Jesuit-run vehicle for the propagation of Catholic, Counter-Reformation ideals. Despite resistance from Protestant nobles, the King of Poland and Lithuania **Stefan Bathory** upgraded the college to university status ten years later. Tuition was initially in Latin, but by the early nineteenth century the university enjoyed a growing reputation as one of the Polish-speaking world's leading educational institutions. It also became a hotbed of Polish resistance to Tsarist rule: students formed conspiratorial societies such as the Philomaths (Towarzystwie Filomatów), dedicated to raising the anti-Russian consciousness of the locals by the promotion of Polish and Lithuanian culture. However, it was broken up by the authorities in November 1823 and its leading lights – including young poet **Adam Mickiewicz** (see box, p.312) – exiled from the city. The Russians closed the university down altogether in 1832 in the wake of the failed anti-Tsarist rebellion of 1830–31, and it wasn't reopened until after World War I when it once more resumed its position as one of Poland's top universities. Before long it was back in the political fray: right-wing students periodically mounted anti-Semitic raids on the nearby Jewish districts of town, while nonconformists gravitated towards left-of-centre groupings such as the Vagabonds' Club (Akademicky klub Włóczęgów), whose members, among them future Nobel laureate **Czesław Miłosz**, advertised their bohemian leanings by wearing floppy black berets. Thoroughly "Lithuanianized" after World War II, the university survived the Soviet era with its academic reputation intact, and is now the country's undisputed centre of learning, with over fourteen thousand students.

The university's **main entrance** is on Universiteto gatvė, where a small office beside the main gate sells tickets (4Lt) and hands out plans. You're then free to wander around the courtyards and visit St John's Church (see below), but you're not supposed to peek inside any of the university interiors unless you've pre-booked a place on a guided tour (℡8-5/268 7103; price depends on numbers). If you do opt for the tour – and it's definitely worth doing – make sure you ask to see the barrel-vaulted **Smugliewicz Hall** (originally the refectory, now the university library's rare books department), decorated with Smugliewicz frescoes depicting Jesuit theologians sheltering under the Virgin Mary's cape; and the Neoclassical **White Hall** of the **observatory**, crammed with old telescopes and celestial globes, and featuring an ornate portal by Carlo Sampari straddled by figures of Diana and Urania.

Assuming you're going it alone, the first courtyard you come to is the Sarbievijus courtyard (Sarbijevijaus kiemas), named after Jesuit theologian and university lecturer **Mattheus Sarbiewski** (1595–1640), who was widely admired throughout Europe for his Latin-language verse. From here you can move off to the left in search of some of the smaller courtyards, or head right through an archway to the **Grand Courtyard** (Didysis kiemas), an arcaded quadrangle dominated by the scrumptious wedding-cake facade of **St John's Church** (Šv Jono bažnyčia), its three custard-coloured tiers seemingly held aloft by slender Corinthian pilasters arranged in clusters of two or three. Although of fourteenth-century origin, the church's outer appearance is due to a mid-eighteenth-century facelift by Jan Krzysztof Glaubitz, architect of more than a few of Vilnius's Baroque buildings. Placed in the care of first the Jesuits, and then the university authorities, the church was closed in 1948 and pressed into service as a warehouse for the newpaper *Tiesa* ("Truth"), the Lithuanian Communist Party's answer to *Pravda*. Vilnius University managed to get the church back in 1963, and turned it into a science museum. It wasn't reconsecrated until 1991.

Inside, a group of altars in no-holds-barred Baroque clusters at the far end of the church. The high altar resembles a vast gateway, guarded by statues of St John Chrysostom, St Gregory the Great, St Anselm and St Augustine, and through which a small statue of the Virgin is barely visible on the far side. Archways on either side of the nave lead off to richly decorated chapels – often locked – some of which still hold books and manuscripts left over from the church's days as a science museum. Over to the left as you face the altar is the **Guild of Musicians' Chapel**, with a fresco of robed academic figures in the cupola, and a richly gilded Madonna, credited with miracle-working powers, on the altar. Cherubs wrestling with pointy-eared demons frame the doorway to the adjacent **St Anne's Chapel**, which houses a brightly painted, eighteenth-century wooden altar showing Christ on the Cross, with the disciples represented as bunches of grapes.

Turning to leave the church, you'll see the slender pipes of the organ high above the main door, topped by trumpeting angels and fronted by a bust of Stanisław Moniuszko (1819–72), the Polish composer who worked as the organist here before becoming a big-time conductor in Warsaw, and penning *Halka*, Poland's first important national opera. Standing apart from the main body of the church is the bell tower,

△ St John's Church

a stout structure capped with a collection of tiny urns that look like sporting trophies. At 68m, it's the tallest belfry in the Old Town. Next to the tower is a stately, barrel-roofed structure that looks as if it ought to be a chapel or an oratory; actually it's a rather swish daytime café for university students.

The Presidential Palace

Stretching west of Universiteto gatvė, the neat, flagstoned triangle of **Daukanto aikštė** is overlooked by the regal facade of the **Presidential Palace** (Prezidentūra), a former merchant's house remodelled in its present Neoclassical form at the end of the eighteenth century, when it served as the comfortable downtown residence of the Bishop of Vilnius. It became the home of the Russian governor general soon afterwards, and it's likely that Adam Mickiewicz was interrogated here prior to his imprisonment in the Basilian monastery. The building's most despised denizen was Governor General Muravyev, nicknamed "the hangman" for his brutal suppression of the anti-Tsarist revolt of 1863–64. Salt was rubbed into local wounds by establishing a Muravyev Museum in the palace after his departure. There was also a statue of the man in front of the palace, but this was dismantled – along with a bombastic Catherine the Great memorial that graced Cathedral Square – and evacuated by retreating Russian troops in 1915, never to return. Despite being right at the heart of the Lithuanian state, the square is a restrained, sober place free of ideological or national symbols – save for the orange, red and green Lithuanian tricolours fluttering gamely from a trio of flagpoles.

The Pyatnitskaya Church and Šlapelis House

From the university you can cut back east along the broad, park-like space of Syrvido skveras to the northern end of Pilies, which culminates in a triangular piazza occupied by a year-round craft market selling paintings, amber jewellery and wicker baskets. Hidden behind the street stalls is the Orthodox **Pyatnitskaya Church** (Pjatnickajos cerkvė), a modest piece of mid-nineteenth-century architecture, rather like a domed brick shed. A Russian-language inscription on the outside wall relates the (admittedly apocryphal) tale that the poet Alexander Pushkin's grandfather Hannibal – an African slave presented to Tsar Peter the Great by the Turkish sultan – was baptized here in

1704. Hugging the eastern side of the street at no. 40 is **Šlapelis House** (Šlapelių namai; Wed–Sun 11am–4pm; free), the former home of Jurgis and Marija Šlapelis, the husband-and-wife team who energetically promoted Lithuanian literature throughout the first half of the twentieth century – a time when Lithuanians were a small minority in a largely Polish- and Yiddish-speaking city. The pair were galvanized into action by the sudden lifting of the ban on printing Lithuanian in the Latin script in 1904: Jurgis threw himself enthusiastically into publishing, while Marija opened Vilnius's first Lithuanian bookshop. Upstairs, there's a display of old photographs evoking life in Vilnius in the early twentieth century, while downstairs is a re-creation of the bookshop (the original was at Dominikonų 13), where self-help pamphlets like *How to Live Without Vodka* and *Health for Mothers and Children* can be found alongside Lithuanian editions of Shakespeare.

Vilnius Picture Gallery

Further south, Pilies gives way to **Didžioji gatvė** or "Main Street". Kicking off the sights along here is the Chodkiewicz Palace at no. 4, an opulent pied-à-terre built three centuries ago for one of the Grand Duchy's most prominent families and now occupied by the **Vilnius Picture Gallery**, home to the permanent collection of the Lithuanian Art Museum (Tues–Sat noon–6pm, Sun noon–5pm; 4Lt; free Wed in winter). Second-Empire furnishings and creaky parquet floors provide an elegant backdrop to the somewhat patchy overview of local painters through the ages. **Franciszek Smugliewicz** (1745–1807), the doyen of Vilnius's Neoclassicists, is particularly well represented, with numerous overblown canvases depicting biblical and historical subjects – look out for the pseudo-oriental pantomime costumes worn by the protagonists of his *Scythian Messengers with Darius, King of Persia*. Most of the other nineteenth- and twentieth-century artists featured here are pretty second-rate, save perhaps for **Ferdynand Ruszczycz**, whose dreamy, Post-Impressionist *Golden Room* (1913) is the most modernist work in a largely conservative display.

South of the gallery, it would be difficult to miss the eye-catching jumble of architectural styles that makes up the Orthodox **Church of St Nicholas** (Šv Mikalojaus cerkvė), remodelled in the wake of the brutal suppression of the 1863–64 rebellion by the Tsar's governor general in Vilnius, General Muravyev, to serve as a propagandist statement of the virtues of Russian culture. Framed by a squat, Byzantine-style chapel on one side and a tapering Muscovite spire on the other, the church's facade is resplendently decked out in bright ochre with brick-red trimmings.

Rotušės aikštė

Immediately beyond the Church of St Nicholas, Didžioji opens out into **Rotušės aikštė**, or "Town Hall Square", very much the hub around which life in the Old Town revolves and crammed with craft stalls during the annual Kaziukas Fair (see p.307). Little changed since the late eighteenth century, the square is a pretty assemblage of two- and three-storey town houses colourwashed in blue, orange and burgundy. Standing at its southern end is the old **Town Hall** (Rotušė) itself, an imposing, off-white pile fronted by a dignified colonnade, built in 1799 by Laurynas Stuoka Gucevičius, the architect of Vilnius Cathedral. Nowadays, the erstwhile council chamber is reserved for art exhibitions and occasional concerts.

On the western side of the square, **Stiklių gatvė** ("Glassmakers' Street" – a reference to the glass-making workshops established here in the mid-sixteenth century) winds its way back towards the university area, passing craft shops stocked with upmarket linen souvenirs. On the eastern side of the square, a seventeenth-century merchant's house at Didžioji 26 provides the suitably atmospheric venue for the **Kazys Varnėlis Museum** (Tues–Sat 9am–5pm but prior booking necessary; ☎8-5/279 1644), a rambling collection of prints, furniture and sculpture collected by artist and art teacher Varnėlis (born in 1917, he emigrated to the US after World War II), alongside the striking abstract paintings he produced himself. Highlights include Dürer and Goya engravings in barrel-vaulted rooms near the entrance, and nineteenth-century Japanese woodcuts in the high-ceilinged galleries upstairs. Varnėlis's own work, involving organic and geometric shapes painted in bright pop-art colours, ranges from the hypnotic to the headache-inducing.

A short detour east along Savičiaus gatvė leads after two minutes to the **Čiurlionis House** (Čiurliono namai; Mon–Fri 10am–4pm; donation requested) at no. 11. It's here that Lithuania's most celebrated artist and composer, Mikalojus Konstantinas Čiurlionis (see box, p.366), spent the winter of 1907–8 trying to promote Lithuanian culture in the city. He helped to organize the first-ever group exhibitions by Lithuanian artists and was disheartened by the low cultural horizons of the people who came to the shows, but failed to buy any of his paintings: "As far as art is concerned," he notoriously grumbled, "Vilnius is still in nappies!" There's not a great deal to see here, though, apart from a few prints, family photographs and coffee-table books showing reproductions of his artwork.

A few paces beyond the Čiurlionis House at Savičaus 5, the five-storey, rocket-like belfry of the eighteenth-century **Augustine Church** (Augustijonų bažnyčia; currently closed for restoration) is one of the most exhilarating architectural sights in the city.

The Contemporary Art Centre

The pale, concrete building marking the southwest corner of Rotušės aikštė, just behind the Town Hall, is the **Contemporary Art Centre** (Šiuolaikinio Meno Centras; ⓦ www.cac.lt; Tues–Sun 11am–7pm; 4Lt, free Wed in winter), which hosts high-profile exhibitions featuring artists from Lithuania and elsewhere. The building initially served as the main exhibition space for the Soviet-era Artists' Union, many members of which were accustomed to having their works displayed here, whatever the quality, and found themselves excluded after the centre's post-1991 transformation into a showcase for challenging contemporary work. The Art Centre's ground-floor café (see "Bars and pubs", p.335) is the main city-centre gathering point for Vilnius bohemians.

St Casimir's Church

Hogging the eastern shoulder of Rotušės aikštė, **St Casimir's Church** (Šv Kazimiero bažnyčia; Mon–Fri 4–6.30pm, Sun 8am–2pm) boasts an arresting facade of homely pink broken up by vertical cream stripes. Built for the Jesuits in the early seventeenth century, the church was turned into a grain store by the Napoleonic French, transformed into an Orthodox church by Tsarist Russia, handed over to the Lutheran congregation by the Germans in World War I and used to house a museum of atheism by the Soviets after World War II, before being finally returned to the Catholic Church in 1987. The church's most striking exterior feature is the elaborate crown and cross on top of the central dome. Representing the ducal crown of the Grand Duchy of Lithuania, it was placed here in 1942 to symbolize Lithuanian sovereignty over the city of Vilnius – which was under Nazi occupation at the time. The towers flanking the building house a series of bells which chime gently whenever the striking mechanism is stirred by the wind – a sound sculpture designed by erstwhile giant of the Soviet jazz scene Vladimir Tarasov. Unsurprisingly, given the church's chequered history, the interior is largely bare, save for a trio of lovingly restored eighteenth-century altars, their gilded capitals appearing to drip down the sombre, grey pillars. The recently restored **organ** is one of the city's finest – and frequently features in weekend concerts (see posters at the church entrance for dates and times).

Along Didžioji and Aušros Vartų

Continuing south along Didžioji, you come to the **Philharmonic building**, whose sober, grey-green Neoclassical front hides a charmingly old-fashioned, chandelier-studded interior. It was here in 1909 that Jascha Heifetz gave his famous performance of Mendelssohn's Violin Concerto in E minor at the age of 8, before leaving his native Vilnius for St Petersburg, then the West, where he became one of the most celebrated virtuosi of the twentieth century – a musician so perfect that George Bernard Shaw once advised him to play "one wrong note every night before you go to bed". Now the home of the Lithuanian National Philharmonic Orchestra, the building has hosted an impressive number of top international soloists and conductors since 1990; before this all visiting artists had to be approved by the stiflingly bureaucratic ministry of culture in Moscow.

The Basilian Gate and the Church of the Holy Trinity

Didžioji gives way to **Aušros Vartų gatvė**, which curves gently southwards past the **Basilian Gate**, an ornate coffee-and-cream archway which leads through to the courtyard of the long-defunct Basilian monastery. The monastery was a major centre of learning in the sixteenth and seventeenth centuries, when it served as the headquarters of the Uniate (also known as Greek-Catholic) community. Created by the Union of Brest in 1596 to accommodate those Orthodox believers prepared to accept the primacy of the pope, the Uniate Church was conceived as a handy way of allowing the Grand Duchy's many Russian and Belorussian nobles access to the country's Catholic-dominated elite. The hulking grey form of the monastery's **Church of the Holy Trinity** (Šv Trejybės cerkvė) still serves the city's small community of Ukranian Greek-Catholics, although it's currently undergoing long-term restoration and only one of its chapels is open for prayer. The surrounding monastery buildings (some of which are still occupied by monks, although most belong to a technical college) were used as a prison during the Tsarist period – the poet Adam Mickiewicz (see box, p.312) was one of the many Polish intellectuals incarcerated here following the roundups of October 1823.

The Church of the Holy Spirit

A short distance further south, a gateway on the left-hand side of the street leads through to the **Church of the Holy Spirit** (Šv Dvasios cerkvė), one of the oldest Orthodox churches in Lithuania and the most popular city-centre place of worship for Vilnius Russians. Inside the church's lofty, light-filled interior, rich with the smell of incense and candles, you're immediately drawn to the Baroque iconostasis in three stunning tiers of frivolous bright greens, blues and pinks, designed by the city's outstanding architect of the time, Jan Krzystof Glaubitz. In front of the iconostasis, the bodies of three fourteenth-century martyrs, Anthony, Ioan and Eustachius, are displayed in a glass casket, dressed in red velvet robes (white at Christmas, and black during Lent). According to tradition, the trio were hanged from an oak tree on the orders of the rigidly pagan Grand Duke Algirdas in 1347, although the latter subsequently married an Orthodox Russian princess, converted to Christianity, and ordered the construction of a chapel (the forerunner of today's church) on the execution site before retiring to become a monk.

St Theresa's Church

A little further along Aušros Vartų gatvė, on the left, rises the stately orange-and-grey **St Theresa's Church** (Šv Teresės bažnyčia), another soaring testament to the city's dominant architectural style. Founded in the mid-1600s by the Grand Duchy's treasurer, Stephen Christopher Pac, the church didn't receive its vibrant, salmon-pink rococo interior until over a century later, when local painter Mateusz Sūszczański provided the exuberant ceiling frescoes depicting scenes from the life of St Theresa.

The Gate of Dawn

The end of Aušros Vartų is marked by the **Gate of Dawn** (Aušros Vartai), the sole survivor of nine city gates that once studded the walls of Vilnius. In 1671, Carmelite monks from nearby St Theresa's Church built a **chapel** inside the gate to house the most revered of the city's many sacred images, the **Madonna of the Gate of Dawn** (Aušros vartų Marija), and the gate has been a place of pilgrimage for both Lithuanians and Poles ever since. The Madonna is just about visible through a trio of arched windows directly above the gate, and it's rare to see locals who don't look up at the image and cross themselves as they pass underneath it.

Entrance to the chapel is via a doorway at the rear end of St Theresa's, from where a narrow staircase leads up to the chamber where the image is kept. It's a small and intimate space, filled with kneeling supplicants whispering prayers, the aura of sanctity strangely undisturbed by the steady shuffle of visitors' footsteps. Her slender fingers splayed in a stylized gesture of grace, the Madonna herself is all but hidden by an extravagant silver-plated covering that emits a beckoning sparkle to those approaching the gate along the street below. The air of glittering opulence is enhanced by the panels on either side of the image, covered with the heart-shaped plaques left by grateful pilgrims.

The southern side of the gate is surprisingly plain, save for a relief depicting a horse-borne knight known as the **Vytis**, which served as the symbol of the Grand Duchy of Lithuania from the times of Vytautas the Great onwards, and was resurrected after 1991 to feature on the newly independent republic's coat of arms.

The Artillery Bastion

Two minutes' walk east of Aušros Vartų gatvė at Boksto 20/18 is the **Artillery Bastion** (Artilerijos Bastėja; Tues–Sun 10am–5pm; 4Lt), a semicircular, red-brick cannon battery built in the seventeenth century to defend the (no longer standing) Subačiaus gate nearby. There's a modest display of weapons and armour inside, although the museum is more interesting for its setting than its contents: visitors descend via a long brick passageway into the bowels of the building, where cannons similar to those used to defend the city have been placed in the embrasures. A door at the top of the passageway leads outside to a viewing terrace, from where you can gaze across towards the crowd of Old Town belfries to the northwest and the narrow streets of the hilly Užupis district to the northeast.

The Old Town's western fringes: the old Jewish quarter, Pylimo gatvė and Vilniaus gatvė

Before World War II, Vilnius was one of the most important centres of Jewish life and culture in Eastern Europe and was known as the "Jerusalem of the North" – a name allegedly bestowed on it by Napoleon Bonaparte when he paused in the city in 1812. First invited to settle in 1410 by Grand Duke Vytautas, the Jews made up a third of the city's population by the nineteenth century, inhabiting a sizeable chunk of the Old Town. The **Jewish quarter** was concentrated in the warren of alleyways either side of **Vokiečių gatvė**, an area vividly remembered by Czesław Miłosz in his book *Beginning with my Streets* (see "Books", p.459) as "a labyrinth of absolutely medieval, narrow little streets, the houses connected by arcades, the uneven pavements two or three metres wide". Little of this world now survives: the 70,000-strong community that once lived here was almost totally wiped out during the Nazi occupation, and few survivors chose to move back after 1945. A handful of the Jewish quarter's streets still retain something of their pre-World War II appearance, although most were reduced to rubble during the war and overlaid with parking lots and office blocks in the years that followed.

The Jewish quarter was carved into two separate **ghettos** by the Germans in 1941, with the streets north of Vokiečių becoming the so-called **Ghetto no. 1** (which was cleared in September 1941), and those to the south becoming **Ghetto no. 2** (cleared in September 1943). The ghettos were rebuilt and repopulated with Lithuanians from the countryside after the war's end, and the area's past was quietly forgotten. The Soviet regime drew a discreet veil over the true extent of Jewish suffering, preferring to present the "Soviet people" as the sole victim of Nazi terror. Vilnius's Jews remained without monuments or memorials until the 1990s, when a scattering of inconspicuous plaques were put up to help fill the yawning gap in the city's collective memory.

Vokiečių and around

Vokiečių gatvė curves northwestwards from Rotušės aikštė, its name (literally "German Street") a relic of the medieval period when merchants from various countries were allowed to settle in different quarters of the city. The Vokiečių of today, however, has little in common with its pre-World War II incarnation, when it served as the main commercial artery of Vilnius's Jewish community and would have been a chaotic jumble of carts, stalls and bilingual Yiddish and Polish shop signs. A broad, tree-lined boulevard with a slim ribbon of park running down the middle, it's busy on summer evenings, when young Vilniusites congregate round the tables of open-air cafés or sprawl on park benches to swig their takeout beers.

Something of the Jewish quarter's original warren-like street plan has been preserved off the southwestern side of Vokiečių, where Mėsinių ("Butchers' Street") leads into the heart of the former site of **Ghetto no. 2**. About 150m up the street, near the junction with Ašmenos, a modest, easy-to-miss granite memorial bears a Hebrew and Lithuanian text reading: "In remembrance of those who suffered and struggled in the Vilnius ghetto". Across a grassy park to the east lies Rūdninkų gatvė, where the main gate to Ghetto no. 2 was located – it was through here that work details left in the morning, and were locked back in at night. A wall plaque bearing a map of the ghetto marks the spot.

West of Mėsinių, take Ašmenos gatvė and its extension, Žemaitijos gatvė, and you'll see a plaque at no. 12 marking the location where the armed Jewish underground put up barricades on September 1, 1943, in a desperate attempt to prevent German troops from clearing the ghetto. From here, Šv Mikalojaus gatvė spins back north to rejoin Vokiečių, on the way passing **St Nicholas's Church** (Šv Mikalojaus bažnyčia), whose red-brick, stepped gable peers over a white courtyard wall. During the inter-war period this was the only Lithuanian-speaking church in Vilnius – services in all the other Catholic establishments were conducted in Polish. The interior is currently being restored, although it's usually open around Mass times.

Immediately opposite St Nicholas's, Pranciškonų darts north towards the eighteenth-century **Franciscan Church** (Pranciškonų bažnyčia), whose impressively lofty interior is once more open for worship after serving as a storehouse during the communist period. Harbouring little else besides a marble statue of the Madonna, this draughty, semi-devastated space packs a spiritual punch more powerful than many of the better-preserved places of worship.

Žydų gatvė and around

The historical heart of Jewish Vilnius lay on the northeastern side of Vokiečių around **Žydų gatvė**, or "Jews' Street" ("Yidishe gas" to its pre-World War II inhabitants), site of the **Great Synagogue** and the labyrinth of courtyards and alleyways that once surrounded it. Seriously damaged in World War II, the synagogue was levelled by the Soviets, and its place is now occupied by a kindergarten tucked between post-war apartment blocks. Outwardly unassuming, the synagogue was built slightly under-ground, possibly as a ruse to prevent its grandeur from inviting the envy of local Christians. "It took my breath away, for I had never expected it to be so grand," wrote Lucy Dawidowicz, whose book *At that Time and Place* (see "Books", p.460) describes the year she spent as an American student in pre-World War II Vilnius. "Outside, the synagogue looked to be about three stories tall, but inside it soared to over five stories." It's said that congregations of five thousand people crammed the synagogue's cavern-ous, domed interior on major religious holidays.

There's no plaque marking the location of the synagogue, but squeezed between the kindergarten and a neighbouring house is a bust of the **Gaon of Vilnius**, Elijah ben Solomon (1720–97), the renowned Talmudic scholar who lived and taught here. The Gaon was one of the main opponents of Hasidism (the ecstatic, mystical sect which spread throughout the Jewish communities of Eastern Europe in the mid-eighteenth century), and his reputation as an authority on all aspects of doctrine added to Vilnius's prestige as a centre of Jewish learning.

Between Žydų and Antokolskio to the east there once existed a warren of court-yards and tiny alleys (now it's just a car park), home to the poorest of Vilnius's Jewish poor, who would eke out a living by selling old clothes and flea-market junk from makeshift stalls. It was here that Lucy Dawidowicz came across the "Durkhoyf" or "Through-Yard", which she called "the most dismal place of poverty I knew in Vilna", where the air "was close, musty and fetid with the odor of old clothes, the stink of refuse, and the rank odor emanating from the buildings' moldering walls".

The Dominican Church

At the northern end of Vokiečių, Dominikonū heads back east into the heart of the Old Town, passing after 100m or so the **Dominican Church** (Dominikonų bažnyčia), yet another medieval edifice rebuilt in Baroque style by the ubiquitous Jan Krzystof Glaubitz in the 1770s. Given the narrowness of the street, it's difficult to get a good look at the church's most arresting external feature – the broad cupola squatting atop a hefty octagonal drum – without viewing it from some distance away. Approaching or leaving along Stiklių gatvė, just to the southeast, should do the trick.

The macabre Last Judgement scenes covering the walls of the porch provide little advance warning of the show-off pink and mauve tones of the church's effervescent interior. Beyond a pulpit decked with sprightly angels and cherubs lies a vivacious cluster of altars, from which gesticulating saints appear poised to leap into the congregation. Up above, a dizzying swirl of frescoes depicting the Apotheosis of the Holy Spirit run around the cupola in celestial comic-strip style.

The church's congregation is largely drawn from the city's Polish community, many of whom come to linger in the side chapels dedicated to a generous assortment of supposedly miracle-working Virgins and saints. Most, however, gravitate towards an unremarkable-looking painting, roughly halfway down the nave, which portrays a robed Christ with divine rays emanating from his chest – a work inspired by the visions experienced by Sister Faustyna Helena Kowalska, a celebrated Catholic mystic of the inter-war period. A local rector encouraged Sister Faustyna to describe what she'd seen to the painter Eugeniusz Kazimirowski in 1934, and the resulting canvas has been the focus of a cult ever since. Sister Faustyna herself was beatified in April 1993 on the occasion of Pope John Paul II's visit to Vilnius.

Pylimo gatvė and the State Vilnius Gaon Jewish Museum

Running parallel to Vokiečių to the southwest, **Pylimo gatvė** follows the line of the former town walls, and still acts as an unofficial boundary between the Old Town and the nineteenth-century Naujamiestis (see p.327) beyond. A slightly scruffy thoroughfare traversed by lumbering trolleybuses, it's nevertheless rich in memories of Jewish Vilnius, not least because of the synagogue and the three sites of the **State Vilnius Gaon Jewish Museum** that lie on or near the street.

At Pylimo's northern end, the **main branch of the Jewish Museum** at no.4 (Valstybinis Vilniaus Gaono Žydų muziejus; Mon–Thurs 9.30am–5.30pm, Fri 9.30am–4.30pm; 1Lt, free Wed in winter) occupies a labyrinthine building housing numerous Jewish cultural organizations. A fragmentary display located in several rooms in different parts of the building kicks off with a tribute to the anti-Nazi resistance groups in the wartime ghettos of Vilnius and Kaunas, and the smuggling operations that allowed a small number of Jews to escape to the forests where they could link up with the partisans. Elsewhere, there are words-and-pictures displays devoted to Vilnius-born cultural figures, notably Yiddish writer Avrom Karpinowicz (1918–2004), and the fiddle-playing phenomenon Jascha Haifetz. Upstairs is the Gallery of the Righteous (Teisuolių galerija), a large hall containing photographs of Lithuanians who were honoured by post-war Israel for their help in sheltering Jews from the Germans, alongside the moving testimonies of those they saved.

Two minutes northwest at Pamėnkalnio 12 is another site of the Jewish Museum, the **Catastrophe Exhibition** (ekspozicija "Katastrofa"; Mon–Thurs 9am–5pm, Fri 9am–4pm; same ticket). Housed in a building colloquially known as the "**Green House**" on account of its colourful timber construction, this contains a harrowing display about the fate of Lithuania's Jews during the war. An English-language leaflet will guide you round the collection of photographs and documents – most chilling of the latter are the matter-of-fact reports submitted by Einsatzkommando leaders in December 1941, detailing how the killing of Jews had been organized and the numbers involved. Most of Lithuania's Jews were murdered within months of the Nazi takeover, although a few exhibits hint at the remarkable tales of the few who survived: there are scale models of the underground hideaways into which people retreated in order to avoid Nazi round-ups and diagrams of the sewer system used by resistance fighters to make their way in and out of the Vilnius ghettos.

Back on Pylimo, walking south and uphill onto Naugarduko you'll find another branch of the Jewish Museum, the so-called **Tolerance Centre** (Tolerancijos centras; Mon–Thurs 10am–6pm, Sun 10am–4pm), which occupies a former Yiddish-language theatre. The display begins on the uppermost of three floors with artworks by Lithua-nian-Jewish artists, including a fine set of abstract lithographs by Druskininkai-born Jacques Lipchitz (see p.324). Nearby are items rescued from the Vilnius Great Syna-gogue, including the doors of the Aron Ha Kodesh (the ark in which the Torah scrolls are kept) and fragments of the reader's lectern. The most delightful exhibit is the series of puppets made by Aaron Chasit of Kelmė in the early twentieth century. Depicting King Solomon and members of his court, they are a unique example of Lithuanian-Jewish folk art. There is a chronological words-and-pictures account of the history of Jews in Lithuania on the second floor, and a space used for temporary art exhibitions on the first.

Further south at no. 39 is the city's one surviving **synagogue** (Mon–Thurs 8am–10am, Sun 7pm–9pm), a Moorish-style structure put up in 1903 to serve a congregation that belonged to the Haskalah ("Enlightenment") tradition – a nineteenth-century movement which aimed to bring Judaism into line with mod-ern secularism. Originally known as the Choral Synagogue, owing to the (then innovative) use of a boys' choir during services, it was a popular place of worship for wealthier, westernized Jews in pre-World War II days, and now serves the whole of Vilnius's remaining Jewish community.

The Frank Zappa Statue

Backtracking north along Pylimo and turning west onto Kalinausko brings you to one of the city's more unexpected cultural monuments. Tucked away in the car park of an ear, nose and throat hospital, and mounted on a soaring pillar, is a bust of the American rock avant-gardist **Frank Zappa**, erected in 1995 on the initiative of local jazz musician Saulius Paukstys. The choice of Zappa – a widely understood symbol of nonconformity perhaps, but hardly a Lithuanian icon – seemed to be a wryly ironic gesture in a country that had seen enough of ideologically charged public monuments, and the project was supported by many people who had never even heard a note of the man's music.

Vilniaus gatvė

If you don't fancy the idea of trudging down Pylimo, an alternative route through the western fringes of the Old Town is offered by Vilniaus gatvė, a sinuous street which starts at the northwestern end of Vokiečių and works its way up towards the bustling shops of Gedimino prospektas. There's a smattering of sights along its length, begin-ning with the gorgeous strawberries-and-cream exterior of **St Catherine's Church** (Šv Kotrynos bažnyčia), an elegant twin-towered structure, the interior of which still awaits renovation. Opposite the church, the two-storey town house at no. 41 provides a suitably refined home for the **Lithuanian Theatre, Music and Film Museum** (Lietuvos teatro, muzikos ir kino muziejus; Tues–Fri noon–6pm, Sat 11am–4pm; 4Lt), which harbours an alluring jumble of posters, costumes and antiquated cameras. Many of Lithuania's leading artists found work designing costumes and sets for the theatre, and the selection of their sketches on show here – including the work of mid-twenti-eth-century modernists such as Adomas Varnas and Stasys Ušinskas – beats anything in the city's picture galleries.

A little further along, at no. 39, the **Teachers' House** (Mokytojų namai), overlook-ing the junction of Vilniaus and Klaipėdos, is occupied by a multitude of cultural

△ Vilnius Old Town

organizations – including the **Vartai Art Gallery** on the second floor (Mon–Fri 1–6pm; free), which quite apart from putting on some of the best contemporary art shows in the capital, retains some spectacular Art Nouveau stucco work in its high-ceilinged rooms. Five minutes further north, a squat, ochre-plastered block at no. 22 is the one surviving wing of the seventeenth-century **Radvila Palace** (Radvilų rūmai; Tues–Sat 11am–6pm; 4Lt), the downtown pad of one of the Grand Duchy of Lithuania's leading aristocratic families. Rising to prominence in the fifteenth century, the Radvilas (more widely known by their Polonized name of Radziwiłł) went on to provide the duchy with many of its most outstanding military commanders, diplomats and bishops. Their palace now contains a rather mundane collection of paintings and furniture, enlivened only by occasional visiting exhibitions, and a downstairs room plastered with 165 oddly compelling prints from the Radvila family album. Commissioned by Mykolas "My Dear Fishy" Radvila (depicted in portrait no. 157, he was so nicknamed because those were the over-familiar words he used to address bemused fellow aristocrats), the series portrays all the prominent family members through the ages, starting with mysterious, semi-mythical founder of the Radvila dynasty, Vaišunda, and culminating with Karol Stanisław Radvila (1734–90), who – despite being pictured here as a foppish aristocrat – was a shaven-headed drunkard and hooligan accused by contemporary chroniclers of shooting his own servants for sport.

Gedimino prospektas

Gedimino prospektas, running west from Cathedral Square, was the main thoroughfare of nineteenth-century Vilnius, and remains the city's most important commercial street. A broad, cobbled boulevard, overlooked by trolleybus wires and spruced-up, stuccoed buildings, it has been named after St George, Mickiewicz, Stalin and Lenin in

On the eve of World War II the Jewish community constituted the biggest single ethnic group in Vilnius, making the city one of the most important centres of Jewish culture in northeastern Europe. Although they had been present in the city since at least the time of Vytautas the Great, their numbers rose significantly after 1795, when the western territories of the Tsarist Empire (of which Lithuania was now a part) were specifically earmarked for Jewish colonization – a ruse designed to keep them out of the Russian heartlands of the east.

As the main urban centre for Jews living in the territories of present-day Lithuania and northern Belarus, Vilnius became a hot-house of intellectual activity towards the end of the nineteenth century. In 1897, the city saw the birth of the **Bund**, the international Jewish socialist movement which had a major influence on the development of left-wing ideas in the Tsarist Empire and beyond. The city also enjoyed a rich artistic life: both the painter **Chaim Soutine** and the sculptor **Jacques Lipchitz** passed through Vilnius Art School in the years before World War I, while violin virtuoso **Jascha Heifetz** was groomed by the city's Music Academy.

The inter-war period saw an upsurge in Yiddish culture, Yiddish being the first language of the majority of Vilnius Jews. In the 1930s, the literary periodical **Yung Vilne** ("Young Vilnius") provided an outlet for a new generation of Jewish poetry and prose writers, of whom Chaim Grade (best known for the autobiographical short-story collection *My Mother's Sabbath Days*; see "Books" p.461) is the most famous representative. The idea of Yiddish as a national Jewish language equal in importance to Hebrew was promoted by the **YIVO** (Yidisher Visnshaflekher Institut or Yiddish Scientific Institute), founded here in 1925 to conduct research into the ethnology and folklore of Yiddish-speaking communities throughout Eastern Europe.

However, Vilnius was not immune from the waves of **anti-Semitism** that swept across Central Europe in the wake of World War I. Already in 1919, units of the Polish Legion – in Vilnius to defend the region against the Bolsheviks – had run amok in the Jewish-inhabited parts of the Old Town, leaving many dead. In the late 1930s, Jewish students at Vilnius University were made to sit on special benches at the back of the lecture hall, in order to prevent them from "contaminating the morals" of their Catholic classmates.

None of this, however, prepared Vilnius's Jews for the fate that lay ahead under the **Nazi occupation**, which began with the German army's arrival in the city on June 24, 1941. Within weeks of taking control of the city, the Nazi authorities were joined by special units known as the Einsatzkommandos, who were specifically charged with the job of ridding the German-controlled areas of Eastern Europe of their Jewish inhabitants. From July 8 onwards, the Einsatzkommando responsible for the Vilnius region – aided by Lithuanian auxiliaries – started taking an average of five hundred Jews a day to the Paneriai forest on the outskirts of Vilnius (see p.332), where they were shot and thrown into pits. On September 6, 1941, the Jewish quarter of Vilnius's Old Town was divided into two **ghettos**, in which the city's surviving Jews were confined. The smaller of the two ("Ghetto no. 1"), comprising the narrow streets on the northeastern side of Vokiečių gatvė, contained about 11,000 people, most of whom were killed over the next two weeks. The larger ghetto ("Ghetto no. 2"), which occupied the streets

the past, reflecting the succession of different regimes. It's a place to come and shop or do business rather than sightsee, although few of its buildings are without deep historical associations.

Around 600m west of Cathedral Square is the **Hotel Neringa**, whose restaurant was the favoured haunt of the city's artistic elite during the brief golden age of relative cultural freedom in the late 1960s and early 1970s. The Russian dissident poet and Nobel Prize winner, Jozef Brodsky, whiled away the evenings here when visiting Lithuanian literary colleague Tomas Venclova, and the avant-garde Ganelin-Tarasov-Chekasin southwest of Vokiečių, initially held 29,000 inhabitants (mostly able-bodied Jews considered fit for work, together with their families), although this number was gradually reduced over the next two years as more and more people were taken away – either to provide slave labour elsewhere, or to be killed at Paneriai.

Despite the constant lack of food and the spirit-sapping fear of Nazi round-ups, Ghetto no. 2 continued to function as an urban community with a semblance of normality, boasting a hospital (jammed between Ligoninės and Pylimo), a public library and sports club (both located at Žemaitijos 4) and even a theatre (at Arklių 3), where a drama troupe, choir and symphony orchestra performed. The ghetto also had a **resistance movement** in the shape of the United Partisan Organization (Fareinikte Partisaner Organizatsie or **FPO**), formed in January 1942 with the aim of smuggling Jews out of the ghetto and into the forests outside Vilnius, where partisan groups were active throughout the war. After an escape attempt in summer 1943, in which twelve made it out of the ghetto (another nine were caught and shot), the Germans announced that they would execute all family members of anyone who tried to flee. The FPO henceforth concentrated on arming itself, which it did by bringing in weapons through the sewer system. In July 1943, the Germans declared that they would liquidate the ghetto forthwith unless the FPO leader, Iztak Witenberg, was handed over to the Gestapo. He gave himself up immediately in order to save the rest of the community.

On September 1, increased military activity around the ghetto persuaded the remaining FPO leaders that the ghetto was about to be cleared and its inhabitants relocated to concentration camps. Barricades were set up at either end of Žemaitijos gatvė in an attempt to protect the FPO headquarters (at Žemaitijos 4) and buy time. Approaching German troops were fired on from a building at the eastern end of Žemaitijos and forced to retreat before returning to blow the building up. This act of resistance was no more than a minor inconvenience to the Germans, but it did persuade them to postpone the full clearing of the ghetto for a couple of weeks, allowing several FPO members and other young Jews to escape (either through the sewers, or via gates in the ghetto wall which were supervised by slack Lithuanian police). One of those who got away was Abraham Sutskever, a member of the pre-war Yung Vilne literary set who went on to become one of the major post-war writers in the Yiddish language.

However, the vast majority of the ghetto's remaining 10,000 inhabitants were rounded up on September 23 and dispatched to a variety of destinations: able-bodied adults were sent to labour camps in Estonia and Latvia; most of the women and children were delivered to the death camps. Those too sick to be transported were taken straight to the Paneriai forest to be shot.

Today, Vilnius has a Jewish population of around 3000, although most of these belong to families who moved to the city from other parts of Lithuania after 1945. Many of the Vilnius-born Jews who survived the Holocaust simply couldn't bear the pain of living here after 1945 and left for North America or Israel – consigning the cosmopolitan world of pre-war Vilnius to the realm of history books and reminiscences.

jazz trio (which went on to achieve world renown) played four-hour sets to appreciative crowds of coffee-swilling intellectuals. Perhaps inevitably, the *Neringa* was also a stronghold of the local KGB: foreign visitors to the restaurant were invariably ushered towards private booths fitted with listening devices. The trend-setting crowd moved away from the *Neringa* decades ago, and the restaurant nowadays caters to fat cats rather than hep cats, but it still preserves much of its original decor, notably the famous murals featuring idealized scenes of fisherfolk from Neringa, the sandy peninsula after which the hotel is named.

Another 400m brings you to the broad open space of **Lukiškių aikštė**, a square which has long played an infamous role in the city's history. After the 1863–64 uprising against the Tsarist regime, a number of rebels were publicly hanged here by the hardline Russian governor Muravyev. From 1952 to 1991 it was graced by a monumental **statue of Lenin**, unceremoniously carted away in August 1991 as the collapse of the Moscow coup signalled the final break-up of the Soviet Union. Preserved as a warning to future generations, the statue can still be seen in the Grūtas sculpture park outside Druskininkai (see p.389).

The Lithuanian Genocide Museum

On the southern side of Lukiškių aikštė, the forbiddingly grey, Neoclassical building at no. 40 is the former site of Lithuania's KGB headquarters and now the educative and moving **Lithuanian Genocide Museum** (Lietuvos genocido aukų muziejus; entrance on Aukų 2A; mid-May to mid-Sept Tues–Sun 10am–6pm; mid-Sept to mid-May Tues–Sun 10am–4pm; donation expected; English-language leaflet 2Lt, tape commentary 8Lt). Originally built in 1899 to serve as the city courthouse, the building was taken over by the NKVD (as the KGB was initially known) during the first Soviet occupation of Lithuania in 1940. It then served as the HQ of the Gestapo when the Germans took over in July the following year, and reverted to the Soviets in 1944. The ground floor contains a imaginative multimedia display relating the history of the Soviet occupation, complete with English-language captions. Down in the basement, the dank cells where the KGB incarcerated and tortured their prisoners have been preserved in their pre-1991 state. There are texts and photographs relating to some of the more famous prisoners to have passed through here – notably the Catholic Bishop Borisevičius, shot in the basement in 1946; and partisan leaders Jonas Žemaitis and Adolfas Ramanauskas, who survived for years in the forests of Soviet Lithuania before being captured – and executed – in the mid-1950s. Particularly chilling are the water isolation cells, in which prisoners had to stand on precarious concrete perches for hours on end – or risk falling into a dirty pool of freezing water below. On the first floor, the reassembled remnants of the KGB's own museum (a propagandistic affair which was only open to KGB members) illustrate the self-celebratory mindset of the Soviet Union's secret police.

The Music Academy and the Parliament Building

Next door to the Genocide Museum at no. 42 looms the Neoclassical bulk of the **Lithuanian Music Academy** (Lietuvos muzikos akademija), where vast pictures of Lenin were hung on Soviet state holidays such as May Day and November 11 (the anniversary of the Bolshevik revolution), and terracing erected so that party leaders could observe the bombastic parades with which such occasions were marked.

At the extreme western end of Gedimino prospektas stands Lithuania's **Parliament Building** (Seimas), a graceless modern structure built in the 1980s to serve as the home of the Lithuanian republic's Supreme Soviet – a toothless assembly of party appointees. The first free elections to the Soviet in February 1990 transformed this bastion of communist authority into a focus of Lithuanian patriotism overnight, and it was here that the restoration of Lithuanian independence was declared on March 11 of the same year – to the intense annoyance of Mikhail Gorbachev, who was on an official visit to Vilnius at the time. When the Kremlin moved to crush the Lithuanian independence movement on January 13,1991, thousands of ordinary citizens descended on the parliament to prevent its capture by Soviet forces, who had already killed twelve unarmed civilians while storming Vilnius's TV Tower. On the side of the parliament facing the river some of the barricades built to defend the building have been preserved, complete with anti-Soviet graffiti; there's also a moving memorial of traditional wooden crosses commemorating those who died at the TV Tower, and the seven border guards killed at Medeninkai by Soviet special forces six months later.

On the opposite bank of the river, the glimmering gunmetal domes of the Orthodox **Znamensky Church** (Znamenskio cerkvė) provide the Gedimino strip with one final architectural flourish, although the bare interior is hardly worth venturing across the bridge for.

Naujamiestis

Extending over the hilly terrain which overlooks the Old Town from the west, the **Naujamiestis**, or "New Town", began life in the mid- to late nineteenth century, when a grid-pattern of broad boulevards and sturdy apartment blocks was laid out in order to accommodate the city's growing middle class.

The few real attractions here begin with the modest display at the **Lithuanian Railway Museum** (Lietuvos Geležinkelių muziejus; 2.50Lt), just uphill to the west of Pylimo gatvė at Mindaugo 15. It contains models of old locomotives, photographs of the building of the Warsaw–St Petersburg line (which connected Vilnius to the Tsarist train network in 1862), and a model train layout with no noticeable Lithuanian connection. It's a short walk north from here to Basanavičiaus, the main artery of the Naujamiestis and home to the Orthodox **All Saints' Church**, one of the city's prettiest. Shaming the street's drab office blocks with its sparkling array of green onion domes, the church was built in 1913 to celebrate the three-hundredth anniversary of the Romanov dynasty's accession to the Russian throne. It's pretty bare and gloomy inside, though, save for an intricate, filigree-effect brass iconostasis.

Marking the western border of the Naujamiestis is **Vingis Park** (Vingio parkas), the city's largest, a gently undulating area of pine forest traversed by asphalt paths. A popular strolling area all year round, it's also the site of a large open-air stage where pop concerts are held in the summer. A full 2km from the Old Town, it's best accessed by walking west along M.K. Čiurlionio gatvė, which runs roughly parallel to Basanavičiaus to the north.

East of the Old Town

From Maironio gatvė, which marks the eastern boundary of the Old Town, a narrow bridge leads over the fast-flowing Vilnia River towards the district of **UŽUPIS** (literally "beyond the river"), a shabby hillside heap of crumbling nineteenth-century houses that seems a world away from the Vilnius of the tourist brochures. However, this former urban backwater is changing fast, not least because the faded charms of its alleyways and courtyards have recently attracted two very different groups of incomers: nouveaux-riches eager to buy and renovate houses on the cheap, and impoverished bohemians on the lookout for low-rent accommodation and squats. It's the latter who are largely responsible for the creation of the so-called **Užupis Republic** (Užupio respublika), which declared its independence from the rest of Vilnius on April Fool's Day 2000. Intended as a wry comment on the very notion of independence in the era of globalization, the "republic" also represents a serious attempt to build a sense of community in the district and to stimulate the activities of the numerous artists and nonconformists who have gathered here. Annual fashion shows, art exhibitions and chaotic summer regattas on the River Vilnia have all been organized here in recent years, alongside a whole host of more impromptu happenings. Unfortunately for the outsider, events tend to be publicized on a word-of-mouth basis, and it's difficult to find out about them unless you have local contacts. The best place to start is probably the *Užupio kavinė* (see "Bars and pubs" p.335), just over the bridge from the Old Town, where many of the republic's leading lights are wont to congregate. Beyond here, a short walk along the gently ascending Užupio gatvė should be enough to give you a flavour of the district; after some 200m it passes a small, triangular piazza, dominated by a tall pillar topped by a trumpet-blowing bronze angel – unveiled in April 2001 to mark the first birthday of the republic.

One of the more infamous former residents of this part of town was **"Iron" Felix Dzerzhinsky**, the Lithuanian-born Pole who went on to become a committed Bolshevik and one of Lenin's closest collaborators. Dzerzhinsky lived at Užupio 14 (roughly level with the angel) while a high-school student, before moving on to become a socialist agitator in Kaunas. After the Russian revolution Dzerzhinsky was entrusted

Romain Gary (1914–1980)

Lists of famous Vilniusites often fail to include the French war hero, novelist and dip-lomat **Romain Gary**, who spent the early 1920s living at Basanavičiaus 16, just to the west of Pylimo gatvė. The nineteenth-century apartment block is still standing and has probably changed little since his time, save for the unobtrusive plaque attached to the wall in his honour.

Gary was a complex character who frequently hid behind aliases and fabricated biographical details, and much about his early life remains obscure. The way he tells it, he arrived in Vilnius in 1921 – the first stage in what his Russian Jewish mother hoped would be a passage to a better life in France. In the meantime she eked out a living making women's hats, which she then passed off as expensive imports from Paris. She even went as far as to organize a promotional party at which a failed actor from Warsaw was drafted in to impersonate a top French couturier. The ladies of Vilnius fell for the ruse, and the business prospered for a time, leaving Gary's ambi-tious mother free to invest in her son's education by hiring a whole roster of private teachers. When he wasn't being tutored in etiquette or horsemanship, Romain spent his days playing in the communal yard behind Basanavičiaus 16, or hovering beside a nearby alley where he frequently caught the local baker indulging in adventurous al-fresco sex with a serving girl – an experience wistfully recounted in the 1960 account of his childhood, *La Promesse de l'Aube*.

After a year in Vilnius, the hat business collapsed and the family moved on, first to Warsaw, and then to France, where Gary passed through the Foreign Legion and the French Air Force before joining up with General de Gaulle's Free French. While in London he met and married the writer, journalist and *Vogue* editor, Lesley Blanch.

Just after the war, Gary burst onto the French literary scene with his first novel, *Education Européene* (a story of World War II Polish partisans in the forests near Vilnius), received with critical acclaim. At around the same time, he entered the French diplomatic service and was immediately posted to Sofia, where the Bul-garian secret service set him up with a local girl and secretly filmed the results. Not surprisingly, his next foreign posting was in politically uneventful Switzerland, from where Gary mischievously filed reports on snow conditions to unamused superiors in Paris.

In 1956, Gary won France's most prestigious literary prize, the Prix Goncourt, for his macho tale of elephant hunters in Africa, *Les Racines du Ciel* (subsequently filmed by John Huston and starring Errol Flynn, Juliet Greco and Trevor Howard). The same year he became consul general in Los Angeles and entertained the Hollywood elite at lavish receptions. A reputation for paying more attention to film starlets than to French economic interests led one newspaper to dub him the "French sexual atta-ché". It was in LA that he met his second wife, Jean Seberg, a young film star 25 years his junior.

Gary quit the diplomatic service in 1961 in order to concentrate on writing, churning out film scripts for big studio producers like Daryll Zanuck and David Selznick. He even directed features himself, few of which made it into the annals of cinema history – although 1972's *Kill* earned notoriety by being banned in the UK for its excessive use of violence.

In 1975, writing under the pseudonym Emile Ajar, Gary again won the Prix Goncourt – the only person to win it twice – for *La Vie Devant Soi*. The Académie Goncourt decided to award the prize without knowing the real identity behind the pseudonym. Gary's cousin, Paul Pavlowitch, posed as the author for a while, and it was only in his posthumous work, *Vie et Mort d'Emile Ajar*, that Gary revealed the truth.

Although they divorced, Gary and Jean Seberg remained close, and some months after Seberg committed suicide, on December 2, 1980, Gary, too, took his own life.

with setting up the Cheka, the much-feared state security service which later metamorphosed into the KGB – hardly an organization remembered with great affection by the majority of Lithuanians. Unsurprisingly, there's no commemorative plaque.

The Hill of Three Crosses

Pathways on the northern side of the Užupis district lead up onto a group of sandy, pine-covered knolls known by the collective name of Kalnų parkas ("Hill Park"), a peaceful area which seems light years away from the bustle of the city below. The most prominent – and most visited – of the heights here is the **Hill of Three Crosses** (Tryų kryžių kalnas), reached more conveniently from its northern side, where an asphalted road climbs up from Kosciuškos gatvė, near to the Applied Art Museum (see p.309). According to popular tradition, it's here that Jogaila erected three crosses in memory of the seven Franciscan monks executed on this spot by his grandfather, Grand Duke Algirdas. Whatever their origins, a trio of crosses did exist here until Russian Governor General Muravyev's decision to remove them – a reprisal for the 1863–64 uprising. Vilnius town council celebrated the departure of the Russians in 1915 by building three new crosses in gleaming white stone, a much-loved landmark on the city's eastern skyline until the Soviets dynamited them in 1950. The replicas erected after 1990 have quickly re-established themselves as popular targets for weekend strollers. Those who make it up here are rewarded with excellent views of the city, with the Old Town laid out in the foreground and more distant landmarks, such as the bright green cupolas of All Saints' Church and the spear-like form of the TV Tower, further away to the east.

The Church of SS Peter and Paul and Antakalnis cemetery

Past the Hill of Three Crosses, Kosciuškos continues 800m northeast towards the **Church of SS Peter and Paul** (Šv Petro ir Povilo bažnyčia), its twin-towered facade presiding over a busy traffic roundabout. Of fifteenth-century origin, the church was rebuilt as a three-aisled basilica in 1668 on the initiative of Lithuania's Grand Hetman (military commander-in-chief and second only to the Grand Duke in times of war), Michael Casimir Pac. Pac intended the church to be a celebration of Vilnius's deliverance from the Russians, who had just vacated the city after a thirteen-year occupation.

The **interior** looks cold and grey at first sight, but on closer inspection comes alive with gloriously over-the-top stucco work, featuring cavorting cherubs, rich foliage and exotic plants laden with fruit. The whole ensemble was conceived by Italian craftsmen Pietro Perti and Giovanni Maria Galli, who spent eleven years cramming every available centimetre of the upper walls and ceiling with over two thousand mouldings. Some of the most complex work is around the dome, where angels twang away on musical instruments and contorted human forms appear to be holding up the central lantern. Of the several richly decorated chapels on either side of the nave, the most famous is the altar of the Madonna of Misericord in the left-hand transept, where an image of the Virgin supposedly protects parishioners from ill health and disease. Donated to the church by Bishop Jerzy Tyszkiewicz in 1647, it became the focus of a serious cult during the plague epidemic of 1708–10, when Bishop Brzostowski began holding forty-hour Masses at the altar in an attempt to soothe the anxieties of his flock. On leaving the church, look out for the stucco figure of Death prancing mischievously on one side of the main doorway – a memento mori said to mark the grave of Pac himself.

Northeast of the church lies the low-key suburb of **Antakalnis**, worth venturing into if only to explore the peaceful, park-like terrain of **Antakalnis cemetery** (Antakalnio kapinės) about 800m beyond – follow Antakalnio gatvė past the church and then bear right along Sapiegos, from where the cemetery is well signed. Ranged across pine-covered hills, the cemetery bears the mark of all the regimes to have ruled over Vilnius during the last two centuries. The tombs of wealthy Tsarist families dot the area near the entrance, while over to the left lies a vale of neatly laid-out crosses honouring the Poles who died defending the Vilnius region from the Red Army in 1919–20. The

△ The Church of SS Peter and Paul

eastern end of the cemetery is overlooked by an angular Soviet-era war memorial and a terraced hillside occupied by the graves of Lithuania's post-1945 communist elite – a uniformly poker-faced bunch if the accompanying busts and reliefs are to be taken seriously. Finally, providing a focus for contemporary patriotism in the central part of the cemetery, a semicircular memorial remembers the thirteen Lithuanian victims of Soviet aggression in January 1991, twelve of whom died defending the Vilnius TV Tower (see p.443).

Antakalnis cemetery has recently been earmarked as the site of a new memorial to the French war dead of winter 1812, when the Grande Armée (deserted by Napoleon himself) retreated in disarray through Vilnius – a city Napoleon had entered in triumph only five months earlier. Renewed interest in the period arose in 2001, when a building site northeast of the city centre yielded the remains of over two thousand soldiers, most of whom had succumbed to a lethal mixture of hunger, typhus and cold weather. Many of the dead were not French nationals, but volunteers picked up in Poland and Lithuania during Napoleon's march eastwards. Once they've been fully examined by archeologists, their remains will be laid to rest here.

The outskirts

Outside central Vilnius, there's a handful of isolated attractions, each of which could be seen in a morning or an afternoon. On the eastern margins of the city, both the **Alexander Pushkin Museum** in Markučiai and the **cemetery** in the suburb of **Rasos** are reasonably short hops from the centre and provide a glimpse of the semi-rustic, forest-fringed outskirts which girdle the city centre. Further to the west, the **Television Tower** is an engaging tourist attraction in its own right, as well as a powerful reminder of Lithuania's resistance to the Soviet aggression of January 1991. Historical memories of an altogether more harrowing kind are attached to the forest of **Paneriai**, 10km southwest of town, where the bulk of Vilnius's pre-war Jewish population were brutally murdered by the Nazis.

The Alexander Pushkin Museum

Situated in the suburb of Markučiai, 2km east of the Old Town, the **Alexander Pushkin Museum** (Aleksandro Puškino muziejus; Wed–Sun 10am–5pm; 4Lt) is a bit of a fake, bearing in mind that it was the home of Pushkin's son rather than that of the great Russian poet himself. Such details shouldn't put you off, however – the timber building in which the museum is housed harbours the best-preserved nineteenth-century interior in the city, and the surrounding woods make it a lovely place for a short stroll. Built for the Russian General Melnikov in 1867, the house was inherited by his daughter, Varvara, who subsequently married Pushkin's youngest son Grigorii. Chunky period furniture and reproduction wallpaper provide the backdrop to a words-and-pictures display (texts in Lithuanian and Russian only) about the poet's life and work, including several references to Adam Mickiewicz (see p.312); the poets knew each other in Moscow, and Pushkin's enthusiasm for his colleague's writings contributed greatly to Mickiewicz's growing international reputation. Outside the house, pathways lead through deciduous forest to the small onion-domed chapel beside which Grigorii and Varvara lie buried. To get to the museum, take bus #10 from the Užupio stop on Mairono gatvė to the Markučiai terminus – the house is on a knoll straight ahead.

Rasų cemetery

A forest of predominantly nineteenth-century funerary monuments ranged across tree-shaded hillocks, **Rasų cemetery** is an important place of pilgrimage for Lithuanians and Poles alike, owing to the unusually large number of historical figures buried here. It lies in otherwise undistinguished suburbs about 1600m southeast of the Old Town: from Rotušės aikštė, walk east along Subačiaus then south along Rasų gatvė; otherwise take bus #31 from the train station. Prime among the remains laid to rest here is the **heart of Marshal Józef Piłsudski**, leader of the Polish independence movement at the beginning of the twentieth century and the country's first president after 1918. Born into an impoverished gentry family in the Polish-Lithuanian borderlands, Piłsudski went to school in Vilnius, and owned land outside the town in the 1920s. He long entertained the romantic notion that the Polish-Lithuanian Commonwealth of old could be restored (a Commonwealth in which the Poles, of course, would play the leading role), and was genuinely disappointed that the strength of Lithuanian national sentiment after World War I rendered such a dream impossible. He gave tacit support to the Żeligowski coup that restored Vilnius to Poland in 1920, and remained sentimentally attached to the Vilnius region throughout his life – hence the desire to have at least one portion of himself laid to rest here. Buried with much pomp on May 12, 1936, the marshal's heart lies underneath a black granite slab just to the left of the cemetery's main entrance, surrounded by the graves of Polish soldiers who defended Vilnius against Bolshevik forces in 1919. Piłsudski's remaining body parts can be found in the crypt of Kraków's Wawel Cathedral.

One of the few prominent Lithuanians who chose to stay in Vilnius during the Piłsudski era was **Jonas Basanavičius** (1851–1927), the publicist and patriot who had become the leader of the Lithuanian national movement at the close of the nineteenth century. A simple obelisk marks his final resting place opposite the cemetery's main chapel, which is uphill and to the right of the Piłsudski memorial. Basanavičius was one of the prime movers behind the Lithuanian Declaration of Independence on February 16, 1918, and wreaths are laid here on the anniversary. A Lithuanian cultural icon of equal stature – the painter and composer **Mikalojus Konstantinis Čiurlionis** (see p.366) – lies a short distance away in the northern part of the cemetery, marked by an angular grey tombstone.

The Television Tower

Perched on high ground 3km west of the centre in the suburb of Karoliniškės, the slender form of the 326-metre **Television Tower** (Televizijos bokštas; daily 10am–9pm; 22Lt) soars gracefully above the surrounding pines. On January 13, 1991, the Kremlin ordered its troops to seize control of the TV Tower and other key public buildings in a ham-fisted attempt to reassert authority over the wayward republic. When unarmed civilians gathered to defend the tower, twelve of them died under the wheels of Soviet tanks. Once in control of the tower, the Soviets closed down the Lithuanian TV service – which simply continued broadcasting from its studios in Kaunas. Fearful of causing further casualties, the Soviets backed off from their plans to storm the Seimas, where many thousands more civilians had gathered. The events of January 13 provoked international outrage (irredeemably tarnishing the image of Soviet leader Mikhail Gorbachev) and only served to boost the prestige of the Lithuanian independence movement.

Today, the dead are commemorated by a group of **wooden crosses** at the tower's base, while a photographic exhibition on the ground floor inside vividly captures the drama and heroism of the time. Lifts convey visitors to the rather drab café-restaurant near the tower's summit, although the trip is rewarded with the chance to savour a superb panorama of the city from the slowly revolving viewing deck.

To get to the tower take trolleybus #16 or bus #54 from the train station, or trolleybus #11 from Lukiškių aikštė; alight at the Televizijos bokštas stop on Sausio 13-Osios gatvė.

Paneriai

PANERIAI, the forested site where the Nazis and their Lithuanian accomplices murdered one hundred thousand people during World War II, lies among nondescript suburbs 10km southwest of the centre. The site was initially used by the Soviet army, who dug oil storage pits here in 1941. The Nazis, who arrived in July the same year, found the pits especially convenient. Political undesirables from all over Europe were among those killed and buried here, although the vast majority (an estimated 70,000) were the Jews of Vilnius, who were systematically exterminated from July 8, 1941 onwards, the biggest waves of killing taking place in September 1941 and September 1943.

The killing grounds are about 1km into the woods due west of Paneriai train station and marshalling yards. The entrance to the site is marked by two stone slabs dating from the communist period, whose Russian and Lithuanian inscriptions refer to murdered "Soviet citizens" rather than Jews – a typical example of how the Soviet authorities exploited the Holocaust for their own political ends, failing to spell out who its real victims were. A central slab with an inscription in Hebrew commemorating "seventy thousand Jewish men, women and children" was only added in 1990. From the memorial, a path leads to the **Paneriai Memorial Museum** (Panerių memorialinis muziejus,

Agrastų 15; official times are Mon & Wed–Fri noon–6pm, Sat & Sun 11am–6pm, but ring ☎8-5/260 2001 to check that it's open), which holds a small display detailing what happened here. From the museum, paths lead to the pits into which the Nazis initially threw their victims; the bodies of many were later exhumed and burned when the advance of Soviet armies prompted the Germans to start hiding the evidence of their crimes. This latter task was carried out by an eighty-man, corpse-burning team composed of Jews and Russian POWs. They were kept chained at all times and slept in a heavily defended bunker accessible by a ladder that was removed at night. After spending three months digging a tunnel with spoons and bare hands, forty of the corpse burners escaped on April 15, 1944. Twenty-five of them were caught and killed straight away, while the rest broke through to join partisan groups in the forest. The forty corpse burners who had stayed behind were executed five days later.

To get to Paneriai, take a southwest-bound suburban train from Vilnius station and alight at Paneriai. From the station platform descend onto Agrastų gatvė, turn right and follow the road through the woods for about 1km.

Eating and drinking

Vilnius has a rapidly growing choice of **restaurants**, offering everything from Lithuanian to Lebanese cuisine, with prices to suit all budgets. There's plenty in the way of **café culture** in the city, although this tends to revolve around smallish places offering snacks and cheap meals, as well as the full range of alcoholic and non-alcoholic drinks. Such cafés may stay open until late evening, although most night-time drinking takes place in the ever-growing range of **bars**, many of which keep going until the early hours. Most bars and restaurants are concentrated around Gedimino or in the Old Town, and there's little point in straying outside this area unless you're looking for one of the few characterful suburban establishments listed below.

Picnic supplies and other **foodstuffs** can be purchased from big stores like Rimi, opposite the town hall at Didžioji 28 (daily 8am–10pm); Iki, in the same building as the bus station (daily 8am–10pm); or from the mega-supermarket Maxima, just west of the Old Town at Mindaugo 11 (daily 8am–midnight).

Restaurants

Many Vilnius **restaurants** serve the kind of cuisine you come across in most northern European countries: solid meat-and-potato fare, schnitzels and chops. An increasing number of establishments, however, are starting to serve up traditional Lithuanian food, such as *cepelinai*, *koldūnai* and *blynai*, in folksy, wood-furnished surroundings. In addition, there's no end of pizzerias and a handful of ethnic restaurants around the centre.

Apart from a few upscale, starched-napkin restaurants in the pricier hotels, most places cultivate an air of relaxed informality. **Prices** for main courses usually fall into the 20–35Lt bracket, although speciality dishes, especially in the posher places, often cost more. In some restaurants it's a good idea to book a table in advance at weekends; telephone numbers are included below where necessary.

Old Town

The restaurants listed below are marked on the "Vilnius Old Town" map on p.310.

Balti drambliai Vilniaus 41. Vegetarian restaurant with a loyal clientele of mildly bohemian youth, located in a many-chambered, red-brick basement decorated with pictures of the Buddha, Shiva, the moon and other deities. Tasty, inexpensive tofu-based stews with couscous or rice form the backbone of the menu. The tusk-like sculpture emerging from the bar is a reference to the restaurant's name, which means "White Elephant". Mon–Fri 11am–midnight, Sat & Sun noon–midnight.

Čili kaimas Vokiečių 8 ☎8-5/231 2536, ⓦwww .cili.lt. Labyrinthine Lithuanian theme restaurant decorated with antlers, saddles, antiquated brass instruments, a whole tree and even a fishpond. The menu features everything from boiled pigs' ears to roast chicken breast, with national dishes like *cepelinai* and *koldūnai* also prominently featured. The food is on the ordinary side, but the fun factor keeps locals and tourists coming back in their droves – be prepared to reserve, or queue, at weekends. Sun–Thurs 10am–midnight, Fri & Sat 10am–2pm.

Čili pica Didžioji 5, also at Gedimino 23 and other locations in town. A popular place for a quick, inexpensive bite, offering a wide choice of thin-crust and deep-pan pizzas in bright and breezy surroundings. Home delivery available on ☎8-5/233 3555. Daily 8am–midnight.

Freskos Didžioji 31 ☎8-5/261 8133. Imaginative, well-presented modern European cuisine in a barrel-vaulted chamber occupying the rear end of the Town Hall. Dishes are expensive and not all as brilliantly prepared as the menu seems to promise, but this is still an enjoyable and characterful place to eat. Good-value lunchtime salad buffet. Daily 11am–midnight.

Gabi Šv Mykolo 6. Solid home cooking in a relaxed and cosy atmosphere. Alongside the standard Lithuanian pork- and chicken-based meals, Gabi serves up serviceable steaks and some delicious potato pancakes. Outdoor seating in a courtyard strewn with agricultural implements. Main courses in the 8–15Lt range. Daily 11am–10pm.

Keisti ženklai Trakų 15. With moody lighting and cushioned-bench seating, Keisti ženklai ("Strange Signs") looks like a cool coffee bar at first sight, an impression bolstered by the avant-garde Russian artworks used to illustrate the menu. In fact, Lithuanian meat-and-potatoes fare is the order of the day, making this a pleasantly quirky place in which to fill up on inexpensive, home-style cooking. Daily 11am–11pm.

Lokys Stiklių 8/10 ☎8-5/262 9046, ⓦwww.lokys.lt. Long-established Lithuanian cellar restaurant serving wild boar, elk and a wide range of pork and beef standards in atmospheric, almost dungeon-like surroundings. Prices are creeping up but remain on the affordable side. Daily noon–midnight.

Markus ir Ko Antokolskio 11 ☎8-5/262 3185. Cosy restaurant set in informal, bar-like surroundings, drawing a loyal clientele of eager carnivores with its superb steaks – filet mignon being the house speciality, plus generous salads. With mains hovering in the region of 30–40Lt, it's not ruinously expensive. Reserve at weekends, when there's live jazz or piano music. Daily noon–midnight.

La Provence Vokiečių 22 ☎8-5/262 0257, ⓦwww.laprovence.lt. French and south European cuisine in a formal environment. Faultless standards of cooking and service, and a more extensive (and pricey) wine list than is usual for Vilnius. Twice as expensive as anything else in the Old Town, but probably worth the treat. Daily 11am–midnight.

Šauni vietelė Pranciškonų 3. Hidden away behind the Franciscan monastery church, Šauni vietelė's

illuminated-panel interior looks like a cross between a nightclub and a video game (without being as noisy as either). The inexpensive menu features pretty much everything in the pork-chop-and-chips line, alongside some excellent potato pancakes. A pleasant place to drink as well as eat, it's popular with a youngish and laid-back clientele. Daily noon–midnight.

Sorena Islandijos 4. Moderately priced Azeri restaurant serving up a high standard of Caucasian cuisine, with fresh salads, big sheets of lavash (Caucasian flat bread) and shashlik-style skewer-grilled kebabs predominant dishes. The mixed grill platter, featuring succulent chunks of veal, lamb and chicken, will satisfy two or three people eating together. Hubble-bubbles for hire in the cushion-seated alcove. Mon–Thurs 11am–10pm, Fri 11am–midnight, Sat noon–midnight.

Steak House Helios Didžioji 28 ☎8-5/260 9009, ⓦwww.steakhouse.lt. Main-street location, lounge-bar furnishings and piano-tinkling live music conspire to make this one of the city's most popular weekend dining spots. The steaks are the star attraction, although the grilled fish dishes shouldn't be overlooked either. And with mains hovering around the 45Lt mark, it's not wildly expensive either. Daily noon–midnight.

Stikliai Gaono 7 ☎8-5/262 4501. French food in the posh restaurant upstairs, homely, somewhat cheaper Lithuanian fare in the beer-cellar-style restaurant downstairs. The latter hosts live Lithuanian folk music every evening bar Sunday. Daily noon–midnight.

Žemaičiai Vokiečių 24 ☎8-5/261 6573, ⓦwww.zemaiciai.lt. Subterranean labyrinth specializing in Žemaitijan (west Lithuanian) cuisine. An excellent place to try cepelinai, smoked fish or Žemaičiū blynai (potato pancakes stuffed with mincemeat), as well as some tasty pork and beef dishes. The drinks list features some strong speciality beers, as well as an array of Lithuanian spirits. Head for the wooden-bench courtyard out the back in summer. Something of a tourist favourite, but prices remain affordable. Daily 1pm–midnight.

Outside the Old Town

The restaurants listed below are marked on the "Vilnius" map on p.302.

Joanos Carinovos smuklė Belmonto 17 ☎8-686 14 656, ⓦwww.belmontas.lt. Lithuanian theme restaurant with folksy trinkets adorning the rooms and a lengthy menu of pork and potato dishes. Located in a renovated old mill in the Belmontas district, a leafy park area 3km east of the Old Town, it makes for a highly enjoyable excursion. Daily noon–1pm.

Marceliukės Klėtis Tuskulėnų 35 ☎ 8-5/272 5087, ⓦ www.marceliuke.lt. Traditional Lithuanian favourites in a folksy tavern-style pavilion jammed between tower blocks north of the River Neris. The food is top quality and not too expensive, and there's live folk music most nights. Daily 11am–midnight.

Tores Užupio 40 ☎ 8-5/262 9309, ⓦ www .tores.lt. Modern European cuisine with the emphasis on steaks and grilled fish. Renowned for

the panoramic view of Vilnius's Old Town from its outdoor terrace. Daily 11am–11pm.

Vandens Malūnas Verkių 100, ☎ 8-5/271 1666, ⓦ www.vandensmalunas.lt. Traditional Lithuanian meaty fare and quality international dishes in an old mill 6km north of the centre, set between suburban houses and meadows. Three storeys of wooden-beamed rooms, with antiquated milling machines dotted around the place and dried herbs hanging from the rafters. Daily 11am–midnight.

Cafés

Many of Vilnius's **cafés** offer much the same fare as those establishments that class themselves as restaurants, but in more informal surroundings and at sometimes significantly cheaper prices. All of the cafés listed below are marked on the Vilnius Old Town map on p.310.

Delano Gedimino 24. Basement self-service restaurant decorated to look like a medieval castle crossed with a village barn. Pile your plate high with salads, marinated-herring snacks and all manner of main courses ranging from the inevitable pork chops to the fancier fillets of fish. Mon–Fri 10am–7pm, Sat & Sun 11am–6pm.

Gusto blyninė Aušros vartų 6. Pancakes with a huge choice of sweet or savoury fillings, in utilitarian but pleasant surroundings. Daily 9am–10pm.

Mano kavinė Bokšto 7. Located on a quiet Old Town street, this café with chic, modernist decor serves an extensive range of speciality teas, generously served by the potful, plus a range of cakes, snacks and full meals, including decent pancakes (*blynai*) and salads. Daily 10am–11pm.

Pieno Baras Didžioji 21. An old-fashioned milk bar bang on Town Hall Square, offering dirt-cheap pastries and non-alcoholic drinks. Best place in the

Old Town for an early-morning breakfast. Mon–Sat 8am–8pm, Sun 9am–7pm.

Pilies Menė Pilies 8. Flash, modern café-bar renowned for its extensive menu of sweet and savoury pancakes. Good place for a daytime coffee or night-time drink. Daily 10am–midnight.

Ponių Laimė Stiklių. One of the more refined order-at-the-counter cafés, perfectly located for a quick Old Town coffee break or lunch. Treats include a salad bar, savoury pastries and pies (including the excellent *daržovių pyragas* or vegetable bake), and a colourful array of cakes. Mon–Fri 9am–10pm, Sat 10am–10pm, Sun 11am–6pm.

Skonis ir Kvapas Trakų 8. Supremely relaxing café occupying an elegant suite of barrel-vaulted rooms, and offering big pots of properly brewed tea, excellent coffee and an affordable range of hot meals. The cakes are top-notch too. Daily 9.30am–midnight.

Drinking

There are innumerable watering holes in central Vilnius, especially in the Old Town, ranging in style from faux-rustic taverns with wooden-bench seating, to swish, modern, designer bars with minimalist decor. Several of them call themselves "pubs", although few really try to ape British or Irish styles directly, preferring instead to cultivate a cosmopolitan, fun atmosphere that wouldn't be out of place in any large, hedonism-driven city. Most drinking venues serve a wide range of food, and the locals are as likely to visit them for lunch or dinner as for a session of serious imbibing. A few hostelries close at 11pm or midnight, although the majority are now open into the early hours of the morning, especially at weekends. All of the places listed below are marked on the Vilnius Old Town map on p.310.

Bars and pubs

Absento fėjos Aušros vartų 11. Classy cocktails, absinthe and all manner of international spirits, in an Art-Nouveau-meets-science-fiction interior. Crammed at weekends, when the young and

beautiful spill out onto the tiny patio-style courtyard. Tues–Thurs 6pm–2am, Fri & Sat 7pm–5am.

Amatininkų Užeiga Didžioji 19/2. A comfy café-pub on the Old Town's main square, the "Artisans'

Inn" has been a popular meeting point ever since the 1980s, when it was central Vilnius's trendiest bar. Still well patronized due to its prime location and late opening hours, it features homely rustic design touches and an extensive range of Lithuanian food. Daily 11am–5am.

Avylis Gedimino 5 ⓦwww.avilys.lt. A smartish but atmospheric brick-clad basement with beer brewed on site and Lithuanian food. Mon–Thurs noon–midnight, Fri & Sat noon–1am, Sun noon–11pm.

Bix Etmonų 6. Named after legendary 1990s alternative rock band Bix, this was the first designer bar in Vilnius and its village-inn-meets-intergalactic-spaceship interior is still very much a one-off. With a full menu of hot meals, and sporting events shown on the big screen, it's a good place to kick off an evening. Daily 11am–2am.

Brodvėjus (aka "Broadway") Mėsinių 4 ⓦwww.brodvejus.lt. Something of a Vilnius classic, this popular drinking-and-dancing venue is built around a long, galleried space packed with tables – with a stage at one end for live bands (Thurs–Sun) and bopping. Full menu of snacks and hot meals; lunchtime specials are chalked up on a board outside. Sun & Mon noon–2am, Tues noon–3am, Wed–Sat noon–4am.

Café de Paris Didžioji 1. The café next to the French Cultural Centre functions fairly well as a coffee-and-crepes venue during the day, but turns into a mildly arty DJ bar at night, featuring offbeat styles of music that you might not hear elsewhere, and occasional acoustic gigs. Oddly shaped and impossible to navigate without bumping into people, but it's an enjoyable crush. Sun–Tues noon–midnight, Wed–Sat noon–2am or later.

Cozy Dominikonų 10 ⓦwww.cozy.lt. One of those wonderfully multi-functional Vilnius locales that serves as a relaxing café during the day and cool DJ bar in the evening. The matt-black floor and tangerine-coloured chairs might have you jotting down interior-design notes. Daily 9am–2am or later.

Grasas Vokiečių 2 ⓦwww.grasas.lt. Spacious stone cellar with artificial grass stuck to the ceiling and the odd mirror ball, attracting a healthy cross-section of Vilnius youth. Either DJs or live rock and jazz gigs are laid on at the weekends, and the food menu covers most dishes in the Lithuanian culinary repertoire. Sun–Tues noon–midnight, Wed & Thurs noon–2am, Fri & Sat noon–3am.

Ibish Lounge Aušros vartų 11 ⓦwww.ibishlounge.net. Snug, two-room bar with Sixties-inspired furniture, DJs on most nights of the week and a tank full of tropical fish. There's also a menu of salads, pastas and meaty main courses. Mon, Thurs–Sat noon–3am, Tues, Wed & Sun noon–midnight.

In Vino Aušros vartų 7 ⓦwww.invino.lt. Wine bar and much more besides, with candlelight and wooden chairs and tables creating a nineteenth-century French-farmhouse-kitchen feel in the main room, and a more loungey area around the corner. Background music of the jazz or chanson variety creates a bit of extra class. Sun–Thurs 4pm–2am, Fri & Sat 4pm–4am.

The Pub Dominikonų 9. Enduringly popular bar with wooden interior and pub-grub food menu that takes in everything from shepherd's pie to chicken curry. The covered courtyard frequently hosts live music, discos and big-screen basketball. Sun–Thurs 11am–1am, Fri & Sat 11am–3am or later.

Savas Kampas Vokiečių 4. A long-standing favourite with a broad cross-section of drinkers, not least because of its prime location. Choose between the front room with mildly rustic wooden tables, and the two back rooms with their sofas, standard lamps and an olde-worlde living-room feel. Food-wise, there are passable pizzas and a plentiful choice of both sweet and savoury pancakes. Mon–Thurs 8.30am–1am, Fri 8.30am–4am, Sat 10am–4am, Sun 10am–1am.

Sole Luna Universiteto 4. With its lemon-yellow walls and bright orange chairs and settees, entering *Sole Luna* is a bit like walking into a huge citrus fruit. It's a good place in which to relax over coffee during the day (the place is run by Italians so the espresso is reassuringly strong), and warms up with DJs and decadence-seeking drinkers at night. Outdoor seating in a gorgeous Renaissance courtyard is the other main draw. Mon–Thurs noon–midnight, Fri & Sat till 2am or later.

Šuolaikinio Meno Centras (ŠMC) Inside the Contemporary Art Centre at Vokiečių 2. This dark, minimally decorated café-bar has long been a prime meeting point for arty types and nonconformists of all ages. The lunches and light meals are cheap and tasty, although it's as an offbeat evening drinking venue that *ŠMC* really comes into its own. Mon–Thurs 11am–midnight, Fri & Sat 11am–1am or later, Sun noon–midnight.

Užupio kavinė Užupio 2. A comfortable café-bar just over the Užupio bridge from the Old Town, catering for a mixed crowd of youngish professionals and the arty denizens of the bohemian Užupis district (see p.327). The moderately priced food menu covers ribs, fish, a couple of vegetarian offerings and above-average potato pancakes. The *Stebuklas* ("Miracle") apple pie fully deserves its moniker and is well worth leaving room for. Madly popular in summer, with a tree-shaded outdoor terrace overlooking the Vilnia River. Daily 10am–11pm.

Woo Vilniaus 22. Basement bar and diner with a white-walled, minimalist interior and DJ-driven club events at weekends. Alongside a good selection of cocktails and a solid wine list there's a full menu of Asian-influenced foods – with Vietnamese soups, Japanese sushi and Thai curries geared to suit most appetites and pockets. Mon–Thurs noon–2am, Fri noon–5am, Sat 5pm–5am, Sun 5pm–midnight.

Nightlife and entertainment

Vilnius is a major centre for high culture, with three full-size **orchestras**, two chamber orchestras and a clutch of quartets pulling in appreciative crowds all year round. Groundbreaking contemporary **drama** is also a regular feature of the cultural calendar, alongside a regular diet of classical theatre. More sybaritic tastes are catered for by the city's ever-changing roster of **clubs** and discos. There are always a few local bars or restaurants hosting gigs by local **jazz** musicians; decent live rock, on the other hand, is hard to find.

The tourist office will have upcoming programme details for the main classical music and drama venues. Otherwise, *Vilnius in your Pocket* or the *Baltic Times* are your most likely source of theatre and concert **listings**, unless you can read Lithuanian, in which case the back pages of local daily *Lietuvos Rytas* or cerebral arts weekly *Literatūra ir menas* carry more detailed information.

Clubbing and live music

Vilnius has several large **mainstream clubs** attracting a friendly, relaxed crowd with an unsophisticated mixture of Western, commercial dance tunes and Lithuanian and Russian techno. In addition, many of the establishments listed under "Bars and pubs" (see 335life venues come and go with alarming regularity. Prices are on the whole reasonable: expect to pay anything between 10 and 35Lt, depending on who is spinning the discs.

Local **rock** and **jazz** bands play at venues such as Brodvėjus/*Broadway* (see "Bars and pubs"; opposite), or *Tamsta* (see "Clubs", p.338); details of upcoming events are posted on the door. Alternative bands occasionally appear in unlicensed, unofficial spaces, but you'll need local knowledge to find out what's on (checking out the excellent punk/ alternative site ⓦwww.hardcore.lt will help). Goth and pagan-metal bands have their own festival in the shape of **Kunigunda Lunaria**, in late April or early May (ⓦwww .dangus.net).

Traditional **folk** music is conspicuous by its absence in Vilnius unless you head for one of the more touristy eateries (see "Restaurants"; p.333), although there's one annual festival in the shape of **Skamba Skamba Kankliai**, when bands from all over Lithuania play in Old Town courtyards and parks in late May.

Clubs

Gravity Jasinskio 16 ⓦwww.clubgravity.lt. Minimalist decor and DJs from the wilder frontiers of dance culture have made this something of a Mecca for contemporary young hedonists who know a thing or two about cutting-edge house and techno. Fri & Sat 10pm–4/5am.
Helios Didžioji 28 ⓦwww.heliosclub.lt. A reliably enjoyable place, in the centre of the Old Town, catering for a good-natured, dressed-up crowd with a largely mainstream menu of dance music. Face control keeps the hoi polloi outside. Thurs–Sat 10pm–4/5am.
Intro Maironio 3 ⓦwww.intro.lt. A minimally decorated, warehouse-style club with a young,

alternative clientele and a wide-ranging programme of specialist DJ nights – anything from dancehall reggae to hip-hop or hardcore punk. Daily noon–2am or later.
Life Club Lukiškių 5 ☎8-5/212 7800, ⓦwww.rhgroup.lt. A mellow venue for the more mature clubber, eschewing house and hip-hop in favour of something that the average twenty- and thirty-something can shake a leg to. Frequent jazz-pop-rock performances add to the classy profile. Thurs–Sat 9pm–3am or later.
Neringa Gedimino 23. An elegant and intimate dance-bar beneath the *Neringa* hotel attracting a stylish twenty-something crowd. Broad range

of danceable pop classics and occasional cover bands. Mon–Sat noon–3am.

Pabo Latino Trakų 3/2 ☎8-5/262 1045, ⓦwww .pabolatino.lt. Hugely enjoyable Latin music club attracting a healthy cross-section of students, business types and vivacious clubbers. Door staff can be choosy at weekends, and if you want to find a seat you'll have to reserve a table in advance. Wed–Sun 8pm–3am or later.

Tamsta Subačiaus 11a ☎8-5/212 4498. Live music club where leading lights of the local rock-pop scene play to good-natured audiences who know their music. It's a chairs-and-tables kind of place, so arrive early if you want a seat. Gig schedule posted on the door. Wed–Sat 7pm–2am or later.

Classical music, opera and ballet

Vilnius can boast two symphony orchestras, of which the **Lithuanian National Philharmonic Orchestra** (Lietuvos nacionalinis simfoninis orkestras) is marginally the more prestigious, receiving the lion's share of visiting soloists and also embarking on major international tours in its own right. The **Lithuanian State Symphony Orchestra** (Lietuvos valstybinis simfoninis orkestras) is a newer outfit that doesn't have quite the same pedigree, but it is also of the highest quality, as is the other jewel in Vilnius's musical crown, the **Lithuanian National Opera and Ballet Theatre** (Nacionalinis operos ir baleto teatras). All three perform concerts throughout the year, except for short periods (notably in July and/or August) when they are either touring abroad or on holiday. In addition, look out for the numerous chamber concerts and solo recitals which round out the programmes of the main venues listed opposite.

A wide range of national and international musicians pack the programme of the **Vilnius Festival** (various venues around town; late May to early July), and the **St Christopher**

Summer Music Festival in July features local and international chamber ensembles, with most performances taking place in St Ignatius's Church on Šv Ignoto gatvė. In August, city folk head out to the summer festival in the nearby town of **Trakai** (see p.342) to enjoy concerts, opera and ballet in the romantic setting of the castle courtyard. The biggest events of the autumn are the **Vilnius Jazz Festival** (October; ⓦwww.vilniusjazz.lt); and the **Gaida Festival of Contemporary Classical Music** in October, to which composers come from far and wide to hear their music performed in a variety of venues across town. For further information on festivals in the city, see ⓦwww .vilniusfestivals.lt.

△ Vilnius Folk Festival

Concert halls

Music Academy (Muzikos akademija) Gedimino 42 ☏ 8-5/261 2691. Venue for recitals by local music students. Tickets available on the night of the performance.

National Philharmonic (Nacionalinė filharmonija) Aušros Vartų 5 ☏ 8-5/266 5233 & 266 5216, ⊛ www.filharmonija.lt. The elegant but not over-formal home of the country's premier orchestra, the Lithuanian National Philharmonic. Symphonic concerts on most Saturdays throughout the year, frequently featuring guest appearances by international soloists and conductors. Also "family" concerts of popular classics on Sunday lunchtimes, and a regular programme of chamber music. Box office Tues–Sat 11am–7pm, Sun 10am–noon.

Opera and Ballet Theatre (Operos ir baleto teatras) Vienuolio 1 ☏ 8-5/262 0727, ⊛ www.opera.lt. A modern auditorium with a busy programme of top-notch productions. Performances take place four or five times a week and are hugely popular, so book well in advance. Box office Mon–Fri 10am–7pm, Sat 10am–6pm, Sun 10am–3pm.

St John's Church (Šv Jono Bažnyčia) Vilnius University main courtyard. Organ and choral concerts every Sunday: check posters in and around the university, or ask at the tourist office for details.

Vilnius Congress Hall (Vilniaus kongresų rūmai) Vilniaus 6/16 ☏ 8-5/261 8828, ⊛ www.lvso.lt. A modern venue hosting performances by the Lithuanian State Symphony Orchestra about once a fortnight, as well as chamber concerts and occasional musicals. Box office Mon–Fri noon–7pm, Sat 11am–4pm.

Theatre

Vilnius's theatre scene is interesting and varied, although performances are invariably in Lithuanian (or Russian) except on the rare occasions when visiting companies are in town. However, the language barrier shouldn't prevent you from enjoying shows by the best of the contemporary drama companies, for whom movement and stagecraft are often just as important as the text. Three Lithuanian directors of worldwide renown whose performances should not be missed are Eimundas Nekrošius, Rimas Tuminas and Oskaras Koršunovas – new productions by all of them are often staged at the nation's most prestigious venue, the National Drama Theatre.

The **Lithuanian International Theatre Festival**, or LIFE (advance information from LIFE, Basanavičiaus 5; ☏ 8-5/262 5158), brings a number of foreign drama companies to town for a fortnight between late May and early June. With the emphasis on young and experimental directors, it offers a good mix of avant-garde craziness and more mainstream drama, with performances taking place at outdoor locations or at some of the venues listed below.

Lėlė Puppet Theatre (Lėlių teatras) Arklių 5 ☏ 8-5/262 8678. Top-quality children's entertainment featuring superbly designed puppets and enchanting stage sets. Performances take place at lunchtime or mid-afternoon. Box office Tues–Sun 10am–4pm.

Lithuanian National Drama Theatre (Lietuvos nacionalinis dramos teatras) Gedimino 4 ☏ 8-5/262 9771, ⊛ www.teatras.lt. Flagship of Lithuanian theatre with a comfortable, modern auditorium. As well as being home to the state drama company, it also hosts productions by prestigious independent drama troupes and high-profile performances from abroad. Some performances take place in the Small Hall (Mažoji salė), entered via Odminių gatvė round the back. Box office Mon & Fri 11am–2pm & 3–7pm, Tues–Thurs 11am–6pm, Sat & Sun 11am–1pm & 2–6pm.

Russian Drama Theatre (Rusų dramos teatras) Basanavičiaus ☏ 8-5/262 7133. Mixed programme of Russian-language classics and modern experimental work in a lovely 150-year-old building in sore need of renovation. It's an atmospheric place with good acoustics, but the glitzy theatre crowd tends to hang out elsewhere. Box office Tues–Sun 1–7pm.

Vilnius Little Theatre (Vilniaus mažasis teatras) Gedimino 22 ☏ 8-5/249 9869, ⊛ www.vmt.lt. Serious contemporary work in a small studio theatre. Box office Tues–Sat 11am–6.30pm, Sun 1–6.30pm.

Youth Theatre (Jaunimo teatras) Arklių 5 ☏ 8-5/261 6126, ⊛ www.jaunimoteatras.lt. A mixture of classical and experimental productions performed by youth companies. Box office Tues–Sun 11am–2pm & 3.30–7.30pm.

Cinema

Films are usually shown in the original language with Lithuanian subtitles. Tickets cost around 12–20Lt except on Mondays, when most cinemas drop their prices. The only **film festival** of real note is Kino Pavasaris ("Cinema Spring"), which falls in the last week of March and screens the odd new Lithuanian film alongside recent international releases.

Coca Cola Plaza Savanorių 7 ⓦwww .forumcinemas.lt. A modern multiscreen showing mainstream, first-run movies. The only drawback is that it's about 2km west of the centre in an area with few other nightlife attractions. Buses #4, #6, #11, #12, #14, #21 and #22.

Forum Akropolis Akropolis shopping centre, Ozo 25 ⓦwww.forumcinemas.lt. A state-of-the-art multiplex 2.5km northwest of the centre, in a retail complex packed with restaurants and bars. Minibus #2 from Pylimo.

Ozo Kino salė Ozo 4. A repertory cinema showing movie classics, stranded in a residential area 2.5km north of the centre. Minibus #2 from Pylimo.

Skalvija Goštauto 2/15. A good place to catch international art-house movies, if you can put up with the hard seats, muggy sound and general lack of atmosphere.

Shopping

Retail culture has wrought major changes on central Vilnius over the last decade, and streets like Gedimino prospektas, Pilies gatvė and Vokiečių gatvė are lined with the kind of clothes, footwear and other high-street stores that you'd expect to find in any European city. However, many locals still buy foodstuffs and household essentials from vast, bustling **markets**, where regular stallholders sell top-quality farm produce alongside small-time traders dealing in all manner of contraband. The most central of these are on Bazilionų gatvė (daily till 1/2pm), just north of the train and bus stations, and on Kalvarijų gatvė (Tues–Sun till 1/2pm), north of the River Neris but still within walking distance of the centre. The biggest of the lot, however, attracting bargain-hunters from all over the Baltic States, is at Gariūnai, 4km west of the centre (Tues–Sun till 1/2pm; bus #29 from Savanorių), where you'll find everything from cooking pots to car parts.

For souvenirs, you should head first to the outdoor **crafts market** at the junction of Didžioji and Pilies, where a gaggle of stalls sell traditional items like wicker baskets, wooden handicrafts and amber jewellery. The goods on display here are of variable quality, but may well be cheaper than those in souvenir shops, of which there are a growing number in the more tourist-trodden streets of the Old Town. Typical **opening hours of shops** are Monday to Friday from 10/11pm to 6/7pm, and Saturdays from 10/11pm to 3/4pm.

Souvenirs and gifts

Amber Museum Gallery Šv Mykolo 8. Amber shops are ten a penny in Vilnius, but this one is a bit special, presenting well-designed (and pricey) jewellery and rare stones in a chic, gallery-style environment. Daily 9am–6pm.

Linen and Amber Studio Stiklių 3, ⓦwww .lgstudija.lt. Linen shirts and dresses, as well as bed sheets and tablecloths, alongside other traditional textiles. Mon–Sat 10am–7pm, Sun 10am–5pm.

Sauluva Šv Mykolo 4 and Literatų 3. Sells a range of gifts, including a wide selection of

verbos, or "palms", the wand-like bundles of dried flowers and grasses which are used to decorate homes in the run-up to Palm Sunday. Mon–Sat 10am–7pm.

Šokoladino namai Trakų 13. A highly individual range of locally produced gourmet chocolates, in a variety of flavours and shapes, ideal for presents. Mon–Fri 10am–8pm, Sat & Sun 11am–6pm.

Verpstė Žydų 2. A good selection of linen, wooden toys and pottery. Mon–Fri 10am–6pm, Sat 11am–3pm.

Bookstores

Akademinė Knyga Universiteto 4. An academic bookstore with English-language books about Lithuania on the ground floor and English-language

fiction in the basement. Mon–Fri 10am–7pm, Sat 10am–3pm.

Littera Šv Jono 12. In the main courtyard of Vilnius University. Worth checking out for the neo-Baroque ceiling paintings as well as the books. Mon–Fri 9am–6pm, Sat 10am–3pm.

Prie Halės Corner of Pylimo and Sodų. Good choice of guidebooks and large-format art titles. Mon–Fri 11am–6pm, Sat 10am–3pm.

Music shops

Muzikos Bomba Corner of Jakšto and Goštauto. A wide selection of Lithuanian classical CDs, as well as international rock and pop. Mon–Fri 10am–7pm, Sat 10am–4pm.

Thelonious Second Hand Music Stiklių 12 ⓦ www.omnitel.net/thelonious. This shop has

Vaga Gedimino 50. One of the bigger downtown bookstores, with a small selection of English-language fiction and tourist-oriented titles. Mon–Fri 10am–7pm, Sat 11am–4pm.

a cellar-full of secondhand CDs and old vinyl – a good place to browse for local jazz and folk. Mon–Fri 11am–7pm, Sat 11am–3pm.

Listings

Airlines Aeroflot, Pylimo 8/2 ⓣ 8-5/212 4189, ⓦ www.aeroflot.ru; Air Baltic, Universiteto 10-7 ⓣ 8-5/243 0618 and at the airport ⓣ 8-5/235 6000; Austrian Airlines, Basanavičiaus 11 ⓣ 8-5/231 3137, ⓦ www.austrianairlines.lt; Finnair, at the airport ⓣ 8-5/261 9339, ⓦ www.finnair.com; FlyLAL, Gustaičio 4 ⓣ 8-5/252 5555, ⓦ www.flylal .lt; LOT, at the airport ⓣ 8-5/273 9020, ⓦ www .lot.com; Lufthansa, at the airport ⓣ 8-5/232 9292, ⓦ www.lufthansa.com; SAS, handled by Air Baltic (see above) and at the airport ⓣ 8-5/235 6000, ⓦ www.sas.lt.

Airport 5km south of the centre at Rodūnios kelias 2. Bus #1 from the train station (roughly hourly) or bus #2 from Lukiškių aikštė (roughly 2 per hour). Information ⓣ 8-5/230 6666, ⓦ www .vilnius-airport.lt.

Car rental A & A Litinterp, Bernardinų 7-2 ⓣ 8-5/212 3850, ⓦ www.litinterp.lt; Atlas, Asanavičiūtės 17 ⓣ 8-5/240 2380, ⓦ www .atlas.lt; Aunela, Vytenio 6-110 ⓣ 8-5/233 0318, ⓦ www.aunela.lt; Avis, at the airport ⓣ 8-5/232 9316, ⓦ www.avis.lt; Budget, at the airport ⓣ 8-5/230 6708, ⓦ www.budget.lt; Europcar, Stuokos-Gucevičiaus 9-1 ⓣ 8-5/212 0207, and at the airport ⓣ 8-5/216 3442, ⓦ www.europcar.lt; Hertz, Kalvarijų 14 ⓣ 8-5/272 6940, ⓦ www.hertz.lt; Sixt, at the airport ⓣ 8-5/239 5636, ⓦ www.sixt.lt.

Embassies and consulates Australia, Vilnius 23 ⓣ 8-5/212 3369; Belarus,: Muitinės 41 ⓣ 8-5/213 2255, ⓦ www.belarus.lt; Canada, Jogailos 4 ⓣ 8-5/249 0950, ⓦ www.canada.lt; Estonia, Mickevičiaus 4A ⓣ 8-5/278 0200, ⓦ www.estemb.lt; Ireland, Gedimino 1 ⓣ 8-5/262 9460; Latvia, Čiurlionio 76 ⓣ 8-5/213 1260, ⓦ www.latvia.lt; Poland, Smėlio 22A ⓣ 8-5/270

9001, ⓦ www.polandembassy.lt; Russia, Latvių 53/54 ⓣ 8-5/272 1763, ⓦ www.rusemb.lt (visas Mon–Fri 8.30am–noon); UK, Antakalnio 2 ⓣ 8-5/246 2900, ⓦ www.britain.lt; Ukraine, Teatro 4 ⓣ 8-5/212 1536; US, Akmenų 6 ⓣ 8-5/266 5500, ⓦ www.usembassy.lt. The nearest New Zealand embassy is in Warsaw, Poland ⓣ +48 22/521 0500.

Exchange Of the high-street banks, DNB Nord, Didžioji 25 (Mon–Fri 8am–7pm, Sat & Sun 10am–5pm) has the longest opening hours. The Parex Bankas exchange office outside the train station at Geležinkelio 8 is open 24hr.

Hospitals The main emergency department is at Vilnius University Emergency Hospital (Vilniaus universitetinė greitosios pagalbos ligoninė) Šiltnamių 29 ⓣ 8-5/216 9140. For private, English-speaking care, Baltic-American Clinic, Nemenčinės 54A ⓣ 8-5/234 2020, ⓦ www.bak.lt.

Internet access Collegium, Pilies 22 (Mon–Fri 8am–10pm, Sat & Sun 11am–10pm).

Laundry Joglė, in the Maxima supermarket at Mindaugo 11, for service washes and dry-cleaning (Mon–Fri 10am–10pm, Sat 10am–6pm).

Left luggage At the bus station (Mon–Sat 5.30am–9.45pm, Sun 7am–9.45pm). Luggage lockers (2Lt/12hr) can be found in the basement of the train station.

Libraries American Center Library, Akmenų 7 ⓣ 8-5/266 5300, ⓦ www.usembassy.lt (Mon–Fri 10am–5pm); British Council Library, Jogailos 4 ⓣ 8-5/264 4890, ⓦ www.britishcouncil.lt (Tues–Sat 11am–6pm).

Pharmacies Gedimino Vaistinė, Gedimino 27 (open 24hr); Vokiečių Vaistinė, Didžioji 13 (Mon–Fri 8am–7pm, Sat & Sun 10am–6pm).

Phones Public telephones are located throughout the city. Buy cards from kiosks or from the Central Phone and Telegraph Office, Vilniaus 33. For information on how to make a call, see "Basics".

Photographic developing and supplies Foto servisas, Pilies 23, process holiday snaps, sell film and offer professional developing services (Mon–Fri 10am–7pm, Sat 10am–5pm, Sun 11am–4pm).

Police ☎02.

Post office The main post office is at Gedimino 7 (Mon–Fri 7am–7pm, Sat 9am–4pm).

Taxis Taxi ranks are located on Rotūšés aikštė, although be warned that overcharging of foreigners

is rife. You stand a better chance of securing a fair price by ringing for a taxi in advance – try Vilniaus taxi (☎8-5/266 6662).

Travel agents AAA Wrislit, Rūdninkū 16 (☎8-5/212 2081, ⓦwww.wrislit.lt), deals in tickets for international airlines and ferries from Klaipėda to Scandinavia; Gintarinė Sala, Vokiečių 9 (☎8-5/212 0722, ⓦwww.gintarinesala.lt), sells plane tickets; and Lithuanian Student and Youth Travel Bureau, Basanavičiaus 30 (☎8-5/239 7397, ⓦwww.jaunimas.lt) offers student cheapies.

Around Vilnius

An appealing mixture of gently rolling agricultural land, pine forests and lakes, the countryside around Vilnius is fairly typical of much of Lithuania and makes a good introduction to the country as a whole. Within easy day-trip distance of the capital are **Trakai**, the much-visited site of a major medieval fortress; the Iron Age site of **Kernavė**; and the open-air sculpture park which goes under the modest name of the **Museum of the Centre of Europe**, just under 20km north. Trakai and Kernavė are easily accessible by bus; to get to the Museum of the Centre of Europe, however, you really need your own transport.

Trakai

Twenty-five kilometres west of the capital, lakeside **TRAKAI** once rivalled Vilnius as a hub of political and military power. The town's imposing island castle, completed during the reign of Vytautas the Great, is arguably the single best-known monument in the country – an instantly recognizable national symbol that receives a year-round stream of visitors. The lakes and forests surrounding the settlement further enhance Trakai's status as a beauty spot, and it's an ideal place for a lazy day of swimming, boating or water's-edge strolling.

Served by regular **buses** and minibuses from Vilnius, Trakai is an easy day-trip from the capital, though the soothing beauty of the surrounding countryside – coupled with a decent range of accommodation choices – makes it a good spot for a longer rural break. Indeed the growing range of **accommodation** available here means that you can quite easily use Trakai as a touring base in preference to Vilnius.

Some history

Together with Vilnius and Kernavė, Trakai was one of the earliest military strongholds in Lithuania, and occupied a crucial position in the ring of castles that protected the heartland of the Grand Duchy from the expansionist forays of the Teutons. The first fortified settlement here was located 3km southeast of the current town, where the village of Senieji Trakai ("Old Trakai") now stands. Senieji Trakai was the ruling stronghold of **Grand Duke Gediminas** before he moved his capital to Vilnius, and it is also thought to be the birthplace of Gediminas's grandson, **Vytautas the Great**, under whom Lithuanian power reached its apogee in the early fifteenth century. It was Vytautas's father, Kęstutis, who founded modern-day Trakai, choosing an island in Lake Galvė to build his impressive **castle**. Vytautas the Great resided here when not on campaign, and invited the **Karaim** (a Judaic sect from the Crimea; see box, p.344) to settle here and serve as his personal bodyguards. A couple of hundred Karaim still live in Trakai, their distinctive wooden cottages lining the town's main street. After the reign of Vytautas, Trakai continued to be second only to Vilnius in political importance: the whole of south-central Lithuania was governed from here, and whoever controlled Trakai castle was effectively the vice-ruler of the Lithuanian state.

The town's significance declined in the sixteenth century, and the castle itself was abandoned after being sacked by the Cossacks in the war of 1654–67, to be rediscovered in the twentieth century as a potent symbol of the country's medieval greatness.

Arrival and information

Trakai's friendly **tourist office** (Mon–Fri 8am–noon & 1–5pm, Sat 10am–3pm; ☏8-528/51934, ⓦwww.trakai.lt), about 800m north of the train and bus stations at Vytauto 69, sells local maps.

Bikes can be rented from the tourist office, *Hotel Trasalis*, or the *Slėnyje* campsite (see below).

Accommodation

There's a fair selection of hotel and guesthouse accommodation in Trakai and its environs, although visitors will need their own transport to access the out-of-town places. The tourist office can organize **bed-and-breakfast** accommodation (①) with local families in both Trakai and the surrounding villages, although vacancies disappear fast in summer. The two **campsites** listed below also offer **guesthouse** accommodation.

Hotels and guesthouses

Akmeninė Rezidencija Bražuolės village ☏8-528/25186, ⓦwww.akmenineuzeiga.lt. Swish waterside retreat on the shores of Lake Akmeninė, 5km north of town just beyond the turn-off for Užutrakis. A central, thatched-roof cottage offers snug doubles with log-cabin decor, iron bedsteads and modern bathrooms. Outlying two-person villas offer self-catering, and super-stylish modern furnishings made from natural materials. There's a restaurant on site (see p.346), and a separate bathhouse with a Russian-style, log-fired sauna. Villas from 795Lt, hotel rooms ⑥

Karaimų 13 Karaimų 13 ☏8-528/51911, ☏8-656 24 562. Six-room guesthouse offering simple but supremely comfy en-suite rooms featuring pine floors and ceiling beams, unobtrusive colour schemes and small TV. Breakfast is not included in the room price, but can be ordered from the downstairs café – which boasts an outdoor lake-facing terrace. ④

Margis Penkininkai village ☏8-528/21717, ⓦwww.margis.lt. Classy option located in pinewoods beside Lake Margis, some 8km west of Trakai on the Aukštadvaris road. Rooms feature designer furniture, earthy or pastelly colour schemes, plenty of desk space and modern bathrooms. Outlying bungalows contain two- or three-person split-level apartments with snazzy modern furnishings, classy fabrics, and floor-to-ceiling windows. Bungalows 900–1250Lt, double rooms depending on size and position ⑤–⑥

Salos Kranto ☏8-528/53990, ⓦwww .salos.lt. Small, central hotel on the shores of Lake

Totoriškų, offering simple, cosy en suites with TV or swanky split-level studios with wooden beams. There's a sauna and plunge-pool on the premises (100Lt/hr) and a basement DJ bar that opens at weekends. ④–⑤

Trasalis Gedimino 26 ☏8-528/51588, ⓦwww.trasalis.lt. Relatively new hundred-room hotel 1km south of the bus and train stations, primarily intended for visiting tour groups. The en-suite doubles are comfortable and fully equipped but the hotel's long corridors are a touch impersonal. With restaurant and bike hire on site, it's otherwise a perfectly good place to rest up. ⑤

Campsites

Antanas Gedvilas ☏8-528/74494, ⓔg.antanas @is.lt. Family farmstead 8km northwest of town in the village of Jovariškes, offering camping in a field overlooking Lake Akmena (Akmenos ežeras), and a handful of two- or three-person self-catering apartments (①). Dinghies, rowing boats and windsurfing boards available for guests.

Kempingas Slėnyje Slėnio 1 ☏8-528/53880 & 8-686/11136, ⓦwww.camptrakai.lt. Seven kilometres by road from Trakai on the far side of Lake Galvė, this is a well-equipped affair with plenty of camping space, electric power points for trailers, an on-site restaurant and access to lovely lakeside walks. It also has two small guesthouses offering en-suite rooms with TV, one with wooden floors, rustic furnishings and lake-ward views (④), the other with slightly chintzier decor (③).

The Town

Trakai extends over a long, narrow peninsula which touches on three lakes: Bernardinų to the east, Totoriškų to the west and the biggest, Galvė, to the north. From the **train**

The Karaim

A Turkic-speaking group practising a branch of Judaism, the **Karaim** are thought to be descended from the **Khazars**, a Central Asian people who held sway over a steppe empire stretching between the Black and Caspian seas in the seventh and eighth centuries AD. It's thought that the Khazar rulers invited Christian, Islamic and Jewish missionaries to their court, and eventually chose Judaism as the religion of the Khazarian elite. Although the Khazar empire was swallowed up by rivals some time in the ninth century, the Khazar language and culture were preserved by individual groups, one of which is believed to be the Karaim.

Whatever their origins, Karaim had by the eleventh century settled in the **Crimea**, which was then ruled by the Tatars – another Central Asian group who spoke a similar language. It was here that they came into contact with the Lithuanian ruler **Vytautas**, who after campaigning in the region in 1397 invited several Karaim and Tatar families to **Trakai** in order to form an elite guard loyal only to the Grand Duke. Karaim migration to the Grand Duchy of Lithuania continued over the next few centuries, with families often coming to Trakai first before moving on to new centres. One such place was **Lutsk** (now in the Ukraine), which became an important centre of Karaim learning and book publishing.

At the beginning of the twentieth century there were thought to be over 5000 Karaim in the Crimea and about 800 in Lithuania. Since then numbers have steadily declined, largely owing to intermarriage and assimilation. The preservation of Karaim culture in Trakai was given some encouragement during the inter-war period, when the Vilnius region found itself in Poland, and any non-Lithuanian minorities were given support, but under the Soviets the community's religious and cultural activities were discouraged. Karaim tended to assimilate into larger ethnic groups, abandoning their language in favour of the more dominant Lithuanian and Russian tongues. Only with the weakening of communist control was there a gradual reawakening of Karaim consciousness, with a Karaim conference in Lithuania in 1989 and a further conference in the Crimea in 1995. There are now an estimated 300 Karaim in Lithuania, just over a hundred of whom are in Trakai – numbers so small that any real Karaim cultural renaissance must remain outside the realms of possibility.

and **bus stations** follow Vytauto gatvė north to reach the main sights, which kick off after about 1000m with the Orthodox **Church of the Holy Mother of God** (Skaisčiausios dievo motinos gimimo cerkvė), a creamy-brown building topped with a Russian spire. Squatting on high ground a couple of hundred metres further on is the twin-towered **Church of the Visitation** (Šv Mergelės Marijos apsilankymo bažnyčia), a fairly unprepossessing place rebuilt many times since its original foundation by Grand Duke Vytautas in 1407. Inside, the garish pulpit and side altars look as if they've been given an over-generous coat of glossy house paint. The church is an important pilgrimage site thanks to the presence of a fourteenth-century icon of the Virgin, presented to Vytautas the Great by Byzantine Emperor Manuel II Paleologos in 1391.

After another 500m, turn right down Kęstučio gatvė to find the remains of the **Peninsula Castle** (Pusiašalio pilis), thought to have been built by Duke Kęstutis, son of Gediminas and father of Vytautas. These days only the walls, rebuilt to a height of about 1–2m, remain, penning in an inner courtyard given over to wild grasses. A restored tower is nowadays occupied by the **Trakai Sacral Art Museum** (Sakralinio meno ekspozicija; Wed–Sun 10am–6pm; 4Lt), which boasts a small display of church silver and priestly regalia.

From here the main street changes its name to Karaimų gatvė and continues north through the part of town traditionally inhabited by the Karaim, their bright-yellow and -green, timber-clad houses set end-on to the road, each sporting three ground-floor windows – "one for God, one for oneself, and one for Grand Duke Vytautas", as the